Cases and Commentary on Constitutional and Administrative Law

THIRD EDITION

John Marston LLB, Solicitor

Principal Lecturer, School of Law, De Montfort University, Leicester

Richard Ward LLB, Solicitor

Professor of Public Law, School of Law, De Montfort University, Leicester

PITMAN PUBLISHING
128 Long Acre, London WC2E 9AN

A Division of Pearson Professional Limited

© Pearson Professional Limited 1995

First published in Great Britain 1991
Second edition 1993
Third edition 1995

British Library Cataloguing in Publication Data
A catalogue record for this book is available from the British Library.

ISBN 0 273 61063 5

10 9 8 7 6 5 4 3 2 1

Printed by Bell and Bain Ltd, Glasgow

The Publishers' policy is to use paper manufactured from sustainable forests.

Contents

Preface

This third edition has been expanded to take into account the changes in Constitutional and Administrative law which have continued to take place at a rapid pace. In particular, developments in European Community law and public order law are reflected in the text. Judicial review continues to provide stimulating case law in quantities sufficient to make the editorial task as difficult as ever.

Although the basic philosophy and focus of the book remain unchanged, we have taken into account the valuable comments from our colleagues and students, and other users of the book.

We would like to thank our publishers for their continued support and guidance, and for the opportunity, yet again, to expand the content. Any errors and omissions are ours.

Particular thanks are owed to Virginia Marston and to Richard McKeown, who provided assistance in the latter stages of the editorial process.

We have endeavoured to state the law as we understand it at 1 January 1995, although we have been able to reflect certain more recent developments, if not always in the detail which we would wish.

John Marston
Richard Ward

Acknowledgments

We would like to express our thanks to the following copyright owners who willingly gave permission for the publishing of extracts:

The Incorporated Council of Law Reporting for England and Wales.
The New Zealand Council of Law Reporting.

Extracts from the All England Law Reports and the English Reports are reproduced with the permission of Butterworth Law Publishers Ltd.

Extracts from the Common Market Law Reports, Criminal Appeal Reports and European Human Rights Reports, are reproduced with the permission of Sweet & Maxwell Ltd.

The extract from reference re Amendment of the Constitution of Canada is reproduced with the permission of Canada Law Book Ind., 240 Edward Street, Aurora, Ontario L4G 3S9.

The extract from *Moss* v *Maclachlan* is reproduced with the permission of Eclipse Publications Ltd.

Extracts from the Commonwealth Law Reports are reproduced with the permission of the publishers, The Law Book Company Limited, North Ryde, Australia.

Table of cases

1 Introduction

Much about the British constitution needs to be stated in negative form. There is no written constitution to create the structures of state, supply ultimate constitutional authority, provide mechanisms to prevent abuse of legal or political power, or to define the role of the courts. There is no rigid separation of functions, and legislative, executive and judicial functions overlap. The separation of powers in Britain in reality largely means an independent judicial process (see p.193). There are no fundamental individual rights protected against executive, legislative or judicial encroachment: the individual has freedom to do anything not prohibited by law, but no legal claim can succeed based solely upon an argument that the basic rights of the individual have been infringed (see p.8).

All this reflects historical and political development, as is the case with all constitutions. The constitutional system that emerged from the upheavals of the seventeenth century has proved sufficiently flexible to respond to the demands made by universal suffrage, a modern constitutional monarchy and the adoption of significant international obligations, though not always without stresses and strains. Yet the issues and challenges that face the modern constitutional lawyer are very different from those that dominated constitutional thinking some years ago. Today, membership of the European Community, the developing European Union, and the increasingly all-embracing nature of judicial review raise issues and problems very different from those reflected in older case law. In the 1990s, openness of government, and particularly of the decision-making process, is recognised as important – a trend which is reflected in the principles of fairness that are applied by the courts (p.322).

The source of authority

The absence of a written constitutional document as the ultimate source of authority has far-reaching implications. With no such ultimate authority, power comes from statute or from common law, though the constitutionally proper means of exercising that power may sometimes be circumscribed by non-legal but constitutionally binding constitutional conventions. This is particularly so in respect of the common law powers unique to the Crown – the Royal Prerogative (see p.50). Not only is the source of power affected by the absence of such a written constitution, so too are the key issues of legal accountability and the role of the courts, which cannot strike down executive or legislative action as 'unconstitutional'. Above all, it forces us to look elsewhere for the underlying principles of British constitutional law.

Studies in British constitutional law do not progress very far without some consideration of the exposition of Dicey's account of constitutional principle in *An Introduction to the Study of the Law of the Constitution*. Written at the turn of the century, his analysis can be shown today in significant respects not to reflect key modern constitutional realities. It has, though, much influenced successive generations of constitutional lawyers, and its influence permeates many of the cases extracted in this section. Dicey identified the doctrine of Parliamentary supremacy as 'the dominant characteristic' of the constitution. By that he meant that 'Parliament . . . has, under the constitution, the right to make or unmake any law whatsoever; and, further, that no person or body is recognised by the law of England as having a right to override or set aside the legislation of Parliament.' Thus legislation is the source of ultimate authority (see *Pickin* v *BRB*, p.26). Parliament can do anything without legal challenge, for no basis to justify challenge exists. Of course this tells us little about possible political or moral challenges. This principle flows inevitably from the triumph of Parliament over the Monarchy in the seventeenth century, and is implicit in Article 9 of the Bill of Rights 1688 (p.16), which prevents judicial investigation into 'proceedings in Parliament'. It also dictates the role of the courts which is confined, in the context of legislation, to an interpretive function (p.190). Yet it cannot be regarded as the sole underlying constitutional principle. Alongside it is another: the principle of legality. Together they dominate British constitutional theory, guiding both executive action and the development of individual liberties, and profoundly dictating the role of the courts. Between them these two principles represent both the strengths and weaknesses of the British constitution.

The principle of legality

Executive bodies have either inherent legal personality (e.g. the Crown) or have been created by statute or Royal Charter. They have the capacity to act as legal persons, e.g. to enter into contracts, and undertake other functions through their officers, employees or agents. Yet the principle of legality governs their actions: where an executive body interferes with the rights of the individual it must be able to point to some legal authority that entitles it so to do. That authority may come from statute, from the Royal Prerogative or simply from the common law, but exist it must. The attempted requisitioning of property in times of war (cf. *Attorney-General* v *De Keysers Royal Hotel*, p.51), the imposition of taxation (cf. *Attorney-General* v *Wilts United Dairies*, p.33), the termination of a television licence (cf. *Congreve* v *Home Office*, p.34), the entry into property (cf. *Entick* v *Carrington*, p.8) are all situations in which we see the principle in action. The great cases concerning claims of royal power in the seventeenth century (see *Ashby* v *White*, *Godden* v *Hales*, *The Case of Shipmoney*) are as much examples of the principle as modern cases concerning police powers where a successful prosecution may depend upon the legality of a policeman's interference with the liberty of the individual (see *Collins* v *Wilcock*, p.383). No mere plea of 'state necessity' will suffice (p.17). The principle is an articulation of a key element of any concept of the Rule of Law, the doctrine through which Dicey sought to identify the qualities we should regard as minimum standards for the law to meet. The extent to which Dicey's analysis of the concept can withstand close scrutiny is limited: whatever merits it may have had in other times, the necessary growth of a body of administrative law, the inevitable spread of discretionary powers and other constitutional developments of the twentieth century have deprived the analysis of much validity. Yet one element still is all-pervading: accountability of the Executive through the courts, which is of course central to the principle of legality. Executive actions are tested for their legal validity in actions for damages, injunctions, and through the process of judicial review of executive action (see *M* v *Home Office*, p.184).

Important though the principle of legality is, it has distinct limitations. It emphasizes the need for executive bodies to follow due process – the limits that the law expressly or impliedly sets out. It tells us nothing about the quality of that law. The infamous House of Lords ruling in *Liversidge* v *Anderson* (p.12) adopted an interpretation of emergency regulations that subordinated the interests of the individual to those of the State, and effectively put beyond challenge the basis of the appellant's detention. It is the dissent of Lord Atkin that is best remembered for his rejection of executive-minded interpretations and his quest for independent judicial scrutiny of the basis upon which the appellant was being detained. Many other examples can be found illustrating the drawbacks of the principle of legality as a constitutional principle (see *R* v *Inland Revenue Commissioners, ex parte Rossminster*, p.11; *Duncan* v *Jones*, p.408).

Even more fundamentally, the combined effect of the Parliament Acts 1911 and 1949 (p.66) and constitutional convention is to give control of the legislative process to the government of the day, through its control of the House of Commons. Since the duty of the courts is to give effect to Acts of Parliament, and since there are no limits upon legislative competence, then the principle of legality will be ineffectual in preventing encroachment upon the rights and liberties of the individual. The absence of fundamental constitutional sources conferring powers which enable judicial protection of individual rights is a crucial weakness.

Statutory power aside, the common law will often confer powers, for example the power inherent in the police officer in respect of breach of the peace (p.401). The Crown itself will claim common law powers through the Royal Prerogative (p.50). As a result of the doctrine of legislative supremacy, the Royal Prerogative can be limited, abolished or, indeed, preserved by statute; for illustrative cases see *Laker Airways* v *Department of Trade* (p.57) and *R* v *Secretary of State for the Home Department ex parte Northumbria Police Authority* (p.55). Whilst the factual conclusions in each of those cases depend upon the courts' view of parliamentary intention, in essence the argument is a simple one: has Parliament sought to limit the prerogative power? The courts' acceptance of Parliament as the ultimate authority makes this pre-eminence of legislation inevitable, and provides the explanation as to why pre-1688 case law (which told us the courts could in some circumstances disregard an Act of Parliament) cannot now be regarded as sound law. In the absence of a written constitution, the courts have found the 'grundnorm' – the fundamental authority – in Parliament. Once again, though, the principle of legality runs in parallel – it is only Acts of Parliament which command this 'blind obedience'. Delegated legislation, resolutions and any other form of activity may all be tested in the courts to ensure that the requirements of the enabling Act, or of some common law legal principle, have been fulfilled (see *R* v *HM Treasury ex parte Smedley*, p.27).

The doctrine of the legislative supremacy of Parliament

Though Dicey and many other authors refer to Parliamentary sovereignty, such terminology often serves to confuse. Debates as to whether Parliament is sovereign or is supreme are interesting but, for our purposes, sterile. The term 'legislative supremacy of Parliament' focuses attention on the important point that it is Acts of Parliament that are supreme. The question is often put by those unfamiliar with the quirks of the British constitution: how can Parliament do anything it likes? In one sense it plainly cannot; there are many limits of a practical nature. The significance of the doctrine is that it describes the attitude of the courts to legislation. In that sense it does not strain credulity to talk of Parliament as being omnicompetent. But what are the implications of such a fundamental doctrine?

The inability to challenge legislation provides a significant limit on accountability through the courts, though that can sometimes be achieved through creative statutory interpretation. The doctrine weakens the protections that are given to the individual through legislation, since one statute may repeal another, expressly or by implication. There are no legal limits on legislative power. It also provides a strait-jacket into which modern constitutional developments must fit. No better illustration of that can be found than our membership of the European Community. Treaty obligations to the Community, including the obligation to observe and apply Community laws, were accepted through accession to the Treaty of Rome in 1972. That action, taken under Royal Prerogative, was given legal effect by the passage of the European Communities Act 1972 (p.83), which incorporates Community law into the United Kingdom. There remains the thorny problem as to how Community obligations can be given effect whilst preserving legislative power. The resulting case law provides a vivid example of the ability of the British constitution to adapt, by creating and adopting presumptions of interpretation which allow effect to be given to our Community obligations whilst maintaining the theoretical position of upholding legislative supremacy. It is by such flexibility that the British constitution has managed to develop whilst maintaining in essence the same structures.

The doctrine also dictates that no challenge can be mounted as to how an Act was passed. This is inevitably so in the light of Article 9, Bill of Rights, and is illustrated by cases such as *Pickin* v *BRB* (p.26). Interesting theoretical arguments arise as to whether, and, if so, how, the courts may determine what is an Act of Parliament. More importantly, the inability of the courts to examine the legislative process creates significant difficulties in the effective protection of individual rights. The twin principles of legislative supremacy and legality leave individual rights at the mercy of the legislative body, and of the courts. In the absence of the courts recognizing a change in the constitutional order through a new constitutional settlement, any attempt to protect individual rights through procedural limitation against change – entrenchment – will be fraught with difficulty.

Individual rights

Is there a need for such an attempt? Mechanisms for accountability exist, either to Parliament through concepts of ministerial responsibility and answerability, or to other structures created to provide checks and means of scrutiny. The constitutional lawyer should not be blind to the fact that legal accountability is only one form of accountability within the British constitution: Parliamentary Committees and procedures, the Parliamentary and Local Commissioners for Administration, the Police Complaints Authority, the Press Complaints Commission, the Advertising Standards Authority are but a few of the mechanisms and means of scrutiny that exist. Constitutional law has as its primary concern power: its distribution, and the safeguards (or lack of them) against misuse. Whilst these mechanisms are important, the basic question for the lawyer is whether legal remedy is available to prevent abuse. That presupposes not only effective means of scrutiny, but positive rights to be protected, whether in the courts or in other forums.

Historically, English law has rejected broadly stated individual rights. Dicey claimed that the writ of habeas corpus was worth 'a hundred' Bills of Rights. The operation of the twin principles of supremacy and legality may cause the modern student to take a different view: the individual is dependent upon legislative power being used reasonably, and with restraint, and upon the courts interpreting statutes and developing the common law in ways that achieve a fair balance between the different interests involved. The existence and appropriateness of wider protections will emerge from consideration of some of the cases dealt with later and from the acceptance of international obligations through accession to the European Convention on Human Rights (p.135). That accession, through Royal Prerogative, is an illustration of one further principle – that Treaties do not form part of the law unless and until incorporated into law by Act of Parliament. Again, then, the legislative process – or the lack of it – is crucial. No Act of Parliament has been passed to incorporate the Convention into English law. The impact of the Convention has to be viewed in that light.

The non-legal rules

Discussion has thus far centred upon legal sources of power, and means of legal accountability. The non-legal framework should be borne in mind. Conduct may indeed be legal, but nevertheless be regarded as unconstitutional. Non-legal rules, known as constitutional conventions, permeate the constitution: these rules are regarded as binding by those to whom they apply, and regulate how legal powers are in fact to be exercised, and by whom.

The *Canadian Reference Case* (p.41) shows that constitutional conventions are not unique to Britain: they arise even in states such as Canada which have the formal fundamental constitution that we lack.

However, they play a particularly important role in the British constitution, and have been crucial in the evolution of our constitution to its modern reality within a framework established some 300 years ago. Their impact is particularly important in relation to the Monarchy, in respect of which we may draw clear distinctions between where legal power lies and what it is proper for the Monarch to do, i.e. between legal theory and constitutional reality. The Monarch must, save in rare instances, act always on the advice of Her Ministers. The legal powers may be those of the Monarch, but it is Her Majesty's Government that in reality exercises such powers, or directs how the Monarch may exercise them, and which, in either case, is answerable to Parliament in respect of their exercise.

By definition conventions are not directly enforceable in law, but neither are many other matters. Certain actions are regarded by the courts as 'non-justiciable' (i.e. not amenable to consideration by the courts) because of the high policy content or other factors – see, for example, the doctrine of parliamentary privilege (p.165) or affairs of state such as foreign or defence policy. Conventions have much the same nature – they involve judgments as to what is politically and constitutionally proper – and accountability in such matters may be more appropriate through Parliament than through the courts. Convention itself imposes both collective and individual responsibility upon government and ministers to Parliament. The non-enforceability of constitutional conventions in law, though an essential definitional element, is therefore not crucial: what is important is a realization that though unenforceable they may command legal recognition, provide an underpinning rationale for legal doctrine, and, on occasion, even provide the motivation for judicial application of legal rules (see *Attorney-General* v *Jonathan Cape Ltd*, p.45). Thus, for example, judicial attitudes to national security matters are at least in part influenced by the courts' recognition that constitutional accountability to Parliament, through the doctrine of ministerial responsibility, exists. Of course that tells us little about the effectiveness of such constitutional accountability.

2 The control of power

Constitutional and administrative law is primarily concerned with the control of power. Inherent in this is the identification of both the existence and the scope of lawful power, and the rejection of mere assertions of power. *Entick* v *Carrington* (below) is the classic illustration of this but see also *A* v *Hayden* (p.17) and *Fitzgerald* v *Muldoon* (p.18). The executive did not always regard itself as subordinate to Parliamentary power, and the Stuart monarchs' persistence in suspending or dispensing with the operation of laws was a major factor contributing to the revolution of 1688, although arguably the royal prerogative provided lawful authority for such actions.

Today, when statutory powers predominate, the focus has shifted to the control of statutory discretionary powers within the overall framework of the legislative supremacy of Parliament (see p.60 and *Congreve* v *Post Office*, p.34). This still requires the courts to identify the scope of any relevant statutory provision, a task which is fraught with potential for controversy – see *Liversidge* v *Anderson* (p.12), R v *Inland Revenue Commissioners, ex parte Rossminster* (p.11) and *McCarthy & Stone (Developments) Ltd* v *Richmond Upon Thames LBC* (p.30). This aspect of the judicial function may raise difficulties within the doctrine of the separation of powers (see p.183). Judicial review (see p.209 and p.288) or private law proceedings may control the actions of the executive, but judicial review is not always available (see Chapter 12) and private law does not always provide a remedy, e.g. see *Malone* v *Metropolitan Police Commissioner* (p.141).

Entick v *Carrington*

(1765) 19 St Tr 1030 · Court of Common Pleas

The defendants, King's Messengers, entered the plaintiff's house, seized his papers and detained him. The plaintiff brought an action in trespass. The defendants maintained that they had lawful power for their actions since they had been granted a general warrant by the Secretary of State. It was held that the Secretary of State had no power to issue the warrant to search for and seize seditious papers since there was no statute or common law power to issue such warrants. The warrant was therefore 'illegal and void' and the actions of the defendants constituted a trespass.

Lord Camden: '. . . [I]f this point should be determined in favour of [the Secretary of State] the secret cabinets and bureaus of every subject in this kingdom will be thrown open to the search and inspection of a messenger, whenever the Secretary of State shall think fit to charge, or even to suspect, a person to be the author, printer or publisher of a seditious libel . . . If it is law, it will be found in our books. If it is not to be found there, it is not law. The great end, for which men entered into society, was to secure their property. That right is preserved sacred and incommunicable in all instances, where it has not been taken away or abridged by some public law for the good of the whole. The cases where this right of property is set aside by positive law, are various . . . By the laws of England, every invasion of private property, be it ever so minute is a trespass. No man can set his foot upon my ground without my licence, but he is liable to an action, though the damage be nothing . . . If he admits the fact, he is bound to show by way of justification, that some positive law has empowered or excused him. The justification is submitted to the judges, who are to look into the books . . . If no such excuse can be found or produced, the silence of the books is an authority against the defendant, and the plaintiff must have judgement . . . It is then said, that it is necessary for the ends of government to lodge such a power with a state officer . . . [W]ith respect to the argument of state necessity, or a distinction that has been aimed at between State offences and others, the common law does not understand that kind of reasoning, nor do the books take notice of any such distinctions.'

Comment

(1)   *Entick* v *Carrington* 'is perhaps the central case in English Constitutional law' (Keir and Lawson). One of a series of cases involving John Wilkes, it decided for the first time that there was no power to issue the warrant claimed but at the same time it did not set out restrictions concerning the issue or criteria for the granting of a warrant. The fact that over a long period many such warrants had been issued and executed did not deter the court from its forceful enquiry into the legality of executive actions.

(2)   The 'Entick' principle presupposes interference with a pre-existing legal right. *Malone* v *Metropolitan Police Commissioner (No.2)* (p.141) demonstrates the weakness of this principle; the court decided that telephone tapping on the authority of the Home Secretary's warrant infringed no legally protected rights.

(3)   The principle that officials cannot without lawful authority authorize what would otherwise amount to a breach of the law is critical to an assessment of the nebulous concept of the Rule of Law. This concept has been perceived in modern times as requiring that laws should have minimum standards (see the European Convention on Human Rights, p.137) but more traditionally the Rule of Law has been regarded as demanding the absence of arbitrary powers in the hands of the Executive. Similarly, it is not for officials, or anyone else, to decide which laws to obey. The Rule of Law was cited by both the House of Lords and the Court of

Appeal in *M* v *Home Office* as being endangered should the courts be unable to grant injunctions against Ministers of the Crown and enforce them by way of contempt of court (see further p.184). See also *Bennett* v *Horseferry Road Magistrates' Court* (p.20) and *X Ltd* v *Morgan Grampian Ltd* (p.24). If a law provides an unwelcome impediment to official aims or objectives then the law should be subjected to the normal scrutiny by Parliament. See further The Bill of Rights, p.16, *A* v *Hayden*, p.17 and *Fitzgerald* v *Muldoon*, p.18.

(4) Statute may create a power of entry with or without warrant. In the case of entry pursuant to warrant Parliament usually grants to judges or magistrates power to issue search warrants, but there are examples of the grant of powers to the Executive. Section 3, Security Service Act 1989 provides that:

> (1) No entry on or interference with property shall be unlawful if it is authorised by a warrant issued by the Secretary of State under this section.
>
> (2) The Secretary of State may on an application made by the Service issue a warrant under this section authorising the taking of such action as is specified in the warrant in respect of any property so specified if the Secretary of State –
>
> > (a) thinks it is necessary for the action to be taken in order to obtain information which –
> >
> > > (i) is likely to be of substantial value in assisting the Service to discharge any of its functions; and
> > >
> > > (ii) cannot reasonably be obtained by other means; and
> > >
> > > (iii) [relates to certain arrangements for non-disclosure of the product of searches].

See also the Intelligence Services Act 1994, s.5, for a similar provision in respect of the Secret Intelligence Service and Government Communications Headquarters, although s.5(1) of the 1994 Act states that 'no entry on or interference with property or with wireless telegraphy shall be unlawful if . . . '.

(5) Although the 'interests of the state' do not of themselves provide lawful justification for executive action infringing the personal or property rights of the citizen, statute may provide justification on that basis. For example, in connection with the search of premises for material which would assist the investigation of terrorist offences, schedule 17, para. 7(1), Prevention of Terrorism (Temporary Provisions) Act 1989, provides that the normal safeguard of a warrant issued by a justice of the peace or a circuit judge need not apply:

> If a police officer of at least the rank of superintendent has reasonable grounds for believing that the case is one of great emergency and that in the interests of the state immediate action is necessary, he may by a written order signed by him give to any constable the authority which may be given by a search warrant under paragraph 2 or 5 above.

R v Inland Revenue Commissioners, ex parte Rossminster

[1980] AC 952 · House of Lords

The House of Lords considered the proper interpretation of a statutory power under which a judge might grant to the Revenue a search warrant and held that the warrant need not disclose the offences in respect of which the application was made; the court commented upon the judicial approach to warrants.

Lord Diplock: '. . . What has to be disclosed upon the face of the search warrant depends upon the true construction of the statute. The construing court ought, no doubt, to remind itself . . . that entering a man's house or office, searching it and seizing his goods against his will are tortious acts against which he is entitled to the protection of the court unless the acts can be justified either at common law or under some statutory authority. So if the statutory words relied upon as authorising the acts are ambiguous or obscure, a construction should be placed upon them that is least restrictive of individual rights which would otherwise enjoy the protection of the common law. But judges, in performing their constitutional function of expounding what words used by Parliament in legislation mean, must not be over zealous to search for ambiguities or obscurities in words which on the face of them are plain simply because the members of the court are out of sympathy with the policy to which the Act appears to give effect.

My Lords, it does not seem to me that in construing s.20C of the Taxes Management Act 1970 any assistance is to be gained from a consideration of those mid-eighteenth century cases centering on John Wilkes and culminating in *Entick* v *Carrington*, which established the illegality of "general warrants" . . . their invalidity was more fundamental; a Secretary of State, it was held, did not have any power at common law or under the prerogative to order the arrest of any citizen or the seizure of any of his property for the purpose of discovering whether he was guilty of publishing as seditious libel. . .'

Lord Wilberforce: '. . . A formidable number of officials now have powers to enter people's premises, and to take property away, and these powers are frequently exercised, sometimes on a large scale. Many people, as well as the respondents, think that this process has gone too far; that is an issue to be debated in Parliament and the press.

The courts have a duty to supervise, I would say critically, even jealously, the purported exercise of these powers. They are the guardians of the citizens' right to privacy. But they must do this in the context of the times, i.e. of increasing Parliamentary intervention, and of the modern power of judicial review . . . [A]ppeals to eighteenth century precedents of arbitrary action by Secretaries of State and references to general warrants do nothing to throw light on the issue. Furthermore, while the courts may look critically at legislation which impairs the rights of citizens and should resolve any doubt in their favour, it is no part of their duty, or power, to restrict or impede the working of legislation, even of unpopular legislation; to do so would be to weaken rather than to advance the democratic process . . .'

Liversidge v *Anderson*

[1942] AC 206 · House of Lords

Regulation 18B of the Defence (General) Regulations 1939 provided that: 'If the Secretary of State has reasonable cause to believe any person to be of hostile origin or associations . . . he may make an order directing that he shall be detained'. The Home Secretary made an order under Regulation 18B detaining the plaintiff who brought an action claiming false imprisonment and sought a declaration that the detention was unlawful. The House of Lords decided by a majority (Lord Atkin dissenting) that the words 'reasonable cause to believe' as used in Regulation 18B bore a subjective meaning; that the grounds upon which the Home Secretary made the order were not open to challenge in judicial proceedings; and that the Home Secretary could not be compelled to disclose particulars of those grounds.

Lord Wright: 'What is involved is the liberty of the subject. Your Lordships have had your attention called to the evils of the exercise of arbitrary powers of arrest by the Executive and the necessity of subjecting all such powers to judicial control. Your Lordships have been reminded of the great constitutional conflicts in the seventeenth century, which culminated in the famous constitutional charters, the Petition of Right, the Bill of Rights, and the Act of Settlement. These struggles did, indeed, involve the liberty of the subject and its vindication against arbitrary and unlawful power. They sprang (to state it very broadly) from the Stuart theory that the King was King by divine right and that his powers were above the law . . . But by the end of the seventeenth century the old common law rule of the supremacy of law was restored and substituted for any theory of royal supremacy. All the courts today, and not least this House, are as jealous as they have ever been in upholding the liberty of the subject. But that liberty is a liberty confined and controlled by law, whether common law or statute. It is, in Burke's words, a regulated freedom. It is not an abstract or absolute freedom. Parliament is supreme. It can enact extraordinary powers of interfering with personal liberty. If an Act of Parliament, or a statutory regulation, like reg. 18B, which has admittedly the force of a statute, because there is no suggestion that it is *ultra vires* or outside the Emergency Powers (Defence) Act, under which it was made, is alleged to limit or curtail the liberty of the subject or vest in the Executive extraordinary powers of detaining a subject, the only question is what is the precise extent of the powers given. The answer to that question is only to be found by scrutinizing the language of the enactment in the light of the circumstances and the general policy and object of the measure. I have ventured on these elementary and obvious observations because it seems to have been suggested on behalf of the appellant that this House was being asked to countenance arbitrary, despotic or tyrannous conduct. But in the constitution of this country there are no guaranteed or absolute rights. The safeguard of British liberty is in the good sense of the people and in the system of representative and responsible government which has been evolved. If extraordinary powers are here given, they are given because the emergency is extraordinary and are limited to the period of the emergency.

I confess that, notwithstanding all my prejudices in favour of upholding the liberty of the subject, I have come to a clear conclusion that the courts below were right in refusing the particulars asked for . . .'

Lord Atkin: 'They are simple words and as it appears to me obviously give only a conditional authority to the minister to detain any person without trial, the condition being that he has reasonable cause for the belief which leads to the detention order. The meaning, however, which for the first time was adopted by the Court of Appeal . . . and appears to have found favour with some of your Lordships is that there is no condition, for the words "if the Secretary of State has reasonable cause" merely mean "if the Secretary of State thinks that he has reasonable cause." The result is that the only implied condition is that the Secretary of State acts in good faith. If he does that – and who could dispute it or disputing it proves the opposite? – the minister has been given complete discretion whether he should detain a subject or not. It is an absolute power which, so far as I know, has never been given before to the Executive, and I shall not apologize for taking some time to demonstrate that no such power is in fact given to the minister by the words in question . . .

It is surely incapable of dispute that the words "if A has X" constitute a condition the essence of which is the existence of X and the having of it by A. If it is a condition to a right (including a power) granted to A, whenever the right comes into dispute the tribunal whatever it may be that is charged with determining the dispute must ascertain whether the condition is fulfilled. In some cases the issue is one of fact, in others of both fact and law, but in all cases the words indicate an existing something the having of which can be ascertained. And the words do not mean and cannot mean "if A thinks that he has." "If A has a broken ankle" does not mean and cannot mean "if A thinks that he has a broken ankle." . . . "Reasonable cause" for an action or a belief is just as much a positive fact capable of determination by a third party as is a broken ankle . . . If its meaning is the subject of dispute as to legal rights, then ordinarily the reasonableness of the cause, and even the existence of any cause is in our law to be determined by the judge and not by the tribunal of fact if the functions deciding law and fact are divided. Thus having established, as I hope, that the plain and natural meaning of the words "has reasonable cause" imports the existence of a fact or state of facts and not the mere belief by the person challenged that the fact or state of facts existed, I proceed to show that this meaning of the words has been accepted in innumerable legal decisions for many generations that "reasonable cause" for a belief when the subject of legal dispute has been always treated as an objective fact to be proved by one or other party and to be determined by the appropriate tribunal. I will go further and show that until June or July of this year in connection with this reg. 18B, there never has been any other construction even submitted to the courts in whatever context the words are found . . .

I have pointed out that the words in question have a plain and natural meaning, that that meaning has been invariably given to them in statements of the common law and in statutes, that there has been one invariable construction of them in the courts, and that the Defence Regulations themselves clearly recognize that meaning, using different words where it is intended that the executive officer should have unqualified discretion . . .

In the present case . . . even if it were open to a judge to consider the question of expediency, what are the suggested grounds which compel him to adopt the hitherto unheard of "subjective" construction? It is said that it could never have been intended to substitute the decision of judges for the decision of the minister, or, as has been said, to give an appeal from the minister to the courts. But no one proposes either a substitution or an appeal. A judge's decision is not substituted for the constable's on the question of unlawful arrest, nor does he sit on appeal from the constable. He has to bear in mind that the constable's authority is limited and that he can only arrest on reasonable suspicion, and the judge has the duty to say whether the conditions of the power are fulfilled. If there are reasonable grounds, the judge has no further duty of deciding whether he would have formed the same belief any more than, if there is reasonable evidence to go to a jury, the judge is concerned with whether he would have come to the same verdict. For instance, the minister may have reasonable grounds on the information before him for believing that a person is of "hostile origin." If so, any ruling by the courts either in an action for false imprisonment or by way of habeas corpus is impossible though it should subsequently be proved beyond doubt that the minister's information was wrong and that the person was of purely British origin . . .

I view with apprehension the attitude of judges who on a mere question of construction when face to face with claims involving the liberty of the subject show themselves more Executive-minded than the Executive. Their function is to give words their natural meaning, not, perhaps, in war time leaning towards liberty, but . . . "In a case in which the liberty of the subject is concerned, we cannot go beyond the natural construction of the statute." In this country, amid the clash of arms, the laws are not silent. They may be changed, but they speak the same language in war as in peace. It has always been one of the pillars of freedom, one of the principles of liberty for which on recent authority we are now fighting, that the judges are no respecters of persons and stand between the subject and any attempted encroachments on his liberty by the Executive, alert to see that any coercive action is justified in law. In this case I have listened to arguments which might have been addressed acceptably to the Court of King's Bench in the time of Charles I.

I protest, even if I do it alone, against a strained construction put on words with the effect of giving an uncontrolled power of imprisonment to the minister . . .

I know of only one authority which might justify the suggested method of construction: ' "When I use a word,' Humpty Dumpty said in rather a scornful tone, 'it means just what I choose it to mean, neither more nor less.' 'The question is,' said Alice, 'whether you can make words mean so many different things.' 'The question is,' said Humpty Dumpty, 'which is to be master – that's all.' " (*Through the Looking Glass*, Chapter 6.) After all this long discussion the question is whether the words "If a man has" can mean "If a man thinks he has." I am of opinion that they cannot, and that the case should be decided accordingly . . .'

Comment

(1) This notorious case (described by Lord Reid in *Ridge* v *Baldwin* as a 'very peculiar decision') is recalled most often for the vigorous dissent of Lord Atkin which is now accepted as containing the correct interpretation of the relevant words (see *R* v *Inland Revenue Commissioners, ex parte Rossminster* and *R* v *Secretary of State for the Home Department, ex parte Khawaja*).

(2) There may be areas of executive action which are beyond the scope of the courts' powers of review. Once it is accepted that Parliament can create, by appropriate formulae, unreviewable powers then the courts, despite their interpretive skills, are powerless to intervene (see p.267: ouster provisions, and the subjectively worded s.3, Security Service Act 1989, p.10).

(3) The objective assessment in the condition precedent of 'reasonable suspicion', see *Holgate Mohammed* v *Duke* p.373, may be omitted, thus leaving the courts with the simple question whether the person possessed of the power honestly held the belief or suspicion (see, e.g. *McKee* v *Chief Constable*). Parliament may sanction search without the need for suspicion – see s.60 Criminal Justice and Public Order Act 1994 where in certain instances relating to offensive weapons or dangerous instruments:

> A constable may ... stop any person or vehicle and make any search he thinks fit whether or not he has any grounds for suspecting that the person or vehicle is carrying weapons or articles of that kind.

Attorney-General v *Guardian Newspapers Ltd (No. 2)*

[1988] 3 WLR 776 · Court of Appeal

Sir John Donaldson MR: 'Lord Denning's Report into the Profumo affair (Cmnd 2152 (1963)) stressed that: "The members of the Service are, in the eye of the law, ordinary citizens with no powers greater than anyone else. They have no special powers of arrest such as the police have. No special powers of search are given to them. They cannot enter premises without the consent of the householder, even if they may suspect a spy is there". He went on to say that this deficiency of powers was made up for by close co-operation with the police forces.

It would be a sad day for democracy and the rule of law if the service were ever to be considered to be above or exempt from the law of the land. And it is not. At any time any member of the service who breaks the law is liable to be prosecuted. But there is a need for some discretion and common sense. Let us suppose that the service has information which suggests that a spy may be operating from particular premises. It needs to have confirmation. It may well consider that, if he proves to be a spy, the interests of the nation are better served by letting him continue with his activities under surveillance and in ignorance that he has been detected by arresting him. What is the service expected to do? A secret search of the premises is the obvious answer. Is this really "wrongdoing"? . . .

Even in the context of the work of the security service which, I must stress, is the defence of the realm, there must be stringent limits to what breaches of the law can be considered excusable. Thus I cannot conceive of physical violence ever coming within this category. Or physical restraint, other than in the powers of arrest enjoyed by every citizen or under the authority of a lawful warrant of arrest. But covert invasions of privacy, which I think is what Mr Wright means by "burglary", may in some circumstances be a different matter.

It may be that the time has come when Parliament should regularise the position of the service. It is certainly a tenable view. The alternative view, which is equally tenable, is that the public interest is better served by leaving the members of the service liable to prosecution for any breach of the law at the instance of a private individual or of a public prosecuting authority, but they may expect that prosecuting authorities will exercise a wise discretion and that in an appropriate case the Attorney-General would enter a *nolle prosequi*, justifying his action to Parliament if necessary. In so acting, the Attorney-General is not acting as a political minister or as a colleague of ministers. He acts personally and in a quasi-judicial capacity as representing the Crown . . . It is not for me to form or express any view on which is the most appropriate course to adopt in the interests of the security of the nation and the maintenance of the rule of law. However that problem is resolved, it is absurd to contend that any breach of the law, whatever its character, will constitute such "wrongdoing" as to deprive the service of the secrecy without which it cannot possibly operate.'

Comment

(1) For the facts, and the decision of the House of Lords, see p.160. A *nolle prosequi* is a procedural means by which the Attorney-General may terminate any prosecution. The Crown Prosecution Service now has the power to take over and discontinue a prosecution. Neither action affects the rights in tort of any victim.

(2) Lord Donaldson MR was speaking only of wrongdoing as a type of conduct which would deprive the wrongdoer of the confidentiality which might otherwise reside in the relevant information. This does not mean that other remedies (e.g. in trespass) would not be available.

(3) The Security Service Act 1989 and the Intelligence Services Act 1994 regularize the constitutional position of the security service and the secret intelligence service. Whether they do so with sufficient safeguards for the individual or groups is another matter.

The Bill of Rights 1688

(1 Will. & Mar. sess. 2c. 2)

. . . And . . . the . . . lords spirituall and temporall and commons . . . being now assembled in a full and free representative of this nation . . . declare

(1) That the pretended power of suspending of laws or the execution of laws by regall authority without consent of Parlyament is illegall.
(2) That the pretended power of dispensing with laws or the execution of laws by regall authoritie as it hath been assumed and exercised of late is illegall.
(3) That the commission for erecting the late court of commissioners for ecclesiastical causes and all other commissions and courts of like nature are illegal and pernicious.
(4) That levying money for or to the use of the Crowne by pretence of prerogative without grant of Parlyament for longer time or in other manner then the same is or shall be granted is illegal.
(5) That it is right of the subjects to petition the King and all commitments and prosecutions for such petitioning are illegal.
(6) That the raising or keeping a standing army within the kingdome in time of peace unless it be with consent of Parlyament is against law.
(7) That the subjects which are protestants may have arms for their defence suitable to their conditions and as allowed by law.
(8) That election of members of Parlyament ought to be free.

(9) That the freedome of speech and debates or proceedings in Parlyament ought not to be impeached or questioned in any court or place out of Parlyament.

(10) That excessive baile ought not to be required nor excessive fines imposed nor cruell and unusuall punishments inflicted.

(11) That jurors ought to be duly impannelled and returned . . .

(12) That all grants and promises of fines and forfeitures of particular persons before conviction are illegal and void.

(13) And that for redresse of all grievances and for the amending strengthening and preserving of the lawes Parlyaments ought to be held frequently . . .

Comment

(1)   Despite its constitutional importance the Bill of Rights can nonetheless be repealed or amended as any other Act. It does not have that special sanctity accorded to Bills of Rights in other countries, e.g. in the United States of America (and see also *Cormack* v *Cope*, p.63). It is fundamental only inasmuch as it illustrates the reasons for the constitutional struggles of the eighteenth century and the nature of the solution. Despite its antiquity, it is of continuing importance: see *Congreve* v *Home Office*. (p.34), *McCarthy & Stone (Developments) Ltd* v *Richmond Upon Thames LBC* (p.30), *Woolwich Building Society* v *IRC (No.2)*, *Attorney-General* v *Wilts United Dairies* (p.33), *Fitzgerald* v *Muldoon* (p.18).

(2)   The revolutionary settlement saw a transfer of much of the power in the state from the monarch to Parliament and was the culmination of the struggle between the Stuart Kings and Parliament. The latter achieved a position of dominance, partly through legal means and partly through political means. The desire for legitimacy was predominant and Parliament clearly felt that it was a lawfully constituted body despite the absence of the motive power of the Crown. The Crown and Parliament Recognition Act 1689 legalized retrospectively the activities of a Parliament which had summoned itself (rather than through the 'lawful' medium of the Royal Writ). Articles 1 and 2 rejected the suspending and dispensing power, and were needed to prevent the extension of regal power which would have threatened parliamentary power.

(3)   Article 10 prohibits 'cruell and unusuall punishments'. In *Williams* v *Home Office (No. 2)* this was shown to be capable of amounting to a right, breach of which would permit an individual to sue for damages. A modern counterpart may be seen in art. 3, European Convention on Human Rights (p.137).

A v Hayden

[1985] LRC (Const) 365 · High Court of Australia

The plaintiffs were Australian Secret Intelligence Service (ASIS) operatives who took part in a covert training exercise which involved, *inter alia*, the carrying of guns through a hotel. The police believed that serious offences had been committed and sought the plaintiffs' identities. The Court refused the plaintiffs' application for an injunction to prevent the defendants (the Minister of State for Foreign Affairs, the Director General and the Assistant Director General of ASIS) from revealing the plaintiffs' identities.

Murphy J: 'The Executive power of the Commonwealth must be exercised in accordance with the Constitution and the laws of the Commonwealth. The Governor-General, the Federal Executive Council and every officer of the Commonwealth are bound to observe the laws of the land. If necessary, constitutional and other writs are available to restrain apprehended violations and to remedy past violations. I restate these elementary principles because astonishingly one of the plaintiffs asserted through counsel that it followed from the nature of the executive government that it is not beyond the executive power, even in a situation other than war, to order one of its citizens to kill another person. Such a proposition is inconsistent with the rule of law. It is subversive of the Constitution and the laws. It is, in other countries, the justification for death squads . . . [I]t is entirely clear that neither ASIS nor the Minister nor the Executive Government could confer authority upon any of the plaintiffs to commit an offence or immunity from prosecution for an offence once committed. The incapacity of the Executive Government to dispense its servants from obedience to laws made by Parliament is the corner-stone of a parliamentary democracy. A prerogative to dispense from the laws was exercised by mediaeval kings, but it was a prerogative "replete with absurdity, and might be converted to the most dangerous purposes" (Chitty, *Prerogatives of the Crown*). James II was the last King to exercise the prerogative dispensing power . . . and the reaction to his doing so found expression in the Declaration of Right . . . By the Bill of Rights the power to dispense from any statute was abolished. Whatever vestige of the dispensing power then remained, it is no more. The principle, as expressed in the Act of Settlement, is that all officers and ministers ought to serve the Crown according to the laws. It is expressed more appropriately for the present case by Griffith CJ in *Clough* v *Leahy*: "If an act is unlawful – forbidden by law – a person who does it can claim no protection by saying that he acted under the authority of the Crown."

   This is no obsolete rule; the principle is fundamental to our law, though it seems sometimes to be forgotten when Executive Governments or their agencies are fettered or frustrated by laws which affect the fulfilment of their policies.'

Comment

The principle in *A* v *Hayden* was specifically approved by the Privy Council in *Yip Chiu Cheung* v *R*, and see also *R* v *Clegg*.

Fitzgerald v Muldoon

[1976] 2 NZLR 615 · New Zealand Supreme Court

The pension arrangements for teachers in New Zealand were governed by statute which required deductions to be made from salary. With a view shortly to changing the scheme, the Premier of New Zealand, in a series of public announcements including a press statement, indicated that the pension scheme would stop immediately and that legislation would be ultimately introduced to that effect. This announcement ran counter to the provisions of the relevant Act. The plaintiff, a teacher opposed to the abolition of the old scheme, brought an action to challenge the legality of the announcement on the basis that it was in breach of the Bill of Rights 1688. The court held that there was a breach of the Bill of Rights and granted a declaration to that effect, but concluded that various other remedies sought would be rejected in pursuance of the court's discretion since there was evidence that the new provisions would be enacted and that it would be an unwarranted step to set in motion again the machinery of the Act.

Wild CJ: 'It is a graphic illustration of the depth of our legal heritage and the strength of our constitutional law that a statute passed by the English Parliament nearly three centuries ago to extirpate the abuses of the Stuart Kings should be available on the other side of the earth to a citizen of this country which was then virtually unknown in Europe and on which no Englishman was to set foot for almost another hundred years. And yet it is not disputed that the Bill of Rights is part of our law. The fact that no modern instance of its application was cited in argument may be due to the fact that it is rarely that a litigant takes up such a cause as the present, or it may be because governments usually follow established constitutional procedures. But it is not a reason for declining to apply the Bill of Rights where it is invoked and a litigant makes out his case . . . That leaves for consideration the Prime Minister's public announcement as evidenced by his press statement of 15 December . . . The first sentence of the third paragraph, however, and the fourth paragraph, amount together to an unequivocal pronouncement that the compulsory requirement for employee deductions and employer contributions were to cease as stated. That was reiterated in unmistakable terms in the second paragraph of the statement made on 23 December. The Act of Parliament in force required that those deductions and contributions must be made, yet here was the Prime Minister announcing that they need not be made. I am bound to hold that in so doing he was purporting to suspend the law without consent of Parliament. Parliament had made the law. Therefore the law could be amended or suspended only by Parliament or with the authority of Parliament.

The question whether "the pretended power of suspending" was "by regall authority" within the meaning of s.1 of the Bill of Rights is, I think, to be determined by reference to the powers of the Prime Minister and the position occupied by him, which are of fundamental importance in our system of government. He is the Prime Minister, the leader of the government elected to office, the chief of the executive government. He had lately received his commission by royal authority, taken the oaths of office, and entered on his duties. In my opinion his public announcement of 15 December, made as it was in the course of his official duties as Prime Minister, must therefore be regarded as made "by regall authority" within the meaning of s.1. The authority accorded it by the officials concerned is abundantly evident from the resolution of the Superannuation Board, and the decision of the State Services Co-ordinating Committee and the various branches of the state services. While I reject the allegation that the Prime Minister gave instructions to these officials I think it is perfectly clear that they acted because of his public announcement of 15 December. Had it not been made they would have continued as before . . . In my view it was implicit in the statement, coming as it did from the Prime Minister, that what was being done was lawful and had legal effect . . .'

Comment

(1)   The seventeenth century had seen the Crown asserting, and the courts largely conceding, a prerogative power to suspend or dispense with laws. Dispensing meant lifting the operation of an Act with regard to one specific person or persons; suspending meant lifting the operation of an Act in every respect. In *Godden* v *Hales* the court seemed to accept the powers as operating without restraint: ''tis an inseparable prerogative in the Kings of England to dispense with penal laws in particular cases, and upon particular necessary reasons. That of those reasons and those necessities, the King himself is the sole judge.' See also *Thomas* v *Sorrell, Case of Prohibitions* and *Case of Proclamations*. The power of the courts not to apply statutory provisions contrary to European Community law has been termed disapplication. The important point is that such power is not pursuant to regal authority but derives from a statutory source, the European Communities Act 1972.

(2)   See also *Professional Promotions & Services* v *Attorney-General*, and *R* v *London County Council, ex parte The Entertainment Protection Association* where Scrutton LJ was driven to observe that '. . . I take it that the London County Council is in no better position than James II and that laws cannot be dispensed with by the authority of the London County Council, when they cannot by royal authority.'

(3)   The real constitutional danger now is the capacity of the executive to promote legislation overturning unwelcome decisions of the courts, either prospectively or retrospectively (see p.xx). Special attention needs to be paid to so-called 'Henry VIII' powers in Acts. These grant to the executive, usually ministers, the power to repeal or amend statutory provisions, subject normally to Parliamentary scrutiny. Although commonly used to alter financial limits in Acts or similar minor amendments, such provisions are a convenient and sometimes necessary way of implementing complex statutory schemes, for example, s.78 National Insurance Act 1911. A modern example is s.8(1) Consumer Protection Act 1987:

> Her Majesty may by Order in Council make such modifications of this Part and of any other enactment (including an enactment contained ... in an Act passed after this Act) as appear to Her Majesty in Council to be necessary or expedient in consequence of any modification of the product liability Directive which is made at any time after the passing of this Act.

The extensive legislative powers granted in s.2(2) and (4) European Communities Act 1972 to Her Majesty in Council should be noted (see p.83).

Bennett v Horseferry Road Magistrates' Court

[1993] 3 All ER 138 · House of Lords

The appellant, a New Zealand citizen living in South Africa, was wanted in the United Kingdom to stand trial on criminal charges. There was no extradition treaty between South Africa and the United Kingdom. For the purposes of deciding the appropriate law, the House of Lords assumed that the English police had colluded with the South

African police to arrest and forcibly return the appellant to the United Kingdom under the pretext of deporting him to New Zealand via Heathrow airport. It was also assumed that the Crown Prosecution Service had been consulted and had approved of these steps. The issue for the House of Lords was whether, in the exercise of its supervisory jurisdiction, the Divisional Court had power to inquire into the circumstances by which a person had been brought within the jurisdiction and, if so, what remedy was available to prevent his trial where he had been lawfully arrested within the jurisdiction for a crime committed within the jurisdiction. The House of Lords, Lord Oliver dissenting, held that the Divisional Court had power to stay the prosecution and order the release of the prisoner.

Lord Griffiths: '. . . Your lordships are now invited to extend the concept of abuse of process a stage further. In the present case there is no suggestion that the appellant cannot have a fair trial, nor could it be suggested that it would have been unfair to try him if he had been returned to this country through extradition procedures. If the court is to have the power to interfere with the prosecution in the present circumstances it must be because the judiciary accept a responsibility for the maintenance of the rule of law that embraces a willingness to oversee executive action and to refuse to countenance behaviour that threatens either basic human rights or the rule of law.

My Lords, I have no doubt that the judiciary should accept this responsibility in the field of criminal law. The great growth of administrative law during the latter half of this century has occurred because of the recognition by the judiciary and Parliament alike that it is the function of the High Court to ensure that executive action is exercised responsibly and as Parliament intended. So also should it be in the field of criminal law and if it comes to the attention of the court that there has been a serious abuse of power it should, in my view, express its disapproval by refusing to act upon it.

Let us consider the position in the context of extradition. Extradition procedures are designed not only to ensure that criminals are returned from one country to another but also to protect the rights of those who are accused of crimes by the requesting country. Thus sufficient evidence has to be produced to show a prima facie case against the accused and the rule of speciality protects the accused from being tried for any crime other than that for which he was extradited.

If a practice developed in which the police or prosecuting authorities of this country ignored extradition procedures and secured the return of an accused by a mere request to police colleagues in another country they would be flouting the extradition procedures and depriving the accused of the safeguards built into the extradition process for his benefit. It is to my mind unthinkable that in such circumstances the court should declare itself to be powerless and stand idly by; I echo the words of Lord Devlin in *Connelly* v *DPP*:

> The courts cannot contemplate for a moment the transference to the executive of the responsibility for seeing that the process of law is not abused.

The courts, of course, have no power to apply direct discipline to the police or the prosecuting authorities, but they can refuse to allow them to take advantage of abuse of power by regarding their behaviour as an abuse of process and thus preventing a prosecution.

In my view your Lordships should now declare that where process of law is available to return an accused to this country through extradition procedures our courts will refuse to try him if he has been forcibly brought within our jurisdiction in disregard of those procedures by a process to which our own police, prosecuting or other executive authorities have been a knowing party.

If extradition is not available very different considerations will arise on which I express no opinion . . .'

Lord Lowry: ' . . . The philosophy which inspires the proposition that a court may stay proceedings brought against a person who has been unlawfully abducted in a foreign country is expressed, so far as existing authority is concerned, in the passages cited by . . . Lord Bridge of Harwich. The view there expressed is that the court, in order to protect its own process from being degraded and misused, must have the power to stay proceedings which have come before it and have only been made possible by acts which offend the court's conscience as being contrary to the rule of law. Those acts by providing a morally unacceptable foundation for the exercise of jurisdiction over the suspect taint the proposed trial and, if tolerated, will mean that the court's process has been abused. Therefore, although the power of the court is rightly confined to its inherent power to protect itself against the abuse of its own process, I respectfully cannot agree that the facts relied on in cases such as the present case (as alleged) "have nothing to do with that process" just because they are not part of the process. They are the indispensable foundation for the holding of the trial.

The implications for international law, as represented by extradition treaties, are significant. If a suspect is extradited from a foreign country to this country, he cannot be tried for an offence which is different from that specified in the warrant and, subject always to the treaty's express provisions, cannot be tried for a political offence. But, if he is kidnapped in the foreign country and brought here, he may be charged with any offence, including a political offence. If British officialdom at any level has participated in or encouraged the kidnapping, it seems to represent a grave contravention of international law, the comity of nations and the rule of law generally if our courts allow themselves to be used by the executive to try an offence which the courts would not be dealing with if the rule of law had prevailed.

It may be said that a guilty accused finding himself in the circumstances predicated is not deserving of much sympathy, but the principle involved goes beyond the scope of such a pragmatic observation and even beyond the rights of those victims who are or may be innocent. It affects the proper administration of justice according to the rule of law and with respect to international law . . . If proceedings are stayed when wrongful conduct is proved, the result will not only be a sign of judicial disapproval but will discourage similar conduct in future and thus will tend to maintain the purity of the stream of justice. No "floodgates" argument applies because the executive can stop the flood at source by refraining from impropriety.

I regard it as essential to the rule of law that the court should not have to make available its process and thereby indorse (on what I am confident will be a very few occasions) unworthy conduct when it is proved against the executive or its agents, however humble in rank. And, remembering that it is not jurisdiction which is in issue but the exercise of a discretion to stay proceedings, while speaking of "unworthy conduct", I would not expect a court to stay the proceedings of every trial which has been preceded by a venial irregularity . . . '

Comment

(1)   In order to act effectively within their jurisdiction, all courts have inherent power to prevent abuse of their process although such power is strictly confined and should be exercised rarely. According to the House of Lords, in the case of magistrates' courts the power is restricted to cases involving the risk to a fair trial (see for example *R* v *Telford Justices, ex parte Badhan*) and in other instances a decision of the High Court should be obtained.

(2)   For an example of 'venial irregularity' see *Schmidt* v *Federal Republic of Germany* where it was said, *obiter*, that no stay would be appropriate since the defendant had merely been tricked into returning to England and not forcibly abducted. In *Schmidt* it was held that the '*Bennett* principle' does not apply to proceedings for extradition under the Extradition Act 1989. Lord Janucey said:

> . . . the position in relation to a pending trial in England is wholly different to that in relation to pending proceedings for extradition from England. In the former case the High Court in its supervisory jurisdiction is the only bulwark against any abuse of process resulting in injustice or oppression which may have resulted in the accused being brought to trial in England. In the latter case, not only has the Secretary of State power to refuse to surrender the accused in such circumstances but the courts of the requesting authority are likely to have powers similar to those held to exist in *Bennett* v *Horseferry Road Magistrates' Court*. An accused fugitive is thus likely to have not one but two safeguards against injustice and oppression before being brought to trial in the requesting state.

It may be questioned whether reliance on an executive whose agents or officers are implicated in the wrongdoing, and on the likelihood of foreign laws coinciding with English law, really are a bulwark against abuse.

(3)   Reliance on the Rule of Law as the foundation for developing legal principle emphasizes its continued importance. The House of Lords invests the idea of the Rule of Law with the notion of requiring both the executive to achieve the moral high ground and, in this instance, the courts to protect their own independence from the executive. In other contexts, the Rule of Law has been used to require obedience to the law by the citizen – see for example *X Ltd* v *Morgan Grampian Ltd*, p.24.

(4)   For an application of the rule of law to systematic and widespread abuses of individual liberty by the executive see the Commission of Enquiry concerning certain activities of the Royal Canadian Mounted Police, vol. I: *Freedom and Security under the Law* (the MacDonald Report) where it was said that:

> . . . when we insist on the rule of law as an absolute principle we have in mind the absolute prohibition of institutionalized unlawfulness . . . What is completely intolerable is to permit police and security forces, as a matter of institutionalized practice, to condone certain legal violations by their members as a necessary means of carrying out the responsibilities of their organizations.
>
>   If governments and police forces do not strictly apply the rule of law to

themselves it will become increasingly difficult for them to persuade private organisations and individuals in our society to respect the law. It is essential that those whose function it is to uphold the law should adhere to it themselves . . .

X Ltd v *Morgan Grampian Ltd*

[1990] 2 All ER 1 · House of Lords

A source had supplied G, the defendant journalist, with details of the plaintiffs' business plan; G planned to write an article for his employers, the defendant publishers. The plaintiff sought an injunction to prevent publication of the confidential information and an order requiring G to disclose his notes which would reveal the name of the source. G disobeyed a court order requiring him to lodge the notes in a sealed letter at court pending the outcome of the proceedings, and was thus in contempt of court. G and the defendant publishers relied on s.10 of the Contempt of Court Act 1981:

> No court may require a person to disclose, nor is any person guilty of contempt of court for refusing to disclose, the source of information contained in a publication for which he is responsible, unless it be established to the satisfaction of the court that disclosure is necessary in the interests of justice or national security or for the prevention of disorder or crime.

The decision of the judge at first instance applying s.10, Contempt of Court Act was upheld because disclosure of the source was 'necessary in the interests of justice'.

Lord Bridge: ' . . . [In the case of the interests of national security and the prevention of crime] it is difficult to imagine that any judge would hesitate to order disclosure. These two public interests are of such overriding importance that once it is shown that disclosure will serve one of those interests, the necessity of disclosure follows almost automatically . . . But the question whether disclosure is necessary in the interests of justice gives rise to a more difficult problem of weighing one public interest against another . . . To construe "justice" as the antonym of "injustice" in s.10 would be far too wide. But to confine it to "the technical sense of the administration of justice in the course of legal proceedings in a court of law" seems to me . . to be too narrow. It is . . . "in the interests of justice", in the sense in which this phrase is used in s.10, that persons should be enabled to exercise important legal rights and to protect themselves from serious legal wrongs whether or not resort to legal proceedings in a court of law will be necessary to attain these objectives . . .

Construing the phrase . . . in this sense immediately emphasises the importance of the balancing exercise. It will not be sufficient, *per se*, for a party seeking disclosure of a source protected by s.10 to show merely that he will be unable without disclosure to exercise the legal right or avert the threatened legal wrong on which he bases his claim in order to establish the necessity of disclosure. The judge's task will always be to weigh in the scales the importance of enabling the ends of justice to be attained in the circumstances of the particular case on the one hand against the importance of protecting the source on the other hand. In this balancing exercise it is only if the judge is satisfied that disclosure in the interests of justice is of such preponderating importance as to override the statutory privilege against disclosure that the threshold of necessity will be reached . . .

The importance to the plaintiffs of obtaining disclosure lies in the threat of severe damage to their business, and consequentially to the livelihood of their employees, which would arise from disclosure of the information contained in their corporate plan while their refinancing negotiations are still continuing. This threat . . . can only be defused if they can identify the source either as himself the thief of the stolen copy of the plan or as a means to lead to the identification of the thief and thus put themselves in a position to institute proceedings for the recovery of the missing document. The importance of protecting the source on the other hand is much diminished by the source's complicity, at the very least, in a gross breach of confidentiality which is not counterbalanced by any legitimate interest which publication of the information was calculated to serve. Disclosure in the interests of justice is . . . clearly of preponderating importance so as to override the policy underlying the statutory protection of sources and the test of necessity for disclosure is satisfied. . . .

[Lord Bridge then addressed the position of G:]

The maintenance of the rule of law is in every way as important in a free society as the democratic franchise. In our society the rule of law rests on twin foundations: the sovereignty of the Queen in Parliament in making the law and the sovereignty of the Queen's courts in interpreting and applying the law. While no one doubts the importance of protecting journalists' sources, no one, I think, seriously advocates an absolute privilege against disclosure admitting of no exceptions. Since the enactment of s.10 of the 1981 Act both the protection of journalists' sources and that limited grounds on which it may exceptionally be necessary to override the protection have been laid down by Parliament. I have not heard of any campaign in the media suggesting that the law itself is unjust or that the exceptions to the protection are too widely drawn. But if there were such a campaign, it should be fought in a democratic society by persuasion, not by disobedience to the law. Given the law as laid down by s.10 who, if not the courts, is to interpret it . . . ?The journalist cannot be left to be judge in his own cause and decide whether or not to make the disclosure. This would be an abdication of the role of Parliament and the courts . . . Of course the courts . . . are fallible and a journalist ordered to disclose his source may . . . feel that the court's decision was wrong. But to contend that the individual litigant . . . has a right of "conscientious objection" which entitles him to set himself above the law if he does not agree with the court's decision, is a doctrine which directly undermines the rule of law and is wholly unacceptable in a democratic society . . . freedom of speech is itself a right which is dependent on the rule of law for its protection and it is paradoxical that a serious challenge to the rule of law should be mounted by responsible journalists . . .'

Comment

(1)   For application of the other criteria in s.10, see *Secretary of State for Defence v Guardian Newspapers Ltd* and *Re an Inquiry under Company Security (Insider Dealing) Act 1985.*

(2)   In the Court of Appeal, Lord Donaldson MR also emphasized the rule of law:

The constitutional position is clear. Parliament makes the law and it is the duty of the courts to enforce the law, whether or not they agree with it. Every citizen, every corporate body and every authority, whether national or local, is entitled to campaign to change the law, but until the law is changed it is their duty to obey it. That is what parliamentary democracy and the rule of law is all about. Each one of us surrenders a part of his personal freedom of action and choice and in return is protected by the law from the consequences of others seeking to exercise an unfettered freedom of action and choice.

Pickin v British Railways Board

[1974] AC 765 · House of Lords

The respondent alleged that he had been deprived of an interest in land by the terms of the British Railways Act 1968, a private Act of Parliament. He claimed that Parliament had been misled by certain recitals in the preamble to the Act. Accordingly, he alleged that the Act was to that extent ineffective to deprive him of his interest in land. The House of Lords held that the court had no powers to impugn the validity of an Act of Parliament or to enquire into the manner in which the Bill had passed through the procedures of Parliament.

Lord Reid: '... First [the respondent] says that s.18 confers a benefit on the appellants and that if he can prove that Parliament was fraudulently misled into enacting this benefit the court can and should disregard the section ... The idea that a court is entitled to disregard a provision in an Act of Parliament on any ground must seem strange and startling to anyone with any knowledge of the history and law of our constitution, but a detailed argument has been submitted to your Lordships and I must deal with it.

I must make it plain that there has been no attempt to question the general supremacy of Parliament. In earlier times many learned lawyers seem to have believed that an Act of Parliament could be disregarded in so far as it was contrary to the law of God or the law of nature or natural justice, but since the supremacy of Parliament was finally demonstrated by the Revolution of 1688 any such idea has become obsolete.

The respondent's contention is that there is a difference between a public and a private Act. There are of course great differences between the methods and procedures followed in dealing with public and private Bills, and there may be some differences in the methods of construing their provisions. But the respondent argues for a much more fundamental difference. There is little in modern authority that he can rely on ... In my judgment the law is correctly stated by Lord Campbell in *Edinburgh and Dalkeith Railway Co.* v *Wauchope*, Mr. Wauchope claimed certain wayleaves. The matter was dealt with in a private Act. He appears to have maintained in the Court of Session that the provisions of that Act should not be applied because it had been passed without his having had notice as required by Standing Orders. This contention was abandoned in this House. Lord Brougham and Lord Cottenham said that want of notice was no ground for holding that the Act did not apply. Lord Campbell based his opinion on more general grounds. He said:

My Lords, I think it right to say a word or two before I sit down, upon the point that has been raised with regard to an Act of Parliament being held inoperative by a court of justice because the forms, in respect of an Act of Parliament, have not been complied with. There seems great reason to believe that [sic] notion has prevailed to a considerable extent in Scotland, . . . I must express some surprise that such a notion should have prevailed. It seems to me there is no foundation for it whatever; all that a court of justice can look to is the parliamentary roll; they see that an Act has passed both Houses of Parliament, and that it has received the royal assent, and no court of justice can inquire into the manner in which it was introduced into Parliament, what was done previously to its being introduced, or what passed in Parliament during the various stages of its progress through both Houses of Parliament. I therefore trust that no such inquiry will hereafter be entered into in Scotland, and that due effect will be given to every Act of Parliament, both private as well as public, upon the just construction which appears to arise upon it.

No doubt this was *obiter* but, so far as I am aware, no one since 1842 has doubted that it is a correct statement of the constitutional position . . .'

R v HM Treasury, ex parte Smedley

[1985] QB 657 · Court of Appeal

An undertaking was entered into by Representatives of the Governments of Member States of the EEC to make community budget payments. That undertaking was specified by the Chancellor of the Exchequer in a draft Order in Council as a Community Treaty within the meaning of s.1(2) of the European Communities Act 1972. Section 1(2) included within the meaning of 'Community Treaty' 'any other treaty . . . entered into . . . as a treaty ancillary to any of the Treaties . . . by the United Kingdom'. 'The Treaties' referred to specific treaties. Section 1(3) of the Act required that a treaty could not be regarded as a Community Treaty unless it was laid in draft before each House of Parliament and approved. The effect of the Order in Council, if approved and promulgated, would have been to authorize payments to be made to the European Community. The draft Order in Council had been laid before both Houses of Parliament at the time of the challenge but had not been approved. Mr Smedley sought judicial review of the determination of the Chancellor of the Exchequer that the undertaking could properly be regarded as a 'Community Treaty' within s.1(2).

The Court of Appeal held that the court could, where appropriate, intervene by way of judicial review even before the matter had been approved by Parliament but that the most likely remedy would be a declaration, and, further, that the Order in Council if made would not be *ultra vires*.

Slade LJ: '. . . I therefore think it inevitable that this court should carefully address its mind to the question whether or not a decision on the legal issues now before it, given at this present moment, would constitute an interference with the functions of Parliament. If it would, this court should simply dismiss the appeal on the ground that this application was premature and say nothing further on the interesting and important legal issues involved.

The answer to this question must, I think, depend on an analysis of the respective functions of Parliament, Her Majesty in Council and the courts in the context of s.1 of the European Communities Act 1972 and the proposed Order in Council. The operative part of the draft Order in Council simply provides:

> 2. The treaty specified in the Schedule to this Order is to be regarded as a Community Treaty as defined in s.1(2) of the European Communities Act 1972.

The Schedule refers to the "Undertaking made by the representatives of the governments of the member states of the European Community, meeting within the Council on 2 and 3 October 1984, to make payments to the Community in 1984 to finance supplementary and amending budget No. 1 . . ."

The reasons why an Order in Council is considered necessary are these. In view of the wording of s.1(2) of the Act of 1972 the Undertaking can qualify as a "Community Treaty" within that subsection only if it amounts to 'any other treaty entered into . . . as a treaty ancillary to any of the Treaties, by the United Kingdom."

Section 1(3) of the Act of 1972 provides: "If Her Majesty by Order in Council declares that a treaty specified in the Order is to be regarded as one of the Community Treaties as herein defined, the Order shall be conclusive that it is to be so regarded; but a treaty entered into by the United Kingdom after 22 January 1972, other than a pre-accession treaty to which the United Kingdom accedes on terms settled on or before that date, shall not be so regarded unless it is so specified, nor be so specified unless a draft of the Order in Council has been approved by resolution of each House of Parliament."

It follows that by virtue of s.1 the Undertaking, not being a pre-accession treaty within this exception, (a) is incapable of being regarded as one of "the Community Treaties" unless it is specified in an Order in Council; (b) is incapable of being specified in an Order in Council unless a draft of the Order in Council has first been approved by resolution of each House of Parliament.

The function conferred on the two Houses of Parliament by s.1(3) in relation to the Undertaking will be, in effect, simply that of deciding whether or not to approve the draft Order in Council. If Parliament were to give a negative decision by withholding its approval, that would be that, the Order in Council could not be made. If, however, Parliament were to give its approval then, at least according to the wording of s.1 of the Act of 1972, two consequences would follow: (1) Her Majesty by Order in Council would have the power to specify the Undertaking as one which was to be regarded as a Community Treaty as defined in s.1(2); (2) any such Order in Council would be "conclusive" that the Undertaking was to be so regarded.

I have somewhat laboured these distinctions between the respective functions of Parliament and Her Majesty in Council in the present case, for the purpose of demonstrating the somewhat limited role which is allotted to Parliament by s.1(3) of the Act of 1972. This role is analogous to a power of veto. If it withholds its approval from the draft Order in Council, the Order cannot be made. If, however, the approval of Parliament is given, Her Majesty in Council is left with a discretion whether or not to make the Order. There is no possible question of the court seeking or being able to control the exercise of the Parliamentary power of veto. However, I can see no reason why the exercise of the last-mentioned discretion given to Her Majesty in Council should not be open to attack in the courts by the process of judicial review, subject to the stringent restrictions on any such attack imposed by what has come to be known as the Wednesbury principle . . . Equally, if the analysis of the position set out earlier in this judgment is correct, I can see no good reason why a decision by the courts given at the present stage and relating to the proposed exercise of the discretion of Her Majesty in Council should be said to usurp or interfere with what I conceive to be the function of Parliament in this present context, namely that of deciding whether or not to exercise what is in substance a power of veto over the proposed Order in Council. Indeed, if this court were to consider that the proposed order would be beyond the legal powers of Her Majesty in Council, I would anticipate that, to echo the words of Younger LJ in *R* v *Electricity Commissioners Co.*: "the interference of the court in such a case as this, and at this stage, so far from being even in the most diluted sense of the words a challenge to its supremacy, will be an assistance to Parliament."

The latter decision seems to me good authority for the proposition that where some administrative order or regulation is required by statute to be approved by resolution of both Houses of Parliament, the court can in an appropriate case intervene by the way of judicial review before the Houses have given their approval, even though I conceive that in at least most such cases the only appropriate form of relief (if any) could be by way of declaration. This is a jurisdiction which must of course be exercised with great circumspection and with close regards to the dangers of usurping or encroaching on any function which statute has specifically conferred on Parliament or on the functions of Parliament in general. In the present case, however, I am satisfied that a decision on Mr Smedley's application will involve no such usurpation or encroachment. I should add that it is common ground that the mere existence of these present proceedings need place no fetter on the course of the impending debate in Parliament. For these reasons, I would reject [the] submission that the application is premature and that no decision should be made in relation to it at the present stage.

However, from what has already been said, two points are in my opinion clear. First, any attack . . . on the proposed Order in Council has to be based on the proposed exercise of the discretion of Her Majesty in Council. Secondly, if it is to succeed, it must be shown that it falls within the Wednesbury principle.'

Comment

(1)   Legislative supremacy is the cornerstone of the constitution (see p.60). The role of the courts *vis–à–vis* Acts of Parliament is limited and there is no basis for distinguishing private Acts from public-general Acts. Procedurally Parliament may choose to treat each differently, but that is a matter for Parliament. (See, generally, Chapter 8 on parliamentary privilege.)

(2)   Judicial impotence in the face of legislation extends only to Acts of Parliament, it does not extend to subordinate legislation the validity of which is a matter into which the courts may enquire in the same way as in respect of administrative action. This is so even where Parliament may be considering whether to approve the draft of that subordinate legislation (see *Nottinghamshire County Council* v *Secretary of State for the Environment*, p.212).

(3)   An Order in Council may be one of two things. Where the Order in Council is

an exercise of the Royal Prerogative then it is regarded as primary legislation (see *GCHQ* case per Lord Fraser, p.216). Where an Act empowers the making of subordinate legislation by way of Order in Council then that Order in Council will be a form of Statutory Instrument (see s.1, Statutory Instruments Act 1946). In *ex parte Smedley* the Order in Council fell into the latter category.

(4) Legislative supremacy of Parliament ensures that governments need only be temporarily hindered by the actions of the courts and can take steps to remedy or limit any 'damage' caused, e.g. the War Damage Act 1965 reversed the effect of the decision in *Burmah Oil* v *Lord Advocate*. In *R* v *Londonderry JJ, ex parte Hume* the court decided that the powers granted to the armed forces operating in Northern Ireland by a series of subordinate legislative provisions were *ultra vires* the parent Act, and that the armed forces had operated unlawfully in arresting Mr Hume. In order to regularize the activities, both past and future, the Northern Ireland Act 1972 was passed:

> 1. The limitations imposed by para (3) of s.4(1) of the Government of Ireland Act 1920 on the powers of the Parliament of Northern Ireland to make laws shall not have effect, and shall be deemed never to have had effect, to preclude the inclusion in laws made by that Parliament for the peace, order or good government of Northern Ireland of all provision relating to members of Her Majesty's forces as such or to things done by them when on duty, and in particular shall not preclude, and shall be deemed never to have precluded, the conferment on them by, under or in pursuance of any such law of powers, authorities, privileges or immunities in relation to the preservation of the peace or maintenance of order in Northern Ireland.

(5) Retrospective legislation is often regarded as contrary to the rule of law, e.g. as when reversing the consequences of an independent court's decision, interfering with substantive rights, or imposing liability. But the courts do not regard it as necessarily unfair: see, generally, *Phillips* v *Eyre, Azam* v *Home Secretary,* and *Plewa* v *Chief Adjudication Officer.* Despite *dicta* in *Waddington* v *Miah,* Parliament has now, arguably, passed retrospective criminal legislation. See the War Crimes Act 1991 which appears to be acceptable within the scope of the European Convention on Human Rights Article 7 (see p.138). For a comparative approach see the decision of the Australian High Court in *Polyukhovich* v *The Commonwealth.* In some instances retrospective legislation will be contrary to European Community law which regards the principle that penal provisions may not have retroactive effect as a fundamental right the observance of which is guaranteed by the Court of Justice. See *R* v *Kirk.*

McCarthy & Stone (Developments) Ltd v Richmond Upon Thames LBC

[1991] 4 All ER 897 · House of Lords

The applicants sought judicial review of the levying of charges by the local authority in respect of consultations held prior to applications for planning permission. The only possible source of the authority to charge was to be found in s.111(1), Local Government Act 1972, which stated that '. . . a local authority shall have power to do any thing . . . which is calculated to facilitate, or is conducive or incidental to, the discharge of any of their functions.' The House of Lords held that the charges were unlawful.

Lord Lowry: '. . . The basis for the proposition, which was accepted by both sides, that statutory authority to charge is required is the well-known principle exemplified by the *ratio decidendi* of *Att-Gen* v *Wilts United Dairies Ltd*:

> In these circumstances, if an officer of the executive seeks to justify a charge upon the subject made for the use of the Crown (which includes all the purposes of the public revenue), he must show, in clear terms, that Parliament has authorised the particular charge. The intention of the Legislature is to be inferred from the language used, and the grant of powers may, though not expressed, have to be implied as necessarily arising from the words of a statute; but in view of the historic struggle of the Legislature to secure for itself the sole power to levy money upon the subject, its complete success in that struggle, the elaborate means adopted by the Representative House to control the amount, the conditions and the purposes of the levy, the circumstances would be remarkable indeed which would induce the Court to believe that the Legislature had sacrificed all the well-known checks and precautions, and, not in express words, but merely by implication, had entrusted a Minister of the Crown with undefined and unlimited powers of imposing charges upon the subject for purposes connected with his department. (See per Atkin LJ.)

Atkin LJ further observed:

> It makes no difference that the obligation to pay the money is expressed in the form of an agreement. It was illegal for the Food Controller to require such an agreement as a condition of any licence. It was illegal for him to enter into such an agreement. The agreement itself is not enforceable against the other contracting party; and if he had paid under it he could, having paid under protest, recover back the sums paid, as money had and received to his use. . .

It is further conceded by the Council that the principle applies whether the money is to be received by the Crown or central government or by a local authority such as the council here. . . . [S]peaking generally . . . it is for the local authority to show that it has the right to charge for the service provided. . . . the power to charge a fee for the relevant service must, if it exists, be found in s.111(1) either expressly or by necessary implication. This provision, as both sides agree, gives statutory recognition to the common law rule governing the activities of local authorities and other statutory corporations . . . A local authority could at common law do anything which was reasonably incidental to its functions and the council here relies on the proposition that to impose a charge for pre-application advice is reasonably incidental, not merely to the giving of that advice, but also to the council's function of considering and determining applications for planning permission.

The definition of "function" is important and I would therefore refer at this point to the recent case of *Hazell* v *Hammersmith and Fulham London BC*, where certain local authorities had engaged in speculative financial transactions and their power to do so was in question. . . . In this House Lord Templeman said:

> In *A-G* v *Great Eastern Rly Co.* Lord Blackburn said: ". . . where there is an Act of Parliament creating a corporation for a particular purpose, and giving it powers for that particular purpose, what it does not expressly or impliedly authorise is to be taken to be prohibited. . ." In the same case Lord Selbourne LC said that the doctrine of *ultra vires* – "ought to be reasonably, and not unreasonably, understood and applied, and that whatever may fairly be regarded as incidental to, or consequential upon, those things which the Legislature has authorised, ought not (unless expressly prohibited) to be held, by judicial construction, to be *ultra vires*." In the same vein Lord Blackburn said: ". . . those things which are incident to, and may reasonably and properly be done under the main purpose, though they may not be literally within it, would not be prohibited." Section 111 embodies these principles. I agree with the Court of Appeal that in s.111 the word "functions" embraces all the duties and powers of a local authority: the sum total of the activities Parliament has entrusted to it. Those activities are its functions.

. . . It is, accordingly, clear that the consideration and determining of planning applications is a function of the council, but the giving of pre-application advice, although it facilitates, and is conducive and incidental to, the function of determining planning applications, is not itself a function of the council.

Thus, it is one thing to say that the giving of pre-application planning advice facilitates or is conducive or incidental to the council's planning functions but it is quite another thing to say that for the council to charge for that advice also facilitates or is conducive or incidental to those functions. The council presented its case on the basis that charging for the service facilitates, or is conducive or incidental to, the giving of the pre-application advice; but, even assuming that to be a fact, this way of presenting the case would simply amount to saying that imposing a charge facilitates, or is conducive or incidental to, a service which in its turn facilitates, or is conducive or incidental to, the council's planning functions. The developers, on the other hand, submit that, in order to qualify as something which is authorised by s.111(1) the imposition of a charge for pre-application advice must facilitate, or be conducive or incidental to, the planning functions themselves. If not, the developers contend, the charge is not within the powers of the council, since it is admittedly not authorised by any provision outside s.111. In this connection the argument that something which is incidental to the incidental (but not incidental to the function) does not pass the test is not a novelty: see *A-G* v *Manchester Corp*, cited in *Hazell* v *Hammersmith and Fulham London BC*.

My Lords, let me now turn to another argument for the council which found favour in the courts below. In its judgement the Court of Appeal has contrasted functions, such as planning, which the council has a duty to provide, with those, such as providing a museum, a library or a public park, which it has power to provide, on the basis that without statutory authority the council cannot charge for the provision of a function which it has a duty to provide, whereas it can charge for a function which it has merely power to provide (or not to provide) at its discretion. Thus, it is said, the council can charge for a service which at its discretion it provides by virtue of s.111(1), as facilitating or being conducive or incidental to the relevant function (in this case the function of considering and determining planning applications) . . .

I consider [that] reasoning to be mistaken, because it does not by any means follow that all of the discretionary functions of the council or all of the facilitating or incidental activities contemplated or possibly contemplated by s.111 are services for which it is permissible to charge in the absence of express authority to do so. The rule is that a charge cannot be made unless the power to charge is given by express words or by necessary implication. These last words impose a rigorous test going far beyond the proposition that it would be reasonable or even conducive or incidental to charge for the provision of a service. Furthermore, as it seems to me, the relevance of the contrast attempted to be drawn, with respect to the power of a council to charge, between duty functions and discretionary functions is vitiated when one has regard to the large number of discretionary functions for the provision of which express statutory authority to charge has been enacted. I am not impressed by the submission that an express power to charge for the performance of discretionary functions may have been conferred "for the sake of clarity".

. . . My Lords, I come back to s.111(1), the relevant provision. The council admits that it cannot without express authority charge for a "duty function", but it still has to say that the ability to charge for pre-application advice is based on the "power to do any thing" which is "incidental . . . to the discharge of any of [the council's] functions". To charge for performing a function (subject always to *Wednesbury* considerations (see *Associated Provincial Picture Houses Ltd* v *Wednesbury Corp.*), which do not arise here) must always be incidental to the provision of the service provided. Therefore the council's interpretation of s.111(1) would allow it to charge for the performance of every function, both obligatory and discretionary, which provided a service. . . Such a construction of the subsection cannot possibly be justified, and I say this before even considering the point that, in the absence of express statutory authority, the power to charge can only be implied, in the words of Atkin LJ in *A-G* v *Wilts United Dairies Ltd*, "as necessarily arising from the words of a statute".

There is yet a further point, to which I have already adverted. As the Court of Appeal has said, the power to give pre-application advice is neither a duty nor a discretionary express power, but is a subsidiary power arising by virtue of s.111(1) (which has codified the common law), because it is calculated to facilitate, or is conducive or incidental to, the discharge of one of the council's functions. To charge for the exercise of that power is, at best, incidental to the incidental and not incidental to the discharge of the functions.

A further point which commended itself to the Court of Appeal was the argument that, since the council was not obliged to provide the service in question, it could state on a "take it or leave it" basis that it was willing to provide it for a reasonable fee, as if entering into a contract. I consider this to be an untenable proposition which, if correct, would justify a local authority in charging for any discretionary service, but which in reality is in conflict with the second principle enunciated by Atkin LJ in *A-G* v *Wilts United Dairies Ltd.* . . '

Comment

(1) In *Attorney-General* v *Wilts United Dairies* the Court of Appeal was

concerned with the grant of a licence to purchase milk. The Food Controller imposed a levy upon milk transported from one area to another. The defendants then refused to pay and the Food Controller sued. The Court of Appeal held that the demand was unlawful since there was no statutory authority for the actions of the Food Controller and the House of Lords subsequently dismissed his appeal. Lord Atkin's judgment (cited by Lord Lowry) is regarded as the classic statement of the applicable principles.

(2)   For the process and grounds of judicial review, see pp.209–347.

Congreve v *Home Office*

[1976] 1 QB 629 · Court of Appeal

On January 29th the Home Secretary announced that TV licences would be increased from £12 to £18 on April 1st. The plaintiff took out for £12 a new licence despite holding a licence which would expire shortly after April 1st (the new licence was called by the court 'an overlapping licence'). The Home Office demanded from all such individuals the additional fee of £6, and, in the event of failure to pay, threatened revocation of the licence without reimbursement of the £12 paid. At a later date the Home Office modified the threat by proposing a revocation after 8 months. The plaintiff refused to pay the £6 and brought an action for a declaration that the revocation would be unlawful. He failed at first instance but on appeal it was held that the revocation would be unlawful (a) as an abuse of power since the overlapping licences were lawfully granted and the need to raise money was not a good reason for revocation of a licence, and (b) the demand was an attempt to levy taxation without Parliament's approval and thus contrary to the Bill of Rights 1688.

Lord Denning MR: '. . . [The] statutory provisions give the Minister a discretion as to the issue and revocation of licences. But it is a discretion which must be exercised in accordance with the law, taking all relevant considerations into account, omitting irrelevant ones, and not being influenced by any ulterior motives. One thing which the Minister must bear in mind is that the owner of a television set has a right of property in it; and, as incident to it, has a right to use it for viewing pictures in his own home, save in so far as that right is prohibited or limited by law. Her Majesty's subjects are not to be delayed or hindered in the exercise of that right except under the authority of Parliament. The statute has conferred a licensing power on the Minister: but it is a very special kind of power. It invades a man in the privacy of his home, and it does so solely for financial reasons so as to enable the Minister to collect money for the revenue. It is a ministerial power which is exercised automatically by clerks in the post office. They cannot be expected to exercise a discretion. They must go by the rules. The simple rule – as known to the public – is that if a man fills in the form honestly and correctly and pays his money, he is to be issued with a licence . . . [Lord Denning concluded that an overlapping licence was lawful] . . .

But now the question comes: can the Minister revoke the overlapping licence which was issued so lawfully? He claims that he can revoke it by virtue of the discretion given him by s.1(4) of the Act. But I think not. The licensee has paid £12 for the 12 months. If the licence is to be revoked – and his money forfeited – the

Minister would have to give good reasons to justify it. Of course, if the licensee had done anything wrong – if he had given a cheque for £12 which was dishonoured, or if he had broken the conditions of the licence – the Minister could revoke it. But when the licensee has done nothing wrong at all, I do not think the Minister can lawfully revoke the licence, at any rate, not without offering him his money back, and not even then except for good cause. If he should revoke it without giving reasons, or for no good reason, the courts can set aside his revocation and restore the licence. It would be a misuse of the power conferred on him by Parliament: and these courts have the authority – and, I would add, the duty – to correct a misuse of power by a Minister or his department, no matter how much he may resent it or warn us of the consequences if we do. *Padfield* v *Minister of Agriculture, Fisheries and Food* is proof of what I say. It shows that when a Minister is given a discretion – and exercises it for reasons which are bad in law – the courts can interfere so as to get him back on to the right road. . . .

What then are the reasons put forward by the Minister in this case? He says that the increased fee of £18 was fixed so as to produce enough revenue for future requirements. It was calculated on previous experience that no one would take out an overlapping licence before April 1, 1975 – or, at any rate, that no appreciable number of people would do so . . . His policy would be thwarted, he says, and the revenue rendered insufficient, if large numbers of people were allowed to take out overlapping licences. He says, too, that other licence holders (being the vast majority) would have a legitimate grievance. So he considered it proper to revoke the overlapping licences of those who had acted contrary to his policy . . .

I cannot accept those reasons for one moment. The Minister relies on the intention of Parliament. But it was not the policy of Parliament that he was seeking to enforce. It was his own policy. And he did it in a way which was unfair and unjust. The story is told in the Seventh Report of the Parliamentary Commissioner for Administration, Session 1974–75. Ever since February 1, 1975, the newspapers had given prominence to the bright idea. They had suggested to readers that money could be saved by taking out a new colour licence in March 1975 instead of waiting till after April 1, 1975. The Minister did nothing to contradict it. His officials read the articles and drew them to his attention. They raised the query: Should a letter be written to "The Times," or should an inspired question be put in Parliament, so as to put a stop to the bright idea? But the Minister decided to do nothing. He allowed the bright idea to circulate without doing anything to contradict it. And all the time he kept up his sleeve his trump card – to revoke all overlapping licences. Thousands of people acted on the bright idea: only to be met afterwards by the demand: "Pay another £6."

The conduct of the Minister, or the conduct of his department, has been found by the Parliamentary Commissioner to be maladministration. I go further. I say it was unlawful. His trump card was a snare and a delusion. He had no right whatever to refuse to issue an overlapping licence, or, if issued, to revoke it. His original demand, "Pay £6 or your licence will be revoked," was clearly unlawful – in the sense that it was a misuse of power – especially as there was no offer to refund the £12, or any part of it. His later demand, "Pay £6 or your licence will be revoked after eight months," was also unlawful. Suppose that, owing to mistaken calculation, the original £12 had been found inadequate. Would it be legitimate for the Minister to say after eight months: "I am going to revoke your licence now and you must take out a new licence"? I should think not. The licence is granted for 12 months and cannot be revoked simply to enable the Minister to raise more money. Want of money is no reason for revoking a licence. The real reason, of course, in this case was that the department did not like people taking out overlapping licences so as to save money. But there was nothing in the Regulations to stop it. It was perfectly lawful: and the department's dislike of it cannot afford a good reason for revoking them. So far as other people (who did not have the foresight to take out overlapping licences) are concerned I doubt whether they would feel aggrieved if these licences remain valid. They might only say: "Good luck to them. We wish we had done the same."

There is yet another reason for holding the demands for £6 to be unlawful. They were made contrary to the Bill of Rights. They were an attempt to levy money for the use of the Crown without the authority of Parliament: and that is quite enough to damn them: see *Attorney-General* v *Wilts United Dairies Ltd.*

My conclusion is that the demands made by the Minister were unlawful. So were the attempted revocations. The licences which were issued lawfully before April 1, 1975, for £12 cannot be revoked except for good cause: and no good cause has been shown to exist. They are, therefore, still in force and the licensees can rely on them until they expire at the date stated on them . . .'

Comment

(1) Assertions of unfettered discretionary powers are regarded by the courts with extreme caution. The '*Wednesbury* Principles', summarized by Lord Denning, govern the exercise of such powers – see p.291.

(2) The raising of money provides a fruitful source of case law – see, for example, the *Case of Shipmoney*, *Darnell's Case*, *Bowles* v *Bank of England* (p.65).

(3) Non-legal remedies include recourse to the Parliamentary and Local Government Commissioners (better known as 'ombudsmen', from their Swedish equivalent); other Commissioners include the Health Service Commissioner. The Commissioners enquire into injustices caused by alleged maladministration. This term is undefined, but during the passage of the Parliamentary Commissioner Bill, the responsible Minister, Richard Crossman, described it as including 'neglect, inattention, delay, incompetence, ineptitude, perversity and arbitrariness' (the 'Crossman Catalogue'). See *R* v *Local Commissioner for the North and East Area of England ex parte Bradford MCC* where the court identified 'maladministration' as concerning the manner of decision-making, and the manner of decision implementation. On the other hand, the courts concern themselves with the legality of the action. In the light of the grounds of challenge by way of judicial review (p.288), the two enquiries are not necessarily mutually exclusive – see *Congreve* v *Home Office*. The recommendations of the ombudsmen are not legally binding.

(4) Some forms of conduct can best be scrutinized through the political process. Much of the debate preceding the passage of the Interception of Communications Act 1985 and the Security Service Act 1989 was on the respective merits of political accountability and legal regulation. The Intelligence Services Act 1994 created the Intelligence and Security Committee to examine the expenditure, administration and policy of the Security and Secret Intelligence Services, and the

Government Communications Headquarters (GCHQ). The Committee members are appointed by the Prime Minister after consultation with the Leader of the Opposition, and must be drawn from the House of Commons or House of Lords, but they may not be Ministers of the Crown. Annual or special reports are made to the Prime Minister who then lays the report before Parliament, subject to the exclusion of any matter which would be prejudicial to the functions of the Services or GCHQ.

R v *Parliamentary Commissioner for Administration, ex parte Dyer*

[1994] I All ER 375 · Queen's Bench Division

D applied for judicial review of a decision of the Parliamentary Commissioner for Administration (the 'PCA') not to reopen his investigation into her complaints against the Department of Social Security alleging maladministration in the handling of her claims for state benefits. The PCA regarded the investigation as having been completed when he sent a report of its results to the MP who had referred the complaint to him and to the department concerned. The report had found D's complaint to be justified and noted that the Permanent Secretary to the department had apologised to D and that an *ex gratia* payment had been made. D also challenged the manner in which the PCA carried out the original investigation.

Simon Brown LJ: ' . . . The first question . . . concerns the proper ambit of this court's supervisory jurisdiction over the PCA. [Counsel] on his behalf submits to us that, certainly so far as the PCA's discretionary powers are concerned, this court has no review jurisdiction whatever over their exercise. In the alternative he submits that the court should intervene only in the most exceptional cases of abuse of discretion, essentially on the same limited basis held by the House of Lords in *Nottinghamshire CC* v *Secretary of State for the Environment* and *Hammersmith and Fulham London BC* v *Secretary of State for the Environment* to be appropriate in the particular area of decision-making there in question.

The resolution of this initial jurisdictional issue clearly depends essentially on the legislation which created the PCA's office and governs the discharge of his functions. To these provision I now turn. They are to be found in the Parliamentary Commissioner Act 1967. Most relevant for present purposes are these sections:

5. (1) Subject to the provisions of this section, the Commissioner may investigate any action taken by or on behalf of a government department or other authority to which this Act applies, being action taken in the exercise of administrative functions of that department or authority, in any case where –
(a) a written complaint is duly made to a member of the House of Commons by a member of the public who claims to have sustained injustice in consequence of maladministration in connection with the action so taken; and
(b) the complaint is referred to the Commissioner, with the consent of the person who made it, by a member of that House with a request to conduct an investigation thereon . . .

(5) In determining whether to initiate, continue or discontinue an investigation under this Act, the Commissioner shall, subject to the foregoing provisions of this

section, act in accordance with his own discretion; and any question whether a complaint is duly made under this Act shall be determined by the Commissioner . . .

7. (1) Where the Commissioner proposes to conduct an investigation pursuant to a complaint under this Act, he shall afford to the principal officer of the department or authority concerned, and to any person who is alleged in the complaint to have taken or authorised the action complained of, an opportunity to comment on any allegations contained in the complaint.

(2) Every such investigation shall be conducted in private, but except as aforesaid the procedure for conducting an investigation shall be such as the Commissioner considers appropriate, in the circumstances of the case; and without prejudice to the generality of the foregoing provision the Commissioner may obtain information from such persons and in such manner, and make such inquiries, as he thinks fit, and may determine whether any person may be represented, by counsel or solicitor or otherwise, in the investigation . . .

10. (1) In any case where the Commissioner conducts an investigation under this Act or decides not to conduct such an investigation, he shall send to the member of the House of Commons by whom the request for investigation was made . . . a report of the results of the investigation or, as the case may be, a statement of his reasons for not conducting an investigation.

(2) In any case where the Commissioner conducts an investigation under this Act, he shall also send a report of the results of the investigation to the principal officer of the department or authority concerned and to any other person who is alleged in the relevant complaint to have taken or authorised the action complained of.

(3) If, after conducting an investigation under this Act, it appears to the Commissioner that injustice has been caused to the person aggrieved in consequence of maladministration and that the injustice has not been, or will not be, remedied, he may, if he thinks fit, lay before each House of Parliament a special report upon the case.

(4) The Commissioner shall annually lay before each House of Parliament a general report on the performance of his functions under this Act and may from time to time lay before each House of Parliament such other reports with respect to those functions as he thinks fit . . .

Shortly after the 1967 Act came into force, we are told, a select committee was appointed specifically with regard to the PCA, to examine his reports and consider any matters in connection with them.

As to his wider proposition – that this court has literally no right to review the PCA's exercise of his discretion under the 1967 Act (not even, to give the classic illustration, if he refused to investigate complaints by red-headed complainants) – [counsel] submits that the legislation is enacted in such terms as to indicate an intention that the PCA should be answerable to Parliament alone for the way he performs his functions. The PCA is, he suggests, an officer of the House of Commons, and, the argument runs, the parliamentary control provided for by the statute displaces any supervisory control by the courts. [Counsel] relies in particular on these considerations: first, the stipulation under s.5 that a complaint must be referred to the PCA by a member of Parliament before even his powers of investigation are engaged; second, the requirement under s.10(1) to report back to the member of Parliament (and, in certain circumstances, to each House of

Parliament – see s.10(3)); third, the requirement under s.10(4) annually to lay a general report before Parliament; fourth, the provision under s.1(3) of the Act for the PCA's removal from office only in the event of addresses from both Houses of Parliament. [Counsel] points also to the PCA being always answerable to the select committee.

Despite these considerations I, for my part, would unhesitatingly reject this argument. Many in government are answerable to Parliament and yet answerable also to the supervisory jurisdiction of this court. I see nothing about the PCA's role or the statutory framework within which he operates so singular as to take him wholly outside the purview of judicial review.

I turn next, therefore, to [counsel]'s alternative and narrower submission that, by analogy with the two House of Lords cases already mentioned, the courts should regard their powers as restricted with regard to reviewing the PCA's exercise of the discretions conferred upon him by this legislation.

I need cite one passage only from the speeches in those two cases, this from Lord Bridge's speech in *Hammersmith and Fulham London BC* v *Secretary of State for the Environment.*

[The extract from Lord Bridge's speech cited by Simon Brown LJ is to be found at p. 215, he continued:]

[Counsel] concedes that the analogy between the position considered there and that arising here is not a very close one. He submits, however, that the underlying rationale for restricting the scope of judicial review in those cases applies also here. Although, as counsel recognises, the PCA's functions are manifestly not political, nevertheless, he submits, the provisions here for parliamentary control afford this case a comparable dimension.

This submission, too, I would reject. There seems to me no parallel whatever between, on the one hand, decisions regarding the formulation and implementation of national economic policy – decisions "depending essentially on political judgment . . . for politicians to take . . . in the political forum of the House of Commons" – and, on the other hand, decisions of the PCA regarding the matters appropriate for investigation and the proper manner of their investigation.

All that said, however, and despite my rejection of both [counsel]'s submissions on the question of jurisdiction, it does not follow that this court will readily be persuaded to interfere with the exercise of the PCA's discretion. Quite the contrary. The intended width of these discretions is made strikingly clear by the legislature: under s.5(5), when determining whether to initiate, continue or discontinue an investigation, the commissioner shall "act in accordance with his own discretion"; under s.7(2) "the procedure for conducting an investigation shall be such as the commissioner considers appropriate in the circumstances of the case". Bearing in mind too that the exercise of these particular discretions inevitably involves a high degree of subjective judgment, it follows that it will always be difficult to mount an effective challenge on what may be called the conventional ground of Wednesbury unreasonableness (see *Associated Provincial Picture Houses Ltd* v *Wednesbury Corp*).

Recognising this, indeed, one may pause to wonder whether in reality the end result is much different from that arrived at by the House of Lords in the two cases referred to, where the decisions in question were held "not open to challenge on the grounds of irrationality short of the extremes of bad faith, improper motive or manifest absurdity". True, in the present case "manifest absurdity" does not have to be shown; but inevitably it will be almost as difficult to demonstrate that the PCA has exercised one or other of his discretions unreasonably in the public law sense . . .'

Comment

(1)   The court considered that none of the allegations made by D were made out and that her application should fail. For *Nottinghamshire CC v Secretary of State for the Environment*, see p.212, and *Hammersmith and Fulham London BC v Secretary of State for the Environment*, see p.214. For the grounds of challenge by way of judicial review see Chapter 13. The willingness and ability of the courts to review the work of the Parliamentary and Local Government Commissioners may be contrasted with the rejection by the courts of jurisdiction to review the work of non-governmental ombudsmen – see p.233.

(2)   The Local Government Commissioner is also subject to judicial review, see *R v Commissioner for Local Administration, ex parte Croydon London BC* and *R v Commissioner for Local Administration, ex parte Eastleigh BC* where Lord Donaldson MR said:

> . . . Parliament has not created a right of appeal against the findings in an ombudsman's report. It is this very fact, coupled with the public law character of the ombudsman's office and powers which is the foundation of the right to relief by way of judicial review.

In each case, the court examined the scope of the Local Commissioner's powers but not the exercise of his discretion; the extent of review of that will be the same as for the Parliamentary Commissioner.

(3)   Note the growth of self-regulatory authorities and the extent to which their activities may be subject to judicial review – see *R v Panel on Takeovers and Mergers, ex parte Datafin plc*, p.224.

3 Constitutional conventions

Legal sources alone do not present a clear picture of the working of the constitution since the operation of purely legal powers is frequently dependent upon the operation of non-legal rules of the constitution known as constitutional conventions. Dicey suggested that:

> The rules which make up constitutional law . . . include two sets of principles or maxims of a totally distinct character. The one set of rules are in the strictest sense 'laws' since they are rules which . . . are enforced by the courts; these rules constitute 'constitutional law' in the proper sense of that term, and may . . . be called collectively 'the law of the constitution'. The other set of rules consist of conventions, understandings, habits, or practices which, though they may regulate the conduct of the several members of the sovereign power, of the ministry, or other officials, are not in reality laws at all since they are not enforced by the courts. This portion of constitutional law may . . . be termed the 'conventions of the constitution', or constitutional morality.

Conventions are often of greater practical significance than the rules to which they relate, e.g. the legal power of the Monarch to refuse assent to a Bill is illusory given the convention that the Monarch cannot refuse assent. The attitude of the courts to conventions is of importance and, in brief, involves recognition but not enforcement.

Reference Re Amendment of the Constitution of Canada

(1982) 125 DLR (3rd) 1 · Supreme Court of Canada

In order to achieve the complete patriation of the Canadian constitution from the residual control of the United Kingdom, the Canadian federal government made proposals which were opposed by a significant number of the provincial governments who alleged that to proceed with the proposals would be to act contrary to a fundamental convention. The Canadian Supreme Court was asked, *inter alia*:

Is it a constitutional convention that the House of Commons and Senate of Canada will not request Her Majesty the Queen to lay before the Parliament of the United Kingdom of Great Britain and Northern Ireland a measure to amend the constitution of Canada affecting federal–provincial relationships or the powers, rights or privileges granted or secured by the constitution of Canada to the provinces, their legislatures or governments without first obtaining the agreement of the provinces?

The majority in the Supreme Court found that there was a convention to the effect that the consent of the provincial governments was required and answered the question, 'Yes'.

Martland J and others: 'Those parts of the Constitution of Canada which are composed of statutory rules and common law rules are generically referred to as the law of the Constitution. In cases of doubt or dispute, it is the function of the Courts to declare what the law is and since the law is sometimes breached, it is generally the function of the Courts to ascertain whether it has in fact been breached in specific instances and, if so, to apply such sanctions as are contemplated by the law, whether they be punitive sanctions or civil sanctions such as a declaration of nullity. Thus, when a federal or a provincial statute is found by the Courts to be in excess of the legislative competence of the Legislature which has enacted it, it is declared null and void and the Courts refuse to give effect to it. In this sense it can be said that the law of the Constitution is administered or enforced by the Courts.

But many Canadians would perhaps be surprised to learn that important parts of the Constitution of Canada, with which they are the most familiar because they are directly involved when they exercise their right to vote at federal and provincial elections, are nowhere to be found in the law of the Constitution. For instance it is a fundamental requirement of the Constitution that if the Opposition obtains the majority at the polls, the Government must tender its resignation forthwith. But fundamental as it is, this requirement of the Constitution does not form part of the law of the Constitution . . .

Yet none of these essential rules of the Constitution can be said to be a law of the Constitution. It was apparently Dicey who . . . called them "the conventions of the constitution" . . . an expression which quickly became current. What Dicey described under these terms are the principles and rules of responsible government, several of which are stated above and which regulate the relations between the Crown, the Prime Minister, the Cabinet and the two Houses of Parliament. These rules developed in Great Britain by way of custom and precedent during the nineteenth century and were exported to such British colonies as were granted self government.

Dicey first gave the impression that constitutional conventions are a peculiarly British and modern phenomenon. But he later recognised . . . that different conventions are found in other constitutions. As Sir William Holdsworth wrote . . .: "In fact conventions must grow up at all times and in all places where the powers of government are vested in different persons or bodies – where in other words there is a mixed constitution . . . Necessarily conventional rules spring up to regulate the working of the various parts of the constitution, their relations to one another, and to the subject".

Within the British Empire, powers of government were vested in different bodies which provided a fertile ground for the growth of new constitutional conventions unknown to Dicey whereby self-governing colonies acquired equal and independent status within the Commonwealth. Many of these culminated in the Statute of Westminster, 1931 . . .

A federal constitution provides for the distribution of powers between various Legislatures and Governments and may also constitute a fertile ground for the growth of constitutional conventions between those Legislatures and Governments. It is conceivable for instance that usage and practice might give birth to conventions in Canada relating to the holding of federal–provincial conferences, the appointment of Lieutenant-Governors, the reservation and disallowance of provincial legislation ...

The main purpose of constitutional conventions is to ensure that the legal framework of the Constitution will be operated in accordance with the prevailing constitutional values or principles of the period . . .

Being based on custom and precedent, constitutional conventions are usually unwritten rules. Some of them, however, may be reduced to writing and expressed in the proceedings and documents of Imperial conferences, or in the preamble of statutes such as the Statute of Westminster, 1931, or in the proceedings and documents of federal–provincial conferences. They are often referred to and recognized in statements made by members of governments.

The conventional rules of the Constitution present one striking peculiarity. In contradistinction to the laws of the Constitution, they are not enforced by the Courts. One reason for this situation is that, unlike common law rules, conventions are not judge-made rules. They are not based on judicial precedents but on precedents established by the institutions of government themselves. Nor are they in the nature of statutory commands which it is the function and duty of the Courts to obey and enforce. Furthermore, to enforce them would mean to administer some formal sanction when they are breached. But the legal system from which they are distinct does not contemplate formal sanctions for their breach.

Perhaps the main reason why conventional rules cannot be enforced by the Courts is that they are generally in conflict with the legal rules which they postulate and the Courts are bound to enforce the legal rules. The conflict is not of a type which would entail the commission of any illegality. It results from the fact that legal rules create wide powers, discretions and rights which conventions prescribe should be exercised only in a certain limited manner, if at all . . .

This conflict between convention and law which prevents the Courts from enforcing conventions also prevents conventions from crystallizing into laws, unless it be by statutory adoption.

It is because the sanctions of convention rest with institutions of government other than Courts, such as the Governor General or the Lieutenant-Governor, or the Houses of Parliament, or with public opinion and ultimately, with the electorate that it is generally said that they are political.

We respectfully adopt the definition of a convention given by the learned Chief Justice of Manitoba, Freedman CJM . . . :

What is a constitutional convention? There is a fairly lengthy literature on the subject. Although there may be shades of difference among the constitutional lawyers, political scientists and Judges who have contributed to that literature, the essential features of a convention may be set forth with some degree of confidence. Thus there is general agreement that a convention occupies a position somewhere in between a usage or custom on the one hand and a constitutional law on the other. There is general agreement that if one sought to fix that position with greater precision he would place convention nearer to law than to usage or custom. There is also general agreement that "a convention is a rule which is regarded as obligatory by the officials to whom it applies", Hogg, *Constitutional Law of Canada* (1977). There is, if not general agreement, at least weighty authority, that the sanction for breach of a convention will be political rather than legal.

It should be borne in mind, however, that, while they are not laws, some conventions may be more important than some laws. Their importance depends on that of the value or principle which they are meant to safeguard. Also they form an integral part of the Constitution and of the constitutional system . . .

That is why it is perfectly appropriate to say that to violate a convention is to do something which is unconstitutional although it entails no direct legal consequence. But the words "constitutional" and "unconstitutional" may also be used in a strict legal sense, for instance with respect to a statute which is found *ultra vires* or unconstitutional. The foregoing may perhaps be summarized in an equation: constitutional conventions plus constitutional law equal the total Constitution of the country. [The court then considered whether the question should be answered. It concluded that it should and continued by asking if the convention existed.]

The requirements for establishing a convention bear some resemblance with those which apply to customary law. Precedents and usage are necessary but do not suffice. They must be normative. We adopt the following passage of Sir W. Ivor Jennings in *The Law and the Constitution* . . . "We have to ask ourselves three questions: first, what are the precedents; secondly, did the actors in the precedents believe that they were bound by a rule; and thirdly, is there a reason for the rule? A single precedent with a good reason may be enough to establish the rule. A whole string of precedents without such a reason will be of no avail, unless it is perfectly certain that the persons concerned regarded them as bound by it."

[After detailed consideration of 22 precedents where change to provincial legislative powers had occurred and, several others where, in the face of provincial opposition, proposed changes were not proceeded with, the court concluded that: a convention did exist although one which fell short of requiring unanimity; the court identified the 'actors' in the precedents and considered that they regarded themselves as bound by a convention that a substantial measure of provincial support was necessary; finally, the court identified the reason for the rule as being the maintenance of the federal structure of Canada. The court finally concluded:]

We have reached the conclusion that the agreement of the Provinces of Canada, no views being expressed as to its quantification, is constitutionally required for the passing of the "Proposed Resolution for a joint Address to Her Majesty respecting the Constitution of Canada" and that the passing of this Resolution without such agreement would be unconstitutional in the conventional sense.'

Comment

(1) In its role as a constitutional court the Supreme Court had jurisdiction to decide the extent of the convention, even if, by definition, conventions are unenforceable in law. No such role is permitted to any English court – see *Attorney-General* v *Jonathan Cape*, below.

(2) The conventions governing the relationship of the United Kingdom and Canada extended to both sides of the Atlantic. Thus, when a large majority of the Canadian Provinces agreed to redrafted proposals of the Federal government, these proposals were approved by the United Kingdom Parliament without demur, as convention demanded, in the shape of the Canada Act 1982 (as to which see *Manuel* v *Attorney-General*, p.60).

(3) For examples of conventions incorporated into statute see Statute of Westminster 1931 and the Northern Ireland Constitution Act 1971. The latter recognizes that the consent of the majority in Northern Ireland is required before Northern Ireland may cease to be part of the United Kingdom; whether this is binding in any formal legal sense must be doubted.

Attorney-General v *Jonathan Cape Ltd*

[1976] QB 752 · Queen's Bench Division

Mr Crossman kept diaries of cabinet matters during his period of office as a cabinet minister which it was his intention to publish during his lifetime but after leaving office. Mr Crossman died and his literary executors proposed that his diaries should be published as a book and serialized in *The Sunday Times* newspaper. It was proposed that publication should take place without fulfilling the requirements of informal rules governing the publication of such material. The Attorney-General sought an injunction prohibiting publication in either form. The court held that there was a convention governing collective cabinet responsibility and that in appropriate instances publication might be restrained by the application to that convention of the equitable doctrine of confidentiality. However, on the facts, an injunction was refused since the public interest did not require that publication should be restrained.

Lord Widgery CJ: 'It has always been assumed by lawyers and, I suspect, by politicians, and the Civil Service, that Cabinet proceedings and Cabinet papers are secret, and cannot be publicly disclosed until they have passed into history. It is quite clear that no court will compel the production of Cabinet papers in the course of discovery in an action, and the Attorney-General contends that not only will the court refuse to compel the production of such matters, but it will go further and positively forbid the disclosure of such papers and proceedings if publication will be contrary to the public interest.

The basis of this contention is the confidential character of these papers and proceedings, derived from the convention of joint Cabinet responsibility whereby any policy decision reached by the Cabinet has to be supported thereafter by all members of the Cabinet whether they approve of it or not, unless they feel compelled to resign. It is contended that Cabinet decisions and papers are confidential for a period to the extent at least that they must not be referred to outside the Cabinet in such a way as to disclose the attitude of individual Ministers in the argument which preceded the decision. Thus, there may be no objection to a Minister disclosing (or leaking, as it was called) the fact that a Cabinet meeting has taken place, or, indeed, the decision taken, so long as the individual views of Ministers are not identified ... If the Attorney-General were restricted in his argument to the general proposition that Cabinet papers and discussion are all under the seal of secrecy at all times, he would be in difficulty. It is true that he has called evidence from eminent former holders of office to the effect that the public interest requires a continuing secrecy, and he cites a powerful passage from the late Viscount Hailsham to this effect . . .

The defendants . . . have also called distinguished former Cabinet Ministers who do not support this view of Lord Hailsham, and it seems to me that the degree of protection afforded to Cabinet papers and discussion cannot be determined by a single rule of thumb. Some secrets require a high standard of protection for a short time. Others require protection until a new political generation has taken over. In the present action . . . the Attorney-General asks for a perpetual injunction to restrain further publication of the Diaries in whole or in part. I am far from convinced that he has made out a case that the public interest requires such a Draconian remedy when due regard is had to other public interests, such as the freedom of speech . . .

I have read affidavits from a large number of leading politicians, and the facts, so far as relevant, appear to be these. In 1964, 1966 and 1969 the Prime Minister . . . issued a confidential document to Cabinet Ministers containing guidance on certain questions of procedure. Paragraph 72 of the 1969 edition provides: "The principle of collective responsibility and the obligation not to disclose information acquired whilst holding Ministerial office apply to former Ministers who are contemplating the publication of material based upon their recollections of the conduct of Cabinet and Cabinet committee business in which they took part."

The general understanding of Ministers while in office was that information obtained from Cabinet sources was secret and not to be disclosed to outsiders.

There is not much evidence of the understanding of Ministers as to the protection of such information after the Minister retires. It seems probable to me that those not desirous of publishing memoirs assumed that the protection went on until the incident was 30 years old, whereas those interested in memoirs would discover on inquiry at the Cabinet Office that draft memoirs were normally submitted to the Secretary of the Cabinet for his advice on their contents before publication. Manuscripts were almost always submitted to the Secretary of the Cabinet in accordance with the last-mentioned procedure. Sir Winston Churchill submitted the whole of his manuscripts concerned with the war years, and accepted the advice given by the Secretary of the Cabinet as to publication.

In recent years, successive Secretaries of the Cabinet, when giving advice on the publication of a Minister's memoirs, were much concerned about (a) disclosure of individual views of Members of the Cabinet in defiance of the principle of joint responsibility; (b) disclosure of advice given by civil servants still in office; (c) disclosure of discussions relating to the promotion or transfer of senior civil servants.

Mr Crossman . . . disapproved of the submission of manuscripts to the Secretary of the Cabinet. He made no attempt to admit the three categories of information just referred to, and expressed the intention to obtain publication whilst memories were green.

Mr Crossman made no secret of the fact that he kept a diary which he intended to use for the writing of his memoirs. It was contended on behalf of the literary executors that any bond of confidence or secrecy normally attending upon Cabinet material had been lifted in Mr. Crossman's case by consent of his colleagues. Even if, as a matter of law, a Minister can release himself from a bond of secrecy in this way, I do not find that Mr. Crossman effectively did so. It is not enough to show that his colleagues accepted the keeping of the diary. It was vital to show that they accepted Mr Crossman's intention to use the diary whether it passed the scrutiny of the Secretary of the Cabinet or not ... I have already indicated some of the difficulties which face the Attorney-General when he relied simply on the public interest as a ground for this action. That such ground is enough in extreme cases is shown by the universal agreement that publication affecting national security can be restrained in this way. It may be that in the short run (for example, over a period of weeks or months) the public interest is equally compelling to maintain joint Cabinet responsibility and the protection of advice given by civil servants, but I would not accept without close investigation that such matters must, as a matter of course, retain protection after a period of years.

However, the Attorney-General has a powerful reinforcement for his argument in the developing equitable doctrine that a man shall not profit from the wrongful publication of information received by him in confidence. This doctrine, said to have its origin in *Prince Albert* v *Strange*, has been frequently recognised as a ground for restraining the unfair use of commercial secrets transmitted in confidence. Sometimes in these cases there is a contract which may be said to have been breached by the breach of confidence, but it is clear that the doctrine applies independently of contract ... [I]n *Coco* v *AN Clark (Engineers) Ltd* Megarry J ... said: "In my judgement three elements are normally required if, apart from contract, a case of breach of confidence is to succeed. First, the information itself, in the words of Lord Greene MR ... must 'have the necessary quality of confidence about it.' Secondly, that information must have been imparted in circumstances importing an obligation of confidence. Thirdly, there must be an unauthorised use of that information to the detriment of the party communicating it."

It is not until the decision in *Argyll* v *Argyll*, that the same principle was applied to domestic secrets such as those passing between husband and wife during the marriage. It was there held by Ungoed-Thomas J. that the plaintiff wife could obtain an order to restrain the defendant husband from communicating such secrets ... This extension of the doctrine of confidence beyond commercial secrets has never been directly challenged ... I am sure that I ought to regard myself ... as bound by the decision of Ungoed-Thomas J.

Even so, these defendants argue that an extension of the principle of the Argyll case to the present dispute involves another large and unjustified leap forward, because in the present case the Attorney-General is seeking to apply the principle to public secrets made confidential in the interests of good government. I cannot see why the courts should be powerless to restrain the publication of public secrets, while enjoying the Argyll powers in regard to domestic secrets. Indeed, as already pointed out, the court must have power to deal with publication which threatens national security, and the difference between such a case and the present case is one of degree rather than kind. I conclude, therefore, that when a Cabinet Minister receives information in confidence the improper publication of such information can be restrained by the court, and his obligation is not merely to observe a gentleman's agreement to refrain from publication.

It is convenient next to deal with [the] third submission, namely, that the evidence does not prove the existence of a convention as to collective responsibility, or adequately define a sphere of secrecy. I find overwhelming evidence that the doctrine of joint responsibility is generally understood and practised and equally strong evidence that it is on occasion ignored. The general effect of the evidence is that the doctrine is an established feature of the English form of government, and it follows that some matters leading up to a Cabinet decision may be regarded as confidential. Furthermore, I am persuaded that the nature of the confidence is that spoken for by the Attorney-General, namely, that since the confidence is imposed to enable the efficient conduct of the Queen's business, the confidence is owed to the Queen and cannot be released by the members of Cabinet themselves. I have been told that a resigning Minister who wishes to make a personal statement in the House, and to disclose matters which are confidential under the doctrine obtains the consent of the Queen for this purpose. Such consent is obtained through the Prime Minister. I have not been told what happened when the Cabinet disclosed divided opinions during the European Economic Community referendum. But even if there was here a breach of confidence (which I doubt) this is no ground for denying the existence of the general rule. I cannot accept the suggestion that a Minister owes no duty of confidence in respect of his own views expressed in Cabinet. It would only need one or two Ministers to describe their own views to enable experienced observers to identify the views of others . . .

The Cabinet is at the very centre of national affairs, and must be in possession at all times of information which is secret or confidential. Secrets relating to national security may require to be preserved indefinitely. Secrets relating to new taxation proposals may be of the highest importance until Budget day, but public knowledge thereafter. To leak a Cabinet decision a day or so before it is officially announced is an accepted exercise in public relations, but to identify the Ministers who voted one way or another is objectionable because it undermines the doctrine of joint responsibility.

It is evident that there cannot be a single rule governing the publication of such a variety of matters. In these actions we are concerned with the publication of diaries at a time when 11 years have expired since the first recorded events. The Attorney-General must show (a) that such publication would be a breach of confidence; (b) that the public interest requires that the publication be restrained; and (c) that there are no other facts of the public interest contradictory of and more compelling than that relied upon. Moreover, the court, when asked to restrain such a publication, must closely examine the extent to which relief is necessary to ensure that restrictions are not imposed beyond the strict requirement of public need.

Applying those principles to the present case, what do we find? In my judgment, the Attorney-General has made out his claim that the expression of individual opinions by Cabinet Ministers in the course of Cabinet discussion are matters of confidence, the publication of which can be restrained by the court when this is clearly necessary in the public interest.

The maintenance of the doctrine of joint responsibility within the Cabinet is in the public interest, and the application of that doctrine might be prejudiced by premature disclosure of the views of individual Ministers.

There must, however, be a limit in time after which the confidential character of the information, and the duty of the court to restrain publication, will lapse. Since the conclusion of the hearing in this case I have had the opportunity to read the whole of volume one of the Diaries, and my considered view is that I cannot believe that the publication at this interval of anything in volume one would inhibit free discussion in the Cabinet of today, even though the individuals involved are the same, and the national problems have a distressing similarity with those of a decade ago. It is unnecessary to elaborate the evils which might flow if at the close of a Cabinet meeting a Minister proceeded to give the press an analysis of the voting, but we are dealing in this case with a disclosure of information nearly 10 years later.

It may, of course, be intensely difficult in a particular case, to say at what point the material loses its confidential character, on the ground that publication will no longer undermine the doctrine of joint Cabinet responsibility. It is this difficulty which prompts some to argue that Cabinet discussions should retain their confidential character for a longer and arbitrary period such as 30 years, or even for all time, but this seems to me to be excessively restrictive. The court should intervene only in the clearest of cases where the continuing confidentiality of the material can be demonstrated. In less clear cases – and this, in my view, is certainly one – reliance must be placed on the good sense and good taste of the Minister or ex-Minister concerned . . .'

Comment

(1) The Attorney-General had to demonstrate that the publication should be restrained in the public interest, that there were no other public interest issues of greater importance and that any restriction was only to the extent strictly required by that public necessity. The ordinary litigant trying to protect confidential information would not be faced with such obstacles. The Attorney-General failed because by the time of the case the material had lost its confidential nature since the convention could not be said to be damaged by the opening up of those particular materials to the public gaze. But the result might have been different had the material been of a different nature or if the publication had been threatened at an earlier stage. For a further discussion, see p.161.

(2) The case concerns an insider trying to publish material; what of an outsider trying to gain access to government material? Openness of government, including local government, is desirable but access is governed by a multitude of piecemeal statutes which form no comprehensive whole – see, e.g., Local Government (Access to Information) Act 1985. Where the outsider is a litigant who needs access to government papers to support his case, even if the 'government' is not a party to the litigation, then he is faced with other difficulties – see public interest immunity, p.348.

(3) For other examples of conventions influencing judicial decisions see *R* v *Secretary of State for Home Department, ex parte Hosenball* where the court relaxed the rules of natural justice relying in part on the responsibility of the minister to answer for his actions on a matter of national security before the House of Commons, cf. *Liversidge* v *Anderson*, p.12. In the *GCHQ* case (p.215) the House of Lords recognized the practical political reality that although prerogative power is legally vested in the Crown it is exercised in accordance with convention by the Crown's ministers; accordingly, the Court should recognize that reality when considering whether to change its attitude to the reviewability of the exercise of the prerogative. See also the principle in *Carltona* v *Commissioner for Works* which depends upon the convention of ministerial responsibility.

4 The Royal Prerogative

The Royal Prerogative amounts to the residue of the Crown's unique common law powers, traditionally those powers which were above and beyond those shared with other legal persons. They are residual because it has long since been recognized that the Crown cannot create new prerogative powers and that statute can curtail prerogative powers. The Royal Prerogative was defined by Blackstone as: 'that special pre-eminence which the King hath, over and above all other persons, and out of the ordinary course of the common law, in right of his regal dignity'. Dicey regarded it as: 'the residue of discretionary or arbitrary authority, which at any given time is legally left in the hands of the Crown.'

Blackstone tends to suggest a stricter view of what can properly be said to be prerogative, but recent judicial authority has tended to cite Dicey with approval. The distinction is important in the context of the potential for judicial review of the exercise of prerogative powers but recent cases suggest that the courts favour a test of reviewability based upon the nature of the function rather than on the strict identification of a power (see p.215).

The history of the prerogative illustrates the struggle for power within the United Kingdom between the Crown and Parliament. The *Case of Prohibitions* established that certain prerogatives were exercisable only through the courts; the power of the Monarch to judge in his own courts was delegated irretrievably to the courts. The *Case of Proclamations* confirmed that the King might encourage subjects to keep laws but that he might not make laws generally by way of proclamation. It also decided that whether or not a prerogative exists is a matter for the courts and not for the Crown. To have decided otherwise would have been to have made the Crown the judge of its own power.

One issue has only recently been resolved. The traditional view had been that the court would decide the precise scope and extent of the prerogative, in the same way as it decides what any rule of the common law is – see *Burmah Oil* v *Lord Advocate* (p.53), *Attorney-General* v *De Keyser's Royal Hotel* (p.51) and *R* v *Secretary of State for the Home Department, ex parte*

Northumbria Police Authority (p.55). But, was it permissible for the Courts to enquire into the mode of exercise of the particular prerogative power? The traditional view was that this was not a matter into which the courts might properly enquire – see, e.g., *Case of Saltpetre, Bates' Case, Darnell's Case* and the *Case of Shipmoney*. The effect of these early cases was that once a prerogative power was found to exist then the Crown's exercise of it, together with any assertion that what was done was done for the purposes of the prerogative power, were unchallengeable in the Courts. Despite *dicta* to the contrary in *Laker Airways* v *Department of Trade* (p.57) this view prevailed until 1984 – see the *GCHQ* case (p.215), when it was decided that, providing the subject matter of the particular prerogative power is suitable for judicial review, then its exercise may be reviewed.

Attorney-General v De Keyser's Royal Hotel

[1920] AC 508 · House of Lords

The War Office took over hotel premises for the purposes of housing military personnel and purported to act under statutory powers which gave the owners a right to compensation. At a later date the War Office claimed to have acted under the Royal Prerogative which (in the view of their lordships) gave the owners no automatic right to compensation but simply the possibility of applying to a specially created commission for an ex gratia payment. The commission's jurisdiction extended only to cases where compensation was 'not otherwise provided for'. The owners, the 'suppliants', submitted a Petition of Right claiming compensation as of right under the terms of the Act. The House of Lords decided that the War Office had been expressly acting under the terms of the legislation, which granted very wide and unchallengeable powers, and accordingly the suppliants were entitled to compensation under that legislation. The House of Lords went on to examine the question of whether or not the Crown could have chosen to act under the Royal Prerogative instead of the Act if it had so wished. The House of Lords analysed the scope of the Royal Prerogative to seize property in an emergency in defence of the realm, and the effect of the legislation upon this prerogative. It concluded that where the subject matter of an Act was coincident with the subject matter of the prerogative then the latter must yield to the former in the absence of express provision.

Lord Dunedin: '. . . Inasmuch as the Crown is a party to every Act of Parliament it is logical enough to consider that when the Act deals with something which before the Act could be effected by the prerogative, and specially empowers the Crown to do the same thing, but subject to conditions, the Crown assents to that, and by that Act, to the prerogative being curtailed . . .'

Lord Atkinson: '. . . It is quite obvious that it would be useless and meaningless for the legislature to impose restrictions and limitations upon, and to attach conditions to, the exercise by the Crown of the powers conferred by a statute, if the Crown were free at its pleasure to disregard these provisions, and by virtue of its prerogative do the very thing the statutes empowered it to do. One cannot in the construction of a statute attribute to the legislature (in the absence of compelling words) an intention so absurd. It was suggested that when a statute is passed empowering the Crown to do a certain thing which it might theretofore have done by virtue of its prerogative, the prerogative is merged in the statute. I confess I do not think the word "merged" is happily chosen. I should prefer to say that when such a statute, expressing the will and intention of the King and of the three estates of the realm, is passed, it abridges the Royal Prerogative while it is a force to this extent: that the Crown can only do the particular thing under and in accordance with the statutory provisions, and that its prerogative power to do that thing is in abeyance. Whichever mode of expression be used, the result intended to be indicated is, I think, the same – namely, that after the statute has been passed, and while it is in force, the thing it empowers the Crown to do can thenceforth only be done by and under the statute, and subject to all the limitations, restrictions and conditions by it imposed, however unrestricted the Royal Prerogative may theretofore have been . . .'

Lord Parmoor: '. . . The constitutional principle is that when the power of the executive to interfere with the property or liberty of subjects has been placed under Parliamentary control, and directly regulated by statute, the executive no longer derives its authority from the Royal Prerogative of the Crown but from Parliament, and that in exercising such authority the executive is bound to observe the restrictions which Parliament has imposed in favour of the subject. I think that the statutory provisions applicable to the interference by the executive with the land and buildings of the respondents bring the case within the above principle. It would be an untenable proposition to suggest that courts of law could disregard the protective restrictions imposed by statute law where they are applicable. In this respect the sovereignty of Parliament is supreme. The principles of construction to be applied in deciding whether the Royal Prerogative has been taken away or abridged are well ascertained. It may be taken away or abridged by express words, by necessary implication, or, as stated in Bacon's Abridgement, where an Act of Parliament is made for the public good, the advancement of religion and justice, and to prevent injury and wrong . . . I am further of opinion that where a matter has been directly regulated by statute there is a necessary implication that the statutory regulation must be obeyed, and that as far as such regulation is inconsistent with the claim of a Royal Prerogative right, such right can no longer be enforced . . .'

Comment

Doubts remain as to the exact effect of any relevant statutory measure upon the Royal Prerogative, but it is quite clear that the executive is precluded, whilst the Act is in force, from referring back to the prerogative. Thus, if the executive wishes to maintain a particular prerogative power it should ensure that Parliament legislates in an appropriate fashion so that the particular prerogative power is not put into abeyance – see, e.g., Immigration Act 1971.

Burmah Oil v *Lord Advocate*

[1965] AC 75 · House of Lords

The British Government ordered the destruction of the company's oil installations in order to stop them falling into enemy hands. Despite receiving an ex gratia payment the company sought compensation and the House of Lords had to decide on the scope of the prerogative power relied on by the Crown. In particular, it had to decide whether compensation was payable in respect of property taken or destroyed in time of war in order to deny its use to the enemy, other than battle damage, i.e. accidental or deliberate damage done in the course of fighting operations e.g. to hamper the enemy's advance. By a majority of 3:2 the House of Lords held that compensation was payable, although the basis of compensation was left open.

Lord Reid: ' . . . What we have to determine in this case is whether or when, in a case not covered by any statute, property can be taken by virtue of the prerogative without any compensation. That could only be an exceptional case, because it would be impracticable to conduct a modern war by use of the prerogative alone, whether or not compensation was paid. The mobilization of the industrial and financial resources of the country could not be done without statutory emergency powers. The prerogative is really a relic of a past age, not lost by disuse, but only available for a case not covered by statute. So I would think the proper approach is a historical one; how was it used in former times and how has it been used in modern times? As regards modern times, extensive investigation in connection with the *De Keyser* case failed to disclose a single instance of taking or interfering with land without payment . . . Negative evidence may not amount to proof, but it is so strong that I would hold it established that prerogative was never used or attempted to be used in that way in modern times before 1914.

As regards earlier times I think that the *Shipmoney Case* deserves rather more consideration than it received in the *De Keyser* case or than it has received in this case . . . Without further investigation I would not rely too much on this case, but it does seem to indicate that, even at the zenith of the Royal Prerogative, no one thought that there was any general rule that the prerogative could be exercised, even in times of war or imminent danger, by taking property required for defence without making any payment for it . . . '

Comment

(1)   The specific point was reversed by the War Damage Act 1965. The case remains important as an example of the traditional approach of the courts to the identification of prerogative powers.

(2)   In *BBC* v *Johns* Diplock LJ observed that 'it is 350 years and a civil war too late for the Queen's courts to broaden the prerogative. The limits within which the executive government may impose obligations or restraints on citizens of the United Kingdom without any statutory authority are now well settled and incapable of extension.' A distinction has to be drawn between the identification of a particular prerogative and the means adopted for its implementation (see *R* v

Secretary of State for the Home Department, ex parte Northumbria Police Authority, p.55).

(3) *R* v *Secretary of State for the Home Department, ex parte Fire Brigades' Union* concerned the Criminal Injuries Compensation Scheme created by exercise of the royal prerogative (see *R* v *Criminal Injuries Compensation Board, ex parte Lain*). The Criminal Justice Act 1988, ss.108–117, had placed that particular scheme on a statutory footing and the Secretary of State had power under s.171 to bring those sections into force but had so far decided not to do so. Instead, he chose to exercise the prerogative power in such a way as to create a new scheme based on radically different principles.

The Court of Appeal, Hobhouse and Morritt LJJ, Bingham MR dissenting on that point, held that the discretion to implement the Act was not open to review. Bingham MR held that it was open to review but that it had not been shown that the discretion had been exercised improperly. The Court of Appeal, Bingham MR and Morritt LJ, Hobhouse LJ dissenting, went on to hold that the prerogative had been fettered to the extent that it was inconsistent with the will of Parliament as expressed by the Criminal Justice Act. *Laker Airways* (p.57) and *De Keyser's Royal Hotel* were not authorities directly on the particular point since they had involved Acts which had been brought into force. Bingham MR observed that:

'. . . the Home Secretary's argument gives too little weight to the overriding legislative role of Parliament. It has approved detailed provisions governing the form which, underpinned by statute, the scheme would take. Sections 108–117 and schs 6 and 7 are not a discussion paper but a blueprint approved in the most solemn form for which our constitution provides. It was, of course, open to the Home Secretary to invite Parliament to repeal those provisions . . . if the 1988 provisions were simply repealed he could have exercised his prerogative powers to introduce the tariff scheme, the field then being once more unoccupied by statute. What in my judgment he could not lawfully do, so long as the 1988 provisions stood unrepealed as an enduring statement of Parliament's will, was to exercise prerogative powers to introduce a scheme radically different from what Parliament had authorised . . .

Morritt LJ emphasised the role of s. 171, which was in force:

. . . it seems to me immaterial that ss.108–117 and schs 6 and 7 have not been brought into force and that the Secretary of State is under no statutory duty to do so. The essence of the principle is that Parliament should, by statute, have empowered the Crown to Act in the same field as that in which it is claimed that the prerogative power still exists. In my judgment that principle is satisfied even though it takes the unusual form of a discretionary statutory power conferred on the Crown to bring the statutory provisions into force . . . it seems to me that the prerogative continues to warrant the old scheme . . . but cannot continue so as to justify the introduction of a new scheme which is wholly inconsistent with those statutory provisions . . .

R v *Secretary of State for the Home Department, ex parte Northumbria Police Authority*

[1988] 2 WLR 590 · Court of Appeal

The Home Secretary issued a Circular to the effect that certain types of riot control equipment would be made available to Chief Officers of Police and that such equipment would be obtainable from a central store. The normal course of events would be that the Chief Officer would purchase the equipment with the approval of his Police Authority. In the event that the Police Authority would not permit this then para. 4 of the Circular provided that it would be possible for the Chief Officer to obtain the equipment from the central store direct and without the approval of the Police Authority. Section 4(4) of the Police Act 1964 authorized the Police Authority to maintain vehicles, apparatus and other equipment as required for police purposes. Section 41 authorized the Secretary of State to provide and maintain such things as forensic science laboratories and such other organizations and services as he considered necessary and expedient for promoting the efficiency of the police.

The Court of Appeal held that (a) as a matter of construction, s.41 did authorize the Home Secretary to supply the equipment from the central store without the approval of the Police Authority, as described in para. 4 of the circular; and (b) even assuming that s.41 did not have that effect, s.4 did not grant, either expressly or impliedly, the Police Authority a monopoly to the exclusion of the Royal Prerogative power, accordingly s.4 did not restrict the power of the Royal Prerogative.

Purchas LJ: 'My judgment on the issues relating to the Act is sufficient to dispose of this appeal. I will, however, add some words of my own on the issue relating to Royal prerogative . . . I find this a more difficult topic. As I have already said . . . the Act is mainly a consolidating Act and does not, in my judgment affect any prerogative power otherwise enjoyed by the Crown any more than any of the enactments in whose place it now stands . . . The continued existence of prerogative has never been questioned. Indeed the police authority conceded that it still exists in the case of national emergency – although as a concept this was difficult to define beyond the obvious extremes of war or threat of war, civil or otherwise. So far as I know, it has never been suggested that in assenting to any of the enactments referred to in this judgment the Monarch has in any way derogated from the Royal prerogative to maintain the peace of the realm . . . one must distinguish between the existence of the prerogative and the machinery set up to enable the expeditious and efficient use of that prerogative. Thus it was seen in *R v Pinney* the magistrate was called on to act in accordance with his duties to preserve the peace. It was held that he sufficiently discharged this duty by calling on the armed forces, and constables and by appointing special constables. Having done this the manner in which those whom he marshalled discharged their respective duties, was no concern of the magistrate – but at no point was the existence of the prerogative of keeping the King's peace as the origin of the resulting duties and powers put in question . . . I am unaware that the statutory provisions for organising the police or their predecessors the constables or custodians of the law or for appointing commissions for the appointment of justices in the Statute of Winchester or the many subsequent Acts of Parliament, have in any way eroded or derogated from the prerogative in the Crown to protect the peace of the realm. [After extensive citation from *Attorney-General v De Keyser's*

Royal Hotel Ltd he continued:]

These speeches are authority for the proposition that where the Crown has assented to statutory rights of compensation to the subject of expropriation in a national emergency, then the Crown cannot use prerogative powers to avoid its statutory liability to pay such compensation . . . In *Attorney-General* v *De Keyser's Royal Hotel* and *Burmah Oil Co. Ltd* v *Lord Advocate*, the courts were dealing with the purported exercise of the war or defence prerogative to avoid a liability to compensate the subject. As Lord Reid pointed out in the *Burmah Oil* case . . . the exercise of the prerogative in the circumstances must be rare because, in recent times, powers to requisition were available under the emergency legislation. It is well established that the courts will intervene to prevent executive action under prerogative powers in violation of property or other rights of the individual where this is inconsistent with statutory provisions providing for the same executive action. Where the executive action is directed towards the benefit or protection of the individual, it is unlikely that its use will attract the intervention of the courts. In my judgment, before the courts will hold that such executive action is contrary to legislation, express and unequivocal terms must be found in the statute which deprive the individual from receiving the benefit or protection intended by the exercise of prerogative power.

In the present case the Secretary of State contended that if he does not have the power to make equipment available to police forces under the Act, he must have this power under the Royal Prerogative for the purpose of promoting the efficiency of the police. In order to dispute this the police authority had to contend that the combined effect of ss.4(1)(4) and 41 is to prevent the Secretary of State from supplying equipment unless it is requested by the police authority. These sections have already been considered in this judgment. Even if I am not justified in holding that these sections afford positive statutory authority for the supply of equipment, they must fall short of an express and unequivocal inhibition sufficient to abridge the prerogative powers, otherwise available to the Secretary of State, to do all that is reasonably necessary to preserve the peace of the realm.

[The Appellant] referred us to Chitty's *Prerogatives of the Crown* (1820) for the purposes of demonstrating that there was then no recognisable "prerogative to provide or equip a police force." With respect . . . this argument begs the question. One is not seeking a prerogative right to do this. The prerogative power is to do all that is reasonably necessary to keep the Queen's peace. This involves the commissioning of justices of the peace, constables and the like. The author clearly identifies the prerogative powers inherent in the Crown in relation to the duty placed on the Sovereign to protect his dominions and subjects . . . [and] turns to the question of the protection of the realm . . . "The duties arising from the relation of sovereign and subject are reciprocal. Protection, that is, the security and governance of his dominions according to law, is the duty of the sovereign; and allegiance and subjection, with reference to the same criterion, the constitution and laws of the country, form, in return, the duty of the governed, as will be more fully noticed hereafter. We have already partially mentioned this duty of the sovereign, and have observed that the prerogatives are vested in him for the benefit of his subjects, and that His Majesty is under, and not above, the laws." . . .

The passing of the Act did nothing to affect the duties and powers of police constables including chief officers of police forces. In my judgment, the prerogative powers to take all reasonable steps to preserve the Queen's peace remain unaffected by the Act and these include the supply of equipment to police forces which is reasonably required for the more efficient discharge of their duties . . .'

Comment

(1) For the relationship of police authorities and chief officers, see p.364.

(2) In *Laker Airways* v *Department of Trade*, Laker Airways had been granted a licence by the Civil Aviation Authority, which operated a statutory scheme, to run a service to the United States of America. In pursuance of the Bermuda Treaty the government had nominated Laker Airways as a designated carrier thus entitling them to land in the United States subject only to the approval of the President. As a result of a change of government, and thus government policy, the current Secretary of State sought to prevent the service operating by purporting to use the statutory machinery. Under the relevant Act he issued 'guidance' requiring the CAA to withdraw the licence in circumstances which Laker Airways said did not fall within the ambit of the Act. The Secretary of State also claimed that in performance of the prerogative he could withdraw the designation of Laker Airways under the Bermuda Treaty. The majority of the Court of Appeal (Roskill and Lawton LJJ) adopted the approach in *De Keyser* and held that the statutory scheme had by necessary implication fettered the prerogative power of the Crown under the Treaty. Further, the exercise of the statutory power itself had been *ultra vires* since the terms of the 'guidance' amounted to the giving of 'directions' and the criteria in the Act for the issuing of directions had not been made out by the Secretary of State.

Lord Denning took a radical view and considered that 'seeing that the prerogative is a discretionary power to be exercised for the public good, it follows that its exercise can be examined by the courts just as any other discretionary power which is vested in the executive . . . [W]hen discretionary powers are entrusted to the executive by statute, the courts can examine the exercise of those powers to see that they are used properly, and not improperly or mistakenly. By "mistakenly" I mean under the influence of a misdirection in fact or in law. Likewise it seems to me that when discretionary powers are entrusted to the executive by the prerogative – in pursuance of the treaty-making power – the courts can examine the exercise of them so as to see that they are not used improperly or mistakenly . . .'. Compare the approach adopted by Lord Fraser in the *GCHQ* case, p.216.

(3) Lord Denning's approach in *Laker Airways* was described as 'too wide' by Lord Roskill in the *GCHQ* case where, nonetheless, the House of Lords did develop the power to challenge the exercise of the Royal Prerogative – see p.217. In the light of the *GCHQ* case, once the precise scope of the particular prerogative power has been identified, the questions for a court will be threefold: (a) is this particular prerogative power susceptible to judicial review; (b) if so, what grounds of review are appropriate to that particular exercise of the prerogative; (c) if review is undertaken, are there features which will persuade the court to discontinue its review?

(4)   Even though the role of the courts in identifying prerogative powers, and the extent of any overlap with statutory powers, remain, the development in *R* v *Panel on Takeovers and Mergers, ex parte Datafin* (see p.224), and the willingness of the courts to review judicially the exercise of a wide range of bodies, means that definitions are now less important. Thus, in the *Datafin* case the court alluded to the vagueness of the definition of prerogative powers and preferred to look at the nature of the duty imposed rather than the nature of the power.

R v *Secretary of State for Foreign & Commonwealth Affairs, ex parte Rees Mogg*

[1994] 1 All ER 457 · Divisional Court

The applicant sought, by way of judicial review, an order of certiorari to quash the decision by the Foreign Secretary to ratify the Treaty on European Union, an order of prohibition to prevent him from proceeding to ratify that treaty, and a declaration that such ratification would be unlawful. That application was based upon three grounds, the first two of which turned upon the decision by the United Kingdom Government not to adopt the Protocol on Social Policy in the Maastricht treaty. The third ground was that the Treaty on European Union amounted to a transfer of the royal prerogative to community institutions without statutory authority. The applications were dismissed.

Lloyd LJ: ' . . . Title V of the Union treaty establishes a common foreign and security policy among the member states . . . Title V is not, of course included in s.1(1) [of the European Communities (Amendment) Act 1993], since it is an inter-governmental agreement, which could have no impact on United Kingdom domestic law. The arguments advanced [by counsel for the applicant] are therefore of a very different nature from the arguments so far considered. By English common law, the Crown is, he says, incapable of abandoning, or transferring, any of its ancient prerogative powers, without statutory enactment. In support of his general proposition, [counsel] quotes a number of old authorities, starting with the *King's Prerogative in Saltpetre* (1606) . . . [counsel] submits that . . . the effect of Title V of the Union Treaty is, or will be, that the Crown has transferred its prerogative power in relation to foreign policy, security, and ultimately defence, to the Council without statutory enactment . . .

[Counsel for the respondent's] first answer is that the questions under this head are simply not justiciable in the English courts. A similar point arose in *Blackburn v Att-Gen* . . . The authority of *Blackburn* v *Att-Gen* has recently been confirmed by the House of Lords in *Maclaine Watson & Co* v *Department of Trade and Industry* . . . [Counsel for the respondents] submits that what was true in 1971 before the EEC Treaty was signed is as true today in relation to Title V of the Union Treaty. Since no question of domestic law is involved, the court has no jurisdiction even to consider the questions raised by [counsel for the applicant] . . .

[Counsel for the applicant] pointed out that the principle of non justiciability is not universal and absolute. There are exceptions. Thus it is clear from s.6 [of the European Elections Act 1978] that the court would be entitled, and indeed bound, if required, to consider whether any treaty which the government proposed to ratify involved an increase in the powers of the European Parliament . . .

Similarly in *ex parte Molyneaux* Taylor J considered the text of the intergovernmental conference established between the government of the United Kingdom and the government of the Republic of Ireland in November 1985 to see if it contravened any statute or rule of common law, or any constitutional convention. He held that it did not.

So we will assume . . . that we are entitled to consider the questions raised . . . We will also assume (what was not in dispute) that the government could not lawfully transfer any part of the crown's prerogative powers in relation to foreign affairs without statutory enactment. Where does that take us? . . . Even if one reads Title V with an eye most favourable [to the appellant] it cannot be regarded as a transfer of prerogative powers. [It] does not entail an abandonment or transfer of prerogative powers, but an exercise of those power. So far as we know, nobody has ever suggested that the Charter of the United Nations, for example, or of the North Atlantic Treaty Organisation, involves a transfer of prerogative powers. Title V should be read in the same light. In the last resort . . . it would presumably be open to the Government to denounce the Union Treaty, or at least to fail to comply with its international obligations under Title V . . . '.

Comment

For *Blackburn v Att-Gen* see p.81. The court rejected the suggested description that the case was 'the most important constitutional case for 300 years', but it was careful to restrict its enquiries to the legality of government action and did not consider the proceedings in Parliament – compare *R v HM Treasury, ex parte Smedley*, p.27. The court also applied the principle in *Att-Gen v De Keyser's Royal Hotel Ltd* and held that s.6, European Parliamentary Elections Act 1978, had not restricted the Crown's prerogative to alter or add to the EEC Treaty, and that in any event the Protocol on Social Policy was technically not a treaty within s.2(1) of the European Communities Act 1972 and thus was incapable of altering United Kingdom law.

5 Legislative supremacy of Parliament

The meaning of 'the legislative supremacy of Parliament' has already been seen (p.4). By 'Parliament' we mean the Monarch acting with the House of Commons and the House of Lords, subject to the Parliament Acts 1911–1949 (p.66). There are no limits to the subject matter upon which Parliament may legislate, nor can any other body override or set aside that legislation. According to the doctrine, Parliament cannot legislate to fetter this legislative omnicompetence, nor can it successfully impose procedural restrictions. Whilst the doctrine has been recognized and discussed by the courts, its foundation is not purely legal. It reflects the political and constitutional realities that fundamental power in the British constitution is conceded by the courts to Parliament. This proposition is still true although significant inroads into the doctrine have been made since membership of the European Community.

Manuel v *Attorney-General*

[1983] Ch 77 · Court of Appeal

In order to achieve total independence (patriation) the Senate and the House of Commons of Canada requested the Queen to lay a Bill before the United Kingdom Parliament. That Bill would amend the constitution of Canada so that the United Kingdom would have no further part to play in that constitution. The Bill became the Canada Act 1982 and Canadian Indian Chiefs sought a declaration that the Act was *ultra vires*. The basis of the claim was that the Act removed the entrenchment of certain protective provisions of an earlier Act. Although the substantive rights were not affected by the 1982 Act the protection afforded to such rights was diminished.

It was held at first instance in the Chancery Division that the doctrine of the legislative supremacy of Parliament applied and that since the 1982 Act was undoubtedly an Act of Parliament it was applicable to Canada. The Court of Appeal held that even if it was accepted that one Parliament could legally restrict the scope of a successor's legislative power by imposing a procedural requirement, nonetheless the successor Parliament in this case had complied with the procedure laid down in the earlier Act. The following extract is from the Chancery Division only.

Megarry V-C: 'On the face of it, a contention that an Act of Parliament is *ultra vires* is bold in the extreme. It is contrary to one of the fundamentals of the British Constitution . . . In the end, [counsel for the Attorney-General] encapsulated his submissions in the proposition that the only question was whether the Canada Act 1982 was an Act of Parliament. If it was, that was the end of the matter; for the courts could not declare that Parliament had no power to pass it, or that it was *ultra vires*. In particular, [counsel] relied on *Pickin v British Railways Board*. In that case the House of Lords unanimously held that a private Act of Parliament was not open to attack in the courts on the ground that the promoters of the Act had fraudulently inserted a false recital in the preamble. As was said by Lord Morris of Borth-y-Gest, it is not for the courts to proceed "as though the Act or some part of it had never been passed"; there may be argument on the interpretation of the Act, but "there must be none as to whether it should be on the Statute Book at all." Any complaint on such matters is for Parliament to deal with and not the courts . . . Accordingly, in that case the paragraphs of a reply which raised such a point were struck out.

[Counsel for Manuel] was, of course, concerned to restrict the ambit of the decision in *Pickin v British Railways Board*. He accepted that it was a binding decision for domestic legislation, but he said that it did not apply in relation to the Statute of Westminster 1931 or to the other countries of the Commonwealth. He also contended that it decided no more than that the courts would not inquire into what occurred in the course of the passage of a bill through Parliament, relying on what Lord Reid said. This latter point is, I think, plainly wrong, since it ignores the words "what was done previously to its being introduced" which Lord Reid cited with approval on that page. The wider point, however, is founded upon the theory that Parliament may surrender its sovereign power over some territory or area of land to another person or body . . . After such a surrender, any legislation which Parliament purports to enact for that territory is not merely ineffective there, but is totally void, in this country as elsewhere, since Parliament has surrendered the power to legislate; and the English courts have jurisdiction to declare such legislation *ultra vires* and void.

Before I discuss this proposition, and its application to Canada, I should mention one curious result of this theory which emerged only at a late stage. In response to a question, [counsel for Manuel] accepted that as the theory applied only to territories over which Parliament had surrendered its sovereignty, it did not affect territories over which Parliament had never exercised sovereignty. Thus if one adapts an example given by Jennings . . . an English statute making it an offence to smoke in the streets of Paris or Vienna would be valid, though enforceable only against those who come within the jurisdiction, whereas an English statute making it an offence to smoke in the streets of Bombay or Sydney would be *ultra vires* and void, and an English court could make a declaration to this effect. At this stage I need say no more than that I find such a distinction surprising . . . The subject, of course, is constitutionally fundamental; and it is also susceptible to much theoretical speculation and contention which would be out of place in a judgment, however appropriate to textbooks or articles. My duty is merely to reach a decision in this case and not to explore side issues, however interesting they are. If I leave on one side the European Communities Act 1972 and all that flows from it, and also the Parliament Acts 1911 and 1949, which do not affect this case, I am bound to say that from first to last I have heard nothing in this case to make me doubt the simple rule that the duty of the court is to obey and apply every Act of Parliament, and that the court cannot hold any such Act to be *ultra vires*. Of course there may be questions about what the Act means, and of course there is power to hold statutory instruments and other subordinate legislation *ultra vires*. But once an instrument is recognised as being an Act of Parliament, no English court can refuse to obey it or question its validity.

In the present case I have before me a copy of the Canada Act 1982 purporting to be published by Her Majesty's Stationery Office. After reciting the request and consent of Canada and the submission of an address to Her Majesty by the Senate and House of Commons of Canada, there are the words of enactment: "Be it therefore enacted by the Queen's Most Excellent Majesty, by and with the advice and consent of the Lords Spiritual and Temporal, and Commons, in this present Parliament assembled, and by the authority of the same, as follows . . ."

There has been no suggestion that the copy before me is not a true copy of the Act itself, or that it was not passed by the House of Commons and the House of Lords, or did not receive the Royal Assent. The Act is therefore an Act of Parliament and the court cannot hold it to be invalid. The case is not one which raises any question under the Parliament Acts 1911 and 1949 . . . In the words of Lord Campbell in *Edinburgh and Dalkeith Railway Co.* v *Wauchope*: "All that a court of justice can do is to look to the Parliamentary roll: if from that it should appear that a bill has passed both Houses and received the Royal Assent, no court of justice can inquire into the mode in which it was introduced into Parliament, nor into what was done previous to its introduction, or what passed in Parliament during its progress in its various stages through both Houses." . . .

The Canada Act 1982 is an Act of Parliament, and sitting as a judge in an English court I owe full and dutiful obedience to that Act.

I do not think that, as a matter of law, it makes any difference if the Act in question purports to apply outside the United Kingdom. I speak not merely of statutes such as the Continental Shelf Act 1964 but also of statutes purporting to apply to other countries. If that other country is a colony, the English courts will apply the Act even if the colony is in a state of revolt against the Crown and direct enforcement of the decision may be impossible: see *Madzimbamuto* v *Lardner-Burke*. It matters not if a convention had grown up that the United Kingdom Parliament would not legislate for that colony without the consent of the colony. Such a convention would not limit the powers of Parliament, and if Parliament legislated in breach of the convention, "the courts could not hold the Act of Parliament invalid". Similarly if the other country is a foreign state which has never been British, I do not think that any English court would or could declare the Act *ultra vires* and void. No doubt the Act would normally be ignored by the foreign state and would not be enforced by it, but that would not invalidate the Act in this country. Those who infringed it could not claim that it was void if proceedings within the jurisdiction were taken against them. Legal validity is one thing, enforceability is another . . . Parliament in fact legislates only for British subjects in this way; but if it also legislated for others, I do not see how the English courts could hold the statute void, however impossible it was to enforce it, and no matter how strong the diplomatic protests.

I do not think that countries which were once colonies but have since been granted independence are in any different position. Plainly once statute has granted independence to a country, the repeal of the statute will not make the country dependent once more; what is done is done, and is not undone by revoking the authority to do it . . . But if Parliament then passes an Act applying to such a country,

I cannot see why that Act should not be in the same position as an Act applying to what has always been a foreign country, namely, an Act which the English courts will recognise and apply but one which the other country will in all probability ignore . . . In my view, it is a fundamental of the English constitution that Parliament is supreme. As a matter of law the courts of England recognise Parliament as being omnipotent in all save the power to destroy its own omnipotence. Under the authority of Parliament the courts of a territory may be released from their legal duty to obey Parliament, but that does not trench on the acceptance by the English courts of all that Parliament does. Nor must validity in law be confused with practical enforceability.'

Comment

(1)   Early dicta suggesting moral or other limits to the scope of Parliamentary power enforceable by the courts are no longer good law. In *Day* v *Savadge* it was said that 'even an Act of Parliament, made against natural equity, as to make a man judge in his own case, is void in itself'; and in *Dr Bonham's Case* it was said that 'when an Act of Parliament is against common right and reason, or repugnant, or impossible to be performed, the common law will control it, and adjudge such an act to be void.' These dicta were rejected in *Lee* v *Bude & Torrington Junction Railway Co.*

(2)   In *Madzimbamuto* v *Lardner-Burke* it was suggested that the Southern Rhodesia Act 1965 had been passed contrary to constitutional convention. Lord Reid observed that:

> It is often said that it would be unconstitutional for the United Kingdom Parliament to do certain things, meaning that moral, political and other reasons against doing them are so strong that most people would regard it as highly improper if Parliament did these things. But that does not mean that it is beyond the power of Parliament to do such things. If Parliament chose to do any of them the courts could not hold the Act of Parliament invalid.

(3)   'Unconstitutional' may mean many different things. In the United Kingdom it does not always follow that what is unconstitutional is illegal. In countries where there is a written constitution there will usually be a closer correlation between unconstitutional behaviour and illegality.

(4)   The function of the courts in countries with a written constitution is different: powers must be exercised in accordance with the written constitution and the function of the courts is to ensure compliance with the constitution. For example, see *Liyanage* v *Queen*, p.189. In *Cormack* v *Cope* the Privy Council had to consider the effect of s.57 of the Australian Constitution which provided for a special form of law-making:

> We are not here dealing with a Parliament whose laws and activities have the paramountcy of the Houses of Parliament in the United Kingdom. The law-making process of the Parliament in Australia is controlled by a written Constitution. This is particularly true of the special law-making process for which

s.57 makes provision. It has been pointed out by the Privy Council in unequivocal language in the case of *Bribery Commissioner* v *Ranasinghe* that where the law-making process of a legislature is laid down by its constating instrument, the courts have a right and duty to ensure that that law-making process is observed . . . Whilst it may be true the Court will not interfere in what I would call the intra-mural deliberative activities of the Parliament, it has both a right and a duty to interfere if the constitutionally required process of law-making is not properly carried out.

. . . it is not the case in Australia, as it is in the United Kingdom, that the judiciary will restrain itself from interference in any part of the law-making process of the Parliament. Whilst the Court will not interfere in what I have called the intra-mural deliberative activities of the House, including what Isaacs J called 'intermediate procedure' and the 'order of events between the Houses' there is no parliamentary privilege which can stand in the way of this Court's right and duty to ensure that the constitutionally provided methods of law-making are observed.

(5)   The distinction between different judicial functions may be seen from the views expressed, in the context of the European Community, in *Stoke on Trent City Council* v *B & Q* (see p.97) where Hoffmann J said:

The power to review Acts of Parliament [on the grounds of proportionality] is new to the courts of this country but familiar in any country, like the United States, Canada and Australia, which has a constitution containing limitations on the powers of an otherwise sovereign legislature. In some cases it will be apparent to the court that the legislative power has been used for an ulterior and impermissible purpose. In others exercise of the power will be clearly invalidated by some basic error of reasoning. But in cases in which different views were reasonably tenable, the courts have not attempted to usurp the functions of the legislature . . .

(6)   One Act may be repealed by a later Act, either expressly or by implication (implied repeal): see *Vauxhall Street Estates* v *Liverpool Corporation*. In *Ellen Street Estates* v *Minister of Health* Maugham LJ observed:

[Counsel] contends that as regards subsequent legislation, in the absence of an express repeal of this provision of the Acquisition of Land (Assessment of Compensation) Act 1919, the provisions of that Act must apply, however clear the intention of Parliament, expressed in the subsequent Act, is to modify the provisions of the Act of 1919. I am quite unable to accept that view. The legislature cannot, according to our constitution, bind itself as to the form of subsequent legislation, and it is impossible for Parliament to enact that in a subsequent statute dealing with the same subject matter there can be no implied repeal. If in a subsequent Act Parliament chooses to make it plain that the earlier statute is being to some extent repealed, effect must be given to that intention just because it is the will of the Legislature.

(7) The Parliamentary Roll no longer exists. It was not suggested that the Canada Act was anything other than what it purported to be, i.e. an Act of Parliament. The reference to the passage of the Act through the constituent parts of Parliament tends to suggest that the courts will be prepared to examine a document to see if it is an Act of Parliament, in other words the courts have a rule, or rules, by which they recognize what an Act is. Once satisfied that the document in question is an Act then they give it 'full and dutiful obedience', subject only to their powers of interpretation.

(8) Legislative supremacy demands that only an Act of Parliament is supreme. The courts will not accord primacy to a measure that falls short of being an Act. In *Bowles* v *Bank of England* the Chancery Division did not regard a resolution of the House of Commons as having the force of law and thus the demand for tax pursuant to that resolution was unlawful. Parker J said:

> . . . Does a resolution of the Committee of the House of Commons for Ways and Means, either alone or when adopted by the House, authorize the Crown to levy on the subject an income tax assented to by such resolution but not yet imposed by Act of Parliament? . . . this question can, in my opinion, only be answered in the negative. By . . . the Bill of Rights it was finally settled that there could be no taxation in this country except under authority of an Act of Parliament. The Bill of Rights still remains unrepealed, and no practice or custom, however prolonged, or however acquiesced in on the part of the subject, can be relied on by the Crown as justifying any infringement of its provisions. It follows that, with regard to the powers of the Crown to levy taxation, no resolution, either of the Committee for Ways and Means or of the House itself, has any legal effect whatever. Such resolutions are necessitated by a parliamentary procedure adopted with a view to the protection of the subject against the hasty imposition of taxes, and it would be strange to find them relied on as justifying the Crown in levying a tax before such tax is actually imposed by Act of Parliament.
>
> I did not, however, understand that the Attorney-General on behalf of the Crown really dissented from this position. His contention was that in the case of income tax there is statutory authority for its collection by the Crown after the resolution of the Committee of the House of Commons for Ways and Means assenting in its imposition and before the passing of the Act by which it is subsequently imposed. This contention necessitates consideration of the Acts regulating the collection of income tax, and in particular of s.30 of the Customs and Inland Revenue Act, 1890.

The court considered the effect of various statutory matters. It concluded that they did not confer the power alleged and that the demand for tax had thus been improperly made. This deficiency was remedied by legislation.

(9) Legislative supremacy also underpins judicial review of executive action. In *R* v *Secretary of State for Home Department, ex parte Brind* (see p.293) Sir John Donaldson MR remarked:

It will undoubtedly strike some people as strange that, the directives having been approved by Parliament, the courts should be prepared to entertain applications to judicially review them, since Parliament is supreme under our constitution . . . Parliament is indeed supreme, subject to immaterial exceptions stemming from European Community law . . . If Parliament had passed an Act containing the restrictions imposed by the Home Secretary's directives, the courts could and would have had nothing to consider or say. However, where Parliament authorises ministers to take executive action, it is the duty of the courts in appropriate cases to consider whether ministers have exceeded that authority.

(10)   The suggestion rejected by the House of Lords in *Pickin* v *British Railways Board* (p.26) was that the Act had been passed in a manner which was procedurally defective. There was no suggestion that it was not an Act of Parliament.

(11)   The principle that Parliament cannot impose binding procedural fetters is supported by authority only in so far as internal Parliamentary procedures are concerned. The cases on implied repeal do not address the issues directly and do not assist since they refer to inconsistent Acts of Parliament, thus begging the question under discussion. There is a body of opinion which suggests that the views of Dicey and others are wrong – see, e.g., Jennings and Heuston. Authorities from the Commonwealth – notably *Bribery Commissioners* v *Ranasinghe, Attorney-General for NSW* v *Trethowan, Harris* v *Minister of Interior* – are often cited in support of the view that one Parliament can impose binding manner and form provisions upon another. Opponents of that view point to the fact that in each case the procedural requirement was imposed by the instrument conferring legislative competence, and thus can be distinguished from the self-imposed nature of any potential limit set by a United Kingdom statute. H.W.R. Wade's important article at [1955] CLJ 172, received favourable judicial comment in both *Manuel* v *Attorney-General* and *Blackburn* v *Attorney-General.*

(12)   The principle of the legislative supremacy of Parliament must be assessed in the light of membership of the European Community. Recent judicial observations suggest that reappraisal will be radical – see p.108.

Parliament Acts 1911–1949

1.   (1)   If a Money Bill, having been passed by the House of Commons, and sent up to the House of Lords at least one month before the end of the session, is not passed by the House of Lords without amendment within one month after it is so sent up to that House, the Bill shall, unless the House of Commons direct to the contrary, be presented to His Majesty and become an Act of Parliament on the Royal Assent being signified, notwithstanding that the House of Lords have not consented to the Bill.

     (2)   A Money Bill means a Public Bill which in the opinion of the Speaker of the House of Commons contains only provisions dealing with all or any of the following subjects, namely, the imposition, repeal, remission, alteration or regulation of taxation; the imposition for the payment of debt or other

financial purposes of charges on the Consolidated Fund, or on money provided by Parliament, or the variation or repeal of any such charges; supply; the appropriation, receipt, custody, issue or audit of accounts of public money; the raising or guarantee of any loan or the repayment thereof; or subordinate matters incidental to those subjects or any of them. In this subsection the expressions 'taxation', 'public money', and 'loan' respectively do not include any taxation, money, or loan raised by local authorities or bodies for local purposes.

(3) There shall be endorsed on every Money Bill when it is sent up to the House of Lords and when it is presented to His Majesty for assent the certificate of the Speaker of the House of Commons signed by him that it is a Money Bill. Before giving his certificate, the Speaker shall consult, if practicable, two members to be appointed from the Chairmen's Panel at the beginning of each Session by the Committee of Selection.

2. (1) If any Public Bill (other than a Money Bill or a Bill containing any provision to extend the maximum duration of Parliament beyond five years) is passed by the House of Commons in [TWO] successive sessions (whether the same Parliament or not), and, having been sent up to the House of Lords at least one month before the end of the session, is rejected by the House of Lords in each of those sessions, that Bill shall, on its rejection for the [SECOND] time by the House of Lords, unless the House of Commons direct to the contrary, be presented to His Majesty and become an Act of Parliament on the Royal Assent being signified thereto, notwithstanding that the House of Lords have not consented to the Bill: Provided that this provision shall not take effect unless [ONE YEAR HAS] elapsed between the date of the second reading in the first of those sessions of the Bill in the House of Commons and the date on which it passes the House of Commons in the [SECOND SESSION].

(2) When a Bill is presented to His Majesty for assent in pursuance of the provisions of the section, there shall be endorsed on the Bill the certificate of the Speaker of the House of Commons signed by him that the provisions of this section have been duly complied with . . .

3. Any certificate of the Speaker of the House of Commons given under this Act shall be conclusive for all purposes, and shall not be questioned in any court of law.

4. (1) In every Bill presented to His Majesty under the preceding provisions of this Act, the words of enactment shall be as follows, that is to say:–

'Be it enacted by the King's most Excellent Majesty, by and with the advice and consent of the Commons in this present Parliament assembled, in accordance with the provisions of the Parliament Acts 1911 and 1914, and by authority of the same, as follows.' . . .

Comment

(1) The 1949 Parliament Act added the words in square brackets. It was passed under the 1911 Act procedure. For other Acts passed under these procedures see the

Welsh Church Act 1914, the Government of Ireland Act 1914 and the War Crimes Act 1990.

(2)   The usual words of enactment are:

Be it enacted by the Queen's most Excellent Majesty, by and with the advice and consent of the Lords Spiritual and Temporal, and Commons, in this present Parliament assembled, and by the authority of the same, as follows:

(3)   These provisions lend some support to the view that Parliament can alter the manner and form of legislating; if Parliament can make it easier to legislate, can it also make it more difficult? The courts will surely recognize the 1949 Act as an Act even though it did not receive the approval of the House of Lords. If it is not an Act then what else is it? It has been suggested that because it did not receive the approval of the House of Lords it must be regarded as delegated legislation. It has also been suggested that since the 1911 Act did not permit the House of Commons and the Crown to enlarge its own powers the 1949 Act was invalid. If this view is correct then it may be possible to entrench legislation, i.e. make it proof against repeal except in a particular way. Such a method might be used to protect a Bill of Rights. It should not be forgotten that it could also be used to protect undesirable legislative provisions.

6 The European Community

Few constitutional or legal developments are more fundamental to the United Kingdom constitutional lawyer than the membership by the United Kingdom of the European Union. This is, for the moment, essentially an internationally agreed inter-governmental structure, based largely upon the European Community, but also upon treaty obligations relating to a common foreign and security policy, and upon provisions relating to co-operation in the fields of justice and home affairs. Further expansion of the role of the European Union will be of considerable importance in respect of the relationship between the Union and its constituent members.

Unlike the European Union, the European Community is a supra-national body, having its own institutions. These are: the Council (now known as the Council of the European Union, the functions of which are set out in arts 145–148, p.74); the Commission, which essentially has a policy development and administrative role (see p.74); the Parliament (which has powers of debate, scrutiny and some participative role in the legislative process); the Court of Justice (which has the power to interpret Community law, and to judicially review actions of the Community institutions and, in the European context, of Member States (see p.104)).

The breadth of the Community now is much greater than that of the European Economic Community established by the Treaty of Rome in 1957, and which the United Kingdom joined in 1972. Although the preamble to that treaty speaks of an aim of creating an 'ever closer union' among the peoples of Europe, the powers of the Community were essentially economic and focused on the creation of fair and equal freedom of trade between Member States. A perusal of arts 2, 3, 3a and 3b (p.71) demonstrates how the aims and objectives of the Community have broadened. The Community has increased in membership (there are currently 15 member states. The role of the Community has likewise broadened, a change achieved through the major extensions of Community power contained in the Single European

Act of 1986 (a treaty, not a United Kingdom Act of Parliament), which created a single market, and by the Treaty on European Union (the Maastricht Treaty) of 1992.

The importance of the Maastricht Treaty can scarcely be underestimated. Not only did it change the name of the European Economic Community to the European Community (and thus formally recognized pre-existing practice), it strengthened the powers of the European institutions, particularly by giving to the European Parliament a greater role in the legislative process and in the scrutiny of other Community institutions. Substantively, it envisages the creation of that 'ever closer union' through economic and monetary union, and through the development of a single currency. The European Union is created to co-ordinate foreign, security and defence policies, and envisages a common citizenship. Not every expansion of function envisaged by the treaty has been accepted by the United Kingdom. In particular, the Social protocol has not been adopted by the United Kingdom, and the introduction of art. 3b, which sets out the principle of subsidiarity (p.73) is indicative of the strong debate that has occurred, and which will continue, as to the proper distribution of functions and powers between Community and Member States.

The constitutional significance of membership of the Community and, now, Union, cannot be denied. The Court of Justice of the Community regards community law as prevailing over incompatible national law (*Costa* v *ENEL*, p.80). Treaty provisions and regulations made by the Community take effect automatically, without the need for implementation by Member States (the doctrine of direct applicability). Even laws which do require implementation by Member States (directives) can sometimes have legal consequences (the doctrine of direct effects, see p.116). The Treaty of Rome gives the ultimate power to interpret Community law to the Court of Justice of the Community (art. 177, see p.76), and imposes on Member States an obligation to ensure that national law complies with Community obligations (art. 5: see p.72). Breach of that obligation may even on occasion confer rights upon an individual which can be enforced in domestic courts (*Francovich* v *Republic of Italy*, see p.131). All these principles now are part of English law, because Parliament has said that shall be. It is trite law that treaties do not form part of United Kingdom law unless and until incorporated into United Kingdom law by Act of Parliament. This has been done. The European Communities Act 1972 (see p.83) creates the legal basis for the application and enforcement of Community law in the United Kingdom. Individuals may rely on Community law in cases before domestic courts. The Single European Act gained legal effect in the United Kingdom by virtue of the European Communities (Amendment) Act 1986, and the

Maastricht Treaty by virtue of the bitterly contested European Communities (Amendment) Act 1993 (see R v *Secretary of State for Foreign and Commonwealth Affairs, ex parte Rees-Mogg*, p.58).

That Parliament has the power to do these things is beyond doubt. Parliament is legislatively supreme (see *Blackburn* v *Attorney-General*, p.81). Once part of our law, however, Community law does in clear respects subordinate Acts of Parliament to the conflicting will of European law, with the result that Acts of Parliament may have to be disapplied to the extent of any conflict with Community legislation or decisions of the Court of Justice of the Community. On many occasions the theoretical constitutional issues can be disguised by approaches to interpretation that avoid direct conflict (see *Garland* v *BRE*, p.127). Yet the very clear subordination of Parliament to European law has been recognized by the United Kingdom courts themselves (see *Factortame* v *Secretary of State for Transport*, p.108). This subordination cannot be disguised by the assertion that it is so because Parliament has willed it and that legislative supremacy remains pure and intact. Literally true, it has constitutional meaning only in the theoretically possible but practically unlikely scenario of the withdrawal of the United Kingdom from the Community and Union.

More problematic in constitutional terms are the provisions of the Treaty on European Union regarding a common foreign and defence policy, and co-operation on Justice and Home Affairs. Such matters domestically often fall within the scope of the Royal Prerogative (see p.50). The courts have, rightly, said that international co-operation in such matters is not a diminution of the prerogative but its exercise in particular ways (*R* v *Secretary of State for Foreign and Commonwealth Affairs, ex parte Rees-Mogg*, p.58). Yet, though practical and constitutional fetters on the exercise of the Royal Prerogative are, of course, well recognized (see, e.g., constitutional conventions) the reasoning here adopted bears some resemblance to that initially adopted in relation to United Kingdom membership of the European Economic Community. The European Union may, in the future, prove to be an important fetter on the powers theoretically available to the Crown and its Ministers.

Treaty of Rome

Article 2:   The Community shall have as its task, by establishing a common market and an economic and monetary union and by implementing the common policies or activities referred to in articles 3 and 3a, to promote throughout the Community a harmonious and balanced development of economic activities, sustainable and non-inflationary growth respecting the environment, a high degree of convergence of economic performance, a high level of employment and of social protection, the raising of the standard of living and quality of life, and economic and social cohesion and solidarity among Member States.

Article 3: For the purposes set out in Article 2, the activities of the Community shall include, as provided in this Treaty and in accordance with the timetable set out therein:

(a) the elimination, as between Member States, of customs duties and quantitative restrictions on the import and export of goods, and of all other measures having equivalent effect;
(b) a common commercial policy;
(c) an internal market characterised by the abolition, as between Member States, of obstacles to the free movement of goods, persons, services and capital;
(d) measures concerning the entry and movement of persons in the internal market as provided for in Article 100c;
(e) a common policy in the sphere of agriculture and fisheries;
(f) a common policy in the sphere of transport;
(g) a system ensuring that competition in the internal market is not distorted;
(h) the approximation of the laws of Member States to the extent required for the functioning of the common market;
(i) a policy in the social sphere comprising a European Social Fund;
(j) the strengthening of economic and social cohesion;
(k) a policy in the sphere of the environment;
(l) the strengthening of the competitiveness of Community industry;
(m) the promotion of research and technological development;
(n) encouragement for the establishment and development of trans-European networks;
(o) a contribution to the attainment of a high level of health protection;
(p) a contribution to education and training of quality and to the flowering of the cultures of the Member States;
(q) a policy in the sphere of development co-operation;
(r) the association of the overseas countries and territories in order to increase trade and promote jointly economic and social development;
(s) a contribution to the strengthening of consumer protection;
(t) measures in the spheres of energy, civil protection and tourism.

Article 3a
(1) For the purposes set out in Article 2, the activities of the Member States and the Community shall include, as provided in this Treaty and in accordance with the timetable set out therein, the adoption of an economic policy which is based on the close co-ordination of Member States' economic policies, on the internal market, and on the definition of common objectives, and conducted in accordance with the principle of an open market economy with free competition.
(2) Concurrently with the foregoing, and as provided in this Treaty and in accordance with the timetable and the procedures set out therein, these activities shall include the irrevocable fixing of exchange rates leading to the introduction of a single currency, the Ecu, and the definition and conduct of a single monetary policy and exchange rate policy the primary objective of both of which shall be to maintain

price stability and, without prejudice to this objective, to support the general economic policies in the Community, in accordance with the principle of an open market economy with free competition . . .

Article 3b: The Community shall act within the limits of the powers conferred upon it by this Treaty and of the objectives assigned to it therein.

In areas which do not fall within the exclusive competence, the Community shall take action, in accordance with the principle of subsidiarity, only if and in so far as the objectives of the proposed action cannot be sufficiently achieved by the Member States and can therefore, by reason of the scale or effects of the proposed action, be better achieved by the Community.

Any action by the Community shall not go beyond what is necessary to achieve the objectives of this Treaty.

Article 5: Member States shall take all appropriate measures, whether general or particular, to ensure fulfilment of the obligations arising out of this Treaty or resulting from action taken by the institutions of the Community. They shall facilitate the achievement of the Community's tasks.

They shall abstain from any measure which could jeopardise the attainment of the objectives of this Treaty.

Article 6: Within the scope of application of this Treaty, and without prejudice to any special provisions contained therein, any discrimination on grounds of nationality shall be prohibited.

The Council, acting in accordance with the procedure referred to in Article 189c, may adopt rules designed to prohibit such discrimination.

Article 100: The Council shall, acting unanimously on a proposal from the Commission and after consulting the European Parliament and the Economic and Social Committee, issue directives for the approximation of such laws, regulations or administrative provisions of the Member States as directly affect the establishment or functioning of the common market.

Article 137: The European Parliament, which shall consist of representatives of the peoples of the States brought together in the Community, shall exercise the powers conferred upon it by this Treaty.

Article 138b: In so far as provided in this Treaty, the European Parliament shall participate in the process leading up to the adoption of Community acts by exercising its powers under the procedures laid down in Articles 189b and 189c and by giving its assent or delivering advisory opinions.

Article 138d: Any citizens of the Union, and any natural or legal person residing or having its registered office in a Member State, shall have the right to address, individually or in association with other citizens or persons, a petition to the European Parliament on a matter which comes within the Community's fields of activity and which affects him, her or it directly.

Article 138e: The European Parliament shall appoint an Ombudsman empowered to receive complaints from any citizen of the Union or any natural or legal person residing or having its registered office in a Member State concerning instances of maladministration in the activities of the Community institutions or bodies, with the exception of the Court of Justice and the Court of First Instance acting in their judicial role . . .

Article 144: If a motion of censure on the activities of the Commission is tabled before it, the European Parliament shall not vote thereon until at least three days after the motion has been tabled and only by open vote.

If the motion of censure is carried by a two-thirds majority of the votes cast, representing a majority of the members of the European Parliament, the members of the Commission shall resign as a body . . .

Article 145: To ensure that the objectives set out in this Treaty are attained, the Council shall, in accordance with the provisions of this Treaty:

- ensure co-ordination of the general economic policies of the Member States;
- have power to take decisions;
- confer on the Commission, in the acts which the Council adopts, powers for the implementation of the rules which the Council lays down . . .

Article 146: The Council shall consist of a Representative of each Member State at ministerial level, authorised to commit the government of that Member State . . .

Article 148:
(1) Save as otherwise provided in this Treaty, the Council shall act by a majority of its members . . .

Article 151:
(1) A committee consisting of the Permanent representatives of the Member States shall be responsible for preparing the work of the Council and for carrying out the tasks assigned to it by the Council . . .

Article 155:
In order to ensure the proper functioning and development of the common market, the Commission shall:

- ensure that the provisions of this Treaty and the measures taken by the institutions pursuant thereto are applied;
- formulate recommendations or deliver opinions on matters dealt with in this Treaty, if it expressly so provides or if the Commission considers it necessary;
- have its own power of decision and participate in the shaping of measures taken by the Council and by the European Parliament in the manner provided for in this Treaty;
- exercise the powers conferred on it by the Council for the implementation of the rules laid down by the latter.

Article 164: The Court of Justice shall ensure that in the interpretation and application of this Treaty the law is observed.

Article 168a:
(1) A Court of First Instance shall be attached to the Court of Justice with jurisdiction to hear and determine at first instance, subject to a right of appeal to the Court of Justice on points of law only and in accordance with the conditions laid down by the Statute, certain classes of action or proceeding defined in accordance with the conditions laid down in paragraph 2. The Court of First Instance shall not be competent to hear and determine questions referred for a preliminary ruling under Article 177 . . .

Article 169: If the Commission considers that a Member State has failed to fulfil an obligation under this Treaty, it shall deliver a reasoned opinion on the matter after giving the State concerned the opportunity to submit its observations.

If the State concerned does not comply with the opinion within the period laid down by the Commission, the latter may bring the matter before the Court of Justice.

Article 170: A Member State which considers that another Member State has failed to fulfil an obligation under this Treaty may bring the matter before the Court of Justice. Before a Member State brings an action against another Member State for an alleged infringement of an obligation under this Treaty, it shall bring the matter before the Commission.

The Commission shall deliver a reasoned opinion after each of the States concerned has been given the opportunity to submit its own case and its observations on the other party's case both orally and in writing.

If the Commission has not delivered an opinion within three months of the date on which the matter was brought before it, the absence of such opinion shall not prevent the matter from being brought before the Court of Justice.

Article 171:
(1) If the Court of Justice finds that a Member State has failed to fulfil an obligation under this Treaty, the State shall be required to take the necessary measures to comply with the judgment of the Court of Justice.
(2) If the Commission considers that the Member State concerned has not taken such measures it shall, after giving that State the opportunity to submit its observations, issue a reasoned statement specifying the points on which the Member State concerned has not complied with the judgment of the Court of Justice.

If the Member State concerned fails to take the necessary measures to comply with the Court's judgment within the time-limit laid down by the Commission, the latter may bring the case before the Court of Justice. In so doing it shall specify the amount of the lump sum or penalty payment to be paid by the Member State concerned which it considers appropriate in the circumstances. If the Court of Justice finds that the Member State concerned has not complied with its judgment it may impose a lump sum or penalty payment on it.

This procedure shall be without prejudice to Article 170.

Article 173: The Court of Justice shall review the legality of acts of the Council and the Commission other than recommendations or opinions. It shall for this purpose have jurisdiction in actions brought by a Member State, the Council or Commission on grounds of lack of competence, infringement of an essential procedural requirement, infringement of this Treaty or of any rule of law relating to its application, or misuse of powers.

Any natural or legal person may, under the same conditions, institute proceedings against a decision addressed to that person or against a decision which, although in the form of a regulation or decision addressed to that person, is of direct and individual concern to the former.

The proceedings provided for in this Article shall be instituted within two months of the publication of the measure, or of its notification to the plaintiff, or in the absence thereof, of the day on which it came to the knowledge of the latter, as the case may be.

Article 174:   If the action is well founded the Court of Justice shall declare the act concerned to be void. In the case of a regulation, however, the Court of Justice shall, if it considers this necessary, state which of the effects of the regulation which it has declared void shall be considered as definitive.

Article 175:   Should the Council or the Commission, in infringement of this Treaty, fail to act the Member States and the other institutions of the Community may bring an action before the Court of Justice to have the infringement established.

The action shall be admissible only if the institution concerned has first been called upon to act. If, within two months of being so called upon, the institution concerned has not defined its position, the action may be brought within a further period of two months.

Any natural or legal person may, under the conditions laid down in the preceding paragraphs, complain to the Court of Justice that an institution of the Community has failed to address to that person any act other than a recommendation or an opinion.

Article 176:   The institution or institutions whose act has been declared void or whose failure to act has been declared contrary to this Treaty shall be required to take the necessary measures to comply with the judgment of the Court of Justice.

This obligation shall not affect any obligation which may result from the application of the second paragraph of Article 215 . . .

Article 177:   The Court of Justice shall have jurisdiction to give preliminary rulings concerning:

- (a)   the interpretation of this Treaty;
- (b)   the validity and interpretation of acts of the institutions of the Community;
- (c)   the interpretation of the statutes of bodies established by an act of the Council, where those statutes so provide.

Where such a question is raised before any court or tribunal of a Member State, that court or tribunal may, if it considers that a decision on the question is necessary to enable it to give judgment, request the Court of Justice to give a ruling thereon.

Where any such question is raised in a case pending before a court or tribunal of a Member State, against whose decisions there is no judicial remedy under national law, that court or tribunal shall bring the matter before the Court of Justice.

Article 186: The Court of Justice may in any cases before it prescribe any necessary interim measures.

Article 189: In order to carry out their task, the Council and the Commission shall, in accordance with the provisions of this Treaty, make regulations, issue directives, take decisions, make recommendations or deliver opinions. A Regulation shall have general application. It shall be binding in its entirety and directly applicable in all Member States.

A Directive shall be binding, as to the result to be achieved, upon each Member State to which it is addressed, but shall leave to the national authorities the choice of form and methods.

A Decision shall be binding in its entirety upon those to whom it is addressed.

Recommendations and Opinions shall have no binding force.

Article 190: Regulations, directives and decisions adopted jointly by the European Parliament and the Council, and such acts adopted by the Council or the Commission, shall state the reasons on which they are based and shall refer to any proposals or opinions which were required to be obtained pursuant to this Treaty.

Article 235: If action by the Community should prove necessary to attain, in the course of the operation of the common market, one of the objectives of the Community and this Treaty has not provided the necessary powers, the Council shall, acting unanimously on a proposal from the Commission and after consulting the European Parliament, take the appropriate measures.

Treaty on European Union

Article J.1:

1. The Union and its Member States shall define and implement a common foreign and security policy, governed by the provisions of the Title, and covering all areas of foreign and security policy.

2. The objectives of the common foreign and security policy shall be:

- to safeguard the common values, fundamental interests and independence of the Union;
- to strengthen the security of the Union and its Member States in all ways;
- to preserve peace and strengthen international security;
- to promote international co-operation;
- to develop and consolidate democracy and the rule of law, and respect for human rights and fundamental freedoms . . .

4. The Member States shall support the Union's external and security policy actively and unreservedly in a spirit of loyalty and mutual solidarity. They shall refrain from any action which is contrary to the interests of the Union or likely to impair its effectiveness as a cohesive force in international relations . . .

Article K.1: For the purpose of achieving the objectives of the Union, in particular the free movement of persons, and without prejudice to the powers of the European Community, Member States shall regard the following areas as matters of common interest:

1. Asylum policy;
2. Rules governing the crossing by persons of the external borders of the Member States and the exercise of controls thereon;
3. immigration policy and policy regarding nationals of third countries: (a) conditions of entry and movement by nationals of third countries on the territory of Member States; (b) conditions of residence by nationals of third countries on the territory of Member States, including family reunion and access to employment; (c) combating unauthorised immigration, residence and work by nationals of third countries on the territory of Member States.
4. Combating drug addiction;
5. Combating fraud on an international scale;
6. Judicial co-operation in civil matters;
7. Judicial co-operation in criminal matters;
8. Customs co-operation;
9. Police co-operation for the purpose of preventing and combating terrorism, unlawful drug trafficking and other serious forms of international crime . . .

Article K.2: 1. The matters referred to in art.K.1 shall be dealt with in compliance with the European Convention for the Protection of Human Rights and Fundamental Freedoms . . .

Comment

(1) The breadth of the objectives stated by art.3 and art.3a is significant. The Treaty contains specific enabling powers in many of these areas, but art.100 and art.235 have the effect of authorizing Community action in pursuit of those general objectives, although the Court of Justice has held that art.235 ought only to be relied upon as a basis for legislative action not otherwise authorized by other provisions: *Commission* v *Council* (Case 45/86). The choice of enabling power will determine the legislative procedure to be followed: see arts 189, 189a, 189b, and *Commission* v *Council* (Case 300/89), where the action of the Council in relying on art.130s as a legal basis for measures which sought to regulate the titanium dioxide industry was held invalid, because its choice of enabling power weakened the participatory role of the European Parliament. The appropriate enabling power, on the facts, was art.100a. Compare *Commission* v *Council* (Case 155/91). The absence of authority provides a ground of challenge under art.173 (see p.104).

(2) The application of the concept of subsidiarity set out in art.3b is far from clear, and likely to lead to considerable dispute. Article 3b does not define the circumstances in which action at Community level is necessary to achieve treaty objectives. Such matters will have to be determined by the Court of Justice, which is the appropriate court for deciding whether enabling power exists under the Treaty. The courts of Member States do not have the power to declare actions of Community institutions invalid: *Firma Foto-Frost* v *Hauptzollamt Lubeck-Ost* (Case 314/85). It is uncertain whether the principle of subsidiarity is to be regarded as justiciable in the Court of Justice, or as a matter where disputes should be resolved by political means.

(3) Article 5 imposes a duty upon Member States to implement Community obligations. This has been used as a justification for the approach taken by the Court of Justice to directives (see the *von Colson* and *Marleasing* cases, p.129). Failure to implement such obligations may lead to a conclusion by the Court of Justice that the Member State is in breach of Community law because it has failed to provide effective remedies for breach of Community rights: see *Factortame* v *Secretary of State for Transport (No. 2)* (p.110).

(4) The Council of the European Community has decided (OJ, November 1993) that henceforth it shall be known as the Council of the European Union. This does not affect the fact that the Council will often be acting pursuant to the Treaty of Rome, not the Treaty of European Union.

(5) Article 6 is a specific example of the Treaty protecting basic human rights. Another is art.119, which seeks to prohibit discrimination on the grounds of gender in employment matters. Community law also recognizes respect for fundamental rights as one of the general principles of law of the Community (see p.102).

(6) The ombudsman remedy in art.138e is in many ways analogous to that which exists in the United Kingdom: see p.36.

(7) The composition of the Court of Justice is set out by art.165. It comprises 13 judges, who may sit in plenary session, or, in some circumstances, in chambers of three or five judges. The classes of action that are dealt with by the Court of First Instance are: (a) disputes between the Community and its servants; (b) actions brought by natural or other legal persons against the Community under art.173.

(8) Article 189 draws a distinction between treaty provisions, regulations and decisions on the one hand, and directives on the other. For an example of a directive, see p.92. Unlike most other sources of Community law, directives do not automatically become legally binding (i.e. are not directly applicable) but require implementation by Member States. Despite this distinction, the Court of Justice has developed principles of Community law that erode this distinction: in particular, directives may attract direct effects (see p.116).

(9) Articles 189a, 189b and 189c create complex procedures for the making of Community legislation. Which procedure applies depends upon the enabling power being relied on. The co-legislation procedure and co-operation procedures in arts 189b and 189c permit the Council to legislate by a qualified majority procedure, the details of which are set out by art.148. This weights the votes of the various Member States, in proportions designed to prevent domination of the legislative process by the largest states.

(10) The provisions of the Treaty of European Union are not directly enforceable by the Court of Justice of the Community, which operates under the powers granted by the Treaty of Rome. However, many matters that fall within the European Union treaty will be relevant to matters arising under the Treaty of Rome (e.g. restrictions

on freedom of movement). They may, therefore, indirectly have some influence upon the jurisprudence of the Court of Justice.

(11)   Note the recognition given by the Treaty of European Union to the European Convention on Human Rights. For discussion of that Convention, see p.135.

Costa v *ENEL* (Case 6/64)

[1964] CMLR 425 · Court of Justice

In proceedings before an Italian court, C claimed that he did not legally owe money to the defendant electricity company. C argued that the statute which created the defendant company infringed both the Italian constitution and art. 37 of the Treaty of Rome (which deals with state monopolies). The court made a reference to the Court of Justice under art.177, to which the Italian government objected, arguing that a national court could not refer a question to the Court of Justice when what was in issue was domestic law, not the meaning of a provision of the Treaty. The Court of Justice rejected this argument.

'By contrast with ordinary international treaties, the EEC Treaty has created its own legal system which, on the entry into force of the Treaty, became an integral part of the legal systems of the Member States and which their courts are bound to apply.

By creating a Community of unlimited duration, having its own institutions, its own personality, its own legal capacity and capacity of representation on the international plane and, more particularly, real powers stemming from a limitation of sovereignty or a transfer of powers from the states to the Community, the Member States have limited their sovereign rights, albeit within limited fields, and have thus created a body of law which binds both their nationals and themselves.

The integration into the laws of each Member State of provisions which derive from the Community, and more generally the terms and the spirit of the Treaty, make it impossible for the states, as a corollary, to accord precedence to a unilateral and subsequent measure over a legal system accepted by them on a basis of reciprocity. Such a measure cannot therefore be inconsistent with that legal system. The executive force of Community law cannot vary from one State to another in deference to subsequent domestic laws, without jeopardising the attainment of the objectives of the Treaty set out in art.5(2) and giving rise to the discrimination prohibited by art.7.

The obligations undertaken under the Treaty establishing the Community would not be unconditional, but merely contingent, if they could be called in question by subsequent legislative acts of the signatories. Wherever the Treaty grants the States the right to act unilaterally, it does this by clear and precise provisions . . .

The precedence of Community law is confirmed by art.189, whereby a regulation 'shall be binding' and 'directly applicable in all Member States'. This provision, which is subject to no reservation, would be quite meaningless if a State could unilaterally nullify its effects by means of a legislative measure which could prevail over Community law.

It follows from all these observations that the law stemming from the Treaty, an independent source of law, could not, because of its special and original nature, be overridden by domestic legal provisions, however framed, without being deprived of its character as Community law and without the legal basis of the Community itself being called into question.

The transfer by the States from their domestic legal system to the Community legal system of the rights and obligations arising under the Treaty carries with it a permanent limitation of their sovereign rights, against which a subsequent unilateral act incompatible with the concept of the Community cannot prevail.'

Comment

(1) It is the duty of Member States to avoid the passage of laws inconsistent with Community obligations: see art.5, and *Commission* v *Council* (Case 22/70).

(2) In *Amministrazione delle Finanze* v *Simmenthal* (Case 106/77), the Court of Justice concluded:

A national court which is called upon, within the limits of its jurisdiction, to apply provisions of Community law is under a duty to give full effect to those provisions, if necessary refusing of its own motion to apply any conflicting provision of national legislation, even if adopted subsequently, and it is not necessary for the court to request or await the prior setting aside of such provisions by legislative or other constitutional means.

See also the *Internationale Handelsgesellschaft* case (p.103).

(3) For the approach of the United Kingdom courts in the application of these principles, see *Factortame Ltd* v *Secretary of State for Transport*, p.108 *et seq.*

Blackburn v Attorney-General

[1971] 1 WLR 1037 · Court of Appeal

The appellant sought, unsuccessfully, to challenge the accession by the United Kingdom to the Treaty of Rome, and to challenge the passage of the European Communities Act 1972.

Lord Denning MR: 'Much of what Mr Blackburn says is quite correct. It does appear that if this country should go into the Common Market and sign the Treaty of Rome, it means that we will have taken a step which is irreversible. The sovereignty of these islands will thenceforward be limited. It will not be ours alone but will be shared with others. Mr Blackburn referred us to . . . *Costa* v *Ente Nazionale Per L'Energia Elettrica (ENEL)* . . . Mr Blackburn points out that many regulations made by the European Economic Community will become automatically binding on the people of this country: and that all the courts of this country, including the House of Lords, will have to follow the decisions of the European Court in certain defined respects, such as the construction of the Treaty.

I will assume that Mr Blackburn is right in what he says on those matters. Nevertheless, I do not think these courts can entertain these actions. Negotiations are still in progress for us to join the Common Market. No agreement has been reached. No treaty has been signed. Even if a treaty is signed, it is elementary that these courts take no notice of treaties as such. We take no notice of treaties until they are embodied in laws enacted by Parliament, and then only to the extent that Parliament tells us ... Mr Blackburn acknowledged the general principle, but he urged that this proposed treaty is in a category by itself, in that it diminishes the sovereignty of Parliament over the people of this country. I cannot accept the distinction. The general principle applies to this treaty as to any other. The treaty-making power of this country rests not in the courts, but in the Crown; that is, Her Majesty acting upon the advice of Her Ministers. When Her Ministers negotiate and sign a treaty, even a treaty of such paramount importance as this proposed one, they act on behalf of the country as a whole. They exercise the prerogative of the Crown. Their action in so doing cannot be challenged or questioned in these courts.

Mr Blackburn takes a second point. He says that, if Parliament should implement the treaty by passing an Act of Parliament for this purpose, it will seek to do the impossible. It will seek to bind its successors. According to the treaty, once it is signed, we are committed to it irrevocably. Once in the Common Market, we cannot withdraw from it. No Parliament can commit us, says Mr Blackburn, to that extent. He prays in aid the principle that no Parliament can bind its successors, and that any Parliament can reverse any previous enactment. He refers to what Professor Maitland said about the Act of Union between England and Scotland ... "We have no irrepealable laws; all laws may be repealed by the ordinary legislature, even the conditions under which the English and Scottish Parliaments agreed to merge themselves in the Parliament of Great Britain."

We have all been brought up to believe that, in legal theory, one Parliament cannot bind another and that no Act is irreversible. But legal theory does not always march alongside political reality. Take the Statute of Westminster 1931, which takes away the power of Parliament to legislate for the Dominions. Can anyone imagine that Parliament could or would reverse that Statute? Take the Acts which have granted independence to the Dominions and territories overseas. Can anyone imagine that Parliament could or would reverse those laws and take away their independence? Most clearly not. Freedom once given cannot be taken away. Legal theory must give way to practical politics. It is as well to remember the remark of Viscount Sankey LC in *British Coal Corporation v The King* " ... the Imperial Parliament could, as a matter of abstract law, repeal or disregard section 4 of the Statute of Westminster. But that is theory and has no relation to realities."

What are the realities here? If Her Majesty's Ministers sign this treaty and Parliament enacts provisions to implement it, I do not envisage that Parliament would afterwards go back on it and try to withdraw from it. But if Parliament should do so, then I say we will consider that event when it happens. We will then say whether Parliament can lawfully do it or not ...'

Comment

(1) The case shows that the treaty making power is one prerogative power that is non-justiciable. See, generally, Lord Roskill in the *GCHQ* case (p.219). The 'checks and balances' upon the use of such powers are political, not legal. In *R v Secretary of State for Foreign and Commonwealth Affairs, ex parte Rees-Mogg* (p.58) unsuccessful challenge was made to the ratification of the Treaty on

European Union. Note the comments of the court that there may be some circumstances in which the legal capacity to make a treaty can be challenged. That is different from a purported challenge to the desirability of making or ratifying that Treaty. For the reviewability of prerogative power, see p.215.

(2) The *dictum* concerning the limits upon the legislative power of Parliament reflects practicalities, not strict constitutional doctrine. For the principle of legislative supremacy, see p.60.

(3) The role of the Community now goes far beyond economic activity. See generally art.3, as amended.

European Communities Act 1972

2. (1) All such rights, powers, liabilities, obligations and restrictions from time to time created or arising by or under the Treaties, and all such remedies and procedures from time to time provided for by or under the Treaties, as in accordance with the Treaties are without further enactment to be given legal effect or used in the United Kingdom shall be recognised and available in law, and be enforced, allowed and followed accordingly; and the expression 'enforceable Community right' and similar expressions shall be read as referring to one to which this subsection applies.

    (2) Subject to Schedule 2 to this Act, at any time after its passing Her Majesty may by Order in Council, and any designated Minister or department may by regulations, make provision –
      (a) for the purpose of implementing any Community obligation of the United Kingdom, or enabling any such obligation to be implemented, or of enabling any rights enjoyed by the United Kingdom under or by virtue of the Treaties to be exercised; or
      (b) for the purpose of dealing with matters arising out of or related to any such obligation or rights or the coming into force, or the operation from time to time, of subsection (1) above;
    and in the exercise of any statutory power or duty, including any power to give directions or to legislate by means of orders, rules, regulations or other subordinate instrument, the person entrusted with the power or duty may have regard to the objects of the Communities and to any such obligation or rights as aforesaid . . .

    (4) The provision that may be made under subsection (2) above includes, subject to Schedule 2 to this Act, any such provision (of any such extent) as might be made by Act of Parliament, and any enactment passed or to be passed, other than one contained in this Part of this Act, shall be construed and have effect subject to the foregoing provisions of this section; but, except as may be provided by any Act passed after this Act, Schedule 2 shall have effect in connection with the powers conferred by this and the following sections of this Act to make Orders in Council and regulations . . .

3. (1) For the purposes of all legal proceedings any question as to the meaning or effect of any of the Treaties, or as to the validity, meaning or effect of any Community instrument, shall be treated as a question of law (and, if

not referred to the European Court, be for determination as such in accordance with the principles laid down by and any relevant decision of the European Court).

(2) Judicial notice shall be taken of the Treaties, of the Official Journal of the Communities and of any decision of, or expression of opinion by, the European Court on any such question as aforesaid; and the Official Journal shall be admissible as evidence of any instrument or other act thereby communicated of any of the Communities or of any Community institution . . .

Schedule 2

1. (1) The powers conferred by s.2(2) of this Act to make provision for the purposes mentioned in s.2(2)(a) and (b) shall not include power –
   (a) to make any provision imposing or increasing taxation; or
   (b) to make any provision taking effect from a date earlier than that of the making of the instrument containing the provision; or
   (c) to confer any power to legislate by means of orders, rules, regulations or other subordinate instrument, other than rules of procedure for any court or tribunal; or
   (d) to create any new criminal offence punishable with imprisonment for more than two years or punishable on summary conviction with imprisonment for more than three months or with a fine . . .

Comment

(1) See also the European Communities (Amendment) Act 1986, giving legal effect to the Single European Act, and the European Communities (Amendment) Act 1993, giving effect to the Treaty on European Union.

(2) By s.2(1) all matters of Community law which do not require further implementing action are given legal effect in the United Kingdom. This includes not only the provisions of the Treaty of Rome, regulations and decisions, but also the principles of European law as laid down from time to time by the Court of Justice. All such matters are said to be directly applicable.

(3) During the passage of the 1972 Act the Minister of State observed that 'there was no question of any erosion of any essential national sovereignty.' In the light of the terms of the Act this must be regarded as a political rather than legal statement. Section 2(4) requires Acts of Parliament to be construed subject to directly applicable Community law: see *Duke* v *Reliance Systems Ltd*, p.129. This may require the disapplication of an Act of Parliament: see *Factortame* v *Secretary of State for Transport (No.2)*, p.108; *Stoke on Trent* v *B & Q*, p.97. Compare this with the power of dispensing with laws invoked by the Monarch before 1688 – see p.17.

(4) Despite Community directives not being directly applicable they can still have legal force if they have direct effects. See p. 116. Where such direct effects exist, s.2(4) requires any inconsistent statute to be applied subject to the directive: see *Duke* v *Reliance Systems Ltd*, p.129.

The Court of Justice

The Court of Justice has a key role within the Community. It has three key functions: (a) dealing with references under art.177; (b) dealing with complaints by the Commission (art.169) or by other Member States (art.170) that Member States are in breach of Community law; (c) judicial review of the actions of Community institutions (arts 173 and 175).

In the exercise of this jurisdiction the Court has been responsible for developing Community law in fundamental ways. Of particular importance is the judicial development of the doctrine of direct effects, under which an individual may in some circumstances rely on a directive against the State (see p.116). The development of the General Principles of Law should also be noted (see p.94).

The effectiveness of the judiciary as a check against executive abuse of power depends upon judicial independence and security of tenure (see p.193). Judges are appointed to the Court of Justice for periods of six years, which may be renewed (art. 167). A judge, or Advocate-General, may only be removed if, in the unanimous opinion of the other judges and Advocates-General, he or she no longer fulfils the conditions of, or meets the obligations of, the office (art. 6, Statute of the Court of Justice).

Enderby v *Frenchay Health Authority* (Case 127/92)

[1994] 1 All ER 495 · Court of Justice

The Court of Justice was considering questions of European law, relating to the equal treatment of men and women, which had been referred to it by the Court of Appeal pursuant to art.177.

'10. The court has consistently held that art.177 of the treaty provides the framework for close co-operation between national courts and the Court of Justice, based upon a division of responsibilities between them. Within that framework, it is solely for the national court before which the dispute has been brought, and which must assume the responsibility for the subsequent judicial decision, to determine in the light of the particular circumstances of each case both the need for a preliminary ruling in order to enable it to deliver judgment and the relevance of the question which it submits to the court (see, in particular, the judgment in *Direccion General de Defensa de la Competencia* v *Asociación Espanola de Banca Privada*, Case 67/91). Accordingly, where the national court's request concerns the interpretation of a provision of Community law, the court is bound to reply to it, unless it is being asked to rule on a purely hypothetical general problem without having available the information as to fact or law necessary to enable it to give a useful reply to the questions referred to it . . .

12. Where, as here, the court receives a request for interpretation of Community law which is not manifestly unrelated to the reality or the subject matter of the main proceedings, it must reply to that request and is not required to consider the validity

of a hypothesis which it is for the referring court to verify subsequently if that should prove to be necessary.'

Comment

In *Telemarsicabruzzo SpA* v *Circostel, Ministero delle Poste e Telecommunicazioni e Ministero della Difesa* (Cases 320-322/90), the Court of Justice held that it was not necessary to rule on the questions posed as the referring national court had not provided the Court of Justice with sufficient information on the case to enable it to give a ruling. This can be distinguished from the Court of Justice questioning the need for a reference: see *Enderby*, above.

Bulmer v *Bollinger*

[1974] Ch 401 · Court of Appeal

An appeal was brought against the refusal by a High Court judge to refer, under art.177, the question whether the use of the term 'champagne' by English cider and perry producers contravened Community law. The appeal was dismissed.

Lord Denning MR: 'The first and fundamental point is that the treaty concerns only those matters which have a European element, that is to say, matters which affect people or property in the nine countries of the Common Market besides ourselves. The treaty does not touch any of the matters which concern solely the mainland of England and the people in it. These are still governed by English law. They are not affected by the treaty. But when we come to matters with a European element, the treaty is like an incoming tide. It flows into the estuaries and up the rivers. It cannot be held back. Parliament has decreed that the treaty is henceforward to be part of our law. It is equal in force to any statute. The governing provision is s.2(1) European Communities Act 1972 . . . In future, in transactions which cross the frontiers, we must no longer speak or think of English law as something on its own. We must speak and think of Community law, of Community rights and obligations, and we must give effect to them. This means a great effort for the lawyers. We have to learn a new system. The treaty, with the regulations and directives, covers many volumes. The case law is contained in hundreds of reported cases both in the European Court of Justice and in the national courts of the nine. Many must be studied before the right result can be reached. We must get down to it . . . Let me put on one side the task of applying the treaty. On this matter in our courts the English judges have the final word. They are the only judges who are empowered to decide the case itself. They have to find the facts, to state the issues, to give judgment for one side or the other, and to see that the judgment is enforced.

Before the English judges can apply the treaty, they have to see what it means and what is its effect. In the task of interpreting the treaty, the English judges are no longer the final authority. They no longer carry the law in their breasts. They are no longer in a position to give rulings which are of binding force. The supreme tribunal for interpreting the treaty is the European Court of Justice at Luxembourg. Our Parliament has so decreed [in s.3] . . . coupled with that section, we must read art.177 of the treaty . . . That article shows that, if a question of interpretation or validity is raised, the European Court is supreme. It is the ultimate authority. Even the House of Lords has to bow down to it. If a question is raised before the House of Lords on the interpretation of the treaty – on which it is necessary to give a ruling – the House of Lords is bound to refer it to the European Court. Article 171(3) of the treaty uses that emphatic word "shall". The House has no option. It must refer the matter to the European Court and, having done so, it is bound to follow the ruling in that particular case in which the point arises. But the ruling in that case does not bind other cases. The European Court is not absolutely bound by its previous decisions . . . It has no doctrine of *stare decisis*. Its decisions are much influenced by considerations of policy and economics; and, as these change, so may their rulings change. It follows from this that, if the House of Lords in a subsequent case thinks that a previous ruling of the European Court was wrong – or should not be followed – it can refer the point again to the European Court, and the European Court can reconsider it. On reconsideration it can make a ruling which will bind that particular case. But not subsequent cases. And so on.

But short of the House of Lords, no other English court is bound to refer a question to the European Court at Luxembourg. Not even a question on the interpretation of the treaty. Article 177(2) uses the permissive word "may" in contrast to "shall" in art.177(3). In England the trial judge has complete discretion. If a question arises on the interpretation of the treaty, an English judge can decide it for himself. He need not refer it to the court at Luxembourg unless he wishes . . . If he does decide it himself, the European Court cannot interfere. None of the parties can go off to the European Court and complain . . . If a party wishes to challenge the decision of the trial judge in England – to refer or not to refer – he must appeal to the Court of Appeal in England . . . They can interpret the treaty themselves if they think fit. If the Court of Appeal do interpret it themselves, the European Court will not rebuke them for doing so. If a party wishes to challenge the decision of the Court of Appeal – to refer or not to refer – he must get leave to go to the House of Lords and go there. It is only in that august place that there is no discretion. If the point of interpretation is one which is 'necessary' to give a ruling, the House must refer it to the European Court at Luxembourg. The reason behind this imperative is this. The cases which get to the House of Lords are substantial cases of the first importance. If a point of interpretation arises there, it is assumed to be worthy of reference to the European Court at Luxembourg . . . Whenever any English court thinks it would be helpful to [refer] there is a condition precedent to be fulfilled. It is a condition which applies to the House of Lords as well as to the lower courts . . . An English court can only refer the matter to the European Court "if it considers that a decision on the question is necessary to enable it to give judgment" . . . On this point again the opinion of the English courts is final, just as it is on the matter of discretion . . .

If the English judge considers it necessary to refer the matter, no one can gainsay it save the Court of Appeal. The European Court will accept his opinion. It will not go into the grounds on which he based it. It will accept the question as he formulates it: it will not alter it or send it back. Even if it is a faulty question, it will do the best it can with it . . . The European Court treats it as a matter between the English courts and themselves – to be dealt with in a spirit of co-operation – in which the parties have no place save that they are invited to be heard . . . If the English judge considers it not necessary to refer a question of interpretation to the European Court – but instead decides it itself – that is the end of the matter . . . Seeing that these matters of "necessary" and "discretion" are the concern of the English courts, it will fall to the English judges to rule on them . . .

The English court has to consider whether "a decision of the question is necessary to enable it to give judgment". That means judgment in the very case which is before the court. The judge must have got to the stage when he says to himself: "This clause of the treaty is capable of two or more meanings. If it means this, I give judgment for the plaintiff. If it means that, I give judgment for the defendant". In short, the point must be such that, whichever way the point is decided, it is conclusive of the case. Nothing more remains but to give judgment . . .

In some cases . . . it may be found that the same point – or substantially the same point – has already been decided by the European Court in a previous case. In that event it is not necessary for the English court to decide it . . . But . . . the European Court is not bound by its previous decisions. So if the English court thinks that a previous decision of the European Court may have been wrong – or if there are new factors which ought to be brought to the notice of the European Court – the English court may consider it necessary to re-submit the point to the European Court. In the event, the European Court will consider the point again . . .

In other cases the English court may consider the point is reasonably clear and free from doubt. In the event there is no need to interpret the treaty but only to apply it, and that is the task of the English court . . . It is to be noticed too, that the word is "necessary". This is much stronger than "desirable" or "convenient". There are some cases where the point, if decided one way, would shorten the trial greatly. But, if decided the other way, it would mean that the trial would have to go its full length. In such a case it might be "convenient" or "desirable" to take it as a preliminary point because it might save much time and expense. But it would not be "necessary" at that stage. When the facts were investigated, it might turn out to have been quite unnecessary. The case would be determined on another ground altogether. As a rule you cannot tell whether it is necessary to decide a point until all the facts are ascertained. So in general it is best to decide the facts first . . .

The national courts of the various member countries have had to consider how to exercise this discretion. The cases show that they have taken into account such matters as the following . . . The length of time which may elapse before a ruling can be obtained from the European Court. This may take months and months. The lawyers have to prepare their briefs; the advocate-general has to prepare his submissions; the case has to be argued; the court has to give its decision . . . Meanwhile, the whole action in the English court is stayed until the ruling is obtained . . . The importance of not overwhelming the European Court by references to it . . . It must be a question of interpretation only of the treaty. It must not be mixed up with the facts. It is the task of the national courts to find the facts and apply the treaty. The European Court must not take that task on themselves. In fairness to them, it is desirable to find the facts and state them clearly before referring the question . . . Unless the point is really difficult and important, it would seem better for the English judge to decide it himself. For in so doing, much delay and expense will be saved . . . The expense to the parties of getting a ruling from the European Court . . . If both parties want the point to be referred to the European Court, the English court should have regard to their wishes, but it should not give them undue weight. The English court should hesitate before making a reference against the wishes of one of the parties, seeing the expense and delay which it involves . . .'

Comment

(1) The view of Lord Denning that only the House of Lords is bound to make a reference, pursuant to art.177(2), is *obiter* and was disapproved by Balcombe LJ in *Chiron Corporation* v *Murex Diagnostics Ltd*.

Community law also provides some support for a contrary approach. In *Costa* v *ENEL* the Court of Justice stated that 'national courts against whose decisions, as in the present case, there is no judicial remedy, must refer the matter . . . '. In cases involving inferior courts or tribunals, their actions are always potentially subject to judicial review, and the requirement to refer will probably not apply: see *Re Holiday in Ireland*.

(2) In *Chiron Corporation* v *Murex Diagnostics Ltd* the Court of Appeal concluded that, in considering whether to grant leave to appeal, the House of Lords acts in a judicial and not administrative capacity. Its power to grant leave to appeal is therefore a judicial remedy within the meaning of art.177. Thus the Court of Appeal is not obliged to make a reference under art.177(3) except in cases where it is the court of last resort.

(3) A court cannot make an art.177 reference once it has given judgment, because it is then *functus officio*: *Pardini* v *Ministero del Commercio L'Estero* (Case 338/85); *SA Magnavision* v *General Optical Council*; *Chiron Corporation* case (supra). Therefore, if an application for leave to appeal is made to the House of Lords, the Appellate Committee should consider whether an issue of Community law is necessary for the decision and whether such issue is *acte clair*.

(4) For other approaches to the meaning of 'necessary', see *R* v *Plymouth JJ, ex parte Rogers*.

(5) In *Slr CILFIT* v *Ministry of Health*, the Court of Justice considered the meaning of the term 'necessary'. Reference was not necessary if (a) the question of Community law was irrelevant; or (b) the point of Community law had already been interpreted by the Court of Justice.

(6) The court in *CILFIT* also stated the doctrine of *acte clair*, when a reference would not be necessary, as follows:

> Finally the correct application of Community law may be so obvious as to leave no scope for any reasonable doubt as to the manner in which the question raised is to be resolved. Before it comes to the conclusion that such is the case, the national court or tribunal must be convinced that the matter was equally obvious to the courts of the other member states and to the Court of Justice.

This should be compared with the weaker formulation of Lord Denning in *Bulmer*: '. . . reasonably clear . . . '. The danger exists that by a too liberal application of *acte clair* national courts may weaken the uniform development of European law. See the contrasting *dictum* of Kerr LJ in *R* v *Pharmaceutical Society of Great Britain, ex parte The Association of Pharmaceutical Importers*, that an English court should 'hesitate long' before declining a reference on this basis.

(7)   Even if the matter is clear, a court must make a reference where the validity of a Community instrument is in issue, because a domestic court has no jurisdiction to declare invalid a Community instrument: *Firma Foto-Frost* v *Hauptzollamt Lubeck-Ost* (Case 314/85).

(8)   Where a reference is made the court will need to consider the grant of interim relief pending disposal of the case following a reference. For the relevant principles, see p.110.

(9)   The decision as to whether it is made is that of the national court. In *Johnson* v *Chief Adjudication Officer* the Court of Appeal found the questions before it uncertain enough to exclude *acte clair*, and confirmed an art.177 reference it had made earlier, despite being invited to withdraw the reference by the Registry of the Court of Justice, in the light of an apparently relevant decision of the Court of Justice.

Customs & Excise Commissioners v ApS Samex

[1983] 1 All ER 1042 · Queen's Bench Division

The defendant company was issued with a licence for the importation of yarn, the licence conditional on the goods being shipped by a given date. The yarn was seized on arrival in the United Kingdom, on the grounds of no valid import licence being in existence. On an application by the plaintiff for the condemnation of the yarn the defendant argued that Community Regulation 3059/78 provided a defence, and sought a reference to the Court of Justice. The court decided to exercise its discretion and make a reference.

Bingham J: 'Lord Denning [in *Bulmer* v *Bollinger*] draws attention to four points relevant to the question of whether the reference is necessary. The first . . . is that the point must be conclusive. On the facts of this case . . . the answer to be given by the Court of Justice will be conclusive in this sense, that if the answers are adverse to the defendant that will admittedly be the end of its case. If the answers are given favourably to the defendant, then depending upon what those answers are and which of them are favourable, there may be some short issues or a short issue to be tried, but there is . . . no doubt that the answer which the Court of Justice will give will be substantially, if not quite totally, determinative of this litigation. The second point raised . . . is previous ruling . . . in this case it is not suggested that there is any previous ruling either on this regulation or on any analogous regulation which yields a clear answer to the present litigation. Third, Lord Denning lists *acte claire* . . . It certainly is of course the task of the English court to apply [the treaty] but it must apply the treaty properly interpreted . . . I do not regard the matter as so free from doubt as to render [the first three points of law] *acte claire*, and I certainly do not regard the fourth point on the principle of proportionality as either reasonably clear or reasonably free from doubt. [Fourthly], Lord Denning MR says, "Decide the facts first". That, with respect, is an injunction of obvious merit. The present case is one in which the essential facts are agreed and on the very minor areas of disagreement or non agreement the facts can no doubt be settled in a form which will enable the relevant question to be answered . . .

I therefore turn to the guidelines which Lord Denning MR has indicated govern the exercise of discretion . . . in endeavouring to follow and respect these guidelines I find myself in some difficulty because it was submitted by [counsel for the defendant] that the issues raised . . . should be resolved by the Court of Justice as the court best fitted to do so . . . sitting as a judge in a national court, asked to decide questions of Community law, I am very conscious of the advantages enjoyed by the Court of Justice. It has a panoramic view of the Community and its institutions, a detailed knowledge of the treaties and of much subordinate legislation made under them, and an intimate familiarity with the functioning of the Community market which no national judge denied the collective experience of the Court of Justice could hope to achieve. Where questions of administrative intention and practice arise the Court of Justice can receive submissions from the Community institutions, as also where relations between the Community and non member states are in issue. Where the interests of member states are affected they can intervene to make their views known. That is a material consideration in this case since there is some slight evidence that the practice of different member states is divergent. Where comparison falls to be made between Community texts in different languages, all texts being equally authentic, the multi-national Court of Justice is equipped to carry out the task in a way no national judge, whatever his linguistic skills, could rival. The interpretation of Community instruments involves very often not the process familiar to common lawyers of laboriously extracting the meaning from words used but the more creative process of supplying flesh to a sparse and loosely constructed skeleton. The choice between alternative submissions may turn not on purely legal considerations, but on a broader view of what the orderly development of the Community requires. These are matters which the Court of Justice is very much better placed to assess and determine than a national court.

It does not follow from this that a reference should be made by a national court of first instance whenever a litigant raises a serious point of Community law . . . for example it [may not be necessary: see *Bulmer* v *Bollinger*] . . . Other considerations may affect the exercise of discretion. Sometimes . . . it may appear that the question is raised mischievously, not in the bona fide hope of success but in order to obstruct or delay an almost inevitable adverse judgment, denying the other party his remedy meanwhile . . . [In this case] while I think the defendant unlikely to succeed, I do not regard its arguments as hopeless . . . so far as I know [the Regulation] has never been considered by the Court of Justice. The defendant is presently denied the possession or use of the yarn but is paying . . . for its storage . . . [The defendant] has already [given] security for the Commissioner's costs . . . and has expressed a willingness to increase [it] . . . [the defendant] has nothing to hope from delay, save the hope of success. The reference to the Court of Justice would be unlikely to take longer than appeals have normally taken to reach the Court of Appeal, at least until recently, and unlikely to cost much more. If, at the Court of Appeal stage, a reference were held to be necessary, the delay and expense would be roughly doubled . . . This does appear to me to be an appropriate case [for a reference] . . .'

Comment

A court has the power to make a reference at the interlocutory stage: *Factortame Ltd* v *Secretary of State for Transport*; *EMI* v *CBS.*; *Polydor* v *Harlequin.* However, note the comments of Jacob J in *South Pembrokeshire DC* v *Wendy Fair Markets Ltd*:

> . . . those cases were where the facts were not in dispute and the question of EC law would be determinative of the whole action either way. (The [last] of these cases also perhaps has an implicit warning to a court at the interlocutory stage not too readily to regard a Euro-point of law as clear, for the Court of Appeal there thought that there was a clear defence but the Court of Justice said not) . . . It is better in my judgment, therefore, to wait for the facts to be determined properly and finally before there is any reference. The Court of Justice will then have the full picture before it . . .

R v *Secretary of State for the National Heritage, ex parte Continental Television BV*

[1993] 2 CMLR 333 · Divisional Court

The applicant sought judicial review of an order made by the Secretary of State pursuant to s.177 of the Broadcasting Act 1990. This section permits the proscription by order of a foreign satellite television service, *inter alia*, in circumstances where the Secretary of State has been notified by the Independent Television Commission that a foreign satellite service is unacceptable because its programmes repeatedly contain matter which offends against good taste or decency. The applicant transmitted direct from the Netherlands on the 'Red Hot Dutch' satellite channel programmes containing explicit, and pornographic, photographs of sexual activity. It was these broadcasts that were subject to the order under s.177.

The appellant contended that the order was unlawful because it contravened the terms of both s.177 and Directive 89/552. The relevant parts of that Directive state:

Article 2(2): Member States shall ensure freedom of reception and shall not restrict retransmission on their territory of television broadcasts from other Member States for reasons which fall within the fields co-ordinated by this directive. Member States may provisionally suspend transmissions of television broadcasts if the following conditions are fulfilled:

(a) a television broadcast coming from another Member State manifestly, seriously and gravely infringes art.22;

(b) during the previous 12 months, the broadcaster has infringed the same provision on at least two prior occasions;

(c) the Member State concerned has notified the broadcaster and the Commission in writing of the alleged infringements and of its intention to restrict retransmission should any such infringements occur again;

(d) consultations with the transmitting State and the Commission have not produced an amicable settlement within 15 days of the notification provided for in point (c), and the alleged infringement persists.

Article 22:   Member States shall take appropriate measures to ensure that television broadcasts by broadcasters under their jurisdiction do not include programmes which might seriously impair the physical, mental or moral development of minors, in particular, those that involve pornography or gratuitous violence. This provision shall extend to other programmes which are likely to impair the physical, mental or moral development of minors, except where it is ensured by selecting the time of the broadcast or by any technical measure, that minors in the area of transmission will not normally hear or see such broadcasts.

   Member States shall also ensure that broadcasts do not contain any incitement to hatred on grounds of race, sex, religion or nationality.

The Divisional Court referred two questions as to the meaning of the Directive to the Court of Justice, and declined to impose an interim injunction on the Minister pending receipt of the rulings of the Court of Justice. The Court declined to refer to the Court of Justice a third question as to whether the actions of the Secretary of State in making an order without consulting the broadcaster, and without considering what other measures to protect minors might be available, infringed the principle of proportionality.

Leggatt LJ: ' . . . this case depends upon Community law. The attitude of the Court in such a case has been aptly summarised by Sir Thomas Bingham in *R* v *International Stock Exchange, ex parte Else* . . . where he said:

> . . . I understand the correct approach in principle of a national court (other than a final court of appeal) to be quite clear: if the facts have been found and the Community law issue is critical to the court's final decision, the appropriate course is ordinarily to refer the issue to the Court of Justice unless the national court can with complete confidence resolve the issue itself. The national court must be fully mindful of the differences between national and Community legislation, of the pitfalls which face a national court venturing into what may be an unfamiliar field, of the need for uniform interpretation throughout the Community and of the great advantages enjoyed by the Court of Justice in construing community instruments. If the national court has any real doubt, it should ordinarily refer.

In the present case there is no dispute about the facts and the issues critical to the Court's final decision are issues of Community law. They are issues that cannot be confidently resolved by this Court. On the one hand, the applicants contend for a narrow, literal interpretation of art.2(2) of a kind which is sometimes adopted in our courts; on the other, the respondent argues that a less restrictive approach is appropriate here so as to implement the manifest objective and scheme of the directive . . . I entertain real doubt which cannot properly be resolved except by reference to the European Court. As [counsel] has submitted "the Court is concerned with the construction of a Community instrument in relation to which the European Commission has expressed strong views which as the Community Institution expressly entrusted with an enforcement role under art.2(20) it should have the opportunity to develop as it would in proceedings before the Court of Justice". I would therefore refer [the two questions] . . . In relation to [the third] I entertain no doubt about its resolution . . . I regard it . . . as peculiarly within the province of the national court to answer [such] questions . . . '

Comment

(1)   The case is a useful example of the role of the Commission in ensuring the development and implementation of Community policy. Note in particular how the court regarded the Commission's views as an important factor in deciding in fact to make the reference. The issues in the case turn on the appropriateness of restrictions on broadcasting under the Treaty of Rome. The same issue is approached from a different perspective by art.10 of the European Convention on Human Rights, which, unlike the Treaty of Rome is not binding in English law. By art.10, any restriction on freedom of expression must be justifiable and proportionate, in the context of the factors identified by art.10(2). See p.150.

Note also the requirement for an anti-discriminatory approach imposed by the directive, an example of how Community law may in fact provide protection for individual rights not specifically identified in the Treaty of Rome.

(2)   The judgment also highlights the differences in approach to questions of statutory interpretation adopted by the Court of Justice. Community provisions should be interpreted in the light of their spirit, general scheme and wording, as well as the legal context in which they arise. This can be determined from the preamble: for the duty to state reasons for the making of a provision, see art. 200.

General principles of law

In the exercise of its jurisdiction the Court of Justice has not confined itself to textual analysis and interpretation of the Treaty and community legislation. The Court has been prepared to develop and apply legal principle. One creature of this judicial activism is the doctrine of direct effects (see p.116). Another is the development by the Court of general principles of Community law, which are applied by the Court whenever appropriate. They owe their origins to concepts developed by national jurisdictions. Many, though not all, of the concepts are mirrored by equivalent rules in English law.

(a)   Proportionality

Obligations may not be imposed on an individual save to the extent that they are necessary to achieve the purpose for which the Community measure or action is undertaken. The principle likewise applies to Member States who are applying provisions of the treaty or community legislation.

R v Intervention Board, ex parte Man (Sugar) Ltd (Case 181/84)

[1986] 2 All ER 115 · Court of Justice

The Board was established at national level to administer certain community legislation. Acting pursuant to a Community regulation the Board ordered the applicant to forfeit a £1.6m security because it was four hours outside the prescribed deadline for the submission of an application for a sugar export licence, a delay caused by staffing problems. The applicant brought judicial review proceedings, arguing that the Community regulation (and thus the actions of the Board) was invalid because it was disproportionate. The Divisional Court referred the question of the validity of the regulation to the Court of Justice under art.177. That Court concluded that art.6(3) of the Regulation was invalid insofar as it prescribed forfeiture of the entire security as the penalty for failure to comply with the time limit.

'. . . in order to establish whether a provision of Community law is in conformity with the principles of proportionality it is necessary to ascertain whether the means which it employs are appropriate and necessary to attain the objective sought. Where Community legislation makes a distinction between a primary obligation, compliance with which is necessary in order to attain the objective sought, and a secondary obligation, essentially of an administrative nature, it cannot, without breaching the principle of proportionality, penalise failure to comply with the secondary obligation as severely as failure to comply with the primary obligation . . .

It is clear from the wording [of the Regulations] . . . from an analysis of the preambles thereto and from the statements made by the Commission in the proceedings before the court that the system of securities is intended above all to ensure that the undertaking, voluntarily entered into by the trader, to export the quantities of sugar in respect of which tenders have been accepted is fulfilled. The trader's obligation to export is therefore undoubtably a primary obligation, compliance with which is ensured by the initial lodging of a security . . .

The Commission considers . . . that the obligation to apply for an export licence within a short period, and to comply with the time-limit strictly, is also a primary obligation and as such is comparable to the obligation to export; indeed, it is that obligation alone which guarantees the proper management of the sugar market . . .

[The Court examined the arguments put by the Commission to justify this submission, and continued:]

However, although it is clear from the foregoing that the obligation to obtain export licences performs a useful administrative function from the Commission's point of view, it cannot be accepted that the obligation is as important as the obligation to export, which remains the essential aim of the Community legislation in question.

Although the Commission was entitled, in the interests of sound administration, to impose a time-limit for the submission of applications for export licences, the penalty imposed for failure to comply with that time-limit should have been significantly less severe for the traders concerned than forfeiture of the entire security and it should have been more consonant with the practical effects of such a failure . . . '

Comment

(1) For the basis of the doctrine, see the *Internationale Handelsgesellschaft* case (Case 11/70). For a similar application of the principle, see *State* v *Watson and*

Belman (Case 111/75), where action by the Italian Government in expelling the defendants from Italy was held by the Court of Justice to be disproportionate, and therefore unlawful. The Italian Government has sought to rely on the provisions of art.48(2) of the Treaty of Rome, which permits derogation on certain grounds from the right of free movement of workers (see *Van Duyn* v *Home Office*, p.116). The expulsion was for failure to comply with relevant administrative procedures required by Italian law. The penalty imposed for breach of these requirements was disproportionate.

(2)   In *Taittinger* v *Allbev Ltd* the Court of Appeal held that the marketing of a non-alcoholic fruit drink under the name 'Elderflower Champagne' infringed EEC Regulation 823/87. This regulation had direct effect (see p.116), and an injunction to prevent the use of such words was not disproportionate to the achievement of the objective of the Regulation. See also *Milk Marketing Board* v *Cricket St Thomas Estate*.

(3)   In judicial review proceedings, the House of Lords has rejected proportionality as a separate and distinct ground of challenge: see *R* v *Secretary of State for the Home Department, ex parte Brind* (p.293). In reality, however, in such proceedings disproportionality is likely to lead to a conclusion of illegality based upon established grounds of challenge (see p.299). For an example of where proportionality has formed part of judicial reasoning, see *R* v *Barnsley MDC, ex parte Hook* (p.332).

Torfaen BC v *B & Q plc* (Case 145/88)

[1990] 1 All ER 129 · Court of Justice.

The Court of Justice considered whether the Shops Act 1950, which restricted shop opening on Sundays, was in breach of art.30 (free movement of goods):

'. . . it is therefore necessary in a case such as this to consider first of all whether rules such as those at issue pursue an aim which is justified with regard to Community law. As far as that question is concerned the Court has already stated (in *Oebel*) . . . that national rules governing the hours of work, delivery and sale in the bread and confectionery industry constitute a legitimate part of economic and social policy, consistent with the objectives of public interest pursued by the treaty.

The same consideration must apply as regards national rules governing the opening hours of retail premises. Such rules reflect certain political and economic choices in so far as their purpose is to ensure that working and non-working hours are so arranged as to accord with national or regional socio-cultural characteristics, and that, in the present state of Community law, is a matter for the Member States . . .

It is necessary to ascertain whether the effects of such national rules exceed what is necessary to achieve the aim in view. As is indicated in [the Directive] . . . the prohibition laid down in art.30 covers national measures governing the marketing of products where the restrictive effect of such measures on the free movement of goods exceeds the effects intrinsic to trade rules.

The question whether the effects of specific national rules do in fact remain within that limit is a question of fact to be determined by the national court . . .'

Comment

(1) In *Stoke-on-Trent City Council* v *B & Q plc* (Case 169/91), the Court of Justice had a further opportunity of considering the same issue. It stated as follows:

Appraising the proportionality of national rules which pursue a legitimate aim under Community law involves weighing the national interest in attaining that aim against the Community interest in ensuring the free movement of goods. In that regard, in order to verify that the restrictive effects on intra-Community trade of the rules at issue do not exceed what is necessary to achieve the aim in view, it must be considered whether those effects are direct, indirect or purely speculative and whether those effects do not impede the marketing of imported products more than the marketing of national products.

It was on the basis of those considerations that in its judgments in the *Conforma* and *Marchandise* cases the court ruled that the restrictive effect on trade of national rules prohibiting the employment of workers on Sundays were not excessive in relation to the aim pursued.

(2) The substantive law in issue in these Sunday trading cases has now been changed: see Sunday Trading Act 1994.

Johnston v *Chief Constable of the Royal Ulster Constabulary*

[1987] QB 129 · European Court of Justice

Article 8 of the Sex Discrimination (Northern Ireland) Order prohibits discriminatory employment practices, subject to certain exceptions for genuine occupational qualifications not applicable in this case. By art.53(2) of that Order, if action taken was certified by the Secretary of State as taken on the grounds of national security, no judicial challenge to that action would be permissible in law.

The Chief Constable directed that women officers were not to be armed, and, for security reasons, therefore were not to be allocated to general police duties. As a result the Chief Constable declined to renew J's contract as part of the RUC Reserve. A complaint of unlawful discrimination was made by J to an industrial tribunal. Reliance was placed upon the terms of Directive 76/207: art.2(1) of the directive prevented discrimination in employment matters on the grounds of sex, subject to exceptions contained in art.2(2) and 2(3). Under art.6 of that directive, all persons were to have an effective remedy for the protection of the rights conferred by the directive.

The tribunal referred questions as to the effect of the directive to the Court of Justice.

8. In the proceedings before the industrial tribunal the Chief Constable produced a certificate issued by the Secretary of State in which that Minister of the United

Kingdom Government certified in accordance with article 53 of the Sex Discrimination (Northern Ireland) Order 1976:

> the act consisting of the refusal of the Royal Ulster Constabulary to offer further full-time employment to Mrs Marguerite I. Johnston in the Royal Ulster Constabulary Reserve was done for the purpose of (a) safeguarding national security; and (b) protecting public safety and public order. . . .

11. Mrs Johnston . . . conceded that the certificate issued by the Secretary of State would deprive her of any remedy if national law was applied on its own; she relied on the provisions of the directive in order to have the effects of art.53 . . . set aside . . .

13. It is therefore necessary to examine in the first place the part of question 6 which raises the point whether . . . [the directive] requires the member states to ensure that their national courts and tribunals exercise effective control over compliance with the provisions of the directive and with the national legislation intended to put it into effect.

14. In Mrs Johnston's view a provision such as art.53(2) . . . is contrary to art.6 of the directive inasmuch as it prevents the competent national court or tribunal from exercising any judicial control.

15. The United Kingdom observes that art.6 of the directive does not require the member states to submit to judicial review every question which may arise in the application of the directive, even where national security and public safety are involved. Rules of evidence such as the rule laid down in art.53(2) . . . are quite common in national procedural law. Their justification is that matters of national security and public safety can be satisfactorily assessed only by the competent political authority namely the minister who issues the certificate in question.

16. The Commission takes the view that to treat the certificate of a minister as having an effect such as that provided for in art.53(2) . . . is tantamount to refusing all judicial control or review and is therefore contrary to a fundamental principle of Community law and to art.6 of the directive.

17. As far as this issue is concerned, it must be borne in mind first of all that art.6 of the directive requires member states to introduce into their internal system such measures as are needed to enable all persons who consider themselves wronged by discrimination 'to pursue their claims by judicial process.' It follows from that provision that the member states must take measures which are sufficiently effective to achieve the aim of the directive and that they must ensure that the rights thus conferred may be effectively relied upon before the national courts by the persons concerned.

18. The requirement of judicial control stipulated by that article reflects a general principle of law which underlies the constitutional traditions common to the member states. That principle is also laid down in articles 6 and 13 [of the ECHR] . . . and as the court has recognised in its decisions the principles on which that Convention is based must be taken into consideration in Community law.

19. By virtue of art.6 . . . interpreted in the light of the general principle stated above, all persons have the right to obtain an effective remedy in a competent court against measures which they consider to be contrary to the principle of equal

treatment for men and women laid down in the directive. It is for the member states to ensure effective judicial control as regards compliance with the applicable provisions of Community law and of national legislation intended to give effect to the rights for which the directive provides.

20. A provision which, like art.53(2) . . . requires a certificate such as the one in question in the present case to be treated as conclusive evidence that the conditions for derogating from the principle of equal treatment are fulfilled allows the competent authority to deprive an individual of the possibility of asserting by judicial process the rights conferred by the directive. Such a provision is therefore contrary to the principle of effective control laid down in art.6 of the directive . . .

[The Court then went on to consider whether the Chief Constable's derogation from the rights in the directive could be justified in Community law, under art.2(2) of that directive.]

38. It must also be borne in mind that, in determining the scope of any derogation from an individual right such as the equal treatment of men and women provided for by the directive, the principle of proportionality, one of the general principles of law underlying the Community legal order, must be observed. That principle requires that derogations remain within the limits of what is appropriate and necessary for achieving the aim in view and requires the principle of equal treatment to be reconciled as far as possible with the requirements of public safety which constitute the decisive factor as regards the context of the activity in question.

39. By reason of the division of jurisdiction provided for in art.177 of the EEC Treaty, it is for the national court to say whether the reasons on which the Chief Constable based his decision are in fact well founded and justify the specific measure taken in Mrs Johnston's case. It is also for the national court to ensure that the principle of proportionality is observed and to determine whether the refusal to renew Mrs Johnston's contract could not be avoided by allocating to women duties which without jeopardising the aims pursued, can be performed without firearms . . .

(b) Procedural rights

The Court of Justice has developed a variety of procedural rights. These include:

(a) the principle of equal treatment, namely that persons in similar circumstances should not be treated differently, unless that different treatment can be justified objectively;
(b) the principle of legal certainty;
(c) the principle that there should be an adequate statement of reasons for action taken;
(d) the principle that Community law should not be retroactive;

(e) the principle that Community law should respect the legitimate expectations of individuals.

Officier van Justitie v *Kolpinghuis Nijmegen* (Case 80/86)

[1987] ECR 3969 · Court of Justice

A Dutch cafe owner was prosecuted by the Dutch authorities, who sought to rely on the provisions of a directive that had not been implemented by the Netherlands. The question as to whether they were entitled to rely on the directive was referred to the Court of Justice under art.177:

'6. The first two questions concern the possibility whether the provisions of a directive which has not yet been implemented in national law in the Member State in question may be applied as such.

7. In this regard it should be recalled that, according to the established case-law of the Court (in particular . . . *Becker v Finanzamt Munster-Innenstadt*) wherever the provisions of a directive appear, as far as their subject matter is concerned, to be unconditional and sufficiently precise, those provisions may be relied upon by an individual against the State where that State fails to implement the directive in national law by the end of the period prescribed or where it fails to implement the directive correctly.

8. That view is based on the consideration that it would be incompatible with the binding nature which art.189 confers on a directive to hold as a matter of principle that the obligation imposed thereby cannot be relied on by those concerned. From that the Court deduced that a Member State which has not adopted the implementing measures required by the directive within the prescribed period may not plead, as against individuals, its own failure to perform the obligations which the directive entails.

9. In *Marshall* v *Southampton & South-West Hampshire Area Health Authority*, the Court emphasised . . . that according to art.189 . . . the binding nature of a directive, which constitutes the basis for the possibility of relying on the directive before a national court, exists only in relation to 'each member state to which it is addressed'. It follows that a directive may not of itself impose obligations on an individual and that the provisions of a directive may not be relied upon as such against such a person before a national court . . .

[Having concluded that the national authority could not rely on the directive as against an individual, the Court continued:]

12. As the Court stated . . . in *von Colson and Kamamn* v *Land Nordrhein-Westfalen*, the Member State's obligation arising from a directive to achieve the result envisaged by the directive and their duty under art.5 . . . to take all appropriate measures, whether general or particular, to secure the fulfilment of that obligation, is binding on all the authorities of Member States including, for matters within their jurisdiction, the courts. It follows that, in applying the national law and in particular the provisions of a national law specifically introduced in order to implement the directive, national courts are required to interpret their

national law in the light of the wording and the purpose of the directive in order to achieve the result referred to in the third paragraph of art.189.
13. However, that obligation . . . is limited by the general principles of law which form part of Community law and in particular the principles of legal certainty and non-retroactivity. Thus the Court ruled . . . in *Pretore di Salo* (Case 14/86) that a directive cannot, of itself and independently of a national law adopted by a Member State for its implementation, have the effect of determining or aggravating the liability in criminal law of persons who act in contravention of the provisions of that directive . . .'

Comment

(1) The principle that a directive may be relied upon by an individual against the State is known as the doctrine of direct effects (see p.116). Although the defendant's criminal liability could not be aggravated by reliance on a directive that had not been implemented in law, he himself might have been able to rely on that directive against the State if it had been appropriate for him to do so.

(2) In *R* v *Kirk* (Case 63/83), the defendant, a fishing boat skipper, was prosecuted by the United Kingdom under certain regulations. The Court of Justice was of the opinion that those regulations infringed the principle of legal certainty and non-retroactivity. The Court stated:

21. Without embarking on an examination of the general legality of the retroactivity of art.6(1) of [regulation 170/83], it is sufficient to point out that such retroactivity may not, in any event, have the effect of validating *ex post facto* national measures of a penal nature which impose penalties for an act which, in fact, was not punishable at the time at which it was committed. That would be the case where, at the time of the act incurring a criminal penalty, the national measure was invalid because it was incompatible with Community law.
22. The principle that penal provisions may not have retroactive effect is one which is common to all the legal orders of the Member States and is enshrined in art.7 of the European Convention on Human Rights and Fundamental Freedoms . . . as a fundamental right; it takes its place among the general principles of law whose observance is ensured by the Court of Justice.
23. Consequently the retroactivity provided for in art.6(1) [of the regulation] cannot be regarded as validating *ex post facto* national measures which imposed criminal penalties, at the time of the conduct at issue, if those measures were not valid.
24. It follows from the foregoing considerations that Community law regarding fishing did not authorize a Member State, at the time of the adoption of the 1982 order, to prohibit vessels registered in another named Member State from fishing within a coastal zone specified by that order and not covered by conservation measures.

(3)   For a good example of the application and interaction of these principles, see *R v Minister of Agriculture, Fisheries and Food, ex parte Fédération Européene de la Santé Animale.*

Defrenne v *Sabena* (Case 43/75)

[1976] 2 CMLR 98 · Court of Justice

Having concluded that art.119 of the Treaty, which has been held to require equal pay for equal work without regard to gender, conferred directly enforceable rights on an individual, the Court considered the date from which this liability arose.

'[The Court's attention has been drawn] to the possible economic consequences of attributing direct effect to the provisions of art.119, on the ground that such a decision might, in many branches of economic life, result in the introduction of claims dating back to the time at which such effect came into existence. In view of the huge number of people concerned such claims, which undertakings might not have foreseen, might seriously affect the financial situation of such undertakings and even drive some of them to bankruptcy.

Although the practical consequences of any judicial decision must be carefully taken into account, it would be impossible to go so far as to diminish the objectivity of the law and compromise its future application on the ground of the possible repercussions which might result, as regards the past, from such a judicial decision. However, in the light of the conduct of several of the Member States and the views adopted by the Commission and repeatedly brought to the notice of the circles concerned, it is appropriate to take exceptionally into account the fact that, over a prolonged period, the parties concerned have been led to continue with practices which were contrary to art.119, although not yet prohibited in their national law. The fact that, in spite of the warning given, the Commission did not institute proceedings under art.169 against the Member States concerned on the grounds of failure to fulfil an obligation was likely to consolidate the incorrect impression ... In these circumstances, it is appropriate to hold that ... important considerations of legal certainty affecting all the interests involved, both public and private, make it impossible in principle to reopen the question as regards the past. Therefore, the direct effect of art.119 cannot be relied on in order to support claims concerning pay periods prior to the date of this judgment ...'

(c)   Fundamental rights

The Community attaches importance to the protection of fundamental rights. In *Stauder* v *Ulm* (Case 29/69) the Court of Justice concluded that nothing in the particular Community legislation prejudiced the fundamental human rights enshrined in the general principles of Community law. In *Nold* v *Commission* (Case 4/73) the Court of Justice held that the constitutions of Member States can themselves supply guidelines that should be followed. The Court cannot 'uphold measures which are incompatible with fundamental rights recognized and protected by the constitutions of Member

States'. More recently, in 1977, a joint declaration was made by the Commission, Council and Parliament (OJ 1977, C103/1) in which the role of the European Convention on Human Rights (as to which see p.135, *et seq*) was stressed.

Internationale Handelsgesellschaft v *Einführ-und-Vorratsstelle für Getreide* (Case 11/70)

[1972] CMLR 255 · Court of Justice

Recourse to the legal rules or concepts of national law in order to judge the validity of measures adopted by the Institutions of the Community would have an adverse effect on the uniformity and efficacy of Community law. In fact, the law stemming from the Treaty, an independent source of law, cannot because of its very nature be overridden by rules of national law, however framed, without being deprived of its character as Community law and without the legal basis of the Community itself being called in question. Therefore the validity of a Community measure or its effect within a Member State cannot be affected by allegations that it runs counter to either fundamental rights as formulated by the constitution of the State, or the principles of a national constitutional structure. However, an examination should be made as to whether or not any analogous guarantee inherent in Community law has been disregarded. In fact, respect for fundamental rights forms an integral part of the general principles of law protected by the Court of Justice. The protection of such rights, whilst inspired by the constitutional traditions common to the Member States, must be ensured within the framework of the structure and objectives of the Community.

Comment

(1)   In *Nold* v *Commission* the Court of Justice observed that some rights are subject to limitations necessary in the public interest, and stated:

> Within the Community legal order it likewise seems legitimate that these rights should, if necessary, be subject to certain limits justified by the overall objectives pursued by the Community, on condition that the substance of these rights is left untouched.

(2)   In *Prais* v *Council* the Court of Justice was asked by the plaintiff to conclude that her right of freedom of religion (protected by art.9 of the European Convention on Human Rights) was infringed by the EC Council failing to take account of her religious convictions when setting the date of a recruitment test. The claim failed on its facts, but the ECJ observed that if the Council had been informed of the difficulty the plaintiff faced in good time, it would have been obliged to take reasonable steps to avoid fixing a date which would make it impossible for a person of a particular religious persuasion to undergo the test.

(3)   The protection of fundamental rights overlaps with the application of other General Principles of Law. In the *FEDESA* case (see p.102) the Court of Justice

recognized that the principle of non-retroactivity was a fundamental right. See also *R* v *Kirk* (p.101); *Johnston* v *Chief Constable of the RUC* (p.121).

(4) In *Cinéthèque* v *Fédération Nationale des Cinémas Français* the Court of Justice observed:

> Although . . . it is the duty of this court to ensure observance of fundamental rights in the field of Community law, it has no power to examine the compatibility with the European Convention of national legislation which concerns as in this case an area which falls within the jurisdiction of the national legislation.

Judicial review

Certain actions of the Community are reviewable by the Court of Justice under arts 173–175. Control of Member States is achieved through the procedures set out in arts 169–170.

Plaumann v *Commission* (Case 25/62)

[1964] CMLR 29 · Court of Justice

The applicant sought to challenge a decision made by the Commission in the context of customs duties upon the importation of clementines. A request by the German government that the customs duty on such importation be only 10% was rejected in a decision by the Commission.

'Under the second paragraph of art.173 of the EEC Treaty "any natural or legal person may . . . institute proceedings against a decision . . . which, although in the form of . . . a decision addressed to another person, is of direct and individual concern to the former". The defendant contends that the words "other person" in this paragraph do not refer to Member States in their capacity as sovereign authorities and that individuals may not therefore bring an action for annulment against the decisions of the Commission or of the Council addressed to Member States.

However, the second paragraph of art.173 does allow an individual to bring an action against decisions addressed to "another person" which are of direct and individual concern to the former, but this Article neither defines nor limits the scope of these words. The words and the natural meaning of this provision justify the broadest interpretation. Moreover provisions of the Treaty regarding the right of interested parties to bring an action must not be interpreted restrictively. Therefore, the Treaty being silent on this point, a limitation in this respect may not be presumed. It follows that the defendant's argument cannot be regarded as well-founded. The defendant further contends that the contested decision is by its very nature a regulation in the form of an individual decision and therefore action against it is no more available to individuals than in the case of legislative measures of general application.

It follows however from arts 189 and 191 of the EEC Treaty that decisions are characterised by the limited number of persons to whom they are addressed. In order to determine whether or not a measure constitutes a decision one must enquire whether that measure concerns specific persons. The contested decision was addressed to the government of the federal republic of Germany and refuses to grant it authorisation for the partial suspension of customs duties on certain products imported from third countries. Therefore the contested measure must be regarded as a decision referring to a particular person and binding that person alone.

Under the second paragraph of art.173 of the Treaty, private individuals may institute proceedings for annulment against decisions which, although addressed to another person, are of direct and individual concern to them, but in the present case the defendant denies that the contested decision is of direct and individual concern to the applicant.

It is appropriate in the first place to examine whether the second requirement of admissibility is fulfilled because, if the applicant is not individually concerned by the decision, it becomes unnecessary to enquire as to whether he is directly concerned.

Persons other than those to whom a decision is addressed may only claim to be individually concerned if that decision affects them by reason of certain attributes which are peculiar to them or by reason of circumstances in which they are differentiated from all other persons and by virtue of these factors distinguishes them individually just as in the case of the person addressed. In the present case the applicant is affected by the disputed Decision as an importer of clementines, that is to say, by reason of a commercial activity which may at any time be practised by any person and is not therefore such as to distinguish the applicant in relation to the contested decision as in the case of the addressee . . .'

Comment

(1)   A considerable body of case-law exists in respect of the requirement for 'direct and individual concern'. See generally, *International Fruit Company* v *Commission* (Cases 41–44/70); *Calpack SpA* v *Commission* (Cases 789-790/79). The principles often are difficult to apply.

(2)   In *Parti Ecologiste 'Les Verts'* v *Parliament* (Case 294/83), the Green Party was held to have individual concern in respect of the allocation of funds by the European Parliament to reimburse election expenses. This may be regarded as an exceptional case.

(3)   The first part of the test of standing in art.173 is 'direct concern'. A matter has 'direct concern' if the national authorities do not enjoy any discretion in respect of the decision impugned. See *Municipality of Differdange* v *Commission* (Case 222/83).

(4)   In deciding whether an action can be brought under art.173. the Court of Justice will examine the nature, rather than the form, of the action in question, to establish whether it is intended to have legal effects. In *Luxembourg* v *European Parliament* (Case 213/88 & 39/89) the Court of Justice held that a resolution of the European Parliament could be regarded as an act within the meaning of art.173.

Re Bathing Water Directive: Commission v United Kingdom (Case 56/90)

[1994] 1 CMLR 760 · Court of Justice.

The Commission brought proceedings under art.169 of the Treaty of Rome, alleging that the United Kingdom was in breach of Directive 76/160, which required Member States to achieve specified standards of quality of bathing water on the coastlines of Member States. The period for compliance in the United Kingdom expired on 31 December 1977. The objections raised by the United Kingdom at the Court of Justice were rejected, the action by the Commission succeeding.

'11. The United Kingdom says that on 19 October 1979 it advised the Commission of the precise criteria which were essential for the identification of bathing waters falling within the scope of the directive. The communication in question was sent to [the responsible local authorities] . . . On the basis of that communication . . . 27 areas were identified as falling within the scope of the directive and were notified to the Commission by a letter of 18 December 1979 . . .

12. On 18 July 1980 the Commission addressed to the United Kingdom a reasoned opinion concerning an alleged failure to implement the directive in Northern Ireland and Scotland. The United Kingdom replied . . . pointing out that in those parts of the United Kingdom no stretch of water came within the criteria laid down and [in relation to bathing water in England and Wales] no changes or additions had been found to be necessary.

13. The United Kingdom maintains that, since the Commission raised no objection following that reply, it was entitled to take the view that the Commission was satisfied with the manner in which the directive was being implemented. By raising objections only much later concerning the exclusion of the bathing waters at issue from the scope of the directive, the Commission created a situation of legal uncertainty and infringed art.5 EEC, which imposes on it a duty of co-operation with the Member States. Accordingly, this application, it maintains, should be declared inadmissible.

14. That argument cannot be upheld.

15. The United Kingdom was not entitled to draw from the Commission's initial inaction the inference that the Commission approved the criteria notified and the manner in which they had been applied. Neither art.5 . . . nor the provisions of the directive obliged the Commission to express a view within a given period on the manner in which the United Kingdom was implementing . . . the directive. The Commission was therefore entitled to formulate its objections at such time as it deemed appropriate and there was nothing to prevent it from subsequently instituting these proceedings under art.169 . . .

16. The United Kingdom raises a second plea of admissibility to the effect that it was physically impossible for it to adopt the measures necessary to ensure that the quality of the waters at issue complied with the requirements of the directive within the period of two months laid down in the reasoned opinions of 2 February 1988.

17. That argument cannot be upheld either.

18. According to . . . Case 293/85, *EC Commission* v *Belgium*, in determining

whether the period allowed in the reasoned opinion is reasonable, account must be taken of all the circumstances of the case.

19. Suffice it to observe that the Commission drew the United Kingdom's attention to the situation concerning the bathing waters in Blackpool and adjacent to Formby and Southport by letters of 3 April and 30 July 1986 respectively, that is to say almost two years earlier to the date of the reasoned opinion. In those circumstances the contested period must be regarded as reasonable. Moreover, the United Kingdom could in any event have prohibited bathing in the areas in question. As the Commission observed . . . other Member States took such action in respect of certain of the waters whose quality was not in conformity with the directive . . .

40. According to the United Kingdom, the directive merely requires the Member States to take all practicable steps to comply with the limit values set [under the directive] . . .

41. That argument cannot be upheld.

42. It is clear [from the directive] that the Member States are to take all necessary measures to ensure that, within ten years following the notification of the directive, bathing water conforms to the . . . values set . . .

43. The only derogations from the obligation incumbent upon Member States to bring their bathing waters into conformity with the requirements of the directive are those provided for [therein] . . . It follows that the directive requires the Member States to take steps to ensure that certain results are attained and, apart from these derogations, they cannot rely on particular circumstances to justify a failure to fulfil that obligation.

44. Consequently, the United Kingdom's argument that it took all practicable steps cannot afford a further ground, in addition to the derogations expressly permitted, justifying the failure to fulfil the obligations to bring the waters into conformity . . .

46. Even assuming that absolute physical impossibility to carry out the obligations may justify failure to fulfil them, the United Kingdom has not . . . succeeded in establishing the existence of such impossibility . . .'

Comment

(1) The case is a good illustration of the interaction of Commission with Member States, of the role directives play in developing long-term Community goals, and the long-winded formal enforcement process.

(2) For the need for a reasoned opinion and the opportunity to make representations, see the terms of art.169.

(3) The fact that other Member States, or the Commission, are in breach of Community obligations does not prevent the Court of Justice making a ruling against a Member State on the same matter: see *EC Commission* v *Belgium and Luxembourg*, Case 90-91/63. It is not a defence to an art.169 application that the Member State was prevented from fulfilling its obligations by factors outside its control: see *EC Commission* v *Belgium*, Case 77/69; *EC Commission* v *United Kingdom*, Case 128/78.

(4) A Member State may bring an action against another Member State, under art.170. Such actions are rare. For an example, see *France* v *United Kingdom*, Case 141/78, where a successful action was brought by France in respect of illegal fishing net mesh sizes.

(5) For available remedies where a Member State is found in breach, see art.171.

Relationship between Community law and the legislative supremacy of Parliament

Factortame Ltd v *Secretary of State for Transport*

[1990] 2 AC 85 · House of Lords

The question arose during a judicial review application whether the Merchant Shipping Act 1988 (and regulations made under it) deprived the applicants of rights under Community law. The Divisional Court decided to refer the matter to the Court of Justice and to grant an interim injunction restraining the enforcement of the Act. The Court of Appeal allowed an appeal against the grant of the injunction. The House of Lords decided that the court had no power to restrain the effect of a statutory provision or to grant an interim injunction against the Crown, but referred to the Court of Justice the question whether, in Community law, it was bound to grant such interim relief.

Lord Bridge: ' . . . By virtue of s.2(4) of the Act of 1972 Part II of the Act of 1988 is to be construed and take effect subject to directly enforceable Community rights and those rights are, by s.2(1) of the Act of 1972, to be "recognised and available in law, and . . . enforced, allowed and followed accordingly; . . . ". This has precisely the same effect as if a section were incorporated in Part II of the Act of 1988 which in terms enacted that the provisions with respect to registration of British fishing vessels were to be without prejudice to the directly enforceable Community rights of nationals of any member state of the EEC. Thus it is common ground that, in so far as the applicants succeed before the ECJ in obtaining a ruling in support of the Community rights which they claim, those rights will prevail over the restrictions imposed on registration of British fishing vessels by Part II of the Act of 1988 and the Divisional Court will, in the final determination of the application for judicial review, be obliged to make appropriate declarations to give effect to those rights.

It is difficult to envisage a parallel situation arising out of the disputed construction of an English statute not involving any question of Community law which would call for a decision as to whether or not the court could grant interim relief of the kind which the applicants are seeking here. Suppose that an English statute contained two sections allegedly in conflict with each other, one clear and unambiguous in its terms, the other of doubtful import. If an English court were faced with a claim by a party litigant to rights granted by the doubtful section which were denied by the unambiguous section, the court confronted with the issue at any level would decide it and no question of interim relief could possibly arise.

The nearest parallel arises where subordinate legislation which in its terms is clear and unambiguous is challenged as *ultra vires* and a question arises as to the enforcement of the subordinate legislation before the challenge to the *vires* has been resolved. This indeed was the question which arose in *Hoffmann-La Roche & Co.* v *Secretary of State for Trade and Industry* . . . The primary question in issue was whether the Secretary of State could be required to give an undertaking in damages as a condition of the grant of an interim injunction pending trial of the action at which the issue as to the validity of [a] statutory order would be determined. But the House also had to determine whether it was appropriate to grant an interim injunction to enforce the terms of the statutory order at a time when a challenge to the *vires* of [an] order had not been resolved.

The House in *Hoffmann-La Roche* affirmed by a majority . . . the decision of the Court of Appeal that the interim injunction should be granted without requiring the Secretary of State to give any cross-undertaking. The Solicitor-General relies on passages in the speeches of the majority as establishing the principle that the unambiguous terms of delegated legislation, and . . . a fortiori of an Act of Parliament, must be presumed to be the law and must be enforced as such unless and until declared to be invalid in the one case or declared to be incompatible with Community law in the other. Lord Reid said: "It must be borne in mind that an order made under statutory authority is as much the law of the land as an Act of Parliament unless and until it has been found to be *ultra vires* . . . But I think that it is for the person against whom the interim injunction is sought to show special reason why justice requires that the injunction should not be granted or should only be granted on terms." . . .

I accept that the court may in its discretion properly decline to exercise its jurisdiction to grant an interim order in aid of the enforcement of disputed legislative measures in a situation where, as in *Hoffmann-La Roche*, it is necessary to invoke the court's jurisdiction in order to secure their enforcement.

The application of this principle in relation to the enforcement of the provisions of Part II of the Act of 1988 admits of a simple illustration. Section 22 . . . creates certain "offences relating to, and liabilities of, unregistered fishing vessels." If any of the applicants were to be prosecuted for an offence in relation to an unregistered fishing vessel or if proceedings for forfeiture of the vessel were instituted under s.22 and the rights under Community law now claimed were relied on in defence, it is very properly conceded by the Solicitor-General that the court before which the prosecution or forfeiture proceedings were brought, if it decided to refer questions of Community law to the ECJ, could grant a stay of the prosecution or forfeiture proceedings pending the preliminary ruling of the ECJ. This would be a proper case of the court staying its hand until the issue as to the claim of Community rights was settled. The prosecution or the forfeiture proceedings would not be frustrated but suspended. If eventually the claimed Community rights were not upheld by the ECJ, there could still be a conviction or a forfeiture of the vessel . . .

I do not believe that *Hoffmann-La Roche* provides the conclusive answer, as a matter of English law, to the applicants' claim for interim relief. But this brings me to what I believe to be the nub of the appeal, in so far as it depends on English law, and to the second critical distinction between the claim to interim relief advanced by the applicants and any claim to interim relief which an English court has ever previously entertained. Unlike the statutory order which the Secretary of State for Trade and Industry sought to enforce by interim injunction against Hoffmann-La Roche, the provisions of Part II of the Act of 1988 require no assistance from the court for their enforcement. Unambiguous in their terms, they simply stand as a barrier to the continued enjoyment by the applicants' vessels of the right to registration as British fishing vessels. In this situation the difficulty which confronts the applicants is that the presumption that an Act of Parliament is compatible with Community law unless and until declared to be incompatible must be at least as strong as the presumption that delegated legislation is valid unless and until declared invalid. But an order granting the applicants the interim relief which they seek will only serve their purpose if it declares that which Parliament has enacted to be the law from 1 December 1988, and to take effect in relation to vessels previously registered under the Act of 1894 from 31 March 1989, not to be the law until some uncertain future date. Effective relief can only be given if it requires the Secretary of State to treat the applicants' vessels as entitled to registration under Part II of the Act in direct contravention of its provisions. Any such order, unlike any form of order for interim relief known to the law, would irreversibly determine in the applicants' favour for a period of some two years rights which are necessarily uncertain until the preliminary ruling of the ECJ has been given. If the applicants fail to establish the rights they claim before the ECJ, the effect of the interim relief granted would be to have conferred upon them rights directly contrary to Parliament's sovereign will and correspondingly to have deprived British fishing vessels, as defined by Parliament, of the enjoyment of a substantial proportion of the United Kingdom quota of stocks of fish protected by the common fisheries policy. I am clearly of the opinion that, as a matter of English law, the court has no power to make an order which has these consequences . . .'

Comment

(1)   For *Hoffman-La Roche*, see p.211. That case is also discussed in *Kirklees BC* v *Wickes Building Supplies*, p.131.

(2)   In 1990 in *R* v *Secretary of State for Transport, ex parte Factortame*, the Court of Justice ruled that where the only obstacle to the granting of interim relief was a rule of national law, then that national law should be set aside by the national court. Thus European law required that interim relief be granted to prevent the operation of the Merchant Shipping Act 1988 pending a final ruling on the question of European law by the Court. The Court noted the attitude of the Court of Justice as to the precedence of directly applicable rules of Community law (see *Amministrazione delle Finanze dello Stato* v *Simmenthal SpA*) and the need to ensure the full effectiveness of Community law. This would be impaired if a national court, having made a reference under art.177, did not grant interim relief until the reply of the Court of Justice.

(3)   The case demonstrates the duty on Member States to grant remedies to protect rights arising in Community law.

Factortame v *Secretary of State for Transport (No. 2)*

[1991] 1 AC 603 · House of Lords

The House of Lords considered the ruling of the Court of Justice in regard to the reference and applied the following principles to the question whether or not to grant an interim injunction: (a) the balance of convenience, (b) whether damages would be an adequate remedy, (c) the importance of upholding the law of the land and the obligation on certain authorities to enforce the law, (d) the fact that the challenge was prima facie so firmly based as to justify so exceptional a course. On the facts of the case the House of Lords granted an interim injunction.

Lord Bridge of Harwich: 'My Lords, when this appeal first came before the House in 1989 your Lordships held that, as a matter of English law, the courts had no jurisdiction to grant interim relief in terms which would involve either overturning an English statute in advance of any decision by the Court of Justice of the European Communities that the statute infringed Community law or granting an injunction against the Crown. It then became necessary to seek a preliminary ruling from the Court of Justice as to whether Community law itself invested us with such jurisdiction. In the speech I delivered on that occasion . . . I explained the reasons which led us to those conclusions. It will be remembered that, on that occasion, the House never directed its attention to the question how, if there were jurisdiction to grant the relief sought, discretion ought to be exercised in deciding whether or not relief should be granted.

In June 1990 we received the judgment of the Court of Justice . . . affirming that we had jurisdiction, in the circumstances postulated, to grant interim relief for the protection of directly enforceable rights under Community law and that no limitation on our jurisdiction imposed by any rule of national law could stand as the sole obstacle to preclude the grant of such relief. In the light of this judgment we were able to conclude the hearing of the appeal in July and unanimously decided that relief should be granted in terms of the orders which the House then made, indicating that we would give our reasons for the decision later . . . Lord Goff . . . has given a very full account of all the relevant circumstances arising since our decision last year in the light of which our final disposal of the appeal fell to be made. I gratefully adopt this account. I also agree with his exposition of the principles applicable in relation to the grant of the interim injunctive relief where the dispute involves a conflict between private and public interests and where damages are not a remedy available to either party, leading in the circumstances of this case, to the conclusion that it was appropriate to grant interim relief in terms of the orders made by the House. But I add some observations of my own in view of the importance of the subject matter.

Some public comments on the decision of the Court of Justice, affirming the jurisdiction of the courts of member states to override national legislation if necessary to enable interim relief to be granted in protection of rights under Community law, have suggested that this was a novel and dangerous invasion by a Community institution of the sovereignty of the United Kingdom Parliament. But such comments are based upon a misconception. If the supremacy within the European Community of Community law over the national law of member states was not always inherent in the EEC Treaty it was certainly well established in the jurisprudence of the Court of Justice long before the United Kingdom joined the Community. Thus, whatever limitation of its sovereignty Parliament accepted when it enacted the European Communities Act 1972 was entirely voluntary. Under the terms of the 1972 Act it has always been clear that it was the duty of a United Kingdom court, when delivering final judgment, to override any rule of national law found to be in conflict with any directly enforceable rule of Community law. Similarly, when decisions of the Court of Justice have exposed areas of United Kingdom statute law which failed to implement Council directives, Parliament has always loyally accepted the obligation to make appropriate and prompt amendments. Thus there is nothing in any way novel in according supremacy to rules of Community law in those areas to which they apply and to insist that, in the protection of rights under Community law, national courts must not be inhibited by rules of national law from granting interim relief in appropriate cases is no more than a logical recognition of that supremacy.

Although affirming our jurisdiction, the judgment of the Court of Justice does not fetter our discretion to determine whether an appropriate case for the grant of an interim relief has been made out . . . '

Comment

(1)   For the ruling of the ECJ on the substantive issues in this dispute, see *R* v *Secretary of State for Transport, ex parte Factortame (No. 3)*.

(2)   The litigation is a clear demonstration of the legal and practical realities of membership of the Community. Lord Bridge reconciles the decision with the doctrine of legislative supremacy by relying on the intent of Parliament in passing the 1972 Act. This argument places a distinct limitation upon the doctrine of implied repeal (see p.64). It requires English courts to ignore the plain words of a statute in favour of the obligation to apply Community law inherent within s.2 and s.3 of the 1972 Act.

(3)   Whilst this decision answers conclusively most of the constitutional arguments about the relationship of United Kingdom and Community law, it does not provide an answer as to the appropriate judicial response should Parliament expressly indicate that an Act of Parliament should prevail over inconsistent Community law. In these circumstances, arguably the doctrine of implied repeal prevents the operation of s.2(4) of the 1972 Act.

In *Macarthys Ltd* v *Smith* the Court of Appeal had an opportunity of considering how conflicts were to be resolved. Lord Denning favoured an approach which assumed that Parliament intended to legislate in accordance with its Community obligations. However, he stated:

I pause here . . . to make one observation on a constitutional point. Thus far I have assumed that our Parliament, whenever it passes legislation, intends to fulfil its obligations under the Treaty. If the time should come when our Parliament deliberately passes an Act – with the intention of repudiating the treaty or any provision in it – or intentionally of acting inconsistently with it – and says so in express terms – then I would have thought that it would be the duty of our courts to follow the statute of our Parliament. I do not however envisage any such situation . . .

For further discussion of this case, see p.127.

(4)   Although at first sight this may seem an example of dispensation with laws, this is not so. Disapplication is by authority of Parliament. By contrast the constitutional objections raised in *Godden* v *Hales* arose precisely because there was no legal authority for such action.

(5)   See also *Stoke on Trent City Council* v *B & Q*, where the court accepted the role of determining the proportionality of legislation. To a limited degree, this amounts to judicial review of legislation. Hoffman J stated:

> The Treaty of Rome is the supreme law of this country, taking precedence over Acts of Parliament. Our entry into the Community meant that (subject to our undoubted but probably theoretical right to withdraw from the Community altogether) Parliament surrendered its sovereign right to legislate contrary to the provisions of the Treaty on the matters of social and economic policy which it regulated. The entry into the Community was in itself a high act of social and economic policy . . . the partial surrender of sovereignty was seen as more than compensated [for] by the advantages of membership.

Equal Opportunities Commission v Secretary of State for Employment

[1994] 1 All ER 910 · House of Lords

The appellant Commission was created by the Sex Discrimination Act 1975. Section 53(1) of the 1975 Act gave to it the duties of working to eliminate discrimination on the grounds of sex, to promote equality of opportunity between men and women, to keep under review the workings of the Act and, when required to do so or when it thinks necessary, to draw up and submit to the Secretary of State proposals for the amendment of the 1975 Act and Equal Pay Act 1970.

The appellant formed the view that certain provisions of the Employment Protection (Consolidation) Act 1978 dealing with the rights of part-time workers did not comply with obligations under European Community law, arising by virtue of art.119 of the Treaty of Rome, Directive 75/117 (the equal pay directive) and Directive 76/207 (the equal treatment directive). In a letter dated 23 April 1990, the Secretary of State for Employment indicated that he had concluded that United Kingdom law did not conflict with European law. The EOC brought an application for judicial review under RSC ord. 53, seeking declarations that the United Kingdom was in breach of Community law, and an order of mandamus requiring the Secretary of State to introduce legislation to amend the law to provide equal pay for equal work. Declarations were also sought by D, who was employed by a local authority as a part-time worker and had been made redundant. Those applications were dismissed, as were appeals against that dismissal to the Court of Appeal and House of Lords.

Lord Keith: '. . . It is convenient first to consider whether [D] is properly joined in the present proceedings. Redundancy pay is "pay" within the meaning of art.119 of the EEC Treaty . . . If the discriminatory measures in the 1978 Act are not objectively justified, [D] has a good claim for redundancy pay against her employers, the

Hertfordshire Area Health Authority, under art.119, which by virtue of s.2(1) of the [European Communities Act 1972] prevails over the discriminatory provisions of the 1978 Act. She would also have a good claim under the equal pay directive and the equal treatment directive, which are directly applicable against her employers as being an emanation of the state: *Marshall* v *Southampton and South West Hampshire Area Health Authority (Teaching)*. [D]'s claim against her employers is a private law claim, and indeed she has already started proceedings to enforce it in the appropriate industrial tribunal . . . I see no good reason why a purely private law claim should be advanced in the Divisional Court against the Secretary of State, who is not the claimant's employer and is not liable to meet the claim, if sound. The determination of such claims has been entrusted by statute to the industrial tribunal, which is fully competent to deal with them . . .

[Lord Keith then turned to the case of the Commission, dealing first with the question of *locus standi*:]

If the admittedly discriminatory provisions of the 1978 Act as regards redundancy pay and compensation for unfair dismissal are not objectively justified, then steps taken by the EOC towards securing that these provisions are changed may very reasonably be regarded as taken in the course of working towards the elimination of discrimination. The present proceedings are clearly such a step. In a number of cases the EOC has been the initiating party to proceedings designed to secure the elimination of discrimination. The prime example is *Equal Opportunities Commission* v *Birmingham City Council* where the EOC successfully challenged the policy of the council as regards the relative availability of grammar school places for girls and for boys, in proceedings which reached this House and in which it was not suggested at any stage that the EOC has lacked *locus standi*. In *R* v *Secretary of State for Defence, ex parte Equal Opportunities Commission* it was common ground that the EOC had *locus standi*. Another instance is *R* v *Secretary of State for Social Security, ex parte Equal Opportunities Commission* Case C-9/91, which went to the European Court. In my opinion it would be a very retrograde step now to hold that the EOC has no *locus standi* to agitate in judicial review proceedings questions related to sex discrimination which are of public importance and affect a large section of the population . . . I would hold that the EOC has sufficient interest to bring these proceedings and hence the necessary *locus standi*.

The next question is whether there exists any decision or justiciable issue susceptible of judicial review. The EOC's application sets out the Secretary of State's letter of 23 April 1990 as being the reviewable decision. In my opinion that letter does not constitute a decision. It does no more than state the Secretary of State's view that the threshold provisions of the 1978 Act regarding redundancy pay and compensation for unfair dismissal are justifiable and in conformity with Community law. The real object of the EOC's attack is these provisions themselves. The question is whether judicial review is available for the purpose of securing a declaration that certain United Kingdom primary legislation is incompatible with Community law. It is argued for the Secretary of State that ord.53, r.1(2), which gives the court power to make declarations in judicial review proceedings, is only applicable where one of the prerogative orders would be available under r.1(1), and if there is no decision in respect of which one of these writs might be issued a declaration cannot be made. I consider that to be too narrow an interpretation of the court's powers. It would mean that while a declaration that a statutory instrument is compatible with Community law could be made, since such an instrument is capable of being set aside by certiorari, no such declaration could be made as regards primary legislation . . .

[Lord Keith cited the *Factortame* series of cases, as to which see p.108, and continued:]

The effect [of these cases] was that certain provisions of United Kingdom primary legislation were held to be invalid in their purported application to nationals of Member States of the European Community, but without any prerogative order being available to strike down the legislation in question, which of course remained valid as regards nationals of non-Member States. At no stage in the course of the litigation . . . was it suggested that judicial review was not available for the purpose of obtaining an adjudication upon the validity of the legislation in so far as it affected the applicants.

The *Factortame* case is thus a precedent in favour of the EOC's recourse to judicial review for the purpose of challenging as incompatible with Community law the relevant provisions of the 1978 Act. It also provides an answer to the third procedural point taken by the Secretary of State, who maintains that the Divisional Court has no jurisdiction to declare that the United Kingdom or the Secretary of State is in breach of obligations under Community law. There is no need for any such declaration. A declaration that the threshold provisions of the 1978 Act are incompatible with Community law would suffice for the purposes sought to be achieved by the EOC and is capable of being granted consistently with the precedent afforded by *Factortame*. This does not involve, as contended for the Secretary of State, any attempt by the EOC to enforce the international treaty obligations of the United Kingdom. The EOC is concerned simply to obtain a ruling which reflects the primacy of Community law enshrined in s.2 of the 1972 Act and determines whether the relevant United Kingdom law is compatible with the equal pay directive and the equal treatment directive.

Similar considerations provide the answer to the Secretary of State's fourth procedural point, by which it is maintained that the Divisional Court is not the appropriate forum to decide the substantive issues at stake. The issues at stake are similar in character to those which were raised in *Factortame*. The Divisional Court is the only English forum in which the EOC, having the capacity and sufficient interest to do so, is in a position to secure the result which it desires. It is said that the incompatibility issue could be tested in proceedings before the European Court instituted by the European Commission against the United Kingdom under art.169 of the EEC Treaty. That may be true, but it affords no reason for concluding that the Divisional Court is an inappropriate forum for the application of the EOC designed towards a similar end and, indeed, there are grounds for the view that the Divisional Court is the more appropriate forum, since the Court of Justice of the European Communities has said that it is for the national court to determine whether an indirectly discriminatory pay practice is founded on objectively justified economic grounds: see *Bilka-Kaufhaus GmbH* v *Weber von Hartz*, Case 170/84 . . . '

Comment

(1) D's private law claim arose by virtue of the doctrine of direct effects: see p.116. Judicial review should not be used for the enforcement of private law rights, as opposed to public law rights: see p.244. Nor will leave to apply for judicial review usually be granted if another procedure or remedy is more appropriate: see p.268. The decision of the court in respect of D might well have been different if her employer had not been a public authority, because then the doctrine of direct effects would have conferred enforceable individual rights: see p.120.

(2) For discussion of the doctrine of *locus standi* in judicial review, see pp.255–64. Note that, on this point only, Lord Jauncey dissented. He distinguished the cases cited by Lord Keith, on the grounds that while the EOC may properly institute proceedings against local authorities or other Secretaries of State, it could not do so against the Secretary of State for Employment. Section 53 of the 1975 Act gives an advisory function to the EOC *vis-à-vis* the Secretary of State for Employment, it being no part of its functions to institute proceedings against him.

(3) The EOC is an example of an independent body being created by statute to achieve certain objectives, in this case the general reduction in sex discrimination. For its powers and duties, see Part VI of the 1975 Act. Consider how such a body may itself be held accountable.

(4) The general jurisdiction of the court to grant declarations on judicial review was explained by Lord Browne-Wilkinson, extracted at p.279.

Direct effects

Direct effects arise where a provision is clear and precise, unconditional, and where it requires no further implementation by the Member State (see *Van Gend en Loos* v *Nederlandse Administratie de Belastingen*). Despite the terms of art.189, directives can have direct effects, and thus be relied upon by individuals.

Van Duyn v *Home Office*

[1975] Ch 383 · European Court of Justice

V was a Dutch citizen seeking entry to this country to take up employment with the Church of Scientology. Leave to enter was refused, the activities of the Church of Scientology being regarded as harmful and undesirable. V brought an action in challenge of that decision, relying on the freedom of movement for workers within the Community, conferred by art.48, the exceptions to which were regulated by Directive 64/221. Questions were referred to the Court of Justice under art.177, including as to the status and application of the directive upon which V relied.

9. The second question asks the court to say whether EEC Directive 64/221 . . . on the co-ordination of special measures concerning the movement and residence

of foreign nationals which are justified on grounds of public policy, public security or public health is directly applicable so as to confer on individuals rights enforceable by them in the courts of a member state.

10. It emerges from the order making the reference that the only provision of the directive which is relevant is that contained in art.3(1) which provides: 'Measures taken on grounds of public policy or public security shall be based exclusively on the personal conduct of the individuals concerned.'

11. The United Kingdom observes that, since art.189 of the EEC Treaty distinguishes between the effects ascribed to regulations, directives and decisions, it must therefore be presumed that the Council, in issuing a directive rather than making a regulation, must have intended that the directive should have an effect other than that of a regulation and accordingly that the former should not be directly applicable.

12. If, however, by virtue of the provisions of art.189 regulations are directly applicable and consequently, may by their very nature have direct effects, it does not follow from this that other categories of acts mentioned in that article can never have similar effects. It would be incompatible with the binding effect attributed to a directive by art.189 to exclude, in principle, the possibility that the obligation which it imposes may be invoked by those concerned. In particular, where the Community authorities have, by directive, imposed on member states the obligation to pursue a particular course of conduct, the useful effect of such an act would be weakened if individuals were prevented from relying on it before their national courts and if the latter were prevented from taking it into consideration as an element of Community law. Article 177, which empowers national courts to refer to the Court questions concerning the validity and interpretation of all acts of the Community institutions, without distinction, implies furthermore that these acts may be invoked by individuals in the national courts. It is necessary to examine, in every case, whether the nature, general scheme and wording of the provision in question are capable of having direct effects on the relations between member states and individuals.

13. By providing that measures taken on grounds of public policy shall be based exclusively on the personal conduct of the individual concerned, art.3(1) of EEC Directive 64/221 is intended to limit the discretionary power which national law generally confers on the authorities responsible for the entry and expulsion of foreign nationals. First, the provision lays down an obligation which is not subject to any exception or condition and which, by its very nature, does not require the intervention of any act on the part either of the institutions of the Community or of member states. Secondly, because member states are thereby obliged, in implementing a clause which derogates from one of the fundamental principles of the EEC Treaty in favour of individuals, not to take account of factors extraneous to personal conduct. Legal certainty for the persons concerned requires that they should be able to rely on this obligation even though it has been laid down in a legislative act which has no automatic direct effect in its entirety.

14. If the meaning and exact scope of the provision raise questions of interpretation, these questions can be resolved by the courts, taking into account also the procedure under art.177 of the EEC Treaty . . .

Comment

(1) Note that the directive was being relied upon against the state: this is known as 'vertical direct effects'.

(2) Although, subject to the conditions for direct effects being satisfied, an individual can rely on the directive against the state, the converse is not true. A state cannot rely on the doctrine of direct effects to create liability where none would otherwise exist. See *Officier van Justitie* v *Kolphinghuis Nijmegen*. Not only would this not be within the justification given in *Van Duyn* for attributing direct effects to directives, it would also infringe the principle of legal certainty. See also *Wychavon DC* v *Secretary of State for the Environment and Velcourt Ltd.*

Marshall v *Southampton & South West Hampshire Area Health Authority*

[1986] QB 401 · European Court of Justice

M (a woman) was required by her employer to retire at the age of 62. The retirement age for men was 65. She claimed sexual discrimination in employment, contrary to art.119 and the Equal Treatment Directive 76/207. Her application had been dismissed by an industrial tribunal and by the Employment Appeal Tribunal, on the basis that such discrimination was permitted by s.6(4), Sex Discrimination Act 1975. Her employer was conceded to be a public body. The Court of Appeal referred to the Court of Justice the question of whether the conduct complained of fell within the directive and, if so, whether M could rely on it. These questions were answered in the affirmative.

39. Since the first question has been answered in the affirmative, it is necessary to consider whether art.5(1) of Directive 76/207 may be relied on by an individual before national courts and tribunals.

40. Miss Marshall and the Commission consider that that question must be answered in the affirmative. They contend in particular, with regard to arts.2(1) and 5(1) of Directive 76/207, that those provisions are sufficiently clear to enable national courts to apply them without legislative intervention by member states, at least so far as overt discrimination is concerned.

41. In support of that view, Miss Marshall points out that directives are capable of conferring rights on individuals which may be relied on directly before the courts of the member states; national courts are obliged by virtue of the binding nature of a directive, in conjunction with art.5 of the EEC Treaty, to give effect to the provisions of directives where possible, in particular when construing or applying relevant provisions of national law (see *von Colson and Kamann* v *Land Nordrhein-Westfalen*. . .). Where there is any inconsistency between national law and Community law which cannot be removed by means of such a construction, Miss Marshall submits that a national court is obliged to declare that the provision of national law which is inconsistent with the directive is inapplicable.

42. The Commission is of the opinion that the provisions of art.5(1) of Directive 76/207 are sufficiently clear and unconditional to be relied on before a national

court. They may therefore be set up against s.6(4), Sex Discrimination Act 1975, which, according to the decisions of the Court of Appeal, has been extended to the question of compulsory retirement and has therefore become ineffective to prevent dismissals based on the difference in retirement ages for men and for women.

43. The authority and the United Kingdom propose, conversely, that the second question should be answered in the negative. They admit that a directive may, in certain specific circumstances, have direct effect as against a member state in so far as the latter may not rely on its failure to perform its obligations under the directive. However, they maintain that a directive can never impose obligations directly on individuals and that it can only have direct effect against a member state qua public authority and not against a member state qua employer. As an employer a state is no different from a private employer. It would not therefore be proper to put persons employed by the state in a better position that those who are employed by a private employer.

44. With regard to the legal position of the authority's employees the United Kingdom states that they are in the same position as the employees of a private employer. Although according to United Kingdom constitutional law . . . health authorities . . . are Crown bodies and their employees are Crown servants, nevertheless the administration of the National Health Service by the health authorities is regarded as being separate from the government's central administration and its employees are not regarded as civil servants.

45. Finally, both the authority and the United Kingdom take the view that the provisions of Directive 76/207 are neither unconditional nor sufficiently clear and precise to give rise to direct effect. The directive provides for a number of possible exceptions, the details of which are to be laid down by the member states. Furthermore, the wording of art.5 is quite imprecise and requires the adoption of measures for its implementation.

46. It is necessary to recall that, according to a long line of decisions of the court (in particular *Becker* v *Finanzamt Munster-Innenstadt*), wherever the provisions of a directive appear, as far as their subject matter is concerned, to be unconditional and sufficiently precise, those provisions may be relied on by an individual against the state where that state fails to implement the directive in national law by the end of the period prescribed or where it fails to implement the directive correctly.

47. That view is based on the consideration that it would be incompatible with the binding nature which art.189 of the EEC Treaty confers on the directive to hold as a matter of principle that the obligation imposed thereby cannot be relied on by those concerned. From that the court deduced that a member state which has not adopted the implementing measures required by the directive within the prescribed period may not plead, as against individuals, its own failure to perform the obligations which the directive entails.

48. With regard to the argument that a directive may not be relied on against an individual, it must be emphasised that according to art.189 of the EEC Treaty the binding nature of a directive, which constitutes the basis for the possibility of relying on the directive before a national court, exists only in relation to 'each Member State to which it is addressed'. It follows that a directive may not of itself impose obligations on an individual and that a provision of a directive may not be relied on as such against such a person. It must therefore be examined

whether, in this case, the authority must be regarded as having acted as an individual.

49. In that respect it must be pointed out that where a person involved in legal proceedings is able to rely on a directive as against the state he may do so regardless of the capacity in which the latter is acting, whether employer or public authority. In either case it is necessary to prevent the state from taking advantage of its own failure to comply with Community law.

50. It is for the national court to apply those considerations to the circumstances of each case; the Court of Appeal has, however, stated in the order for reference that the Southampton and South West Hampshire Area Health Authority (Teaching) is a public authority.

51. The argument submitted by the United Kingdom that the possibility of relying on provisions of the directive against the authority qua organ of the state would give rise to an arbitrary and unfair distinction between the rights of state employees and those of private employees does not justify any other conclusion. Such a distinction may easily be avoided if the member state concerned has correctly implemented the directive in national law.

52. Finally, with regard to the question whether the provision contained in art.5(1) of Directive 76/207, which implements the principle of equality of treatment set out in art.2(1) of the directive, may be considered, as far as its contents are concerned, to be unconditional and sufficiently precise to be relied on by an individual as against the state, it must be stated that the provision, taken by itself, prohibits any discrimination on grounds of sex with regard to working conditions governing dismissal, in a general manner and in unequivocal terms. The provision is therefore sufficiently precise to be relied on by an individual and to be applied by the national courts.

Comment

(1) If the United Kingdom legislation had been introduced to give effect to the directive, it would have been possible to construe it to give effect to the obligations under the directive: see *Pickstone* v *Freemans plc* (p.128); *Litster* v *Forth Dry Dock & Engineering Ltd* (p.129).

(2) The existence of the distinction between 'vertical' direct effects (i.e. against the state, as in this case) and 'horizontal' direct effects (i.e. against another individual) means that the availability of a remedy in employment cases may depend upon the accident of who the employer is.

(3) For the resulting litigation arising out of this ruling, see *Marshall* v *Southampton & SW Hampshire AHA (No. 2)*.

(4) Even if a directive is not directly effective, this does not mean that it has no legal consequences: see *Marleasing SA* v *La Comercial Internacional De Alimentacion SA* (p.129). However, the United Kingdom courts are not prepared in such circumstances to distort the clear and unambiguous words of a statute: see *Duke* v *Reliance Systems Ltd* (p.129). In *Re Hartlebury Printers Ltd* the High Court held that although it was the duty of the national court, if possible, to construe

national legislation so as to comply with Community obligations arising under a directive, this must be achieved, if possible, by proper processes of construction and not by the equivalent of judicial legislation.

(5) In *Wychavon District Council* v *Secretary of State for the Environment and Velcourt Ltd* the Divisional Court held that directives having direct effect could not be relied upon against a body other than against an emanation of state. A local authority is not an 'individual' for the purposes of Community law, and cannot rely on a directive as against another individual.

Johnston v *Chief Constable of the RUC*

[1987] QB 129 · Court of Justice

[See p.97 for consideration of general principles of law. The following extract deals with the enforceability of directives.]

51. On this point it must be observed first of all that in all cases in which a directive has been properly implemented its effects reach individuals through the implementing measures adopted by the member states concerned. The question whether art.2(1) may be relied upon before a national court therefore has no purpose since it is established that the provision has been put into effect in national law.

52. The derogation from the principle of equal treatment which, as stated above, is allowed by art.2(2) constitutes only an option for the member states. It is for the competent national court to see whether that option has been exercised in provision of national law and to construe the content of those provisions. The question whether an individual may rely upon a provision of the directive in order to have a derogation laid down by national legislation set aside arises only if that derogation went beyond the limits of the exceptions permitted by art.2(2) of the directive.

53. In this context it should be observed first of all that, as the Court has already stated in *von Colson and Kamann* v *Land Nordrhein-Westfalen*, the member states' obligation under a directive to achieve the result envisaged by that directive and their duty under article 5 of the EEC Treaty to take all appropriate measures, whether general or particular, to ensure the fulfilment of that obligation, is binding on all the authorities of member states including, for matters within their jurisdiction, the courts. It follows that, in applying national law, and in particular the provisions of national legislation specifically introduced in order to implement [the directive], national courts are required to interpret their national law in the light of the wording and the purpose of the directive in order to achieve the result referred to in the third paragraph of art.189 of the EEC Treaty. It is therefore for the industrial tribunal to interpret the provisions of . . . art.53(1) . . . in the light of the provisions of the directive, as interpreted above, in order to give it its full effect.

54. In the event that, having regard to the foregoing, the question should still arise whether an individual may rely on the directive as against a derogation laid down by national legislation, reference should be made to the established case law of the Court: see in particular its judgment in *Becker* v *Finanzamt Munster-Innenstadt* . . . More particularly, the court recently held in *Marshall* v

Southampton and South West Hampshire Area Health Authority (Teaching) that certain provisions of [the directive] are, as far as their subject matter is concerned, unconditional and sufficiently precise and that they may be relied upon by individuals as against a member state where it fails to implement it correctly . . .

56. The Court also held in that case that individuals may rely on the directive as against an organ of the state whether it acts qua employer or qua public authority. As regards an authority like the Chief Constable, it must be observed that, according to the industrial tribunal's decision, the Chief Constable is an official responsible for the direction of the police service. Whatever its relations may be with other organs of the state, such a public authority, charged by the state with the maintenance of public order and safety, does not act as a private individual. It may not take advantage of the failure of the state, of which it is an emanation, to comply with Community law.

57. The answer should therefore be that individuals may claim the application, as against a state authority charged with the maintenance of public order and safety acting in its capacity of an employer, of the principle of equal treatment for men and women laid down in art.2(1) of [the directive] to the matters referred to in arts.3(1) and 4 concerning the conditions for access to posts and to vocational training and advanced vocational training in order to have a derogation from that principle under national legislation set aside in so far as it exceeds the limits of the exceptions permitted by art.2(2).

58. As regards art.6 of the directive which . . . is also applicable in this case, the court has already held in *von Colson and Kamann* v *Land Nordrhein-Westfalen* that that article does not contain, as far as sanctions for any discrimination are concerned, any unconditional and sufficiently precise obligation which may be relied upon by an individual. On the other hand, in so far as it follows from that article, construed in the light of a general principle which it expresses, that all persons who consider themselves wronged by sex discrimination must have an effective judicial remedy, that provision is sufficiently precise and unconditional to be capable of being relied upon as against a member state which has not ensured that it is fully implemented in its internal legal order . . .

Comment

The *von Colson* case cited in *Johnston* demonstrates the duty on national courts to interpret implementing legislation in such a way as to comply with Community law. See *Garland* v *BRE*, p.127. For expansion of the *von Colson* principle, see the *Marleasing* case (p.129). Under s.3, ECA 1972, it is the duty of English courts to adopt this approach to interpretation.

Foster v British Gas

[1991] QB 405 · European Court of Justice

[1991] 2 AC 306 · House of Lords

The female appellants claimed that their compulsory retirement at age 60 infringed the Equal Treatment Directive 76/207 (see *Marshall*, p.118). Whilst the ruling of the

ECJ in *Marshall* had led to legislative change, that was not retrospective, and the appellants sought to rely on the direct effects of that directive. A reference was made to the Court of Justice. The ECJ ruled as to the nature of state bodies against which a directive might be directly effective. This ruling was applied by the House of Lords, who decided that the British Gas Corporation (BGC) (at that time a state-owned public corporation) was a state body for these purposes.

Court of Justice:

16. As the court has consistently held (see *Becker* v *Finanzamt Munster-Innenstadt*), where the Community authorities have, by means of a directive, placed member states under a duty to adopt a certain course of action, the effectiveness of such a measure would be diminished if persons were prevented from relying on it in proceedings before a court and national courts were prevented from taking it into consideration as an element of Community law. Consequently, a member state which has not adopted the implementing measures required by the directive within the prescribed period may not plead, as against individuals, its own failure to perform the obligations which the directive entails. Thus, wherever the provisions of a directive appear, as far as their subject matter is concerned, to be unconditional and sufficiently precise, those provisions may, in the absence of implementing measures adopted within the prescribed period, be relied upon as against any national provision which is incompatible with the directive or in so far as the provisions define rights which individuals are able to assert against the state.

17. The court further held in *Marshall*'s case that where a person is able to rely on a directive as against the state he may do so regardless of the capacity in which the latter is acting, whether as employer or as public authority. In either case it is necessary to prevent the state from taking advantage of its own failure to comply with Community law.

18. On the basis of these considerations, the court has held in a series of cases that unconditional and sufficiently precise provisions of a directive could be relied on against organisations or bodies which were subject to the authority or control of the state or had special powers beyond those which result from the normal rules applicable to relations between individuals.

19. The court has accordingly held that the provisions of a directive could be relied on against tax authorities (see the judgments in *Becker*'s case . . .), local or regional authorities (see *Flli Costanzo SpA* v *Comune di Milano*), constitutionally independent authorities responsible for the maintenance of public order and safety (see *Johnston* v *Chief Constable of the Royal Ulster Constabulary*) and public authorities providing public health services (see *Marshall*'s case).

20. It follows from the foregoing that a body, whatever its legal form, which has been made responsible, pursuant to a measure adopted by the state, for providing a public service under the control of the state and which has for that purpose special powers beyond those which result from the normal rules applicable in relations between individuals is included in any event among the bodies against which the provisions of a directive capable of having direct effect may be relied upon.

House of Lords:

Lord Templeman: ' . . . It falls to this House now to determine whether the BGC was a body which was made responsible, pursuant to a measure adopted by the state, for providing a public service under the control of the state and had for that purpose special powers beyond those which result from the normal rules applicable in relations between individuals.

By the Gas Act 1972, replacing the Gas Act 1965 and since repealed by the Gas Act 1986 and orders made thereunder, the BGC was established as a body corporate. The Secretary of State was authorised to make regulations with regard to the appointment and tenure and vacation of office by members of the corporation. Section 2 provided:

(1) It shall be the duty of the Corporation to develop and maintain an efficient, co-ordinated and economical system of gas supply for Great Britain, and to satisfy, so far as it is economical to do so, all reasonable demands for gas in Great Britain . . . .

Thus the BGC was a body which was made responsible, pursuant to a measure adopted by the state, for providing a public service.

By s.4 the BGC was directed to report to the minister, who was authorised (by sub-s.(3)) to –

give to the Corporation such directions as he considers appropriate for securing that the management of the activities of the Corporation and their subsidiaries is organised in the most efficient manner; and it shall be the duty of the Corporation to give effect to any such directions.

By s.7(1) the Secretary of State was authorised to –

give to the Corporation directions of a general character as to the exercise and performance by the Corporation of their functions . . . in relation to matters which appear to him to affect the national interest, and the Corporation shall give effect to any such directions.

By s.8 the BGC was ordered to make an annual report to the minister, if so directed by the minister, in such form as might be specific in the direction on the exercise by the BGC of its functions, and on its policy and programmes. Under Pt II of the 1972 Act the Secretary of State was given general control over the finances of the corporation and, in particular, was authorised to direct the corporation to pay over to him so much of excess revenue of the corporation as appeared to him surplus to the corporation's requirements . . .

By these provisions the BGC performed its public service of providing a gas supply under the control of the state. The corporation was not independent: its members were appointed by the state, the corporation was responsible to the minister acting on behalf of the state and the corporation was subject to directions given by the Secretary of State.

By s.29(1) of the 1972 Act:

. . . no person other than the Corporation shall . . . supply gas to any premises except with the consent of the Corporation and in accordance with such conditions as may be attached to that consent.

This section conferred on BGC 'special powers beyond those which result from the normal rules applicable in relations between individuals'.

Accordingly, the BGC was, in my opinion, a body which was made responsible, pursuant to a measure adopted by the state, for providing a public service under the control of the state and had, for that purpose, special powers beyond those which resulted from the normal rules applicable in relations between individuals and therefore the BGC cannot take advantage of the failure of the state to comply with the equal treatment directive . . .

Before the European Court and before this House the respondent repeated the arguments which had found favour with the courts below; the BGC, it was submitted, was a statutory corporation engaged in commercial activities; the BGC did not perform any of the traditional functions of the state and was not the agent of the state. The European Court could not have intended to make the equal treatment directive enforceable against a commercial concern. These submissions were ignored by the European Court and are irrelevant to the tests laid down by the European Court in its ruling . . . counsel urged that the rulings of the European Court . . . indicated that there were two categories of state bodies, first, bodies which performed some of the traditional functions of the state and, secondly, bodies such as the health authority in *Marshall*'s case which were expressly appointed agents of the state or of a minister to carry out functions assumed by the state. The European Court in its present ruling, it was now submitted, had not clearly provided that nationalised industries carrying out commercial functions were to be regarded as organs of the state.

My Lords, the principle laid down by the European Court is that the state must not be allowed to take advantage of its own failure to comply with Community law. The policy of the BGC, which involved discrimination against women in breach of the equal treatment directive, was no doubt thought to be in the financial and commercial interests of the BGC. The advantages of the policy would accrue indirectly to the state, which provided through the BGC a supply of the gas for all citizens generally and which was entitled to the surplus revenue of the BGC. If the BGC were allowed to escape the consequences of an admitted breach of the equal treatment directive the state would be taking advantage of its own failure to comply with Community law. In these circumstances I can see no justification for a narrow or strained construction of the ruling of the European Court which applies to a body 'under the control of the state'. That control was exercised by the Secretary of State, who could give general and special directions and to whom the BGC was accountable. The day-to-day control exercised by the BGC over its activities did not render the BGC independent. In the final analysis the BGC was under the control of the state and nobody else. Similarly, I can see no justification for a narrow or strained construction of the ruling of the European Court which applies to a body which has 'special powers beyond those which result from the normal rules applicable in relations between individuals'. The 1972 Act conferred on the BGC an express power to prevent anyone else from supplying gas in the United Kingdom. That power was special power which could not have resulted from transactions between individuals. I decline to apply the ruling of the European Court, couched in terms of broad principle and purposive language characteristic of Community law in a manner which is, for better or worse, sometimes applied to enactments of the United Kingdom Parliament. I can find no warrant in the present circumstances for the limited and speculative approach of the respondent and have no means of judging whether the relevant provisions of the equal treatment directive are enforceable against the BGC save by applying the plain words of the ruling of the European Court . . .'

Comment

(1)   *Foster* v *British Gas* was considered in *Doughty* v *Rolls-Royce*. In that case the government was the controlling shareholder in the company. This did not have the consequence of making the company a state body for the purposes of the doctrine of direct effects. The court in *Doughty* left open the question as to whether the *Foster* test was the right one in all circumstances.

(2)   In *Griffin v South West Water Services Ltd*, the High Court decided that a privatized water company is an 'emanation of the state' within the principles stated by the Court of Justice in *Foster*. The defendant company, created by the Water Act 1989, had a clear public service function, laid down in the Water Industry Act 1991, namely to develop and maintain an efficient and economical system of water supply. It also possessed a range of statutory powers to facilitate the performance of that function. In respect of the key test as to whether the company was 'under the control of the State', the crucial question was whether the public service in question was under such control, not whether that body was so controlled. The fact that the body in question was a commercial body, not controlled in its day-to-day activities by the State, was irrelevant.

Applying this test, Blackburne J concluded that the defendant company was performing 'its public service as a water and sewerage undertaker under the control of the State'. It could therefore be the subject of direct effects of a directive, but was held not to be liable in that way, because the directives in question were insufficiently precise.

(3)   Some comparison can be made with the approach to whether matters are 'governmental' for the purposes of judicial review: see p.224.

The relationship between Community law and United Kingdom statutes

The relationship between the two sources of law has already been seen: p.108. In cases of conflict, directly applicable Community law will prevail. The approach by way of interpretation is, though, still important. Not only will there be a wish to avoid conflict where possible; the approach to interpretation is still of vital importance in the treatment of non-directly effective directives.

Garland v *British Rail Engineering*

[1983] 2 AC 751 · House of Lords

Following a reference to the ECJ the House of Lords held that the Sex Discrimination Act 1975 should be construed subject to the provisions of art.119.

Lord Diplock: 'My Lords, even if the obligation to observe the provisions of art.119 were an obligation assumed by the United Kingdom under an ordinary international treaty or convention and there were no question of the treaty obligation being directly applicable as part of the law to be applied by the courts in this country without need for any further enactment, it is a principle of construction of United Kingdom statutes, now too well established to call for citation of authority, that the words of a statute passed after the Treaty has been signed and dealing with the subject matter of the international obligation of the United Kingdom, are to be construed if they are reasonably capable of bearing such a meaning, as intended to carry out the obligation, and not to be inconsistent with it. A fortiori is this the case where the treaty obligation arises under one of the Community treaties to which s.2, European Communities Act 1972, applies.

The instant appeal does not present an appropriate occasion to consider whether, having regard to the express direction as to the construction of enactments "to be passed" which is contained in s.2 (4) anything short of an express positive statement in an Act of Parliament passed after January 1, 1973, that a particular provision is intended to be made in breach of an obligation assumed by the United Kingdom under a Community treaty, would justify an English court in construing that provision in a manner inconsistent with a Community treaty obligation of the United Kingdom, however wide a departure from the prima facie meaning of the language of the provision might be needed in order to achieve consistency. For, in the instant case the words of s.6(4), Sex Discrimination Act 1975, that fall to be construed, "provision in relation to . . . retirement," without any undue straining of the ordinary meaning of the language used, are capable of bearing either the narrow meaning accepted by the Employment Appeal Tribunal or the wider meaning preferred by the Court of Appeal but acknowledged by that court to be largely a matter of first impression. Had the attention of the court been drawn to art.119 of the EEC Treaty and the judgment of the European Court of Justice in *Defrenne* v *Sabena*, I have no doubt that, consistently with statements made by Lord Denning MR in previous cases, they would have construed s.6(4) so as not to make it inconsistent with art.119 . . .'

Comment

(1) The most important of the statements made by Lord Denning was in *Macarthys Ltd* v *Smith*. In that case the Court of Appeal considered a claim for equal pay brought by a woman employee. Lord Denning considered that Community law should be used as an aid to construction of the English statute, and concluded that the claim for equal pay was capable of succeeding on that basis. This approach differed markedly from that of Lawton and Cumming-Bruce LJJ, who concluded that the words of the United Kingdom Act were clear and unambiguous but then concluded that the question of whether claims of this type should succeed on the basis of European law was unclear. A reference was made to

the ECJ under art.177, the responses to which formed the basis for the claim for equal pay for equal work succeeding.

The approach of Lord Denning is that taken in *Garland*. Since the *Factortame* case, whichever approach is taken will, in most cases, not affect the result.

(2) The wider application of *Garland* to treaty provisions was discussed in *R* v *Secretary of State for the Home Department, ex parte Brind*: see p.293.

Pickstone v *Freemans plc*

[1989] AC 66 · House of Lords

The court was considering the interpretation of a statutory provision (inserted by regulation into an earlier Act) to give effect to an obligation imposed by Community directive. In the Court of Appeal the words of the statute were found to be clear and unambiguous, but over which Community law prevailed. (Cf. Lawton and Cumming-Bruce LJJ in *Macarthys Ltd* v *Smith*.) By contrast, the House of Lords held that a purposive approach to interpretation should be taken.

Lord Oliver: ' . . . It must, I think, be recognised that so to construe a provision which, on its face, is unambiguous involves a departure from a number of well-established rules of construction. The intention of Parliament has, it is said, to be ascertained from the words which it has used and those words are to be construed according to their plain and ordinary meaning. The fact that a statute is passed to give effect to an international treaty does not, of itself, enable the treaty to be referred to in order to construe the words used in other than in their plain and unambiguous sense. Moreover, even in the case of ambiguity, what is said in Parliament in the course of the passage of the Bill, cannot ordinarily be referred to assist in construction. I think, however, that it has also to be recognised that a statute which is passed in order to give effect to the United Kingdom's obligations under the EEC Treaty falls into a special category and it does so because, unlike other treaty obligations, those obligations have, in effect, been incorporated into English law by the European Communities Act 1972 . . .

Those regulations having been passed with the manifest and express purpose of producing a full compliance with the United Kingdom's obligation, they fall to be construed accordingly and that which I have suggested as falling to be implied into s.1(2)(c) is necessary to achieve that purpose . . . In the instant case, the strict and literal construction of the section does indeed involve the conclusion that the regulations, although purporting to give full effect to the United Kingdom's obligations under art.119, were in fact in breach of those obligations. The question, following Lord Diplock's formulation of principle, is whether they are reasonably capable of bearing a meaning which does in fact comply with the obligations imposed by the EEC Treaty. I was, initially, in some doubt . . . that doubt removed, I am satisfied that the words of s.1(2)(c), whilst on the face of them unequivocal, are reasonably capable of bearing a meaning which will not put the United Kingdom in breach of its treaty obligations. This conclusion is justified, in my judgment, by the manifest purpose of the legislation, by its history, and by the compulsive provision of s.2(4) of the 1972 Act. It is comforting indeed to find, from the statement made by the minister to which my noble and learned friend has referred, that this construction does in fact conform not only with what clearly was the parliamentary intention but also with what was stated to be the parliamentary intention.'

Comment

(1) In *Litster* v *Forth Dry Dock and Engineering Co. Ltd* the House of Lords indicated that, in construing a United Kingdom measure intended to give effect to a non-directly effective Community measure, the court would construe not simply in accordance with that measure, but also consistently with the interpretations placed upon it by the ECJ. This is an application of the principle in the *von Colson* case, p.100.

(2) The Court of Justice has extended the operation of the *von Colson* principle. See *Marleasing SA* v *La Comercial Internacional De Alimentacion SA* (Case C–196/89), where the court stated at paragraphs 6–8:

> With regard to the question whether an individual may rely on the directive against a national law, it should be observed that . . . a directive may not of itself impose obligations on an individual and, consequently, a provision of a directive may not be relied upon as against such a person [*Marshall*, p.118].
>
> However, it is apparent [in this case] that the national court seeks in substance to ascertain whether a national court hearing a case which falls within the scope of Directive 68/151 is required to interpret its national law in the light of the wording and the purpose of the directive . . .
>
> In order to reply to that question, it should be observed that, as the Court pointed out in . . . *von Colson and Kamann* v *Land Nordrhein Westfalen*, the Member States' obligation arising from a directive to achieve the result envisaged by the directive and their duty under art.5 EEC to take all appropriate measures, whether general or particular, to ensure the fulfilment of that obligation, is binding on all the authorities of Member States including, for matters within their jurisdiction, the courts. It follows that, in applying national law, whether the provisions in question were adopted before or after the directive, the national court called upon to interpret it is required to do so, so far as possible, in the light of the wording and the purpose of the directive in order to achieve the result pursued by the latter and thereby comply with the third paragraph of Article 189. . . .

This has not been applied by the United Kingdom courts. See *Duke* v *Reliance Systems* (below); *Webb* v *EMO Air Cargo*.

Duke v *Reliance Systems Ltd*

[1988] 1 AC 618 · House of Lords

R, a company, had a policy where the retirement age for women was 60 compared with 65 for men. A was dismissed shortly after attaining 60 years. She complained to an industrial tribunal, on the grounds she had been discriminated against contrary to s.6(2) of the Sex Discrimination Act 1975. Her complaint was dismissed on the grounds that s.6(4) did not operate in respect of discriminatory retirement ages. An appeal to the Employment Appeal Tribunal was dismissed. A further appeal to the Court of Appeal was dismissed since the Sex Discrimination Act 1975 was not passed to give effect to the Equal Treatment Directives. That decision was upheld by the House of Lords. At the time of the passage of the legislation the United Kingdom government considered that the law was in conformity with Community obligations: the Act was not passed to give effect to a directive, and must therefore be given its ordinary and natural meaning.

Lord Templeman: 'The United Kingdom, pursuant to its obligations under the EEC Treaty to give effect to Community legislation as construed by the European Court of Justice and following the decision in *Marshall*'s case, enacted the Sex Discrimination Act 1986 . . . so as to render unlawful discriminatory retirement ages as between men and women. The Act of 1986 was not retrospective and does not avail the appellant.

Marshall's case decided that the Equal Treatment Directive required member states to prohibit discrimination with regard to retirement or dismissal in accordance with an employer's policy. In the present case therefore, the appellant can show that her forcible retirement before reaching the age of 65 years was discrimination contrary to the requirements of the Equal Treatment Directive. But *Marshall*'s case also decided that the Equal Treatment Directive did not possess direct effect as between individuals, so that the appellant cannot claim damages against the respondent simply for breach of the directive . . .

Of course a British court will always be willing and anxious to conclude that United Kingdom law is consistent with Community law. Where an Act is passed for the purpose of giving effect to an obligation imposed by a directive or other instrument a British court will seldom encounter difficulty in concluding that the language of the Act is effective for the intended purpose. But the construction of a British Parliament is a matter of judgment to be determined by British courts and to be derived from the language of the legislation considered in the light of the circumstances prevailing at the date of enactment. The circumstances in which the Equal Pay Act 1970 and the Sex Discrimination Act 1975 were enacted are set forth . . .

The Acts were not passed to give effect to the Equal Treatment Directive and were intended to preserve discriminatory retirement ages. Proposals for the Equal Treatment Directive . . . were in circulation when the Bill for the Sex Discrimination Act 1975 was under discussion but it does not appear that these proposals were understood by the British Government or the Parliament of the United Kingdom to involve the prohibition of differential retirement ages linked to differential pensionable ages.

[Lord Templeman cited Lord Diplock in *Garland*, p.127, and continued:]

On the hearing of this appeal, your Lordships have had the advantage, not available to Lord Diplock, of full argument which has satisfied me that the Sex Discrimination Act 1975 was not intended to give effect to the Equal Treatment Directive as subsequently construed in the *Marshall* case and that the words of s.6(4) are not reasonably capable of being limited to the meaning ascribed to them by the appellant. Section 2(4), European Communities Act 1972, does not in my opinion enable or constrain a British court to distort the meaning of a British statute in order to enforce against an individual a Community directive which has no direct effect between individuals. Section 2(4) applies and only applies where Community provisions are directly applicable.'

Comment

(1) This case should be compared with *Pickstone* v *Freemans plc* (p.128), where the court applied the principle in *von Colson*. In *Duke* v *Reliance Systems*, essentially the argument is that the test stated in *von Colson* does not apply. The duty to interpret consistently with Community obligations only extends 'in so far as it is given discretion to do so under national law'. Lord Templeman is saying that there is no discretion. See also *Webb* v *EMO Air Cargo*; *Re Hartlebury Printers Ltd* (p.120).

(2) The reasoning of the court is to an extent circular. There is no discretion because the House of Lords says there is none, relying on s.2(4), ECA 1972. Arguably the duty to apply principles of European law requires the court to take a different view, and is given precedence by virtue of s.2(4). So to reason would, however, virtually eliminate the distinction between regulations and directives.

(3) The distinction between regulations and directives is further eroded by *Francovich* v *Italian Republic* where the ECJ stated that in some circumstances an individual may be able successfully to claim damages from the state for failure to implement a directive. In that case the directive was intended to confer individual rights, the rights of the claimant were quantifiable from the directive, and the directive would have had direct effect but for the discretion remaining in the hands of the state as to which body within the state should bear liability. It would be an overstatement to say that damages can be claimed for any failure found to exist. However, where there is a deliberate failure to implement a directive, or disregard of a Court of Justice ruling, damages may be a distinct possibility.

(4) The remedy for breach of Community law in cases like *Duke* where no direct effects exist is to seek action against the United Kingdom in the Court of Justice. This will usually be by the Commission, under art.169, since no right of individual petition arises other than to a limited extent against the actions of the Community institutions (art.173).

Kirklees BC v Wickes Building Supplies

[1992] 3 WLR 170 · House of Lords

The House of Lords considered whether a cross-undertaking in damages was required of a local authority seeking an interim injunction to prevent stores trading illegally on Sundays. The injunction was being sought pending a ruling from the Court of Justice as to the compatibility of the relevant statutory provision with art.30, Treaty of Rome. The House ruled that no cross-undertaking was required.

Lord Goff: 'I turn next to the question of the undertaking in damages . . . [and] first consider the point under English domestic law. This depends upon a proper understanding of the decision of this House in *F. Hoffman-La Roche & Co* v *Secretary of State for Trade and Industry* . . . It was decided, first, that in actions brought by the Crown to enforce or protect its proprietary or contractual rights, it should be in no different a position from the ordinary citizen and so should be required to give an undertaking in the normal way. But second, it was held that different principles applied in cases where the Crown brought a law enforcement action, in which an injunction was sought to restrain a subject from breaking a law where the breach would be harmful to the public or a section of it . . .

[Lord Goff then cited from the judgment of Lord Diplock in *Hoffman-La Roche*, described its application by the Court of Appeal in the instant case, and continued:]

I do not read the speeches in the *Hoffman-La Roche* case as conferring a privilege on the Crown in law enforcement proceedings. On the contrary I read them as dismantling an old Crown privilege and substituting for it a principle upon which, in certain limited circumstances, the court has a discretion whether or not to require an undertaking in damages from the Crown as law enforcer . . .

It follows that, apart from the question of the impact of Community law, such is the discretion which the courts should have exercised in the present case. I turn therefore to the issue of Community law . . .

[Lord Goff identified and discussed the relevant case law on this matter. He continued:]

It is against that background that I return to the conclusion of the majority of the Court of Appeal that the mere fact that [the defendant] may be able to advance [an argument that the statute was contrary to art.30, EEC Treaty] which was not at least a groundless argument, compelled the Court of Appeal to require an undertaking in damages from the council. In so holding, the court relied in particular upon the decision of the European Court in *Amministrazione delle Finanze dello Stato* v *Simmenthal SpA* in which the court ruled:

> A national court which is called upon, within the limits of its jurisdiction, to apply provisions of Community law is under a duty to give full effect to those provisions, if necessary refusing of its own motion to apply any conflicting provisions of national legislation, even if adopted subsequently, and it is not necessary for the court to request or await the setting aside of such provisions by legislative or other constitutional means.

I only pause to observe . . . that the decision, although obviously of great importance, was not concerned with the terms upon which interim relief in the form of an interlocutory injunction should be granted . . .

[Counsel for the local authority] submitted . . . that, if a national court is considering whether to grant an interlocutory injunction in a case such as the present, where the validity of the law sought to be enforced is challenged by the defendant on the ground that it is inconsistent with Community law, the question whether the court should require an undertaking in damages from the plaintiff as a condition of the grant of an injunction is to be decided . . . [under national law], being a question of procedure which . . . is left to national law [by Community law: *Factortame Ltd* v *Secretary of State for Transport (No. 2)*] . . .

[This submission] is too sweeping in its effect . . . [it] cannot . . . necessarily be regarded as a matter of procedure for the national law where the imposition of the term under consideration is directed towards preserving rights which may arise under Community law . . . [Counsel for the defendants submits] that the function of the undertaking in damages required of the council by the Court of Appeal was to protect the right of [the defendant] which flowed from the direct effect of art.30, in the event of the European Court holding, on the reference to it . . . that s.47 . . . was invalid because it was inconsistent with art.30 . . . This submission . . . appears to me . . . to be misconceived.

I approach the matter as follows. In *Bourgoin SA* v *Ministry of Agriculture, Fisheries & Food* it was held by the Court of Appeal . . . that a breach of art.30 would not of itself give rise to a claim in damages by the injured party. However, since the decision of the European Court in *Francovich* v *Italian Republic* . . . there must now be doubt whether the *Bourgoin* case was correctly decided. It is true that *Francovich*'s case was concerned with the situation where a member state fails to implement an EEC directive, the court holding that in such a case the member state is obliged to make good damage suffered by individuals as a result of its failure so to do. But the court in its judgment spoke in more general terms:

33. It should be stated that the full effectiveness of Community provisions would be affected and the protection of rights they recognise undermined if individuals were not able to recover damages when their rights were infringed by a breach of Community law attributable to a member state.
34. The possibility of obtaining damages from the state is particularly essential where, as in the present case, the full effect of Community provisions is conditional upon the state taking certain action, and, in consequence, in the absence of such action being taken, individuals cannot rely on the rights accorded to them by Community law before national courts.
35. It follows that the principle of the liability of the state for damage to individuals caused by a breach of Community law for which it is responsible is inherent in the scheme of the Treaty.
36. The obligation on member states to make good the damage is also based on art.5 of the Treaty, under which the member states are bound to take all appropriate measures, whether general or particular, to ensure fulfilment of the obligations arising under Community law . . .
37. It follows from the foregoing that Community law lays down a principle according to which a member state is obliged to make good the damage to individuals caused by a breach of Community law for which it is responsible.

It is not necessary [for this case] to decide whether the *Bourgoin* case was correctly decided . . . but, having regard to the [cited passages] . . . it is in my opinion right that in the present case Your Lordships should proceed on the basis that if, on the reference to it in the *Stoke on Trent* case the court should hold that s.47, Shops Act 1950 is invalid as being in conflict with art.30 . . . the United Kingdom may be obliged to make good damage caused to individuals by the breach of art.30 for which it is responsible.

It does not, however, follow that, in the present case, the council should be obliged to give an undertaking in damages as a condition of the grant of an injunction . . . This is because the obligation (if any) on the United Kingdom to make good any damage suffered by [the defendant] will arise irrespective of any undertaking in damages given by the council . . . But there are two other subsidiary matters which reinforce the conclusion that the council should not be required to give such an undertaking. The first is that the effect of such an undertaking would be to impose an obligation on the council to indemnify [the defendant] . . . irrespective of whether in such circumstances [the defendant] has a right to damages, i.e. irrespective of whether the *Bourgoin* case was wrongly decided. In other words, that question is pre-empted by the requirement of such an undertaking from the council. The second is that, if, following *Francovich*'s case, there was held to be a right to damages in such circumstances, the effect of requiring an undertaking from the council would be to impose liability in damages on the council instead of on the United Kingdom [government] . . .'

Comment

(1) The availability of damages in national law for breach of Community obligations is uncertain. In *Garden Cottage Foods* v *Milk Marketing Board* the availability of damages was accepted. This was distinguished in *Bourgoin SA* v *Ministry of Agriculture, Fisheries & Food* as being confined to where the alleged breach was by an individual. The majority of the court in *Bourgoin* were of the view that the failure of the state to implement its obligations was a public law matter for which judicial review, not damages, was the appropriate remedy. It may well be that the duty to provide effective remedies (see *R* v *Secretary of State for Transport, ex parte Factortame*, p.108) will require reconsideration of the *Bourgoin* ruling.

(2) Lord Goff also considered the right of an individual to seek civil remedies to prevent breach of the criminal law. See, generally, *Gouriet* v *Union of Post Office Workers* (p.260).

(3) In *R* v *HM Treasury, ex parte British Telecommunications plc* a Divisional Court assumed (without deciding) that damages might be available to a British company which had sought judicial review of legislation allegedly in breach of a Community directive.

(4) In *Faccini Dori* v *Recreb Srl* (Case 91/92) the Court of Justice stated that Community law required the Member State to make good damage caused to individuals through failure to transpose a directive, provided three conditions were fulfilled: (1) that the directive was intended to confer individual rights; (2) it must be possible to identify the content of those rights on the basis of the provisions of that directive; (3) there has to be a causal link between the breach of the state's obligation and the damage suffered.

Where damage has been suffered and that damage was caused by that state's failure, it was for the national court to uphold the right of aggrieved persons in accordance with national law on liability.

7 The European Convention on Human Rights

The common law tends to recognize residual liberties rather than rights, and starts from the basis that the citizen is free to do anything except that which is forbidden by law; the common law has not created any fundamental rights which are inviolate. In the absence of a constitutional document or Bill of Rights guaranteeing basic liberties and rights, and in the light of the inability of the Courts to control the legislative power of Parliament other than by interpretation, we must look elsewhere for the standards of rights and freedoms which are to exist in the United Kingdom.

The European Convention on Human Rights (ECHR) has not been incorporated into United Kingdom law and thus does not form part of the law of the United Kingdom – see *Blackburn* v *Attorney-General* (p.81) and *R* v *Secretary of State for the Home Department ex parte Brind* (p.150 and p.293). In *Maclaine Watson* v *Department of Trade* Lord Templeman said:

> A treaty is a contract between the governments of two or more sovereign states. International law regulates the relations between sovereign states and determines the validity, the interpretation and the enforcement of treaties. A treaty to which Her Majesty's government is a party does not alter the laws of the United Kingdom. A treaty may be incorporated into and alter the laws of the United Kingdom by means of legislation. Except to the extent that a treaty becomes incorporated into the laws of the United Kingdom by statute, the courts of the United Kingdom have no power to enforce treaty rights and obligations at the behest of a sovereign government or at the behest of a private individual.

The Courts may use the ECHR to construe United Kingdom legislation and will presume that Parliament intended to legislate in accordance with it; but this presumption must yield to a contrary intention being discovered either by express or necessary implication. In *Birdi* v *Secretary of State for Home Affairs* Lord Denning observed that: 'The courts could and should take the Convention into account in interpreting the Statute. An Act of

Parliament should be construed as to conform with the Convention.' Later, in *R* v *Secretary of State for Home Affairs, ex parte Singh*, he said:

> I said [in *Birdi*] that if an Act of Parliament did not conform to the convention I might be inclined to hold that it was invalid. That was a very tentative statement, but it went too far. There are many cases in which it has been said, as plainly as can be, that a Treaty does not become part of English law except and insofar as it is made so by Parliament.

Although the ECHR cannot fetter the legislative power of Parliament, it can influence the development of the common law, for example to discover where policy demands that a particular line be drawn (see, e.g., *Attorney-General* v *Guardian Newspapers (No. 1)* and *(No. 2)* and *Lord Advocate* v *Scotsman Publications Ltd*, p.163).

Where United Kingdom law or executive action has been found to be in breach of the ECHR there is an obligation under the convention to take action to secure compliance. There are many examples of this, e.g. after the finding in *Sunday Times* v *United Kingdom* that aspects of the law on contempt of court were in breach of art.10, the law on contempt was altered by the Contempt of Court Act 1981; after adverse findings in *Silver* v *United Kingdom* and *Golder* v *United Kingdom*, the Prison Rules were amended; after the adverse finding in *Campbell & Cosans* v *United Kingdom*, the law relating to the chastisement of schoolchildren was amended by the Education (No. 2) Act 1986; as a result of the finding in *Home Office* v *Harman*, statutory provision was made to permit access by journalists to material read out or referred to in open court.

Even where a likely breach of the ECHR is pointed out judicially action may not follow and the government may wait for an adverse finding in the European Court of Human Rights – see *Malone* v *Metropolitan Police Commissioner (No. 2)* (p.141). However, there are instances where the United Kingdom government has taken steps prior to action in the European Court of Human Rights, e.g. certain interrogation techniques used in Northern Ireland were criticized as unlawful in an extra-judicial inquiry by Lord Parker (Cmnd 4901) – see in particular the dissenting view of Lord Gardiner. These techniques were abandoned when the report was published. Six years later, in *Ireland* v *United Kingdom* the United Kingdom was found to be in breach of art.3.

Submission to the requirements of the ECHR may take the form of a derogation under art.15, e.g. the derogation in respect of certain emergency powers in Northern Ireland (considered in *Ireland* v *United Kingdom*) and the derogation in connection with the Prevention of Terrorism (Temporary Provisions) Act 1984 as a result of the case of *Brogan* v *United Kingdom.*

European Convention on Human Rights and Fundamental Freedoms

Article 1

The high contracting parties shall secure to everyone within their jurisdiction the rights and freedoms defined in Section 1 of this Convention.

Section 1
Article 2

1. Everyone's right to life shall be protected by law. No one shall be deprived of his life intentionally save in the execution of a sentence of a court following his conviction of a crime for which this penalty is provided by law.

2. Deprivation of life shall not be regarded as inflicted in contravention of this article when it results from the use of force which is no more than absolutely necessary:
    a. in defence of any person from unlawful violence;
    b. in order to effect a lawful arrest or to prevent the escape of a person lawfully detained;
    c. in action lawfully taken for the purpose of quelling a riot or insurrection.

Article 3

No one shall be subjected to torture or to inhuman or degrading treatment or punishment.

[Article 4 relates to slavery]

Article 5

1. Everyone has the right to liberty and security of person. No one shall be deprived of his liberty save in the following cases and in accordance with a procedure prescribed by law:
    a. the lawful detention of a person after conviction by a competent court;
    b. the lawful arrest or detention of a person for non-compliance with the lawful order of a court or in order to secure the fulfilment of any obligation prescribed by law;
    c. the lawful arrest or detention of a person effected for the purpose of bringing him before the competent legal authority on reasonable suspicion of having committed an offence or fleeing after having done so; . . .
2. Everyone who is arrested shall be informed promptly, in a language which he understands, of the reasons for his arrest and of any charge against him.

3. Everyone arrested or detained in accordance with the provisions of paragraph 1 (c) of this article shall be brought promptly before a judge or other officer authorised by law to exercise judicial power and shall be entitled to trial within a reasonable time or to release pending trial. Release may be conditioned by guarantees to appear for trial.

4. Everyone who is deprived of his liberty by arrest or detention shall be entitled to take proceedings by which the lawfulness of his detention shall be decided speedily by a court and his release ordered if the detention is not lawful.

5. Everyone who has been the victim of arrest or detention in contravention of the provisions of this article shall have an enforceable right to compensation.

Article 6

1. In the determination of his civil rights and obligations or of any criminal charge against him, everyone is entitled to a fair and public hearing within a reasonable time by an independent and impartial tribunal established by law. Judgement shall be pronounced publicly but the press and public may be excluded from all or part of the trial in the interests of morals, public order or national security in a democratic society, where the interests of juveniles or the protection of the private life of the parties so require, or to the extent strictly necessary in the opinion of the court in special circumstances where publicity would prejudice the interests of justice . . .

Article 7

1. No one shall be held guilty of any criminal offence on account of any act or omission which did not constitute a criminal offence under national or international law at the time when it was committed. Nor shall a heavier penalty be imposed than the one that was applicable at the time the criminal offence was committed.

2. This article shall not prejudice the trial and punishment of any person for any act or omission which, at the time when it was committed, was criminal according to the general principles of law recognised by civilised nations.

Article 8

1. Everyone has the right to respect for his private and family life, his home and his correspondence.

2. There shall be no interference by a public authority with the exercise of this right except such as is in accordance with the law and is necessary in a democratic society in the interests of national security, public safety or the economic well-being of the country, for the prevention of disorder or crime, for the protection of health or morals, or for the protection of the rights and freedoms of others.

Article 9

1. Everyone has the right to freedom of thought, conscience and religion; this right includes freedom to change his religion or belief and freedom, either alone or in community with others and in public or private, to manifest his religion or belief, in worship, teaching, practice and observance.

2. Freedom to manifest one's religion or beliefs shall be subject only to such limitations as are prescribed by law and are necessary in a democratic society in the interests of public safety, for the protection of public order, health or morals, or for the protection of the rights and freedoms of others.

Article 10

1. Everyone has the right to freedom of expression. This right shall include freedom to hold opinions and to receive and impart information and ideas without interference by public authority and regardless of frontiers. This article shall not prevent States from requiring the licensing of broadcasting, television or cinema enterprises.

2. The exercise of these freedoms, since it carries with it duties and responsibilities, may be subject to such formalities, conditions, restrictions or penalties as are prescribed by law and are necessary in a democratic society, in the interests of national security, territorial integrity or public safety, for the prevention of disorder or crime, for the protection of health or morals, for the protection of the reputation or rights of others, for preventing the disclosure of information received in confidence, or for maintaining the authority and impartiality of the judiciary.

Article 11

1. Everyone has the right to freedom of peaceful assembly and to freedom of association with others, including the right to form and to join trade unions for the protection of his interests.

2. No restrictions shall be placed on the exercise of these rights other than such as are prescribed by law and are necessary in a democratic society in the interests of national security or public safety, for the prevention of disorder or crime, for the protection of health or morals or for the protection of the rights and freedoms of others . . .

[Article 12 relates to a right to marry and found a family]

Article 13

Everyone whose rights and freedoms as set forth in this Convention are violated shall have an effective remedy before a national authority notwithstanding that the violation has been committed by persons acting in an official capacity.

[Article 14 relates to the enjoyment of the rights free from discrimination]

Article 15

1.   In time of war or other public emergency threatening the life of the nation, any High Contracting Party may take measures derogating from its obligations under this Convention to the extent strictly required by the exigencies of the situation, provided that such measures are not inconsistent with its other obligations under international law.

2.   No derogation from Article 2, except in respect of deaths resulting from lawful acts of war, or from Articles 3, 4 (paragraph 1) and 7 shall be made under this provision . . .

Comment

(1)   For art.8 see *Malone* v *Metropolitan Police Commissioner No. 2* (p.141); for art.9 see *Ahmad* v *ILEA* (p.148); for art.10 see *Attorney-General* v *Guardian Newspapers (No. 1)* and *(No. 2)* (p.157) and *Gleaves* v *Deakin* (below); for art.5 see *Hone* v *Maze Prison Board of Prison Visitors* (p.343).

(2)   Consider: art.2 in the context of *Attorney-General for Northern Ireland's Reference No. 1 of 1975* (p.404); art.10 in the context of open justice (p.199); art.5 in the context of the Police and Criminal Evidence Act 1984 (p.392).

(3)   The jurisprudence of the European Community demands consistency between Community law and international obligations. Thus, fundamental rights form part of the general principles of Community law – see *Nold* v *Commission*. For the European Community, see p.102.

Gleaves v Deakin

[1980] AC 477 · House of Lords

The House of Lords considered the elements of the offence of criminal libel and concluded that it required only an intention to publish the particular matter. The House of Lords commented upon the requirements of the ECHR.

Lord Diplock: '. . . this particular offence has retained anomalies which involve serious departures from accepted principles . . . [which] are difficult to reconcile with international obligations which this country has undertaken by becoming a party to the [ECHR] . . . [U]nder art.10.2 . . .the exercise of the right of freedom of expression may be subjected to restrictions or penalties by a contracting state, only to the extent that those restrictions or penalties are necessary in a democratic society for the protection of what (apart from the reputation of individuals and the protection of information received in confidence) may generically be described as the public interest. In contrast to this the truth of the defamatory statement is not in itself a defence to a charge of defamatory libel under our criminal law; so here is a restriction on the freedom to impart information which states that are parties to the

Convention have expressly undertaken to secure to everyone within their jurisdiction. No onus lies upon the prosecution to show that the defamatory matter was of a kind that it is necessary in a democratic society to suppress or penalise in order to protect the public interest. On the contrary, even though no public interest can be shown to be injuriously affected by imparting to others accurate information about seriously discreditable conduct of an individual, the publisher of the information must be convicted unless he himself can prove to the satisfaction of a jury that the publication of it was for the public benefit.

This is to turn art.10 . . . on its head. Under our criminal law a person's freedom of expression, wherever it involves exposing seriously discreditable conduct of others, is to be repressed by public authority unless he can convince a jury *ex post facto* that the particular exercise of the freedom was for the public benefit; whereas art.10 requires that freedom of expression shall be untrammelled by public authority except where its interference to repress a particular exercise of the freedom is necessary for the protection of the public interest . . .'

Comment

The Law Commission called for a change in the law, but no changes have yet taken place.

Malone v *Metropolitan Police Commissioner (No. 2)*

[1979] Ch 344 · Chancery Division

During a trial of the plaintiff on a theft charge a police officer inadvertently revealed that the plaintiff's telephone had been 'tapped'. The plaintiff brought an action in which he challenged the legality of the telephone tapping. The telephone tap was assumed to have been carried out by the Post Office on Post Office premises at the request of the police acting on just cause in connection with a criminal matter and authorized by a warrant issued by the Home Secretary. The Chancery Division held that there was no specific provision of law authorizing the tapping of telephones in those circumstances but that none was required since the various rights alleged by the plaintiff did not exist in respect of telephonic communications. Accordingly the court found against the plaintiff.

Sir Robert Megarry V-C: '. . . [The Plaintiff's] first main contention was that by reason of the right of privacy and the right of confidentiality it was unlawful to tap a telephone, even under the authority of a warrant of the Home Secretary . . . First, I do not think that any assistance is obtained from the general warrant cases, or other authorities dealing with warrants. At common law, the only power to search premises under a search warrant issued by a justice of the peace is to search for stolen goods: see *Entick* v *Carrington*. However, many statutes authorise searches under search warrants for many different purposes; and there is admittedly no statute which in terms authorises the tapping of telephones, with or without a warrant. Nevertheless, any conclusion that the tapping of telephones is therefore illegal would plainly be superficial in the extreme. The reason why a search of premises which is not authorised by law is illegal is that it involves the tort of trespass to those premises: and any trespass, whether to land or goods or the person, that is made without legal authority is prima facie illegal. Telephone tapping by the Post Office, on the other hand, involves no act of trespass . . . There is no question of there being any trespass on the plaintiff's premises for the purpose of attaching anything either to the premises themselves or to anything on them: all that is done is done within the Post Office's own domain. As Lord Camden CJ said in *Entick* v *Carrington*, "the eye cannot by the laws of England be guilty of a trespass"; and, I would add, nor can the ear.

Second, I turn to the warrant of the Home Secretary. This contrasts with search warrants in that it is issued by one of the great officers of state as such, and not by a justice of the peace acting as such. Furthermore, it does not purport to be issued under the authority of any statute or of the common law. From the Birkett Report [1957 Cmnd 283] it appears that the power to tap telephones has been exercised "from time to time since the introduction of the telephone", but that not until 1937 were any warrants issued . . .

[After tracing the history of telephone tapping, Megarry VC continued] . . . That, however, does not alter the fact that by the Post Office Act 1969 Parliamentary recognition to such warrants was given. Accordingly, I leave this part of the case on the footing that by that Act Parliament has provided a clear recognition of the warrant of the Home Secretary as having an effective function in law, both as providing a defence to certain criminal charges, and also as amounting to an effective requirement for the Post Office to do certain acts . . .

Third, there is the right of privacy. Here the contention is that although at present no general right of privacy has been recognised by English law, there is a particular right of privacy, namely, the right to hold a telephone conversation in the privacy of one's home without molestation. This, it was said, ought to be recognised and declared to be part of English law, despite the absence of any English authority to this effect . . . I am not unduly troubled by the absence of English authority: there has to be a first time for everything, and if the principles of English law, and not least analogies from the existing rules, together with the requirements of justice and common sense, pointed firmly to such a right existing, then I think the court should not be deterred from recognising the right.

On the other hand, it is no function of the courts to legislate in a new field. The extension of the existing laws and principles is one thing, the creation of an altogether new right is another. At times judges must, and do, legislate; but as Holmes J once said, they do so only interstitially, and with molecular rather than molar motions. Anything beyond that must be left for legislation. No new right in the law, fully-fledged with all the appropriate safeguards, can spring from the head of a judge deciding a particular case: only Parliament can create such a right.

Where there is some major gap in the law, no doubt a judge would be capable of framing what he considered to be a proper code to fill it; and sometimes he may be tempted. But he has to remember that his function is judicial, not legislative, and that he ought not to use his office to legislate in the guise of exercising his judicial powers.

One of the factors that must be relevant in such a case is the degree of particularity in the right that is claimed. The wider and more indefinite the right claimed, the greater the undesirability of holding that such a right exists. Wide and indefinite rights, while conferring an advantage on those who have them, may well gravely impair the position of those who are subject to the rights. To create a right for one person, you have to impose a corresponding duty on another. In the present case, the alleged right to hold a telephone conversation in the privacy of one's own home without molestation is wide and indefinite in its scope, and in any case does not seem to be very apt for covering the plaintiff's grievance. He was not "molested" in holding his telephone conversations: he held them without "molestation", but without their retaining the privacy that he desired. If a man telephones from his own home, but an open window makes it possible for a near neighbour to overhear what is said, and the neighbour, remaining throughout on his own property, listens to the conversation, is he to be a tortfeasor? . . . Why is the right that is claimed confined to a man's own home, so that it would not apply to private telephone conversations from offices, call boxes or the houses of others? If they were to be included, what of the greater opportunities for deliberate overhearing that they offer? In any case, why is the telephone to be subject to this special right of privacy when there is no general right?

That is not all. Suppose that there is what for brevity I may call a right to telephonic privacy, sounding in tort. What exceptions to it, if any, would there be? Would it be a breach of the right if anyone listened to a telephone conversation in which some act of criminal violence or dishonesty was being planned? Should a listener be restrained by injunction from disclosing to the authorities a conversation that would lead to the release of someone who has been kidnapped? There are many, many questions that can, and should, be asked . . .

In the result, therefore, I can find nothing in the authorities or contentions that have been put before me to support the plaintiff's claim based on the right of privacy . . .

Fourth, there is the right of confidentiality. [Megarry V-C considered the requirements for confidentiality set out in *CoCo* v *AN Clark* (see *Attorney-General* v *Jonathan Cape*, p.45).]

It seems to me that a person who utters confidential information must accept the risk of any unknown overhearing that is inherent in the circumstances of communication. Those who exchange confidences on a bus or a train run the risk of a nearby passenger with acute hearing or a more distant passenger who is adept at lip-reading . . .

I do not see why someone who has overheard some secret in such a way should be exposed to legal proceedings if he uses or divulges what he has heard. No doubt an honourable man would give some warning when he realises that what he is hearing is not intended for his ears; but I have to concern myself with the law, and not with moral standards. There are, of course, many moral precepts which are not legally enforceable.

When this is applied to telephone conversations, it appears to me that the speaker is taking such risks of being overheard as are inherent in the system. As I have mentioned, the Younger Report referred to users of the telephone being aware that there were several well-understood possibilities of being overheard, and stated that a realistic person would not rely on the telephone system to protect the confidence of what he says. That comment seems unanswerable . . . No doubt a person who uses a telephone to give confidential information to another may do so in such a way as to impose an obligation of confidence on that other: but I do not see how it could be said that any such obligation is imposed on those who overhear the conversation, whether by means of tapping or otherwise.

Even if any duty of confidentiality were, contrary to my judgment, to be held to bind those who overhear a telephone conversation, there remains the question of the limits to that duty . . .

I think that one has to approach these matters with some measure of balance and common sense. The rights and liberties of a telephone subscriber are indeed important; but so also are the desires of the great bulk of the population not to be the victims of assault, theft or other crimes. The detection and prosecution of criminals, and the discovery of projected crimes, are important weapons in protecting the public. In the nature of things it will be virtually impossible to know beforehand whether any particular telephone conversation will be criminal in nature. The question is not whether there is a certainty that the conversation tapped will be iniquitous, but whether there is just cause or excuse for the tapping for the use made of the material obtained by the tapping.

If certain requirements are satisfied, then I think that there will plainly be just cause or excuse for what is done by or on behalf of the police . . . I am not, of course, saying that nothing else can constitute a just cause or excuse: what I am saying is that if these requirements are satisfied, then in my judgment there will be a just cause or excuse. I am not, for instance, saying anything about matters of national security: I speak only of what is before me in the present case, concerning tapping for police purposes in relation to crime.

So far as the evidence goes, it seems to me that the process of tapping, as carried out on behalf of the police in relation to crime, fully conforms with these requirements: indeed, there are restrictions on tapping, and safeguards, which go beyond these requirements . . .

Accordingly, in my judgment, if, contrary to my opinion, telephone tapping on behalf of the police is a breach of any duty of confidentiality, there is just cause or excuse for that tapping in the circumstances of this case . . .

Fifth there is [the plaintiff's] second main head, based on the [ECHR] and the *Klass* case. The first limb of this relates to the direct rights conferred by the Convention. Any such right is . . . a direct right in relation to the European Commission of Human Rights and the European Court of Human Rights, and not in relation to the courts of this country; for the Convention is not law here . . . The United Kingdom . . . has thus long been under an obligation to secure these rights and freedoms to everyone. That obligation, however, is an obligation under a treaty which is not justiciable in the courts of this country. Whether that obligation has been carried out is not for me to say. It is, I suppose, possible to contend that the *de facto* practice in this country sufficiently secures these rights and freedoms, without legislation for the purpose being needed. It is also plainly possible to contend that, among other things, the existing safeguards against unbridled telephone tapping, being merely administrative in nature and not imposed by law, fall far short of making any rights and freedoms "secure" to anyone, However, as I have said, that is not for me to decide. All that I do is to hold that the Convention does not, as a matter of English law, confer any direct rights on the plaintiff that he can enforce in the English courts.

Sixth, there is the second limb of [the plaintiff's] contentions, based on the Convention and the *Klass* case as assisting the court to determine what English law is on a point on which authority is lacking or uncertain. Can it be said that in this case two courses are reasonably open to the court, one of which is inconsistent with the Convention and the other consonant with it? . . . I readily accept that if the question before me were one of construing a statute enacted with the purpose of giving effect to obligations imposed by the Convention, the court would readily seek to construe the legislation in a way that would effectuate the Convention rather than frustrate it. However, no relevant legislation of that sort is in existence. It seems to me that where Parliament has abstained from legislating on a point that is plainly suitable for legislation, it is indeed difficult for the court to lay down new rules of common law or equity that will carry out the Crown's treaty obligations, or to discover for the first time that such rules have always existed.

Now the West German system that came under scrutiny in the *Klass* case was laid down by statute, and it contained a number of statutory safeguards. There must be imminent danger; other methods of surveillance must be at least considerably more difficult; both the person making the request for surveillance and the method of making it are limited; the period of surveillance is limited in time, and in any case must cease when the need has passed; the person subjected to surveillance must be notified as soon as this will not jeopardise the purpose of surveillance; no information is made available to the police unless an official qualified for judicial office is satisfied that it is within the safeguards; all other information obtained must be destroyed; the process is supervised by a Parliamentary board on which the opposition is represented; and there is also a supervising commission which may order that surveillance is to cease, or that notification of it is to be given to the person who has been subjected to it. Not a single one of these safeguards is to be found as a matter of established law in England, and only a few corresponding provisions exist as a matter of administrative procedure.

It does not, of course, follow that a system with fewer or different safeguards will fail to satisfy art.8 in the eyes of the European Court of Human Rights. At the same time, it is impossible to read the judgment in the *Klass* case without its becoming abundantly clear that a system which has no legal safeguards whatever has small chance of satisfying the requirements of that court, whatever administrative provisions there may be. Broadly, the court was concerned to see whether the German legislation provided "adequate and effective safeguards against abuse". Though in principle it was desirable that there should be judicial control of tapping, the court was satisfied that the German system provided an adequate substitute in the independence of the board and Commission from the authorities carrying out the surveillance. Further, the provisions for the subsequent notification of the surveillance when this would not frustrate its purpose were also considered to be adequate. In England, on the other hand, the system in operation provides no such independence, and contains no provision whatever for subsequent notification. Even if the system were to be considered adequate in its conditions, it is laid down merely as a matter of administrative procedure, so that it is unenforceable in law, and as a matter of law could at any time be altered without warning or subsequent notification. Certainly in law any "adequate and effective safeguards against abuse" are wanting. In this respect English law compares most unfavourably with West German law: this is not a subject on which it is possible to feel any pride in English law.

I therefore find it impossible to see how English law could be said to satisfy the requirements of the Convention, as interpreted in the *Klass* case, unless that law not only prohibited all telephone tapping save in suitably limited classes of case, but also laid down detailed restrictions on the exercise of the power in those limited classes. It may perhaps be that the common law is sufficiently fertile to achieve what is required by the first limb of this; possible ways of expressing such a rule may be seen in what I have already said. But I see the greatest difficulty in the common law framing the safeguards required by the second limb. Various institutions or offices would have to be brought into being to exercise various defined functions. The more complex and indefinite the subject matter, the greater the difficulty in the court doing what it is really appropriate, and only appropriate, for the legislature to do. Furthermore, I find it hard to see what there is in the present case to require the English courts to struggle with such a problem. Give full rein to the Convention, and it is clear that when the object of the surveillance is the detection of crime, the question is not whether there ought to be a general prohibition of all surveillance, but in what circumstances, and subject to what conditions and restrictions, it ought to be permitted. It is those circumstances, conditions and restrictions which are at the centre of this case; and yet it is they which are the least suitable for determination by judicial decision.

It appears to me that to decide this case in the way that [the plaintiff] seeks would carry me far beyond any possible function of the Convention as influencing English law that has ever been suggested; and it would be most undesirable. Any regulation of so complex a matter as telephone tapping is essentially a matter for Parliament, not the courts; and neither the Convention nor the *Klass* case can, I think, play any proper part in deciding the issue before me. Accordingly, the second limb of [the plaintiff's] second main contention also fails.

I would only add that, even if it was not clear before, this case seems to me to make it plain that telephone tapping is a subject which cries out for legislation. Privacy and confidentiality are, of course, subjects of considerable complexity. Yet however desirable it may be that they should at least to some extent be defined and regulated by statute, rather than being left for slow and expensive evolution in individual cases brought at the expense of litigants and the legal aid fund, the difficulty of the subject matter is liable to discourage legislative zeal. Telephone tapping lies in a much narrower compass; the difficulties in legislating on the subject ought not to prove insuperable; and the requirements of the Convention should provide a spur to action, even if belated. This, however, is not for me to decide. I can do no more than express a hope, and offer a proleptic welcome to any statute on the subject. However much the protection of the public against crime demands that in proper cases the police should have the assistance of telephone tapping, I would have thought that in any civilised system of law the claims of liberty and justice would require that telephone users should have effective and independent safeguards against possible abuses. The fact that a telephone user is suspected of crime increases rather than diminishes this requirement: suspicions, however reasonably held, may sometimes prove to be wholly unfounded. If there were effective and independent safeguards, these would not only exclude some cases of excessive zeal but also, by their mere existence, provide some degree of reassurance for those who are resentful of the police or believe themselves to be persecuted. I may perhaps add that it would be wrong to allow my decision in this case to be influenced by the consideration that if the courts were to hold that all telephone tapping was illegal, this might well offer a strong and prompt inducement to the government to persuade Parliament to legislate on the subject . . .'

Comment

(1) On a complaint by Mr Malone the European Court of Human Rights in *Malone* v *UK* held that the United Kingdom practices were in breach of art.8 since they were not 'in accordance with the law':

... it cannot be said with any reasonable certainty what elements of the powers to intercept are incorporated in legal rules and what elements remain within the discretion of the executive. In view of the attendant obscurity and uncertainty as to the state of the law in this essential respect, the Court cannot but reach a similar conclusion to that of the Commission. In the opinion of the Court, the law of England and Wales does not indicate with reasonable clarity the scope and manner of exercise of the relevant discretion conferred on public authorities. To that extent, the minimum degree of legal protection to which citizens are entitled under the rule of law in a democratic society is lacking.

That Court did not consider the content of the rules relating to telephone tapping to see if they were in accordance with the Convention.

(2) In the Report of a Committee of Privy Councillors on the Interception of Communications (the 'Birkett' Report) Cmnd 283 the practice of government telephone tapping was examined for the first time. The Report could find no legal basis for telephone tapping but suggested that prerogative power to intercept mails was one remote possibility. The Birkett Report was updated by a White Paper (*The Interception of Communications in Great Britain*, Cmnd 7873 (April 1980)) which was followed by a report by Lord Diplock into the practice of telephone tapping, Cmnd 8191 (March 1981). On 1 April 1980 the Home Secretary rejected the call for legislation and instead created a scheme of judicial oversight of telephone tapping, but with no judicial remedy. In February 1985, in the light of the judgment of the European Court of Human Rights, the White Paper *The Interception of Communications in Great Britain*, Cmnd 9438, outlined the government's proposals for legislation which formed the basis of the Interception of Communications Act 1985. Note the provision ousting the jurisdiction of the court (p.268) and the similar section in the Security Service Act 1989. Compare *Anisminic* v *Foreign Compensation Commission*, p.267.

(3) Megarry V-C specifically restricted his decision to government authorized tapping. In the case of non-governmental tapping remedies have been forthcoming, e.g. in *Francome* v *Mirror Newspapers* the plaintiff obtained an injunction for breach of confidence where his telephone conversations had been improperly taped.

(4) In *R* v *Khan*, the Court of Appeal, an aural surveillance device was placed by police on the exterior of the defendant's house and was conceded to have been a trespass. The use of such devices was governed by Home Office guidelines but there was no statutory or common law authority for their use. Even though there was a trespass, in the light of the seriousness of the offences under investigation and the slight damage involved, the court refused to exercise its discretion so as to exclude the evidence obtained. The Court of Appeal did suggest that consideration be given to whether or not the administrative procedures should be placed on a statutory footing as in the case of telephone tapping.

In the absence of a positive authorization in law, particularly in the light of the trespass, there will almost inevitably be a breach of art.8 because the procedure could not be said to have been authorized by law. As with telephone tapping, the principles concerning the safeguards for the individual would still have to meet the standards required by the European Court of Human Rights in order to be capable of being described as necessary in a democratic society.

Ahmad v *ILEA*

[1978] QB 36 · Court of Appeal

Mr Ahmad was employed as a full-time teacher and moved to a school which was close enough to a mosque to enable him to attend prayers on a Friday afternoon which resulted in him being late for his afternoon class. He resigned when he was told that if he continued to be late for classes he would be required to apply for a part-time post. Mr Ahmad sued in the Industrial Tribunal for unfair (constructive) dismissal and relied upon s.30 of the Education Act 1944: '... no person shall be disqualified by reason of his religious opinions, or of his attending or omitting to attend religious worship, from being a teacher ... and no teacher ... shall ... receive any less emolument or be deprived of, or disqualified for, any promotion or other advantage ... by reason of his religious opinions or of his attending or omitting to attend religious worship'. The Court of Appeal, Scarman LJ dissenting, held that s.30 should not be construed so as to permit Mr Ahmad to take time off work.

Lord Denning: '[After referring to art.9, ECHR he continued:] The convention is not part of our English law, but, as I have often said, we will always have regard to it. We will do our best to see that our decisions are in conformity with it. But it is drawn in such vague terms that it can be used for all sorts of unreasonable claims and provoke all sorts of litigation. As so often happens with high-sounding principles, they have to be brought down to earth. They have to be applied in a work-a-day world. I venture to suggest that it would do the Muslim community no good – or any other minority group no good – if they were to be given preferential treatment over the great majority of the people. If it should happen that, in the name of religious freedom, they were given special privileges or advantages, it would provoke discontent, and even resentment among those with whom they work. As, indeed, it has done in this very case. And so the cause of racial integration would suffer. So, whilst upholding religious freedom to the full, I would suggest that it should be applied with caution, especially having regard to the setting in which it is sought. Applied to our educational system, I think that Mr. Ahmad's right to "manifest his religion in practice and observance" must be subject to the rights of the education authorities under the contract and to the interests of the children whom he is paid to teach. I see nothing in the European Convention to give Mr Ahmad any right to manifest his religion on Friday afternoons in derogation of his contract of employment: and certainly not on full pay.'

Lord Scarman: '[Section 30] has ... never been considered by the courts. The reasons for its 30 years of immunity from judicial interpretation are not hard to see. First, and foremost, local education authorities, like the ILEA in this case, have treated it as no more than of negative intent – forbidding discrimination on the ground of religion in the selection and employment of teachers, but not obliging them to ensure that religious minorities are represented amongst their teachers. The ILEA, we have been told, have sought to comply with the section by not asking questions, the theory being that, if you do not know a man's religion, you cannot discriminate against him on that ground. Secondly, there were until recently no substantial religious groupings in our country which fell outside the broad categories of Christian and Jew. So long as there was no discrimination between them, no problem was likely to arise. The five-day school week, of course, takes care of the Sabbath and of Sunday as days of special religious observance. But with the advent of new religious groups in our society s.30 assumes a new importance. Is it an infringement of s.30 for a local education authority to refuse a Muslim time off to go to the Mosque on Friday unless he accepts less pay than a full-time teacher earns?

When the section was enacted, the negative approach to its interpretation was, no doubt, sufficient. But society has changed since 1944: so also has the legal background. Religions such as Islam and Buddhism, have substantial followings among our people. Room has to be found for teachers and pupils of the new religions in the educational system, if discrimination is to be avoided. This calls not for a policy of the blind eye but for one of understanding. The system must be made sufficiently flexible to accommodate their beliefs and their observances: otherwise, they will suffer discrimination – a consequence contrary to the spirit of s.30, whatever the letter of that law. The change in legal background is no less momentous. Since 1944 the United Kingdom has accepted international obligations designed to protect human rights and freedoms, and has enacted a series of statutes designed for the same purpose in certain critical areas of our society. These major statutes include the Trade Union and Labour Relations Act 1974, the Employment Protection Act 1975, the Sex Discrimination Act 1975, and the race relations legislation.

They were enacted after the United Kingdom had ratified the ECHR . . . and in the light of our obligations under the Charter of the United Nations. Today, therefore, we have to construe and apply s.30 not against the background of the law and society of 1944 but in a multi-racial society which has accepted international obligations and enacted statutes designed to eliminate discrimination on grounds of race, religion, colour or sex. Further, it is no longer possible to argue that because the international treaty obligations of the United Kingdom do not become law unless enacted by Parliament our courts pay no regard to our international obligations. They pay very serious regard to them: in particular, they will interpret statutory language and apply common law principles, wherever possible, so as to reach a conclusion consistent with our international obligations: see *Salomon* v *Customs and Excise Commissioners* . . . With these general considerations in mind, I conclude that the present case, properly considered, begins but does not end with the law of contract. It ends with a very different problem – the application to the particular circumstances of this appellant of the new law associated with the protection of the individual's human rights and fundamental freedoms.

The broad construction, for which Mr. Ahmad contends, is as follows. The section, it is submitted, is concerned quite generally with the religious opinions and practice of the teacher: he is to suffer no financial or career disadvantage by reason of his religion. No problem arises either in respect of the teacher's religious opinions or in respect of religious instruction. Opinions are not capable of spatial or temporal limitation. Contrariwise, it is obvious that the reference to giving religious instruction is a reference to something occurring at school in school hours. The words "by reason . . . of his attending or omitting to attend religious worship" are clearly also a reference to an event occurring in school hours. Are they also limited to "a single act of worship" with which the school day is to begin? See s.25(1) of the Act. There is no such express limitation in the section. Is it, then, necessary to read it into the section?

The ILEA submits that because of its context, coming as it does as a final saving for the position of teachers at the end of a set of sections dealing with religious education in schools, the section is to be read as limited to attending, or omitting to attend worship in school. Further, the authority submits, it would be unfair on the teacher's colleagues, who will have to stand in for him while away, to read the section otherwise.

Although I see the force of the submission, I reject it; because fundamentally a narrow construction of the section is in conflict with the developments in our society to which I have already referred – developments which are protected by the statutes to which I have also referred. A narrow construction of the section would mean that a Muslim, who took his religious duty seriously, could never accept employment as a full-time teacher, but must be content with the lesser emoluments of part-time service. In modern British society, with its elaborate statutory protection of the individual from discrimination arising from race, colour, religion or sex, and against the background of the European Convention, this is unacceptable, inconsistent with the policy of modern statute law, and almost certainly a breach of our international obligations. Unless, therefore, the language of s.30 forces one to adopt the narrow construction, I would think it wrong to do so. But it does not: the section, linguistically speaking, can be construed broadly or narrowly. No doubt, Parliament in 1944 never addressed its mind to the problem of this case. But, if the section lends itself, as successful human rights or constitutional legislation must lend itself, to judicial interpretation in accordance with the spirit of the age, there is nothing in this point, save for the comment that Parliament by refusing to be too specific was wiser than some of us have subsequently realised. The choice of construction, while it must be exercised judicially, is ours . . .'

R v Secretary of State for the Home Department, ex parte Brind

[1991] 2 WLR 588; [1991] 1 All ER 720 · House of Lords

The Secretary of State was empowered by s.29(3) of the Broadcasting Act 1981 and cl.13(4) of the BBC's licence and operating agreement to issue directives. One such directive prohibited the broadcasting of statements by representatives of organizations proscribed under other legislation. The applicant journalists sought judicial review of the Secretary of State's actions, *inter alia*, on the basis that the power should be exercised in accordance with the provisions of the ECHR, art.10. The House of Lords upheld the legality of the directives.

Lord Bridge of Harwich: ' . . . this appeal has been argued primarily on the basis that the power of the Secretary of State . . . may only be lawfully exercised in accordance with art.10 of the ECHR. Any exercise by the Secretary of State of the power in question necessarily imposes some restriction on freedom of expression. The obligations of the United Kingdom, as a party to the convention, are to secure to every one within its jurisdiction the rights which the convention defines . . . It is accepted, of course, by the appellants that, like any other treaty obligations which have not been embodied in the law by statute, the convention is not part of the domestic law, that the courts accordingly have no power to enforce convention rights directly and that, if domestic legislation conflicts with the convention, the courts must nevertheless enforce it. But it is already well settled that, in construing any provision in domestic legislation which is ambiguous in the sense that it is capable of a meaning which either conforms to or conflicts with the convention, the courts will presume that Parliament intended to legislate in conformity with the convention, not in conflict with it. Hence, it is submitted, when a statute confers upon an administrative authority a discretion capable of being exercised in a way which infringes any basic human right protected by the convention, it may similarly be presumed that the legislative intention was that the discretion should be exercised within the limitations which the convention imposes. I confess that I found considerable persuasive force in this submission. But in the end I have been convinced that the logic of it is flawed. When confronted with a simple choice between two possible interpretations of some specific statutory provision, the presumption whereby the courts prefer that which avoids conflict between our domestic legislation and our international treaty obligations is a mere canon of construction which involves no importation of international law into the domestic field. But where Parliament has conferred on the executive an administrative discretion without indicating the precise limits within which it must be exercised, to presume that it must be exercised within convention limits would be to go far beyond the resolution of an ambiguity. It would be to impute to Parliament an intention not only that the executive should exercise the discretion in conformity with the convention, but also that the domestic courts should enforce that conformity by the importation into domestic administrative law of the text of the convention and the jurisprudence of the European Court of Human Rights in the interpretation and application of it. If such a presumption is to apply to the statutory discretion exercised by the Secretary of State under s.29(3) of the 1981 Act in the instant case, it must also apply to any other statutory discretion exercised by the executive which is capable of involving an infringement of convention rights. When Parliament has been content for so long to leave those who complain that their convention rights have been infringed to seek their remedy in Strasbourg, it would be surprising suddenly to find that the judiciary had, without Parliament's aid, the means to incorporate the convention into such an important area of domestic law and I cannot escape the conclusion that this would be a judicial usurpation of the legislative function.

But I do not accept that this conclusion means that the courts are powerless to prevent the exercise by the executive of administrative discretions, even when conferred, as in the instant case, in terms which are on their face unlimited, in a way which infringes fundamental human rights. Most of the rights spelled out in terms in the convention, including the right to freedom of expression, are less than absolute and must in some cases yield to the claims of competing public interests . . . In exercising the power of judicial review we have neither the advantages nor the disadvantages of any comparable code to which we may refer or by which we are bound. But again, this surely does not mean that in deciding where the Secretary of State, in the exercise of his discretion, could reasonably impose the restriction he has imposed on the broadcasting organizations, we are not perfectly entitled to start from the premise that any restriction of the right to freedom of expression requires to be justified and that nothing less than an important competing public interest will be sufficient to justify it. The primary judgment as to whether the particular competing public interest justifies the particular restriction imposed falls to be made by the

Secretary of State to whom Parliament has entrusted the discretion. But we are entitled to exercise a secondary judgment by asking whether a reasonable Secretary of State, on the material before him, could reasonably make that primary judgment.

Applying these principles to the circumstances of the case, . . . I find it impossible to say that the Secretary of State exceeded the limits of his discretion. In any civilized and law-abiding society the defeat of the terrorist is a public interest of the first importance. That some restriction on the freedom of the terrorist and his supporters to propagate his cause may well be justified in support of that public interest is a proposition which I apprehend the appellants hardly dispute. Their real case is that they, in the exercise of their editorial judgment, may and must be trusted to ensure that the broadcasting media are not used in such a way as will afford any encouragement or support to terrorism and that any interference with that editorial judgment is necessarily an unjustifiable restriction on the right to freedom of expression. Accepting, as I do, their complete good faith, I nevertheless cannot accept this proposition. The Secretary of State, for the reasons he made so clear in Parliament, decided that it was necessary to deny to the terrorist and his supporters the opportunity to speak directly to the public through the most influential of all the media of communication and that this justified some interference with editorial freedom. I do not see how this judgment can be categorized as unreasonable. What is perhaps surprising is that the restriction imposed is of such limited scope. There is no restriction at all on the matter which may be broadcast, only on the manner of its presentation. The viewer may see the terrorist's face and hear his words provided only that they are not spoken in his own voice. I well understand the broadcast journalist's complaint that to put him to the trouble of dubbing the voice of the speaker he has interviewed before the television camera is an irritant which the difference in effect between the speaker's voice and the actor's voice hardly justifies. I well understand the political complaint that the restriction may be counter-productive in the sense that the adverse criticism it provokes outweighs any benefit it achieves. But these complaints fall very far short of demonstrating that a reasonable Secretary of State could not reasonably conclude that the restriction was justified by the important public interest of combating terrorism . . .'

Comment

For further extracts see p.293. The obligations of the Crown under international law are a relevant consideration for the purposes of judicial review (see *Wednesbury* principles, p.291) but the scope of the power to legislate is governed by the terms of the parent Act.

Derbyshire County Council v Times Newspapers Ltd and others

[1992] 3 All ER 65   ·   Court of Appeal
[1993] 1 ALL ER 1011   ·   House of Lords

The House of Lords and Court of Appeal considered whether local authorities have the right to sue for defamation. The Court of Appeal thought that the law was unclear and applied art.10 of the ECHR in deciding that there should be no right. The House of Lords held that the law was certain, and that in the public interest there should be no such right, accordingly the law was consistent with the provisions of the ECHR. The extracts are taken from the Court of Appeal.

Balcombe LJ: 'It has been stated on high authority that art.10 is in effect the same as the English common law . . . *Att-Gen* v *Guardian Newspapers Ltd (No. 2)* . . . So art.10 does not establish any novel proposition under English Law. Nevertheless, since it states the right to freedom of expression and the qualifications to that right in precise terms, it will be convenient to consider the question by reference to art.10 alone.

Article 10 has not been incorporated into English domestic law. Nevertheless it may be resorted to in order to help resolve some uncertainty or ambiguity in municipal law . . . Thus (1) art.10 may be used for the purpose of the resolution of an ambiguity in English primary or subordinate legislation (see *Brind's* case . . .). (2) Article 10 may be used when considering the principles upon which the court should act in exercising a discretion, e.g. whether or not to grant an interlocutory injunction (see *A-G* v *Guardian Newspapers Ltd* . . .); *Re W (a minor) (wardship: restriction on publication)*. (3) Article 10 may be used when the common law . . . is uncertain. In *A-G* v *Guardian Newspapers Ltd (No. 2)* the courts at all levels had regard to the provisions of art.10 in considering the extent of the duty of confidence. They did not limit the application of art.10 to the discretion of the court to grant or withhold an injunction to restrain a breach of confidence.

Even if the common law is certain, the courts will still, when appropriate, consider whether the United Kingdom is in breach of art.10. Thus in *R* v *Chief Metropolitan Stipendiary Magistrate, ex parte Choudhury*, where the issue was whether the common law offence of blasphemy is restricted to Christianity, Watkins LJ . . . said:

> [Counsel for the respondent publishers] accepted that the obligations imposed on the United Kingdom by the convention are relevant sources of public policy where the common law is uncertain. But, he maintained, the common law of blasphemy is, without doubt, certain. Accordingly, it is not necessary to pay any regard to the convention. Nevertheless, he thought it necessary, and *we agree*, in the context of this case, to attempt to satisfy us that the United Kingdom is not in any event in breach of the convention. (My emphasis.)

This approach of English law to art.10 is wholly consistent with the jurisprudence of the European Court of Human Rights. That court has, on more than one occasion, held that a decision of the English courts has violated a litigant's rights under art.10 and this on occasion has led to Parliament having to change the substantive law . . . Of more immediate relevance to the present case the European Court of Human Rights has held in *Lingens* v *Austria* that the prosecution and conviction, under the Austrian law of criminal defamation, of a magazine publisher in Vienna for printing two articles critical of the Austrian Chancellor, was a violation of art.10.

In my judgment, therefore, where the law is uncertain, it must be right for the court to approach the issue before it with a predilection to ensure that our law should not involve a breach of art.10 . . . The law on this very important point is . . . uncertain. The issue is whether a civil action for defamation lies at the suit of a corporate authority. This court is in a position to define the extent of this common law tort in such a way as not to require a positive amendment of the law by Parliament. In my judgment we both can and should consider the effect of art.10. This I now proceed to do.

Article 10(1) in terms expresses an absolute right, that of freedom of expression. That right to freedom of expression includes freedom to impart information and ideas without interference by public authority. Prima facie that right will be interfered with by a public authority if the maker of the statement is sued for defamation. In the normal case the interfering public authority is the court which entertains the suit for defamation. (Here the interference by public authority is twofold since the council, which has initiated the suit, is itself a public authority.) That an action for defamation is a prima facie interference with the right is recognised by art.10(2) which provides that the exercise of the freedoms referred to in art.(10)(1) may be subject to such restrictions "as are prescribed by law and are *necessary in a democratic society . . .* for the protection of the reputation . . . of others".

Thus art.10 requires a balancing exercise to be conducted: the balance in this case is between the right to freedom of expression and such restrictions as are necessary in a democratic society for the protection of the reputation of a non-trading corporation which is also a public authority.

Before I consider that balancing exercise in the present case, I remind myself that it is not only local authorities which are public authorities with corporate status. We were helpfully provided by [counsel] with a schedule listing eight examples of government departments with corporate status: they include the Secretaries of State for Defence, Education and Science, Energy, Environment and Social Services. If the council can sue for libel, then so can those departments.

The law reports, both of this country and of other jurisdictions, contain many statements emphasising the importance of the right, in a democratic society, to be able to criticise freely the conduct of affairs by public authorities. I cite only a few.

In *Hector* v *A-G of Antigua and Barbuda* Lord Bridge of Harwich said:

> In a free democratic society it is almost too obvious to need stating that those who hold office in government and who are responsible for public administration must always be open to criticism. Any attempt to stifle or fetter such criticism amounts to political censorship of the most insidious and objectionable kind.

In *Commonwealth of Australia* v *John Fairfax & Sons Ltd* Mason J said:

> It is unacceptable in our democratic society that there should be a restraint on the publication of information relating to government when the only vice of that information is that it enables the public to discuss, review and criticise government action.

This passage is part of a longer passage cited with approval by Lord Keith of Kinkel, Lord Griffiths and Lord Goff of Chieveley in A-G v *Guardian Newspapers Ltd (No.2)*. In the United States of America it has long been held that a municipal authority cannot sue in the tort of libel. While this rule depends upon the provisions of the Federal and state constitutions, the reasoning has universal application. In *City of Chicago* v *Tribune Co* Thomson CJ of the Supreme Court of Illinois . . . said:

> The fundamental right of freedom of speech is involved in this litigation and not merely the right of liberty of the press. If this action can be maintained against a newspaper it can be maintained against every private citizen who ventures to criticise the ministers who are temporarily conducting the affairs of his government. Where any person by speech or writing seeks to persuade others to

violate existing law or to overthrow by force or other unlawful means the existing government he may be punished ... but all other utterances or publications against the government must be considered absolutely privileged. While in the early history of the struggle for freedom of speech the restrictions were enforced by criminal prosecutions, it is clear that a civil action is as great, if not a greater, restriction than a criminal prosecution. If the right to criticise the government is a privilege which, with the exceptions above enumerated, cannot be restricted, then all civil as well as criminal actions are forbidden. A despotic or corrupt government can more easily stifle opposition by a series of civil actions than by criminal prosecutions ... It follows, therefore, that every citizen has a right to criticise an inefficient or corrupt government without fear of civil as well as criminal prosecution. This absolute privilege is founded on the principle that it is advantageous for the public interest that the citizen should not be in any way fettered in his statements, and where the public service or due administration of justice is involved he shall have the right to speak his mind freely ... Municipal corporations, however, exist primarily for governmental purposes, and they are permitted to enter the commercial field solely for the purpose of subserving the interests of the public which they represent. A city is no less a government because it owns and operates its own water system, its own gas and electric system and its own transportation system ... It is manifest that the more so-called private property the people permit their governments to own and operate, the more important is the right to freely criticise the administration of the government. As the amount of property owned by the city and the amount of public business to be transacted by the city increase, so does the opportunity for inefficient and corrupt government increase and the greater will be the efforts of the administration to remain in control of such a political prize. The richer the city the greater the incentive to stifle opposition. In so far as the question before us is concerned, no distinction can be made with respect to the proprietary and the governmental capacities of a city.

This judgment, which demonstrates the "chilling effect" which the ability to sue for libel may have on the right to criticise a public authority, was cited with approval by Brennan J delivering the opinion of the United States Supreme Court in New York Times Co v Sullivan ... If a corporate public authority is unable to sue for libel it is, however, by no means without remedy. First, and probably of most practical significance, its actions will necessarily be those of its members or officers since, being a legal fiction, it can only act through the instrumentality of human beings. They, if defamed, will have the right to sue for libel and, in the case of a libel upon the authority's officers acting in the course of their duties, it may be that the authority will subvert their actions. It is not without significance that in the present case [the council leader's] action for libel is based upon the same complaints as those made by the council. Then in an appropriate case the public authority may be able to secure the institution of a prosecution for criminal libel. Where, as here, the alleged libel has been published in a newspaper, the prosecution may not be commenced without the leave of a judge under s. 8 of the Law of Libel Amendment Act 1888, a very important safeguard when the freedom of the press is in issue. Finally, the authority may have an action for malicious (sometimes called 'injurious') falsehood ...

Bearing in mind the words of art.10(2), in my judgment the right to sue for malicious falsehood gives to a corporate public authority all such rights as are "necessary in a democratic society", i.e. for which there exists a pressing social need, for the protection of its reputation. It does not need, for that protection, to have the right to sue in defamation and thereby be able to stifle legitimate public criticism of its activities . . .'

Comment

(1)   The approach of the Court of Appeal demonstrates the correct approach to the ECHR albeit that the House of Lords were able to reach the same conclusion as to the appropriate state of the law by a different route. In the House of Lords Lord Keith said:

'. . . It is of the highest public importance that a democratically elected governmental body, or indeed any governmental body, should be open to uninhibited public criticism. The threat of a civil action for defamation must inevitably have an inhibiting effect on freedom of speech . . . [As] is shown by the decision in *A-G v Guardian Newspapers Ltd (No.2)* . . . there are rights available to private citizens which institutions of central government are not in a position to exercise unless they can show that it is in the public interest to do so. The same applies . . . to local authorities. In both cases I regard it as right for this House to lay down that not only is there no public interest favouring the right of organs of government, whether central or local, to sue for libel, but that it is contrary to the public interest that they should have it. It is contrary to the public interest because to admit such actions would place an undesirable fetter on freedom of speech . . .'

(2)   In *Rantzen v Mirror Group Newspaper Plc* art.10 was applied to re-examine the scope of judicial discretion. The defendants appealed against an award of damages in defamation proceedings and asked the Court of Appeal to exercise its power to order a new trial or substitute an amount of damages under s.8 of the Courts and Legal Services Act 1990. Prior to the Act the Court of Appeal had no power to disturb the amount of damages but it did have power to order a re-trial on the basis that the amount was 'so excessive that no twelve men could reasonably have given them' or that 'it was divorced from reality'. In the light of the statutory changes and the scope of art.10 of the ECHR the court adopted a more searching test to decide whether the award of damages had been excessive: 'could a reasonable jury have thought that this award was necessary to compensate the plaintiff and to re-establish his reputation?'

(3)   In *R v Secretary of State for the Home Department, ex parte Leech*, the Court of Appeal held that r.33(3) Prison Rules 1964, which created an unrestricted right for a prison governor to intercept and read prisoners' letters, was *ultra vires* the Prison Act 1952 since it amounted to interference with the right of a prisoner to seek legal advice and unimpeded access to the courts which the Court of Appeal described as 'a constitutional right'. The court noted that the decision meant that the

law was consistent with the view of the European Court of Human Rights in *Campbell* v *UK* on the scope of art.8.

Attorney-General v *Guardian Newspapers (No. 1)*

[1987] 1 WLR 1248 · House of Lords

A book entitled *Spycatcher* was written by Peter Wright, a retired member of the Intelligence Services living outside the jurisdiction of the English courts, in Australia. In the book he discussed his career and alleged wrong-doing by members of those Services (including himself) in the form of both illegal activities and improper interference with the political process. The allegations were not wholly new, but this was the first attempt at disclosure of them by a member of the Security Services. The British government sought to prevent publication, not only in England, but in Scotland, Australia, New Zealand and other jurisdictions, relying upon a claimed duty upon Wright of life-long secrecy in respect of his work as part of the intelligence community, and upon the confidentiality of the information proposed to be disclosed. Some of the allegations to be made in the book were already in the public domain, and copies of the book were increasingly available in England through publication in other jurisdictions, particularly the United States.

No prosecution under the Official Secrets Act 1911 was attempted, bearing in mind that Wright was outside the jurisdiction. Nor, on the same basis, was injunctive relief sought against Wright himself. The remedies sought were against those who intended either to serialize extracts from the book (*The Sunday Times*) or to report allegations made in the book (*The Observer* and *Guardian* newspapers), thus raising fundamental questions about freedom of expression and its limits, scrutiny of alleged wrong-doing, and upon the standards imposed upon English law by art.10, European Convention on Human Rights. Interim injunctions were granted by the Divisional Court (the Millett injunctions), and eventually upheld by the House of Lords in *Guardian Newspapers (No. 1)*; on the trial of the issues the injunctions were discharged – see *Guardian Newspapers (No. 2)*, p.118. In the light of the widespread knowledge of the allegations both at home and abroad and publication overseas it could not be shown that the public interest demanded that publication be restrained.

Lord Bridge (dissenting): 'The basis of the claim for the Millett injunctions was to prevent disclosure of the *Spycatcher* allegations in breach of the life-long obligation of confidence which Mr Wright, as a former officer of the Security Service, owed to Her Majesty's Government. So long as any of the *Spycatcher* allegations remained undisclosed, I should have been wholeheartedly in favour of maintaining the injunctions in the interests of national security for all the reasons so cogently deployed in the affidavit of Sir Robert Armstrong. But it is perfectly obvious and elementary that, once information is freely available to the general public, it is nonsensical to talk about preventing its "disclosure." Whether the *Spycatcher* allegations are true or false is beside the point. What is to the point is that they are now freely available to the public or, perhaps more accurately, to any member of the public who wants to read them. I deliberately refrain from using expressions such as "the public domain" which may have technical overtones. The fact is that the intelligence and security services of any country in the world can buy the book

Spycatcher and read what is in it. The fact is that any citizen of this country can buy the book in America and bring it home with him or order the book from America and receive a copy by post . . . If, as I have always thought, the interest of national security in protecting sensitive and classified information is to conceal it from those who might make improper use of it, it is manifestly now too late for the Millett injunctions to serve that interest. If the confidence of friendly countries in the ability of this country to protect its secrets has been undermined by the publication in the United States of America of *Spycatcher*, the maintenance of the Millett injunctions can do nothing to restore that confidence. So much, I believe, is obvious and incontrovertible . . .

The legal basis for the Attorney-General's claim to enjoin the newspapers is that any third party who comes into possession of information knowing that it originated from a breach of confidence owes the same duty to the original confider as that owed by the original confidant. If this proposition is held to be of universal application, no matter how widely the original confidential information has been disseminated before reaching the third party, it would seem to me to lead to absurd and unacceptable consequences. But I am prepared to assume for present purposes that the Attorney-General is still in a position to assert a bare duty binding on the conscience of newspaper editors which is capable of surviving the publication of *Spycatcher* in America.

The key question in the case, to my mind, is whether there is any remaining interest of national security which the Millett injunctions are capable of protecting and, if so, whether it is of sufficient weight to justify the massive encroachment on freedom of speech which the continuance of the Millett injunctions in present circumstances necessarily involves . . .

What of the other side of the coin and the encroachment on freedom of speech? Having no written constitution, we have no equivalent in our law to the First Amendment to the Constitution of the United States of America. Some think that puts freedom of speech on too lofty a pedestal. Perhaps they are right. We have not adopted as part of our law the [ECHR]. Many think that we should. I have hitherto not been of that persuasion, in large part because I have had confidence in the capacity of the common law to safeguard the fundamental freedoms essential to a free society including the right to freedom of speech which is specifically safeguarded by art.10 of the Convention. My confidence is seriously undermined by your Lordships' decision. All the judges in the courts below in this case have been concerned not to impose any unnecessary fetter on freedom of speech. I suspect that what the Court of Appeal would have liked to achieve, and perhaps set out to achieve by their compromise solution, was to inhibit "The Sunday Times" from continuing the serialisation of *Spycatcher*, but to leave the press at large at liberty to discuss and comment on the *Spycatcher* allegations. If there were a method of achieving these results which could be sustained in law, I can see much to be said for it on the merits. But I can see nothing whatever, either in law or on the merits, to be said for the maintenance of a total ban on discussion in the press of this country of matters of undoubted public interest and concern which the rest of the world now knows all about and can discuss freely. Still less can I approve your Lordships' decision to throw in for good measure a restriction on reporting court proceedings in Australia which the Attorney-General had never even asked for.

Freedom of speech is always the first casualty under a totalitarian regime. Such a regime cannot afford to allow the free circulation of information and ideas among its citizens. Censorship is the dispensable tool to regulate what the public may and what they may not know. The present attempt to insulate the public in this country from information which is freely available elsewhere is a significant step down that very dangerous road. The maintenance of the ban, as more and more copies of the book *Spycatcher* enter this country and circulate here, will seem more and more ridiculous. If the Government are determined to fight to maintain the ban to the end, they will face inevitable condemnation and humiliation by the European Court of Human Rights in Strasbourg. Long before that they will have been condemned at the bar of public opinion in the free world.'

Lord Ackner: 'In the *Sunday Times* v *United Kingdom*, the European Court of Human Rights decided by a majority of 11 to 9 that there had been a violation of the convention by reason of the judgment of this House in *Attorney-General* v *Times Newspapers Ltd* which restrained "The Sunday Times" from publishing . . . The European Court pointed out that this House applying domestic law had balanced the public interest in freedom of expression and the public interest in the due administration of justice. But the European Court "is faced not with a choice between two conflicting principles, but with a principle of freedom of expression that is subject to a number of exceptions which must be narrowly interpreted . . . It is not sufficient that the interference involved belongs to that class of exceptions listed in art.10(2) which has been invoked; neither is it sufficient that the interference was imposed because its subject matter fell within a particular category or was caught by a legal rule formulated in general or absolute terms: the court has to be satisfied that the interference was necessary having regard to the facts and circumstances prevailing in the specific case before it." . . .

The question is therefore whether the interference with freedom of expression constituted by the Millett injunctions was, on 30 July 1987 when they were continued by this House, necessary in a democratic society in the interests of national security, for protecting the reputation or rights of others, for preventing the disclosure of information received in confidence or for maintaining the authority and impartiality of the judiciary having regard to the facts and circumstances prevailing on 30 July 1987 and in the light of the events which had happened. The continuance of the Millett injunctions appears to me to be necessary for all these purposes.

My Lords, in my opinion a democracy is entitled to take the view that a public servant who is employed in the Security Service must be restrained from making any disclosures concerning the Security Service and that similar restraints must be imposed on anybody who receives those disclosures knowing that they are confidential.

There are safeguards. No member of the Security Service is immune from criminal prosecution or civil suit in respect of his actions. Instructions from superior officers are no defence. In addition, anyone, whether public servant, newspaper editor or journalist who is aware that a crime has been committed or is dissatisfied with the activities of the Security Service is free to report to the police in relation to crime and in other matters is free to report to the Prime Minister who is charged with the responsibility of the security services and to the Security Commission which advises the Prime Minister. The Security Services are not above the law. In the present case there is not the slightest evidence that these safeguards have failed. Furthermore there is nothing to prevent the press investigating all the allegations made by Mr Wright and reporting the results of their investigations to the public. It is only unlawful for the press to publish information unlawfully disclosed by Mr Wright and which may or may not be true . . .'

Comment

(1)   The attitude of Lords Bridge and Oliver (dissenting) reflect the belief that the interim injunctions could not be shown to be justifiable in terms of the ECHR. This belief was supported in part by the decision of the European Court of Human Rights to the effect that up until the decision of the House of Lords the interim injunctions could be justified but that thereafter, in the light of the widespread availability of the book and the absence of any threat to national security, the continuation of the interim injunctions could not be justified.

(2)   The breadth of the decision was increased by the ruling in *Attorney-General* v *Newspaper Publishing PLC*. The Court of Appeal ruled that *The Independent* newspaper was in contempt of court for publishing information which was the subject of the interim injunctions against *The Observer* and *The Guardian*, despite the fact that it was not a party to, or bound directly by, those injunctions. The effect of the ruling is to prevent publication where an interim injunction, based on an 'arguable case' approach, has been granted. It is likely that the breadth of this restriction is in breach of art.10.

(3)   The House of Lords held in *Attorney-General* v *Times Newspapers Ltd*, that *The Sunday Times* was in contempt of court for having published material from *Spycatcher* in breach of the injunction first obtained against other newspapers.

(4)   In *Attorney-General* v *Observer Ltd, re an Application by Derbyshire CC*, Knox J ruled that the applicant local authority was not entitled to purchase and make available to the public through its public libraries copies of the book purchased overseas: the statutory duty to provide an efficient library service was qualified by a duty not to interfere with the administration of justice. Whilst there was no duty on the authority to examine publications, in this case the harm suffered by delaying making the book available was outweighed by the harm that the loss of protection by the interim orders would cause.

Attorney-General v *Guardian Newspaper (No. 2)*

[1988] 3 WLR 776 · House of Lords

Lord Keith: 'The Crown's case upon all the issues which arise invokes the law about confidentiality . . . as a general rule, it is in the public interest that confidences should be respected, and the encouragement of such respect may in itself constitute a sufficient ground for recognising and enforcing the obligation of confidence even where the confider can point to no specific detriment to himself . . . The position of the Crown, as presenting the continuing government of the country may, however, be regarded as being special. In some instances disclosure of confidential information entrusted to a servant of the Crown may result in a financial loss to the public. In other instances such disclosure may tend to harm the public interest by impeding the efficient attainment of proper governmental ends, and the revelation of defence or intelligence secrets certainly falls into that category. The Crown, however, as representing the nation as a whole, has no private life or personal feelings capable of being hurt by the disclosure of confidential information. In so far as the Crown acts to prevent such disclosure or to seek redress for it on confidentiality grounds, it must necessarily, in my opinion, be in a position to show that the disclosure is likely to damage or has damaged the public interest. How far the Crown has to go in order to show this must depend on the circumstances of each case. In a question with a Crown servant himself, or others acting as his agents, the general public interest in the preservation of confidentiality, and in encouraging other Crown servants to preserve it, may suffice. But where the publication is proposed to be made by third parties unconnected with the particular confidant, the position may be different . . . The general rule is that anyone is entitled to communicate anything he pleases to anyone else, by speech or in writing or in any other way. That rule is limited by the law of defamation and other restrictions similar to those mentioned in art.10 of the [ECHR]. All those restrictions are imposed in the light of considerations of public interest such as to countervail the public interest in freedom of expression. A communication about some aspect of government activity which does no harm to the interests of the nation cannot, even where the original disclosure has been made in breach of confidence, be restrained on the ground of a nebulous equitable duty of conscience serving no useful purpose.

There are two important cases in which the special position of a government in relation to the preservation of confidence has been considered. The first of them is *Attorney-General* v *Jonathan Cape Ltd* . . . in the result [that] decision turned on [the judge's] view that it had not been shown that publication of the diaries would do any harm to the public interest.

The second case is *Commonwealth of Australia* v *John Fairfax & Sons Ltd.* That was a decision of Mason J in the High Court of Australia, dealing with an application by the Commonwealth for an interlocutory injunction to restrain publication of a book containing the texts of government documents concerned with its relations with other countries, in particular the government of Indonesia in connection with the "East Timor Crisis." The documents appeared to have been leaked by a civil servant. Restraint of publication was claimed on the ground of breach of confidence and also on that of infringement of copyright. Mason J granted an injunction on the latter ground but not on the former. Having mentioned . . . an argument for the Commonwealth that the government was entitled to protect information which was not public property, even if no public interest is served by maintaining confidentiality, he continued . . .

> "However, the plaintiff must show, not only that the information is confidential in quality and that it was imparted so as to import an obligation of confidence, but also that there will be "an unauthorised use of that information to the detriment of the party communicating it" (*Coco* v *A N Clark (Engineers) Ltd*). The question then, when the executive government seeks the protection given by equity, is: What detriment does it need to show?
>
> The equitable principle has been fashioned to protect the personal, private and proprietary interests of the citizen, not to protect the very different interests of the executive government. It acts, or is supposed to act, not according to standards of private interest, but in the public interest. This is not to say that equity will not

protect information in the hands of the government, but it is to say that when equity protects government information it will look at the matter through different spectacles.

It may be a sufficient detriment to the citizen that disclosure of information relating to his affairs will expose his actions to public discussion and criticism. But it can scarcely be a relevant detriment to the government that publication of material concerning its actions will merely expose it to public discussion and criticism. It is unacceptable in our democratic society that there should be a restraint on the publication of information relating to government when the only vice of that information is that it enables the public to discuss, review and criticise government action.

Accordingly, the court will determine the government's claim to confidentiality by reference to the public interest. Unless disclosure is likely to injure the public interest, it will not be protected.

The court will not prevent the publication of information which merely throws light on the past workings of government, even if it be not public property, so long as it does not prejudice the community in other respects. Then disclosure will itself serve the public interest in keeping the community informed and in promoting discussion of public affairs. If, however, it appears that disclosure will be inimical to the public interest because national security, relations with foreign countries or the ordinary business of government will be prejudiced, disclosure will be restrained. There will be cases in which the conflicting considerations will be finely balanced, where it is difficult to decide whether the public's interest in knowing and in expressing its opinion, outweighs the need to protect confidentiality."

I find myself in broad agreement with this statement by Mason J. In particular I agree that a government is not in a position to win the assistance of the court in restraining the publication of information imparted in confidence by it or its predecessors unless it can show that publication would be harmful to the public interest . . .'

Comment

(1)   At first instance Scott J thought that national courts should endeavour to reach decisions consistent with the ECHR; compare *R v Secretary of State for Home Department ex parte Brind* (p.150).

(2)   The House of Lords regard members of the Security Services as owing a life-long duty of confidentiality to the Crown; this has been reinforced by the Official Secrets Act 1989. The doctrine of confidentiality allows disclosure in the public interest and wrong-doing is not an essential. In considering the position of Wright, note that the allegations in his book were not wholly new or unknown; also consider the other avenues open to him to expose wrong-doing, e.g. by handing his information to the police. There has long been a custom of government declining to answer questions concerning the Security Services in Parliament. For the views of the Court of Appeal on the meaning of 'wrong-doing' in the context of the Security Services, see p.15.

(3) For the structure and accountability of the Service now see Security Service Act 1989. That Act provides in s.4 for judicial scrutiny of the work of the Security Service but the judge appointed to supervise the Service (the Security Service Commissioner) reports to the Prime Minister who then presents the Commissioner's report to Parliament subject, at his or her discretion, to exclusion of any matter which 'would be prejudicial to the continued discharge of the functions of the Service'. The Act in s.5 creates a tribunal for the investigation of complaints but the decisions of that body are not subject to judicial review (s.5(4)). See also the similar provision in the Intelligence Services Act 1994.

(4) For the position of disclosure of information by persons working, or who have worked, for the Security Services, and also the liability in law of those who transmit such information, see Official Secrets Act 1989. This has the practical effect of preventing members of the Security Services from publishing non-authorized disclosures. Whether this will be an effective deterrent against those outside the jurisdiction is a matter of conjecture. The willingness of juries to convict under the new provisions (cf. *R* v *Ponting*) has also to be seen.

(5) In *Lord Advocate* v *The Scotsman Publications Ltd*, the newspaper had received from a third party a copy of a privately printed book distributed to 279 prominent individuals and containing the memoirs of C, a retired member of the Security Services. The newspaper published an article containing extracts and refused to undertake not to publish further articles. The Crown conceded that the material sought to be restrained was not damaging to the Security Services. The House of Lords upheld the decision at first instance to refuse an injunction. Had the 1989 Act been in force then C would have committed an offence because the disclosure of any material is prohibited. But the newspaper would not have committed an offence because the disclosure would not have been damaging within the meaning of s.5, which creates the relevant offence for third parties. Lord Templeman said:

[Any restraint on publication] is an interference with the right of expression safeguarded by art.10 [the ECHR] ... The question therefore is whether the restraint sought to be imposed on the respondents is "necessary in a democratic society in the interests of national security." Similar questions were considered in *Attorney-General* v *Guardian Newspapers Ltd (No. 2)* ("the *Spycatcher* case") but at that time Parliament had not provided any answer to the questions posed by the conflict between the freedom of expression and the requirement of national security.

In my opinion, it is for Parliament to determine the restraints on freedom of expression which are necessary in a democratic society. The courts of this country should follow any guidance contained in a statute. If that guidance is inconsistent with the requirements of the Convention then that will be a matter for the Convention authorities and for the United Kingdom Government. It will not be a matter for the courts.

The guidance of Parliament has now been provided in the Official Secrets Act 1989 . . . In my opinion the civil jurisdiction of the courts of this country to grant an injunction restraining a breach of confidence at the suit of the Crown should not, in principle, be exercised in a manner different from or more severe than any appropriate restriction which Parliament has imposed in the Act of 1989 and which, if breached, will create a criminal offence as soon as the Act is brought into force . . .

The information itself does not fall within a class or description of information the unauthorised disclosure of which would be likely to be damaging. Nevertheless, the Crown contend that they are entitled to restrain the respondents from publishing this harmless information because the information is contained in the memoirs of a security employee. It is said that the publication of harmless information derived from a former security employee and protected by s.1 against disclosure by him, though not damaging in itself, would cause harm by encouraging other security employees to make disclosures in breach of s.1 of the Act of 1989 and by raising doubts as to reliability of the Security Service.

My Lords, it is well known, at home and abroad, that every security service suffers from time to time from an employee who is disloyal for ideological or other reasons which may derive from the desire for profit or notoriety. The motives of Cavendish are irrelevant if he is in breach of the duty of life-long confidence of security employees accepted in the *Spycatcher* case and imposed by s.1 of the Act of 1989. If the Act of 1989 had been in force when Cavendish circulated his book to a chosen band of readers, he would have committed an offence under s.1 of the Act notwithstanding that the information disclosed in his book is harmless. But it does not follow that the third parties commit an offence if they disclose harmless information. Were it otherwise, the distinction between an offence by a security employee and an offence by a third party which appears from the Act of 1989 would be eradicated. A security employee can commit an offence if he discloses any information. A third party is only guilty of an offence if the information is damaging in the sense defined by the Act.

If the Crown had asserted that future publication by "The Scotsman" would be likely to damage the work of the Security Services, then difficult questions might have arisen as to the nature of the damage feared, as to whether an injunction was necessary within the meaning attributed to that expression by the European Court of Human Rights and as to whether the restriction of freedom of expression constituted by the injunction sought was "proportionate to the legitimate aim pursued" as required by the European Court in *Handyside* v *United Kingdom* and *The Sunday Times* v *United Kingdom*. These difficult questions do not, however, arise since the Crown conceded that future publication would not be likely to cause damage other than the indirect damage which I have already rejected . . .

8 Parliamentary privilege

The ability of Parliament to carry out its functions depends in part on the privileges claimed on behalf of each House at the beginning of each Parliament. Interference with those privileges by the Crown was a major cause of the discontent leading up to the revolutionary settlement of 1688. In modern terms, the most important privileges are freedom of speech and Parliament's right to control its own internal affairs. Other privileges have tended to lose their significance, e.g. freedom from arrest in civil matters.

The current relationship between the Courts and Parliament was reached only after considerable struggle, but even so the position is far from clear. The issues in the nineteenth century cases were resolved in the end by neither the courts nor Parliament pursuing their theoretical claims. *Stockdale* v *Hansard* (p.166) and *Bradlaugh* v *Gossett* (p.176) are important for more than mere historical interest; they highlight the potential for disagreement between Parliament and the Courts, and the need for one body to avoid trespassing into the domain of another. See also *Rost* v *Edwards*, p.168, and *Pickin* v *British Railways Board*, p.177. There are serious implications both in respect of freedom of speech outside the House, e.g. to criticize or comment on government activity, and the ability to mount an effective defence to defamation proceedings, as *Prebble* v *Television New Zealand Ltd* shows, p.173

As parliamentary privilege demonstrates, there are areas into which the Courts do not enquire, and the Courts will exercise self-restraint in matters which they see as falling within the remit of Parliament – see Lord Simon in *Pickin* v *BRB* (p.177). Once a matter falls within Parliament's own jurisdiction the Courts will not enquire further. Thus, for example, the Courts recognize that Parliament has sole control of its internal affairs and it may punish anyone for contempt of Parliament free from the interference of the Courts (*Case of the Sheriff of Middlesex*, p.187). On the other hand, the Courts will decide upon the existence and extent of a claimed privilege (*Stockdale* v *Hansard* and *Pepper* v *Hart*).

The power of Parliament to punish for contempt is one aspect of the power to regulate its own affairs. Every breach of privilege is a contempt. In addition, there are other matters which relate to obstructing or impeding either House in the performance of its functions which are punishable by either House as contempts, such as improperly threatening an MP to compel the MP to vote in a particular way, or disturbing the proceedings of the House. The courts will not enquire into the exercise of the power to punish – see *Case of the Sheriff of Middlesex*.

Stockdale v *Hansard*

(1839) 9 A & E 1 · Queen's Bench Division

There was a series of actions in defamation brought by Stockdale against Hansard. These arose out of the publication by the defendant of an allegation that certain books had been published by the plaintiff and that those books were obscene. In the first action the defendant succeeded on the basis that the allegation was true. Upon a further publication of the allegation the plaintiff brought another action. In the second action, the defendant simply stated that the document containing the allegations had been printed pursuant to a resolution of the House of Commons to the general effect (a) that the publishing of reports was an essential element in the function of the House and was protected by privilege; (b) that the House of Commons 'has the sole and exclusive jurisdiction to determine upon the existence and extent of its privileges'; (c) that for any other body to decide upon matters inconsistently with the House would be contrary to law and a breach of privilege and contempt.

 The court held that it was a proper function of the court to enquire into the existence and extent of any alleged privilege, that the resolution of the House was incapable of changing the law and could not prevent the enquiry of the court. The court concluded that there was no such alleged privilege and gave judgment for the plaintiff.

Lord Denman CJ: '. . . The grievance complained of appears to be an act done by order of the House of Commons, a court superior to any court of law, and none of whose proceedings are to be questioned in any way. This principle the learned counsel for the defendant repeatedly avowed in his long and laboured argument . . . It is a claim for an arbitrary power to authorise the commission of any act whatever on behalf of a body which in the same argument is admitted not to be the supreme power in the State. The supremacy of Parliament, the foundation upon which the claim is made to rest, appears to me to completely overturn it, because the House of Commons is not the Parliament, but only a co-ordinate and component part of the Parliament. That sovereign power can make or unmake the laws; but the concurrence of the three legislative estates is necessary; the resolution of any one of them cannot alter the law or place anyone beyond its control. The proposition is, therefore, wholly untenable, and abhorrent to the first principles of the constitution of England.

 The next defence . . . is that the defendant committed the grievance by order of the House of Commons in a case of privilege, and that each House of Parliament is the sole judge of its own privileges . . .

 Parliament is said to be supreme; I must fully acknowledge its supremacy. It follows . . . that neither branch of it is supreme when acting by itself. It is also said that the privilege of each House is the privilege of the whole Parliament. In one sense I agree to this, because whatever impedes the proper action of either impedes those functions which are necessary for the performance of their joint duties . . . But it by no means follows that the opinion that either House may entertain of the extent of its own privileges is correct, or its declaration of them binding . . . To the assertion that the courts have always acquiesced in the unlimited claim of privilege, I have already stated enough to authorise me in opposing the contrary assertion . . . The other concession [of the Attorney-General] . . . is that when matter of privilege comes before the courts not directly but incidentally, they may, because they must, decide it. Otherwise, said the Attorney-General, there would be a failure of justice . . . Since, then, the courts may give judgement on matters of privilege incidentally, it is plain that they have the means of arriving at a correct conclusion, and that they may differ from the Houses of Parliament . . .

I come at length to consider whether this privilege of publication exists . . . The Attorney-General would preclude us from commencing this enquiry . . . But, having convinced myself that the mere order of the House will not justify an act otherwise illegal, and that the simple declaration that that order is made in the exercise of a privilege does not prove the privilege, it is no longer optional with me to decline to accept the office of deciding whether this privilege exists in law . . . It is said the House of Commons is the sole judge of its own privileges; and so I admit so far as the proceedings in the House and some other things are concerned; but I do not think it follows that they have a power to declare what their privileges are, so as to preclude enquiry what they declare are part of their privileges. The Attorney-General admits that they have not the power to create new privileges; but they declare this to be their privilege. But how are we to know that this is part of their privileges, without enquiring into it, when no such privilege was declared before? We must therefore be enabled to determine whether it be part of their privileges or not . . . '

Comment

(1)   The court held that the privilege asserted did not exist. The case is authority for the proposition that it is the Queen in Parliament and not the separate parts of the legislature which can change the law – see *Bowles* v *Bank of England* (p.65). The Parliamentary Papers Act 1840 was passed to give effect to the resolution of the House which caused the problem in *Stockdale* v *Hansard*; Parliament thereby implicitly recognized that it is the role of the Courts to decide the scope of any alleged privilege – and see *Pepper* v *Hart* (p.171).

(2)   When Stockdale successfully obtained judgment in his third action the House of Commons imprisoned him. In *The Case of the Sheriff of Middlesex*, the Sheriff of Middlesex (an office held by Evans and Wheelton) had recovered £600 from the defendant in the third action between Stockdale and Hansard. The Sheriff was ordered to hand over the money to the House but refused; the office holders were committed for contempt of the House and breach of privilege. In habeas corpus proceedings, the return to the writ stated that Evans and Wheelton were held by virtue of a warrant issued by the Speaker for contempt and a breach of privilege. It

was alleged that the return to the writ was bad and the prisoners should be released. The court refused to intervene and held that the return to the writ made by Parliament need not specify the grounds of imprisonment and that there was an undoubted power in the House to punish for contempt. Parliament has control of its internal affairs and it would be improper for the courts to interfere.

Rost v Edwards

[1990] 2 WLR 1280 · Queen's Bench Division

The plaintiff MP was said by the defendant journalist to have failed to disclose certain consultancies in the Register of Members' Interests. On the same day as the article appeared the plaintiff was de-selected from the Standing Committee on which he served, and an opposition MP wrote to the Speaker complaining of the plaintiff's conduct. The plaintiff sued in defamation and wished (a) to call evidence that the article had caused his de-selection; (b) to put in evidence the latter; and (c) to give evidence of the criteria for registration of interests. The court held that the letter and membership of the committee were protected by parliamentary privilege as proceedings in Parliament, but the register of interests was not.

Popplewell J: ' . . . The courts must always be sensitive to the rights and privileges of Parliament and the constitutional importance of Parliament retaining control over its own proceedings. Equally . . . the House will be anxious to confine its own or its members' privileges to the minimum infringement of the liberties of others. Mutual respect for and understanding of each other's respective rights and privileges are an essential ingredient in the relationship between Parliament and the courts.

Lawyers have always been well aware of the necessity to treat claims for parliamentary privilege with great respect and the consequences if they do not . . . [Popplewell J then referred to Jay and Topham's Case and R v Paty] . . .

I turn now to the conflicting principles involved in this case, and I deal first with the privileges of Parliament.

The privileges of Parliament have evolved by custom, resolutions of Parliament, by decisions of the courts and by Acts of Parliament. In Stockdale v Hansard Lord Denman CJ said: "The Commons of England are not invested with more of power and dignity by their legislative character than by that which they bear as the grant inquest of the nation. All the privileges that can be required to get energetic discharge of the duties inherent in that high trust are conceded without a murmur or a doubt." . . . Coleridge J said in Stockdale v Hansard: ". . . that the House should have exclusive jurisdiction to regulate the course of its own proceedings, and animadvert upon any conduct there in violation of its rules, or delegation from its dignity, stands upon the clearest grounds of necessity."

It is not necessary to trace the history of parliamentary privilege before the seventeenth century save to mention Strodes' Act (the Privilege of Parliament Act 1512) . . .

Article 9 of the Bill of Rights (1688) provides: "That the freedome of speech and debates or proceedings in Parlyament ought not to be impeached or questioned in any court or place out of Parlyament."

The question of what are "proceedings in Parliament" and the meaning of the word "questioned" are the matters on which argument in the instant case has been presented . . .

It might have been thought that the juxtaposition of the word "questioned" with the word "impeached" in the Bill of Rights would have led the courts to construe it as meaning "adversely question" or "criticise" or "attribute improper motive". This was not, however, how the law developed. Blackstone said (1 B1 Com (17th edn) 163, quoting from 4 Co Inst 15): " . . . whatever matter arises concerning either house of parliament, ought to be examined, discussed, and adjudged in that house to which it relates, and not elsewhere." In *Stockdale* v *Hansard* Lord Denman CJ said: " . . . whatever is done within the walls of either assembly must pass without question in any other place." Littledale J said "It is said the House of Commons is a sole judge of its own privileges: and so I admit as far as the proceedings in the House and some other things are concerned . . . " Patteson J said "Beyond all dispute it is necessary that the proceedings of each House of Parliament should be entirely free and unshackled; that whatever is said or done in either House should not be liable to examination elsewhere . . . "

[Popplewell J cited *Bradlaugh* v *Gossett* (see p.176), *Dingle* v *Associated Newspapers Ltd* and *Church of Scientology* v *Johnson Smith* (see p.178) and continued:]

 . . . There is nothing, says [counsel for the plaintiff] to support on the simple construction of the Bill of Rights the contention that "questioned" means "examined". If it was intended simply to prevent any discussion about what was said in Parliament it would have been quite unnecessary to use the word "impeach". He observed that all the cases cited involved some criticism either of individual members of Parliament or the Houses of Parliament as a whole. Thus in *Bradlaugh* v *Gossett* what was sought to be impugned was an order of the House on the ground that it was beyond their power and jurisdiction to grant the order. In *Dingle* v *Associated Newspapers Ltd* what was being sought to attack was the report of the select committee on the ground of some defect of procedure. In the *Church of Scientology* case what was being suggested was some improper motive on the part of a member of Parliament and in *R* v *Secretary of State for Trade, ex p Anderson Strathclyde plc* what was being sought was in some way adversely to criticise what the Secretary of State had said in the House of Commons.
Counsel for the plaintiff says that he does not wish in this case to criticise anybody. He simply wants to call as a factual witness a chairman of the committee of selection to say (a) that the plaintiff had been selected to sit on the standing committee and (b) that as a result of the article he had deen deselected. He is not asking the court to draw any inference; he is merely seeking to lead evidence of fact which in no possible sense could affect the dignity of the House or infringe the right of free speech in proceedings in the House. . . .
I have some sympathy for the interpretation of counsel for the plaintiff of the word "questioned" and if I were faced for the first time with interpreting the word "questioned" in the Bill of Rights I confess that I might well have concluded that it involved some allegation of improper motive. But what is clear is that, given the views of the large number of judges (and, more particularly, their quality) who have interpreted the Bill of Rights, it is simply not open to this court to take that view. Counsel for the plaintiff asks, rhetorically, how is freedom of speech and the dignity of the House affected by ascertaining not only what happened but why it happened? I have to say that the weight of authority is such that if it is now sought to challenge

the unanimous view of those judges who have expressed their views on this subject it can only be resolved by a court at a higher level than this one. . . .

The result of the principles on which the Solicitor General relies, will prevent the plaintiff without leave of the House from calling any evidence as to his appointment or deselection as a member of the standing committee. Nor can the plaintiff simply say, "I was appointed; on the day of the article I was deselected," and invite the jury to draw the inference for which the plaintiff contends. The reason for the deselection would involve discussing and examining the proceedings of the House because the appointment and deselection of members of a committee of the House form part of the proceedings of that House. Likewise in relation to the anticipated election of the plaintiff to be chairman of the Select Committee on Energy, that would constitute a direct inquiry into and examination and discussion of the appointment of a member of a committee of the House and inferences about that could also not be drawn. Additionally, there is the difficulty evidentially that one member of the committee would not be a proper person to give evidence of the views of the whole committee.

For the reasons that I have given above I am clearly of the view that if counsel for the plaintiff wishes to call evidence at the trial in relation to the appointment and deselection of the plaintiff in relation to the standing committee for the Electricity Bill and in relation to his disappointment in relation to the chairmanship of the Select Committee on Energy it will be necessary for him to petition the House . . .

Lord Reid said in *British Railways Board* v *Pickin*: "For a century or more both Parliament and the courts have been careful not to act so as to cause conflict between them."

I have sought to interpret the conflicting principles in the light of those observations. I hope, therefore, I may be permitted to say this, that the effect of this judgment if the House declines the petition may (and I emphasise the word may) be to deprive a litigant of his proper rights. This has particular importance in a case where, as far as one can see, neither freedom of speech nor the dignity of the House will have been affected. No question, as I understand it, arises of questioning the validity of any decision of the House or its committee or making any suggestion of improper motive. Accordingly, in so far as it is appropriate for me to make any comment on the exercise of the House's judgment about a matter over which they have exclusive jurisdiction, as I have ruled, I express the hope that they will approach the matter sympathetically.

The third issue which arises for consideration is the letter written by one of the opposition members both to the plaintiff and to the Speaker in relation to questions which he subsequently raised in the House about the plaintiff's conduct. I have already ruled that the questions asked by members of Parliament are inadmissible. In my judgment the letters themselves add nothing to the evidence in this case, whether covered by privilege or not. If I have to decide whether the letters are governed by parliamentary privilege I have no hesitation in saying that they are.

I turn now to the question of the Register of Members' Interests. . . .

The approach I have to this aspect of the case is this. There are clearly cases where Parliament is to be the sole judge of its affairs. Equally there are clear cases where the courts are to have exclusive jurisdiction. In a case which may be described as a grey area a court, while giving full attention to the necessity for comity between the courts and Parliament, should not be astute to find a reason for ousting the jurisdiction of the court and for limiting or even defeating a proper claim by a party to litigation before it. If Parliament wishes to cover a particular area with privilege it has the ability to do so by passing an Act of Parliament giving itself the right to exclusive jurisdiction. Ousting the jurisdiction of the court has always been regarded as requiring the clearest possible words. Nothing in the authorities, as I have indicated, in any way covers the instant situation. It is true that courts have over the years enlarged the definition of "proceedings" from the formal speeches in the House to other matters, as appears from the various authorities to which I have been referred.

But, as counsel for the defendants pointed out, there are plenty of areas which are not covered by "proceedings in Parliament". It is clearly not possible to arrive at an exhaustive definition. Counsel for the defendants referred by way of example to *Stockdale* v *Hansard*, where it was held that no privilege attached at common law to a report by the Inspector of Prisons even though the publication of the report had been made by order of the House of Commons. As a result the Parliamentary Papers Act 1840 had to be passed. This is an example, says counsel for the defendants, of what is ancillary to the operation of Parliament . . .

In the result, I conclude that claims for privilege in respect of the Register of Members' Interests do not fall within the definition of "proceedings in Parliament", and accordingly I rule that it is open to the plaintiff to give the evidence that he seeks to do in relation to the registration of members' interests and it is open to the defendants to challenge that evidence.'

Comment

(1) In *Jay and Topham*'s case, judges had ruled in a civil case against Topham, an officer of the House of Commons, despite a plea that he had been arresting the plaintiffs in that action for a breach of parliamentary privilege. Two of the judges attended the House when required to do so, and after being heard were ordered to be taken into custody for breach of privilege.

(2) In *R* v *Paty* five Aylesbury men had challenged the returning officer in an election for refusing their votes. After that case they had been committed to prison by the House of Commons for breach of privilege, and applied for habeas corpus. When that was refused, they petitioned the Queen for a writ of error. The House of Commons resolved that a number of attorneys who had pleaded in the habeas corpus proceedings were guilty of breach of privilege and accordingly were in contempt.

(3) Note that on the issue of the use of Hansard to prove a fact, the Privy Council in *Prebble* v *Television New Zealand Ltd*, p.173, cast doubt on *Rost* v *Edwards*, and the House of Lords in *Pepper* v *Hart* considered that *R* v *Secretary of State for Trade, ex parte Anderson Strathclyde* was wrongly decided.

Pepper v *Hart*

[1993] 1 All ER 42 · House of Lords

The House of Lords considered whether a court when interpreting an Act might have regard to parliamentary materials. The House of Lords decided to depart from the previous practice and permit reference in cases of ambiguous or obscure statutes or where the literal meaning would lead to absurdity, and where the material relied on was a clear statement by a minister or promoter of a Bill.

Lord Browne-Wilkinson: '. . . The Attorney-General was not contending that the use of parliamentary material by the courts for the purposes of construction would constitute an "impeachment" of freedom of speech since impeachment is limited to cases where a member of Parliament is sought to be made liable, either in criminal or civil proceedings, for what he has said in Parliament.

. . . The submission was that the use of *Hansard* for the purpose of construing an Act would constitute a "questioning" of the freedom of speech or debate. The process, it is said, would involve an investigation of what the minister meant by the words he used and would inhibit the minister in what he says by attaching legislative effect to his words. This, it was submitted, constituted "questioning" the freedom of speech or debate.

Article 9 [of the Bill of Rights] is a provision of the highest constitutional importance and should not be narrowly construed. It ensures the ability of democratically elected members of Parliament to discuss what they will (freedom of debate) and to say what they will (freedom of speech). But, even given a generous approach to this construction, I find it impossible to attach the breadth of meaning to the word "question" which the Attorney-General urges. It must be remembered that art.9 prohibits questioning not only "in any court" but also in any "place out of Parliament". If the Attorney-General's submission is correct, any comment in the media or elsewhere on what is said in Parliament would constitute "questioning" since all members of Parliament must speak and act taking into account what political commentators and others will say. Plainly art.9 cannot have effect so as to stifle the freedom of all to comment on what is said in Parliament, even though such comment may influence members in what they say.

In my judgment, the plain meaning of art.9, viewed against the historical background in which it was enacted, was to ensure that members of Parliament were not subjected to any penalty, civil or criminal, for what they said and were able, contrary to the previous assertions of the Stuart monarchy, to discuss what they, as opposed to the monarch, chose to have discussed. Relaxation of the rule will not involve the courts in criticising what is said in Parliament. The purpose of looking at *Hansard* will not be to construe the words used by the minister but to give effect to the words used, so long as they are clear. Far from questioning the independence of Parliament and its debates, the courts would be giving effect to what is said and done there.

Moreover, the Attorney-General's contentions are inconsistent with the practice which has now continued over a number of years in cases of judicial review. In such cases, *Hansard* has frequently been referred to with a view to ascertaining whether a statutory power has been improperly exercised for an alien purpose or in a wholly unreasonable manner. In *Brind* v *Secretary of State for the Home Department*, it was the Crown which invited the court to look at *Hansard* to show that the minister in that case had acted correctly. This House attached importance to what the minister had said. The Attorney-General accepted that references to *Hansard* for the purposes of judicial review litigation did not infringe art.9. Yet reference for the purposes of judicial review and for the purposes of construction are indistinguishable. In both types of case, the minister's words are considered and taken into account by the court; in both, the use of such words by the courts might affect what is said in Parliament. . . .

In *R* v *Secretary of State for Trade, ex parte Anderson Strathclyde plc* an applicant for judicial review sought to adduce parliamentary materials to prove a fact. The Crown did not object to the Divisional Court looking at the materials but the court itself refused to do so on the grounds that it would constitute a breach of art.9. In view of the Attorney-General's concession and the decision of this House in *Brind's* case, in my judgment *ex parte Anderson Strathclyde plc* was wrongly decided on this point.

Accordingly in my judgment the use of clear ministerial statements by the court as a guide to the construction of ambiguous legislation would not contravene art.9. No doubt all judges will be astute to ensure that counsel does not in any way impugn or criticise the minister's statements or his reasoning. . .'

Prebble v *Television New Zealand Ltd*

[1994] 3 All ER 407 · Privy Council

In New Zealand, the defendant alleged in a television programme that the plaintiff, the Minister for State Owned Enterprises, had secretly conspired with businessmen and public officials to promote statutes to implement the sale of state assets in order to allow the businessmen the opportunity to obtain assets on unduly favourable terms. The plaintiff sued in libel, and the defence of justification was based in part on statements made in Parliament which it was said were misleading. The plaintiff applied for these parts of the defence to be struck out on the basis that they infringed parliamentary privilege.

Lord Browne-Wilkinson: ' . . . an action for libel cannot be brought against a member based on words said by him in the House.

In this action, the position is reversed: the libel action is brought, not against, but by a member of the legislature. The defendants wish to allege that allegedly defamatory statements made by them were true and are seeking to demonstrate such truth by relying on things said and acts done in Parliament, i.e. the defendants wish to use parliamentary materials not as a sword but as a shield. The question is whether art.9 precludes such deployment of parliamentary material . . . There are two types of allegation in the particulars which might infringe parliamentary privilege. First, there are allegations that the plaintiff and other ministers made statements in the House which were misleading in that they suggested that the government did not intend to sell off state-owned assets when in fact the spokesman was, it is alleged, conspiring to do so. The second type of allegation is that the conspiracy was implemented by introducing and passing legislation in the House . . . When the defence was amended to plead justification, the plaintiff after consulting the parliamentary authorities applied to strike out those particulars which it was thought infringed parliamentary privilege . . .

If art.9 is looked at alone, the question is whether it would infringe the Article to suggest that the statements made in the House were improper or the legislation procured in pursuance of the alleged conspiracy, as constituting impeachment or questioning of the freedom of speech of Parliament.

In addition to art.9 itself, there is a long line of authority which supports a wider principle, of which art.9 is merely one manifestation, viz that the courts and Parliament are both astute to recognise their respective constitutional roles. So far as the courts are concerned they will not allow any challenge to be made to what is said or done within the walls of Parliament in performance of its legislative functions and protection of its established privileges: *Burdett* v *Abbot, Stockdale* v *Hansard, Bradlaugh* v *Gossett, British Railways Board* v *Pickin, Pepper* v *Hart.* As Blackstone said (1 Bl Com (17th edn) 163):

> The whole of the law and custom of Parliament has its original from this one maxim, that whatever matter arises concerning either House of Parliament ought to be examined, discussed, and adjudged in that House to which it relates, and not elsewhere.

According to conventional wisdom, the combined operation of art.9 and that wider principle would undoubtedly prohibit any suggestion in the present action (whether by way of direct evidence, cross-examination or submission) that statements were made in the House which were lies or motivated by a desire to mislead. It would also prohibit any suggestion that proceedings in the House were initiated or carried through into legislation in pursuance of the alleged conspiracy. However, it is the defendants' case that the principle has a more limited scope. The defendants submit, first, that the principle only operates to protect the questioning of statements made in the House in proceedings which seek to assert legal consequences against the maker of the statement for making that statement. Alternatively, the defendants submit that parliamentary privilege does not apply where it is the member of Parliament himself who brings proceedings for libel and parliamentary privilege would operate so as to prevent a defendant who wishes to justify the libel from challenging the veracity or bona fides of the plaintiff in making statements in the House.

The first of those submissions is based on the decision in the New South Wales Supreme Court *R* v *Murphy* . . . In their Lordships' view the law as stated by Hunt J [in that case] was not correct so far as the rest of the Commonwealth is concerned. First, his views were in conflict with the long line of dicta that the courts will not allow any challenge to what is said or done in Parliament. Second, as Hunt J recognised, his decision was inconsistent with the decision of Browne J in *Church of Scientology of California* v *Johnson-Smith* (subsequently approved by the House of Lords in *Pepper* v *Hart*) and *Comalco Ltd* v *Australian Broadcasting Corp*, in both of which cases it was held that it would be a breach of privilege to allow what is said in Parliament to be the subject matter of investigation or submission.

Finally, Hunt J based himself on a narrow construction of art.9, derived from the historical context in which it was originally enacted. He correctly identified the mischief sought to be remedied in 1688 as being, *inter alia*, the assertion by the King's courts of a right to hold a member of Parliament criminally or legally liable for what he had done or said in Parliament. From this he deduced the principle that art.9 only applies to cases in which a court is being asked to expose the maker of the statement to legal liability for what he has said in Parliament. This view discounts the basic concept underlying art.9, viz the need to ensure so far as possible that a member of the legislature and witnesses before committees of the House can speak freely without fear that what they say will later be held against them in the courts. The important public interest protected by such privilege is to ensure that the member or witness *at the time he speaks* is not inhibited from stating fully and freely what he has to say. If there were any exceptions which permitted his statements to be questioned subsequently, at the time when he speaks in Parliament he would not know whether or not there would subsequently be a challenge to what he is saying. Therefore he would not have the confidence the privilege is designed to protect.

Moreover to allow it to be suggested in cross-examination or submission that a member or witness was lying to the House could lead to exactly that conflict between the courts and Parliament which the wider principle of non-intervention is designed to avoid. Misleading the House is a contempt of the House punishable by the House: if a court were also to be permitted to decide whether or not a member or witness had misled the House there would be a serious risk of conflicting decisions on the issue.

The defendants' second submission (that the rules excluding parliamentary material do not apply when the action is brought by a member of Parliament) is based on the decision of the Supreme Court of South Australia in *Wright and Advertiser Newspapers Ltd* v *Lewis* . . . Although their Lordships are sympathetic with the concern felt by the South Australian Supreme Court, they cannot accept that the fact that the maker of the statement is the initiator of the court proceedings can affect the question whether art.9 is infringed. The privilege protected by art.9 is the privilege of Parliament itself. The actions of any individual member of Parliament, even if he has an individual privilege of his own, cannot determine whether or not the privilege of Parliament is to apply. The wider principle encapsulated in Blackstone's words quoted above prevents the courts from adjudicating on issues arising in or concerning the House, viz whether or not a member has misled the House or acted from improper motives. The decision of an individual member cannot override that collective privilege of the House to be the sole judge of such matters . . .

Their Lordships are acutely conscious (as were the courts below) that to preclude reliance on things said and done in the House in defence of libel proceedings brought by a member of the House could have a serious impact on a most important aspect of freedom of speech, viz the right of the public to comment on and criticise the actions of those elected to power in a democratic society: see *Derbyshire CC* v *Times Newspapers Ltd.* If the media and others are unable to establish the truth of fair criticisms of the conduct of their elected members in the very performance of their legislative duties in the House, the results could indeed be chilling to the proper monitoring of members' behaviour. But the present case and *Wright*'s case illustrate how public policy, or human rights, issues can conflict. There are three such issues in play in these cases: first, the need to ensure that the legislature can exercise its powers freely on behalf of its electors, with access to all relevant information; second, the need to protect freedom of speech generally; third, the interests of justice in ensuring that all relevant evidence is available to the courts. Their Lordships are of the view that the law has been long settled that, of these three public interests, the first must prevail. But the other two public interests cannot be ignored and their Lordships will revert to them in considering the question of a stay of proceedings.

For these reasons . . . their Lordships are of the view that parties to litigation, by whomsoever commenced, cannot bring into question anything said or done in the House by suggesting (whether by direct evidence, cross-examination, inference or submission) that the actions or words were inspired by improper motives or were untrue or misleading. Such matters lie entirely within the jurisdiction of the House, subject to any statutory exception . . .

However, their Lordships wish to make it clear that this principle does not exclude all references in court proceedings to what has taken place in the House. In the past, Parliament used to assert a right, separate from the privilege of freedom of speech enshrined in art.9, to restrain publication of its proceedings. Formerly the procedure was to petition the House for leave to produce Hansard in court. Since 1980 this right has no longer been generally asserted by the United Kingdom Parliament and their Lordships understood from the Attorney-General that in practice the House of Representatives in New Zealand no longer asserts the right. A number of the authorities on the scope of art.9 betray some confusion between the right to prove the occurrence of parliamentary events and the embargo on questioning their propriety. In particular, it is questionable whether *Rost* v *Edwards* was rightly decided.

Since there can no longer be any objection to the production of Hansard, the Attorney-General accepted (in their Lordships' view rightly) that there could be no objection to the use of Hansard to prove what was done and said in Parliament as a matter of history. Similarly, he accepted that the fact that a statute had been passed is admissible in court proceedings. Thus, in the present action, there cannot be any objection to it being proved what the plaintiff or the Prime Minister said in the House . . . or that the State-Owned Enterprises Act 1986 was passed . . . It will be for the trial judge to ensure that the proof of these historical facts is not used to suggest that the words were improperly spoken or the statute passed to achieve an improper purpose.

It is clear that, on the pleadings as they presently stand, the defendants intend to rely on these matters not purely as a matter of history but as part of the alleged conspiracy or its implementation. Therefore, in their Lordships' view, Smellie J was right to strike them out. But their Lordships wish to make it clear that if the defendants wish at the trial to allege the occurrence of events or the saying of certain words in Parliament without any accompanying allegation of impropriety or any other questioning there is no objection to that course . . . '

Bradlaugh v *Gossett*

(1884) 12 QBD 271 · Queen's Bench Division

Bradlaugh, an atheist, was elected as Member of Parliament but the Speaker would not call upon him to take the oath. The House of Commons resolved to exclude Bradlaugh from the House. He tried to re-enter at a later stage and was ejected by the Sergeant at Arms. Bradlaugh sought an injunction to prevent the Sergeant at Arms from excluding him and a declaration that the resolution of the House was void. The court held that it had no power to interfere in the internal management of the House since as a matter of privilege that fell within the sole jurisdiction of the House.

Lord Coleridge CJ: '. . . What is said or done within the walls of Parliament cannot be enquired into in a court of law . . . The jurisdiction of the Houses over their own members, their right to impose discipline within their walls, is absolute, and exclusive. To use the words of Lord Ellenborough, "They would sink into utter contempt and inefficiency without it." . . . '

Stephen J: '[*Clarke* v *Bradlaugh*] appears to me to illustrate exactly the true relation between the House of Commons and this court as regards the interpretation of statutes affecting them, and the effect of their resolutions on our proceedings. A resolution of the House permitting Mr Bradlaugh to take his seat on making a statutory declaration would certainly never have been interfered with by this court. If we had been moved to declare it void and to restrain Mr Bradlaugh from taking his seat until he had taken the oath, we should certainly have refused to do so. On the other hand, if the House had resolved ever so decidedly that Mr Bradlaugh was entitled to make the statutory declaration instead of taking the oath, and had attempted by resolution or otherwise to protect him against an action for penalties, it would have been our duty to disregard such resolution, and if an action for penalties were brought, to hear and determine it according to our own interpretation of the statute. Suppose, again, that the House had taken the view of the statute ultimately arrived at by this court, that it did not enable Mr Bradlaugh to make the statutory promise, we should certainly not have entertained an application to declare their resolution void. We should have said that for the purpose of determining on a right to be exercised in the House itself, and in particular the right of sitting and voting, the House, and the House only, could interpret the statute; but that as regarded rights to be exercised out of and independently of the House, such as the right of suing for a penalty for having sat and voted, the statute must be interpreted by this court independently of the House.'

Comment

(1) At an earlier stage the House had resolved to permit Bradlaugh, subject to any legal penalties which he might incur, to make a declaration instead of taking the oath. In *Clarke* v *Bradlaugh* the court concluded that the Parliamentary Oaths Act 1866 did not permit Bradlaugh to make a statutory declaration instead of taking the oath. That case had been brought by a common informer with a view to compelling the payment of a penalty for having improperly sat and voted.

(2) See *Church of Scientology* v *Johnson Smith* (p.178). Interference by the courts with the internal affairs of the House would be a contempt of the House. The power to control its own internal affairs also permits Parliament to punish for contempt of the House MPs who abuse their privileges as well as outsiders who are in breach of privilege.

(3) The case also confirms that a resolution of either House, or both, cannot alter the law – see *Bowles* v *Bank of England* (p.65), and *Stockdale* v *Hansard* (p.166).

Pickin v British Railways Board

[see p.26]

Lord Simon '. . .A second concomitant of the sovereignty of Parliament is that the Houses of Parliament enjoy certain privileges. These are vouchsafed so that Parliament can fulfil its key function in our system of democratic government. To adapt the words of Lord Ellenborough CJ in *Burdett* v *Abbot* "they [the Houses] would sink into utter contempt and inefficiency without [them]." Parliamentary privilege is part of the law of the land . . . Among the privileges of the Houses of

Parliament is the exclusive right to determine the regularity of their own internal proceedings . . .

I have no doubt that the respondent . . . is seeking to impeach proceedings in Parliament, and that the issues raised by those paragraphs cannot be tried without questioning proceedings in Parliament.

It is well known that in the past there have been dangerous strains between the law courts and Parliament – dangerous because each institution has its own particular role to play in our constitution, and because collision between the two institutions is likely to impair their power to vouchsafe those constitutional rights for which citizens depend on them. So for many years Parliament and the courts have each been astute to respect the sphere of action and the privileges of the other . . .

The respondent . . . claimed that he could discharge the onus of proving the allegations . . . merely by reliance on presumptions, so that proceedings in Parliament need not, so far as he was concerned, be forensically questioned. Even if this were so, it would still leave unanswered how the appellant could proceed in rebuttal without calling parliamentary proceedings in question. I am quite clear that the issues would not be fairly tried without infringement of the Bill of Rights and of that general parliamentary privilege which is part of the law of the land.

The respondent claims, however, that, whatever may be the position as regards a public Act of Parliament, it is open to a litigant to impugn the validity (or, at least, by invoking jurisdiction in equity, nullify the operation) of an enactment in a private Act of Parliament. But the considerations of parliamentary privilege to which I have referred would undoubtedly seem to extend to private Bill procedure; and the authorities to which my noble and learned friends have adverted are clearly contrary to the respondent's submissions . . .

A further practical consideration is that if there is evidence that Parliament may have been misled into an enactment, Parliament might well – indeed, would be likely to – wish to conduct its own inquiry. It would be unthinkable that two inquiries – one parliamentary and the other forensic – should proceed concurrently, conceivably arriving at different conclusions; and a parliamentary examination of parliamentary procedures and of the actions and understandings of officers of Parliament would seem to be clearly more satisfactory than one conducted in a court of law – quite apart from considerations of Parliamentary privilege . . . If the respondent thinks that Parliament has been misled into an enactment inimical to his interests, his remedy lies with Parliament itself, and nowhere else.'

Church of Scientology of California v *Johnson Smith*

[1972] 1 QB 522 · Queen's Bench Division

The defendant, a Member of Parliament, was alleged to have published a libel during the course of a television interview about the plaintiff, the Church of Scientology. He had previously asked a question of the Minister of Health in the House of Commons. The plaintiff sought to rebut the defendant's plea of fair comment by referring to proceedings in Parliament. The High Court held that parliamentary privilege extended not only to excluding a cause of action based upon what was said or done in the course of proceedings in Parliament but also to excluding the examination of proceedings in Parliament to support a cause of action arising out of something done outside the House.

Browne J referred to *Bradlaugh* v *Gosset* (see p.176) and *Stockdale* v *Hansard* (see p.166), and continued:

' . . . It is quite clear therefore that no action for defamation could be brought in respect of anything said in the House of Commons itself. The Attorney-General says that the privilege goes further and that what is said or done in the House in the course of any proceedings there cannot be examined outside Parliament for the purpose of supporting a cause of action, even though the cause of action itself arises out of something done outside the House . . . The defendant in his defence here pleaded fair comment and privilege. Privilege, of course, in the ordinary sense of which that word is used in the law of defamation and not Parliamentary privilege. And the purpose of paragraph 4 of the reply is that the plaintiffs are alleging malice in order to defeat those pleas. The particulars under paragraph 4 of the reply, including sub-paragraphs (ix) and (x), are particulars of the facts on which the plaintiffs intend to rely as establishing that the defendant acted with malice, in other words, that he acted with some sort of improper motive.

In my view sub-paragraphs (ix) and (x) must involve a suggestion that the defendant was, in one way or another, acting improperly or with an improper motive when he did and said in Parliament the things referred to in those sub-paragraphs. I accept the Attorney-General's argument that the scope of Parliamentary privilege extends beyond excluding any cause of action in respect of what is said or done in the House itself. And I accept his proposition . . . that what is said or done in the House in the course of proceedings there cannot be examined outside Parliament for the purpose of supporting a cause of action even though the cause of action itself arises out of something done outside the House. In my view this conclusion is supported by both principle and authority . . .

[T]he basis on which Blackstone puts it . . . is that anything arising concerning the House ought to be examined, discussed, and adjudged in that House and not elsewhere. The House must have complete control over its own proceedings and its own members. I also accept the other basis for this privilege which the Attorney-General suggested, which is, that a member must have a complete right of free speech in the House without any fear that his motives or intentions or reasoning will be questioned or held against him thereafter. So far as the authorities are concerned it will be seen that the words used are very wide. In the Bill of Rights 1688 itself the word is "questioned": "freedom of Speech, and debates or proceedings in Parliament ought not to be impeached or questioned in any court or place out of Parliament." Blackstone uses the words "examined, discussed, and adjudged," they ought not to be examined, discussed or adjudged elsewhere than in the House. In Lord Denman CJ's judgment in *Stockdale* v *Hansard* . . . the words are that "whatever is done within the walls of either assembly must pass without question in any other place," and in the same case Patteson J said "that whatever is done or said in either House should not be liable to examination elsewhere." . . . I am quite satisfied that in these proceedings it is not open to either party to go directly, or indirectly, into any question of the motives or intentions of the defendant . . . or the then Minister of Health or any other Member of Parliament in anything they said or did in the House . . . '

Wason v Walter

[1868] 4 QB 73 · House of Lords

The plaintiff petitioned the House of Lords alleging highly improper conduct and asking that a committee of the House should investigate Sir Fitzroy Kelly. The defendant published in *The Times* a detailed report of the debate which ensued and the plaintiff sued the defendant in respect of that report. For the first time the question arose whether or not a faithful report in a public newspaper of a debate in either House of Parliament which contained matter disparaging to the character of another was actionable. The House of Lords held that it was not and that the report if fair and honest, and not motivated by malice, was protected by qualified privilege in the law of defamation.

Lord Cockburn CJ: 'It is now well established that faithful and fair reports of the proceedings of courts of justice, though the character of individuals may incidentally suffer, are privileged, and that for the publication of such reports the publishers are neither criminally nor civilly responsible.

The immunity thus afforded in respect of the publication of the proceedings of courts of justice rests upon a twofold ground. In the English law of libel, malice is said to be the gist of an action for defamation. And though it is true that by malice, as necessary to give a cause of action in respect of a defamatory statement, legal, and not actual malice, is meant, while by legal malice . . . is meant no more than the wrongful intention which the law always presumes as accompanying a wrongful act without any proof of malice in fact, yet the presumption of law may be rebutted by the circumstances under which the defamatory matter has been uttered or published, and, if this should be the case, though the character of the party concerned may have suffered, no right of action will arise . . . It is thus that in the case of reports of proceedings of courts of justice, though individuals may occasionally suffer from them, yet, as they are published without any reference to the individuals concerned, but solely to afford information to the public and for the benefit of society, the presumption of malice is rebutted, and such publications are held to be privileged.

The other and the broader principle on which this exception to the general law of libel is founded is, that the advantage to the community from publicity being given to the proceedings of courts of justice is so great, that the occasional inconvenience to individuals arising from it must yield to the general good . . .

Both the principles, on which the exemption from legal consequences is thus extended to the publication of the proceedings of courts of justice, appear to us to be applicable to the case before us. The presumption of malice is negatived in the one case as in the other by the fact that the publication has in view the instruction and advantage of the public, and has no particular reference to the party concerned. There is also in the one case as in the other a preponderance of general good over partial and occasional evil . . . It seems to us impossible to doubt that it is of paramount public and national importance that the proceedings of the Houses of Parliament shall be communicated to the public, who have the deepest interest in knowing what passes within their walls, seeing that on what is there said and done, the welfare of the community depends. Where would be our confidence in the government of the country or in the legislature by which our laws are framed, and to whose charge the great interests of the country are committed – where would be our attachment to the constitution under which we live – if the proceedings of the great council of the realm were shrouded in secrecy and concealed from the knowledge of the nation? How could the communications between the representatives of the people and their constituents, which are so essential to the working of the representative system, be usefully carried on, if the constituencies were kept in ignorance of what their representatives are doing? What would become of the right of petitioning on all measures pending in Parliament, the undoubted right of the subject, if the people are to be kept in ignorance of what is passing in either House? Can any man bring himself to doubt that the publicity given in modern times to what passes in Parliament is essential to the maintenance of the relations subsisting between the government, the legislature, and the country at large? . . .

It is to be observed that the analogy between the case of reports of proceedings of courts of justice and those of proceedings in Parliament being complete, all the limitations placed on the one to prevent injustice to individuals will necessarily attach on the other: a garbled or partial report, or of detached parts of proceedings, published with intent to injure individuals, will equally be disentitled to protection. Our judgement will in no way interfere with the decisions that the publication of a single speech for the purpose or with the effect of injuring an individual will be unlawful . . . At the same time it may be as well to observe that we are disposed to agree with what was said in *Davison* v *Duncan*, as to such a speech being privileged if bona fide published by a member for the information of his constituents. But whatever would deprive a report of the proceedings in a court of justice of immunity will equally apply to a report of proceedings in Parliament.'

Comment

(1) As to communications by and with an MP, see *Beech* v *Freeson*, and *Re Parliamentary Privilege Act 1770*. Correspondence by Members of Parliament has sometimes been given absolute privilege in the law of defamation – see, for example, s.10, Parliamentary Commissioner Act 1967.

(2) In *Cook* v *Alexander*, the plaintiff was a teacher at an approved school who made allegations about the way in which the school had been run. These were investigated and some were found to be true. In a debate in the House of Lords a bishop criticized the plaintiff. The *Daily Telegraph* carried a full report of the proceedings on an inside page and also carried on its back page a 'parliamentary sketch'. This sketch emphasized the attack by the bishop on the plaintiff who sued for libel. The Court of Appeal held that qualified privilege in the law of defamation extended to the sketch provided it was a fair and honest report of the proceedings. Lord Denning MR said:

> When making a sketch, a reporter does not summarize all the speeches. He selects a part of the debate which appears to him to be of special public interest and then describes it and the impact which it made on the House. I think that a parliamentary sketch is privileged if it is made fairly and honestly with the intention of giving an impression of the impact made on the hearers . . . It is sufficient if it is a fair presentation of what took place so as to convey to the reader the impression which the debate itself would have made on a hearer of it .

.. Even if it is defamatory of some one, it is privileged because the public interest in the debate counterbalances the private interest of the individual . . . I would emphasize that it has to be fair . . . But fairness in this regard means a fair presentation of what took place as it impressed the hearers. It does not mean fairness in the abstract as between [the plaintiff] and those who were attacking him. Applying that test, it seems to me that this parliamentary sketch is protected by the qualified privilege. It gives a fair presentation of the impression on the hearers. The bishop's speech made the most impact: so it was given particular prominence. If it had been unfairly distorted, it would not have been a fair presentation. If Lord Longford's rebuttal had been omitted, it would not have been a fair presentation.

9 Separation of powers

The separation of powers concerns the division of state power as between the executive, the legislature and the judiciary. The prominence given to this doctrine in modern constitutions may be traced to Montesquieu, but it undoubtedly has more ancient origins. The scope of the doctrine is a matter of considerable debate and is capable of widely differing interpretations. Statements about the existence and importance of a separation of powers in the United Kingdom must be treated with caution. Whilst it is easy to point to examples where the different functions merge (such as the office of Lord Chancellor) there are a series of checks and balances in the constitution, e.g. through the courts and parliamentary scrutiny. This does not mean that these checks and balances are always effective.

In the United Kingdom the separation of powers plays a secondary role, the lead being taken by the legislative supremacy of Parliament. A strict separation of powers is impossible given the particular importance of that doctrine; the nature of the separation of powers within the United Kingdom reflects the development of the constitution. In strict constitutional theory the three functions are derived from the Crown. Although the courts recognize that as a legal fiction, they will not permit anything to turn upon it (see *M v Home Office*, p.184) save perhaps the privileged position of the Monarch.

In matters where Parliament remains supreme it may interfere successfully with the judicial function. Consider, for example, the passing of legislation retrospectively to validate earlier invalid executive acts (*R v Londonderry JJ, ex parte Hume*, p.30) or to deal with unwelcome judicial decisions (e.g. the War Damage Act 1965, reversing *Burmah Oil v Lord Advocate*, p.53).

As the constitution evolves so too does the separation of powers. Within the European Community the separation of powers is developing as a major feature. And, even within the United Kingdom, the demands of membership occasion a review of the separation of powers. Thus, a court has questioned the continued validity of a legislative provision (see *Stoke on Trent City*

Council v *B & Q*, p.113) as a proper exercise of the function thrust upon it by European law.

The judicial function

The Crown has long since yielded the power to make law (*Case of Proclamations*) or to decide cases (*Case of Prohibitions*). But, even now, there are areas where there is executive interference in the administration of justice, e.g. the prerogative of mercy, the power to discontinue criminal proceedings, and executive early release of prisoners.

The separation of powers has influenced judicial thinking in a wide range of contexts, and the courts are conscious of the doctrine and of their proper constitutional function (see *M* v *Home Office*, and *Duport Steels Ltd* v *Sirs*, p.190). There are occasions when the courts will by choice refuse to adjudicate upon matters. Thus, the courts will not interfere where there is an executive decision made on the grounds of national security (p.264) provided that there was power to do what was done.

M v *Home Office*

[1993] 3 All ER 537 · House of Lords

M alleged that he had been wrongly deported. During a series of hearings a judge believed that an undertaking not to deport had been given on behalf of the Secretary of State; in breach of that apparent undertaking M was deported. At a later hearing the judge ordered that M should be returned to the United Kingdom. Despite this order, the Secretary of State cancelled return arrangements which had been made.

M commenced committal proceedings against the Home Office and the Secretary of State in respect of the breach of undertaking and the failure to comply with the mandatory interim injunction. At first instance Simon Brown J held that the undertaking and injunction were not enforceable by any process of compulsion. The Court of Appeal held, *obiter* in respect of the alleged undertaking, that they were so enforceable but only against ministers personally. The House of Lords held that there was power to grant injunctions, including interim injunctions, against ministers acting in their official capacity. In addition, the court was entitled to enforce injunctions by way of contempt proceedings against ministers, or relevant government departments, in their official capacity.

Lord Templeman: 'Parliament makes the law, the executive carry the law into effect and the judiciary enforce the law. The expression "the Crown" has two meanings, namely the monarch and the executive. In the seventeenth century Parliament established its supremacy over the Crown as monarch, over the executive and over the judiciary. Parliamentary supremacy over the Crown as monarch stems from the fact that the monarch must accept the advice of a Prime Minister who is supported by a majority of Parliament. Parliamentary supremacy over the Crown as executive stems from the fact that Parliament maintains in office the Prime Minister, who appoints the ministers in charge of the executive. Parliamentary supremacy over the judiciary is only exercisable by statute. The judiciary enforce the law against individuals, against institutions and against the executive. The judges cannot enforce the law against the Crown as monarch because the Crown as monarch can do no wrong but judges enforce the law against the Crown as executive and against the individuals who from time to time represent the Crown. A litigant complaining of a breach of the law by the executive can sue the Crown as executive bringing his action against the minister who is responsible for the department of state involved, in the present case the Secretary of State for Home Affairs. To enforce the law the courts have power to grant remedies including injunctions against a minister in his official capacity. If the minister has personally broken the law, the litigant can sue the minister, in this case Mr Kenneth Baker, in his personal capacity. For the purpose of enforcing the law against all persons and institutions, including ministers in their official capacity and in their personal capacity, the courts are armed with coercive powers exercisable in proceedings for contempt of court.

In the present case, counsel for the Secretary of State argued that the judge could not enforce the law by injunction or contempt proceedings against the minister in his official capacity. Counsel also argued that in his personal capacity Mr Baker the Secretary of State for Home Affairs had not been guilty of contempt.

My Lords, the argument that there is no power to enforce the law by injunction or contempt proceedings against a minister in his official capacity would, if upheld, establish the proposition that the executive obey the law as a matter of grace and not as a matter of necessity, a proposition which would reverse the result of the Civil War. For the reasons given by my noble and learned friend, Lord Woolf, and on principle, I am satisfied that injunctions and contempt proceedings may be brought against the minister in his official capacity and that in the present case the Home Office for which the Secretary of State was responsible was in contempt. I am also satisfied that Mr Baker was throughout acting in his official capacity, on advice which he was entitled to accept and under a mistaken view as to the law. In these circumstances I do not consider that Mr Baker personally was guilty of contempt. I would therefore dismiss this appeal substituting the Secretary of State for Home Affairs as being the person against whom the finding of contempt was made.'

Lord Woolf: ' . . . The Court of Appeal were of the opinion that a finding of contempt could not be made against the Crown, a government department or a minister of the Crown in his official capacity. Although it is to be expected that it will be rare indeed that the circumstances will exist in which such a finding would be justified, I do not believe there is any impediment to a court making such a finding, when it is appropriate to do so, not against the Crown directly, but against a government department or a minister of the Crown in his official capacity. Lord Donaldson MR considered that a problem was created in making a finding of contempt because the Crown lacked a legal personality. However, at least for some purposes, the Crown has a legal personality. It can be appropriately described as a corporation sole or a corporation aggregate (per Lord Diplock and Lord Simon of Glaisdale respectively in *Town Investments Ltd* v *Dept of the Environment*). The Crown can hold property and enter into contracts. On the other hand, even after the Crown Proceedings Act 1947, it cannot conduct litigation except in the name of an authorised government department or, in the case of judicial review, in the name of a minister. In any event it is not in relation to the Crown that I differ from Lord Donaldson MR, but as to a government department or a minister.

Nolan LJ considered that the fact that proceedings for contempt are "essentially personal and punitive" meant that it was not open to a court, as a matter of law, to make a finding of contempt against the Home Office or the Home Secretary . . . While contempt proceedings usually have these characteristics and contempt proceedings against a government department or a minister in an official capacity would not be either personal or punitive (it would clearly not be appropriate to fine or sequest the assets of the Crown or a government department or an officer of the Crown acting in his official capacity), this does not mean that a finding of contempt against a government department or minister would be pointless. The very fact of making such a finding would vindicate the requirements of justice. In addition an order for costs could be made to underline the significance of a contempt. A purpose of the court's powers to make findings of contempt is to ensure the orders of the court are obeyed. This jurisdiction is required to be co-extensive with the courts' jurisdiction to make orders which need the protection which the jurisdiction to make findings of contempt provides. In civil proceedings the court can now make orders (other than injunctions or for specific performance) against authorised government departments or the Attorney-General. On applications for judicial review orders can be made against ministers. In consequence of the developments identified already such orders must be taken not to offend the theory that the Crown can supposedly do no wrong. Equally, if such orders are made and not obeyed, the body against whom the orders were made can be found guilty of contempt without offending that theory, which would be the only justifiable impediment against making a finding of contempt.

In cases not involving a government department or a minister the ability to punish for contempt may be necessary. However, as is reflected in the restrictions on execution against the Crown, the Crown's relationship with the courts does not depend on coercion and in the exceptional situation when a government department's conduct justifies this, a finding of contempt should suffice. In that exceptional situation, the ability of the court to make a finding of contempt is of great importance. It would demonstrate that a government department has interfered with the administration of justice. It will then be for Parliament to determine what should be the consequences of that finding. In accord with tradition the finding should not be made against the "Crown" by name but in the name of the authorised department (or the Attorney-General) or the minister so as to accord with the body against whom the order was made. . . . [The] object of the exercise is not so much to punish an individual as to vindicate the rule of law by a finding of contempt. This can be achieved equally by a declaratory finding of the court as to the contempt against the minister as representing the department. By making the finding against the minister in his official capacity the court will be indicating that it is the department for which the minister is responsible which has been guilty of contempt. The minister himself may or may not have been personally guilty of contempt. The position so far as he is personally concerned would be the equivalent of that which needs to exist for the court to give relief against the minister in proceedings for judicial review. There would need to be default by the department for which the minister is responsible . . .

However, although the injunction was granted by Garland J against Mr Baker in his official capacity this does not mean that he is in the same position as a third party. To draw a distinction between his two personalities would be unduly technical.

While he was Home Secretary the order was one binding upon him personally and one for the compliance with which he as the head of the department was personally responsible. He was, therefore, under a strict liability to comply with the order. However, on the facts of this case I have little doubt that if the Court of Appeal had appreciated that they could make a finding against Mr Baker in his official capacity this is what the court would have done. The conduct complained of in this case which justified the bringing of contempt proceedings was not that of Mr Baker alone and he was acting on advice. His error was understandable and I accept that there is an element of unfairness in the finding against him personally . . .

It is for these reasons that I would dismiss this appeal with costs save for substituting the Secretary of State for the Home Department as being the person against whom the finding of contempt was made . . .'

Comment

(1)   For the decision of the House of lords on the availability of injunctive relief, see p.281.

(2)   Obedience to the law is an aspect of the rule of law and in the Court of Appeal Lord Donaldson MR observed that:

. . . I agree with the judge that this is a matter of high constitutional importance. Indeed I would say of the very highest. I agree with him that the day to day relationship between the judiciary and all governments and ministers in modern times has been based upon trust. In a sense the same is true of its relationship with all who resort to the courts for justice in civil disputes. The system would be put under intolerable strain and would be likely to break down if a significant number of citizens treated the courts' orders as mere requests which could be complied with or ignored as they thought appropriate. I share his confidence that in the foreseeable future governments and ministers will recognise their obligations to their opponents, to the courts and to justice. Where I have somewhat less confidence is in the suggestion that were it ever otherwise there would be a heavy political price to pay. There might well be, but I am not sure that there would be if, in particular circumstances, popular opinion was firmly on the side of the government and against the person who had obtained the order. Yet it is precisely in those circumstances that individual citizens should be able to look to the judiciary for protection under the law. I therefore do indeed think that it would be a black day for the rule of law and for the liberty of the subject if Simon Brown J has correctly interpreted the law. I have reached the firm conclusion that he was mistaken.

(3)   At first instance the court alluded to the historical foundation of the state:

The Crown's first main argument . . . is that the very source of the contempt jurisdiction . . . is itself the Crown and the Crown cannot be in contempt of itself . . . The Crown's submissions overlook, the applicant submits, the constitutional realities of today: Parliament, the executive and the judiciary, albeit by constitutional fiction three manifestations of the Crown, have long been recognised as three distinct elements of a single state, each exercising their separate powers, their relationship to each other controlled by convention and the rule of law. I believe this response to be sound: the mere fact that the contempt jurisdiction emanates from the Crown cannot of itself decide the issue whether a separate institution of state is amenable to that jurisdiction.

In the Court of Appeal Lord Donaldson MR placed great emphasis on the separation of powers:

> Our unwritten constitution rests upon a separation of powers. It also rests upon a mutual recognition of those powers. It is for Parliament to make new laws and to amend old laws, including the common law. It is for the courts to interpret and enforce the law. It is for the government to govern within the law. Each in its own sphere is supreme. Ultimate supremacy lies with Parliament, but only to the extent that it can control the government by its votes and that it can control the courts by using the full legislative procedure for changing the law, either generally or with a view to reversing a particular decision by the courts.

(4)   There is risk of confusion over the legal personality of 'the Crown'. Although the Monarch personally can do no wrong, the organs of executive government derived from the Crown personally are not in such a happy position, as *M* v *Home Office* shows. Lord Donaldson's observation that the Crown had no legal personality was rejected by the House of Lords where Lord Woolf relied on *Town Investments Ltd* v *Department of the Environment*.

In that case a lease of premises was granted to a minister 'for and on behalf of Her Majesty'. It was held by the House of Lords that the Crown was the tenant, accordingly the premises were occupied for the business purposes of the Crown and were protected by a rent freeze imposed under counter-inflation legislation. Lord Diplock said:

> . . . it is not private law but public law that governs the relationship between Her Majesty acting in her political capacity, the government departments among which the work of Her Majesty's government is distributed, the Ministers of the Crown in charge of the various departments and civil servants of all grades who are employed in those departments. These relationships have in the course of centuries been transformed with the continuous evolution of the constitution of this country from that of personal rule by a feudal landowning monarchy to the constitutional monarchy of today; but the vocabulary used by lawyers in the field of public law has not kept pace with this evolution and remains more apt to the constitutional realities of the Tudor or even the Norman monarchy than to the constitutional realities of the 20th century. To use as a metaphor the symbol of royalty, 'the Crown', was no doubt a convenient way of denoting and distinguishing the monarch when doing acts of government in his political capacity from the monarch when doing private acts in his personal capacity, at a period when legislative and executive powers were exercised by him in accordance with his own will. But to continue nowadays to speak of 'the Crown' as doing legislative or executive acts of government, which, in reality as distinct from legal fiction, are decided on and done by human beings other than the

Queen herself, involves risk of confusion. We very sensibly speak today of legislation being made by Act of Parliament – though the preamble to every statute still maintains the fiction that the maker was Her Majesty and that the participation of the members of the two Houses of Parliament had been restricted to advice and acquiescence. Where ... we are concerned with the legal nature of the exercise of the executive powers of government, I believe that some of the more Athanasian like features of the debate ... could have been eliminated if instead of speaking of the Crown we were to speak of the government – a term appropriate to embrace both collectively and individually all of the ministers of the Crown and parliamentary secretaries under whose direction the administrative work of government is carried on by the civil servants ... It is through them that the executive powers of Her Majesty's government in the United Kingdom are exercised, sometimes in the more important administrative matters in Her Majesty's name, but most often under their own official designation. Executive acts of government that are done by any of them are acts done by 'the Crown' in the fictional sense in which that expression is now used in English public law ... In my opinion, the tenant was the government acting through its appropriate member or, expressed in the term of art in public law, the tenant was the Crown.

(5)   In *Lord Advocate* v *Dumbarton DC*, the House of Lords had to decide whether or not the Crown was bound by statutory provisions relating to planning law and after a detailed analysis of the relevant legislation held that the Crown was not bound either expressly or by necessary implication. Lord Keith approved the view of the law as laid down by Diplock LJ in *BBC* v *Johns (Inspector of Taxes)*:

... The question is ... one of construction of a statute. Since laws are made by rulers for subjects, a general expression in a law such as 'any person' descriptive of those on whom the law imposes obligations or restraints is not to be read as including the ruler himself. Under our more sophisticated constitution the concept of sovereignty has in the course of history come to be treated as comprising three distinct functions of a ruler: executive, legislative and judicial, though the distinction between these functions in the case, for instance, of prerogative powers and administrative tribunals is sometimes blurred. The modern rule of construction of statutes is that the Crown, which today personifies the executive government of the country and is also a party to all the legislation, is not bound by a statute which imposes obligations or restraints on persons or in respect of property, unless the statute says so expressly or by necessary implication.

(6)   Written constitutions often provide for a strict separation of powers which the courts will be vigilant to maintain. Even if a constitution is silent upon this point the courts will address the issue. Thus, in *Liyanage* v *The Queen*, the Privy Council held that the constitution of Ceylon (derived from an Act of the United Kingdom Parliament), although silent upon the division of powers as between the executive and the judiciary, must have been intended to preserve the position prior to the

constitutional document when a strict separation of powers existed. The executive had procured the passage of retrospective legislation aimed at named individuals altering the admissibility of otherwise inadmissible confession evidence, changing the fundamental law of evidence, legalising imprisonment post arrest, and depriving the judges of any discretion in sentence. The Privy Council held that this legislation, intended as it was to obtain the judicial conviction and extended sentence of those named, was invalid as an erosion of the judicial function.

(7)   The impact of the separation of powers can also be seen in the principles underpinning judicial review (p.209); parliamentary privilege (*Pickin* v *BRB*, p.177, and *Rost* v *Edwards*, p.168); European Community and local government finance (*R* v *HM Treasury, ex parte Smedley*, p.27, *Nottinghamshire CC* v *Secretary of State for the Environment*, p.212, and *Hammersmith & Fulham London BC* v *Secretary of State for the Environment*, p.214).

Duport Steels Ltd v Sirs

[1980] 1 WLR 142 · House of Lords

The House of Lords had to consider the meaning of acts done 'in . . . furtherance of a trade dispute' in s.13(1), Trade Union and Labour Relations Act 1974, in respect of strike action aimed at third parties, a highly contentious and politically charged issue in the light of the immunity which would be accorded such acts.

Lord Diplock: ' . . . at a time when more and more cases involve the application of legislation which gives effect to policies that are the subject of bitter public and parliamentary controversy, it cannot be too strongly emphasised that the British constitution, though largely unwritten, is firmly based upon the separation of powers; Parliament makes the laws, the judiciary interpret them. When Parliament legislates to remedy what the majority of its members at the time perceive to be a defect or a lacuna in the existing law . . . the role of the judiciary is confined to ascertaining from the words that Parliament has approved as expressing its intention what that intention was, and to giving effect to it. Where the meaning of the statutory words is plain and unambiguous it is not for the judges to invent fancied ambiguities as an excuse for failing to give effect to its plain meaning because they themselves consider that the consequences of doing so would be inexpedient, or even unjust or immoral. In controversial matters such as are involved in industrial relations there is room for differences of opinion as to what is expedient, what is just and what is morally justifiable. Under our constitution it is Parliament's opinion on these matters that is paramount . . .

It endangers continued public confidence in the political impartiality of the judiciary, which is essential to the continuance of the rule of law, if judges, under the guise of interpretation, provide their own preferred amendments to statutes which experience of their operation has shown to have had consequences that members of the court before whom the matter comes consider to be injurious to the public interest . . . [F]or a judge . . . to pose himself the question: "Can Parliament really have intended that the acts that were done in this particular case should have the benefit of the immunity?" is to risk straying beyond his constitutional role as interpreter of the enacted law and assuming a power to decide at his own discretion whether or not to apply the general law to a particular case. The legitimate questions for a judge in his role as interpreter of the enacted law are: "How has Parliament, by the words that it has used in the statute to express its intentions, defined the category of Acts that are entitled to the immunity? Do the acts done in this particular case fall within that description?" '

Comment

Compare the cases on judicial review of administrative action (pp.288–320) and the approach to the control of such action. Note also that there may be occasions where the courts will regard words within an Act as 'mere surplusage' (see *R* v *R*, and *McMonagle* v *Westminster City Council*).

R v *Registrar General, ex parte Smith*

[1991] 2 QB 393 · Court of Appeal

The applicant for judicial review, who had been adopted, sought the identity of his natural parents. Section 51, Adoption Act 1976, granted an apparently unfettered right to this information. The applicant, who was detained in a secure mental hospital, had twice been convicted of murder, had demonstrated an extreme hatred for his adoptive parents, and one of his victims had been killed in a bout of psychotic illness in the belief that the victim was the adoptive mother. In the light of the medical and social reports, the Registrar General refused to give the information on the grounds of public policy. The applicant's appeal was dismissed.

Staughton LJ: ' . . . It is well established in private law that the courts will not enforce a contract if to do so would enable the plaintiff to benefit from his own crime . . . This rule is not based on any process of interpreting the contract. Be it ever so plain, the courts will refuse to enforce it. However, there may well be . . . an exception . . . Some criminal conduct may not be of a particular serious nature so that it would not be an affront to the public conscience if a plaintiff were to recover a benefit from it by enforcing his contract, but rather an injustice if enforcement were refused.

It is apparent that a similar doctrine has evolved in the enforcement of Acts of Parliament, even when they are apparently absolute in their terms. In *R* v *National Insurance Comr, ex p. Connor*, Mrs Connor was unable to recover the widow's allowance under the Social Security Act 1975 because she had unlawfully killed her husband. In *R* v *Secretary of State for the Home Dept, ex p. Puttick*, Mrs Puttick was denied the benefit of registration as a citizen of the United Kingdom and Colonies under the British Nationality Act 1948, although she was lawfully married to a citizen, because she had committed perjury and forgery in the course of procuring the marriage. Again, the rule is not absolute. Lord Lane CJ said in *Connor*'s case that it is . . .

> not the label which the law applies to the crime which has been committed but the nature of the crime itself which in the end will dictate whether public policy demands the court to drive the applicant from the seat of justice.

Donaldson LJ in *Puttick* 's case referred to *Connor* 's case as authority . . .

> for the proposition that statutory duties which are in terms absolute may nevertheless be subject to implied limitations based on principles of public policy accepted by the courts at the time when the Act is passed.

In the case of statutory duties the rule is, in my opinion, based upon interpretation of the meaning intended by Parliament. It is not a rule imposed *ab extra* as in the case of contracts . . . To hold otherwise would come perilously close to infringing constitutional doctrine of major importance. Our courts have no power to dispense with the laws enacted by Parliament or (as it is now called) to disapply them, subject to the law of the European Community. So the rule is that we must interpret Acts of Parliament as not requiring performance of duties, even when they are in terms absolute, if to do so would enable someone to benefit from his own serious crime.

So much for benefits from past crime. But this case is concerned with an apprehension or risk of crime in the future. No authority has been cited dealing with that situation . . .

A principle that statutory duties, although apparently absolute, will not be enforced if performance of them would enable a person to commit serious crime or to cause serious harm is fraught with difficulty. Other examples were given in the course of the argument. I do not repeat them now for fear of giving unwarranted encouragement to others not to perform their statutory duties. But there is one which can perhaps safely be mentioned: the Second Amendment to the Constitution of the United States provides:

> . . . the right of the people to keep and bear arms, shall not be infringed.

If such a doctrine of interpretation in the name of public policy has been transported with the rest of the common law across the Atlantic, would it impinge upon the Second Amendment?

There is, moreover, a practical distinction between declining to enforce a statute when to do so would enable the person to benefit from serious crime in the past (as in *Connor* 's case and *Puttick* 's case) and declining to enforce a statute because it is apprehended that to do so would facilitate serious crime in the future. In the former case, one can tell with reasonable certainty what the consequence of enforcement would be; in the latter, it may be a matter of speculation.

Nevertheless, I am persuaded that some such principle exists . . . If it be the law that Parliament, even when enacting statutory duties in apparently absolute terms, is presumed not to have intended that they should apply so as to reward serious crime in the past, it seems to me that Parliament must likewise be presumed not to have intended to promote serious crime in the future. That is consistent with the growing tendency, perhaps encouraged by Europe, towards a purposive construction of statutes, at all events if they do not deal with penal or revenue matters.

The principle should not, in my judgment, be limited to statutes passed after it has been authoritatively declared by the courts. It is and always has been public policy to prevent crime. I can see no reason why Parliament should only be presumed to have intended that after, and not before, the presumption has been recognised by the courts.

Nor would I limit the principle . . . to cases where performance of the statutory duty is required for the purpose of a serious crime which the applicant intends to commit. It must be a matter of degree. The likelihood of future crime and the seriousness of the consequences if crime is committed must both be taken into account. For present purposes, it is sufficient to hold that a statutory duty is not to be enforced if there is a significant risk that to do so would facilitate crime resulting in danger to life. Parliament is presumed not to have intended that, unless it has said so in plain terms. That is as far as I would go in this case. Even so, I fear that other cases may require further elucidation.

. . . [T]his is not the exercise of the discretion either by officials with statutory duties to perform or by the court. It is in no way connected with the discretion of the court to refuse relief in judicial review cases. It is a rule of law to be applied in the interpretation of Acts of Parliament, on the facts of each case. No doubt individuals with duties to perform will, when the topic arises, have to make their own assessment of the facts. But if their decision is challenged in court, the assessment of an individual will not be determinative, and it will be for a Court to find the facts.

In this case I am satisfied on the evidence that there is a significant risk that to enforce the duty of the Registrar General under s.51 of the Adoption Act 1976 would facilitate crime resulting in danger to life. . . .

Accordingly, I would hold that the Registrar General has not acted unlawfully; nor, for the reasons just given, has she acted irrationally or unfairly . . .'

Comment

(1)   The cautious approach of the court was necessary to avoid contravening the separation of powers and the legislative supremacy of Parliament, but the case is on the margins of legitimate judicial activism. *R* v *Registrar General, ex parte Smith* was distinguished in *Re X (a minor)(adoption details: disclosure)*.

(2)   The judicial law making role concerns both the interpretive function of the courts (as in *Duport Steels Ltd* v *Sirs, R* v *Registrar General, ex parte Smith*) and the development of the common law. In this latter context the scope of judicial discretion in this context can be seen from *Malone* v *MPC (No.2)* (p.141) where the court decided against developing common law rules to provide better protection for individual privacy.

Independence of judge and jury

Given the absence of a strict separation of powers, and the well-known overlaps between executive and judicial functions, what is important is that the process of judicial scrutiny should be beyond executive interference. Judicial independence, freedom from dismissal (other than in clearly defined situations), and the ability to give rulings free from individual liability are all prerequisites for effective check upon the executive by the judiciary. Only with this protection can judges be demonstrably free to give judgments 'without fear or favour'. This is equally true, though harder to achieve, in respect of the large number of tribunals and inquiries which provide administrative justice, and which, in the context of state and individual, play crucial roles.

Supreme Court of Judicature (Consolidation) Act 1925

12 (1) All the judges of the High Court and of the Court of Appeal, with the exception of the Lord Chancellor, shall hold their offices during good behaviour subject to a power of removal by His Majesty on an address presented to His Majesty by both Houses of Parliament.

Courts Act 1971

16 (1) Her Majesty may from time to time appoint as Circuit judges, to serve in the Crown Court and county courts and to carry out such other judicial functions as may be conferred on them under this or any other enactment, such qualified persons as may be recommended to Her by the Lord Chancellor . . .

17 (1) Subject to subsections (2) to (4) below, a Circuit judge shall vacate his office at the end of the completed year of service in which he attains the age of seventy-two.
   (2) Where the Lord Chancellor considers it desirable in the public interest to retain a Circuit judge in office after the time at which he would otherwise retire in accordance with subsection (1) above, he may from time to time authorise the continuance in office of that judge until such date, not being later than the date on which the judge attains the age of seventy-five, as he thinks fit . . .
   (4) The Lord Chancellor may, if he thinks fit, remove a Circuit judge from office on the ground of incapacity or misbehaviour . . .

Comment

(1)   Section 12 is the successor to the Act of Settlement 1700. Some doubt exists as to its precise meaning. It has been assumed during various Parliamentary proceedings that removal by an Address is the only means of removal.

(2)   No English High Court judge has been removed under these provisions. Circuit judges have been removed – see, for example, the removal of a circuit judge in 1983 for customs offences ([1984] PL 135).

(3)   Magistrates may be removed from office by the Lord Chancellor – see s.1, Administration of Justice Act 1973.

(4)   An independent judicial process also requires freedom from legal action in respect of judicial functions. Superior court judges have absolute protection. For the more limited position of magistrates, see *Sirros* v *Moore*; *Re McC*.

The jury

Jury trial is regarded by many as a key safeguard for the individual against the abuse of the criminal process by the state. In 1956 Lord Devlin described it as 'the lamp that shows that freedom lives'. The extent to which that is, or was true, is a matter of debate. The fundamental precept is that the jury should be selected at random, not that it should be representative. The prosecution has the power to request a juror to 'stand by for the Crown', no reasons need be given; the juror is then not sworn but returns to the panel of potential jurors from which the jury is to be selected. The exercise of the right to stand by is now governed by a Practice Note containing the Attorney-General's guidelines [1988] 3 All ER 1086. Except for the case of information received from jury checks (see below), the power should be exercised only where the juror is manifestly unsuitable and the defence agrees. The extent of the right of the defence to challenge without cause – 'peremptory challenge' – was gradually reduced, and finally removed by the Criminal Justice Act 1988. The rights of both Crown and defence to challenge for cause, e.g. bias, remain, as does the power of the judge to intervene in a proper case, e.g. if it appears that a juror is physically unsuited.

Attorney-General's Guidelines on Jury Checks

Practice Note · [1988] 3 All ER 1086

1. The principles which are generally to be observed are (a) that members of a jury should be selected at random from the panel, (b) the Juries Act 1974 together with the Juries (Disqualification) Act 1984 identified those classes of persons who alone are either disqualified from or ineligible for service on a jury; no other class of person may be treated as disqualified or ineligible, and (c) the correct way for the Crown to seek to exclude a member of the panel from sitting as a juror is by the exercise in open court of the right to request a stand by or, if necessary, to challenge for cause.
2. . . . any search of criminal records for the purpose of ascertaining whether or not a jury panel includes any disqualified person is a matter for the police . . .
3. There are . . . certain exceptional types of case of public importance for which the provisions as to majority verdicts and the disqualification of jurors may not be sufficient to ensure the proper administration of justice. In such cases it is in the interests of both justice and the public that there should be further safeguards against the possibility of bias and in such cases checks which go beyond the investigation of criminal records may be necessary.
4. These classes of case may be defined broadly as (a) cases in which national security is involved and part of the evidence is likely to be heard in camera, and (b) terrorist cases.
5. The particular aspects of these cases which may make it desirable to seek extra precautions are (a) in security cases a danger that a juror, either voluntarily or under pressure, may make an improper use of evidence which, because of its sensitivity, has been given in camera, (b) in both security and terrorist cases that a juror's political beliefs are so biased as to go beyond normally reflecting the broad views and interests in the community to reflect the extreme views of

certain interest or pressure groups to a degree which might interfere with his fair assessment of the facts of the case or lead him to exert improper pressure on his fellow jurors.

6.   . . . [in these instances] it may be necessary to conduct a limited investigation of the panel. In general, such further investigation beyond one of the criminal records made for disqualifications may only be made with the records of police Special Branches. However, in . . . security cases, the investigation may, additionally, involve the security services. No checks other than on these sources and no general enquiries are to be made save to the limited extent that they may be needed to confirm the identity of a juror about whom the initial check has raised serious doubts . . .

Comment

(1)   Checks of the sort mentioned in paragraphs 5 and 6 must be authorized personally by the Attorney-General on application by the Director of Public Prosecutions. The right to stand by on the basis of the check may be exercised only with the authority of the Attorney-General and where there is a 'strong reason for believing that a particular juror might be a security risk, be susceptible to improper advances or be influenced in arriving at a verdict for the reasons given [in paragraph 6]'. Where a check suggests bias against the accused then the defence should be told.

(2)   The Practice Note annexed the recommendations of the Association of Chief Police Officers relating to jury checks. These provide guidelines for the carrying out of checks under paragraph 2 above. In particular they state that the police should undertake a check when the Director of Public Prosecutions or a chief constable considers that it would be in the interests of justice 'namely (i) in any case in which there is reason to believe that attempts are being made to circumvent the statutory provisions . . . (ii) in any case in which it is believed that in a previous related abortive trial an attempt was made to interfere with a juror or jurors, and (iii) in any other case in which in the opinion of the Director of Public Prosecutions or the chief constable it is particularly important to ensure that no disqualified person serves on the jury.'

(3)   There is conflicting judicial opinion on jury checks – see *R* v *Mason* and *R* v *Sheffield Crown Court, ex parte Brownlow*. In the latter, Lord Denning regarded them as generally unconstitutional.

(4)   In *R* v *Ford* in a Crown Court trial, the appellant, who was black, intended during cross-examination of a police officer to impute racial motives, in order for the officer's conduct to be explained. On arraignment, the appellant's application to have a multi-racial jury empanelled was rejected by the judge; his appeal to the Court of Appeal against conviction, based in part on this refusal, was dismissed. Lord Lane CJ emphasized the random nature of jury selection and that the court had no power to interfere with the selection of a jury except in the rarest of cases and for cause, e.g. relating to the physical or mental fitness of the proposed juror. Lord

Lane also distinguished a challenge to the way in which the panel had been selected. That was a matter for the Lord Chancellor and the judge was restricted to considering on a challenge for cause whether the summoning officer had displayed bias or other impropriety.

(5)   In a Practice Note [1988] 3 All ER 177 Lord Lane CJ stated that, 'Jury service is an important public duty which individual members of the public are chosen at random to undertake.' Lord Lane recognized that there may be occasions when circumstances will exclude a person, e.g. 'personal hardship or conscientious objection to jury service'. In *R* v *Crown Court at Guildford, ex parte Siderfin* there was a successful challenge to a refusal by a Crown Court judge to excuse from jury service the applicant, a member of the Plymouth Brethren sect the beliefs of which did not permit jury service. The successful ground of challenge was the failure of the judge to direct his mind to the question of legal representation of the juror seeking excusal, but the court indicated, *obiter*, that although religious beliefs were not *per se* a 'good reason' for excusal, they may in some circumstances prevent the juror from performing his or her duty, and there should be no blanket ground of refusal of applications based on religious beliefs. Each case should be considered on its merits. Section 42 of the Criminal Justice and Public Order Act 1994 grants the right of excusal from jury service, within Schedule 1, Juries Act 1974, to 'A practising member of a religious society or other order the tenets or beliefs of which are incompatible with jury service.'

R v *McKenna*

[1960] 1 QB 411 · Court of Criminal Appeal

A trial judge in a criminal case, who had earlier during the trial indicated particular commitments to which he was subject, told the jury that unless they reached a verdict within ten minutes, they would be kept overnight and the trial resumed the following day. The jury, who until then had been deliberating in excess of two hours, reached a guilty verdict within six minutes. On appeal, the conviction was quashed, because of the improper pressure imposed on the jury.

Cassels J: '. . . It is a cardinal principle of our criminal law that in considering their verdict, concerning, as it does, the liberty of the subject, a jury shall deliberate in complete freedom, uninfluenced by any promise, unintimidated by any threat. They still stand between the Crown and the subject, and they are still one of the main defences of personal liberty. To say to such a tribunal in the course of its deliberations that it must reach a conclusion within ten minutes or else undergo hours of personal inconvenience and discomfort, is a disservice to the cause of justice. In this case the ultimatum no doubt fell with added force upon the jury since two of them were women. It may well be that having regard to the steps he had taken from the outset to ensure that the case should finish by mid-day on the third day, steps which included working beyond the normal hours on the Monday and the Tuesday, the judge was understandably irritated by the inconvenient slowness of the jury in reaching a verdict in what he thought was a plain straightforward case. But juries do at times take much longer than a judge may think necessary to arrive at a verdict; there are, after all, twelve of them who have to be unanimous, and the proper exercise of the judicial office requires that irritation on these occasions must be suppressed or, at any rate, kept severely in check. To experience it is understandable; to express it in the form of such a threat to the jury as was uttered here is insupportable . . .'

Comment

(1)   In *R* v *Rose* a conviction was quashed when a judge indicated that the jury would be discharged if they failed to reach a verdict within a specified time.

(2)   Cassel J refers to the need for unanimity. See now s.17, Juries Act 1974, which permits, in certain circumstances, a majority verdict. For the detailed operation of this provision, and its predecessor, see Practice Direction [1967] 1 WLR 1198, and Practice Direction [1970] 1 WLR 916.

(3)   For the protection given to jurors, see *Bushell's Case* (1670) where in a trial of several Quakers on charges of unlawful assembly, jurors refused to convict. The trial judge declined to accept the verdicts, and ordered the jurors to resume deliberation without food or drink. When they persisted in their refusal they were fined and imprisoned until payment. It was held, by Court of Common Pleas, that the judge had no power to punish the jury for their verdict.

(4)   For modern examples illustrating the independent functioning of a jury, see *R* v *Gent* (applying *DPP* v *Stonehouse*): an accused is entitled to the verdict of the jury, even though only one verdict is possible, and that an acquittal would, in the view of the judge, be perverse. See also *R* v *Ponting*, where a jury acquitted the defendant of charges under s.2, Official Secrets Act 1911, despite the fact that the only live issue was whether disclosure was in the 'interests of state', the judge directing the jury that that was a matter for the government.

(5)   In Northern Ireland, since 1973, trial of 'scheduled offences' has been by judge alone (The Diplock Court) following the recommendations of Lord Diplock in 1972, Cmnd 5185. See now, s.7, Northern Ireland (Emergency Provisions) Act 1978. Section 30 and Sch.4 of that Act define 'scheduled offences' in some detail: they include murder, most serious offences of violence, and offences related to the causing of explosions, even if not connected with terrorism.

(6)   The Report of the Fraud Trials Committee (1986) (the Roskill Report) recommended the abolition of jury trial in serious fraud cases, and its replacement by a fraud trials tribunal comprising a judge and two lay assessors, on the grounds that the complex nature of fraud trials necessitated a different form of tribunal.

(7)   Research into the effectiveness of jury trial has been handicapped by the lack of evidence other than anecdotal, or that of 'shadow' juries. Baldwin and McConville (*Jury Trials*, 1979) considered that trial by jury is an 'arbitrary and unpredictable business'. Note s.8, Contempt of Court Act 1981 (reversing *Attorney-General* v *New Statesman*): '. . . It is a contempt of court to obtain, disclose or solicit any particulars of statements made, opinions expressed, arguments advanced or votes cast by members of a jury in the course of their deliberations in any legal proceedings . . .'

In *Attorney-General* v *Associated Newspapers Ltd*, independent researchers had carried out interviews with jurors involved in a well-publicised fraud trial and the defendant newspaper had obtained and published extracts. The House of Lords held that there had been a contempt of court under s.8, Contempt of Court Act.

Open justice

This is a key concept, because only through the openness of proceedings and the freedom to report what is done in the courts can there be effective scrutiny and accountability of the judicial process. The main principle is stated in *Scott* v *Scott*:

> While the broad principle is that the courts . . . must . . . administer justice in public, this principle is subject to apparent exception . . . But the exceptions are themselves the outcome of a yet more fundamental principle that the chief object of the Courts of Justice must be to secure that justice is done . . . [I]t may well be that justice could not be done at all if it had to be done in public. As the paramount object must always be to do justice, the general rule as to publicity, after all only the means to an end, must accordingly, yield.

Despite statutory intervention in 1981, the common law is still important, particularly since s.11, Contempt of Court Act 1981 does not confer power to prohibit reporting where no power existed at common law. Judicial restrictions upon open justice are permitted only where, and to the extent, necessary for the purposes of the due administration of justice. In these instances the court can take such action as is required – see, for example, the use of screens in child abuse cases to shield the child witness: *R* v *X, Y & Z*.

Attorney-General v *Socialist Worker*

[1975] QB 637 · Divisional Court

At the trial of J on charges of blackmail, the trial judge directed that the two victims of the alleged blackmail should be referred to in court as X and Y, and be allowed to write down their names. The defendant newspaper and its editor published the names of X and Y, and were held in these proceedings to be in contempt of court on the basis: (a) that the conduct was a blatant affront to the authority of the court, and (b) such conduct would deter blackmail victims from coming forward in the future.

Lord Widgery LCJ: '. . . It has for long been recognised that if an action is brought in regard to a secret process and the publicity of the hearing will prevent the process from being secret any longer and thus destroy it, that is a legitimate ground for a hearing in camera. In a sense, as the Attorney-General submitted . . . what is going on here is the same kind of thing. The complainant in the blackmail charge has a secret which he shares with Miss Janie Jones, a secret which he has been paying money to keep a secret. If by coming to court in order to see that she is charged with her offence he must give up his secret, there is, one would think, a parallel of some consequence between the different proceedings.

The matter is conveniently summed up in *Scott* v *Scott* . . . "An aggrieved person, entitled to protection against one man who had stolen his secret, would not ask for it on the terms that the secret was to be communicated to all the world. There would be in effect a denial of justice."

A man who had a secret with a defendant and no other would not seek proceedings on the terms that the secret was to be communicated to the world . . . The great virtue of having the public in our courts is that discipline which the presence of the public imposes on the court itself. When the court is full of interested members of the public . . . it is bound to have the effect that everybody is more careful about what they do, everybody tries just that little bit harder and there is a disciplinary effect on the court which would be totally lacking if there were no critical members of the public or press present . . .

When one has an order for trial in camera, all the public and all the press are evicted at one fell swoop, and the entire supervision by the public is gone. Where one has a hearing which is open, but where the names of the witnesses are withheld, virtually all the desirable features of having the public present are to be seen. The only thing which is kept from their knowledge is the name of the witness . . .'

Attorney-General v *Leveller Magazine*

[1979] AC 440 · House of Lords

In committal proceedings for offences under the Official Secrets Acts magistrates had allowed one witness to be referred to as 'Colonel B', and for his name to be written down and shown only to the court, defendants and counsel. During testimony he gave details which enabled his identity to be ascertained easily. The appellants identified Colonel B in various publications, and proceedings for contempt were commenced by the Attorney-General.

It was held, by the House of Lords, allowing appeals against conviction for contempt, that whilst there was some doubt as to whether the magistrates had the power to make directions that bind those outside the court, publications which frustrated the purpose of the pseudonym might amount to contempt at common law. In this case, though, there was no interference with the administration of justice, since Colonel B's evidence had made his name easily ascertainable.

Lord Diplock: '. . . Although criminal contempts of court may take a variety of forms they all share a common characteristic: they involve an interference with the due administration of justice either in a particular case or more generally as a continuing process. It is justice itself that is flouted by contempt of court, not the individual court or judge who is attempting to administer it.

Of those contempts that can be committed outside the courtroom the most familiar consist of publishing, in connection with legal proceedings that are pending or imminent, comment or information that has a tendency to pervert the course of justice, either in those proceedings or by deterring other people from having recourse to courts of justice in the future for the vindication of their lawful rights or for the enforcement of the criminal law. In determining whether what is published has such a tendency a distinction must be drawn between reporting what actually occurred at the hearing of the proceedings and publishing other kinds of comment or information; for prima facie the interests of justice are served by its being administered in the full light of publicity.

As a general rule the English system of administering justice does require that it be done in public: *Scott* v *Scott.* If the way that courts behave cannot be hidden from the public ear and eye this provides a safeguard against judicial arbitrariness or idiosyncrasy and maintains the public confidence in the administration of justice. The application of this principle of open justice has two aspects: as respects proceedings in the court itself it requires that they should be held in open court to which the press and public are admitted and that, in criminal cases at any rate, all evidence communicated to the court is communicated publicly. As respects the publication to a wider public of fair and accurate reports of proceedings that have taken place in court the principle requires that nothing should be done to discourage this.

However, since the purpose of the general rule is to serve the ends of justice it may be necessary to depart from it where the nature or circumstances of the particular proceeding are such that the application of the general rule in its entirety would frustrate or render impracticable the administration of justice or would damage some other public interest for whose protection Parliament has made some statutory derogation from the rule. Apart from statutory exceptions, however, where a court in the exercise of its inherent power to control the conduct of proceedings before it departs in any way from the general rule, the departure is justified to the extent and to no more than the extent that the court reasonably believes it to be necessary in order to serve the ends of justice. A familiar instance of this is provided by the "trial within a trial" as to the admissibility of a confession in a criminal prosecution. The due administration of justice requires that the jury should be unaware of what was the evidence adduced at the "trial within a trial" until after they have reached their verdict; but no greater derogation from the general rule as to the public nature of all proceedings at a criminal trial is justified than is necessary to ensure this. So far as proceedings in the courtroom are concerned the trial within a trial is held in open court in the presence of the press and public but in the absence of the jury. So far as publishing those proceedings outside the court is concerned any report of them which might come to the knowledge of the jury must be withheld until after they have reached their verdict; but it may be published after that. Only premature publication would constitute contempt of court . . .

[Having identified statutory power to sit in private, Lord Diplock continued:] In substitution for hearing "Colonel B's" evidence in camera which it could have asked for the prosecution was content to treat a much less drastic derogation from the principle of open justice as adequate to protect the interests of national security. The witness's evidence was to be given in open court in the normal way except that he was to be referred to by the pseudonym of "Colonel B" and evidence as to his real name and address was to be written down and disclosed only to the court, the defendants and their legal representatives.

I do not doubt that, applying their minds to the matter that it was their duty to con-sider the interests of the due administration of justice, the magistrates had power to accede to this proposal for the very reason that it would involve less derogation from the general principle of open justice than would result from the Crown being driven to have recourse to the statutory procedure for hearing evidence in camera under s.8 (4) of the Official Secrets Act 1920; but in adopting this particular device which on the face of it related only to how proceedings within the courtroom were to be conducted it behoved the magistrates to make it clear what restrictions, if any, were intended by them to be imposed upon publishing outside the courtroom information relating to those proceedings and whether such restrictions were to be precatory only or enforceable by the sanction of proceedings for contempt of court . . .

[In argument] little attempt was made to analyse the juristic basis on which a court can make a "ruling," "order" or "direction" . . . relating to proceedings taking place before it which has the effect in law of restricting what may be done outside the courtroom by members of the public who are not engaged in those proceedings as parties or their legal representatives or as witnesses . . . It may be that a "ruling" by the court as to the conduct of proceedings can have binding effect as such within the courtroom only, so that breach of it is not *ipso facto* a contempt of court unless it is committed there. Nevertheless where (1) the reason for a ruling which involves departing in some measure from the general principle of open justice within the courtroom is that the departure is necessary in the interests of the due administration of justice and (2) it would be apparent to anyone who was aware of the ruling that the result which the ruling is designed to achieve would be frustrated by a particular kind of act done outside the courtroom, the doing of such an act with knowledge of the ruling and of its purpose may constitute a contempt of court, not because it is a breach of the ruling but because it interferes with the due administration of justice.

So it does not seem to me to matter greatly in the instant case whether or not the magistrates were rightly advised that they had in law no power to give directions which would be binding as such upon members of the public as to what information relating to the proceedings taking place before them might be published outside the courtroom. What was incumbent upon them was to make it clear to anyone present at, or reading an accurate report of, the proceedings what in the interests of the due administration of justice was the result that was intended by them to be achieved by the limited derogation from the principle of open justice within the courtroom which they had authorised, and what kind of information derived from what happened in the courtroom would if it were published frustrate that result.

There may be many cases in which the result intended to be achieved by a ruling by the court as to what is to be done in court is so obvious as to speak for itself; it calls for no explicit statement. Sending the jury out of court during a trial within a trial is an example of this; so may be the common ruling in prosecutions for blackmail that a victim called as a witness be referred to in court by a pseudonym . . . but, in the absence of any explicit statement by [these] magistrates at the conclusion of the colonel's evidence that the purpose of their ruling would be frustrated if anything were published outside the courtroom that would be likely to lead to the identification of "Colonel B" as the person who had given evidence in the case, I do not think that the instant case falls into this class . . .'

Contempt of Court Act 1981

4. (1) Subject to this section a person is not guilty of contempt of court under the strict liability rule in respect of a fair and accurate report of legal proceedings held in public, published contemporaneously and in good faith.

(2) In any such proceedings the court may, where it appears to be necessary

for avoiding a substantial risk of prejudice to the administration of justice in those proceedings, or in any other proceedings pending or imminent, order that the publication of any report of the proceedings, or any part of the proceedings, be postponed for such period as the court thinks necessary for that purpose . . .

11. In any case where a court (having power to do so) allows a name or other matter to be withheld from the public in proceedings before the court, the court may give such directions prohibiting the publication of that name or matter in connection with the proceedings as appear to the court to be necessary for the purpose for which it was so withheld.

R v *Evesham JJ, ex parte McDonagh*

[1988] QB 540 · Divisional Court

D, a former MP, had been charged with a motoring offence. D had indicated to the court that his former wife had been guilty of violent attacks on his motor vehicle and his home, and that he had obtained an injunction to prevent further harassment. Rather than reveal his current home address in open court he had offered as his address the registered address of his company. Instead magistrates accepted his home address written down but not revealed to the press or public. The magistrates wanted to ensure that the press did not have opportunity to publish the address if revealed on later perusal of the court file, and they made an order under s.11, Contempt of Court Act 1981 prohibiting publication of his address. A journalist successfully applied for judicial review of the decision.

Watkins LJ: '. . . There are undoubtedly cases in which it is necessary for the identity of a witness or even a defendant to be protected from publicity. But they are rare and the circumstances of them bear no comparison with those which obtained in the present case. It is also beyond doubt that justices may do what seems to them to be right properly to control procedures in their courts. They may receive information in the form of a document the nature of which they may not be obliged to reveal. This is clear from what Lord Parker CJ said in *R* v *Beckett*:

Only a few days ago another court of this Division was criticised for giving judgement reducing a sentence without making public written statements concerning a prisoner . . . We should like to make it perfectly clear that, in sentence appeals – and we are only talking about sentence appeals – hardly a day goes by on which the court is not asked to look at some document which it would be wholly contrary to the interest of the appellant or, indeed, of the public, to quote in open court. There may be cases where reports are received on some purely personal matter affecting an appellant, some health disability or other matter, publication of which would, we think, result in proper criticism of the court. Another class of cases arises where information is received concerning someone who is not before the court which is highly defamatory of such person, and that person has himself no opportunity of dealing with it. We would like to make it perfectly clear that there can be no impropriety, provided that counsel for the defence is made fully aware of the information and has a full opportunity of dealing with it.

It is not, therefore, right to say that everything which justices receive as evidence has publicly to be revealed. This is because the proper administration of justice commands a measure of confidentiality in respect of certain evidence which, in the public interest, should not be published.

However, I am bound to say that I am impressed with the argument that the action taken by the justices in the present case had nothing to do with the administration of justice. It seems to me that the concern shown by the justices for not giving publicity to [the defendant's] home address was solely motivated by their sympathy for his well-being if his former wife should learn of his home address and harass him yet again. That kind of predicament is not, unfortunately, unique. There are undoubtedly many people who find themselves defending criminal charges who for all manner of reasons would like to keep unrevealed their identity, their home address in particular. Indeed, I go so far as to say that in the vast majority of cases, in magistrates' courts anyway, defendants would like their identity to be unrevealed and would be capable of advancing seemingly plausible reasons why that should be so. But, s.11 was not enacted for the benefit of the comfort and feelings of defendants. The general rule enunciated in . . . *Attorney-General* v *Leveller Magazine Ltd* may not, as is there stated, be departed from save where the nature or the circumstances of proceedings are such that the application of the general rule in its entirety would frustrate or render impracticable the administration of justice. I fail to see how the revelation of [the defendant's] home address could in the circumstances in any sense warrant a departure from observance of the general rule of ensuring open justice.

For those reasons I have come to the conclusion that the justices in the present case misused the provisions of s.11 and further were in error in not causing [the defendant] to give his home address publicly for the purpose of fully identifying himself to the court in the usual way. By the usual way I mean that whilst no statutory provision lays down that a defendant's address has publicly to be given in court, it is well established practice that, save for a justifiable reason, it must be . . .'

R v *Beck, ex parte Daily Telegraph plc*

[1993] 2 All ER 177 · Court of Appeal

Shortly before the trial of the defendants, who were social workers, for very serious sex offences against children in the care of a local authority, a Crown Court judge made an order under s.4(2) because of two proposed trials of the defendants on related offences. It was accepted by the Court of Appeal that there was a substantial risk of prejudice to the administration of justice in the other trials.

Farquharson LJ: ' . . . the problem that we really have to consider is whether it is necessary to avoid that risk [of prejudice] by making the order excluding the press or other organs of the media from reporting the trial. We bear very much in mind the submissions made by counsel representing the three defendants. The horrific nature of the details of the charges against their respective clients are such that there is no possibility, they would contend, of anybody who read about the matter ever forgetting about it. So the difficulties of empanelling a second jury would be great, if not insurmountable. We recognise the force of that argument.

It can be said to be a two-edged argument, because on the other side we have the submissions of the appellants, which seem to us in turn to have great force. The allegations here concern officers of the social services and they are of a grave and horrific nature. Those activities by the persons accused are alleged to have gone on over a very long period of time. There must therefore inevitably be widespread public concern, not only in Leicester but generally, over the circumstances in which those in public service have the opportunity to commit such offences, and why, notwithstanding complaints on the part of the victims, nothing whatever was done about it. Is it right in those circumstances, we ask ourselves, that this trial should proceed without the public having any opportunity of knowing what is going on? In approaching this question, we have balanced those matters with the arguments put forward on behalf of the defendants.

Having regard to the considerations we have put forward, we conclude it was not necessary to make the order, notwithstanding the risk to the administration of justice, and that the order made by the learned judge in respect of the current trial should be reversed . . .'

Comment

(1)   Section 1, Contempt of Court Act 1981, provides that:

In this Act 'the strict liability rule' means the rule of law whereby conduct may be treated as a contempt of court as tending to interfere with the course of justice in particular legal proceedings regardless of intent to do so.

The strict liability rule applies to publications which pose a substantial risk of serious prejudice to proceedings which are active within the meaning of s.2 and Schedule 4 of the Act.

(2)   In *R v Malvern JJ, ex parte Evans* magistrates sat in camera in order to hear mitigation in relation to a driving offence where evidence of mental state indicated that a hearing in open court would inhibit the defendant from making that mitigation. The Court of Appeal held that magistrates had power to sit in camera, but instances where it would be proper to use that power would be rare, and then only in accordance with the principles in *Scott* v *Scott*. The court dismissed the challenge to the order made, but observed *obiter* that, in its view, the exercise of discretion by the magistrates in this case had been erroneous.

(3)   In *R v Horsham JJ, ex parte Farquharson* Lord Denning emphasized that, in the exercise of the s.4(2) postponement power, the sole consideration was the potential prejudice to the administration of justice. In *Re Central Independent Television* the Court of Appeal allowed an appeal against the making of a s.4(2) order which prevented reporting of a trial by radio or television whilst a jury was spending one night during its deliberations at a hotel. The order was made to prevent the inconvenience to the jury of being unable to watch television; this was not enough to justify such an order.

In *R v Dover Justices, ex parte Dover DC*, in criminal proceedings relating to breaches of food hygiene regulations, a restaurateur sought an order under s.11 to prevent publication of his name and that of his restaurant. The justices had accepted his evidence that the publicity would be highly prejudicial and would lead to closure of the restaurant, and had ordered that the information should not be revealed during the trial and not at all in respect of any charges of which he might have been acquitted. In quashing the order Neill LJ acknowledged that exceptions to the general rule of openness did exist but that the case did not fall within them.

(4)   Section 11 only permits prohibition where such could lawfully have occurred at common law. The purpose of s.11 is to allow the making of orders that bind the world at large. Compare the view taken, in the context of s.4, by Lord Denning MR in *R* v *Horsham JJ, ex parte Farquharson.*

(5)   Section 159, Criminal Justice Act 1988, creates a right of appeal against the making of a s.4 or s.11 order. In *Re Crook* the Court of Appeal held that a trial judge was entitled to hear an application for a s.4 or s.11 order in private. Each application had to be considered on its own merits, and until the trial judge knew the reasons for the application it would not be possible to determine whether the administration of justice would be prejudiced by a public hearing. If exclusion of the public is necessary then normally no exception should be made in favour of the press. Magistrates' courts have the discretion to hear press representations before making an order under s.4(2) since the press are 'the best qualified to represent the public interest in publicity which the court has to take into account when performing any balancing exercise' (see *R* v *Clerkenwell Magistrates' Court, ex parte Telegraph plc*).

(6)   Certain statutory restrictions allow hearings in private (e.g. s.8, Official Secrets Act 1920), others restrict publishable material (e.g. s.4, Sexual Offences (Amendment) Act 1976 – identity of rape complainants). There may also be restrictions at common law: see *Re M & another (Wardship: Freedom of publication* and *R* v *Central Television*, p.207).

(7)   In *R* v *Felixstowe JJ, ex parte Leigh* the Divisional Court ruled that magistrates had no power to withhold their identity from public or press. The court cited Lord Denning in *The Road to Justice*: 'Every member of the public must be entitled to report in the public press all that he has seen and heard. The reason for this rule is the very felicitous influence which publicity has for all those who work in the light of it . . .'. Watkins LJ continued:

> These observations . . . emphasise . . . the vital significance of the work of the journalist in reporting Court proceedings, and, within the bounds of impartiality and fairness, commenting on the decision of judges and justices and their behaviour in and conduct of the proceedings. If someone in the seat of justice misconducts himself or is worthy of praise, is the public disentitled at the whim of that person to know his identity?

(8)   Note the terms of art.6, ECHR (p.138), which creates an entitlement to a 'fair and public hearing'. It permits exclusion of press and public from all or part of the trial, in certain circumstances which, to an extent, are wider than those permissible under English law.

(9)   In the *Beck* case, the decision to sever the indictment so as to create three trials was itself made the subject of a s.4(2) order and the public were unaware of the

pending trials. There was no application in respect of that particular order. The defendants were convicted and the other trials did not take place. For a similar discussion on the function of the court and the resilience of juries in the case of a substantial risk of prejudice see *ex parte Telegraph plc* where it was also observed that the criterion of necessity in s.4(2) was 'a statutory recognition of the principle of open justice'.

R v *Central Television plc*

[1994] 3 All ER 641 · Court of Appeal

The mother of a child sought an injunction to prevent a television company broadcasting a programme about the child's father who had been convicted of indecency. She claimed that despite the steps taken by the television company, pictures of him would reveal the identity of the mother and child, and lead to consequential harm for the child. The Court of Appeal refused to grant an injunction. It held that, although a court exercising its supervisory jurisdiction over children may prevent publication of matters relating to the care and upbringing of the child in question, it had no jurisdiction to do so in matters unrelated to care and upbringing.

Hoffmann LJ: 'There are in the law reports many impressive and emphatic statements about the importance of the freedom of speech and the press. But they are often followed by a paragraph which begins with the word "nevertheless". The judge then goes on to explain that there are other interests which have to be balanced against press freedom. And in deciding upon the importance of press freedom in the particular case, he is likely to distinguish between what he thinks deserves publication in the public interest and things in which the public are merely interested. He may even advert to the commercial motives of the newspaper or television company compared with the damage to the public or individual interest which would be caused by publication.

The motives which impel judges to assume a power to balance freedom of speech against other interests are almost always understandable and humane on the facts of the particular case before them. Newspapers are sometimes irresponsible and their motives in a market economy cannot be expected to be unalloyed by considerations of commercial advantage. And, publication may cause needless pain, distress and damage to individuals or harm to other aspects of the public interest. But a freedom which is restricted to what judges think to be responsible or in the public interest is no freedom. Freedom means the right to publish things which government and judges, however well motivated, think should not be published. It means the right to say things which "right-thinking" people regard as dangerous or irresponsible. This freedom is subject only to clearly defined exceptions laid down by common law or statute.

Furthermore, in order to enable us to meet our international obligations under the European Convention for the Protection of Human Rights and Fundamental Freedoms . . . it is necessary that any exceptions should satisfy the tests laid down in art.10(2) . . . It cannot be too strongly emphasised that outside the established exceptions . . . there is no question of balancing freedom of speech against other interests. It is a trump card which always wins . . .

[I]n a series of decisions commencing with *Re C (a minor) (Wardship: Medical treatment)(No.2)* the courts have, without any statutory or ... previous authority, assumed a power to create by injunction what is in effect a right of privacy for children ... [T]he existence of a jurisdiction to restrain publication of information concerning a child and its upbringing is no longer open to dispute in this court.

But this new jurisdiction is concerned only with the privacy of children and their upbringing. It does not extend ... to "injunctive protection of children from publicity which, though inimical to their welfare, is not directed at them or at those who care for them". It cannot therefore apply to publication of the fact that the child's father has been convicted of a serious offence, however distressing it may be for the child to be identified as the daughter of such a man. If such a jurisdiction existed, it could be exercised to restrain the identification of any convicted criminal who has young children ...'

Comment

(1) A wide range of statutory provisions enables the courts to prohibit reporting, e.g. s.39, Children and Young Persons Act 1933. The *Central Television* case demonstrates the development of a common law principle aimed at protecting the court's supervisory functions. In *Re R (a minor)* an injunction granted by a judge in wardship proceedings would have had the effect of preventing the fair and accurate reporting of the trial relating to the abduction of the ward by her father. The Court of Appeal considered that since the injunction interfered with the reporting of the criminal proceedings it went further than the wardship jurisdiction had previously warranted. The principles of open justice required that the criminal trial judge should have been left to make an order under s.39, Children and Young Persons Act 1933 or under s.4, Contempt of Court Act as appropriate.

(2) For an instance where the court does have to balance competing interests see *X Ltd* v *Morgan Grampian Ltd*, p.24.

10 Basis of judicial review

Private law actions may be brought against a public body, based on claims in contract or tort. The legality of the acts of such a body may be raised as a defence to civil or criminal proceedings (see, e.g. *DPP* v *Hutchinson*). The legality of the actions of the European Community institutions can be tested in the Court of Justice (see p.104), although, usually, not by an individual.

More technically, the term 'judicial review' means the procedure under RSC, o.53 which is the normal means of challenge to the public law actions of public bodies (see *O'Reilly* v *Mackman*, p.238). Through this procedure, available to those who can show a 'sufficient interest' and thus establish *locus standi*, a variety of remedies is available, ranging from the old prerogative orders of *certiorari*, prohibition and mandamus to declarations and, sometimes, injunctions.

Judicial review concerns itself with public law matters. Some grounds of challenge, principally natural justice and procedural fairness, are wide enough to reach beyond the public law context in their application. Judicial review does not extend that far. However, the converse is equally true: the scope of judicial review potentially extends to all public law matters, and the cases (particularly the *GCHQ* case, p.215, and *Datafin*, p.224) show an increasing willingness of the courts to review matters perceived to be of a public law nature. They are less concerned with the traditional, and sometimes rigid, classifications that in the past determined whether judicial review was available.

In general, only Acts of Parliament are beyond the reach of the courts (see p.26). Even powers which seemingly confer wide discretion are not immune: the courts seek to give effect to the will of Parliament and determine to prevent where possible unchallengeable discretion. As Wade, *Administrative Law* (5th edn), puts it, in a passage approved by the House of Lords in *Tower Hamlets* v *Chetnik Developments*:

> ... the common theme [of the cases] is that the notion of absolute or unfettered discretion is rejected. Statutory power conferred for public

purposes is conferred as it were upon trust, not absolutely – that is to say, it can validly be used only in the right and proper way which Parliament when conferring it is presumed to have intended . . . [T]he truth is that in a system based on the rule of law, unfettered governmental discretion is a contradiction in terms.

Nor will the fact that what is being questioned is delegated legislation, or has been approved by one House of Parliament, prevent judicial review (see *Attorney-General* v *Wilts Utd Dairies*, p.33, and *Hoffman-La Roche*, p.211). However, in these instances the courts may be less willing to intervene.

Only two limits exist. First, the matter should be suitable for judicial review: some matters are regarded by the courts as matters more suitably determined in the political arena, and therefore regarded as non-justiciable. Some prerogative powers are within this class (see Lord Roskill in the *GCHQ* case, p.215). Secondly, the doctrine of the separation of powers requires that the courts confine themselves to matters of legality, not merits. Given the breadth of the potential grounds of challenge, this distinction is not easily drawn in practice, and on occasion the courts seem dragged into political controversy. In *R* v *Boundary Commissioners for England, ex parte Foot* Sir John Donaldson said:

> . . . There are many Acts of Parliament which give ministers and local authorities extensive powers to take action which affects the citizenry of this country, but give no right of appeal to the courts. In such cases the courts are not concerned or involved so long as ministers and local authorities do not exceed the powers given to them by Parliament. Those powers may give them a wide range of choice on what action to take or to refrain from taking and so long as they confine themselves to making choices within that range the courts will have no wish or power to intervene. But if ministers or local authorities exceed their powers, if they choose to do something or to refrain from doing something in circumstances in which this is not one of the options given to them by Parliament, the courts can and will intervene . . .

For discussion of the general nature of the separation of powers, see pp.183–208.

Padfield v Minister of Agriculture, Fisheries & Food

[1968] AC 997 · House of Lords

The court upheld a challenge to the exercise of a discretionary power conferred upon the Minister by the Agricultural Marketing Act 1958 in seemingly wide and unfettered terms as to whether or not to refer complaints to a Committee of Investigation.

Lord Reid: '. . . It is implicit in the argument for the Minister that there are only two possible interpretations of this provision – either he must refer every complaint or he has an unfettered discretion to refuse to refer in any case. I do not think this is right. Parliament must have conferred the discretion with the intention that it should be used to promote the policy and objects of the Act; the policy and objects of the Act must be determined by construing the Act as a whole and construction is always a matter for the Court. In a matter of this kind it is not possible to draw a hard and fast line, but if the Minister, by reason of his having misconstrued the Act or for some other reason so uses his discretion as to thwart or run counter to the policy and objects of the Act, then our law would be very defective if persons aggrieved were not entitled to the protection of the Court.'

Comment

(1)   In *Tower Hamlets* v *Chetnik Developments* Lord Bridge stated that:

. . . before deciding whether a discretion has been exercised for good or bad reasons, the court must first construe the enactment by which the discretion is conferred. Some statutory discretions may be so wide that they can, for practical purposes, only be challenged if shown to have been exercised irrationally or in bad faith. But if the purpose which the discretion is intended to serve is clear, the discretion can only be validly exercised for reasons relevant to the achievement of that purpose.

See also *R* v *Secretary of State for the Home Department, ex parte Brind* (p.293); *R* v *Somerset CC, ex parte Fewings* (p.314).

(2)   The *Padfield* approach therefore allows the court a wide discretion as to the extent of judicial intervention. Much turns on whether the court perceives a clear parliamentary intention. As to how that intention may on occasion be established, see *Pepper* v *Hart* (p.171).

Hoffmann-La Roche AG v Secretary of State for Trade and Industry

[1975] AC 295 · House of Lords

Lord Diplock: '. . . My Lords, in constitutional law a clear distinction can be drawn between an Act of Parliament and subordinate legislation, even though the latter is contained in an order made by statutory instrument approved by resolutions of both Houses of Parliament. Despite this indication that the majority of members of both Houses of the contemporary Parliament regard the order as being for the common weal, I entertain no doubt that the courts have jurisdiction to declare it to be invalid if they are satisfied that in making it the Minister who did so acted outwith the legislative powers conferred upon him by the previous Act of Parliament under which the order purported to be made, and this is so whether the order is *ultra vires* by reason of its contents . . . or by reason of defects in the procedure followed prior to its being made . . . Under our legal system, however, the courts as the judicial arm of government do not act on their own initiative. Their jurisdiction to determine that a statutory instrument is *ultra vires* does not arise until its validity is challenged in proceedings *inter partes* either brought by one party to enforce the law declared by the instrument against another party or brought by a party whose interests are affected by the law so declared sufficiently directly to give him *locus standi* to initiate proceedings to challenge the validity of the instrument. Unless there is such challenge and, if there is, until it has been upheld by a judgment of the court, the validity of the statutory instrument and the legality of acts done pursuant to the law declared by it are presumed. It would, however, be inconsistent with the doctrine of *ultra vires* as it has been developed in English law as a means of controlling abuse of power by the executive arm of government if the judgment of a court . . . that a statutory instrument was *ultra vires* were to have any lesser consequence in law than to render the instrument incapable of ever having had any legal effect upon the rights or duties of the parties to the proceedings . . . Although such a decision is directly binding only as between the parties to the proceedings in which it was made, the application of the doctrine of precedent has the consequence of enabling the benefit of it to accrue to all other persons whose legal rights have been interfered with in reliance on the law which the statutory instrument purported to declare.'

Comment

For further discussion of this case see *Factortame* v *Secretary of State for Transport*, p.108; *Kirklees BC* v *Wickes Building Supplies*, p.131.

Nottinghamshire CC v Secretary of State for the Environment

[1986] AC 240 · House of Lords

The respondents sought to challenge, on the grounds of unreasonableness, guidance given to local authorities under the Local Government, Planning and Land Act 1980. Pursuant to the statutory requirements this guidance had been approved by the House of Commons.

Lord Scarman: '. . . I think that the courts below were absolutely right to decline the invitation to intervene. I can understand that there may well arise a justiciable issue as to the true construction of the words of the statute and that, if the Secretary of State has issued guidance which fails to comply with the requirement of . . . [the Act] . . . the guidance can be quashed. But I cannot accept that it is constitutionally appropriate, save in very exceptional circumstances, for the courts to intervene on the ground of "unreasonableness" to quash guidance framed by the Secretary of State and by necessary implication approved by the House of Commons, the guidance being concerned with the limits of public expenditure by local authorities and the incidence of the tax burden as between taxpayers and ratepayers. Unless and until a statute provides otherwise, or it is established that the Secretary of State has abused his power, these are matters of political judgment for him and for the House of Commons. They are not for the judges or your Lordships' House in its judicial capacity . . .

In my judgment, therefore, the courts below acted with constitutional propriety in rejecting the so-called "*Wednesbury* unreasonableness" argument in this case. The trial judge [having cited Lord Diplock in *Secretary of State for Education and Science v Tameside Metropolitan Borough Council* – see p.301] . . . concluded, after giving more attention to the detailed arguments as to the financial consequences of the guidance than they were strictly entitled to receive: "In my judgment, although the Secretary of State could, of course, have set different guidance which would perhaps not have caused the applicant authorities to complain, it cannot be said that the approach which he has adopted was unreasonable in the *Wednesbury* sense."

The Court of Appeal adopted the same approach. After referring to [the section of the Act] which requires the Secretary of State, when deciding what guidance to issue, to do what he thinks necessary having regard to general economic conditions, Lawton LJ observed with constitutional propriety: "Parliament has left him to decide what he thinks necessary. He has to make a political and economic judgment. He may make a sound one or a bad one. This court might have been able to make a better one than he made; but we must remind ourselves that Parliament, no doubt for good reason, has not entrusted guidance to us."

The other members of the court had no doubt that no case was made out that the Secretary of State had acted with *Wednesbury* unreasonableness or perversity.

"*Wednesbury* principles" is a convenient legal "shorthand" used by lawyers to refer to the classical review by Lord Greene MR in the *Wednesbury* case of the circumstances in which the courts will intervene to quash as being illegal the exercise of an administrative discretion. No question of constitutional propriety arose in the case, and the Master of the Rolls was not concerned with the constitutional limits to the exercise of judicial power in our parliamentary democracy. There is a risk, however, that [Lord Greene's judgment] may be treated as a complete, exhaustive, definitive statement of the law. The law has developed beyond the limits understood to apply to judicial review as practised by the courts in 1948. The ground upon which the courts will review the exercise of an administrative discretion by a public officer is abuse of power. Power can be abused in a number of ways: by mistake of law in misconstruing the limits imposed by statute (or by common law in the case of a common law power) upon the scope of the power; by procedural irregularity; by unreasonableness in the *Wednesbury* sense; or by bad faith or an improper motive in its exercise. A valuable, and already "classical", but certainly not exhaustive analysis of the grounds upon which courts will embark on the judicial review of an administrative power exercised by a public officer is now to be found in Lord Diplock's speech in [the *GCHQ* case] . . . In an earlier case, in which this House ruled that the Inland Revenue Commissioners were "not immune" from judicial review, Lord Diplock made the comment that they were accountable to Parliament "so far as regards efficiency and policy, and of that Parliament is the only judge; they are responsible to a court of justice for the lawfulness of what they do, and of that the court is the only judge": *IRC* v *National Federation of Self-Employed and Small Businesses Ltd* . . . This approach with its distinction between accountability to Parliament and review by the courts of the lawfulness of the exercise of administrative power was further developed and confirmed by the House in . . . *R* v *IRC ex parte Preston* and *Wheeler* v *Leicester City Council*. In *Preston*'s case . . . Lord Templeman . . . declared the principle of law to be that the courts may intervene to review a power conferred by statute on the ground of unfairness but only if the unfairness in the purported exercise of the power be such as to amount to an abuse of the power. *Wheeler* v *Leicester City Council* is a striking illustration on its facts of circumstances in which the courts may intervene on the ground of abuse of power arising from an improper motive in its exercise.

The present case raises in acute form the constitutional problem of the separation of powers between Parliament, the executive, and the courts. In this case, Parliament has enacted that an executive power is not to be exercised save with the consent and approval of one of its Houses. It is true that the framing of the guidance is for the Secretary of State alone after consultation with local authorities; but he cannot act on the guidance so as to discriminate between local authorities without reporting to, and obtaining the approval of, the House of Commons. That House has, therefore, a role and a responsibility not only at the legislative stage when the Act was passed but in the action to be taken by the Secretary of State in the exercise of the power conferred upon him by the legislation.

To sum it up, the levels of public expenditure and the incidence and distribution of taxation are matters for Parliament, and, within Parliament, especially for the House of Commons. If Parliament legislates, the courts have their interpretative role: they must, if called upon to do so, construe the statute. If a minister exercises a power conferred on him by the legislation, the courts can investigate whether he has abused his power. But if, as in this case, effect cannot be given to the Secretary of State's determination without the consent of the House of Commons and the House of Commons has consented, it is not open to the courts to intervene unless the minister and the House must have misconstrued the statute or the minister has – to put it bluntly – deceived the House. The courts can properly rule that a minister has acted unlawfully if he has erred in law as to the limits of his power even when his action has the approval of the House of Commons, itself acting not legislatively but within the limits set by a statute. But, if a statute, as in this case, requires the House of Commons to approve a minister's decision before he can lawfully enforce it, and if the action proposed complies with the terms of the statute (as, your Lordships, I understand, are convinced that it does in the present case), it is not for the judges to say that the action has such unreasonable consequences that the guidance upon which the action is based and of which the House of Commons had notice was perverse and must be set aside. For that is a question of policy for the minister and the Commons, unless there has been bad faith or misconduct by the minister. Where Parliament has legislated that the action to be taken by the Secretary of State must, before it is taken, be approved by the House of Commons, it is no part of the judges' role to declare that the action proposed is unfair, unless it constitutes an abuse of power in the sense which I have explained; for Parliament has enacted that one of its Houses is responsible. Judicial review is a great weapon in the hands of the judges: but the judges must observe the constitutional limits set by our parliamentary system upon their exercise of this beneficent power . . .'

Comment

(1) In *Hammersmith and Fulham LBC* v *Secretary of State for the Environment* the court considered the *Nottinghamshire* case. Under challenge by way of judicial review in the *Hammersmith* case was the action of the Secretary of State, pursuant to statute, of 'charge-capping' certain local authorities, action which had been approved by the House of Commons. In the Divisional Court it had been doubted

whether actions approved by the House of Commons could be attacked on the ground of irrationality, the court relying on the *Nottinghamshire* case. The judgments of the Court of Appeal appeared to differ on that point.

The House of Lords considered both the meaning of irrationality and its application. For discussion of the former, see p.296. In relation to the latter, Lord Bridge observed:

> The restriction which the *Nottinghamshire CC* case imposes on the scope of judicial review operates only when the court has first determined that the ministerial action in question does not contravene the requirements of the statute, whether express or implied, and only then declares that, since the statute has conferred a power on the Secretary of State which involves the formulation and implementation of national economic policy and which can only take effect with the approval of the House of Commons, it is not open to challenge on the grounds of irrationality short of the extremes of bad faith, improper motive or manifest absurdity. Both the constitutional propriety and the good sense of this restriction seem to me to be clear enough. The formulation and implementation of national economic policy are matters depending essentially on political judgment. The decisions which shape them are for politicians to take and it is in the political forum of the House of Commons that they are properly to be debated and approved or disapproved on their merits. If the decisions have been taken in good faith within the four corners of the Act, the merits of the policy underlying the decisions are not susceptible to review by the courts and the courts would be exceeding their proper function if they presumed to condemn the policy as unreasonable.

(2)   The constitutional role of the courts is well illustrated by Lord Donaldson MR in *R v Secretary of State for the Home Department, ex parte Cheblak*, p.338.

Council of Civil Service Unions v Minister for the Civil Service (the *GCHQ* case)

[1985] AC 374 · House of Lords

Article 4 of the Civil Service Order in Council 1982 (an Order made by the Sovereign under the Royal Prerogative) empowered the Minister for the Civil Service to make regulations or issue instructions in respect of the conditions of service of persons employed in the Home Civil Service. Following industrial action which was taken by staff at the Government Communications Headquarters (GCHQ), and which disrupted the work of this establishment in providing signals intelligence vital to national security, the Minister for the Civil Service, without consultation with the appellant Union, issued an Instruction pursuant to art.4. This Instruction prevented employees at GCHQ from trade union membership, a right enjoyed since 1947. Although no legal right of consultation was contained in art.4, the practice of consultation with staff prior to changes in conditions of service was well established. The appellant sought a declaration that the Instruction was invalid, because of the failure to consult. The respondent argued that the making of the Instruction was not open to review being an emanation of the Prerogative. The application failed. Even if the issue of the Instruction were treated as a direct exercise of prerogative power, that of itself did not prevent judicial review (Lords Scarman, Diplock and Roskill); or, the Instruction was not a direct exercise of prerogative power, but was reviewable as the exercise of delegated power pursuant to lawful authority (Lords Fraser and Brightman). The Union had a legitimate expectation of consultation, but on the facts that was outweighed by competing interests of national security.

Lord Fraser: '. . . The Order in Council was not issued under powers conferred by any Act of Parliament . . . it was issued by the sovereign by virtue of her prerogative, but of course on the advice of the government of the day. In these circumstances [counsel] submitted that the instruction was not open to review by the courts because it was an emanation of the prerogative. This submission involves two propositions: (1) that prerogative powers are discretionary, that is to say they may be exercised at the discretion of the sovereign (acting on advice in accordance with modern constitutional practice) and the way in which they are exercised is not open to review by the courts; (2) that an instruction given in the exercise of a delegated power conferred by the sovereign under the prerogative enjoys the same immunity from review as if it were itself a direct exercise of prerogative power . . .

The first of these propositions is vouched by an impressive array of authority, which I do not propose to cite at all fully . . . they are at one in stating that, within the sphere of its prerogative powers, the Crown has an absolute discretion. In more recent times the best known definition of the prerogative is that given in Dicey, *Law of the Constitution*, 8th ed . . .which is as follows: "The prerogative is the name for the remaining portion of the Crown's original authority, and is therefore, as already pointed out the name for the residue of discretionary power left at any moment in the hands of the Crown, whether such powers be in fact exercised by the King himself or by his ministers."

Dicey's definition was quoted with approval in this House in *Attorney-General* v *De Keyser's Royal Hotel Ltd* by Lord Dunedin and was impliedly accepted by the other Law Lords in that case. In *Burmah Oil Co Ltd* v *Lord Advocate*, Lord Reid referred to Dicey's definition as being "always quoted with approval" although he said it did not take him very far in that case. It was also referred to with apparent approval by Roskill LJ [as he then was] in *Laker Airways Ltd* v *Department of Trade*. As *De Keyser's* case shows, the courts will inquire into whether a particular prerogative power exists or not, and, if it does exist, into its extent. But once the existence and the extent of a power are established to the satisfaction of the court, the court cannot inquire into the propriety of its exercise. That is undoubtedly the position as laid down in the authorities to which I have briefly referred and it is plainly reasonable in relation to many of the most important prerogative powers which are concerned with control of the armed forces and with foreign policy and with other matters which are unsuitable for discussion or review in the law courts. In the present case the prerogative power involved is power to regulate the Home Civil Service, and I recognise there is no obvious reason why the mode of exercise of that power should be immune from review by the courts. Nevertheless to permit such review would run counter to the great weight of authority to which I have briefly referred . . .

I prefer to leave that question open until it arises in a case where a decision upon it is necessary. I therefore assume, without deciding, that his first proposition is correct and that all powers exercised directly under the prerogative are immune from challenge in the courts. I pass to consider his second proposition.

The second proposition depends for its soundness upon whether the power conferred by art.4 of the Order in Council of 1982 on the Minister for the Civil Service of "providing for . . . the conditions of service" of the Civil Service is subject to an implied obligation to act fairly. Such an obligation is sometimes referred to as an obligation to obey the rules of natural justice, but that is a less appropriate description, at least when applied, as in the present case, to a power which is executive and not judicial. There is no doubt that, if the Order in Council of 1982 had been made under the authority of a statute, the power delegated to the Minister by art.4 would have been construed as being subject to an obligation to act fairly. I am unable to see why the words conferring the same powers should be construed differently merely because their source was an Order in Council made under the prerogative . . . There seems to be no sensible reason why the words should not bear the same meaning whatever the source of authority for the legislation in which they are contained. The Order in Council of 1982 was described . . . as primary legislation; that is, in my opinion, a correct description, subject to the qualification that the Order in Council, being made under the prerogative, derives its authority from the sovereign alone and not, as is more commonly the case with legislation, from the sovereign in Parliament. Legislation frequently delegates power from the legislating authority – the sovereign alone in one case, the sovereign in Parliament in the other – to some other person or body and, when that is done, the delegated powers are defined more or less closely by the legislation, in this case by art.4. But, whatever their source, powers which are defined, either by reference to their object or by reference to procedure for their exercise, or in some other way, and whether the definition is expressed or implied, are in my opinion normally subject to judicial control to ensure that they are not exceeded. By "normally" I mean provided that considerations of national security do not require otherwise.

The courts have already shown themselves ready to control by way of judicial review the actions of a tribunal set up under the prerogative. *R v Criminal Injuries Compensation Board, ex parte Lain* was such a case. In that case Lord Parker CJ said:

I can see no reason either in principle or in authority why a board set up as this board was set up is not a body of persons amenable to the jurisdiction of this court. True it is not set up by statute but the fact that it is set up by executive government, ie, under the prerogative, does not render its acts any the less lawful. Indeed, the writ of *certiorari* has issued not only to courts set up by statute but to courts whose authority is derived, *inter alia*, from the prerogative. Once the jurisdiction is extended, as it clearly has been, to tribunals as opposed to courts, there is no reason why the remedy by way of *certiorari* cannot be invoked to a body of persons set up under the prerogative . . .

Accordingly I agree with the conclusion of Glidewell J that there is no reason for treating the exercise of a power under art.4 any differently from the exercise of a statutory power merely because art.4 itself is found in an order issued under the prerogative.'

[Lord Brightman concurred with Lord Fraser.]

Lord Roskill: '. . . The appellants . . . invited the House to consider and if necessary to reconsider the reviewability of executive acts done under the prerogative. [Counsel] for the respondent understandably did not press the argument that no action taken under the prerogative could ever be the subject of judicial review. But, helpfully, he thought it right to make available to your Lordships a selection from the classic pronouncements of many famous writers in this field from Locke through Blackstone and Chitty to Dicey and from the writings of distinguished modern authorities including de Smith, Wade, Hood, Phillips and Heuston designed to show first the historic view that acts done under the prerogative were never reviewable and secondly the extent to which that classic doctrine may at least in this century be said to have been diluted.

Dicey's classic statement in *Law of the Constitution*, 10th ed. that the prerogative is "the residue of discretionary or arbitrary authority, which at any given time is legally left in the hands of the Crown" has the weight behind it not only of the author's own authority but also of the majority of this House in *Burmah Oil Co Ltd* v *Lord Advocate* . . . But as Lord Reid himself pointed out this definition "does not take us very far". On the other hand the attempt by Lord Denning MR in *Laker Airways Ltd* v *Department of Trade* (*obiter* since the other members of the Court of Appeal did not take so broad a view) to assert that the prerogative "if . . . exercised improperly or mistakenly" was reviewable is, with great respect, far too wide. The Master of the Rolls sought to support his view by a quotation from *Blackstone's Commentaries*, 15th ed . . . But unfortunately and no doubt inadvertently he omitted the opening words of the paragraph:

> In the exercise therefore of those prerogatives, which the law has given him, the King is irresistible and absolute, according to the forms of the constitution. And yet, if the consequence of that exertion be manifestly to the grievance or dishonour of the kingdom, the parliament will call his advisers to a just and severe account.

In short the orthodox view was at that time that the remedy for abuse of the prerogative lay in the political and not in the judicial field. But fascinating as it is to explore this mainstream of our legal history, to do so in connection with the present appeal has an air of unreality. To speak today of the acts of the sovereign as "irresistible and absolute" when modern constitutional convention requires that all such acts are done by the sovereign on the advice of and will be carried out by the sovereign's ministers currently in power is surely to hamper the continual development of our administrative law by harking back to what Lord Atkin once called, albeit in a different context, the clanking of mediaeval chains of the ghosts of the past . . . the right of the executive to do a lawful act affecting the rights of the citizen, whether adversely or beneficially, is founded upon the giving to the executive of a power enabling it to do that act. The giving of such a power usually carries with it legal sanctions to enable that power if necessary to be enforced by the courts. In most cases that power is derived from statute though in some cases, as indeed in the present case, it may still be derived from the prerogative. In yet other cases, as the decisions show, the two powers may coexist or the statutory power may by necessary implication have replaced the former prerogative power. If the executive in pursuance of the statutory power does an act affecting the rights of the citizen, it is beyond question that in principle the manner of the exercise of that power may today be challenged on one or more of the three grounds which I have mentioned earlier in this speech. If the executive instead of acting under a statutory power acts under a prerogative power and in particular a prerogative power delegated to the respondent under art.4 of the Order in Council of 1982, so as to affect the rights of the citizen, I am unable to see, subject to what I shall say later, that there is any logical reason why the fact that the source of the power is the prerogative and not statute should today deprive the citizen of that right of challenge to the manner of its exercise which he would possess were the source of the power statutory. In either case the act in question is the act of the executive. To talk of that act as the act of the sovereign savours of the archaism of past centuries. In reaching this conclusion I find myself in agreement with . . . Lord Scarman and Lord Diplock . . .

But I do not think that that right of challenge can be unqualified. It must, I think, depend upon the subject matter of the prerogative power which is exercised. Many examples were given during the argument of prerogative powers which as at present advised I do not think could properly be made the subject of judicial review. Prerogative powers such as those relating to the making of treaties, the defence of the realm, the prerogative of mercy, the grant of honours, the dissolution of Parliament and the appointment of ministers as well as others are not, I think, susceptible to judicial review because their nature and subject matter are such as not to be amenable to the judicial process. The courts are not the place wherein to determine whether a treaty should be concluded or the armed forces disposed in a particular manner or Parliament dissolved on one date rather than another.

In my view the exercise of the prerogative which enabled the oral instructions of 22 December 1983 to be given does not by reason of its subject matter fall within what for want of a better phrase I would call the "excluded categories", some of which I have just mentioned. It follows that in principle I can see no reason why those instructions should not be the subject of judicial review . . .

I find considerable support for the conclusion I have reached in the decision of the Divisional Court . . . in R v *Criminal Injuries Compensation Board, ex parte Lain*, the judgments in which may without exaggeration be described as a landmark in the development of this branch of the law. The board had been set up not by statute but by executive action under, as I think and as Lord Parker CJ stated, the prerogative. It was strenuously argued that the board was not subject to the jurisdiction of the courts since it did not have what was described as legal authority in the sense of statutory authority. This argument . . . was emphatically and unanimously rejected . . .

It follows from what I have said thus far that in principle I am of the clear opinion that the respondent's oral instructions of 22 December 1983 are amenable to judicial review and are not immune from such review because the instructions were given pursuant to prerogative powers.'

Comment

(1) For discussion of the Royal Prerogative, see p.50. Dicey's definition encompasses a variety of matters (e.g. the issue and revocation of passports – see *ex parte Everett*, p.220) which would not have the quality of 'uniqueness to the Crown' stressed by Blackstone. In the light of the trend towards judicial review of governmental matters (see the *Datafin* case, p.224) the distinctions and arguments are probably unimportant.

(2) The significance of *ex parte Lain* is not perhaps as obvious as Lord Roskill suggests. Even if the Criminal Injuries Compensation Board was established under Royal Prerogative, which Wade doubts, what was in issue was not the review of the exercise of prerogative powers (i.e. the establishment of the Board), but rather the issue of *certiorari* to review its actions. See further, the *dicta* of Lord Parker CJ, cited in *ex parte Aga Khan* (p.228).

(3) The *GCHQ* case was applied in *R* v *Secretary of State for Foreign and Commonwealth Affairs, ex parte Everett*: E was refused a passport by the Secretary of State because of a policy that no passport was to be issued in respect of persons wanted by police for serious crime. No details of the outstanding arrest warrant were given to E. The Court of Appeal confirmed that the exercise of the passport power was judicially reviewable; the Secretary of State was under an obligation to give reasons for refusal, and to inform E that the application of the policy would be considered in the light of any exceptional reasons for non-application that E could produce. However, since at the time of the trial E was aware of all the facts and the reason for the refusal, he had suffered no injustice, and the appeal of the Secretary of State was allowed.

(4) In *R* v *Director of Government Communications Headquarters, ex parte Hodges* the applicant (an employee at GCHQ) sought judicial review of the withdrawal of his positive vetting clearance. This action was taken as a result of his own admission of homosexual orientation. The security clearance was withdrawn because of the nature of the relationships he had. The grounds of challenge were the alleged unreasonableness of the decision itself, and procedural unfairness in the hearings. The respondent argued that the action was justified on the grounds of national security. The application was dismissed. Given that evidence of national security existed, the justification for the decision was not justiciable. The ground of challenge based on procedural unfairness was justiciable, but there was not, on the facts, procedural impropriety. This case suggests that whether a matter is justiciable may depend upon the ground of challenge. For discussion of the question of national security, see p.264.

(5) In *R* v *Civil Service Appeal Board, ex parte Bruce* the Court of Appeal held that despite the absence of a contract of service between B (a civil servant) and the Crown, there was a public law element in his dismissal. The Board, which was an independent body established by Royal Prerogative, had upheld B's dismissal, and it was that action that was challenged in these proceedings. The position of the Board is analogous to that of the Criminal Injuries Compensation Board in *ex parte Lain* (see p.217). For the position of civil servants, and the public law element, see p.234.

(6) It should be borne in mind that the process of judicial review owes its origins to the prerogative powers of the Crown in respect of inferior courts and bodies. It goes beyond scrutiny of the actions of executive bodies, to include the actions of inferior courts and tribunals. It does not extend to review of trials on indictment (s.29, Supreme Court Act 1981), but judicial review can occur where the use of the judicial process amounts to an abuse of process. The line is difficult to draw, but the

courts are reluctant to extend judicial review into matters that can be better dealt with by way of appeal. See *DPP* v *Crown Court at Manchester*, and also p.268.

R v Secretary of State for the Home Department, ex parte Bentley

[1993] 4 All ER 442 · Divisional Court

The applicant was the brother of a man who was hanged for murder in 1953. The case caused considerable controversy both at the time and subsequently, because the co-accused of the brother (who fired the fatal shot) was reprieved on the grounds of his age. After a campaign lasting many years, the Home Secretary in 1992 declined to recommend the granting of a posthumous free pardon, pursuant to the Royal Prerogative. The applicant sought to challenge that refusal in an application for judicial review. The application was successful, the Divisional Court concluding that the Home Secretary had directed himself wrongly in law.

Watkins LJ: 'Before the decision in the *CCSU* case it had been thought that the exercise of prerogative power was not susceptible to judicial review and so the earlier cases must be viewed with some caution. We have, however, been referred to a number of them including two which deal specifically with the prerogative of mercy. The first of these is *Hanratty v Butler* where the court had to consider whether to strike out a negligence claim against the Home Secretary for the way in which he had exercised the prerogative of mercy. Lord Denning MR said:

> These courts have had occasion in the past to cut down some of the prerogatives of the Crown: but they have never sought to encroach on the prerogative of mercy. It is not exercised by the Queen herself personally. It is exercised by her on the advice of one of the principal Secretaries of State. He advises her with the greatest conscience and good care. He takes full responsibility for the manner of its exercise. That being so, the law will not inquire into the manner in which the prerogative is exercised. It is outside the competence of the courts to call it into question: nor would they wish to do so.

Salmon LJ said:

> As a matter of constitutional practice it is of course well known that the Crown acted upon the advice of the Home Secretary. But the prerogative was, and still would be the prerogative of the Crown alone. It is well established that the courts have no power to review the exercise by the Crown of its prerogative, providing the Crown is acting within the scope of its powers. Nor are the courts entitled to be informed of, let alone to pass any opinion upon, such advice as may have been given to the Crown.

The second case is *de Freitas* v *Benny*. In that case the appellant claimed he was entitled to have disclosed to him the material furnished to the minister to enable him to advise the Governor-General of Trinidad and Tobago as to the exercise of the prerogative of mercy. In rejecting this claim Lord Diplock said:

> Except in so far as it may have been altered by the Constitution the legal nature of the exercise of the royal prerogative of mercy in Trinidad and Tobago remains the same as it was in England at common law. At common law this has always

been a matter which lies solely in the discretion of the sovereign, who by constitutional convention exercises it in respect of England on the advice of the Home Secretary to whom Her Majesty delegates her discretion. Mercy is not the subject of legal rights. It begins where legal rights end. A convicted person has no legal right even to have his case considered by the Home Secretary in connection with the exercise of the prerogative of mercy. In tendering his advice to the sovereign the Home Secretary is doing something that is often cited as the exemplar of a purely discretionary act as contrasted with the exercise of a quasi-judicial function.

There are no English cases dealing with the prerogative of mercy since 1985. We were referred to *R* v *Secretary of State for Foreign and Commonwealth Affairs, ex parte Everett* in which the Court of Appeal had to consider whether the decision to refuse the applicant a passport was reviewable. Taylor LJ said:

> I am in no doubt that the court has power to review the withdrawal or refusal to grant or renew a passport . . . At the top of the scale of executive functions under the prerogative are matters of high policy, [such as] making treaties, making law, dissolving Parliament, mobilising the armed forces. Clearly those matters, and no doubt a number of others, are not justiciable. But the grant or refusal of a passport is in a quite different category. It is a matter of administrative decision, affecting the rights of individuals and their freedom of travel. It raises issues which are just as justiciable as, for example, the issues arising in immigration cases.

We have also been referred to the New Zealand case of *Burt* v *Governor-General*. The plaintiff sought judicial review of the Governor-General's refusal to grant him a full pardon in the exercise of the prerogative of mercy. At first instance Greig J decided that the decision could not be reviewed. Having considered the effect of the *CCSU* case he concluded a detailed judgment by saying:

> . . . the prerogative of mercy . . . is a unique extra-legal, extra-judicial and extraordinary power that cannot be subject to Court review.

The Court of Appeal . . . dismissed the appeal but in doing so it said:

> The prerogative of mercy is a prerogative power in the strictest sense of that term, for it is peculiar to the crown and its exercise directly affects the rights of persons. On the other hand it would be inconsistent with the contemporary approach to say that, merely because it is a pure and strict prerogative power, its exercise or non-exercise must be immune from curial challenge. There is nothing heterodox in asserting, as counsel for the appellant do, that the rule of law requires that challenge shall be permitted in so far as issues arise of a kind with which the Courts are competent to deal . . . In the end the issue must turn on weighing the competing considerations, a number of which we have stated. Probably it cannot be said that any one answer is necessarily right; it is more a matter of a value or conceptual judgment as to the place in the law and the effectiveness or otherwise of the prerogative of mercy at the present day. In attempting such a judgment it must be right to exclude any lingering thought that the prerogative of mercy is no more than an arbitrary monarchial right of grace and favour. As developed it has become an integral element in the criminal justice system, a constitutional safeguard against mistakes.

It is clear from that judgment that the court would have been prepared to review the exercise of the prerogative of mercy if it felt that justice required it. It concluded however that this was not necessary in New Zealand "at any rate at present".

Finally we have been referred to a passage from Lewis *Judicial Remedies in Public Law* (1992) p.21:

In principle, a failure to consider exercising the power to grant a pardon should be reviewable, at least if an individual can demonstrate that there is some reason why the Home Secretary should consider the case. It is also difficult to see why a decision to refuse a pardon should not also be reviewable in appropriate circumstances, for example, where the allegation is that there has been a failure to consider relevant material, or a failure to act in accordance with any relevant guidelines, or if there is an error of law as to the elements of the offence for which the pardon was sought.

[Counsel] relies on this passage. He argues that the prerogative of mercy is exercised by the Home Secretary on behalf of us all. It is an important feature of our criminal justice system. It would be surprising and regrettable in our developed state of public law were the decision of the Home Secretary to be immune from legal challenge irrespective of the gravity of the legal errors which infected such a decision. Many types of decisions made by the Home Secretary do involve an element of policy (e.g. parole) but are subject to review.

We accept these arguments. The *CCSU* case made it clear that the powers of the court cannot be ousted merely by invoking the word "prerogative". The question is simply whether the nature and subject matter of the decision is amenable to the judicial process. Are the courts qualified to deal with the matter or does the decision involve such questions of policy that they should not intrude because they are ill-equipped to do so? Looked at in this way there must be cases in which the exercise of the royal prerogative is reviewable, in our judgment. If, for example, it was clear that the Home Secretary had refused to pardon someone solely on the grounds of their sex, race or religion, the courts would be expected to interfere and, in our judgment, would be entitled to do so.

We conclude therefore that some aspects of the exercise of the royal prerogative are amenable to the judicial process. We do not think that it is necessary for us to say more than this in the instant case. It will be for other courts to decide on a case by case basis whether the matter in question is reviewable or not.

We do not think that we are precluded from reaching this conclusion by authority. Lord Roskill's passing reference to the prerogative of mercy in the *CCSU* case was *obiter. Hanratty* and *de Freitas* were decided before the *CCSU* case and neither concerned judicial review of an error of law.'

Comment

It has already been noted that whether a court will consider a matter justiciable may depend on the ground on which it is being challenged. *Bentley* confirms this approach, contrasting the justiciability of the legal criteria for the exercise of the prerogative of mercy with the non-justiciability of the merits of such an exercise. However, note that even in respect of its exercise a decision might well be justiciable if no merits whatsoever existed, or the power was exercised in bad faith (see p.318).

R v *Panel on Takeovers & Mergers, ex parte Datafin plc*

[1987] QB 815 · Court of Appeal

The Panel on Takeovers and Mergers, an unincorporated association without legal personality, was the mechanism for self-regulation by the City of London of the processes of takeovers and mergers. It had no direct statutory or common law powers, but its role was recognized and supported by certain statutory powers. The applicants sought judicial review of the rejection by the Panel of a complaint made by them. The Panel contended that its actions were not subject to judicial review, on the basis that it did not derive its powers from statute or prerogative. On appeal, it was held that since the Panel was performing a public duty it was subject to judicial review, but in this case there were no grounds for successful challenge, and therefore the application for judicial review failed.

Sir John Donaldson MR: ' . . . In all the reports it is possible to find enumerations of factors giving rise to the [public law] jurisdiction, but it is a fatal error to regard the presence of all these factors as essential or as being exclusive of other factors. Possibly the only essential elements are what can be described as a public element, which can take many different forms, and the exclusion from the jurisdiction of bodies whose sole source of power is a consensual submission to its jurisdiction . . . [The Panel] is without doubt performing a public duty and an important one. This is clear from the expressed willingness of the Secretary of State for Trade and Industry to limit legislation in the field of takeovers and mergers and to use the Panel as the centrepiece of his regulation market. The rights of citizens are indirectly affected by its decisions . . . At least in its determination of whether there has been a breach of the code it has a duty to act judicially . . . Its source of power is only partly based on moral persuasion . . . the bottom line being the statutory powers exercised by the Department of Trade and Industry and the Bank of England . . . '

Lloyd LJ: 'There have been a number of cases since the decision of the House of Lords in *O'Reilly* v *Mackman* in which it has been necessary for the courts to consider the new-found distinction between public and private law. In most of them, objection has been taken by the defendant that the plaintiff has sought the wrong remedy. By seeking a remedy in private law, instead of public law, the plaintiff has, so it has been said, deprived the defendant of the special protection afforded by RSC o.53. The formalism thus introduced into our procedure has been the subject of strong criticism . . . The curiosity of the present case is that it is, so to speak, the other way round. The plaintiff is seeking a remedy in public law. It is the defendant who asserts that the plaintiff's remedy, if any . . . lies in private law . . . On this part of the case [counsel] has advanced arguments on two levels. On the level of pure policy he submits that it is undesirable for decisions or rulings of the Panel to be reviewable. The intervention of the court would best impede, at worst frustrate, the purposes for which the Panel exists. Secondly, on a more technical level, he submits that to hold that the Panel is subject to the supervisory jurisdiction of the High Court would be to extend that jurisdiction further than it has ever been extended before.

On the policy level, I find myself unpersuaded. [Counsel] made much of the word "self-regulating." No doubt self-regulation has many advantages. But I was unable to see why the mere fact that a body is self-regulating makes it less appropriate for judicial review. Of course there will be many self-regulating bodies which are wholly inappropriate for judicial review. The committee of an ordinary club affords an obvious example. But the reason why a club is not subject to judicial review is not just because it is self-regulating. The Panel wields enormous power. It has a giant's strength. The fact that it is self-regulating, which means, presumably, that it is not subject to regulation by others, and in particular the Department of Trade and Industry, makes it not less but more appropriate that it should be subject to judicial review by the courts.

It has been said that "it is excellent to have a giant's strength, but it is tyrannous to use it like a giant." Nobody suggests that there is any present danger of the Panel abusing its power. But it is at least possible to imagine circumstances in which a ruling or decision of the Panel might give rise to legitimate complaint. An obvious example would be if it reached a decision in flagrant breach of the rules of natural justice. It is no answer to say that there would be a right of appeal in such a case. For a complainant has no right of appeal where the decision is that there has been no breach of the code. Yet a complainant is just as much entitled to natural justice as the company against whom the complaint is made.

Nor is it any answer that a company coming to the market must take it as it finds it. The City is not a club which one can join or not at will. In that sense, the word "self-regulation" may be misleading. The Panel regulates not only itself, but all others who have no alternative but to come to the market in a case to which the code applies.

[Counsel] urged on us the importance of speed and finality in these matters. I accept that submission. I accept also the possibility that unmeritorious applications will be made from time to time as a harassing or delaying tactic. It would be up to the court to ensure that this does not happen. These considerations are all very relevant to the exercise of the court's discretion in particular cases. They mean that a successful application for judicial review is likely to be very rare. But they do not mean that we should decline jurisdiction altogether.

So long as there is a possibility, however remote, of the Panel abusing its great powers, then it would be wrong for the courts to abdicate responsibility. The courts must remain ready, willing and able to hear a legitimate complaint in this as in any other field of our national life. I am not persuaded that this particular field is one in which the courts do not belong, or from which they should retire, on grounds of policy. And if the courts are to remain in the field, then it is clearly better, as a matter of policy, that legal proceedings should be in the realm of public law rather than private law, not only because they are quicker, but also because the requirement of leave under RSC o.53 will exclude claims which are clearly unmeritorious.

So I turn to [counsel's] more technical argument. He starts with the speech of Lord Diplock in *Council of Civil Service Unions* v *Minister for the Civil Service . . .* [Counsel] . . . argues (i) that the sole test whether the body of persons is subject to judicial review is the source of its power, and (ii) that there has been no case where that source has been other than legislation, including subordinate legislation, or the prerogative.

I do not agree that the source of the power is the sole test whether a body is subject to judicial review, nor do I so read Lord Diplock's speech. Of course the source of the power will often, perhaps usually, be decisive. If the source of power is a statute, or subordinate legislation under a statute, then clearly the body in question will be subject to judicial review. If, at the other end of the scale, the source of power is contractual, as in the case of private arbitration, then clearly the arbitrator is not subject to judicial review . . . But in between these extremes there is an area in which it is helpful to look not just at the source of the power but at the nature of the power. If the body in question is exercising public law functions, or if the exercise of its functions have public law consequences, then that may . . . be sufficient to bring the body within the reach of judicial review. It may be said that to refer to "public law" in this context is to beg the question. But I do not think it does. The essential distinction, which runs through all the cases to which we referred, is between a domestic or private tribunal on the one hand and a body of persons who are under some public duty on the other . . . So I would reject [counsel's] argument that the sole test whether a body is subject to judicial review is the source of its power. So to hold would in my judgment impose an artificial limit on the developing law of judicial review . . .

I now turn to the second of [counsel's] two arguments under this head. He submits that there has never been a case when the source of the power has been other than statutory or under the prerogative. There is a certain imprecision in the use of the term "prerogative" in this connection, as Professor Sir William Wade makes clear [at] (1985) 101 LQR 180. Strictly the term "prerogative" should be confined to those powers which are unique to the Crown. As Professor Wade pointed out, there was nothing unique in the creation by the government, out of funds, voted by Parliament, of a scheme for the compensation of victims of violent crime. Any foundation or trust, given sufficient money, could have done the same thing. Nor do I think that the distinction between the Criminal Injuries Compensation Board and a private foundation or trust for the same purposes lies in the source of the funds. The distinction must lie in the nature of the duty imposed, whether expressly or by implication. If the duty is a public duty, then the body in question is subject to public law.

So once again one comes back to what I regard as the true view, that it is not just the source of the power that matters, but also the nature of the duty. I can see nothing in R v Criminal Injuries Compensation Board, ex parte Lain which contradicts that view, or compels us to decide that, in non-statutory cases, judicial review is confined to bodies created under the prerogative, whether in the strict sense, or in the wider sense in which that word has now come to be used . . .

But suppose I am wrong: suppose that the courts are indeed confined to looking at the source of the power, as [counsel] submits. Then I would accept [the submission] that the source of the power in the present case is indeed governmental, at least in part. [Counsel] argued that, so far from the source of the power being governmental, this is a case where the government has deliberately abstained from exercising power. I do not take that view. I agree . . . that there has here been an implied devolution of power. Power exercised behind the scenes is power nonetheless. The express powers conferred on inferior tribunals were of critical importance in the early days when the sole or main ground for intervention by the courts was that the inferior tribunal had exceeded its powers. But those days are long since past. Having regard to the way in which the Panel came to be established, the fact that the Governor of the Bank of England appoints both the chairman and the deputy chairman, and the other matters to which Sir John Donaldson MR has referred, I am persuaded that the Panel was established "under authority of the Government," to use the language of

Diplock LJ in *Lain*'s case. If in addition to looking at the source of power we are entitled to look at the nature of the power, as I believe we are, then the case is all the stronger . . .'

Comment

(1)   In *Gillick* v *West Norfolk and Wisbech Area Health Authority* Lords Fraser and Scarman considered, *obiter*, that judicial review extends to guidance circulars issued by a Department without specific authority.

(2)   The cumulative effect of *ex parte Lain*, *GCHQ* and *Datafin* is to concentrate upon the nature of the power and action of which review is sought, not its source. Provided the matter can be regarded as having, in the context of the particular case, a public law element, then judicial review is potentially available. The 'governmental' test is descriptive rather than analytical, and not altogether helpful. The criteria adopted by Lord Diplock in *GCHQ* (see p.289) are useful pointers to the availability of judicial review. In *R* v *Norfolk CC, ex parte M* Waite J held that the placing of a parent's name upon the children 'at risk' register was susceptible to judicial review because of the disadvantageous consequences it would have on the individual.

(3)   The 'governmental' approach may be contrasted with that taken in *Foster* v *British Gas* as to what is an organ of the state for the purposes of the doctrine of direct effects. See p.122.

(4)   A public law element will not arise simply because the actions are taken by a public body. Where there is the exercise of a statutory or prerogative power, then that public element will generally be present; see, for example, *Ridge* v *Baldwin* (p.323); *Wheeler* v *Leicester City Council* (p.310). The principle is not always easy to apply.

In *R* v *East Berkshire Health Authority, ex parte Walsh*, W was a senior nursing officer employed by a health authority under a contract which incorporated the Whitley Council Agreement arrived at pursuant to statute. W was dismissed for misconduct, and sought judicial review for breach of natural justice. The Court of Appeal allowed the appeal by the authority against a ruling permitting W to proceed under o.53, rather than in private law, because no public law right was being affected. A distinction had to be drawn between infringement of statutory provisions, which would give rise to public law rights, and infringement of a contract of employment, which was a private law matter. By contrast, in *R* v *Secretary of State for Home Department, ex parte Benwell* B was dismissed from his employment as a prison officer for breaches of discipline contrary to a Code which derived its authority from statute. B alleged that there were grounds for judicial review based upon irrelevant considerations and breach of natural justice. The Court of Appeal held that the action had rightly been brought under o.53. The public law element arose from the performance by the Secretary of State of a function pursuant to the statutory terms. The question was not the breach of contractual provisions (cf. *Walsh*) but the exercise of disciplinary functions pursuant to statute.

(5) The 'governmental' test leaves open for judicial consideration the extent to which the Courts will involve themselves in judicial review of contract-making powers. Cases such as *R v Wear Valley DC, ex parte Binks* (termination of tenancy at an informal market) can now be seen in reality as the use of the contract power as a regulatory tool, and thus governmental. See also *R v Lewisham LBC, ex parte Shell UK*, p.313. Although a public law element has in part been created by the Local Government Act 1988, this will not always apply, and the public/private law distinction may be decisive in determining whether an aggrieved person has a legal remedy. See also *R v Somerset CC, ex parte Fewings* (p.314).

As these cases show, particular problems arise in the employment context. See the discussion in *McLaren v Home Office* (p.234).

R v Disciplinary Committee of the Jockey Club, ex parte Aga Khan

[1993] 1 WLR 909 · Court of Appeal

The applicant sought to challenge the actions of the Jockey Club by means of judicial review. The Court of Appeal held that this was not permissible, the Jockey Club not being a public body.

Sir Thomas Bingham MR: 'We were referred to a considerable body of authority relied on as relevant in determining the scope of judicial review and identifying the bodies and decisions which are susceptible to judicial review . . .

In *R v Criminal Injuries Compensation Board, ex parte Lain* Lord Parker CJ . . . made certain general observations which have been much quoted since and are of undoubted authority. He said:

> The position as I see it is that the exact limits of the ancient remedy by way of certiorari have never been, and ought not to be, specifically defined. They have varied from time to time, being extended to meet changing conditions. At one time the writ only went to an inferior court. Later its ambit was extended to statutory tribunals determining a lis *inter partes*. Later again it extended to cases where there was no lis in the strict sense of the word, but where immediate or subsequent rights of a citizen were affected. The only constant limits throughout were that the body concerned was under a duty to act judicially and that it was performing a public duty. Private or domestic tribunals have always been outside the scope of certiorari since their authority is derived solely from contract, that is from the agreement of the parties concerned . . . We have, as it seems to me, reached the position when the ambit of certiorari can be said to cover every case in which a body of persons, of a public as opposed to a purely private or domestic character, has to determine matters affecting subjects provided always that it has a duty to act judicially. Looked at in this way the board in my judgment comes fairly and squarely within the jurisdiction of this court. The board are, as counsel

for the board said, 'a servant of the Crown charged by the Crown, by executive instruction, with the duty of distributing the bounty of the Crown'. The board are clearly, therefore, performing public duties.

Diplock LJ pointed out that the board's performance of quasi-judicial functions as an inferior tribunal:

> is not derived from any agreement between Crown and applicants but from instructions by the executive government, that is, by prerogative act of the Crown. The appointment of the board and the conferring on the board of jurisdiction to entertain and determine applications, and of authority to make payments in accordance with such determinations, are acts of government, done without statutory authority but nonetheless lawful for that.

Thus the court declined to set firm bounds to the grant of public law remedies, but did not extend them beyond acts of government performed by a creature of executive government.

In *Law v National Greyhound Racing Club Ltd* the plaintiff was a trainer whose licence had been suspended because he had had charge of a greyhound which had been found on examination to have prohibited substances in its tissues. He had issued an originating summons seeking a declaration that the stewards' decision was void and *ultra vires* because reached in breach of an implied duty of fairness and an injunction or damages. The National Greyhound Racing Club (the NGRC) moved to strike out the plaintiff's action on the ground that he should have sought judicial review under s.31 of the Supreme Court Act 1981. This contention was rejected . . . at first instance and by the Court of Appeal . . .

The crux of Lawton LJ's judgment is to be found in this passage:

> In my judgment, such powers as the stewards had to suspend the plaintiff's licence were derived from a contract between him and the defendants. This was so for all who took part in greyhound racing in stadiums licensed by the defendants. A stewards' inquiry under the defendants' rules of racing concerned only those who voluntarily submitted themselves to the stewards' jurisdiction. There was no public element in the jurisdiction itself. Its exercise, however, could have consequences from which the public benefited, as for example by the stamping out of malpractices, and from which individuals might have their rights restricted by, for example, being prevented from employing a trainer whose licence has been suspended. Consequences affecting the public generally can flow from the decisions of many domestic tribunals. In the past the courts have always refused to use the order of certiorari to review the decisions of domestic tribunals.

He then quoted from Lord Parker's judgment in *ex parte Lain* and held that s.31 had regulated the court's procedure in judicial review and not extended its scope.

[Sir Thomas Bingham cited similar dicta from Fox LJ and Slade LJ, and continued:]

The parallel between the Jockey Club and the NGRC is not exact. The former is incorporated by royal charter, the latter is a company limited by guarantee. The NGRC's effective monopoly is territorially more limited than that of the Jockey Club.

Its history is shorter and less glamorous. The industry it regulates is smaller and, some would feel, more dispensable. But the two bodies, within their respective spheres, exercise much the same powers in much the same way. The NGRC's rules of racing plainly owe much to those of the Jockey Club. If the NGRC's contentions were rightly rejected in *Law* v *National Greyhound Racing Club Ltd* for the reasons given, the applicant's contentions could not without anomaly be upheld on this appeal, unless the bounds of judicial review have been significantly extended in the years since that case was decided.

In arguing that such extension has indeed occurred, the applicant relies principally on *R v Panel on Takeovers and Mergers, ex parte Datafin plc (Norton Opax plc intervening)* . . .

[Sir Thomas Bingham cited the facts, and extensive passages from the judgments of Sir John Donaldson MR and Lloyd LJ (as to which, see p.224), and continued:]

The effect of this decision was to extend judicial review to a body whose birth and constitution owed nothing to any exercise of governmental power but which had been woven into the fabric of public regulation in the field of takeovers and mergers. *R v Advertising Standards Authority Ltd, ex parte Insurance Service plc* appears to me to be precise application of the principle thus established to analogous facts.

Mention should be made of two cases, both in the Divisional Court and both involving the Jockey Club. The earlier of the two was *R v Disciplinary Committee of the Jockey Club, ex parte Massingberd-Mundy*. In this case the applicant sought judicial review of a decision that his name be removed from the list of those qualified to act as chairman of a panel of local stewards. The Jockey Club challenged the jurisdiction of the court to grant judicial review. Neill LJ observed that if the matter were free from authority he might have been disposed to conclude that some decisions at any rate of the Jockey Club were capable of being judicially reviewed, but found it impossible to distinguish the binding authority of *Law* v *National Greyhound Racing Club Ltd*. Roch J, with some difference of emphasis, reached the same decision. The case may be distinguished from the present on two grounds. First, it does not appear (although this may not be entirely clear) that there was any contract between the applicant and the Jockey Club. Secondly, the question whether the applicant or some other local steward should act as chairman may fairly be seen as a domestic question lacking public significance and involving no exercise of power which could be seen as affecting the public.

The later decision was *R v Jockey Club, ex parte RAM Racecourses Ltd*. In that case the applicant for judicial review was a racecourse management which sought to challenge the Jockey Club's allocation of racing fixtures. The Jockey Club again challenged the court's jurisdiction to grant judicial review. On this issue Stuart-Smith LJ, being unconvinced that the court's decision in *ex parte Massingberd-Mundy* was wrong, felt bound to follow it although adding that he would but for that authority have held that the Jockey Club were amenable to judicial review. Simon Brown J held himself similarly bound to follow *ex parte Massingberd-Mundy*, but in doing so expressed some criticism of the wider grounds of that decision. He thought it possible to distinguish *Law*, in which the applicant had been bound to the club by contract, particularly in the light of *Datafin*. In the course of his judgment he said:

I find myself, I confess, much attracted by [counsel for the applicant's] submissions that the nature of the power being exercised by the Jockey Club in discharging its functions of regulating racecourses and allocating fixtures is strikingly akin to the exercise of a statutory licensing power. I have no difficulty in regarding this function as one of a public law body, giving rise to public law consequences. On any view it seems to have strikingly close affinities with those sorts of decision-making that commonly *are* accepted as reviewable by the courts. And at the same time I certainly cannot identify this particular exercise of power with that of an arbitrator or other domestic body such as would clearly be outside the supervisory jurisdiction.' [My emphasis.]

But he concluded:

Plainly the Jockey Club for the most part take decisions which affect only – or at least essentially – those voluntarily and willingly subscribing to their rules and procedures. The wider public have no interest in all this, certainly not sufficient to make such decisions reviewable. But just occasionally, as when exercising the quasi-licensing power here under challenge, I for my part would regard the Jockey Club as subject to review.

In that case, as in *ex parte Massingberd-Mundy*, but unlike *Law* and the present case, there was no contract between the applicant and the club.

In *R v Football Association Ltd, ex parte Football League Ltd* Rose J had to consider the susceptibility of the Football Association to judicial review. Having reviewed the authorities (including some not touched on here) at some length, the learned judge gave reasons based both on principle and pragmatism for rejecting the application:

I have crossed a great deal of ground in order to reach what, on the authorities, is the clear and inescapable conclusion for me that the FA is not a body susceptible to judicial review either in general or, more particularly, at the instigation of the League, with whom it is contractually bound. Despite its virtually monopolistic powers and the importance of its decisions to many members of the public who are not contractually bound to it, it is, in my judgment, a domestic body whose powers arise from and duties exist in private law only. I find no sign of underpinning directly or indirectly by any organ or agency of the state or any potential government interest, as Simon Brown J put it in *R v Chief Rabbi of the United Hebrew Congregations of GB and the Commonwealth, ex parte Wachmann* nor is there any evidence to suggest that if the FA did not exist the state would intervene to create a public body to perform its functions. On the contrary, the evidence of commercial interest in the professional game is such as to suggest that a far more likely intervener to run football would be a television or similar company rooted in the entertainment business or a commercial company seeking advertising benefits such as presently provides sponsorship in one form or another. I do not find this conclusion unwelcome. Although thousands play and millions watch football, although it excites passions and divides families, and although millions of pounds are spent by spectators, sponsors, television companies and also clubs on salaries, wages, transfer fees and the maintenance of grounds, much the same can also be said in relation to cricket, golf, tennis, racing and other sports. But they are all essentially forms of popular recreation and entertainment and they are all susceptible to control by the courts in a variety of ways. This does not, of itself, exempt their governing bodies from control by judicial review. Each case will turn on the particular circumstances. But, for my part, to apply to the governing body of football, on the basis that it is a public body, principles honed for the control of the abuse of power by government and its creatures would involve what, in today's fashionable parlance, would be called a quantum leap. It would also, in my view, for what it is worth, be a misapplication of increasingly scarce judicial resources. It will become impossible to provide a swift remedy, which is one of the conspicuous hallmarks of judicial review, if the courts become even more swamped with such applications than they are already. This is not, of course, a jurisprudential reason for refusing judicial review, but it will be cold comfort to the seven or eight other substantive applicants and the many more *ex parte* applicants who have had to be displaced from the court's lists in order to accommodate the present litigation to learn that, though they may have a remedy for their complaints about the arbitrary abuse of executive power, it cannot be granted to them yet.

Conclusions

I have little hesitation in accepting the applicant's contention that the Jockey Club effectively regulates a significant national activity, exercising powers which affect the public and are exercised in the interest of the public. I am willing to accept that if the Jockey Club did not regulate this activity the government would probably be driven to create a public body to do so.

But the Jockey Club is not in its origin, its history, its constitution or (least of all) its membership a public body. While the grant of a royal charter was no doubt a mark of official approval, this did not in any way alter its essential nature, functions or standing. Statute provides for its representation on the Horseracing Betting Levy Board, no doubt as a body with an obvious interest in racing, but it has otherwise escaped mention in the statute book. It has not been woven into any system of governmental control of horse racing, perhaps because it has itself controlled horse racing so successfully that there has been no need for any such governmental system and such does not therefore exist. This has the result that while the Jockey Club's powers may be described as, in many ways, public they are in no sense governmental. The discretion conferred by s.31(6) of the Supreme Court Act 1981 to refuse the grant of leave or relief where the applicant has been guilty of delay which would be prejudicial to good administration can scarcely have been envisaged as applicable in a case such as this.

I would accept that those who agree to be bound by the Rules of Racing have no effective alternative to doing so if they want to take part in racing in this country. It also seems likely to me that if, instead of Rules of Racing administered by the Jockey Club, there were a statutory code administered by a public body, the rights and obligations conferred and imposed by the code would probably approximate to those conferred and imposed by the Rules of Racing. But this does not, as it seems to me, alter the fact, however anomalous it may be, that the powers which the Jockey Club exercises over those who (like the applicant) agree to be bound by the Rules of Racing derive from the agreement of the parties and give rise to private rights on which effective action for a declaration, an injunction and damages can be based without resort to judicial review. It would in my opinion be contrary to sound and long-standing principle to extend the remedy of judicial review to such a case.

It is unnecessary for purposes of this appeal to decide whether decisions of the Jockey Club may ever in any circumstances be challenged by judicial review and I do not do so. Cases where the applicant or plaintiff has no contract on which to rely may raise different considerations and the existence or non-existence of alternative remedies may then be material. I think it better that this court should defer detailed consideration of such a case until it arises. I am, however, satisfied that on the facts of this case the appeal should be dismissed.'

Comment

(1)   Farquharson and Hoffman LJJ delivered concurring judgments, although some differences in emphasis exist. The key features in *Aga Khan* were: (a) the lack of integration into a scheme of public regulation (Bingham, Hoffman LJJ); (b) the fact that the Club was not a 'surrogate organ of government' (Hoffman LJ); (c) the fact that its powers derived from consent, and that effective private law remedies existed (Bingham, Farquharson LJJ). Note also that in *Datafin* it was said that no single factor was determinative of jurisdiction.

(2)   In *R v Code of Practice Committee of the British Pharmaceutical Industry, ex parte Professional Counselling Aids Ltd*, the court concluded that the decisions of the committee fell within the *Datafin* principle and therefore were susceptible to judicial review. The Committee was responsible for the Code of Practice, designed to secure standards of conduct in the marketing of medical products. The Code was drawn up in conjunction with the British Medical Association and the Department of Health. Popplewell J followed *Datafin* with reluctance:

firstly because the extension of the law in *Datafin* seems to me to be likely to enlarge enormously the scope of those who are subject to judicial review with the consequential swamping of the courts in what are essentially domestic issues, and an imposition on domestic bodies of a standard and code of conduct which it was never intended they should have. Secondly, the test which existed before *Datafin* was, if not entirely clear, a great deal clearer than the law is now.

See also the criticisms of Sir William Wade, cited by Popplewell J.

(3)   In the *Advertising Standards Authority* case referred to, the actions of the authority in regulating (under a voluntary Code) the content of advertisements were held to be governmental, and thus susceptible to judicial review. By contrast, in *R v Insurance Ombudsman Bureau, ex parte Aegon Life Assurance Ltd*, the actions of the Insurance Ombudsman were held not susceptible to judicial review. The Ombudsman only had jurisdiction over those who agree to be members, and provides what is, in effect, an alternative forum for the resolution of disputes. The public do not have to use the Insurance Ombudsman, and can bring their complaints before the courts. The Divisional Court also observed that the fact that the body whose actions are the subject of challenge was created by another body which was governmental in nature does not inevitably create susceptibility to judicial review.

McClaren v Home Office

[1990] ICR 824 · Court of Appeal

The plaintiff appealed against a ruling at first instance that his claim should be struck out as disclosing no arguable private law claim. The plaintiff was a prison officer, and was claiming the existence of a contractual relationship of employment which would allow a claim to recover salary that had been withheld to succeed. His appeal was allowed, the Court of Appeal accepting that it was arguable that the relationship between the plaintiff and Home Office was contractual, and that the issues raised were private law as opposed to public law matters.

Woolf LJ: 'There are two issues on this appeal. (1) Is the plaintiff required to bring his claim against the Home Office by way of judicial review? (2) If he is not required to bring his proceedings by way of judicial review has he a reasonable cause of action or was his claim correctly struck out as being clearly unsustainable?

In resolving [the first issue] the following principles have to be borne in mind:

(1)   In relation to his personal claims against an employer, an employee of a public body is normally in exactly the same situation as other employees. If he has a cause of action and he wishes to assert or establish his rights in relation to his employment he can bring proceedings for damages, a declaration or an injunction (except in relation to the Crown) in the High Court or the county court in the ordinary way. The fact that a person is employed by the Crown may limit his rights against the Crown but otherwise his position is very much the same as any other employee. However, he may, instead of having an ordinary master and servant relationship with the Crown, hold office under the Crown and may have been appointed to that office as a result of the Crown exercising a prerogative power or, as in this case, a statutory power. If he holds such an appointment then it will almost invariably be terminable at will and may be subjected to other limitations, but whatever rights the employee has will be enforceable normally by an ordinary action. Not only will it not be necessary for him to seek relief by way of judicial review, it will normally be inappropriate for him to do so: see *Kodeeswaran* v *Attorney-General of Ceylon, R* v *East Berkshire Health Authority, ex parte Walsh* and *R* v *Derbyshire County Council, ex parte Noble.*

(2)   There can however be situations where an employee of a public body can seek judicial review and obtain a remedy which would not be available to an employee in the private sector. This will arise where there exists some disciplinary or other body established under the prerogative or by statute to which the employer or the employee is entitled or required to refer disputes affecting their relationship. The procedure of judicial review can then be appropriate because it has always been part of the role of the court in public law proceedings to supervise inferior tribunals and the court in reviewing disciplinary proceedings is performing a similar role. As long as the "tribunal" or other body has a sufficient public law element, which it almost invariably will have if the employer is the Crown, and it is not domestic or wholly informal, its proceedings and determination can be appropriate subjects for judicial review. An example is provided here by the decision of the Divisional Court in *R* v *Civil Service Appeal Board, ex parte Bruce.* If there had not been available the more effective alternative remedy before an industrial tribunal, the Divisional Court would have

regarded the decision of the Civil Service Appeal Board in that case as reviewable upon judicial review. The decision of this court which has just been given in *R* v *Secretary of State for the Home Department, ex parte Attard*, is another example of the same situation. There what was being considered by this court were the powers of a prison governor in connection with disciplinary proceedings in respect of prison officers. The prison governor's disciplinary powers in relation to prisoners are reviewable only on judicial review (see *Leech* v *Deputy Governor of Parkhurst Prison*) and they can also be reviewed on judicial review where they affect a prison officer on the application of that officer.

(3)   In addition if an employee of the Crown or other body is adversely affected by a decision of general application by his employer, but he contends that that decision is flawed on what I loosely describe as *Wednesbury* grounds (*Associated Provincial Picture Houses Ltd* v *Wednesbury Corporation*), he can be entitled to challenge that decision by way of judicial review. Within this category comes *Council of Civil Service Unions* v *Minister for the Civil Service*.

In the House of Lords there was no dispute as to whether the case was appropriately brought by way of judicial review. The House of Lords assumed that it was and I would respectfully suggest that they were right to do so. The decision under challenge was one affecting employees at GCHQ generally. The action which was being challenged was the instruction by the Minister for the Civil Service in the interests of national security to vary the terms and conditions of service of the staff so that they would no longer be permitted to belong to trade unions. Although the decision affected individual members of the staff, it was a decision which was taken as a matter of policy, not in relation to a particular member of staff, but in relation to staff in general and so it could be the subject of judicial review.

(4)   There can be situations where although there are procedures which are applicable they are of a purely domestic nature and therefore, albeit that their decisions might affect the public, the process of judicial review will not be available. However, this does not mean that a particular employee who is adversely affected by those disciplinary proceedings will not have a remedy. The existence of the disciplinary proceedings may be highly material to indicate that the category of employee concerned, unlike an ordinary employee, is not limited to a claim for damages but can in the appropriate circumstances in an ordinary action seek a declaration or an injunction to ensure that the proceedings are conducted fairly. (As to dismissal see *Ridge* v *Baldwin, per* Lord Reid and *Law* v *National Greyhound Racing Club Ltd* and *R* v *British Broadcasting Corporation, ex parte Lavelle*.)

In giving his judgment in this case, Hoffman J . . . was of the view that there was no "arguable distinction between the facts of this case and those of Mr Bruce" – referring to *R* v *Civil Services Appeal Board, ex parte Bruce* – I disagree. In this case, unlike *ex parte Bruce*, which falls within the second category, the plaintiff is not making any complaint about disciplinary proceedings. He is seeking declarations as to the terms of his employment and a sum which he alleges is due for services rendered. If those claims have any merit they fall within the first category set out above. They are private law claims which require private rights to support them. Counsel for the plaintiff firmly disavowed any suggestion that any public law claim is being advanced by the plaintiff. Whether or not he is an employee of the Crown or has a contract of service, or holds an office under the Crown, he is entitled to bring private law proceedings if he has reasonable grounds for contending that his private law rights have been infringed. As his claim is pleaded . . . it is entirely unsuited to judicial review. Unlike continental jurisdictions in which there is a Conseil d'Etat, claims of the kind which are made by the plaintiff have to be brought by ordinary civil proceedings unless they are subsidiary to other public law claims, in which case it may be possible for them now to be disposed of in the same proceedings on an application for judicial review. The first issue must therefore be resolved in favour of the plaintiff.'

Comment

(1)   In relation to the second point, Woolf LJ considered the fact that the plaintiff was dismissible at pleasure did not mean that he did not have a private law right in relation to other matters. For the position of civil servants, see *R* v *Civil Service Appeal Board, ex parte Bruce*, where no contract of employment was held to exist, the public law element coming from the nature of the tribunal dealing with the disciplinary proceedings (see p.220). On the contractual point, *ex parte Bruce* was not followed by the Court of Appeal in *R* v *Lord Chancellor's Department, ex parte Nangle*. In that case the relationship between an individual employed as a clerical officer in the Civil Service and the Crown was held to have all the incidents of a contract of employment. The relationship between himself and the Crown was intended to create legal relations, the parties intending to be governed by private not public law. For that reason, internal disciplinary proceedings were not susceptible to judicial review. Alternatively, the court considered the position if it were wrong on the contractual point. In those circumstances, no public law element would exist. The fact that no private law remedy existed did not mean that public law challenge was permissible. The proceedings were of an internal or domestic nature, not raising public law issues.

(2)   In *R* v *British Coal Corporation and Secretary for Trade and Industry, ex parte Vardy* successful challenge was made to a decision by British Coal to close 31 collieries, despite earlier authority which stated that pit closures were not amenable to judicial review (*R* v *NCB, ex parte NUM*). British Coal was subject to a statutory requirement to consult employees, which they had not done. The court also stated, following *McLaren*, that judicial review will obtain in respect of an employee where there exists some disciplinary or other body to which the employer or employee is entitled or required to refer disputes concerning their relationship. In this case such procedures existed in the form of an Independent Review Board.

11 Procedure for judicial review

Supreme Court Act 1981

31 (1) An application to the High Court for one or more of the following forms of relief, namely –
   (a) an order of mandamus, prohibition or *certiorari* ;
   (b) a declaration or injunction under subsection (2); or
   (c) an injunction under section 30 restraining a person not entitled to do so from acting in an office to which that section applies,
   shall be made in accordance with rules of court by a procedure to be known as an application for judicial review.

   (2) A declaration may be made or an injunction granted under this subsection in any case where an application for judicial review, seeking that relief, has been made and the High Court considers that, having regard to–
   (a) the nature of the matters in respect of which relief may be granted by orders of mandamus, prohibition or *certiorari* ;
   (b) the nature of the persons and bodies against whom relief may be granted by such orders; and
   (c) all the circumstances of the case,
   it would be just and convenient for the declaration to be made or the injunction to be granted, as the case may be.

   (3) No application for judicial review shall be made unless the leave of the High Court has been obtained in accordance with rules of court; and the court shall not grant leave to make such an application unless it considers that the applicant has a sufficient interest in the matter to which the application relates.

   (4) On an application for judicial review the High Court may award damages to the applicant if –
   (a) he has joined with his application a claim for damages arising from any matter to which the application relates; and
   (b) the court is satisfied that, if the claim had been made in an action begun by the applicant at the time of making his application, he would have been awarded damages.

   (5) If, on an application for judicial review seeking an order of *certiorari*, the High Court quashes the decision to which the application relates, the High Court may remit the matter to the court, tribunal or authority concerned, with a direction to reconsider it and reach a decision in accordance with the findings of the High Court.

(6) Where the High Court considers that there has been undue delay in making an application for judicial review, the court may refuse to grant –
  (a) leave for the making of the application; or
  (b) any relief sought on the application,
  if it considers that the granting of the relief sought would be likely to cause substantial hardship to, or substantially prejudice the rights of, any person or would be detrimental to good administration.

(7) Subsection (6) is without prejudice to any enactment or rule of court which has the effect of limiting the time within which an application for judicial review may be made.

Comment

Section 31 is supplemented by the detailed provisions of the revised RSC, o.53.

O'Reilly v Mackman

[1983] 2 AC 237 · House of Lords

In actions commenced by writs and summons, four plaintiffs were alleging that the prison visitors of Hull Prison had acted contrary to the Prison Rules, and in breach of the principles of natural justice. The defendant had at first instance applied to have the action struck out as an abuse of process, arguing that such action could only be undertaken by way of judicial review under RSC, o.53. This application was unsuccessful, but the defendant appealed successfully to the Court of Appeal. The plaintiff's appeal to the House of Lords was dismissed. As a general rule actions by a public body affecting public law matters should be commenced by judicial review under o.53.

Lord Diplock: '... In *Ridge* v *Baldwin* ... Lord Reid said "We do not have a developed system of administrative law – perhaps because until fairly recently we did not need it." By 1977 the need had continued to grow apace and this reproach to English law had been removed. We did have by then a developed system of administrative law, to the development of which Lord Reid himself, by his speeches in cases which reached this House, had made an outstanding contribution. To the landmark cases of *Ridge* v *Baldwin* and *Anisminic Ltd* v *Foreign Compensation Commission* I would add a third, *Padfield* v *Minister of Agriculture, Fisheries and Food* ...

Although the availability of the remedy of orders to quash a decision by *certiorari* had in theory been widely extended by these developments, the procedural disadvantages under which applicants for this remedy laboured remained substantially unchanged until the alteration of o.53 in 1977. Foremost among these was the absence of any provision for discovery. In the case of a decision which did not state the reasons for it, it was not possible to challenge its validity for error of law in the reasoning by which the decision had been reached. If it had been an application for *certiorari* those who were the plaintiffs in the *Anisminic* case would have failed; it was only because by pursuing an action by writ for a declaration of nullity that the plaintiffs were entitled to the discovery by which the minute of the commission's reasons which showed that they had asked themselves the wrong question, was obtained. Again under o.53 evidence was required to be on affidavit. This in itself is not an unjust disadvantage; it is a common feature of many forms of procedure in the High Court, including originating summonses; but in the absence of any express provision for cross-examination of deponents, as your Lordships who are familiar with the pre-1977 procedure will be aware, even applications for leave to cross-examine were virtually unknown . . .

On the other hand as compared with an action for a declaration commenced by writ or originating summons, the procedure under o.53 both before and after 1977 provided for the respondent decision-making statutory tribunal or public authority against which the remedy of *certiorari* was sought protection against claims which it was not in the public interest for courts of justice to entertain.

First, leave to apply for the order was required. The application for leave which was *ex parte* but could be, and in practice often was, adjourned in order to enable the proposed respondent to be represented, had to be supported by a statement setting out, *inter alia*, the grounds on which the relief was sought and by affidavits verifying the facts relied on: so that a knowingly false statement of fact would amount to the criminal offence of perjury. Such affidavit was also required to satisfy the requirement of *uberrima fides*, with the consequence that failure to make on oath a full and candid disclosure of material facts was of itself a ground for refusing the relief sought in the substantive application for which leave had been obtained on the strength of the affidavit. This was an important safeguard, which is preserved in the new o.53 of 1977. The public interest in good administration requires that public authorities and third parties should not be kept in suspense as to the legal validity of a decision the authority has reached in purported exercise of decision-making powers for any longer period than is absolutely necessary in fairness to the person affected by the decision. In contrast, allegations made in a statement of claim or an endorsement of an originating summons are not on oath, so the requirement of a prior application for leave to be supported by full and candid affidavits verifying the facts relied on is an important safeguard against groundless or unmeritorious claims that a particular decision is a nullity. There was also power in the court on granting leave to impose terms as to costs or security.

Furthermore, as o.53 was applied in practice, as soon as the application for leave had been made it provided a very speedy means, available in urgent cases within a matter of days rather than months, for determining whether a disputed decision was valid in law or not. A reduction of the period of suspense was also effected by the requirement that leave to apply for *certiorari* to quash a decision must be made within a limited period after the impugned decision was made, unless delay beyond that limited period was accounted for to the satisfaction of the judge. The period was six months under the pre-1977 o.53; under the current o.53 it is further reduced to three months . . . the exclusion of all right to discovery in application for *certiorari* under o.53, particularly before the passing of the Tribunal and Inquiries Act 1958, was calculated to cause injustice to persons who had no means, if they adopted that procedure, of ascertaining whether a public body, which had made a decision adversely affecting them, had done so for reasons which were wrong in law and rendered their decision invalid. It will be within the knowledge of all of your Lordships that, at any rate from the 1950s onwards, actions for declarations of nullity of decisions affecting the rights of individuals under public law were widely entertained, in parallel to applications for *certiorari* to quash, as means of obtaining an effective alternative remedy . . .

Nevertheless I accept that having regard to disadvantages, particularly in relation to the absolute bar upon compelling discovery of documents by the respondent public authority to an applicant for an order of *certiorari*, and the almost invariable practice of refusing leave to allow cross-examination of deponents to affidavits lodged on its behalf, it could not be regarded as an abuse of the process of the court, before the amendments made to o.53 in 1977, to proceed against the authority by an action for a declaration of nullity of the impugned decision with an injunction to prevent the authority from acting on it, instead of applying for an order of *certiorari*; and this despite the fact that, by adopting this course, the plaintiff evaded the safeguards imposed in the public interest against groundless, unmeritorious or tardy attacks upon the validity of decisions made by public authorities in the field of public law.

Those disadvantages, which formerly might have resulted in an applicant's being unable to obtain justice in an application for *certiorari* under o.53, have all been removed by the new o.53 introduced in 1977. There is express provision in the new rule 8 for interlocutory applications for discovery of documents, the administration of interrogatories and the cross-examination of deponents to affidavits. Discovery of documents (which may often be a time-consuming process) is not automatic as in an action begun by writ, but . . . discovery is obtainable upon application whenever, and to the extent that, the justice of the case requires; similarly o.26 applies to applications for interrogatories; and to applications for cross-examination of deponents to affidavits o.28 r.2(3) applies. This is the rule that deals with evidence in actions begun by originating summons and permits oral cross-examination on affidavit evidence wherever the justice of the case requires. It may well be that for the reasons given by Lord Denning MR in *George* v *Secretary of State for the Environment*, it will only be upon rare occasions that the interest of justice will require that leave be given for cross-examination of deponents on their affidavits in applications for judicial review. This is because of the nature of the issues that normally arise upon judicial review. The facts, except where the claim that a decision was invalid on the ground that the statutory tribunal or public authority that made the decision failed to comply with the procedure prescribed by the legislation under which it was acting or failed to observe the fundamental rules of natural justice or fairness, can seldom be a matter of relevant dispute upon an application for judicial review, since the tribunal or authority's findings of fact, as distinguished from the legal consequences of the facts that they have found, are not open to review by the court in the exercise of its supervisory powers [except in limited circumstances] . . . and to allow cross-examination presents the court with a temptation, not always easily resisted, to substitute its own view of the facts for that of the decision-making body upon whom the exclusive jurisdiction to determine facts has been conferred by Parliament. Nevertheless having regard to a possible misunderstanding of what was said by Geoffrey Lane LJ in *R* v *Board of Visitors of Hull Prison, ex parte St Germain (No. 2)* your Lordships may think this an appropriate occasion on which to emphasise that whatever may have been the position before the rule was altered in 1977 in all proceedings for judicial review that have been started since that date the grant of leave to cross-examine deponents upon applications for judicial review is governed by the same principles as it is in actions begun by originating summons; it should be allowed whenever the justice of the particular case so requires.

Another handicap under which an applicant for a prerogative order under o.53 formerly laboured (though it would not have affected the appellants in the instant cases even if they had brought their actions before the 1977 alteration to o.53) was that a claim for damages for breach of a right in private law of the applicant resulting from an invalid decision of a public authority could not be made in an application under o.53. Damages could only be claimed in a separate action begun by writ; whereas in an action so begun they could be claimed as additional relief as well as a declaration of nullity of the decision from which the damage claimed had flowed. Rule 7 of the new o.53 permits the applicant for judicial review to include in the statement in support of his application for leave a claim for damages and empowers the court to award damages on the hearing of the application if satisfied that such damages could have been awarded to him in an action begun by him by writ at the time of the making of the application.

Finally rule 1 of the new o.53 enables an application for a declaration or an injunction to be included in an application for judicial review. This was not previously the case; only prerogative orders could be obtained in proceedings under o.53. Declarations or injunctions were obtainable only in actions begun by writ or originating summons. So a person seeking to challenge a decision had to make a choice of the remedy that he sought at the outset of the proceedings, although when the matter was examined more closely in the course of the proceedings it might appear that he was not entitled to that remedy but would have been entitled to some other remedy available only in the other kind of proceeding. This reform may have lost some of its importance since there have come to be realised that the full consequences of the *Anisminic* case, in introducing the concept that if a statutory decision-making authority asks itself the wrong question it acts without jurisdiction, have been virtually to abolish the distinction between errors within jurisdiction that rendered voidable a decision that remained valid until quashed, and errors that went to jurisdiction and rendered a decision void *ab initio* provided that its validity was challenged timeously in the High Court by an appropriate procedure. Failing such challenge within the applicable time limit, public policy, expressed in the maxim *omnia praesumuntur rite esse acta*, requires that after the expiry of the time limit it should be given all the effects in law of a valid decision. Nevertheless, there may still be cases where it turns out in the course of proceedings to challenge a decision of a statutory authority that a declaration of rights rather than *certiorari* is the appropriate remedy . . .

So o.53 since 1977 has provided a procedure by which every type of remedy for infringement of the rights of individuals that are entitled to protection in public law can be obtained in one and the same proceeding by way of an application for judicial review, and whichever remedy is found to be most appropriate in the light of what has emerged upon the hearing of the application, can be granted to him. If what should emerge is that his complaint is not of an infringement of any of his rights that are entitled to protection in public law, but may be an infringement of his rights in private law and thus not a proper subject for judicial review, the court has power under rule 9(5), instead of refusing the application, to order the proceedings to continue as if they had begun by writ. There is no such converse power under the RSC to permit an action begun by writ to continue as if it were an application for judicial review . . .

My Lords, at the outset of this speech, I drew attention to the fact that the remedy by way of declaration of nullity of the decisions of the board was discretionary – as are all the remedies available upon judicial review. Counsel for the plaintiffs accordingly conceded the fact that by adopting the procedure of an action begun by writ or by originating summons instead of an application for judicial review under o.53 (from which there have now been removed all those disadvantages to applicants that had previously led the courts to countenance actions for declarations and injunctions as an alternative procedure for obtaining a remedy for infringement of the rights of the individual that are entitled to protection in public law only) the plaintiffs had thereby been able to evade those protections against groundless, unmeritorious or tardy harassment that were afforded to statutory tribunals or decision-making public authorities by o.53, and which might have resulted in the summary, and would in any event have resulted in the speedy disposition of the application, is among the matters fit to be taken into consideration by the judge in deciding whether to exercise his discretion by refusing to grant a declaration; but, it was contended, this he may only do at the conclusion of the trial. So to delay the judge's decision as to how to exercise his discretion would defeat the public policy that underlies the grant of those protections: *viz.*, the need, in the interests of good administration and of third parties who may be indirectly affected by the decision, for speedy certainty as to whether it has the effect of a decision that is valid in public law. An action for a declaration or injunction need not be commenced until the very end of the limitation period; if begun by writ, discovery and interlocutory proceedings may be prolonged and the plaintiffs are not required to support their allegations by evidence on oath until the actual trial. The period of uncertainty as to the validity of a decision that has been challenged upon allegations that may eventually turn out to be baseless and unsupported by evidence on oath, may thus be strung out for a very lengthy period, as the actions of the first three appellants in the instant appeals show. Unless such an action can be struck out summarily at the outset as an abuse of the process of the court the whole purpose of the public policy to which the change in o.53 was directed would be defeated . . .

Order 53 does not expressly provide that procedure by application for judicial review shall be the exclusive procedure available by which the remedy of a declaration or injunction may be obtained for infringement of rights that are entitled to protection under public law; nor does section 31 of the Supreme Court Act 1981 . . . I do not think that your Lordships would be wise to use this as an occasion to lay down categories of cases in which it would necessarily always be an abuse to seek in an action begun by writ or originating summons a remedy against infringement of rights of the individual that are entitled to protection in public law.

The position of applicants for judicial review has been drastically ameliorated by the new o.53. It has removed all those disadvantages, particularly in relation to discovery, that were manifestly unfair to them and had, in many cases, made applications for prerogative orders an inadequate remedy if justice was to be done. This it was that justified the courts in not treating as an abuse of their powers resort to an alternative procedure by way of an action for a declaration or injunction (not then obtainable on an application under o.53), despite the fact that this procedure had the effect of depriving the defendants of the protection to statutory tribunals and public authorities for which for public policy reasons o.53 provided.

Now that those disadvantages to applicants have been removed and all remedies for infringements of rights protected by public law can be obtained upon an application for judicial review, as can also remedies for infringements of rights under private law if such infringements should also be involved, it would in my view as a general rule be contrary to public policy, and as such an abuse of the process of the court, to permit a person seeking to establish that a decision of a public authority infringed rights to which he was entitled to protection under public law to proceed by way of an ordinary action and by this means to evade the provisions of o.53 for the protection of such authorities.

My Lords, I have described this as a general rule; for although it may normally be appropriate to apply it by the summary process of striking out the action, there may be exceptions, particularly where the invalidity of the decision arises as a collateral issue in a claim for infringement of a right of the plaintiff arising under private law, or where none of the parties objects to the adoption of the procedure by writ or originating summons. Whether there should be other exceptions should in my view be left to be decided on a case-by-case basis . . .'

Comment

(1) *O'Reilly* determines the normal method of challenge of public law matters, and its principle was applied in *Cocks* v *Thanet DC*. Order 53 is not, though, the exclusive means of challenge: see *Wandsworth LBC* v *Winder* where the appellant Council was seeking possession of a house, for non-payment of rent. The defendant sought to resist the application for possession by showing that the arrears of rent relied upon were based upon rent increases which were, allegedly, *ultra vires* as contrary to *Wednesbury* principles (see p.291). It was held that the respondents were entitled to raise that invalidity as a defence. (For extensive extracts from these cases, see the judgment of Lord Lowry in *Roy* v *Kensington and Chelsea & Westminster FPC*, p.244.)

(2) *Winder* was itself distinguished in *Avon CC* v *Buscott* where a possession order was sought against trespassing gypsies. The local authority was admittedly in breach of its statutory duty to make appropriate provision for gypsies, and in *West Glamorgan CC* v *Rafferty* the Court of Appeal had held that a decision by a local authority to seek to evict squatters could be challenged on the basis that it was *Wednesbury* unreasonable to apply for a possession order whilst in breach of that statutory duty in respect to gypsies. In *Buscott* the defendants alleged that this breach of statutory duty by the council rendered its possession action *ultra vires*. The Court of Appeal rejected that argument: any challenge based on that failure had to be by means of judicial review. Unlike in *Winder*, where the defence was, in effect, that the money was not owed and that therefore possession could not be lawfully sought, here the defendants had no defence on the merits, but simply were arguing that the eviction proceedings should not have been brought. That type of challenge had to be undertaken through the o.53 procedure. In other words, there was no private law issue in *Buscott*. There was in *Winder*: i.e. the individual liability to pay the rent claimed. See also *Waverley BC* v *Hilden*.

(3) For the impact of this decision on the availability of remedies, see *Equal Opportunities Commission* v *Secretary of State for Employment* (p.279); *M* v *Home Office* (p.281).

Roy v *Kensington and Chelsea & Westminster Family Practitioners Committee*

[1992] 2 WLR 239 · House of Lords

Dr Roy (the respondent) commenced by writ an action against the Family Practitioners Committee in respect of payments that were being withheld from him by the Committee. The Committee concluded that R was failing to devote sufficient time to his general practice under the National Health Service. The terms of his employment by the Committee were statutory, and regulations made pursuant to statute dealt with the payment and withholding of fees. The Committee applied to have the action struck out as an abuse of process: the matters raised were public law matters which could only be challenged by judicial review under o.53. This application succeeded, but an appeal to the Court of Appeal was allowed, that court ruling that R had a contract of services with the Committee. The Committee's appeal to the House of Lords was dismissed: private law rights could be enforced by private law action, even if they involved challenge to a public law decision.

Lord Lowry: '. . . [I come back to] the committee's original contention . . . which was that Dr Roy should have proceeded not by action but by an application for judicial review. The authorities relied on were (and still are) *Cocks* v *Thanet District Council* and *O'Reilly* v *Mackman*, two cases heard consecutively by the same appellate committee, in which the judgments were later delivered on the same day.

Cocks v *Thanet District Council* was a case in which the plaintiff had applied to the council, which was the local housing authority, for permanent accommodation. The council provided temporary accommodation. The plaintiff then sued in the county court for a declaration that the council owed, and was in breach of, a duty to house him permanently under the Housing (Homeless Persons) Act 1977. The case was removed into the High Court for determination of the preliminary issue whether the plaintiff was entitled to proceed in the county court or should go by judicial review. The judge held that the plaintiff could proceed in the county court but, on a leapfrog appeal, this House held that he must proceed by judicial review. The leading opinion was delivered by . . . Lord Bridge . . . He said:

> The procedural issue on which the appeal turns will naturally fall for decision in the light of the principles expounded in the speech of my noble and learned friend, Lord Diplock, in *O'Reilly* v *Mackman*, in which judgment has just been delivered. But before attempting to apply those principles, it is necessary to analyse the functions of housing authorities under the Housing (Homeless Persons) Act 1977. These functions fall into two wholly distinct categories. On the one hand, the housing authority are charged with decision-making functions. It is for the housing authority to decide whether they have reason to believe the matters which will give rise to the duty to inquire or to the temporary housing duty. It is for the housing authority, once the duty to inquire has arisen, to make the appropriate inquiries and to decide whether they are satisfied, or not satisfied as the case may be, of the matters which will give rise to the limited housing duty or the full housing duty. These are essentially public law functions. The power of decision being committed by the statute exclusively to the housing authority, their exercise of the power can only be challenged before the courts on the strictly limited grounds (i) that their decision was vitiated by bias or procedural

unfairness; (ii) that they have reached a conclusion of fact which can be impugned on the principles set out in the speech of Lord Radcliffe in *Edwards* v *Bairstow*, or (iii) that, in so far as they have exercised a discretion (as they may require to do in considering questions of reasonableness under section 17(1)(2) and (4)), the exercise can be impugned on the principles set out in the judgment of Lord Greene MR in *Associated Provincial Pictures Houses Ltd* v *Wednesbury Corporation*. All this is trite law and the contrary has, so far as I know, never been argued in any case which has come before the courts under the Act of 1977. On the other hand, the housing authority are charged with executive functions. Once a decision has been reached by the housing authority which gives rise to the temporary, the limited or the full housing duty, rights and obligations are immediately created in the field of private law. Each of the duties referred to, once established, is capable of being enforced by injunction and the breach of it will give rise to a liability in damages. But it is inherent in the scheme of the Act that an appropriate public law decision of the housing authority is a condition precedent to the establishment of the private law duty.

I refer to two further passages in the speech of my noble and learned friend; first:

I have already indicated my agreement with the views of my noble and learned friend, Lord Diplock, as expressed in *O'Reilly* v *Mackman* and I gratefully adopt all his reasons for the conclusion that: "it would . . . as a general rule be contrary to public policy, and as such an abuse of the process of the court, to permit a person seeking to establish that a decision of a public authority infringed rights to which he was entitled to protection under public law to proceed by way of an ordinary action and by this means to evade the provisions of o.53 for the protection of such authorities." Does the same general rule apply, where the decision of the public authority which the litigant wishes to overturn is not one alleged to infringe any existing right but a decision which, being adverse to him, prevents him establishing a necessary condition precedent to the statutory private law right which he seeks to enforce? Any relevant decision of a housing authority under the Act of 1977 which an applicant for accommodation wants to challenge will be of that character. I have no doubt that the same general rule should apply to such a case.

Secondly:

Even though nullification of a public law decision can, if necessary, be achieved by declaration as an alternative to an order of *certiorari*, *certiorari* to quash remains the primary and most appropriate remedy. Now that all public law remedies are available to be sought by the unified and simplified procedure of an application for judicial review, there can be no valid reason, where the quashing of a decision is the sole remedy sought, why it should be sought otherwise than by *certiorari*. But an unsuccessful applicant for accommodation under the Act of 1977, confronted by an adverse decision of the housing authority as to, say, the question of his intentional homelessness, may strictly need not only an order of *certiorari* to quash the adverse decision but also an order of mandamus to the housing authority to determine the question afresh according to law.

[Lord Lowry then cited extensively from *O'Reilly* v *Mackman*, and from the judgment of Sir John Donaldson MR in *An Bord Bainne Co-Operative Ltd* v *Milk Marketing Board* (the *Irish Dairy Board* case). He then continued:

I would further invite your Lordships' attention to the speech of Lord Fraser . . . in *Winder*'s case, where he said:

It would in my opinion be a very strange use of language to describe the respondent's behaviour in relation to this litigation as an abuse or misuse by him of the process of the court. He did not select the procedure to be adopted. He is merely seeking to defend proceedings brought against him by the appellants. In so doing he is seeking only to exercise the ordinary right of any individual to defend an action against him on the ground that he is not liable for the whole sum claimed by the plaintiff. Moreover, he puts forward his defence as a matter of right, whereas in an application for judicial review, success would require an exercise of the court's discretion in his favour. Apart from the provisions of Order 53 and s.31 Supreme Court Act 1981, he would certainly be entitled to defend the action on the ground that the plaintiff's claim arises from a resolution which (on his view) is invalid . . . I find it impossible to accept that the right to challenge the decision of a local authority in course of defending an action for non-payment can have been swept away by Order 53, which was directed to introducing a procedural reform. As my noble and learned friend Lord Scarman said in *R v Inland Revenue Commissioners, ex parte Federation of Self Employed and Small Businesses Ltd* : "The new RSC o.53 is a procedural reform of great importance in the field of public law, but it does not – indeed, cannot – either extend or diminish the substantive law. Its function is limited to ensuring '*ubi jus, ibi remedium.*' " Lord Wilberforce spoke to the same effect . . . Nor, in my opinion, did s.31 Supreme Court Act 1981 which refers only to "an application" for judicial review have the effect of limiting the rights of a defendant *sub silentio*. I would adopt the words of Viscount Simonds in *Pyx Granite Co. Ltd* v *Ministry of Housing and Local Government* as follows: "It is a principle not by any means to be whittled down that the subject's recourse to Her Majesty's courts for the determination of his rights is not to be excluded except by clear words." The argument of the appellants in the present case would be directly in conflict with that observation.

In this passage the contrast drawn between "a matter of right" and "an exercise of the court's discretion" echoes the observation of Sir John Donaldson MR in the *Irish Dairy Board* case. It will also be seen that Lord Fraser of Tullybelton invoked the *Pyx Granite* principle, as he had already done in *Davy* v *Spelthorne Borough Council*, not merely against barring a subject from the courts, but against excluding him from a particular mode of procedure. The observation attributed to Lord Scarman recalls what he had earlier said in *R v Inland Revenue Commissioners, ex parte Rossminster Ltd*:

The application for judicial review is a recent procedural innovation in our law. It is governed by RSC, o.53, r. 2 which was introduced in 1977. The rule made no alteration to the substantive law; nor did it introduce any new remedy.

Indeed, it seems to me that Lord Scarman, had the occasion demanded it, might well have added the words "or abolish any existing remedy." . . .

[Lord Lowry then discussed *McClaren* v *Home Office*, and then moved to consider whether, in the present case, a contractual relationship existed:]

I am not satisfied that there was. *R* v *East Berkshire Health Authority, ex parte Walsh* does not in my view provide a reliable argument in favour of saying that there was a contract in the present case and *Wadi* v *Cornwall and Isles of Scilly Family Practitioner Committee* indicates the contrary. At the same time, I would be foolish to disregard the fact that all the members of a distinguished Court of Appeal held that a contract for services existed between Dr Roy and the committee. It shows, to say the least, that there are "contractual echoes in the relationship", . . . and makes it almost inevitable that the relationship, as was said of that which arose in *Wadi*'s case, gave rise to "rights and obligations" and that Dr Roy's rights were private law rights. I would here observe that the mere fact that the Act and the Regulations constitute a statutory scheme which lays down the doctor's "terms of service" (an expression which has contractual overtones) and creates the relationship between him and the Committee, is not fatal to the idea of a contract, but that relationship did not need to be contractual. Moreover, the discretion which the scheme confers on the Committee is not typically characteristic of a contractual relationship, and the same can be said of the appellate and supervisory role given to the Secretary of State.

But the actual or possible absence of a contract is not decisive against Dr Roy. He has in my opinion a bundle of rights which should be regarded as his individual private law rights against the Committee, arising from the statute and regulations and including the very important private law right to be paid for the work that he has done. As [the judge] said:

> The rights and duties are no less real or effective for the individual practitioner. Private law rights flow from the statutory provisions and are enforceable, as such, in the courts but no contractual relations come into existence.

The judge, however, held that, even if the doctor's rights to full payments under the scheme were contractually based, the Committee's duty was a public law duty and could be challenged only on judicial review. [Counsel for the Committee] admitted that, if the doctor has a contractual right, he could . . . vindicate it by action. But . . . I go further: if Dr Roy has any kind of private law right, even though not contractual, he can sue for its alleged breach.

In this case it has been suggested that Dr Roy could have gone by judicial review, because there is no issue of fact, but that would not always hold good in a similar type of case. And I do not forget that he might have been faced with the argument which succeeded in *ex parte Walsh*. In any event, a successful application by judicial review could not lead directly, as it would in an action, to an order for payment of the full basic practice allowance. Other proceedings would be needed.

An important point is that the court clearly has jurisdiction to entertain the doctor's action. Furthermore, even if one accepts the full rigour of *O'Reilly* v *Mackman*, there is ample room to hold that this case comes within the exceptions allowed for by Lord Diplock. It is concerned with a private law right, it involves a question which could in some circumstances give rise to a dispute of fact and one object of the plaintiff is to obtain an order for the payment (not by way of damages) of an ascertained or ascertainable sum of money. If it is wrong to allow such a claim to be litigated by action, what is to be said of other disputed claims for remuneration? I think it is right to consider the whole spectrum of claims which a doctor might make against the Committee. The existence of any dispute as to entitlement means that he will be alleging a breach of his private law rights through a failure by the Committee to perform their public duty. If the Committee's argument prevails, the doctor must in all these cases go by judicial review, even when the facts are not clear. I scarcely think that this can be the right answer.

My Lords, whether Dr Roy's rights were contractual or statutory, the observations made by the Court of Appeal concerning their enforcement are important.

[Further citation from the Court of Appeal judgments were made. Lord Lowry continued:]

The judgments to which I have referred effectively dispose of an argument pressed by the Committee that Dr Roy had no right to be paid a basic practice allowance until the Committee had carried out their public duty of forming an opinion under paragraph 12.1(b), with the supposed consequence that, until that had happened, the doctor had no private law right which he could enforce. The answer is that Dr Roy had a right to a fair and legally correct consideration of his claim. Failing that, his private law right has been infringed and he can sue the Committee . . .

Dr Roy's printed case contained detailed arguments in favour of a contract between him and the Committee, but before your Lordships [Counsel for Dr Roy] simply argued that the doctor had a private law right, whether contractual or statutory. With regard to *O'Reilly* v *Mackman* he argued in the alternative. The "broad approach" was that the rule in *O'Reilly* v *Mackman* did not apply generally against bringing actions to vindicate private rights in all circumstances in which those actions involved a challenge to a public law act or decision, but that it merely required the aggrieved person to proceed by judicial review only when private law rights were not at stake. The "narrow approach" assumed that the rule applied generally to all proceedings in which public law acts or decisions were challenged, subject to some exceptions when private law rights were involved. There was no need in *O'Reilly* v *Mackman* to choose between these approaches, but it seems clear that Lord Diplock considered himself to be stating a general rule with exceptions. For my part, I much prefer the broad approach, which is both traditionally orthodox and consistent with the *Pyx Granite* principle, as applied in *Davy* v *Spelthorne Borough Council* and in *Wandsworth London Borough Council* v *Winder*. It would also, if adopted, have the practical merit of getting rid of a procedural minefield. I shall, however, be content for the purpose of this appeal to adopt the narrow approach, which avoids the need to discuss the proper scope of the rule, a point which has not been argued before your Lordships and has hitherto been seriously discussed only by the academic writers.

Whichever approach one adopts, the arguments for excluding the present case from the ambit of the rule or, in the alternative, making an exception of it are similar and to my mind convincing:

1. Dr Roy has either a contractual or a statutory private law right to his remuneration in accordance with his statutory terms of service.
2. Although he seeks to enforce performance of a public law duty . . . his private law rights dominate the proceedings.
3. The type of claim and other claims for remuneration (although not this particular claim) may involve disputed issues of fact.

4. The order sought (for the payment of money due) could not be granted on judicial review.
5. The claim is joined with another claim which is fit to be brought in an action (and has already been successfully prosecuted).
6. When individual rights are claimed, there should not be a need for leave or a special time limit, nor should the relief be discretionary.
7. The action should be allowed to proceed unless it is plainly an abuse of process.
8. The cases I have cited show that the rule in *O'Reilly* v *Mackman*, assuming it to be a rule of general application, is subject to many exceptions based on the nature of the claim and on the undesirability of erecting procedural barriers.

My Lords, I have already disclaimed the intention of discussing the scope of the rule in *O'Reilly* v *Mackman* but, even if I treat it as a general rule, there are many indications in favour of a liberal attitude towards the exceptions contemplated but not spelt out by Lord Diplock. For example:

1. The Law Commission, when recommending the new judicial review procedure, contemplated the continued co-existence of judicial review proceedings and actions for a declaration with regard to public law issues. *Associated Provincial Picture Houses Ltd* v *Wednesbury Corporation* is a famous prototype of the latter.
2. This House has expressly approved actions for a declaration of nullity as alternative to applications for *certiorari* to quash, where private law rights were concerned: *Wandsworth London Borough Council* v *Winder, per* Robert Goff LJ.
3. "The principle remains intact that public authorities and public servants are, unless clearly exempted, answerable in the ordinary courts for wrongs done to individuals. But by an extension of remedies and a flexible procedure it can be said that something resembling a system of public law is being developed. Before the expression 'public law' can be used to deny a subject a right of action in the court of his choice it must be related to a positive prescription of law, by statute or by statutory rules. We have not yet reached the point at which mere characterisation of a claim as a claim in public law is sufficient to exclude it from consideration by the ordinary courts: to permit this would be to create a dual system of law with the rigidity and procedural hardship for plaintiffs which it was the purpose of the recent reforms to remove": *Davy* v *Spelthorne Borough Council, per* Lord Wilberforce.

In conclusion, my Lords, it seems to me that, unless the procedure adopted by the moving party is ill suited to dispose of the question at issue, there is much to be said in favour of the proposition that a court having jurisdiction ought to let a case be heard rather than entertain a debate concerning the form of the proceedings.'

Comment

(1) The passages extracted comprise an important review of the case law in this area, and should be read in that light.

(2) Careful note should be taken of the distinction between the 'broad approach' and 'the narrow approach' to *O'Reilly* v *Mackman* identified by Lord Lowry. He identifies Lord Diplock as having taken a 'narrow' approach, and states his own preference for a 'broad' approach. If adopted by the courts, this would significantly limit the general rule stated in *O'Reilly* v *Mackman*.

(3) The case is decided on the narrow basis. No indication (other than the eight identified factors of this particular case) is given as to what other exceptions to the *O'Reilly* principle will be accepted.

(4) *Wandsworth LBC* v *Winder* was explained by Sir John Donaldson in the *Irish Dairy Board* case as follows:

> An illustration of the fact that the rule in *O'Reilly* v *Mackman* is, indeed, subject to exceptions where, although the principal issue is one of public law, private law rights are involved and it would cause the citizen injustice to be required to use the judicial reveiw procedure. We do not regard it as a decision which turns upon the accident that the citizen was the defendant, although this was important in the sense that the choice of forum had not been his and he was entitled to argue that he should not be penalised for that choice.

Note the specific approval given by the House of Lords in *Roy* to *Davy* v *Spelthorne BC* and *Wandsworth BC* v *Winder*.

(5) In *R* v *Derbyshire CC, ex parte Noble*, Woolf LJ stated that: 'Cross examination and discovery can take place on an application for judicial review, but in the ordinary way judicial review is designed to deal with matters which can be resolved without resorting to these procedures.' In noting that passage Lord Lowry indicated that 'that fact alone must constitute an important qualification of the general theory propounded by Lord Diplock in *O'Reilly* v *Mackman*'. Lord Lowry also noted Woolf LJ's identification of the 'misunderstanding' of *O'Reilly* v *Mackman*.

(6) For further discussion of *R* v *Derbyshire CC, ex parte Noble*, and generally as to the public /private law divide, see p.234.

(7) In *Doyle* v *Northumbria Probation Committee* (decided before *Roy*) Henry J observed of this area of law:

> Looking at these authorities . . . there have been eight reported cases on this topic cited to me. Five of the eight went to the House of Lords . . . The principles that Lord Diplock expected to emerge . . . have clearly not yet fully been worked out, and the reason for this seems to me to be clear, namely that the circumstances in which there may be such a mixture of private and public law claims are infinitely variable and can arise in very disparate situations. But the wealth of authority on this point and the potential for expensive appeals on it leads one to conclude that . . . there is potentially a formidable extra hurdle for plaintiffs in litigation where public law and private law mix. It seems to me that this is at present an area of law where the forms of action abolished by the Common

Law Procedure Act 1854 in the 19th century appear to be in danger of returning to rule us from their graves.

(8) In *Equal Opportunities Commission* v *Secretary of State for Employment* the application for judicial review brought by the Commission (as to which see p.113 and p.279) was joined with an application for judicial review by an ex-employee. The House of Lords held that this individual applicant could not succeed in her application as her claim was a private law claim, which should be pursued through private law means (i.e. through an application to an industrial tribunal).

(9) The Law Commission has supported the 'broad' approach favoured by Lord Lowry in *Roy* (Law Com. 226, para. 3.15).

R v Reading Crown Court, ex parte Hutchinson

[1988] QB 834 · Divisional Court

The defendants were prosecuted under byelaws made to prohibit access to Greenham Common. As part of the defence it was argued that the byelaws were invalid. The court held that the defendants were entitled to raise the validity of the byelaws as a defence, and were not required to bring proceedings under o.53.

Lloyd LJ: '. . . When a defendant in summary proceedings wishes to challenge the validity of a byelaw under which he has been charged, is it open to the justices to decide the issue of validity, or must the defendant proceed first by way of judicial review?

I venture to think that until a few years ago the answer to that question would have been regarded as obvious. But [the court has] held, that they have no jurisdiction to inquire into the validity of a byelaw, unless it is invalid on its face, in which case no inquiry would be necessary. Since the byelaws in question, the RAF Greenham Common Bye-Laws 1985, are not invalid on their face, they adjourned the hearing before them in order that the issue of validity might be determined on an application for judicial review.

I can well understand why the Crown Court at Reading took the course it did, in view of the decision of this court in *Plymouth City Council* v *Quietlynn Ltd.* That case appears to suggest that the long established practice whereby justices have ruled on the validity of byelaws has been overtaken by s.31 of the Supreme Court Act 1981. Justices are no longer to be expected "to assume the function of the Divisional Court" and decide difficult questions of law, which can more readily be decided on judicial review. The question for us is whether the decision in the *Quietlynn* case goes as far as might at first sight appear . . .

I have said that, until a few years ago, the answer to the question would have been self evident. In *Wade on Administrative Law*, 5th ed. (1982) it is said: "The commonest method of resisting an invalid regulation or byelaw is to plead its invalidity in defence to a prosecution or enforcement proceedings."

The note to s.235 of the Local Government Act 1972 in *Stone's Justices Manual 1986* contains a long list of cases in which the courts have had to consider the validity of byelaws . . . I need only mention two . . . the first . . . *R* v *Rose, ex parte Mary Wood*, was not an appeal by way of case stated, but an application for *certiorari.* The applicant had been convicted under a byelaw for failing to clear snow from the footpath in front of her house. Her defence was that the byelaw was invalid. The stipendiary magistrate refused to inquire into the validity of the byelaw. He assumed it to be valid, since it had been approved by the Secretary of State. A strong Divisional Court quashed her conviction. The court held that the byelaw was bad, and that therefore the stipendiary magistrate had no jurisdiction to convict. But it is clear from the opening sentence of Lord Campbell's judgment that in his view the stipendiary magistrate was entitled to inquire into the validity of byelaws; and Crompton J said: "I am disposed to think that the justice had no jurisdiction to enforce a bad byelaw. He had a right to inquire whether it was bad or good, but that is not what he has done." The case is cited in *Stone* as authority for the proposition that justices are bound to decide on any objection to the validity of a byelaw.

The only other case I need mention is *Kruse* v *Johnson* . . . The defendant was charged under a byelaw with singing on a highway, within 50 yards of a dwelling-house, after being required by a constable to desist. The defence was that the byelaw was invalid, on the ground that it was unreasonable. The justices held that the byelaw was reasonable, and convicted accordingly. The defendant's appeal was dismissed . . . Not one of the judges in the Divisional Court suggested that the justices had had no jurisdiction to inquire into the validity of the byelaw.

[Counsel] for the Crown Prosecution Service, submits that *Kruse* v *Johnson* was decided *per incuriam*. He would have to make the same submission with regard to all the many other cases in which byelaws have been considered by justices, and appeals brought before the Divisional Court on a case stated, whether by the prosecution or the defence. In all such cases, says [Counsel] the justices have exceeded their jurisdiction. Their proper course was always to adjourn the hearing before them so as to allow the defendant to apply for a prerogative writ, presumably prohibition.

I cannot accept so bold a submission. Nor can it be sustained by the consideration – which I would certainly accept – that the jurisdiction of justices is statutory. The absence of express statutory authority for justices to inquire into the validity of a byelaw does not mean that they do not have implied authority to do so, when the validity of the byelaw is challenged by the defendant . . .

In my judgment justices have always had jurisdiction to inquire into the validity of a byelaw. They are not only entitled, but bound to do so when the defendant relies on the invalidity of the byelaw by way of defence. Then has the position changed as a result of the new streamlined procedure for judicial review introduced [in 1977]? Or by virtue of s.31 of the Supreme Court Act 1981? Or has it changed as a result of the decision of the House of Lords in *O'Reilly* v *Mackman*? [Counsel] submits that it has. He concedes that there is nothing in any legislation to take away the jurisdiction of justices to inquire into the validity of byelaws, if (contrary to his first submission) they ever had it. But he submits that it is now contrary to public policy, or an abuse of the process of the court, for a defendant to challenge the validity of a byelaw under which he is charged, except by way of separate proceedings in the High Court.

I find [this] submission almost as bold as his first. *O'Reilly* v *Mackman* decides, in broad terms, that it is an abuse of the process of the court for a plaintiff to proceed by writ when he is complaining of an infringement of his rights in public law, since to do so would circumvent the safeguards provided by RSC o.53. But how can that principle possibly apply to a case where the plaintiff is not complaining of anything, but is defending himself against a criminal charge? To use the well worn metaphor, the defendants in the present proceedings are deploying their arguments as a shield, not as a sword. To describe what they are doing as an abuse of the process of the court is fanciful. It is the Crown Prosecution Service who has invoked the process of the court, not them . . .

As a matter of ordinary common sense, it cannot be said that the defendants here are abusing the process of the court unless we are to adopt the principle "cet animal est très mechant – quand on l'attaque, il se défend." It may be more convenient for the Crown Prosecution Service that the validity of byelaws, at any rate these byelaws, be tested by way of judicial review, though I do not accept that it is. But even if it were so, convenience of the Crown Prosecution Service is one thing; an abuse of the process of the court is something quite different.

Even if there were ever any doubt as to the scope of the principle stated in *O'Reilly* v *Mackman* or its irrelevance to a case such as the present, it was removed by the subsequent decision of the House of Lords in *Wandsworth London Borough Council* v *Winder* . . .

So I would reject [these] submissions on principle. Indeed, I hardly think he would have advanced them at all, but for two recent decisions of this court to which I now turn. In the first, *Director of Public Prosecutions* v *Bugg*, the facts were very similar to the present case. The respondent was charged with contravening the RAF Mildenhall Bye-Laws 1986. His defence was that the byelaws were invalid. The justices acquitted the respondent on the ground that the prosecution had not proved beyond reasonable doubt that the byelaws were valid. This was clearly wrong. So the appeal was allowed, and the case remitted with a direction to convict. The importance of the case for present purposes lies in certain observations of Watkins LJ . . . "I feel bound to say, however, that I am not wholly satisfied, despite the existence of the authorities . . . that it is open to a defendant charged with a breach of them to question their validity in a magistrates' court. Not having looked exhaustively at these authorities, I am left wondering whether the right so to do has ever been challenged. If that be so, it seems to me that such a challenge is overdue." . . .

Although one can share . . . fully in the sympathy which Watkins LJ felt for justices who have to grapple with difficult questions of law, the case is obviously no authority for the proposition that they are not obliged to inquire into the validity of byelaws which are challenged by way of defence . . . The difficulty in the *Quietlynn* case lies not so much in the actual decision, as in some of the incidental reasoning employed by Webster J in giving the judgment of the court. After referring to *Wandsworth LBC* v *Winder* and a number of the other cases, Webster J said "But we have been referred to no *dictum* in any of those cases which suggests that challenges to the decisions of local authorities are permissible in criminal proceedings; nor is it possible, in our view, to derive from those decisions a principle that such a challenge is permissible in proceedings of every kind."

With great respect, I find it hard to follow the distinction between civil and criminal proceedings in this context. If the validity of a decision of a local authority is an essential element in the proof of the crime alleged, then I can see no reason why it should not be challenged in the magistrates' court or the Crown Court as the case may be. Indeed, this seems to be contemplated as a proper procedure in an earlier passage in the *Quietlynn* case, where . . . Webster J said: "and, although justices sometimes, for the purpose of the case immediately before them, have to rule upon the validity of a byelaw or the decision of a local authority, that ruling is binding in no other case . . ."

All that the applicants in the present case want is, I suspect, that the Crown Court at Reading should rule upon the validity of the byelaws "for the purposes of the case immediately before them." If so, then the present case is covered by the passage I have just quoted.

It may be said that there is a distinction between challenging a decision of the local authority, and challenging a local authority byelaw. But there is a difficulty in that approach, correct though it would have been on the facts of the *Quietlynn* case, since it is nowhere reflected in the judgment of the court in that case. Indeed the first of the two reasons given by the court for rejecting the company's argument, namely, the need to achieve uniformity between different magistrates' courts and Crown Courts, would seem to have even more force in the case of byelaws which are binding on all, than in the case of decisions of local authorities which operate *in personam.*

Moreover there is another passage . . . which appears to treat byelaws and decisions on the same footing . . . This passage seems to suggest that the right to challenge byelaws in the magistrates' court has been affected by s.31 of the Supreme Court Act 1981. Otherwise it is difficult to see why byelaws are mentioned at all. If that is the implication of the passage, then with great respect I would venture to disagree. Neither s.31 . . . nor RSC o.53, has taken away the right of a defendant in criminal proceedings to challenge the validity of a byelaw under which he has been charged . . .'

Comment

(1)   In *DPP* v *Hutchinson* the House of Lords held the byelaws to be invalid.

(2)   For grounds of challenge to byelaws, and other delegated legislation, see *Kruse* v *Johnson* (p.298). In *DPP* v *Bugg* (1992) a distinction was drawn between delegated legislation invalid on its face and delegated legislation invalid for reasons not so apparent, e.g. because of procedural irregularity. In the former case, the alleged invalidity may be raised as a defence to criminal proceedings. In the latter, challenges must be by way of an application for judicial review.

(3)   In *Quietlynn*, the local authority had commenced proceedings against the applicants for running sex shops, having been refused the licences required by statute in respect of such premises. The applicants had commenced, but withdrawn, an application for judicial review. The Divisional Court concluded it was not permissible to challenge the validity of the decision by the local authority to refuse licences as a defence to prosecutions brought by the local authority: such challenge should be made through the o.53 procedure. This is an illustration of the court's power to correct an abuse of process: see *R* v *Oxford Crown Court, ex parte Smith.*

12 Availability of judicial remedies

Locus standi

The availability of a remedy through judicial review under o.53 depends on the applicant having a sufficient interest. This is not always an easy matter to determine.

Inland Revenue Commissioners v National Federation of Self Employed and Small Businesses

[1982] AC 617 · House of Lords

The respondents, who represented the self-employed and small businesses, sought judicial review of various actions of the Inland Revenue. Large numbers of casual workers in the newspaper industry had used various devices to avoid paying tax on their earnings: the Inland Revenue agreed an arrangement which would lead in future to the proper assessment or deduction of tax, in return for no investigation in respect of tax due for previous years. The respondents sought a declaration that the Revenue had acted unlawfully in granting the tax amnesty, and an order of mandamus compelling them to collect the tax lost. The Divisional Court held that the respondents had no *locus standi* to make application under o.53. This ruling was reversed by the Court of Appeal. On further appeal to the House of Lords, the decision of the Divisional Court was restored.

Lord Diplock: '... Before the new o.53 was substituted for its predecessor, the private citizen who sought redress against a person or authority for acting unlawfully or *ultra vires* in the purported exercise of statutory powers had to choose from a number of different procedures that which was the most appropriate to furnish him the redress that he sought. The major differences in procedure, including *locus standi* to apply for the relief sought, were between the remedies by way of declaration or injunction obtainable by a civil action brought to enforce public law and the remedies by way of the prerogative orders of mandamus, prohibition or certiorari which lay in public law alone; but even between the three public law remedies there were minor procedural differences, and the *locus standi* to apply for them was not quite the same for each, although the divergences were in process of diminishing.
    Your Lordships can take judicial notice of the fact that the main purpose of the new o.53 was to sweep away these procedural differences including, in particular,

differences as to *locus standi*, to substitute for them a single simplified procedure for obtaining all forms of relief, and to leave to the court a wide discretion as to what interlocutory directions including orders for discovery, were appropriate to the particular case.

In the instant case, in [the lower courts], the argument for the Board was put on the footing that notwithstanding this unification of procedure for obtaining the various remedies available in public law, including those which had been available in private law only, the new o.53 had left unchanged the basis on which an applicant was recognised as having *locus standi* to apply for each individual form of relief sought. In the instant case these were a declaration and an order of mandamus.

As respects the claim for a declaration considerable reliance was placed on the recent decision of this House in *Gouriet v Union of Post Office Workers*, which held that a private citizen, except as relator in an action brought by the Attorney-General, has no *locus standi* in private law as plaintiff in a civil action to obtain either an injunction to restrain another private citizen (*in casu* a trade union) from committing a public wrong by breaking the criminal law or a declaration that his conduct is unlawful unless the plaintiff can show that some legal or equitable right of his own has been infringed or that he will sustain some special damage over and above that suffered by the general public. This decision is, in my view, irrelevant to any question that your Lordships have to decide today. The defendant trade union in deciding to instruct its members to take unlawful industrial action was not exercising any governmental powers; it was acting as a private citizen and could only be sued as such in a civil action under private law. It was not amenable to any remedy in public law . . .

In contrast to this, judicial review is a remedy that lies exclusively in public law. In my view the language of r.1(2) and (3) of the new o.53 shows an intention that on an application for judicial review the court should have jurisdiction to grant a declaration or an injunction as an alternative to making one of the prerogative orders, whenever in its discretion it thinks that it is just and convenient to do so, and that this jurisdiction should be exercisable in any case in which the applicant would previously have had *locus standi* to apply for any of the prerogative orders . . .

So if, before the new o.53 came into force, the court would have had jurisdiction to grant to the applicant any of the prerogative orders it may now grant him a declaration or injunction instead, notwithstanding that the applicant would have no *locus standi* to claim the declaration or injunction under private law in a civil action against the respondent to the application because he could not show that any legal right of his own was threatened or infringed.

So I turn first to consider what constituted *locus standi* to apply for one or other of the prerogative orders immediately before the new o.53 came into force. In the earlier cases a more restrictive rule for *locus standi* was applied to applications for the writ of mandamus than for writs of prohibition or certiorari; and since mandamus was the prerogative order sought by the Federation in the instant case your Lordships have been referred to many of them, [including] the extempore judgment of Wright J delivered at the end of the last century in *R v Guardians of Lewisham Union*. He there said that an application for a mandamus "must first of all shew that he has a legal specific right to ask for the interference of the Court". The law has not stood still since 1897. By 1977 this was no longer correct, and I have no hesitation in saying that it is inconceivable that mandamus would have been refused in the circumstances of that case if it had come before a Divisional Court any time during the last twenty years.

The rules as to "standing" for the purpose of applying for prerogative orders, like most of English public law, are not to be found in any statute. They were made by judges; by judges they can be changed, and so they have been over the years to meet the need to preserve the integrity of the rule of law despite changes in the social structure, methods of government and the extent to which the activities of private citizens are controlled by governmental authorities that have been taking place continuously, sometimes slowly, sometimes swiftly, since the rules were originally propounded. Those changes have been particularly rapid since the 1939–45 war. Any judicial statements on matters of public law if made before 1950 are likely to be a misleading guide to what the law is today.

In 1951 the decision of the Divisional Court in *R* v *Northumberland Compensation Appeal Tribunal* resurrected error of law on the face of the record as a ground for granting certiorari. Parliament by the Tribunals and Inquiries Act 1958 followed this up by requiring reasons to be given for many administrative decisions that had previously been cloaked in silence; and the years that followed between then and 1977 witnessed a dramatic liberalisation of access to the courts for the purpose of obtaining prerogative orders against persons and authorities exercising governmental powers. This involved a virtual abandonment of the former restrictive rules as to the *locus standi* of persons seeking such orders. The process of liberalisation of access to the courts and the progressive discarding of technical limitations on *locus standi* is too well known to call for detailed citation of the cases by which it may be demonstrated. They are referred to and discussed in Professor H.W.R. Wade's *Administrative Law* . . .The author points out there that, although lip service continued to be paid to a difference in standing required to entitle an applicant to mandamus on the one hand and prohibition or *certiorari* on the other, in practice the courts found some way of treating the *locus standi* for all three remedies as being the same. A striking example of this is to be found in *R* v *Hereford Corpn, ex parte Harrower*, where the applicants were treated as having *locus standi* in their capacity as ratepayers though their real interest in the matter was as electrical contractors only. For my part I need only refer to *R* v *Greater London Council, ex parte Blackburn*. In that case Mr Blackburn, who lived in London with his wife who was a ratepayer, applied successfully for an order of prohibition against the council to stop them acting in breach of their statutory duty to prevent the exhibition of pornographic films within their administrative area. Mrs Blackburn was also party to the application. Lord Denning MR and Stephenson LJ were of opinion that both Mr and Mrs Blackburn had *locus standi* to make the application: Mr Blackburn because he lived within the administrative area of the council and had children who might be harmed by seeing pornographic films and Mrs Blackburn not only as a parent but also on the additional ground that she was a ratepayer. Bridge LJ relied only on Mrs Blackburn's status as a ratepayer, a class of persons to whom for historical reasons the Court of King's Bench afforded generous access to control *ultra vires* activities of the public bodies to whose expenses they contributed. But now that local government franchise is not limited to ratepayers, this distinction between the two applicants strikes me as carrying technicality to the limits of absurdity having regard to the subject matter of the application in the Blackburn case. I agree in substance with what Lord Denning MR there said . . .

> I regard it as a matter of high constitutional principle that if there is good ground
> for supposing that a government department or a public authority is transgressing

the law, or is about to transgress it, in a way which offends or injures thousands of Her Majesty's subjects, then any one of those offended or injured can draw it to the attention of the courts of law and seek to have the law enforced, and the courts in their discretion can grant whatever remedy is appropriate.

The reference here is to flagrant and serious breaches of the law by persons and authorities exercising governmental functions which are continuing unchecked. To revert to technical restrictions on *locus standi* to prevent this that were current thirty years ago or more would be to reverse that progress towards a comprehensive system of administrative law that I regard as having been the greatest achievement of the English courts in my judicial lifetime.

The reliance by Bridge LJ in *R* v *Greater London Council, ex parte Blackburn* on Mrs Blackburn's status as a ratepayer to give her *locus standi* reflects a special relationship between ratepayers and the rate-levying authority and between one ratepayer and another, which is of ancient origin and antedates by centuries the first imposition of taxes on income. This led the Board in the instant case to seek to rely on the decision of this House in *Arsenal Football Club Ltd* v *Ende* as authority for a proposition of law that a taxpayer lacked a sufficient interest in what the Board did in dealing with the tax affairs of other taxpayers to clothe the court with jurisdiction to entertain his application for an order of mandamus, however flagrantly the Board, in their dealing with those other taxpayers, had flouted the law. So, it was contended, no question of discretion could arise. The *Arsenal Football Club* case had been decided before the new o.53 had been made; but, in any event, it was not concerned with an application for a prerogative order: it turned on whether a ratepayer who complained that the value for the hereditament of another ratepayer published in the valuation list was too low was "person aggrieved" by that low valuation within the meaning of s.69 of the General Rate Act 1967, notwithstanding that, since the raising of the valuation of the hereditament could have no effect on the amount of rates payable by the objecting ratepayer, no financial interest of his own was affected . . . It was held that the objecting ratepayer was a "person aggrieved", not only in his capacity as a ratepayer in the same London Borough as that in which the hereditament that was the subject of his complaint was situated but also as a ratepayer of another London borough within the precepting area of the GLC. The case is thus illustrative of the liberal attitude of the courts in granting access to legal remedies for those complaining of failure of public officers to perform their duties. He was held, however, not to be a person aggrieved in his capacity as a taxpayer despite the fact that any shortfall in the rate yield due to the undervaluation of the hereditament would be made up from central funds to which all taxpayers in Great Britain contribute. A line, it was said, has to be drawn somewhere, and his interest as a taxpayer was too remote to qualify him as a person aggrieved by a single entry in the valuation list for rating purposes of a London borough . . .

[T]he expression "person aggrieved" is of common occurrence in statutes and, in its various statutory contexts, has been the subject of considerable judicial exegesis. In the past, however, it had also sometimes been used by judges to describe those persons who had *locus standi* to apply for the . . . prerogative orders . . . the draftsman of [o.53] avoided using the expression "a person aggrieved", although it lay ready to his hand. He chose instead to get away from any formula that might be thought to have acquired, through judicial exposition, a particular meaning as a term of legal art. The expression that he used in r.3(5) had cropped up sporadically in judgments relating to prerogative writs and orders and consisted of ordinary English words which, on the face of them, leave to the court an unfettered discretion to decide what in its own good judgment it considers to be "a sufficient interest" on the part of an applicant in the particular circumstances of the case before it. For my part I would not strain to give them any narrower meaning.

The procedure under the new o.53 involves two stages: (1) the application for leave to apply for judicial review, and (2) if leave is granted, the hearing of the application itself. The former, or "threshold", stage is regulated by r.3. The application for leave to apply for judicial review is made initially *ex parte*, but may be adjourned for the persons or bodies against whom relief is sought to be represented. This did not happen in the instant case. Rule 3(5) specifically requires the court to consider at this stage whether "it considers that the applicant has a sufficient interest in the matter to which the application relates". So this is a "threshold" question in the sense that the court must direct its mind to it and form a prima facie view about it on the material that is available at the first stage. The prima facie view so formed, if favourable to the applicant, may alter on further consideration in the light of further evidence that may be before the court at the second stage of the hearing of the application for judicial review itself.

The need for leave to start proceedings for remedies in public law is not new. It applied previously to applications for prerogative orders, though not to civil actions for injunctions or declarations. Its purpose is to prevent the time of the court being wasted by busybodies with misguided or trivial complaints of administrative error, and to remove the uncertainty in which public officers and authorities might be left whether they could safely proceed with administrative action while proceedings for judicial review of it were actually pending even though misconceived . . .

I understand that all your Lordships are agreed that . . . the Divisional Court . . . was justified in exercising its discretion in favour of granting the leave sought . . . The analysis to which the relevant legislation has been subjected by some of your Lordships, and particularly the requirement of confidentiality which would be broken if one taxpayer could complain that another taxpayer was being treated by the Revenue more favourably than himself, means that occasions will be very rare on which an individual taxpayer (or pressure group of taxpayers) will be able to show a sufficient interest to justify an application for judicial review of the way in which the Revenue have dealt with the tax affairs of any taxpayer other than the applicant himself. Rare though they may be, however, if, in the instant case, what at the threshold stage was suspicion only had been proved at the hearing of the application for judicial review to have been true in fact (instead of being utterly destroyed), I would have held that this was a matter in which the Federation had a sufficient interest in obtaining an appropriate order, whether by way of declaration or mandamus, to require performance by the Board of statutory duties which for reasons shown to be *ultra vires* they were failing to perform.

It would, in my view, be a grave lacuna in our system of public law if a pressure group, like the Federation, or even a single public spirited taxpayer, were prevented by outdated technical rules of *locus standi* from bringing the matter to the attention of the court to vindicate the rule of law and get the unlawful conduct stopped. The Attorney-General, although he occasionally applies for prerogative orders against public authorities that do not form part of central government, in practice never does so against government departments. It is not, in my view, a sufficient answer to say that judicial review of the actions of officers or departments of central government is unnecessary because they are accountable to Parliament for the way in which they carry out their functions. They are accountable to Parliament for what they do so far as regards efficiency and policy, and of that Parliament is the only judge; they are responsible to a court of justice for the lawfulness of what they do, and of that the court is the only judge.'

Comment

(1)   A relator action is one in which the Attorney-General on the application of an individual brings an action to assert a public right. See *Gouriet v Union of Post Office Workers*, where an application for an injunction to prevent an anticipated breach of the criminal law was held by the House of Lords to be improper except through a relator action.

(2)   The approach of Lord Diplock in the *Small Businesses* case is the most radical of the five Law Lords. Significant variations in emphasis exist, though all agree that the matter turns upon the nature of the statutory duty in question.

(3)   In *R v Secretary of State for the Environment, ex parte Rose Theatre Trust*, the court had to consider, *inter alia*, whether a company established to pursue a campaign to save from redevelopment an important archaeological site, the Globe Theatre site in London, had *locus standi*. In concluding that it did not, Schiemann J identified the following propositions that he perceived to be consistent with the House of Lords ruling:

(a)   Once leave has been given to move for judicial review, the court which hears the application ought still to examine whether the applicant has a sufficient interest.
(b)   Whether an applicant has a sufficient interest is not purely a matter of discretion in the court.
(c)   Not every member of the public can complain of every breach of statutory duty by a person empowered to come to a decision by that statute. To rule otherwise would be to deprive the phrase 'sufficient interest' of all meaning.
(d)   However, a direct financial or legal interest is not required.
(e)   Where one is examining an alleged failure to perform a duty imposed by statute it is useful to look at the statute and see whether it gives an applicant a right enabling him to have that duty performed.
(f)   Merely to assert that one has an interest does not give one an interest.
(g)   The fact that some thousands of people join together and assert they have an interest does not create an interest if the individuals did not have an interest.
(h)   The fact that those without an interest incorporate themselves and give the company in its memorandum power to pursue a particular object does not give the company an interest.

No matter how distinguished citizens were in this particular field, the decision not to schedule the site under statute was a decision for government. In so deciding, Schiemann J recognized that the effect of his ruling might be, if not now then in the future, to leave an unlawful act of a minister uncorrected. Note, however, the reaction of Otton J in the *Greenpeace* case.

(4)   Schiemann J had a further opportunity to consider the question of *locus standi* in *R v Poole BC, ex parte Beebee*. After noting that his earlier judgment in the *Rose Theatre* case had not escaped academic criticism, he concluded that both the World Wildlife Fund (WWF) and the British Heperetological Society (BHS), which are both unincorporated associations, had *locus standi* to challenge the actions of the respondent Council, which had granted planning permission to itself in respect of heathland of special scientific interest. He placed emphasis upon the BHS's close financial interest in the site, and the fact that the WWF had given an undertaking to pay costs if necessary. These are factors not always likely to be present in the context of pressure and amenity groups.

(5)   Although in *ex parte Beebee*, the two unincorporated associations were held to have *locus standi*, in *R v Darlington BC, ex parte Association of Darlington Taxi Owners* a divisional court held that unincorporated associations do not have the legal capacity to bring judicial review proceedings.

(6)   See also: *Covent Garden Community Association v Greater London Council*; *R v Hammersmith & Fulham BC, ex parte People Before Profit Ltd.*

(7)   For consideration of the authorities on the meaning of 'person aggrieved', see *Cook v Southend BC*.

R v HM Inspectorate of Pollution and Ministry of Agriculture Fisheries and Food, ex parte Greenpeace (No. 2)

[1994] 4 All ER 329   ·   Divisional Court

British Nuclear Fuels submitted to the respondent an application to vary an authorization to discharge radioactive waste. The application if granted would have allowed BNF to test a new thermal oxide re-processing plant (THORP) for nuclear waste, constructed at Sellafield. The applicant organization, which has as its objectives the preservation of the environment, was asked to comment on the proposed variation. It sought, unsuccessfully, to challenge the variation on judicial review. The Divisional Court held that the applicant did have *locus standi*, but that the respondents acted lawfully. The extracted passages deal only with the question of *locus standi*.

Otton J: 'The requirement of a sufficient interest emerges from s. 31(3) Supreme Court Act 1981 . . . In reaching my conclusions, I adopt the approach indicated by Lord Donaldson MR in *R v Monopolies and Mergers Commission, ex parte Argyle Group*:

> The first stage test which is applied on the application for leave, will lead to a refusal if the applicant has no interest whatsoever and is, in truth, no more than a meddlesome busybody. If, however, an application appears otherwise to be arguable and there is no other discretionary bar, such as dilatoriness on the part

of the applicant, the applicant may expect to get leave to apply, leaving the test of interest or standing to be re-applied as a matter of discretion on the hearing of the substantive application. At this second stage, the strength of the applicant's interest is one of the factors to be weighed in the balance . . .

This approach was followed and developed by Purchas LJ in *R v Department of Transport, ex parte Presvac Engineering Limited* when after considering the decision of the House of Lords in the [Small Businesses case], he said: "Personally I would prefer to restrict the use of the expression *locus standi* to the threshold exercise and to describe the decision at the ultimate stage as the exercise of discretion not to grant relief as the applicant has not established that he had been or would be sufficiently affected".

Thus I approach this matter primarily as one of discretion. I consider it appropriate to take into account the nature of Greenpeace and the extent of its interest in the issues raised, the remedy Greenpeace seeks to achieve and the nature of that relief sought.

In doing so I take into account the very nature of Greenpeace. Lord Melchett has affirmed thus:

Greenpeace International has nearly five million supporters worldwide; Greenpeace UK has over 400 000 supporters in the United Kingdom and about 2500 of them are in the Cumbria region, where the BNFL plant is situated. Greenpeace is a campaigning organisation which has as its prime objective the protection of the natural environment.

Greenpeace International has also been accredited with consultative status with the United Nations Economic and Social Council (including the United Nations General Assembly). It has accreditation status with the UN Conference on Environment and Development. They have observer status or right to attend meetings of 17 named bodies including Parcom (Paris Convention for the Prevention of Marine Pollution from Land Based Sources). BNFL rightly acknowledge the national and international standing of Greenpeace and its integrity. So must I. I have not the slightest reservation that Greenpeace is an entirely responsible and respected body with a general concern for the environment. That concern naturally leads to a bona fide interest in the activities carried on by BNFL at Sellafield and in particular the discharge and disposal of radioactive waste from their premises and to which the respondent's decision to vary relates. The fact that there are 400 000 supporters in the United Kingdom carries less weight than the fact that 2500 of them come from the Cumbria region. I would be ignoring the blindly obvious if I were to disregard the fact that these persons are inevitably concerned about (and have a genuine perception that there is) a danger to their health and safety from any additional discharge of radioactive waste even from testing. I have no doubt that the issues raised by this application are serious and worthy of determination by this court.

It seems to me that if I were to deny standing to Greenpeace, those it represents might not have an effective way to bring the issues before the court. There would have to be an application either by an individual employee of BNFL or a near neighbour. . . . Consequently, a less well informed challenge might be mounted which would stretch unnecessarily the court's resources and which would not afford the court the assistance it requires in order to do justice between the parties. Further, if the unsuccessful applicant had the benefit of legal aid it might leave the respondents and BNFL without an effective remedy in costs. Alternatively, the individual (or Greenpeace) might seek to persuade HM Attorney-General to commence a relator action which (as a matter of policy or practice) he may be reluctant to undertake against a government department . . . Neither of these courses of action would have the advantage of an application by Greenpeace who, with its particular experience in environmental matters, its access to experts in the relevant realms of science and technology (not to mention the law) is able to mount a carefully selected, focused, relevant and well-argued challenge . . .

I also take into account the nature of the relief sought. In the [Small Businesses] case the House of Lords expressed the view that if mandamus were sought that would be a reason to decline jurisdiction. Here the primary relief sought is certiorari (less stringent) and, if granted, the question of an injunction to stop the testing pending determination of the main applications would still be in the discretion of the court. I also take into account the fact that Greenpeace has been treated as one of the consultees during the consultation process and that they were invited (albeit with other non-consultees) to comment on the "minded to vary" letter.

[Otton J concluded that the nature of the applicants was such as to warrant the granting of *locus standi*, but noted that such a matter was a mixed question of fact and law, to be dealt with on a case-by-case basis. He continued:]

Thus it must not be assumed that Greenpeace (or any other interest group) will automatically be afforded standing in any subsequent application for judicial review . . . I also bear this consideration in mind when I respectfully decline to follow the decision of Schiemann J in the [*Rose Theatre* case]. Suffice it to say that the circumstances were different, the interest group had been formed for the exclusive purpose of saving the Rose Theatre site and no individual member could show any personal interest in the outcome . . .

Comment

(1) In *R* v *Secretary of State for Social Services, ex parte Child Poverty Action Group*, counsel for the Secretary of State was not disposed to argue that the CPAG did not have *locus*, although he reserved the position for argument in future cases. Woolf LJ stated:

The question of *locus standi* goes to the jurisdiction of the court . . . the parties are not entitled to confer jurisdiction which the court does not have, on the court by consent, and if the court had been minded to grant declaratory relief, the respondents would have had to have in advance any arguments which were available to them or accept the consequences of not doing so.

(2) See also *R* v *Secretary of State for the Environment, ex parte Friends of the Earth Ltd*; *R* v *Secretary of State for Foreign Affairs, ex parte World Development Movement*, where the court recognized that the merits of each case were relevant.

(3) The Law Commission has recommended that an application for judicial review should not be allowed to proceed to a substantive hearing unless the court is

satisfied that the applicant has been or would be adversely affected, or the High Court considers that it is in the public interest for the applicant to make the application.

National security

The establishment of grounds of national security may prevent a court intervening.

CCSU v Minister for the Civil Service

[See p.215]

Lord Scarman: '. . . I would dismiss this appeal for one reason only. I am satisfied that the respondent has made out a case on the ground of national security . . . I have no doubt that the respondent refused to consult the unions before issuing her instruction of the 22 December 1983 because she feared that, if she did, union-organised disruption of the monitoring services of GCHQ could well result. I am further satisfied that the fear was one which a reasonable minister in the circumstances in which she found herself could reasonably entertain. I am also satisfied that a reasonable minister could reasonably consider such disruption to constitute a threat to national security . . .

The point of principle in the appeal is as to the duty of the court when in proceedings properly brought before it a question arises as to what is required in the interest of national security . . . however it arises, it is a matter to be considered by the court in the circumstances and context of the case. Though there are limits dictated by law and common sense which the court must observe in dealing with the question, the court does not abdicate its judicial function. If the question arises as a matter of fact, the court requires evidence to be given. If it arises as a factor to be considered in reviewing the exercise of a discretionary power, evidence is also needed so that the court may determine whether it should intervene to correct excess or abuse of the power.

Let me give three illustrations taken from the case law of the 20th century. First, *The Zamora* – surely one of the more courageous of judicial decisions even in our long history. In April 1916 a question of national security came before the Judicial Committee of the Privy Council sitting in Prize. The Crown's role in the Prize Court was that of a belligerent power having by international law the right to requisition vessels or goods in the custody of its Prize Court. A neutral vessel carrying a cargo of copper (contraband) had been stopped at sea by the Royal Navy and taken to a British port. No decree of condemnation of the cargo had yet been made by the Prize Court, when the Crown intervened by summons to requisition the cargo then in the custody of the court. Lord Parker concluded: "A belligerent power has by international law the right to requisition vessels or goods in the custody of its Prize Court pending a decision of the question whether they should be condemned or released, but such right is subject to certain limitations. First, the vessel or goods in question must be urgently required for use in connection with the defence of the realm, the prosecution of the war, or other matters involving national security . . ." . . .

Discussing the first limitation, Lord Parker observed that the judge ought, "as a rule," to treat the statement of the proper officer of the Crown that the vessel or goods were urgently required for national security reasons as conclusive of the fact. And it was in this context that he delivered his famous dictum "Those who are responsible for the national security must be the sole judges of what the national security requires." These words were no abdication of the judicial function, but were an indication of the evidence required by the court. In fact the evidence adduced by the Crown was not sufficient, and the court ruled that the Crown had no right to requisition. The Crown's claim was rejected "because the judge had before him no satisfactory evidence that such a right was exercisable". The Prize Court, therefore, treated the question as one of fact for its determination and indicated the evidence needed to establish the fact. The true significance of Lord Parker's *dictum* is simply that the court is in no position to substitute its opinion for the opinion of those responsible for national security. But the case is a fine illustration of the court's duty to ensure that the essential facts to which the opinion or judgment of those responsible relates are proved to the satisfaction of the court.

My second illustration is *Chandler* v *DPP.* In this case the interest of national security came into court as a matter of fact to be established by evidence to the satisfaction of a jury in a criminal case. The appellants were convicted of conspiring to commit a breach of section 1 of the Official Secrets Act 1911, "namely, for a purpose prejudicial to the safety or interests of the state to enter a Royal Air Force station . . . at Wethersfield." There was evidence from an officer of air rank that the airfield was of importance for national security: and . . . Lord Reid and Viscount Radcliffe treated his evidence as relevant to the dismissal of the appeal. Lord Devlin developed the point taken in the case on national security in a passage . . . which . . . I believe to be sound law. Having referred to the undoubted principle that all matters relating to the disposition and armament of the armed forces are left to the unfettered control of the Crown, he made three comments. First, he put the *Zamora dictum* into its true context. Secondly, he observed that, when a court is faced with the exercise of a discretionary power, inquiry is not altogether excluded: the court will intervene to correct excess or abuse. His third and, as he said, his "most significant" comment was as to the nature and effect of the principle: "Where it operates, it limits the issue which the court has to determine; it does not exclude any evidence or argument relevant to the issue".

As I read the speeches in *Chandler*'s case, the House accepted that the statute required the prosecution to establish by evidence that the conspiracy was to enter a prohibited place for a purpose prejudicial to the safety or interests of the state. As Parliament had left the existence of a prejudicial purpose to the decision of a jury, it was not the Crown's opinion as to the existence of prejudice to the safety or interests of the state but the jury's which mattered: hence, as Lord Devlin remarked, the Crown's opinion on that was inadmissible but the Crown's evidence as to its interests was an "entirely different matter." Here, like Lord Parker in *The Zamora*, Lord Devlin was accepting that the Crown, or its responsible servants, are the best judges of what national security requires without excluding the judicial function of determining whether the interest of national security has been shown to be involved in the case.

Finally, I would refer to *Secretary of State for Defence* v *Guardian Newspapers Ltd*, a case arising under s.10 of the Contempt of Court Act of 1981. As in *Chandler*'s case, the interest of national security had to be considered in proceedings where it arose as a question of fact to be established to the satisfaction of a court. Though the House was divided as to the effect of the evidence, all their Lordships held that evidence was necessary so that the court could be judicially satisfied that the interest of national security required disclosure of the newspaper's source of information . . .

I conclude, therefore, that where a question as to the interest of national security arises in judicial proceedings the court has to act on evidence. In some cases a judge or jury is required by law to be satisfied that the interest is proved to exist: in others, the interest is a factor to be considered in the review of the exercise of an executive discretionary power. Once the factual basis is established by evidence so that the court is satisfied that the interest of national security is a relevant factor to be considered in the determination of the case, the court will accept the opinion of the Crown or its responsible officer as to what is required to meet it, unless it is possible to show that the opinion was one which no reasonable minister advising the Crown could in the circumstances reasonably have held. There is no abdication of the judicial function, but there is a common sense limitation recognised by the judges as to what is justiciable: and the limitation is entirely consistent with the general development of the modern case law of judicial review . . .'

Comment

(1)   For discussion of the concept of justiciability, see p.219.

(2)   Lord Scarman regarded unreasonableness of the opinion of the minister as a possible ground of challenge. This raises questions on the proper boundaries of judicial intervention. For the meaning of unreasonableness, see p.292.

R v Secretary of State for the Home Department, ex parte Ruddock

[See p.327]

Taylor J: '[Counsel] does not challenge here the jurisdiction of the court to decide the issues raised. He bases his submission upon a plea to the court's discretion. In effect the plea amounts to this: the Secretary of State invariably maintains silence in the interests of national security on issues such as are raised here. The court in its discretion should do likewise, and since making findings to decide the case may break that silence, the court should, in Lord Scarman's phrase, abdicate its judicial function. I cannot agree with that, either as a general proposition or in this particular case. I do not accept that the court should never inquire into a complaint against a minister if he says his policy is to maintain silence in the interests of national security. To take an extreme and one hopes unlikely example, suppose an application were put before the court alleging a warrant was improperly issued by a Secretary of State against a political opponent, and suppose the application to be supported by the production of a note in the minister's own hand acknowledging the criteria did not apply but giving instructions that the phone be tapped nevertheless to see if anything discreditable could be learnt. It could not be sensibly argued that the department's invariable policy of silence should require the court meekly to follow suit and decline to decide such a case. At the other extreme, I recognise there could occur a case where the issue raised was so sensitive and the revelations necessarily following its decision so damaging to national security that the court might have to take special measures (for example, sitting in camera or prohibiting the mention of names). Conceivably (although I would reserve the point) in an extreme case the court might have to decline to try the issues. But in all such cases, cogent evidence of potential damage to national security flowing from the trial of the issues would have to be adduced, whether in open court or in camera, to justify any modification of the court's normal procedure. Totally to oust the court's supervisory jurisdiction in a field where *ex hypothesi* the citizen can have no right to be consulted is a draconian and dangerous step indeed. Evidence to justify the court's declining to decide a case (if such a course is ever justified) would need to be very strong and specific . . .'

Comment

The approach is a useful reminder of the dangers of the courts accepting too readily executive claims of national security, and thereby becoming 'more executive-minded than the executive' – see Lord Atkin in *Liversidge* v *Anderson*, p.12.

Restrictions on judicial scrutiny

Anisminic Ltd v *Foreign Compensation Commission*

[1969] 2 AC 147 · House of Lords

The property of Anisminic Ltd had been seized by the Egyptian government along with many other properties. It was then sold by Anisminic to TEDO at a reduced price. A general scheme for compensation was later agreed and the FCC was charged with the distribution of the money. Anisminic Ltd made a claim. The issue for the court was whether or not the 'determination' of the Commission in refusing compensation had been legally correct. The determination had been made on the basis that the compensation was to be paid only if the applicant's successor in title was a British citizen. The House of Lords addressed the issue of the interpretation of the relevant section of the Order in Council and concluded that the Commission had erred. The next point was the 'ouster provision' in s.4(4) of the Act which stated that the determination of the Commission 'shall not be called in question in any court of law.' The House of Lords held that 'determination' meant a real determination and not one where the body had erred in a matter of law or, in some other way, critical to its jurisdiction.

Lord Reid: '. . . It has sometimes been said that it is only where a tribunal acts without jurisdiction that its decision is a nullity. But in such cases the word "jurisdiction" has been used in a very wide sense, and I have come to the conclusion that it is better not to use the term except in the narrow and original sense of the tribunal being entitled to enter on the inquiry in question. But there are many cases where, although the tribunal had jurisdiction to enter on the inquiry it has done or failed to do something in the course of the inquiry which is of such a nature that its decision is a nullity. It may have given its decision in bad faith. It may have made a decision which it has no power to make. It may have failed in the course of the inquiry to comply with the requirements of natural justice. It may in perfect good faith have misconstrued the provisions giving it power to act so that it failed to deal with the questions remitted to it and decided some question which was not remitted to it. It may have refused to take into account something which it was required to take into account. Or it may have based its decision on some matter which, under the provisions setting it up, it has no right to take into account. I do not intend this list to be exhaustive. But if it decides a question remitted to it for decision without committing any of these errors it is as much entitled to decide that question wrongly as rightly. I understand that some confusion has been caused by my having said in *R v Governor of Brixton Prison, ex parte Armah* . . . that if a tribunal has jurisdiction to go right it has jurisdiction to go wrong. So it has, if one uses "jurisdiction" in the narrow original sense. If it is entitled to enter on the inquiry and does not do any of those things which I have mentioned in the course of the proceedings, then its decision is equally valid whether it is right or wrong subject only to the power of the court in certain circumstances to correct an error of law . . .'

Comment

(1) Section 4(4) was replaced by s.3, Foreign Compensation Act 1969, which, subject to exceptions, prevents challenge to any 'purported determination' of the Commission. See also s.7(8), Interception of Communications Act 1985, which provides that 'The decisions of the Tribunal (including any decisions as to their jurisdiction) shall not be subject to appeal or liable to be questioned in any court.' This appears to be wide enough to circumvent the principle in *Anisminic*.

(2) Attempts to limit judicial scrutiny involve conflict between the legislative supremacy of Parliament and accountability of the executive, and considerable case law has developed. Particularly, in the case of time limited provisions, the principle in *Anisminic* does not mean that such clauses will never preclude a court from intervening. See *Smith* v *East Elloe RDC*, *R* v *Secretary of State for the Environment, ex parte Ostler*, cited in *R* v *Cornwall CC, ex parte Huntington*, p.269.

(3) Where a statute provides a right of appeal, the right to proceed by judicial review may be limited. For detailed discussion, see *R* v *Chief Constable of Merseyside, ex parte Calveley*; *R* v *Hillingdon LBC, ex parte Royco Homes*.

(4) Remedies are discretionary. Even if grounds of challenge exist, leave to apply may not be granted. See, for example, *R* v *Harrow LBC, ex parte D*, in the context of judicial review in respect of child abuse register entries: 'All concerned . . . should be allowed to perform their task without looking over their shoulder all the time. The important power of the court to intervene should be kept very much in reserve, perhaps confined to the exceptional case which involves a point of principle which needs to be resolved . . .'. Nor, even if leave is granted and successful grounds of challenge established, will a remedy always be granted. See the decision in *R* v *Secretary of State for Social Services, ex parte AMA*, where the regulations in question were successfully challenged, but no remedy other than a declaration granted because the regulations in question were already in operation. See also s.31(6), Supreme Court Act 1981, p.238.

(5)   An ouster provision may be contrary to the duty in European Community law to provide an effective remedy for breach of a Community obligation – see *Johnston* v *Chief Constable of the RUC*, p.121.

R v *Cornwall CC, ex parte Huntington*

[1992] 3 All ER 566   ·   Divisional Court

The local authority sought the setting aside of the leave to apply for judicial review granted to the applicants. The applicants were seeking to challenge an order made under the Wildlife & Countryside Act 1981. Paragraph 12 of the 1981 Act prescribed that challenges to such orders had to be made within a period of 42 days from the date of publication of a statutory notice, and that 'the validity of an order shall not be questioned' except within this period. The application by the local authority succeeded. The court had no jurisdiction to grant judicial review except as prescribed by para.12, which prevented judicial review outside the statutory period.

Mann LJ: 'Paragraph 12 is a standard form of preclusive clause. There are now many such clauses . . . The draftsmanship varies, but the common features are the prescription of an opportunity for challenge on specified grounds and of the period within which that challenge can be made together with the proscription of any challenge outside that period. Such a clause was before the House of Lords in *Smith* v *East Elloe RDC* and another such was before the Court of Appeal in *R* v *Secretary of State for the Environment, ex parte Ostler*. The latter case was followed by the Court of Appeal in *R* v *Secretary of State for the Environment, ex parte Kent*. Those three authorities are binding on this court and [counsel] submits that they are determinate in his favour for in each the clause was allowed to operate in accord with its terms so as to prevent a challenge outside the prescribed period. [Counsel for the respondent] recognised that the authorities are binding in this court, but seeks to distinguish them on the grounds that they related to administrative and not (as he says, here) quasi-judicial functions, and to decisions which were not (as he says, here) "fundamentally invalid" (his phrase).

The argument as to fundamental invalidity is based upon *Anisminic Ltd* v *Foreign Compensation Commission* but before examining that case I must examine the earlier decision in *Smith* v *East Elloe RDC*. In that case land belonging to the appellant had been the subject of a compulsory purchase order made by the respondent council and confirmed by the respondent minister's predecessor. The making and confirmation of the order were regulated by Sch. I to the Acquisition of Land (Authorisation Procedure) Act 1946, and paras 15 and 16 of Part IV of that schedule were in practically similar terms as respectively sub-paras (1) and (3) of para. 12 of Sch. 15 to the 1981 Act. More than six weeks after the date of confirmation, the appellant commenced an action against the council and the minister claiming amongst other relief a declaration that the order was made wrongfully and in bad faith. The respondents applied to have the writ set aside on the ground that "the writ of summons . . . is invalid for lack of jurisdiction" . . .

The majority in the House . . . were of the opinion that para. 16 of Part IV of Sch. 1 prevented the action from proceeding. Viscount Simonds thought that the plain words of the paragraph ousted the jurisdiction. Lord Morton also thought that the words were clear and deprived "all courts of any jurisdiction to try . . . issues . . . whereby the appellant . . . seeks to question the validity of the order".

Lord Ratcliffe said:

> At one time the argument was shaped into the form of saying that an order made in bad faith was in law a nullity and that, consequently, all references to compulsory purchase orders in para. 15 and para. 16 must be treated as references to such orders only as had been made in good faith. But this argument is, in reality, a play on the meaning of the word nullity. An order, even if not made in good faith, is still an act capable of legal consequences. It bears no brand of invalidity on its forehead. Unless the necessary proceedings are taken at law to establish the cause of invalidity and to get it quashed or otherwise upset, it will remain as effective for its ostensible purpose as the most impeccable of orders. And that brings us back to the question that determines this case: Has Parliament allowed the necessary proceedings to be taken? I am afraid that I have searched in vain for a principle of construction as applied to Acts of Parliament which would enable the appellant to succeed. On the other hand, it is difficult not to recall in the respondents' favour the *dictum* of Lord Bacon: "*non est interpretatio, sed divinatio, quae recedit a litera*".

Smith v *East Elloe RDC* was referred to in *Anisminic Ltd* v *Foreign Compensation Commission* [see p.267]. . . . Lord Reid said:

> Statutory provisions which seek to limit the ordinary jurisdiction of the court have a long history. No case has been cited in which any other form of words limiting the jurisdiction of the court has been held to protect a nullity. If the draftsman or Parliament has intended to introduce a new kind of ouster clause so as to prevent any enquiry, even whether the document relied on was a forgery, I would have expected to find something much more specific than the bald statement that a determination shall not be called in question in any court of law. Undoubtedly such a provision protects every determination which is not a nullity. But I do not think that it is necessary or even reasonable to construe the word "determination" as including everything which purports to be a determination but which is in fact no determination at all. And there are no degrees of nullity. There are a number of reasons why the law will hold a purported decision to be a nullity. I do not see how it could be said that such a provision protects some kinds of nullity but not others; if that were intended it would be easy to say so. The case which gives most difficulty is *Smith* v *East Elloe Rural District Council*, where the form of ouster clause was similar to that in the present case. But I cannot regard it as a very satisfactory case. The plaintiff was aggrieved by a compulsory purchase order. After two unsuccessful actions, she tried again after six years. As this case never reached the stage of a statement of claim we do not know whether her case was that the Clerk of the Council had fraudulently misled the Council and the Ministry, or whether it was that the Council and the Ministry were parties to the fraud. The result would be quite different, in my view, for it is only if the authority which made the order had itself acted in *mala fide* that the order would be a nullity. I think that the case which it was intended to present must have been that the fraud was only the fraud of the Clerk, because almost the whole of the argument was on the question whether a time limit in the Act applied where the

fraud was alleged; there was no citation of the authorities on the question whether a clause ousting the jurisdiction of the court applied when nullity was in question, and there was little about this matter in the speeches. I do not, therefore, regard this case as a binding authority on this question.

[Mann LJ then further quoted from the judgments of Lord Pearce, Lord Wilberforce and Lord Pearson, and continued:]

The decision has a landmark quality because it has been taken (notably by Lord Diplock) as ending any need to distinguish between errors of law that went to jurisdiction and those which did not when considering the decisions of administrative bodies, tribunals and at least some inferior courts: see *Re Racal Communications Ltd*, *O'Reilly v Mackman*, *R v Greater Manchester Coroner, ex parte Tal* and *R v Oxford City Justices, ex parte Berry*.

Any challenge is in practice nowadays regarded as a challenge as to jurisdiction. That said, the speeches from which I have quoted left uncertain the vitality of *Smith v East Elloe RDC*. That uncertainty had to be considered by the Court of Appeal in *ex parte Ostler*. Mr Ostler applied for an order of *certiorari* to quash as invalid two trunk road orders which had been confirmed by the Secretary of State in pursuance of powers conferred by the Highways Act 1959. Schedule 2 to that Act contained provisions in paras 2 and 4 which were in practically similar terms to respectively sub-paragraphs (1) and (3) of paragraph 12 of Sch. 15 to the 1981 Act. Mr Ostler's application was necessarily made more than six weeks after the date of confirmation because the facts giving rise to his challenge on grounds of bad faith and breach of natural justice did not come to his knowledge until after the elapse of that period. The Secretary of State submitted as a preliminary point that the attack on the orders could not be made because of the preclusive provision in the statute.

This court (presided over by Lord Widgery CJ) thought that having regard to the *Anisminic* case "proof that the order was a nullity would be an answer to the type of exclusionary provision with which we are concerned here", and therefore ordered that the application should proceed. The Secretary of State's appeal was allowed. Lord Denning MR commenced his judgment with the remark:

> We are here presented with a nice question. Is *Smith v East Elloe Rural District Council* a good authority or has it been overruled by *Anisminic v Foreign Compensation Commission*?

Lord Denning MR concluded that *Smith v East Elloe RDC* was to be regarded as good and binding on the Court of Appeal. He said:

> It is readily to be distinguished from the *Anisminic* case. The points of difference are these. First, in the *Anisminic* case the Foreign Compensation Act 1959 ousted the jurisdiction of the court altogether. It precluded the court from entertaining any complaint at any time about the determination. Whereas in *Smith v East Elloe Rural District Council* the statutory provision has given the court jurisdiction to enquire into complaints so long as the applicant comes within six weeks. The provision is more in the nature of a limitation period than of a complete ouster. . . . Second, in the *Anisminic* case the House was considering a determination by a truly judicial body, the Foreign Compensation Tribunal, whereas in *Smith v East Elloe Rural District Council* the House was considering an order which was very

much in the nature of an administrative decision. That is a distinction which Lord Reid himself drew in *Ridge* v *Baldwin*. There is a great difference between the two. In making a judicial decision, the tribunal considers the rights of the parties without regard to the public interest. But in an administrative decision (such as a compulsory purchase order) the public interest plays an important part. The question is, to what extent are private interests to be subordinated to the public interest. Third, in the *Anisminic* case the House had to consider the actual determination of the tribunal, whereas in *Smith* v *East Elloe Rural District Council* the House had to consider the validity of the process by which the decision was reached.

Goff LJ found difficulty in distinguishing the *Anisminic* case on the ground that in that case there was an absolute prohibition against recourse to the court, and based himself upon the character of the decision and upon an admittedly difficult distinction between an act without jurisdiction (*Anisminic*) and an act done in bad faith, but within jurisdiction (*Smith* v *East Elloe RDC* and *ex parte Ostler*). Shaw LJ agreed with Lord Denning MR and added some short reasons of his own.

[Counsel for the respondent] seeks to distinguish, as he must, both that case and *Smith* v *East Elloe RDC*.

The ground that the 1991 order is "fundamentally invalid" whilst the orders in neither *Smith* v *East Elloe RDC* nor *ex parte Ostler* were so invalid predicates that there are degrees of invalidity, and that only errors which are not fundamental are immune from review. I am unable to accept that there are degrees of invalidity. I am unaware of any modern authority which suggests that there are, and in particular I do not read the speech[es] . . . in the *Anisminic* case as contemplating the suggestion . . . In my judgment, a decision is either apt to be declared void or it is not.

We heard some argument as to whether "bad faith" was a special ground of invalidity which perhaps specially attracted the ouster clause as in *Smith* v *East Elloe RDC*. In that case the members of the House were divided as to whether a question of bad faith was a question as to statutory empowerment and thus within the prescribed grounds on which a statutory challenge could be made. . . . However, and importantly, I cannot read any of the speeches as suggesting that invalidity by reason of "bad faith" in the local authority or the minister, whether taking the form of impropriety of purpose or of simple dishonesty, did not affect validity. I have no doubt that it does, and I cannot in 1992 differentiate between grounds of jurisdictional invalidity any more than I can between degrees of invalidity. Whether the majority opinion in the House in 1956 can still stand in the light of the development of the law since the *Anisminic* case must await resolution.

"Bad faith" might now be regarded as it was by Lord Radcliffe, and thus available as a ground within the statutory challenge procedure. The statutory ground of challenge that an order "is not within the powers of" the Act might now be regarded as apt to embrace all grounds of challenge to validity. Professor Sir William Wade . . . writes that the phrase "is simply a draftsman's translation of '*ultra vires*' comprising all its varieties". The point does not arise for decision in the present case because the scope of the statutory challenge is not in issue.

[Counsel's] second ground is based upon the distinction between an administrative and a judicial decision to which Lord Denning MR and Goff LJ attached importance. I am doubtful whether a decision to make an order under [the

1981 Act] is to be characterised either as a decision by a judicial body or as a quasi-judicial decision by an administrative body. However, if I assume that it does bear one or other of those characteristics, I would have to construe sub-paragraphs (1) and (3) of paragraph 12 of Sch. 15 to the 1981 Act differently from the practically similar paragraphs 2 and 4 of Sch. 2 to the Highways Act 1959 either in regard to all [such] orders or in regard to such of them as are made after a decision which has judicial characteristics. I cannot find any warrant in the language of the statute for such differentiations.

In my judgment, the decision in *ex parte Ostler* presents the same insuperable obstacle to [the respondent] as it did to the applicant in *ex parte Kent*. The question as to the ouster clause in the 1981 Act is one of construction and so far as this court is concerned it has been authoritatively decided. The intention of Parliament when it uses an *Anisminic* clause is that questions as to validity are not excluded. When paragraphs such as those considered in *ex parte Ostler* are used, then the legislative intention is that questions as to invalidity may be raised on the specified grounds in the prescribed time and in the prescribed manner, but that otherwise the jurisdiction of the court is excluded in the interest of certainty. This was the view of Lord Denning MR . . . and that view is binding on this court. I would, however, have independently formed the same view for the legislative intention seems to me to be plain from the language employed when the two sub-paragraphs of paragraph 12 are taken together. The language does not admit of differentiations between degrees (if such there be) or grounds of invalidity, nor does it admit of differing constructions according as to whether the decision to make an order is judicial or administrative in character.

For the reasons which I have given, I would set aside the leave granted by Otton J.'

R v Cornwall CC, ex parte Huntingdon
R v Devon CC, ex parte Isaacs

[1994] 1 All ER 694   ·   Court of Appeal

The decision of the Divisional Court in *ex parte Huntington* (above), and in a companion case involving Devon CC, was upheld on appeal.

Simon Brown LJ: '. . . I turn to the authorities. Those most directly in point are *Smith v East Elloe RDC*, *Anisminic Ltd v Foreign Compensation Commission*, *R v Secretary of State for the Environment, ex parte Ostler* and *R v Secretary of State for the Environment, ex parte Kent* – the first two decisions of the House of Lords, the last two of this court.

The preclusive clauses in *Smith v East Elloe RDC* and *ex parte Kent* . . . were in substantially similar terms to those of para. 12 of sch. 15 to the 1981 Act. The *Anisminic* case concerned a materially different provision – s. 4(4) of the Foreign Compensation Act 1950, which provided that "the determination by the Commission of any application made to them under this Act shall not be called into question in any court of law".

These decisions, and in particular the first three, were subjected to close analysis by Mann LJ in the Cornwall application . . .

[Simon Brown LJ cited extensively from the judgment of Mann LJ and continued:]

Faced with the Divisional Court's judgments in the Cornwall application (given only days previously), counsel for the applicant in the Devon appeal sought to argue that the court had overlooked the distinction between the situation in the three earlier cases – *Smith* v *East Elloe RDC, ex parte Ostler* and *ex parte Kent* – and the situation arising here, namely that in those three cases the applicants were beyond the statutory time limit in coming to court, whereas in the present cases, the arguments ran, the appellants do not seek to challenge any decision in respect of which there is a right of application. The right to apply to the High Court is a right to challenge the validity of a confirmed order; the challenge proposed here is to the validity of an unconfirmed order. Since, the submission ran, this cannot be done under the statutory right of application to the High Court it can, therefore, as in the *Anisminic* case, be done by way of judicial review.

   McCullough J rejected this argument. The three earlier cases, as he put it, made –

   clear that what prevented the decisions under challenge from being questioned in any legal proceedings except those brought under the provisions enabling an application to be made to this court within six weeks was the existence of the statutory scheme as a whole. It is the intention of Parliament in all these provisions that the High Court should only become involved when all the administrative steps have been completed.

Again I agree. And, indeed, in my judgment it is more rather than less probable that Parliament should intend to preclude the court's jurisdiction in the present situation that where, as in the earlier cases, such jurisdiction is held precluded (in the interests of certainty and finality) even though sometimes that has the unfortunate consequence of denying a person aggrieved any possibility of challenge at all, either because he does not discover the grounds for challenging the decision until after the statutory period has elapsed (as in *Smith* v *East Elloe RDC* and *ex parte Ostler*) or, indeed, because he does not even learn of the decision until after it is too late to challenge it (as in *ex parte Kent* and, a decision on a related issue, in *Griffiths* v *Secretary of State for the Environment*).

   True, as McCullough J recognised in the Devon appeal, it is arguably –

   less than ideal that the opportunity to challenge the order on the basis of the county council's default should only arise after the order has been confirmed, thus risking the possibility that the time and money devoted to the intervening local inquiry will have been wasted.

But, as he then pointed out, the answer to the argument is that this is what Parliament has ordained, and in any event, there are obvious countervailing benefits. First amongst these is that the very fact that an application for judicial review cannot be made at this preliminary stage means that the inquiry will not be delayed thereby. I agree and would furthermore point out that the Secretary of State may in any event refuse to confirm the order, thus making unnecessary any legal challenge whatever . . .

   In expressing the views that I have, I wish to make it plain that I have not overlooked a number of authorities helpfully brought to our attention . . . These cases, on analysis, can all be seen to concern challenges which are excluded from the statutory review procedure and which therefore were held amenable to the process of judicial review. Typically they are cases where what is challenged is not the decision itself but rather (a) a failure by the statutory decision-maker to exercise his jurisdiction – in short a refusal to make a decision (see *Lenlyn Ltd* v *Secretary of State for the Environment)*, (b) the reasoning underpinning the decision which is otherwise in the applicants' favour – such reasoning itself being damaging to some further interest of the applicants (see *Greater London Council* v *Secretary of State for the Environment)* and (c) some antecedent step quite separate and distinct from any eventual decision reviewable under the statute (see *R* v *Camden London BC, ex parte Comyn Ching & Co (London) Ltd* and *R* v *Secretary of State for the Environment, ex parte Stewart)*.

Essentially these applicants seek to bring themselves within this third category of case to which the jurisdictional bar does not apply. But in my judgment they cannot do so. *Ex parte Stewart*, decided under the provisions of the antecedent legislation, had earlier been relied upon to this end by ... the applicants' counsel ... As, however, [he] came to concede before the Divisional Court, the decision sought to be impugned in *ex parte Stewart* proved on analysis not to have been subject to the statutory clause at all.

Here by contrast there can be no doubt that all the complaints which these applicants seek to ventilate can be advanced, if necessary, under the statutory review procedure if and when these modification orders come to be confirmed by the Secretary of State.

The applicants' central quarrel with their respective county council is, as they frankly recognise, upon the facts of the cases and clearly these facts can and will be investigated in full at the public local inquiries yet to be held.'

Comment

(1)   Sometimes there is an overlap between judicial review procedures under RSC o.53 and statutory rights of challenge. The scope of the remedies available, and the standing required to bring such an action, may be greater under o.53 than under the statutory scheme.

(2)   Whether a court will permit an applicant to proceed by o.53 will depend on all the circumstances, including whether the statutory scheme creates an effective remedy: see *R* v *Hillingdon LBC, ex parte Royco Homes Ltd.* In *R* v *Birmingham City Council, ex parte Ferraro Ltd,* the Court of Appeal suggested that where an alternative remedy existed (and particularly where there was a statutory appellate scheme) it was only exceptionally that judicial review would be granted.

R v *Lord President of the Privy Council, ex parte Page*

[1992] 3 WLR 1112   ·   House of Lords

The applicant was made redundant from his lecturing position at a university. He petitioned the visitor to the university, who had jurisdiction under university statutes to determine such disputes. He alleged that his dismissal was contrary to the statutes. The petition was dismissed, and the applicant sought judicial review of that decision. The House of Lords held that the visitor had exclusive jurisdiction in respect of the internal affairs of the university, and could not be successfully challenged on the basis of an error of law made while acting within his jurisdiction.

Lord Browne-Wilkinson: ' . . . Under the modern law, *certiorari* normally lies to quash a decision for error of law. Therefore, the narrow issue in this case is whether . . . *certiorari* lies against the visitor to quash his decision as being erroneous in point of law notwithstanding that the question of law arises under the domestic law of the university which the visitor has "exclusive" jurisdiction to decide . . .

In my judgment this review of the authorities demonstrates that for over 300 years the law has been clearly established that the visitor of an eleemosynary charity has an exclusive jurisdiction to determine what are the internal laws of the charity and the proper application of those laws to those within his jurisdiction. The court's inability to determine those matters is not limited to the period pending the visitor's determination but extends so as to prohibit any subsequent review by the court of the correctness of a decision made by the visitor acting within his jurisdiction and in accordance with the rules of natural justice. This inability of the court to intervene is founded on the fact that the applicable law is not the common law of England but a peculiar or domestic law of which the visitor is the sole judge. This special status of a visitor springs from the common law recognising the right of the founder to lay down such a special law subject to adjudication only by a special judge, the visitor.

How then is it contended that the courts have power to review the visitor's decision as to the effect of the domestic law of the university in this case? The Divisional Court and the Court of Appeal did not consider in any detail the old authorities . . . They started from the position, in my judgment incorrectly, that the references in *Thomas* v *University of Bradford* to the visitor's jurisdiction being exclusive meant simply that the court did not have concurrent jurisdiction with him. Then, since this House in *Thomas's* case had accepted that judicial review by way of *certiorari* did lie to the visitor at least to restrain an abusive process, they held that there was jurisdiction to correct errors of law, since "illegality" is one of the accepted heads of judicial review.

[Counsel] relied upon the great development that has recently taken place in the law of judicial review whereby the courts have asserted a general jurisdiction to review the decisions of tribunals and inferior courts. He points to the way in which the law has developed from a maze of individual sets of circumstances in which one or other of the prerogative writs would lie to a general principle under which courts will review decisions on the three grounds of illegality, irrationality and procedural impropriety: see per Lord Diplock in *Council of Civil Service Unions* v *Minister for the Civil Service*. [He] submits that if judicial review lies at all, then it is not possible to pick and choose between Lord Diplock's three categories: it must lie on all three grounds or not at all. As to illegality, recent developments in the law have shown that any relevant error of law made by the decision maker, whether as to his powers or as to the law he is to apply, may lead to his decision being quashed. In the present case, since the decision in *Thomas* v *University of Bradford* shows that judicial review does lie against the visitor, so his decision is capable of being reviewed on any one of Lord Diplock's three grounds, including illegality. If, therefore, the visitor has made an error in construing the statutes of the university, his decision can be quashed on judicial review.

I accept much of [these] submissions. Over the last 40 years, the courts have developed general principles of judicial review. The fundamental principle is that the courts will intervene to ensure that the powers of public decision-making bodies are exercised lawfully. In all cases, save possibly one, this intervention by way of prohibition or *certiorari* is based on the proposition that such powers have been conferred on the decision maker on the underlying assumption that the powers are to be exercised only within the jurisdiction conferred, in accordance with fair procedures and, in a *Wednesbury* sense . . ., reasonably. If the decision maker exercises his powers outside the jurisdiction conferred, in a manner which is procedurally irregular or is *Wednesbury* unreasonable, he is acting *ultra vires* his powers and therefore unlawfully. . . . The one possible exception to this general rule used to be the jurisdiction of the court to quash a decision taken within the jurisdiction of the decision taker where an error of law appeared on the face of the record: *R v Northumberland Compensation Appeal Tribunal, ex parte Shaw*.

In my judgment the decision in *Anisminic Ltd* v *Foreign Compensation Commission* rendered obsolete the distinction between errors of law on the face of the record and other errors of law on the face of the record by extending the doctrine of *ultra vires*. Thenceforward it was to be taken that Parliament had only conferred the decision-making power on the basis that it was to be exercised on the correct legal basis: a misdirection in law in making the decision therefore rendered the decision *ultra vires*. Professor Wade considers that the true effect of *Anisminic* is still in doubt: *Administrative Law*, 6th ed., p.299 *et seq*. But in my judgment the decision of this House in *O'Reilly* v *Mackman* establishes the law in the sense that I have stated . . . in general any error of law made by an administrative tribunal or inferior court in reaching its decision can be quashed for error of law . . .

Although the general rule is that decisions affected by errors of law made by industrial tribunals or inferior courts can be quashed, in my judgment there are two reasons why that rule does not apply in the case of visitors. First, as I have sought to explain, the constitutional basis of the courts' power to quash is that the decision of the inferior tribunal is unlawful on the grounds that it is *ultra vires*. In the ordinary case, the law applicable to a decision made by such a body is the general law of the land. Therefore, a tribunal or inferior court acts *ultra vires* if it reaches its conclusion on a basis erroneous under the general law. But the position of decisions made by a visitor is different. As the authorities which I have cited demonstrate, the visitor is applying not the general law of the land but a peculiar, domestic law of which he is the sole arbiter and of which the courts have no cognisance. If the visitor has power under the regulating documents to enter into the adjudication of the dispute (i.e. is acting within his jurisdiction in the narrow sense) he cannot err in law in reaching this decision since the general law is not the applicable law. Therefore he cannot be acting *ultra vires* and unlawfully by applying his view of the domestic law in reaching his decision. The court has no jurisdiction either to say that he erred in his application of the general law (since the general law is not applicable to the decision) or to reach a contrary view as to the effect of the domestic law (since the visitor is the sole judge of such domestic law).

The second reason is closely allied to the first. In *Pearlman* v *Keepers and Governors of Harrow School* a statute provided that the decision of the county court as to whether works constituted an "improvement" within the meaning of the Act should be "final and conclusive". A tenant claimed that the installation of a central heating system constituted an "improvement". The county court judge ruled that it did not. The tenant then applied to the Divisional Court by way of judicial review to quash the judge's decision. The majority of the Court of Appeal held that it had jurisdiction to quash the judge's order. However, Geoffrey Lane LJ dissented. He held that the judge had done nothing which went outside the proper area of his inquiry. The question was not whether the judge had made a wrong decision but whether he had inquired into and decided a matter which he had no right to consider. Therefore he held that the court had no jurisdiction to review the decision of the county court judge for error of law.

This dissenting judgment of Geoffrey Lane LJ has been approved by the Privy Council in *South East Asia Fire Bricks Sdn. Bhd.* v *Non-Metallic Mineral Products Manufacturing Employees Union* and by a majority in this House in *Re Racal Communications Ltd.* In the latter case, Lord Diplock pointed out that the decision in *Anisminic Ltd* v *Foreign Compensation Commission* applied to decisions of administrative tribunals or other administrative bodies made under statutory powers: in those cases there was a presumption that the statute conferring the power did not intend the administrative body to be the final arbiter of questions of law. He then contrasted that position with the case where a decision-making power had been conferred on a court of law. In that case no such presumption could exist: on the contrary, where Parliament had provided that the decision of an inferior court was final and conclusive, the High Court should not be astute to find that the inferior court's decision on a question of law had not been made final and conclusive, thereby excluding the jurisdiction to review it.

In my judgment, therefore, if there were a statutory provision that the decision of a visitor on the law applicable to internal disputes of a charity was to be "final and conclusive", courts would have no jurisdiction to review the visitor's decision on the grounds of error of law made by the visitor within his jurisdiction (in the narrow sense). For myself, I can see no relevant distinction between a case where a statute has conferred such final and conclusive jurisdiction and the case where the common law has for 300 years recognised that the visitor's decision on questions of fact and law are final and conclusive and are not to be reviewed by the courts. Accordingly, unless this House is prepared to sweep away long-established law, there is no jurisdiction in the court to review a visitor's decision for error of law committed within his jurisdiction.

[Counsel] urged that the position of a visitor would be anomalous if he were immune from review on the grounds of error of law. He submitted that the concept of a peculiar domestic law differing from the general law of the land was artificial since in practice the charter and statutes of a university are expressed in ordinary legal language and applied in accordance with the same principles as those applicable under the general law. He pointed to the important public role occupied by universities and submitted that it was wrong that they should be immune from the general law of the land: "There must be no Alsatia in England where the King's writ does not run": per Scrutton LJ in *Czarnikow* v *Roth, Schmidt & Co.* He further suggested that to permit review of a visitor's decision for error of law would not impair the effectiveness of the visitor's domestic jurisdiction.

I accept that the position of the visitor is anomalous, indeed unique. I further accept that where the visitor is, or is advised by, a lawyer the distinction between the peculiar domestic law he applies and the general law is artificial. But I do not regard these factors as justifying sweeping away the law which for so long has regulated the conduct of charitable corporations. There are internal disputes which are resolved by a visitor who is not a lawyer himself and has not taken legal advice. It is not only modern universities which have visitors: there is a substantial number of other long-established educational, ecclesiastical and eleemosynary bodies which have visitors. The advantage of having an informal system which produces a speedy, cheap and final answer to internal disputes has been repeatedly emphasised in the authorities, most recently by this House in *Thomas* v *University of Bradford*. . . . If it were to be held that judicial review for error of law lay against the visitor, I fear that, as in the present case, finality would be lost not only in cases raising pure questions of law but also in cases where it would be urged in accordance with the *Wednesbury* principle, *Associated Provincial Picture Houses Ltd* v *Wednesbury Corporation*, that the visitor had failed to take into account relevant matters or taken into account irrelevant matters or had reached an irrational conclusion. Although the visitor's position is anomalous, it provides a valuable machinery for resolving internal disputes, which should not be lost.

I have therefore reached the conclusion that judicial review does not lie to impeach the decisions of a visitor taken within his jurisdiction (in the narrow sense) on questions of either fact or law. Judicial review does lie to the visitor in cases where he has acted outside his jurisdiction (in the narrow sense) or abused his powers or acted in breach of the rules of natural justice. Accordingly, in my judgment the Divisional Court had no jurisdiction to entertain the application for judicial review of the visitor's decision in this case.'

Comment

The principles in this case were applied in *R* v *Visitors to the Inns of Court, ex parte Calder, Persaud*. The Court of Appeal concluded that the decisions of High Court judges acting as Visitors to the Inns of Court were susceptible to judicial review if there was no authority to enter into the adjudication at all, if they had misused power, or committed a breach of the principles of natural justice.

Available remedies

Equal Opportunities Commission v *Secretary of State for Employment*

[1994] 1 All ER 910 · House of Lords

[For facts and decision, see p.113.]

Lord Browne-Wilkinson: 'I . . . wish to add a few words on the procedural question whether the court can make a declaration on an application for judicial review even though in the circumstances of the case the court could not grant one of the prerogative orders.

The question arises in this way. It being established . . . that the Equal Opportunities Commission has *locus standi* to bring proceedings for judicial review but has not demonstrated that there is any "decision" by the Secretary of State which can be quashed, has the court got jurisdiction to make a declaration that the domestic law of the United Kingdom is not in conformity with Community law?

Before 1977 there were two routes whereby relief could be sought from the courts in the field of what is now known as public law. The first was by application to the Queen's Bench Divisional Court for one of the prerogative orders. The second was by way of a civil action in the High Court for a declaration . . . As early as 1911 it was established that, in a civil action brought by a competent plaintiff, the court could grant declaratory relief against the Crown as to the legality of actions which the Crown proposed to take: see *Dyson* v *A-G*. Of course, in such civil proceedings in the High Court there could be no question of the plaintiff being entitled to any of the prerogative orders, which could only be made in proceedings on the Crown side.

Civil proceedings for a declaration as to public rights were a widely adopted method down to 1977. Indeed, many of the most recent developments in public law were made in such civil actions brought to obtain declaratory relief only: see, e.g. *Ridge* v *Baldwin*, *Anisminic* v *Foreign Compensation Commission* . . .

The ability to obtain a declaration of public rights in civil proceedings was restricted by the need to show sufficient *locus standi*. Although the plaintiff did not have to show actual or threatened infringement of his private rights, he did have to show that any actual or threatened infringement of public rights would cause him special damage: see *Gouriet* v *Union of Post Office Workers* . . .

In 1977 the new ord. 53 was introduced, laying down the modern procedure for judicial review. Order 53, r.1(2) expressly provides that an application for a declaration can be made in judicial review proceedings and gives the Divisional Court the power to make a declaration if it considers it just and convenient –

> having regard to – (a) the nature of the matters in respect of which relief may be granted by way of an order of mandamus, prohibition or *certiorari*, (b) the nature of the persons and bodies against whom relief may be granted by way of such an order and (c) all the circumstances of the case.

This rule was given statutory confirmation by s.31 of the Supreme Court Act 1981.

In the period between the introduction of the new ord.53 and the decision in *O'Reilly* v *Mackman* there were therefore two routes whereby a declaration of public rights could be obtained . . . As to the latter, the position remained as it was before 1977. During this period, civil proceedings for a declaration as to public rights continued to be brought. Thus in *Royal College of Nursing of the UK* v *Dept of Health and Social Security* civil proceedings were brought . . . for a declaration as to the correctness in law of a circular from DHSS purporting to explain to the medical profession the effect of the Abortion Act 1967 . . .

Accordingly, right down to the decision of this House in *O'Reilly* v *Mackman* the two procedures for obtaining declaratory relief . . . continued . . . In [that case] . . . this House held that in such public law cases, it is an abuse of process to proceed by way of civil action and that such proceedings must be brought by way of judicial review . . .

[Lord Browne-Wilkinson cited from the speech of Lord Diplock, and continued:]

In my judgment, this passage makes it clear that under ord. 53 any declaration as to public rights which could formerly be obtained in civil proceedings in the High Court can now also be obtained in judicial review proceedings. If this were not so, the effect of the purely procedural decision in *O'Reilly* v *Mackman* requiring all public law cases to be brought by way of judicial review would have had the effect of thenceforward preventing a plaintiff who previously had *locus standi* to bring civil proceedings for a declaration as to public rights (even though there was no decision which could be the subject of a prerogative order) from bringing proceedings for such a declaration. No statutory provision has ever removed the right to seek such a declaration which right has been established and exercised since 1911. Order 53, r.1(2) does not say that a declaration is only to be made in lieu of a prerogative order. All it requires is that the court should have regard to "the nature of the matters in respect of which" prerogative orders can be made. In the second *Factortame* case . . . this House . . . plainly envisaged that a declaration as to public rights could be made, even though on the facts of that case none of the prerogative orders could have been made . . .'

Comment

(1)   For *locus standi*, see p.255.

(2)   The effect of the decision is to provide an important mechanism for challenging English law on the basis that it fails to comply with obligations under European law. See, further, the *Factortame* litigation (p.108) and the obligation to provide effective remedies which is inherent in art.5 of the Treaty of Rome (see p.121).

(3)   For the problems involved in the concept of exclusivity of o.53 procedures, see p.250.

M v Home Office

[1993] 3 All ER 537   ·   House of Lords

[For the facts and decision, see p.184]

Lord Woolf: '[Counsel for M] placed at the forefront of his argument the issue as to whether the courts have jurisdiction to make coercive orders against the Crown or ministers of the Crown . . . In support of their respective submissions as to the correct answer to the issue, [counsel] relied on principles which had been repeatedly reiterated down the centuries since mediaeval times. The principles on which [Counsel for the Home Secretary] founded his argument are that the King can do no wrong and that the King cannot be sued in his own courts. [Counsel for the applicant] on the other hand relied on the equally historic principle which is intimately linked with the name of Professor Dicey that –

> when we speak of the "rule of law" as a characteristic of our country, [we mean] not only that with us no man is above the law, but (what is a different thing) that here every man, whatever be his rank or condition, is subject to the ordinary law of the realm and amenable to the jurisdiction of the ordinary tribunals. In England the idea of legal equality, or the universal subjection of all classes to one law administered by the ordinary courts, has been pushed to its utmost limit. With us every official, from Prime Minister down to a constable or a collector of taxes, is under the same responsibility for every act done without legal justification as any other citizen. The reports abound with cases in which officials have been brought before the courts, and made, in their personal capacity, liable to punishment, or to the payment of damages, for acts done in their official character but in excess of

their lawful authority. A colonial governor, a secretary of state, a military officer, and all subordinates, though carrying out the commands of their official superiors, are as responsible for any act which the law does not authorise as is any private and unofficial person. (See *Introduction to the Study of the Law of the Constitution* (10th edn, 1965) pp. 193–194.)

In the course of argument we were referred to numerous authorities which supported these principles. However, in the present proceedings what is in dispute is not the validity of the principles but the manner in which in practice they were reconciled by the courts. The fact that the Sovereign could do no wrong did not mean that a servant of the Crown could do no wrong. Prior to the Crown Proceedings Act 1947 it was long established that what would now be described as private law rights could be established against the Crown either by bringing a petition of right or, in the case of an action in tort, when a petition of right was not available (*Tobin* v *R* (1864)), by bringing an action for damages against the servant of the Crown responsible for the tort in his own name . . .

The position so far as civil wrongs are concerned, prior to the 1947 Act, can be summarised, therefore, by saying that as long as the plaintiffs sued the actual wrongdoer or the person who ordered the wrongdoing he could bring an action against officials personally, in particular as to torts committed by them and they were not able to hide behind the immunity of the Crown. This was the position even though at the time they committed the alleged torts they were acting in their official capacity. In those proceedings an injunction, including, if appropriate, an interlocutory injunction, could be granted. The problem which existed in seeking a remedy against the Crown was not confined to injunctions. It applied to any form of proceedings and where proceedings were possible by suing the wrongdoer personally then an injunction would be available in the same circumstances as other remedies. If such a position required reconciling with the historic maxim as to the Crown doing no wrong, then this could be achieved by an approach, which [counsel for the Home Office] endorsed in the course of argument, by saying that, as the Crown could do no wrong, the Crown could not be considered to have authorised the doing of wrong, so the tortfeasor was not acting with the authority of the Crown . . .

The difficulty which a plaintiff might have in identifying the appropriate servant of the Crown who was the tortfeasor in practice was overcome by the Crown nominating the individual responsible for the damage and the lack of resources of the defendant did not cause problems since the Treasury would make an *ex gratia* payment of compensation if it was a case where, but for Crown immunity, the Crown would be vicariously liable. In such proceedings, if it was appropriate for an injunction to be granted, there was no reason why this should not be done . . .

It was the criticisms in *Adams* v *Naylor*, and the cases which applied those criticisms, of the practice of the Crown nominating a defendant who might not have been personally guilty of any tort which were the catalysts for the changes which were brought about by the 1947 Act.

However, before referring to that Act it is necessary to draw attention to one additional development in bringing proceedings against the Crown. This involved the grant of declaratory relief against the Crown. In *Dyson* v *A-G* it was decided that it was unnecessary to have a cause of action in order to obtain declaratory relief. This opened the door to proceedings for a declaration against the Crown, at least where the estate of the Crown was not involved, without the necessity of proceeding by petition of right. In such proceedings there would be no question of obtaining an injunction.

So far as civil proceedings were concerned the position was transformed by the 1947 Act. Section 1 enabled the Crown to be sued directly in those situations where prior to the Act a claim might have been enforced by petition of right. Section 2 did not remove the right to sue the actual tortfeasor.

[Lord Woolf examined parts of the 1947 Act, cited the terms of s.21 of the Act, and continued:]

Returning to s.21, what is clear is that in relation to proceedings to which provisos (a) and (b) of s.21(1) apply, no injunction can be granted against the Crown. In addition there is the further restriction on granting an injunction against an officer of the Crown under s.21(2). That subsection is restricted in its application to situations where the effect of the grant of an injunction or an order against an officer of the Crown will be to give any relief against the Crown which could not have been obtained in proceedings against the Crown prior to the Act . . .

There appears to be no reason in principle why, if a statute places a duty on a specified minister or other official which creates a cause of action, an action cannot now be brought for breach of statutory duty claiming damages or for an injunction, in the limited circumstances where injunctive relief would be appropriate, against the specified minister personally by any person entitled to the benefit of the cause of action. If, on the other hand, the duty is placed on the Crown in general, then s. 21(2) would appear to prevent injunctive relief being granted, but as Professor Sir William Wade QC has pointed out ('Injunction relief against the Crown and ministers' (1991) 107 LQR 4) there are likely to be few situations when there will be statutory duties which place a duty on the Crown in general instead of on a named minister. In broad terms therefore the effect of the Act can be summarised by saying that it is only in those situations where prior to the Act no injunctive relief could be obtained that s. 21 prevents an injunction being granted. In other words it restricts the effect of the procedural reforms that it implemented so that they did not extend the power of the courts to grant injunctions. This is the least that can be expected from legislation intended to make it easier for proceedings to be brought against the Crown . . .

[Lord Woolf cites *Merricks* v *Heathcote-Amory*, doubting certain *dicta* suggesting that a minister when acting in his official capacity could not be sued personally and an injunction granted, and that, in any event, those *dicta* were not made in the context of the prerogative orders of judicial review. He continued:]

I now turn to the historical development of relief against the Crown in prerogative proceedings. I do so because the historical development of the two sets of proceedings have been on different lines. Prior to the introduction of judicial review, the principal remedies which were available were certiorari, mandamus, prohibition and habeas corpus. As we are primarily concerned with the possible availability of injunction, I will focus on mandamus and prohibition since they are indistinguishable in their effect from final injunctions . . .

The prerogative remedies could not be obtained against the Crown directly as was explained by Lord Denman CJ in *R* v *Powell* (1841):

... both because there would be an incongruity in the Queen commanding herself to do an act, and also because the disobedience to a writ of mandamus is to be enforced by attachment.

Originally this difficulty could not be avoided by bringing the proceedings against named ministers of the Crown ... But, where a duty was imposed by statute for the benefit of the public upon a particular minister, so that he was under a duty to perform that duty in his official capacity, then orders of prohibition and mandamus were granted regularly against the minister. The proceedings were brought against the minister in his official name and, according to the title of the proceedings, by the Crown. The title of the proceedings would be *R* v *Minister, ex parte the applicant* (as is still the position today), so that unless the minister was treated as being distinct from the Crown the title of the proceedings would disclose the "incongruity" of the Crown suing the Crown. This did not mean that the minister was treated as acting other than in his official capacity and the order was made against him in his official name. In accordance with this practice there have been numerous cases where prerogative orders, including orders of prohibition and mandamus have been made against ministers.

Nonetheless, there were limits at that time ... to the availability of mandamus. It was necessary that there should be a duty which was owed to the applicant as a member of the public. The duty which was required was not a private duty which would give rise to a right to damages in the event of a breach, but a public duty. In addition the duty had to be placed on a named minister. As already indicated, in most situations today statutory duties are conferred on ministers in their own name and not upon the Crown in general: see Professor Sir William Wade QC "Injunctive relief against the Crown and ministers" (1991) 107 LQR 4. Furthermore, by the time of the introduction of the remedy of judicial review the position had developed so that the prerogative orders, including prohibition and mandamus, were being granted regularly against ministers without any investigation of whether a statutory duty, which had not been complied with, was placed upon the minister or some one else in the department for which the minister was responsible ...

After the introduction of judicial review in 1977 it was therefore not necessary to draw any distinction between an officer of the Crown "acting as such" and an officer acting in some other capacity in public law proceedings. The changes made in procedure introduced in 1977 by RCS ord.53 for judicial review were first given statutory authority by primary legislation in s.31 of the Supreme Court Act 1981 ...

In s.31 the jurisdiction to grant declarations and injunctions is directly linked to that which already existed in relation to the prerogative orders. The jurisdiction to award damages by contrast is restricted to those situations where damages are recoverable in an action begun by writ. It has never been suggested that a declaration is not available in proceedings against a minister in his official capacity and if ord.53 and s.31 apply to a minister in the case of declarations then, applying ordinary rules of construction, one would expect the position to be precisely the same in the case of injunctions. As an examination of the position prior to the introduction of judicial review indicates, because of the scope of the remedies of mandamus and prohibition the availability of injunctions against ministers would only be of any significance in situations where it would be appropriate to grant interim relief. Even here the significance of the change was reduced by the power of the court to grant a stay under ord.53, r.3(10). Furthermore, in practice an injunction against a minister would be no more than a peremptory declaration because of the limitations on execution contained in ord.77, r.15 which because of the definition of "order against the Crown" in ord.77, r.1(2) applies to judicial review and proceedings against an officer of the Crown as such.

Lord Bridge in *Factortame Ltd* v *Secretary of State for Transport* acknowledged "the question at issue depends, first, on the true construction of s.31 . . ." Lord Bridge also accepted that if s.31 "were to be construed in isolation" there would be "great force in the reasoning" that s.31 did enable injunctions to be granted for the first time against ministers of the Crown in judicial review proceedings . . . Why then did Lord Bridge come to the conclusion that an injunction could not be granted against a minister in proceedings for judicial review?

A primary cause for Lord Bridge's taking this view was that he concluded that it would be a dramatic departure from what was the position prior to the introduction of judicial review for an injunction to be available against the Crown or a minister of the Crown, so that the change was one which could be expected to be made only by express legislation. His conclusion was not, however, based on as comprehensive an argument of the history of both civil and prerogative proceedings as was available to your Lordships. In particular he did not have an account of the developments which had taken place in the granting of prerogative orders against ministers, which meant that in practical terms the only consequence of treating s.31 as enabling injunctions to be granted against ministers acting in their official capacity would be to provide an alternative in name only to the orders of prohibition and mandamus which were already available and to allow interim relief other than a stay for the first time.

A secondary cause was his reliance upon Upjohn J's judgment in *Merricks* v *Heathcoat-Amory*, a judgment which, as already indicated, should be approached with caution. Lord Bridge was also influenced by the fact that the new ord.53 was introduced following the Law Commission's Report on Remedies in Administrative Law (Law Com. No. 73) (1976) and that that report drew attention to the problem created by the lack of jurisdiction to grant interim injunctions against the Crown and recommended that the problem should be remedied by amending s.21 of the 1947 Act. The report included a draft of the legislation proposed. This proposal of the Law Commission was never implemented. Instead the decision was taken following the Law Commission's report to proceed by amendment of the Rules of the Supreme Court rather than by primary legislation. Lord Bridge in his speech explains why, in his view, this meant that s.31 of the 1981 Act should be given a restricted interpretation.

This is a very closely and carefully argued justification for adopting a narrow approach to the effect of s.31 of the 1981 Act. It deserves very careful attention coming, as it does, from a judge who is acknowledged to have made an outstanding contribution to this area of the law. Nonetheless, I do not regard it as justifying limiting the natural interpretation of s.31 so as to exclude the jurisdiction to grant injunctions, including interim injunctions, on applications for judicial review against ministers of the Crown. I will try to explain why.

First of all it is unsafe to draw any inference from the fact that judicial review was not first introduced by primary legislation. Primary legislation could have led to delay . . . Order 53 undoubtedly extended the circumstances in which a declaration could be granted against the appropriate representative of the Crown. Prior to the change no remedy whatsoever in the nature of a declaration could be obtained in prerogative proceedings. Furthermore, there are situations where no declaration could be obtained in private law proceedings against the Crown without the assistance of the Attorney-General in circumstances in which it is now available on judicial review. It is not suggested that ord.53 was *ultra vires* in allowing declarations against ministers and in my view if it was not *ultra vires* in relation to declarations there is no reason why it should be regarded as being *ultra vires* in relation to injunctions, albeit that the effect is that an injunction cannot be obtained against a minister of the Crown where previously only an order of mandamus or prohibition could be obtained. However, if ord.53 were to be regarded as being open to challenge on this ground, this would explain why the unusual course was taken, a change having been introduced by an amendment to the Rules of the Supreme Court, of confirming the amendment a substantial period later by the 1981 Act. As a matter of construction it is difficult to treat the provisions as to injunctions in ord.53 and s.31 as not applying to ministers, but as doing so in the case of the other remedies . . . RSC ord.53, r.3(10) deals with the grant of interim relief on an application for judicial review. It provides:

> Where leave to apply for judicial review is granted, then – (a) if the relief sought is an order of a prohibition or certiorari and the court so directs, the grant shall operate as a stay of the proceedings to which the application relates until the determination of the application or until the court otherwise orders; (b) if any other relief is sought, the court may at any time grant in the proceedings such interim relief as could be granted in an action begun by writ.

So far as respondents other than ministers are concerned, the provisions of ord.53, r.3(10)(b) have always been treated as giving the court jurisdiction to grant interim injunctions. This is confirmed to be the position by the decision of the Court of Appeal in *R* v *Kensington and Chelsea Royal London BC, ex parte Hammell*. The power of the court to grant interim injunctions is linked to the power of the court to grant final injunctions. If the court has the power to grant a final injunction against a minister it must surely have the power to grant an interim injunction and vice versa. This is confirmed by s.37(1) of the 1981 Act, which provides:

> The High Court may by order (whether interlocutory or final) grant an injunction . . . in all cases which it appears to the court to be just and convenient to do so.

[Lord Woolf examined various technical points, and continued:]

Prior to the introduction of ord.53 there was the same problem of the inability to grant interim injunctions against bodies which had no connection with the Crown. The changes which are reflected in ss.31(2) and (3) and ord.53, r.3(10) provided a solution in relation to those bodies and it must surely follow that if s.31(2) gives the court jurisdiction to grant final injunctions against ministers it must also provide the jurisdiction to grant interim injunctions.

I am, therefore, of the opinion that the language of s.31 being unqualified in its terms, there is no warrant for restricting its application so that in respect of ministers and other officers of the Crown alone the remedy of an injunction, including an interim injunction, is not available. In my view the history of prerogative proceedings against officers of the Crown supports such a conclusion. So far as interim relief is concerned which is the practical change which has been made, there is no justification for adopting a different approach to officers of the Crown from that adopted in relation to other respondents in the absence of clear language such as that contained in s.21(2) of the 1947 Act. The fact that in any event a stay could be granted against the Crown under ord.53, r.3(10) emphasises the limits of the change in the situation which is involved. It would be most regrettable if an approach which is inconsistent with that which exists in Community law should be allowed to persist if this is not strictly necessary. The restriction provided for in s.21(2) of the 1947 Act does, however, remain in relation to civil proceedings.

The fact that, in my view, the court should be regarded as having jurisdiction to grant interim and final injunctions against officers of the Crown does not mean that that jurisdiction should be exercised except in the most limited circumstances. In the majority of situations, so far as final relief is concerned, a declaration will continue to be appropriate remedy on an application for judicial review involving officers of the Crown. As has been the position in the past, the Crown can be relied upon to co-operate fully with such declarations. To avoid having to grant interim injunctions against officers of the Crown, I can see advantages in the courts being able to grant interim declarations. However, it is obviously not desirable to deal with this topic, if it is not necessary to do so, until the views of the Law Commission are known.'

Comment

The decision brings the general position of the law into line with that which has applied where questions of European law are concerned. See *Factortame (No. 2)*, p.287.

13 Grounds for judicial review

The grounds upon which judicial review can be sought successfully were conveniently summarized by Lord Diplock in the *GCHQ* case (p.289) as 'illegality', 'irrationality' and 'procedural impropriety'. These phrases, though useful starting points both for the courts and for the purposes of exposition, should be used with care. The following extracts demonstrate vividly that they are useful headings rather than definitive statements. They provide a useful summary of the current state of the law, but are not always used in precisely the same way, and overlap significantly. Thus, the well-known *Wednesbury* principles (p.291), which provide a starting point for consideration of alleged misuse of executive discretion, fall in part within the concept of illegality, and in part (the concept of 'Wednesbury unreasonableness') within irrationality.

Errors of law as to the meaning or extent of an enabling power will generally create illegality. Historically, there was, and still is, a doctrine of error on the face of the record, whereby a court could intervene to correct any error apparent from the record of proceedings of an administrative or inferior judicial body. This doctrine is, though, now of little importance in the context of executive bodies: the landmark decision of the House of Lords in *Anisminic* v *Foreign Compensation Board* (p.267), and its subsequent application, indicates that there is a presumption by the courts that an executive body has no power to misconstrue a statute: the courts can (subject to possible limits – see p.269) intervene to correct such errors, and the availability of discovery under RSC, o.53 will often enable such errors to be identified. The position with regard to the power of courts or inferior tribunals is more complicated: see *R* v *Lord President of the Privy Council, ex parte Page* (p.275). In respect of executive bodies, misconstruction of enabling power will render a decision challengeable.

It has already been seen that this applies equally to discretionary powers. The courts will imply limits, both in terms of keeping within the policy and intent of the enabling power, but also by an application of *Wednesbury* principles. Above all, the discretion must be genuinely exercised, and in accordance with factors that the law will apply.

Finally, even if a power exists, it must be used in a procedurally correct way. The procedural limits set by the enabling power must be kept within, though the effect of non-compliance will vary depending upon whether the procedural requirement is 'mandatory' or 'directory'. Other procedural requirements may be implied. In particular, there may often, although not always, be a duty to state the reasons why a particular decision was taken (p.333).

CCSU v Minister for the Civil Service

[See p.215]

Lord Diplock: '. . . Judicial review, now regulated by RSC o.53, provides the means by which judicial control of administrative action is exercised. The subject matter of every judicial review is a decision made by some person (or body of persons) whom I will call the "decision-maker" or else a refusal by him to make a decision.

To qualify as a subject for judicial review the decision must have consequences which affect some person (or body of persons) other than the decision-maker, although it may affect him too. It must affect such other person either: (a) by altering rights or obligations of that person which are enforceable by or against him in private law; or (b) by depriving him of some benefit or advantage which either (i) he has in the past been permitted by the decision-maker to enjoy and which he can legitimately expect to be permitted to continue to do until there has been communicated to him some rational grounds for withdrawing it on which he has been given an opportunity to comment; or (ii) he has received assurance from the decision-maker will not be withdrawn without giving him first an opportunity of advancing reasons for contending that they should not be withdrawn. (I prefer to continue to call the kind of expectation that qualifies a decision for inclusion in class (b) a "legitimate expectation" rather than a "reasonable expectation", in order thereby to indicate that it has consequences to which effect will be given in public law, whereas an expectation or hope that some benefit or advantage would continue to be enjoyed, although it might well be entertained by a "reasonable" man, would not necessarily have such consequences. The recent decision of this House in *Re Findlay* presents an example of the latter kind of expectation. "Reasonable" furthermore bears different meanings according to whether the context in which it is being used is that of private law or of public law. To eliminate confusion it is best avoided in the latter.)

For a decision to be susceptible to judicial review the decision-maker must be empowered by public law (and not merely, as in arbitration, by agreement between private parties) to make decisions that, if validly made, will lead to administrative action or abstention from action by an authority endowed by law with executive powers, which have one or other of the consequences mentioned in the preceding paragraph. The ultimate source of the decision-making power is nearly always nowadays a statute or subordinate legislation made under the statute; but in the absence of any statute regulating the subject matter of the decision the source of the decision-making power may still be the common law itself, i.e. that part of the common law that is given by lawyers the label of "the prerogative." Where this is the source of decision-making power, the power is confined to executive officers of central as distinct from local government and in constitutional practice is generally exercised by those holding ministerial rank . . .

Judicial review has I think developed to a stage today when . . . one can conveniently classify under three heads the grounds upon which administrative action is subject to control by judicial review. The first ground I would call "illegality", the second "irrationality" and the third "procedural impropriety." That is not to say that further development on a case by case basis may not in course of time add further grounds. I have in mind particularly the possible adoption in the future of the principle of "proportionality" which is recognised in the administrative law of several of our fellow members of the European Economic Community; but to dispose of the instant case the three already well-established heads that I have mentioned will suffice.

By "illegality" as a ground for judicial review I mean that the decision-maker must understand correctly the law that regulates his decision-making power and must give effect to it. Whether he has or not is *par excellence* a justiciable question to be decided, in the event of dispute, by those persons, the judges, by whom the judicial power of the state is exercisable.

By "irrationality" I mean what can by now be succinctly referred to as "*Wednesbury* unreasonableness" . . . It applies to a decision which is so outrageous in its defiance of logic or of accepted moral standards that no sensible person who had applied his mind to the question to be decided could have arrived at it. Whether a decision falls within this category is a question that judges by their training and experience should be well equipped to answer, or else there would be something badly wrong with our judicial system . . . I have described the third head as "procedural impropriety" rather than failure to observe basic rules of natural justice or failure to act with procedural fairness towards the person who will be affected by the decision. This is because susceptibility to judicial review under this head covers also failure by an administrative tribunal to observe procedural rules that are expressly laid down in the legislative instrument by which its jurisdiction is conferred, even where such failure does not involve any denial of natural justice. But the instant case is not concerned with the proceedings of an administrative tribunal at all . . .

While I see no a priori reason to rule out "irrationality" as a ground for judicial review of a ministerial decision taken in the exercise of "prerogative" powers, I find it difficult to envisage in any of the various fields in which the prerogative remains the only source of the relevant decision-making power a decision of a kind that would be open to attack through the judicial process upon this ground. Such decisions will generally involve the application of government policy. The reasons for the decision-maker taking one course rather than another do not normally involve questions to which, if disputed, the judicial process is adapted to provide the right answer, by which I mean that the kind of evidence that is admissible under judicial procedures and the way in which it has to be adduced tend to exclude from the attention of the court competing policy considerations which, if the executive discretion is to be wisely exercised, need to be weighed against one another – a balancing exercise which judges by their upbringing and experience are ill-qualified to perform. So I leave this as an open question to be dealt with on a case to case basis if, indeed, the case should ever arise.

As respects "procedural propriety" I see no reason why it should not be a ground for judicial review of a decision made under powers of which the ultimate source is the prerogative . . . Indeed, where the decision is one which does not alter rights or obligations enforceable in private law but only deprives a person of legitimate expectations, "procedural impropriety" will normally provide the only ground on which the decision is open to judicial review. But in any event what procedure will satisfy the public law requirement of procedural propriety depends upon the subject matter of the decision, the executive functions of the decision-maker (if the decision is not that of an administrative tribunal) and the particular circumstances in which the decision came to be made . . .'

Comment

Lord Diplock's three-fold classification is a useful summary of the grounds of review, and widely used as such. It does not, though, create new grounds of challenge. The terms used are convenient labels: see Sir John Donaldson in *ex parte Brind*. Note in particular that in respect of discretionary powers the labels 'illegality' and 'irrationality' express different aspects of the principles set out in *APPH* v *Wednesbury Corporation.*

Associated Provincial Picture Houses v Wednesbury Corporation

[1948] 1 KB 223 · Court of Appeal

The Court had to consider the legality of a condition imposed under a statute allowing '. . . such conditions as the authority think fit to impose.' The condition purported to restrict use of the cinema on Sundays. The Court concluded that the authority had not acted outside the limit of its powers.

Lord Greene MR: '. . . What, then, is the power of the courts? They can only interfere with an act of executive authority if it be shown that the authority has contravened the law. It is for those who assert that the local authority has contravened the law to establish that proposition. On the face of it, a condition of the kind imposed in this case is perfectly lawful. It is not to be assumed prima facie that responsible bodies like the local authority in this case will exceed their powers; but the court, whenever it is alleged that the local authority have contravened the law, must not substitute itself for that authority. It is only concerned with seeing whether or not the proposition is made good. When an executive discretion is entrusted by Parliament to a body such as the local authority in this case, what appears to be an exercise of that discretion can only be challenged in the courts in a strictly limited class of case. As I have said, it must always be remembered that the court is not a court of appeal. When discretion of this kind is granted the law recognises certain principles upon which that discretion must be exercised, but within the four corners of those principles the discretion is an absolute one and cannot be questioned in any court of law. What then are those principles? They are well understood. They are principles which the court looks to in considering any question of discretion of this kind. The exercise of such a discretion must be a real exercise of the discretion. If, in the statute conferring the discretion, there is to be found, expressly or by implication, matters which the authority exercising the discretion ought to have regard to, then in exercising the discretion it must have regard to those matters. Conversely, if the nature of the subject matter and the general interpretation of the Act make it clear that certain matters would not be germane to the matter in question, the authority must disregard those irrelevant collateral matters.

There have been in the cases expressions used relating to the sort of things that authorities must not do, not merely in cases under the Cinematograph Act but, generally speaking, under other cases, where the powers of local authorities came to be considered. I am not sure myself whether the permissible grounds of attack cannot be defined under a single head. It has been perhaps a little bit confusing to find a series of grounds set out. Bad faith, dishonesty – those of course, stand by themselves – unreasonableness, attention given to extraneous circumstances, disregard of public policy and things like that have all been referred to, according to the facts of individual cases, as being matters which are relevant to the question. If they cannot all be confined under one head, they at any rate, I think, overlap to a very great extent. For instance, we have heard in this case a great deal about the meaning of the word "unreasonable".

It is true the discretion must be exercised reasonably. Now what does that mean? Lawyers familiar with the phraseology commonly used in relation to exercise of statutory discretions often use the word "unreasonable" in a rather comprehensive sense. It has frequently been used and is frequently used as a general description of the things that must not be done. For instance, a person entrusted with a discretion must, so to speak, direct himself properly in law. He must call his own attention to the matters which he is bound to consider. He must exclude from his consideration matters which are irrelevant to what he has to consider. If he does not obey those rules, he may truly be said, and often is said, to be acting "unreasonably". Similarly, there may be something so absurd that no sensible person could even dream that it lay within the powers of the authority. Warrington LJ in *Short v Poole Corporation* gave the example of the redhaired teacher, dismissed because she had red hair. That is unreasonable in one sense. In another sense it is taking into consideration extraneous matters. It is so unreasonable that it might almost be described as being done in bad faith; and, in fact, all these things run into one another.'

Comment

Note the two aspects of Lord Greene's statement: first, the factors that the discretionary authority must avoid ('the *Wednesbury* principles'); second, the wider, and constitutionally more controversial, notion of absurdity (elsewhere called '*Wednesbury* unreasonableness'). These are not mutually exclusive: most matters challengeable on the latter basis fall, or it could be argued should fall, within the former. A judgment based on absurdity inevitably involves assessment as to merits, or, to put it more accurately, the lack of them. This brings the courts to the very limits of proper judicial interference with executive action, and raises questions as to the separation of powers.

R v *Secretary of State for the Home Department, ex parte Brind*

[1991] 1 All ER 720 · House of Lords

Judicial review was sought by B of two directives made by the Home Secretary requiring the BBC and IBA to refrain from broadcasting specified matters in relation to various organizations engaged in, or believed to support, terrorism in Northern Ireland. The application to quash these directives, made respectively under the BBC Licence and under s.29, Broadcasting Act 1981, was unsuccessful. An appeal against that ruling was dismissed by the Court of Appeal, and again by the House of Lords.

Lord Ackner: . . . 'I now turn to the bases upon which it is contended that the Secretary of State exceeded his statutory powers.

(1) *The directives frustrated the policy and the objects of the 1981 Act* . . .

It is . . . accepted by . . . the Secretary of State that the discretion given to him by s.29(3) is not an absolute or unfettered discretion. It is a discretion which is to be exercised according to law and therefore must be used only to advance the purposes for which it was conferred. It has accordingly to be used to promote the policy and objects of the Act (see *Padfield* v *Minister of Agriculture Fisheries and Food*). It is further accepted on behalf of the Secretary of State that the powers under s.29(3) can be properly categorized as "reserve" powers in the sense that they are to be used infrequently. In fact they have only been used once previously.

In the Divisional Court and Court of Appeal much was made of the words in s.4(1)(*f*): "due impartiality". The argument was not repeated before your Lordships. I can find nothing in para (*f*) to suggest that the policy and objects of s.4(1) are in any way frustrated by the Secretary of State's exercise of his reserve powers where, in the proper exercise of his discretion, he considers it appropriate to do so.

(2) *The directives were unlawful on* "Wednesbury" *grounds*

Save only in one respect, namely the ECHR . . . it is not suggested that the minister failed to call his attention to matters which he was bound to consider, nor that he included in his considerations matters which were irrelevant. In neither of those senses can it be said that the minister acted unreasonably. The failure to mount such a challenge in this appeal is important. In a field which concerns a fundamental human right, namely that of free speech, close scrutiny must be given to the reasons provided as justification for interference with that right. . . .

There remains however the potential criticism under the *Wednesbury* grounds . . . that the conclusion was "so unreasonable that no reasonable authority could ever have come to it". This standard of unreasonableness, often referred to as "the irrationality test", has been criticized as being too high. But it has to be expressed in terms that confine the jurisdiction exercised by the judiciary to a supervisory, as opposed to an appellate, jurisdiction. Where Parliament has given to a minister or other person or body a discretion, the court's jurisdiction is limited, in the absence of a statutory right of appeal, to the supervision of the exercise of that discretionary power, so as to ensure that it has been exercised lawfully. It would be a wrongful usurpation of power by the judiciary to substitute its view, the judicial view, on the merits and on that basis to quash the decision. If no reasonable minister properly directing himself would have reached the impugned decision, the minister has exceeded his powers and thus acted unlawfully and the court, in the exercise of its supervisory role, will quash that decision. Such a decision is correctly, though unattractively, described as a "perverse" decision. To seek the court's intervention on the basis that the correct or objectively reasonable decision is other than the decision which the minister has made, is to invite the court to adjudicate as if Parliament had provided a right of appeal against the decision, that is to invite an abuse of power by the judiciary.

So far as the facts of this case are concerned it is only necessary to read the speeches in the Houses of Parliament . . . to reach the conclusion, that whether the Secretary of State was right or wrong to decide to issue the directives, there was clearly material which would justify a reasonable minister making the same decision. In the words of Lord Diplock in *Secretary of State for Education and Science* v *Tameside Metropolitan Borough* (see p.301) . . .

In his speech in the House of Commons on 2 November 1988 the Secretary of State in emphasizing the significance of imposing a restriction, not on the reporting of the material uttered by terrorists and those supporting them, but on their direct appearance on television, said:

> It is not simply that people are affronted – we can live with affront – by the direct access of men of violence and supporters of violence to television and radio. That direct access gives those who use it an air and appearance of authority which spreads further outwards the ripple of fear that terrorist acts create in a community. The terrorist act creates the fear and the direct broadcast spreads it. The men of violence and their supporters have used this access with skill. They do not hope to persuade – this is where we get into the cosy luxury of discussion which is unreal – but to frighten. So far from being outlaws hunted by the forces of law and order and pursued by the courts, they calmly appear on the screen and, thus, in the homes of their victims and the friends and neighbours of their victims . . .

I entirely agree with McCowan LJ when he said that he found it quite impossible to hold that the Secretary of State's political judgment that the appearance of terrorists on programmes increases their standing and lends them political legitimacy is one that no reasonable Home Secretary could hold. As the learned Lord Justice observed "It is, it should be noted, also the political judgment of the terrorists, or they would not be so anxious to be interviewed by the media or be so against the Home Secretary's ban."

[Counsel for the appellants] contended that in issuing these directives the Secretary of State has used a sledgehammer to crack a nut. Of course that is a picturesque way of describing the *Wednesbury* "irrational" test. The Secretary of State has in my judgment used no sledgehammer. Quite the contrary is the case.

I agree with Lord Donaldson MR who, when commenting on how limited the restrictions were, said in his judgment

> They have no application in the circumstances mentioned in para 3 (proceedings in the United Kingdom Parliament and elections) and, by allowing reported speech either verbatim or in paraphrase, in effect put those affected in no worse a position than they would if they had access to newspaper publicity with a circulation equal to the listening and viewing audiences of the programmes concerned. Furthermore, on the applicants' own evidence, if the directives had been in force during the previous 12 months, the effect would have been minimal

in terms of air time. Thus, ITN say that 8 minutes 20 seconds (including repeats) out of 1,200 hours, or 0.01% of air time would have been affected. Furthermore, it would not have been necessary to omit these items. They could have been recast into a form which complied with the directives.

Thus the extent of the interference with the right to freedom of speech is a very modest one. On the other hand, the vehemence of the criticism of the Secretary of State's decision is perhaps a clear indication of the strength of the impact of the terrorist message when he is seen or heard expressing his views.

(3) *The minister failed to have proper regard to the European Convention for the Protection of Human Rights and Fundamental Freedoms and in particular art.10*
. . . The convention which is contained in an international treaty to which the United Kingdom is a party has not yet been incorporated into English domestic law. The appellants accept that it is a constitutional principle that if Parliament has legislated and the words of the statute are clear, the statute must be applied even if its application is in breach of international law. In *Salomon* v *Customs and Excise Comrs* Diplock LJ stated: "If the terms of the legislation are clear and unambiguous they must be given effect to whether or not they carry out Her Majesty's treaty obligations . . ."

Much reliance was placed upon the observations of Lord Diplock in *Garland* v *British Rail Engineering Ltd* when he said: ". . . it is a principle of construction of United Kingdom statutes . . . that the words of a statute passed after the treaty has been signed and dealing with the subject matter of the international obligation of the United Kingdom, are to be construed, if they are reasonably capable of bearing such a meaning, as intended to carry out the obligation, and not to be inconsistent with it."

I did not take the view that Lord Diplock was intending to detract from or modify what he said in *Salomon's* case.

It is well settled that the convention may be deployed for the purpose of the resolution of an ambiguity in English primary or subordinate legislation. In *R* v *Chief Immigration Officer, Heathrow Airport, ex parte Salamat Bibi* . . . Lord Denning MR said: "The position, as I understand it, is that if there is any ambiguity in our statutes or uncertainty in our law, then these courts can look to the convention as an aid to clear up the ambiguity and uncertainty. . . But I would dispute altogether that the convention is part of our law. Treaties and declarations do not become part of our law until they are made law by Parliament."

. . . [Counsel for the appellant] contends that s.29(3) is ambiguous and uncertain. He submits that although it contains within its wording no fetter upon the extent of the discretion it gives to the Secretary of State, it is accepted that that discretion is not absolute. There is however no ambiguity in s.29(3). It is not open to two or more different constructions. The limit placed upon the discretion is simply that the power is to be used only for the purposes for which it was granted by the legislation (the so-called *Padfield* doctrine) and that it must be exercised reasonably in the *Wednesbury* sense. No question of the construction of the words of s.29(3) arises, as would be the case if it was alleged to be ambiguous or its meaning uncertain.

There is yet a further answer to [counsel's] contention. He claims that the Secretary of State before issuing his directives should have considered not only the convention (it is accepted that he in fact did so) but that he should have properly construed it and correctly taken it into consideration. It was therefore a relevant, indeed a vital, factor to which he was obliged to have proper regard pursuant to the *Wednesbury* doctrine, with the result that his failure to do so rendered his decision unlawful. The fallacy of this submission is however plain. If the Secretary of State was obliged to have proper regard to the convention, i.e. to conform with art.10, this inevitably would result in incorporating the convention into English domestic law by the back door. It would oblige the courts to police the operation of the convention and to ask itself in each case, where there was a challenge, whether the restrictions were "necessary in a democratic society . . ." applying the principles enunciated in the decisions of the European Court of Human Rights. The treaty, not having been incorporated in English law, cannot be a source of rights and obligations and the question – did the Secretary of State act in breach of art.10? – does not therefore arise . . .

(4) *The Secretary of State has acted ultra vires because he has acted "in a disproportionate manner"*
This attack is not a repetition of the *Wednesbury* "irrational" test under another guise. Clearly a decision by a minister which suffers from a total lack of proportionality will qualify for the "*Wednesbury* unreasonable" epithet. It is, *ex hypothesi*, a decision which no reasonable minister could make. This is, however, a different and severer test.

[Counsel for the appellant] is asking your Lordships to adopt a different principle: the principle of "proportionality" which is recognized in the administrative law of several members of the European Economic Community. What is urged is a further development in English administrative law, which Lord Diplock viewed as a possibility in the *GCHQ* case.

[Counsel for the appellant] was at pains to record "that there is a clear distinction between an appeal on the merits and a review based on whether the principle of proportionality has been satisfied". He was prepared to accept that to stray into the realms of appellate jurisdiction involves the courts in a wrongful usurpation of power. Yet in order to invest the proportionality test with a higher status than the *Wednesbury* test, an inquiry into and a decision upon the merits cannot be avoided. [Counsel for the appellant's] formulation – could the minister reasonably conclude that his direction was necessary? – must involve balancing the reasons, pro and con, for his decision, albeit allowing him "a margin of appreciation" to use the European concept of the tolerance accorded to the decision-maker in whom a discretion has been vested. The European test of "whether the interference complained of corresponds to a pressing social need" (see *Sunday Times* v *UK*) must ultimately result in the question – is the particular decision acceptable? – and this must involve a review of the merits of the decision. Unless and until Parliament incorporates the convention into domestic law, a course which it is well known has a strong body of support, there appears to me to be at present no basis upon which the proportionality doctrine applied by the European Court can be followed by the courts of this country. . ." '

Lord Lowry: ' . . . The kind of unreasonableness for which a court can set aside an administrative act or decision is popularly called "*Wednesbury* unreasonableness" from . . . *Associated Provincial Picture Houses Ltd* v *Wednesbury Corp* in which Lord Greene MR spoke of a decision "so absurd that no sensible person could ever dream that it lay within the powers of the authority". In *Secretary of State for*

Education and Science v *Tameside Metropolitan Borough* Lord Denning MR referred to decisions "so wrong that no reasonable person could sensibly take that view". In *Council of Civil Service Unions* v *Minister for the Civil Service* Lord Diplock, having used irrationality as a synonym of *Wednesbury* unreasonableness, said that "It applies to a decision which is so outrageous in its defiance of logic or of accepted moral standards that no sensible person who had applied his mind to the question to be decided could have arrived at it", while in *Nottinghamshire CC* v *Secretary of State for the Environment* Lord Scarman, when invited to examine the detail and consequences of guidance given by the Secretary of State, said:

> Such an examination by a court would be justified only if a prima facie case were to be shown for holding that the Secretary of State had acted in bad faith, or for an improper motive, or that the consequences of his guidance were so absurd that he must have taken leave of his senses.

These colourful statements emphasize the legal principle that judicial review of administrative action is a supervisory and not an appellate jurisdiction. . . .

I believe that the subject is nowhere better discussed than by Sir William Wade in his authoritative textbook *Administrative Law* (6th edn, 1988) . . . The learned author . . . clearly demonstrates that what we are accustomed to call *Wednesbury* unreasonableness is a branch of the abuse, or misuse, of power: the court's duty is not to interfere with a discretion which Parliament has entrusted to a statutory body or an individual but to maintain a check on excesses in the exercise of discretion. That is why it is not enough if a judge feels able to say . . . "I think that is unreasonable; that is not what I would have done." It also explains the emphatic language which judges have used in order to drive home the message and the necessity, as judges have seen it, for the act to be "so unreasonable that no reasonable minister etc would have done it". In that strong, and necessary, emphasis lies the danger. The seductive voice of counsel will suggest . . . that, for example, ministers, who are far from irrational and indeed are reasonable people, may occasionally be guilty of an abuse of power by going too far. And then the court is in danger of turning its back not only on the vigorous language but on the principles which it was intended to support. A less emotive, but, subject to one qualification, reliable test is to ask: "*Could* a decision-maker acting reasonably have reached this decision?" The qualification is that the supervising court must bear in mind that it is not sitting on appeal, but satisfying itself whether the decision-maker has acted within the bounds of his discretion. For that reason it is fallacious for those seeking to quash administrative acts and decisions to call in aid decisions of a Court of Appeal reversing a judge's finding, it may be on a question of what is reasonable. To say what is reasonable was the judge's task in the first place and the duty of the Court of Appeal, after giving due weight to the judge's opinion, is to say whether they agree with him. In judicial review, on the other hand, the task of the High Court is as described above, and the task of the Court of Appeal and, when necessary, this House is to decide whether the High Court has correctly exercised its *supervisory* jurisdiction.

Of course, whichever kind of jurisdiction is being exercised on the subject of reasonableness, there is bound to be a subjective element in the decision. There is no objective standard in either case which would allow the result to be foretold with certainty. The important requirement, however, is to ask the right question. . . .'

Comment

(1) See p.150 for the Court's decision on the applicability of the European Convention on Human Rights.

(2) In the Court of Appeal ruling in *Hammersmith and Fulham LBC* v *Secretary of State for the Environment*, Sir John Donaldson stated:

> [Irrationality] is relevant if it is alleged that the decision taker has taken into account legally irrelevant matters, or has failed to have regard to those which were legally relevant, or that his decision would frustrate the policy of the Act on which he relied for his authority . . . The other limb of the irrationality jurisdiction [is] a decision so unreasonable that no reasonable authority could ever have come to it . . .

This approach cannot be supported since it gives a wider meaning to irrationality than Lord Diplock, and Donaldson MR himself in *Brind*, took. The matters falling within the first limb belong properly within the illegality classification. Irrationality is restricted to what is otherwise called '*Wednesbury* unreasonableness'. This view is confirmed by the decision of the House of Lords in the *Hammersmith* case where Lord Bridge stated:

> I think there is a danger of confusion in terminology here. If the court concludes, as the House did in *Padfield*'s case, that a minister's exercise of a statutory discretion has been such as to frustrate the policy of the statute, that conclusion rests on the view taken by the court of the true construction of the statute which the exercise of the discretion in question is then held to have contravened. The administrative action or inaction is then condemned on the ground of illegality. Similarly, if there are matters which, on the true construction of the statute conferring discretion, the person exercising the discretion must take into account and others which he may not take into account, disregard of those legally relevant matters or regard of those legally irrelevant matters will lay the decision open to review on the ground of illegality.

(3) Delegated legislation is challengeable on the basis of illegality (see p.299). In relation to by-laws it is clear that they may be challenged on the grounds of unreasonableness: see, for example, *Kruse* v *Johnson, per* Lord Russell CJ:

> But unreasonable in what sense? If for instance they were found to be partial and unequal in their operation as between different classes; if they were manifestly unjust; if they disclosed bad faith; if they involved such oppressive or gratuitous interference with the rights of those subject to them as could find no justification in the minds of reasonable men, the Court might well say, 'Parliament never intended to give authority to make such rules; they are unreasonable and *ultra vires*'. But it is in this sense, and in this sense only, as I conceive, that the question of unreasonableness can properly be regarded. A by-law is not unreasonable merely because particular judges may think it goes further than is prudent or necessary or convenient . . .

The Court concluded that it should be slow to hold a by-law invalid for unreasonableness, and upheld a by-law prohibiting the playing of music, or singing, in any public place or highway within 50 yards of any dwelling-house, having been requested by any constable, or any inmate of such house, to desist.

The role and powers of a court when delegated legislation is challenged may vary according to the basis of challenge (see *DPP* v *Bugg*).

Despite *dicta* to the contrary in *Sparks* v *Edward Ash Ltd* there seems no reason in principle why other delegated legislation should not be likewise challengeable for unreasonableness, though Parliamentary approval may make this harder to establish. The statement of Lord Bridge in the *Hammersmith* case is equally applicable in this context.

(4)   The concept of proportionality was first applied tentatively, alongside other grounds of challenge, in *ex parte Hook* where Lord Denning observed that the termination of a licence to trade on Barnsley market was excessive bearing in mind the trivial 'offence' complained of (see p.332). The House of Lords rejects proportionality as a distinct ground of challenge, but accepts that the proportionality may be relevant to deciding whether or not the executive body has gone beyond the intent and purpose of Parliament (the *Padfield* principle), or acted in a way that is *Wednesbury* unreasonable.

(5)   The concept of proportionality is likely to be of increasing importance through the development of European law. *Stoke on Trent City Council* v *B & Q* (see p.97), although not a judicial review case in the technical sense, demonstrates the obligation that proportionality can place upon the courts, and which is likely to be mirrored in judicial review applications. The Divisional Court, following a Court of Justice ruling in respect of the effect of European law upon the restrictions on Sunday trading contained in the Shops Act 1950, had to consider the application of that ruling. The Court of Justice had indicated that the validity of any restrictions in municipal law depended in part upon whether the effect of the law exceeded what was necessary to achieve, and proportionate to, a sufficiently important objective. Hoffman J indicated that it was not his function to carry out a balancing function, or form a view as to whether the objective could be achieved by other means. Those questions involved compromises between competing interests which in a democratic society had to be resolved by the legislature. The duty of the court was to decide no more than whether the view taken by the legislature was a reasonably tenable view as to the importance of the objective, and whether or not it could justify the consequent reduction in Community trade. See also *Johnston* v *Chief Constable of RUC*, p.121.

Illegality

Many examples have already been seen. Note in particular the *GCHQ* case (p.215); *Congreve* v *Home Office* (p.34); *Laker Airways* v *Department of*

Trade (p.57). The ground of challenge applies equally to delegated legislation as well as executive actions under statute or prerogative – see, for example, *Attorney-General* v *Wilts Utd Dairies* (p.33). In determining the scope of the enabling power, the Court will be concerned, in its interpretation and application of the legislative provision, to give effect to the policy explicit or implicit in that enabling power. By this means even the widest discretionary power is potentially the subject of judicial review, as the decision in *Padfield* (p.210) shows. On other occasions the policy underpinning the enabling power is explicit: thus in *Bromley LBC* v *GLC* the actions of the respondent Council in making large grants to the London Transport Executive in order to ensure low fares, and pursuant to a statutory power to make grants 'for any purpose', had to be measured against a stated statutory purpose imposing a duty 'to promote the provision of integrated, efficient and economic transport facilities . . .'.

In interpreting any statutory provision, the Court will imply such powers '. . . that . . . may be fairly regarded as incidental to, or consequential upon, those things which the legislature has authorised . . .'. For a statutory enactment to like effect, see s.111, Local Government Act 1972: a local authority may '. . . do anything . . . which is calculated to facilitate or is conducive, or incidental to, this discharge of any of their functions.' For consideration of this provision see *McCarthy & Stone* v *Richmond LBC*, p.30.

In determining the scope of discretionary powers, the *Wednesbury* principles should be carefully noted. They encompass the failure to have regard to relevant matters, the failure to disregard irrelevances, improper purposes, and bad faith. Other aspects of challenge will be later seen as failure to exercise discretion (p.318), procedural impropriety (p.321) and *Wednesbury* unreasonableness (p.319).

An issue of importance is in respect of the statement of reasons for a decision. The statement of bad reasons may provide evidence which justifies a finding of illegality or irrationality. More often, it may be difficult to establish what the reasons for a decision were, although these may become apparent on discovery, which has been available on judicial review since 1977. There is no general duty to give reasons, although in appropriate cases the failure to do so may form the basis of challenge. A failure to state reasons, or a failure to state adequate reasons, may thus affect a decision on each of the three grounds of challenge identified by Lord Diplock in the *GCHQ* case. For convenience it is dealt with in the context of procedural impropriety (p.333).

Secretary of State for Education and Science v *Tameside MBC*

[1977] AC 1014 · House of Lords

The court had to consider whether the Secretary of State for Education had acted within his powers in the exercise of his default power contained in s.68, Education Act 1944. This entitled him to issue directions to a local education authority where he was satisfied that they were acting unreasonably. The Secretary of State issued a direction when the local education authority, as a result of a change of political power following local elections, sought to reverse decisions to implement a reorganization of secondary education along comprehensive lines. The House of Lords concluded that the Secretary of State had no lawful basis for concluding the Council were acting unreasonably.

Lord Wilberforce: '. . . Analysis of the section brings out three cardinal points. 1. The matters with which the section is concerned are primarily matters of educational administration. The action, which the Secretary of State is entitled to stop, is unreasonable action with respect to the exercise of a power or the performance of a duty; the power and the duty of the authority are presupposed and cannot be interfered with. Local education authorities are entitled under the [1944] Act to have a policy, and this section does not enable the Secretary of State to require them to abandon or reverse a policy just because the Secretary of State disagrees with it. Specifically, the Secretary of State cannot use power under this section to impose a general policy of comprehensive education on a local education authority which does not agree with the policy. He cannot direct them to bring in a scheme for total comprehensive education in their area, and if they have done so he cannot direct them to implement it. If he tries to use a direction under s.68 for this purpose, his direction would be clearly invalid. A direction under s.68 must be justified on the ground of unreasonable action in doing what under the 1944 Act the local authority is entitled to do, and under the Act it has a freedom of choice. I do not think that there is any controversy on these propositions.

The critical question in this case, and it is not an easy one, is whether, on a matter which appears to be one of education administration, namely whether the change of course proposed by the authority in May 1976 would lead to educational chaos or undue disruption, the Secretary of State's judgment can be challenged.

2. The section is framed in a "subjective" form – if the Secretary of State "is satisfied". This form of section is quite well known, and at first sight might seem to exclude judicial review. Sections in this form may, no doubt, exclude judicial review on what is or has become a matter of pure judgment. But I do not think that they go further than that. If a judgment requires, before it can be made, the existence of some facts, then, although the evaluation of those facts is for the Secretary of State alone, the court must enquire whether those facts exist, and have been taken into account, whether the judgment has been made on a proper self-direction as to those facts, whether the judgment has not been made on other facts which ought not to have been taken into account. If these requirements are not met, then the exercise of judgment, however bona fide it may be, becomes capable of challenge . . .

3. The section has to be considered within the structure of the [1944] Act. In many statutes a Minister or other authority is given a discretionary power and in these cases the court's power to review any exercise of the discretion, though still real, is limited. In these cases it is said that the courts cannot substitute their opinion for that

of the Minister: they can interfere on such grounds as that the Minister has acted right outside his powers or outside the purpose of the Act, or unfairly, or on an incorrect basis of fact. But there is no universal rule as to the principles on which the exercise of a discretion may be reviewed: each statute or type of statute must be individually looked at. This Act of 1944, is quite different from those which simply create a ministerial discretion. The Secretary of State, under s.68, is not merely exercising a discretion; he is reviewing the action of another public body which itself has discretionary powers and duties. He, by contrast with the courts in the normal case, may substitute his opinion for that of the authority: this is what the section allows, but he must take account of what the authority, under the statute, is entitled to do. The authority – this is vital – is itself elected, and given specific powers as to the kind of schools it wants in its area. Therefore two situations may arise. One is that there may be a difference of policy between the Secretary of State (under Parliament) and the local authority: the section gives no power to the Secretary of State to make his policy prevail. The other is that, owing to the the democratic process involving periodic elections, abrupt reversals of policy may take place, particularly where there are only two parties and the winner takes all. Any reversal of policy if at all substantial must cause some administrative disruption; this was as true of the 1975 proposals as of those of [Tameside]. So the mere possibility, or probability, of disruption cannot be a ground for issuing a direction to abandon the policy. What the Secretary of State is entitled, by a direction if necessary, to ensure is that such disruptions are not "unreasonable", i.e. greater than a body, elected to carry out a new programme, with which the Secretary of State may disagree, ought to impose on those for whom it is responsible. After all, those who voted for the new programme, involving a change of course, must also be taken to have accepted some degree of disruption in implementing it.

The ultimate question in this case, in my opinion, is whether the Secretary of State has given sufficient, or any, weight to this particular factor in the exercise of judgment . . .'

Comment

Lord Diplock explained unreasonableness:

> My Lords, in public law 'unreasonable' as descriptive of the way in which a public authority has purported to exercise a discretion vested in it by statute has become a term of legal art. To fall within this expression it must be conduct which no sensible authority acting with due appreciation of its responsibilities would have decided to adopt. The very concept of administrative discretion involves a right to choose between more than one possible course of action on which there is room for reasonable people to hold differing opinions as to which is to be preferred.

Oladehinde v *Secretary of State for the Home Department*

[1990] 3 All ER 383 · House of Lords

The applicants were seeking to challenge the issue of notices of intention to deport them, issued by immigration inspectors under powers conferred upon the Secretary of State by the Immigration Act 1971. These inspectors were senior civil servants, and the applicants argued that this amounted to an improper delegation of power by the Secretary of State. The application was successful in the Divisional Court, but an appeal was allowed, the Court of Appeal relying on the principle in *Carltona Ltd* v *Commissioner of Works*. The actual deportation order would be made by the Secretary of State. A further appeal by the applicant to the House of Lords was dismissed.

Court of Appeal

Lord Donaldson MR: 'It may be convenient at this point to cite the passage from the judgment of Lord Greene MR which enshrines and explains the *Carltona* principle:

> In the administration of government in this country the functions which are given to ministers (and constitutionally properly given to ministers because they are constitutionally responsible) are functions so multifarious that no minister could ever personally attend to them. To take the example of the present case no doubt there have been thousands of requisitions in this country by individual ministries. It cannot be supposed that this regulation meant that, in each case, the minister in person should direct his mind to the matter. The duties imposed upon ministers and the powers given to ministers are normally exercised under the authority of the ministers by responsible officials of the department. Public business could not be carried on if that were not the case. Constitutionally, the decision of such an official is, of course, the decision of the minister. The minister is responsible. It is he who must answer before Parliament for anything that his officials have done under his authority, and, if for an important matter he selected an official of such junior standing that he could not be expected competently to perform the work, the minister would have to answer for that in Parliament. The whole system of departmental organisation and administration is based on the view that ministers, being responsible to Parliament, will see that important duties are committed to experienced officials. If they do not do that, Parliament is the place where complaint must be made against them.

Lord Greene MR contemplated that, in devolving authority to take decisions on his behalf, the Secretary of State would only be answerable to Parliament, but it is conceded that, at least in recent times, such a course of action would also be susceptible to judicial review in an appropriate case, the only issue being whether this is such a case.

Woolf LJ held that the *Carltona* principle should be regarded "as an implication which is read into a statute in the absence of any clear contrary indication by Parliament that the implication is not to apply" . . . In this we think he must be mistaken, because it applies equally where the Minister's powers are derived otherwise than from a statute, e.g. from prerogative powers . . . the better view is that this is a common law constitutional power, but one which is capable of being negatived or confined by express statutory provisions, as has been achieved in . . . [the 1971 Act] . . . or by clearly necessary implication. However, so far as implication is concerned, we would expect any challenge to be mounted on the possibly broader basis that the decision to devolve authority was *Wednesbury* unreasonable with, if appropriate, a submission that it involved a contravention of the rules of natural justice or of fairness. Thus we have no doubt that the courts would strike down a decision to authorise a prison governor to deal, on behalf of the Secretary of State, with petitions by prisoners complaining of the conduct of that governor. We hasten to add that no such decision has ever been taken. Consistently with this approach, we think that the present decision needs to be reviewed with the possibility of *Wednesbury* irrationality clearly in mind . . .'

House of Lords

Lord Griffiths: 'It is well recognised that when a statute places a duty upon a minister it may generally be exercised by a member of his department for whom he accepts responsibility; this is the *Carltona* principle. Parliament can . . . limit the minister's power to devolve or delegate the decision and require him to exercise it in person. There are three examples of such a limitation in the [present] Act. . . . Where I find in a statute three explicit limitations on the Secretary of State's power to devolve, I should be very slow to read into the statute a further implicit limitation . . . I can . . . see no reason why he should not authorise members of that service to take decisions under the *Carltona* principle providing they do not conflict or embarrass them in the discharge of their specific statutory duties . . . and that the decisions are suitable to their grading and experience.'

Comment

(1)   The speeches in the House of Lords do not add to the statement of principle, and recognize the right of a minister to devolve decision making, unless limited by Parliament. It had not been so limited in this case. Nor was any procedural unfairness involved. The *Carltona* principle recognizes that ministerial responsibility requires that the minister answers to Parliament for the actions of his officials.

(2)   The *Carltona* principle must be carefully distinguished from improper delegation of power. Whilst in some circumstances a minister can act through his officials, it is not permissible for an executive body to delegate power to another person or body without authority (express or implied) to do so. See p.319.

(3)   In *Doody* v *Secretary of State for the Environment* the House of Lords agreed with the view of the Court of Appeal that decisions under s.61(1) Criminal Justice Act 1967 (power in a Secretary of State to release a life prisoner) need not be taken personally by the Secretary of State but might be taken by a minister of state. Staughton LJ referred to the practice of review of mandatory life sentences and thought that:

> Every such case demands serious consideration, and the burden of considering them all must be substantial. I can see nothing irrational in the Secretary of State devolving the task upon junior ministers. They too are appointed by the Crown to hold office in the department, they have the same advice and assistance from departmental officials as the Secretary of State would have and they too are answerable to Parliament. There is in my judgment no objection to the decisions

attached in this case on the ground that they were or may have been taken by junior ministers rather than by the Secretary of State.

Some office holders may delegate and some may not; for instance the Lord Chief Justice has a part to play in the process whereby release on licence is possible, but, as the House of Lords made clear in *Doody*, the Lord Chief Justice would have to act in person rather than delegate.

(4) In *Local Government Board* v *Arlidge*, a case concerning the nature of procedures to be adopted by an administrative body, Viscount Haldane said:

> . . . I concur in this view of the position of an administrative body to which the decision of a question in dispute between parties has been entrusted. The result of its enquiry must . . . be taken, in the absence of directions in the statute to the contrary, to be intended to be reached by its ordinary procedure. In the case of the Local Government Board it is not doubtful what this procedure is. The Minister at the head of the Board is directly responsible to Parliament like other Ministers. He is responsible not only for what he himself does but for all that is done in his department. The volume of work entrusted to him is very great and he cannot do the great bulk of it himself. He is expected to obtain his materials vicariously through his officials, and he has discharged his duty if he sees that they obtain these materials for him properly. To try to extend his duty beyond this and to insist that he and other members of the Board should do everything personally would be to impair his efficiency. Unlike a judge in a Court he is not only at liberty but is compelled to rely on the assistance of his staff. When, therefore, the Board is directed to dispose of an appeal, that does not mean that any particular official of the Board is to dispose of it . . . Provided the work is done judicially and fairly . . . the only authority that can review what has been done is the Parliament to which the Minister in charge is responsible.

Pickwell v *Camden LBC*

[1983] 2 WLR 583 · Divisional Court

Under s.161, Local Government Act 1972 (then the operative power), the district auditor sought a declaration that sums of money spent were contrary to law. The sums in question were additional sums of money paid by the council to settle an industrial dispute amongst the council's manual workers. The result of the agreement of these payments was that the wages earned were higher than the levels of wages later agreed under a national agreement. For the action to succeed it had to be shown that the payments were unreasonable. The action failed.

Forbes J: '. . . Where the court is exercising a supervisory jurisdiction its approach to the matter in hand is necessarily different from its approach when acting as a Court of Appeal. The approach is often referred to as the *Wednesbury* doctrine because the elements are conveniently summarised in the judgment of Lord Greene MR in *Associated Provincial Picture Houses Ltd* v *Wednesbury Corporation*. Since there has been considerable argument in this case on the extent of the *Wednesbury* principle and its application to the matter before us I should read two passages from that judgment . . .

I might add a very short passage from . . . *Mixnam's Properties Ltd* v *Chertsey Urban District Council.* Diplock LJ said:

> Thus, the kind of unreasonableness which invalidates a by-law is not the antonym of "reasonableness" in the sense of which that expression is used in the common law, but such manifest arbitrariness, injustice or partiality that a court would say: "Parliament never intended to give authority to make such rules; they are unreasonable and *ultra vires.*"

The last sentence in that passage is a quotation from the judgment of Lord Russell of Killowen CJ in *Kruse* v *Johnson.*

I have indicated that the principles enshrined in the *Wednesbury* case are only another way of looking at the approach which the court adopts when exercising a supervisory rather than an appellate jurisdiction. Precisely the same approach is to be found when the Divisional Court is exercising the same kind of jurisdiction in criminal matters . . . The principles of *Wednesbury* can therefore be seen as the corollary of the assertion of a supervisory rather than an appellate jurisdiction and involve, so far as is material here, the three brief propositions: (1) an authority must not be affected by immaterial nor ignore material considerations; (2) an authority must not act in such a way that it can be said of it that no reasonable authority, properly directing itself to what was material, could have concluded that it was entitled so to act; and (3) in reviewing the acts of an authority the court will not substitute its own view of how a discretion should be exercised for that of the authority entrusted by Parliament with the discretion. The principles enshrined in the *Wednesbury* case of course long pre-date that decision. It is possible to argue that there is only one principle, that of "unreasonableness" as that term is used in this context . . . It is possible also to argue . . . that the question to which *Wednesbury* is addressed is simply whether or not the act under scrutiny is *ultra vires.* There is much to be said for these arguments. But I think *Wednesbury* is dealing largely with the question of the exercise of a statutory discretion. It is true that the abuse of a statutory discretion can, if not always then nearly always, be put as an *ultra vires* act, on the basis that the discretion given was not intended to cover the action taken. But while the abuse of a discretionary power can almost be regarded as *ultra vires*, an action which is *ultra vires* is not always the abuse of a discretionary power. There are acts which may not be covered by a statutory power at all and others where some want of form produces an illegality. But the majority of cases which come before the courts are concerned with the abuse of discretionary powers and here it is not helpful to pursue too far a philosophical argument as to whether a disregard of a material consideration is to be regarded as subsumed in the concept of unreasonableness or as a separate ground of challenge. [Counsel for the auditor] puts [his] case on the basis of the relevant/irrelevant argument: [counsel for the authority] says it is merely a question of unreasonableness and therefore *vires.* I think the matter has to be looked at from both points of view, accepting that they may well overlap. The one thing which is beyond question is that the court in the exercise of its supervisory jurisdiction never allows itself to substitute its own discretion for that of the body to whom discretion has been given . . .

The modern position is to be found in s.161, Local Government Act 1972. . . . It is clear that there has been a fundamental change in the position of the district auditor in relation to items in the account which may be contrary to law. The district auditor is no longer under a duty to disallow such items nor to surcharge the amounts on the persons responsible. He has a discretionary power to make an application to the court for a declaration. The court, too, is in a fundamentally different situation. It is not to embark on the process of seeing whether the district auditor was right. It must itself decide all questions which arise, both of fact and law. The onus is also altered: the onus of satisfying the court that the item of account is contrary to law is now on the district auditor . . .

It is plain that the district auditor in this case considered that he was following the guidance given by their Lordships in *Roberts* v *Hopwood*. It should be noted however that, although traces may be found in that case of a consideration by their Lordships of failure to take into account relevant matters, the fact is that the case of the Poplar councillors was that in reality their decision was based on the concept that £4 a week was the minimum wage which they thought – without regard to current wage rates but having regard to the dignity of labour – ought to be paid to an adult worker. Looking at the wage itself and the reasons advanced for paying it the inference was irresistible that no question of whether the remuneration was appropriate for the work required or whether it compared in any way with wage rates paid elsewhere could possibly have been taken into account. The case seems to me to decide no more than this, that where the inevitable inference which must be drawn is that an obviously excessive wage payment was agreed to be paid without any regard to any commercial consideration and solely on some extraneous principle as, for instance, philanthropy, such a payment can only be regarded as a gift and is not covered by a statutory power to pay reasonable wages. Looking back, as we do, over 60 years of progress in the field of social reform and industrial relations some of their Lordships' observations may, with the benefit of this hindsight, appear unsympathetic. But what has changed over those years is our attitudes to what should be regarded as pure philanthropy: the basic legal principle, that a payment is illegal which cannot be justified by reference to the objects for which a statutory power is granted, still remains. . . .

In *Prescott* v *Birmingham Corporation* Jenkins LJ underlines this principle:

> Local authorities are not, of course, trustees for their ratepayers, but they do, we think, owe an analogous fiduciary duty to their ratepayers in relation to the application of funds contributed by the latter. Thus local authorities running an omnibus undertaking at the risk of their ratepayers, in the sense that any deficiencies must be met by an addition to the rates, are not, in our view, entitled, merely on the strength of a general power, to charge different fares to different passengers or classes of passengers, to make a gift to a particular class of persons of rights of free travel on their vehicles, simply because the local authority concerned are of opinion that the favoured class of persons ought, on benevolent or philanthropic grounds, to be accorded that benefit. In other words, they are not, in our view, entitled to use their discriminatory power as proprietors of the transport undertaking in order to confer out of rates a special benefit on some particular class of inhabitants whom they, as the local authority for the town or district in question, may think deserving of such assistance. In the absence of clear statutory authority for such a proceeding (which to our mind a mere general power to charge differential fares certainly is not) we would, for our part, regard it as illegal, on the ground that, to put the matter bluntly, it would amount simply to the making of a gift or present in money's worth to a

particular section of the local community at the expense of the general body of ratepayers.

Of course it is plain that a local authority owes a fiduciary duty to its ratepayers: it also owes a duty, laid on it specifically by Parliament, to provide a wide range of services for its inhabitants, be they ratepayers, electors or neither. It is entitled as an employer to have regard to the interests and welfare of its workforce, as any good employer should. It must therefore often be involved in balancing fairly these interests which may frequently conflict. As it is the ratepayers, ignoring for this purpose grants from central government, who largely find the money which the local authority spends, and it is the account of that money which the district auditor is engaged in checking, it is right to regard the district auditor as the ratepayers' watch-dog. It may be interesting to speculate on what was Parliament's intention when in 1933 it took away the right of a ratepayer or property owner to challenge items of account and transferred that right to local government electors, but I suppose one possible result is to underscore the importance of the district auditor's role in looking after the ratepayers' interests. But I think despite this the district auditor in considering the accounts, and certainly the court in considering any application for a declaration under s.161, must have due regard to the other duties which the local authority has to discharge. If it can be shown, and the onus is now on the district auditor to show it, that a local authority has deliberately topped the balance in favour of one interest over others then, whether this be put as taking into account irrelevant material or as the brand of unreasonableness to which *Wednesbury* refers, it is plainly something beyond the power which was entrusted to it . . .

In deciding whether or not a local authority has acted unreasonably as that term is understood in this jurisdiction it is the court which has to decide on the matter before it whether the action can properly be so regarded. But not infrequently the facts on which the decision was based can be shown at that stage, sometimes with hindsight, to have been other than they appeared to those making the decision. There may be circumstances in which this makes no difference: if a local authority receives legal advice, even from its chief executive, to the effect that a course of action may properly in law be taken, and it subsequently transpires that such advice was wrong, this will not render the act legal. But there are frequently circumstances in which, if an authority honestly and properly (in the sense that there has been no failure to take reasonable steps to discover the truth) believes that the facts are such-and-such and subsequently this turns out to be wrong, it would not be proper to consider that the question of unreasonableness falls to be determined by regarding solely the facts as they turn out to have been . . .

[Forbes J considered submissions on the facts, and continued:]

I desire to make two general observations about these submissions. The first is that when applying the principles of *Associated Provincial Picture Houses Ltd* v *Wednesbury Corporation* which is to say, when exercising its supervisory jurisdiction, the court is not concerned with whether due or proper weight is given to a material consideration: the weight to be given to such a matter is for the body exercising the discretion to determine; the court will no more substitute its own view of the importance of any relevant matter than it will do so for any other matter of statutory discretion. In considering whether it is right to conclude that ineluctably the only inference is that a relevant matter has been ignored the court should, I think, be very wary of coming to that conclusion: to weigh up a relevant matter and to conclude that the weight to be accorded to it is nil lies within the scope of discretion and is not necessarily to be equated with ignoring it. And the second is that, while such a conclusion might sometimes be justified, despite the reluctance of the court to interfere in the exercise by a statutory authority of discretionary powers, where the decision is taken freely, voluntarily, and under no pressure, the position may be very different where an emergency dictates a rapid solution to an urgent and pressing problem.'

Comment

(1)   Ormerod LJ gave a concurring judgment. There are, though, differences of emphasis in the detailed legal analysis. The taking of irrelevancies into account is evidence of illegality, but does not of itself amount to illegality. Forbes J leaves this point open. See also the different analyses of *Roberts* v *Hopwood*.

(2)   In *R* v *Port Talbot BC, ex parte Jones*, the Court upheld a challenge to a decision by a local housing authority to allocate housing to K, a councillor seeking re-election. It was, stated Nolan J, a clear case of irrelevant considerations and abuse of power. What is a relevant/irrelevant purpose will depend upon the view taken by the Court as to the underlying purpose of the legislation. Many cases of irrelevant considerations/failure to have regard to relevances can also be argued in terms of improper purposes. A body acting for improper purposes is almost inevitably having regard to irrelevant matters, and failing to have regard to relevances. Thus in *Roberts* v *Hopwood* the council used its statutory power to fix the level of wages to ensure equality of treatment between male and female workers, and to set wages at a level above the 'going rate'. The Court concluded that the council was using its powers for improper purposes, namely for social rather than economic objectives. By implication, the Court was addressing irrelevant matters. The decision is much criticized both for judicial attitude and for the scope of judicial involvement. Despite some extravagant language and the display of attitudes strange to modern ears, the legal reasoning may remain sound. See Forbes J in *Pickwell* (p.305).

(3)   Local authorities are in a fiduciary relationship to their residents. The interests of these is a factor to which local authorities must have regard: see *Roberts* v *Hopwood*; *Bromley LBC* v *GLC*. For the appropriate *locus standi* to justify judicial intervention, see the *Small Businesses* case, p.255.

(4)   Parliament may on occasion state what may or may not be relevant factors to take into account. See, in the area of local authority commercial contracts, ss.17–19, Local Government Act 1988, which prohibit the taking into account of non-commercial considerations.

(5)   For the propriety of taking into account party political matters, note *R* v

Waltham Forest LBC, ex parte Baxter where Russell LJ said:

> Party loyalty, party unanimity, party policy are all relevant considerations for the individual councillor. The vote only becomes unlawful when the councillor allows these considerations or any other outside influences so to dominate as to exclude other considerations which are required for a balanced judgment.

For election manifestoes, see *Bromley LBC v GLC*; *Secretary of State for Education and Science v Tameside MBC* (p.301). Although their contents may be relevant factors to which regard may be had, they must not be considered by the authority to be binding and thus amount to a fetter on discretion.

(6) Section 161 has now been replaced by ss.19–20, Local Government Finance Act 1982 (see *Lloyd v McMahon*).

Wheeler v Leicester City Council

[1985] AC 1054 · House of Lords

The appellant rugby players and others on behalf of themselves and of the Leicester Rugby Football Club sought judicial review to quash a resolution of the respondent Council which prevented use of a recreation ground by the club for a period of 12 months. Members of the club had been part of a touring side which visited South Africa. The Council put to the club four questions in respect of the club's attitude to the tour and their members who were to participate. The club's response was not acceptable to the Council who passed the resolution stated above. It was held by the House of Lords that the Council had acted unlawfully. The Council in exercising statutory powers under the Public Health and Open Spaces Acts had (*per* Lord Roskill) acted in a manner that was unfair and (*per* Lord Templeman) was misusing its power in seeking to punish the club.

Lord Roskill: '. . . The reasons for the imposition of the ban are clearly set out [by the Leader of the Council] . . . It is important to emphasise that there was nothing illegal in the action of the three members in joining the tour. The government policy recorded in the well-known Gleneagles agreement . . . has never been given the force of law at the instance of any government, whatever its political complexion, and a person who acts otherwise than in accordance with the principles of that agreement, commits no offence even though he may by his action earn the moral disapprobation of large numbers of his fellow citizens. That the club condemns apartheid, as does the council, admits of no doubt. But the council's actions against the club were not taken, as already pointed out, because the club took no action against its three members. They were taken . . . because the club failed to condemn the tour and to discourage its members from playing. The same point was put more succinctly . . . for the council – "The club failed to align themselves whole-heartedly with the council on a controversial issue." The club did not condemn the tour. They did not give specific affirmative answers to the first two questions. Thus, so the argument ran, the council, legitimately bitterly hostile to the policy of apartheid, were justified in exercising their statutory discretion to determine by whom the recreation ground should be used so as to exclude those, such as the club, who would not support the council's policy on the council's terms. The club had, however, circulated to those involved the powerfully reasoned and impressive memorandum which had been sent to the RFU on 12 March 1984 by the anti-apartheid movement. Of the club's own opposition to apartheid as expressed in its memorandum which was given to [the Council Leader], there is no doubt. But the club recognised that those views, like those of the council, however passionately held by some, were by no means universally held, especially by those who sincerely believed that the evils of apartheid were enhanced rather than diminished by a total prohibition of all sporting links with South Africa.

The council's main defence rested on s.71 of the Race Relations Act 1976 . . . "Without prejudice to their obligation to comply with any other provision of this Act, it shall be the duty of every local authority to make appropriate arrangements with a view to securing that their various functions are carried out with due regard to the need – (a) to eliminate unlawful racial discrimination; and (b) to promote equality of opportunity, and good relations, between persons of different racial groups" . . .

It was strenuously argued on behalf of the club that this section should be given what was called a "narrow" construction. It was suggested that the section was only concerned with the actions of the council as regards its own internal behaviour and was what was described as "inward looking." The section had no relevance to the general exercise by the council or indeed of any local authority of their statutory functions, as for example in relation to the control of open spaces or in determining who should be entitled to use a recreation ground and on what terms. It was said that the section was expressed in terms of a "duty." But it did not impose any duty so as to compel the exercise by a local authority of other statutory functions in order to achieve the objectives of the Act of 1976 . . .

I unhesitatingly reject this argument. I think the whole purpose of this section is to see that in relation to matters other than those specifically dealt with, for example, in Part II, employment, and in Part III, education, local authorities must in relation to "their various functions" make "appropriate arrangements" to secure that those functions are carried out "with due regard to the need" mentioned in the section.

It follows that I do not doubt that the council were fully entitled in exercising their statutory discretion under, for example, the Open Spaces Act 1906 and the various Public Health Acts . . . to pay regard to what they thought was in the best interests of race relations.

The only question is, therefore, whether the action of the council of which the club complains is susceptible of attack by way of judicial review. It was forcibly argued . . . for the council, that once it was accepted, as I do accept, that s.71 bears the construction for which the council contended, the matter became one of political judgment only, and that by interfering the courts would be trespassing across that line which divides a proper exercise of a statutory discretion based on a political judgment, in relation to which the courts must not and will not interfere, from an improper exercise of such a discretion in relation to which the courts will interfere.

My Lords . . . in [the *GCHQ* case] Lord Diplock classified three already well established heads or sets of circumstances in which the court will interfere . . . Those three heads are not exhaustive, and as Lord Diplock pointed out, further grounds may hereafter require to be added. Nor are they necessarily mutually exclusive.

To my mind the crucial question is whether the conduct of the council in trying by their four questions, whether taken individually or collectively, to force acceptance by the club of their own policy (however proper that policy may be) on their own terms, as for example, by forcing them to lend their considerable prestige to a public condemnation of the tour, can be said either to be so "unreasonable" as to give rise to "*Wednesbury* unreasonableness" . . . or to be so fundamental a breach of the duty to act fairly which rests upon every local authority in matters of this kind and thus justify interference by the courts.

I do not for one moment doubt the great importance which the council attach to the presence in their midst of a 25 per cent. population of persons who are either Asian or of Afro-Caribbean origin. Nor do I doubt for one moment the sincerity of the view expressed in [the Council Leader's] affidavit regarding the need for the council to distance itself from bodies who hold important positions and who do not actively discourage sporting contacts with South Africa. Persuasion, even powerful persuasion, is always a permissible way of seeking to obtain an objective. But in a field where other views can equally legitimately be held, persuasion, however powerful, must not be allowed to cross that line where it moves into the field of illegitimate pressure coupled with the threat of sanctions. The four questions, coupled with the insistence that only affirmative answers to all four would be acceptable, are suggestive of more than powerful persuasion . . . None of the judges in the courts below have felt able to hold that the action of the [council] was unreasonable or perverse in the *Wednesbury* sense. They do not appear to have been invited to consider whether those actions, even if not unreasonable on *Wednesbury* principles, were assailable on the grounds of procedural impropriety or unfairness by the council in the manner in which, in the light of the facts which I have outlined, they took their decision to suspend for 12 months the use by the club of the Welford Road recreation ground.

I greatly hesitate to differ from four learned judges on the *Wednesbury* issue but for myself I would have been disposed respectfully to do this and to say that the actions of the council were unreasonable in the *Wednesbury* sense. But even if I am wrong in this view, I am clearly of the opinion that the manner in which the council took that decision was in all the circumstances unfair within the third of the [Diplock] principles . . . the Council formulated those four questions in the manner of which I have spoken and indicated that only such affirmative answers would be acceptable. They received reasoned and reasonable answers which went a long way in support of the policy which the council had accepted and desired to see accepted. The views expressed in these reasoned and reasonable answers were lawful views and the views which, as the evidence shows, many people sincerely hold and believe to be correct. If the club had adopted a different and hostile attitude, different considerations might well have arisen. But the club did not adopt any such attitude.

In my view, therefore, this is a case in which the court should interfere because of the unfair manner in which the council set about obtaining its objective . . .'

Lord Templeman '. . . My Lords, the laws of this country are not like the laws of Nazi Germany. A private individual or a private organisation cannot be obliged to display zeal in the pursuit of an object sought by a public authority and cannot be obliged to publish views dictated by a public authority.

The club having committed no wrong, the council could not use their statutory powers in the management of their property or any other statutory powers in order to punish the club. There is no doubt that the council intended to punish and have punished the club . . . In my opinion, this use by the council of its statutory powers was a misuse of power. The council could not properly seek to use its statutory powers of management or any other statutory powers for the purposes of punishing the club when the club had done no wrong . . . [citing *Congreve* v *Home Office* (see p.34)].

Similar considerations apply, in my opinion, to the present case. Of course this does not mean that the council is bound to allow its property to be used by a racist organisation or by any organisation which, by its actions or its words, infringes the letter or the spirit of the Race Relations Act 1976. But the attitude of the club and of the committee of the club was a perfectly proper attitude, caught as they were in a political controversy which was not of their making.'

Comment

(1)   Lord Templeman also agreed with the reasons given by Lord Roskill; and Lord Roskill agreed with the reasons given by Lord Templeman. The remaining three Law Lords agreed with both judgments. The *ratio decidendi* is unclear.

(2)   In *R* v *Lewisham LBC, ex parte Shell UK Ltd* the applicant company sought judicial review of a decision by the Council to boycott all of the company's products where alternative products were available on reasonable terms, because of the South African interests and activities of the group of which the company was a part. The Council argued that it acted in the way it did in order to promote good race relations. The Court upheld the application and quashed the Council resolution, issued an injunction to restrain implementation of the decision, and issued a declaration declaring unlawful the conducting of a campaign urging other authorities to boycott the products of the company. Whilst, following *Wheeler* v *Leicester City Council*, race relations matters were relevant considerations, and whilst the actions of the Council were not *Wednesbury* unreasonable (i.e. irrational) the Council was using its powers to seek to change the policy of the company: this was an improper purpose.

(3)   Where a public body acts for dual purposes, one of which is improper, the action will be *ultra vires* if the improper purpose was a material consideration. In *R* v *Inner London Education Authority, ex parte Westminster City Council* the Council sought judicial review of the decision to mount an advertising campaign in relation to education policy and the views of ILEA about government policy. The ground of challenge was that ILEA had allowed its decision to be affected by an irrelevant consideration, namely the Council's desire to oppose 'ratecapping' by central government. ILEA argued that there was a dual purpose for the advertising campaign, which did not solely depend upon that admittedly irrelevant consideration. It was held that there were dual purposes for their campaign. Since one of these was improper, based as it was on an irrelevant consideration, since it materially affected the making of the decision and was not merely subsidiary, the decision was *ultra vires*.

R v *Somerset County Council, ex parte Fewings*

[1995] 1 All ER 513 · Divisional Court.

The respondent local authority resolved to ban stag-hunting from land owned by it, and appropriated for recreational purposes pursuant to s.120 Local Government Act 1972. It claimed to be entitled to impose such a ban by virtue of its powers as landowner. The applicant sought judicial review of that resolution. The Divisional Court held that such a resolution was *ultra vires*, because it was using powers for an improper purpose and taking irrelevant factors into account.

Laws J: 'The true construction of s.120 is of critical importance in the case, not because of any legalistic pedantry with which Councillors seeking to act in the public interest as they see it may justly feel impatient, but because a major principle of the common law necessarily engages it. The principle is this: a public body, such as a local authority, enjoys no such thing as an unfettered discretion. This is a sinew of the rule of law, and has been described by Sir William Wade . . . [*Administrative Law*, 6th edition] as follows:

> The powers of public authorities are . . . essentially different from those of private persons. A person making his will may, subject to any rights of his dependents, dispose of his property just as he may wish. He may act out of malice or a spirit of revenge, but in law this does not affect his exercise of his power. In the same way a private person has an absolute power to allow who he likes to use his land . . . regardless of his motives. This is unfettered discretion. But a public authority may do none of these things unless it acts reasonably and in good faith and upon lawful and relevant grounds of public interest . . . The whole conception of unfettered discretion is inappropriate to a public authority, which possesses powers solely in order that it may use them for the public good.

The corresponding passage in the previous edition which is much to the same effect was endorsed as a correct statement of basic principle by Lord Bridge in *R* v *Tower Hamlets London Borough Council, ex parte Chetnik Developments Ltd*. Nor . . . is this in the least surprising: a truly unfettered discretion will at once put the decision maker outside or, as I prefer to say, above the law. Public bodies and private persons are both subject to the rule of law; nothing could be more elementary. But the principles which govern their relationships with the law are wholly different. For private persons the rule is that you may do anything you choose which the law does not prohibit. It means that the freedoms of the private citizen are not conditional upon some distinct and affirmative justification for which he must burrow in the law books. Such a notion would be anathema to our English legal traditions. But for public bodies, the rule is opposite, and so of another character altogether. It is that any action to be taken must be justified by positive law. A public body has no heritage of legal rights which it enjoys for its own sake: at every turn all of its dealings constitute the fulfilment of duties which it owes to others; indeed, it exists for no other purpose. I would say that a public body enjoys no rights properly so called; it may in various contexts be entitled to insist that this or that procedure be followed, whether by a person affected by its decision or by a superior body having power over it; it may come to the court as a judicial review applicant to complain of the decision of some other public authority; it may maintain a private law action to enforce a contract or otherwise protect its property (although a local authority, at any rate, may not sue in defamation: see *Derbyshire County Council* v *Times Newspapers Ltd*). But in every such instance, and no doubt many others where a public body asserts claims or defences in court, it does so, if it acts in good faith, only to vindicate the better performance of the duties for whose fulfilment it exists. It is in this sense that it has no rights of its own, no axe to grind beyond its public responsibility: a responsibility which defines its purpose and justifies its existence. Under our law, this is true of every public body. The rule is necessary in order to protect the people from arbitrary interference by those set in power over them. This legal fact underpins our principal rules of substantive judicial review, such as those enshrined in *Padfield* v *Minister of Agriculture, Fisheries and Food* and *Wednesbury* itself . . .

[Laws J cited the principles from these two cases, and continued:]

[Counsel for the applicant] cited a number of cases to me. They included *Wheeler* v *Leicester City Council, R* v *Ealing LBC, ex parte Times Newspapers Ltd* and *R* v *Lewisham LBC, ex parte Shell-UK Ltd.* These last two in particular indicate that in deciding whether a local authority has exceeded its powers the Court may examine the motives underlying its actions; this I think is no more than an application of the *Padfield* rule. *Wheeler*, though striking on its facts, was a *Wednesbury* case. Other authority . . . was cited to support the proposition that the functions of a local authority are analogous to those of a trustee. Leaving aside the particular considerations which may arise as regards such an authority's stewardship of public funds, this analogy is in my judgment no more than another means of articulating, in the context of local government, the principle that a public body may only act in fulfilment of the duty cast upon it by statute, and has no possession of legal rights, akin to those of a private person, which are truly its own . . . The primary question in this case . . . is whether the councillors' moral objections to the practice of hunting are capable of justifying the prohibition as a measure which conduces to "the benefit, improvement or development of their area within [s.120] . . ."

Now, I entertain no doubt that there may be circumstances in which a prohibition on hunting could be said to promote such a statutory purpose . . . If some part of the area being hunted contained rare flora which were so damaged by the hunt that their meagre stocks were at risk of dwindling to extinction, I see no reason why in principle the Council should not regard that circumstance as offering potential justification for a ban. Again, if the animals being hunted were themselves rare and the hunt so reduced in numbers as to threaten their survival, the hunt might perhaps be stopped in the interests of preserving the wildlife of the area . . . all these examples possess an important common feature: it is that the prohibition contemplated would objectively relate to the preservation or betterment of the area's amenities. It would not spring from, nor be fuelled by, the ethical perceptions of the councillors about the rights and wrongs of hunting.

Further, I certainly accept that it is possible to construct instances in which in the exercise of statutory power by a local authority, moralistic considerations would rightly be regarded as relevant or indeed critical to the decision in hand. Depending of course on the precise nature of the power conferred, such a case might arise where for example a local authority was authorised to make by-laws for the preservation of public decency, and some pleasant country spot in the area had become notorious for the undisguised practice of sexual pastimes by young people resorting there. Again, a local authority's power to take proceedings to control

Sunday trading may plainly be said to engage a moral element. So too would a power to regulate the age below which children may not take employment (though in fact, of course, this is done by main legislation). But these examples also possess a common feature: it is that the moral element in the decision is itself part and parcel of the purposes for which the power in question is conferred. It would be an axiom of the Council's statutory function; they would be bound to have regard to it irrespective of their own views; no matter that, for example, the councillors might look warmly (even wistfully) on the uninhibited passions of the young, they would be obliged to consider the degree of offence, entertained it may be on moral grounds, caused to others who resorted to the place in question for altogether less exuberant purposes. What is important here is that the moral element would not arise as a supervening consideration, grafted on to the decision-making process by the decision maker's subjective perceptions of what is morally good or bad: it would be part of his compulsory terms of reference. And it would be indissolubly linked with objective or practical considerations possessing an impetus beyond that generated by the personal moral views of the authority's members . . .

[Laws J then considered arguments based on the meaning of s.120, and concluded that the decision was in fact taken on the basis that hunting was morally repulsive. He continued:]

The true question, therefore is whether the Council was entitled to reach a decision based on a moral position whose rationale had nothing to do with issues of management at all . . . Before directly addressing that question, I should indicate that I reject out of hand one [argument of counsel for the local authority] . . . this was that the elected members of a local authority could not realistically be expected to put such ethical questions as arose in this case out of their minds . . . Apart from the dry legal fact that an assessment of what may be in human terms expected of councillors can hardly be more than a questionable aid to the construction of s.120, I consider . . . that this submission does less than justice to his clients. I entertain no doubt that if it is authoritatively held that the councillors may not have regard to their moral views about hunting as a freestanding consideration when they approach their duties under s.120, the councillors will be well able to abide by such a ruling . . . The real question upon this part of the argument is whether the democratic quality of the respondent Council should colour and affect the true interpretation of s.120 . . .

[Laws J then cited from *Slattery* v *Naylor* and *Kruse* v *Johnson*, and continued:]

These cases do not support the bare proposition . . . that where a body acting under statutory powers is elected by a section of the public, it is a rule of construction that the provision conferring the powers in question should be interpreted more broadly, or more "benevolently" than where the statute's delegate is unelected. *Kruse* v *Johnson* concerned the making of by-laws as to whose contents the promolgating authority enjoyed on any view a wide discretion, controlled by formal safeguards. In *Slattery* there were formal safeguards also. No such measures exist in the instant case, where the impugned decision did not involve by-laws at all. The only safeguard, if that is the right word, to ensure that the Council acted within its power lies in the jurisdiction of this Court . . . The question for the Court is the same as in every case where the use of statutory power is challenged as lying beyond the authority granted by Parliament: what are the limits of the power conferred? To hold that Parliament intended to bestow a greater power upon an elected local authority than it might have given to an unelected body by the same words, which in logic is the burden of the submission [for the Council] is to impute an intention to the legislature which *ex hypothesi* cannot be derived from the language of the Act. Such a conclusion could rest only upon the supposition that on democratic grounds the local authority should in Parliament's view have as much free rein as possible . . . I know of no principle of statutory construction upon which this argument could be supported . . .

If the activity in question is permissible under the general law, as is the practice of deer hunting, it is by no means to be prohibited on grounds only of the decision maker's distaste or ethical objection where the reach of his statutory function on its face requires no more than the making of objective judgments for the management of a particular regime. While, of course, it is open to Parliament to legislate so as to curtail the activities of private individuals on avowedly moral grounds (assuming consistency with the law of the European Union), such restrictions involve a very particular encroachment upon personal liberty; and the Court must be alert to see that any action of that kind is strictly justified by law. Where a right to act is asserted by a subordinate body, whose powers by definition are not large, the Court will presume against it unless the empowering statute positively requires the authority in question to bring its moral views to bear on the subject in hand, and allows or demands that it treat those views as decisive . . . there is no such language here . . .'

Comment

(1)   This case, like the *Lewisham* case (p.313) raises questions as to the basis on which the court intervened. In *Fewings* the local authority argued that it was exercising its powers to regulate the use of land, as any landowner is entitled to do. In *Lewisham*, the local authority argued that it was using its powers to decide with whom, and on what terms, it would contract. In neither case was there misuse of the statutory powers themselves. The court in each case was unimpressed by such arguments, and the availability of judicial review marks a recognition by the courts that local authorities and other public bodies cannot be regarded in the same way as ordinary legal persons. For confirmation of this in another context, see *Derbyshire County Council* v *Times Newspapers*.

(2)   Laws J in *Fewings* regards *Wheeler* as a case of *Wednesbury* unreasonableness. His precise meaning is unclear. This may in fact reflect the uncertainty as to the precise basis of challenge found in *Wheeler*.

Cannock Chase DC v Kelly

[1978] 1 WLR 1 · Court of Appeal

Megaw LJ: '. . . One of the grounds upon which a challenge can be made, and, if established, should certainly succeed, is bad faith. As Lord Greene [in *Wednesbury*] says: "Bad faith, dishonesty – those of course stand by themselves". I would stress . . . that bad faith or, as it is sometimes put, "lack of good faith", means dishonesty; not necessarily for a financial motive, but still dishonesty. It always involves a grave charge. It must not be treated as a synonym for an honest, though mistaken, taking into consideration of a factor which is in law irrelevant . . .'

Comment

A charge of bad faith against a public authority will rarely succeed but in *R v Derbyshire CC, ex parte The Times Supplements* it was held that the council was actuated by bad faith or vindictiveness in moving its advertising of education job vacancies from *The Times Educational Supplement* to another newspaper. The action was not based on any valid educational objective, bearing in mind an obligation on school governors to advertise vacancies, but rather as part of a general ban on papers owned by the newspaper proprietor Rupert Murdoch. Furthermore, the council had sought deliberately to mislead the court as to the true reasons for the decision.

Policy

All discretions must be genuinely exercised in the light of the individual case (see, for example, *Lindley v Rutter*, p.371). That does not preclude the existence of policy.

British Oxygen Co. Ltd v *Board of Trade*

[1971] AC 610 · House of Lords

Lord Reid: ' . . . The general rule is that anyone who has to exercise a statutory discretion must not "shut his ears to an application" . . . I do not think there is any great difference between a policy and a rule. There may be cases where an officer or authority ought to listen to a substantial argument reasonably presented urging a change of policy. What the authority must not do is to refuse to listen at all. But a Ministry or large authority may have had to deal already with a multitude of similar applications and then they will almost certainly have evolved a policy so precise that it could well be called a rule. There can be no objection to that, provided the authority is always willing to listen to anyone with something new to say – of course I do not mean to say that there need be an oral hearing.'

Comment

(1)   The application of this principle is by no means easy in the context of public bodies, principally local authorities, working in reality within a party political context. A manifesto commitment must not be followed blindly: see p.310. In *R v Waltham Forest LBC, ex parte Baxter*, where the Court held that a local authority member had not fettered his discretion by taking into account and weighing in his own mind the party policy of his fellow councillors and the requirements of the party whip, Sir John Donaldson MR stated:

... The duty of an individual councillor ... is to make up his own mind on how to vote, giving such weight as he thinks appropriate to the views of other councillors and to the policy of the group of which he is a member. It is only if he abdicates his personal responsibility that questions can arise as to the validity of his vote. The distinction between giving great weight to the views of colleagues and to party policy on the one hand and voting blindly in support of party policy may on occasion be a fine one, but it is nevertheless very real.

(2) Fettering by policy can also be viewed as bias and thus procedural impropriety: see *Steeples* v *Derbyshire CC*, p.332; *R* v *Amber Valley DC, ex parte Jackson*, p.327.

(3) Even if the policy is legitimately relied upon, and not an improper fetter, that does not prevent challenge to the substance of the policy itself: see *Attorney-General ex rel. Tilley* v *Wandsworth LBC*. In addition, there may be a legitimate expectation that an authority shall apply consistently an announced policy until such time as it is changed: see *R* v *Secretary of State for Home Department, ex parte Asif Khan*, cited at p.329.

(4) A discretion must be exercised by the body upon whom it is conferred, and must not be delegated without authority in law, or otherwise abrogated.

Irrationality

R v Cornwall County Council, ex parte Cornwall & Isles of Scilly Guardian Ad Litem & Reporting Officers Panel

[1992] 2 All ER 471 · Divisional Court

The applicants sought judicial review to quash the decision of the respondent local authority to impose a limit of 65 hours per case that would be paid to guardians *ad litem* in respect of each child care case handled by them.

Sir Simon Brown P: 'The role of the guardian *ad litem* is of primary importance in the implementation of the Children Act 1989. Section 41 [of that Act] requires that the court concerned "shall appoint a guardian *ad litem* for the child concerned unless satisfied that it is not necessary to do so in order to safeguard his interests" ... Accordingly, the position of the guardian has become a matter of greater prominence than hitherto. It is vital that the independence of the guardian in carrying out his or her duties on behalf of the child in any proceedings should be clearly recognised and understood. Since it is the responsibility of each local authority to establish a panel of guardians in its area and to be responsible for the payment of expenses, fees and allowances to the guardians and furthermore to determine within its own area the rates of payment, it is vitally important that the position of the guardian should not be compromised by any restriction placed directly or indirectly upon him or her ...

I can well understand that the guardians felt that they were being treated as if they were, in effect, direct employees of the local authority. This was an instruction or direction issued to them individually by the director of social services. In the context of the necessity to ensure the independence of the guardians in my judgment this exceeded the proper exercise of his authority by the director of social services and is to be categorised as an unreasonable exercise of power in the *Wednesbury* sense. Although the intention so to do is disclaimed, the decision to impose the benchmark system in fact sought to restrict the discretion of the guardian to undertake work which the guardian might consider to be necessary. Further, the director imposed this in an arbitrary manner . . .'

Comment

Successful challenges based on true irrationality will be few. For discussion of principle, see *ex parte Brind* (p.293) and *R* v *GMC, ex parte Coleman*. In *Backhouse* v *Lambeth LBC*, in order to raise the average rent of all council dwellings, the Council resolved to raise the rent of one unoccupied and unfit house by £18,000 p.w. This was held to be a resolution no reasonable authority could have passed. In *Hall* v *Shoreham by Sea UDC* a requirement upon the granting of planning permission to a developer that he provide, at his own expense, what was in effect a new extension to a public highway was held to be a conclusion no planning authority, appreciating its duty and properly applying itself to the facts, could reasonably have reached. *Wheeler* v *Leicester City Council* was ultimately decided on the narrower illegality basis, but it can be argued that almost all irrationality cases could be dealt with on that basis.

14 Procedural impropriety

This ground of challenge provides a means for enforcement of procedural requirements required by statute or common law. Statute may set detailed procedural requirements, or authorize their making in delegated legislation. These, of course, must be followed, but not every breach of a procedural requirement will create invalidity: only where a procedural requirement is 'mandatory' (as opposed to 'directory') will the impugned action be *ultra vires*. Case law shows that the factors which will be considered by the Court in determining the effect of any breach will be the nature of the requirement, its role in relation to the individual, the extent of non-compliance, and the consequence of non-compliance. Examples of actions being quashed for procedural irregularity of this type include *Bradbury* v *Enfield LBC* (failure to publish necessary details of rights of objection in respect of school closures) and *London & Clydesdale Estate Ltd* v *Aberdeen DC* (breach of requirement in planning legislation that notice be given of the existence of rights of appeal).

Agricultural, Horticultural & Forestry Training Board v Aylesbury Mushrooms

[1972] 1 WLR 190 · Queen's Bench Division

A minister wanted to establish a training board pursuant to the Industrial Training Act 1964. Section 1(4) imposed a duty on the minister to consult 'any organisation or association of organisations appearing to him to be representative of substantial numbers of employers engaged in the activities concerned . . .' The Mushroom Growers Association (a subsidiary of the NFU, which was consulted) was not formally consulted despite being included in a draft Schedule of bodies to be consulted. It was held that there had been on the facts a failure to consult within the meaning of the Act.

Donaldson J: '. . . Both parties are agreed that under the terms of s.1(4) of the Act, some consultation by the Minister is mandatory and that in the absence of any particular consultation which is so required, the persons who should have been but were not consulted are not bound by the order, although the order remains effective in relation to all others who were in fact consulted or whom there was no need to consult . . . the Shorter Oxford English dictionary gives as one definition of the verb "to consult", "to ask advice of, seek counsel from; to have recourse to for instruction or professional advice". However, in truth the mere sending of a letter constitutes but an attempt to consult and this does not suffice. The essence of consultation is the communication of a genuine invitation, extended with a receptive mind, to give advice (see Bucknill LJ approving a *dictum* of Morris J in *Rollo* v *Minister of Town & Country Planning*). If the invitation is once received, it matters not that it is not accepted and no advice is proffered. Were it otherwise organisations with a right to be consulted could in effect veto the making of any order by simply failing to respond to the invitation. But without communication and the consequent opportunity of responding, there can be no consultation . . .'

Comment

See also *R* v *Secretary of State for Social Services, ex parte AMA* where Webster J indicated that, 'It is not necessarily to be regarded as the normal practice, where delegated legislation is held to be *ultra vires*, to revoke the instrument . . . ' The converse was the case; revocation is a matter of discretion.

Natural justice and procedural fairness

The standards implied by the Courts have historically been known as the principles of natural justice, summarized in two Latin maxims: *audi alteram partem* (hear both sides), and *nemo judex in causa sua potest* (no one should be judge in their own cause). These maxims reflect appropriate standards to be adopted in the performance of judicial functions, but are less helpful in consideration of the procedural standards to be expected in the performance of executive and administrative functions. For that reason, the hope of Lord Roskill in *GCHQ* that the phrase 'natural justice' may now be allowed to find a permanent resting place and be better replaced by speaking of a duty 'to act fairly' is to be welcomed as a recognition that, whilst fair procedure is highly important, what that may involve will vary from the high 'court-like' standards where a body is under a duty to act judicially to little more than an obligation to act honestly in the case of some executive functions. Indeed, Lord Morris in *Lloyd* v *McMahon* accepted that natural justice was only 'fair play in action'. They also vary in their application (see *Doody* v *Secretary of State for the Home Department*, p.333). These standards are not confined to the actions of public bodies, but cover a range of situations involving, for example, disciplinary or like functions.

The principles of natural justice were described as follows by Lord Bridge in *Lloyd* v *McMahon*:

> . . . the so-called rules of natural justice are not engraved on tablets of stone. To use the phrase which better expresses the underlying concept,

what the requirements of fairness demand when any body, domestic, administrative or judicial, has to make a decision which will affect the rights of individuals depends on the character of the decision-making body, the kind of decision it has to make and the statutory or other framework in which it operates. In particular, it is well established that when a statute has conferred on any body the power to take decisions affecting individuals, the courts will not only require the procedure prescribed by the statute to be followed, but will readily imply so much and no more to be introduced by way of additional procedural safeguards as will ensure the attainment of fairness.

Whilst the applicable principles are common, the extracts here concentrate on the application of the principles in the public law field.

Ridge v *Baldwin*

[1964] AC 40 · House of Lords

The appellant, the Chief Constable of Brighton, was dismissed by the Watch Committee (the forerunner of the modern Police Authority) pursuant to powers contained in s.191, Municipal Corporations Act 1882. He had previously been tried and acquitted on conspiracy charges, but was the subject of significant criticism by the trial judge. He was not asked to attend the meeting of the Committee which determined to dismiss him; at a second meeting, where he was represented, the Committee confirmed its actions. The appellant sought to challenge the dismissal from office on the grounds of breach of natural justice. The House of Lords held that the Watch Committee was in breach of the principles of natural justice, as well as being in breach of the statutory regulations governing police discipline. The major issue for the Court was whether, in the light of authority, the principles of natural justice were to be implied.

Lord Reid: '. . . The appellant's case is that . . . the watch committee were bound to observe what are commonly called the principles of natural justice, that before attempting to reach any decision they were bound to inform him of the grounds on which they proposed to act and give him a fair opportunity of being heard in his own defence. The authorities on the applicability of the principles of natural justice are in some confusion.

[Lord Reid examined the classes of case in respect of dismissal of employees and dismissal from an office. He then continued:]

Stopping there, I would think that authority was wholly in favour of the appellant, but the respondent's argument was mainly based on what has been said in a number of fairly recent cases dealing with different subject-matter. Those cases deal with decisions by ministers, officials and bodies of various kinds which adversely affected property rights or privileges of persons who had had no opportunity or no proper opportunity of presenting their cases before the decisions were given. And it is necessary to examine those cases for another reason. The question which was or ought to have been considered by the watch committee on March 7, 1958, was not a simple question whether or not the appellant should be dismissed. There were three possible courses open to the watch committee – reinstating the appellant as chief constable, dismissing him, or requiring him to resign. The difference between the latter two is that dismissal involved forfeiture of pension rights, whereas requiring him to resign did not. Indeed, it is now clear that the appellant's real interest in this appeal is to try to save his pension rights.

It may be convenient at this point to deal with an argument that, even if as a general rule a watch committee must hear a constable in his own defence before dismissing him, this case was so clear that nothing that the appellant could have said could have made any difference. It is at least very doubtful whether that could be accepted as an excuse. But, even if it could, the respondents would, in my view, fail on the facts. It may well be that no reasonable body of men could have reinstated the appellant. But as between the other two courses open to the watch committee the case is not so clear. Certainly on the facts, as we know them, the watch committee could reasonably have decided to forfeit the appellant's pension rights, but I could not hold that they would have acted wrongly or wholly unreasonably if they had in the exercise of their discretion decided to take a more lenient course.

I would start an examination of the authorities dealing with property rights and privileges with *Cooper* v *Wandsworth Board of Works*. Where an owner had failed to give proper notice to the board they had under an Act of 1855 authority to demolish any building he had erected and recover the cost from him. This action was brought against the board because they had used that power without giving the owner an opportunity of being heard. The board maintained that their discretion to order demolition was not a judicial discretion and that any appeal should have been to the Metropolitan Board of Works. But the court decided unanimously in favour of the owner. Erle CJ held that the power was subject to a qualification repeatedly recognised that no man is to be deprived of his property without his having an opportunity of being heard and that this had been applied to "many exercises of power which in common understanding would not be at all a more judicial proceeding than would be the act of the district board in ordering a house to be pulled down." Willes J said that the rule was "of universal application, and founded upon the plainest principles of justice" and Byles J said that "although there are no positive words in a statute requiring that the party shall be heard, yet the justice of the common law will supply the omission of the legislature . . ." [After citation of further authority, Lord Reid continued:]

I shall now turn to a different class of case – deprivation of membership of a professional or social body. In *Wood* v *Woad* the committee purported to expel a member of a mutual insurance society without hearing him, and it was held that their action was void, and so he was still a member. Kelly CB said of *audi alteram partem*: "This rule is not confined to the conduct of strictly legal tribunals, but is applicable to every tribunal or body of persons invested with authority to adjudicate upon matters involving civil consequences to individuals." . . .

Then there are the club cases, *Fisher* v *Keane* and *Dawkins* v *Antrobus*. In the former, Jessel MR said of the committee: "They ought not, as I understand it, according to the ordinary rules by which justice should be administered by committees of clubs, or by any other body of persons who decide upon the conduct of others, to blast a man's reputation for ever – perhaps to ruin his prospects for life, without giving him an opportunity of either defending or palliating his conduct." . . .

I shall not at present advert to the various trade union cases because I am deliberately considering the state of the law before difficulties were introduced by statements in various fairly recent cases. It appears to me that if the present case had arisen thirty or forty years ago the courts would have had no difficulty in deciding this issue in favour of the appellant on the authorities which I have cited. So far as I am aware none of these authorities has ever been disapproved or even doubted. Yet the Court of Appeal have decided this issue against the appellant on more recent authorities which apparently justify that result. How has this come about?

At least three things appear to me to have contributed. In the first place there have been many cases where it has been sought to apply the principles of natural justice to the wider duties imposed on ministers and other organs of government by modern legislation. For reasons which I shall attempt to state in a moment, it has been held that those principles have a limited application in such cases and those limitations have tended to be reflected in other decisions on matters to which in principle they do not appear to me to apply. Secondly . . . those principles have been held to have a limited application in cases arising out of war-time legislation; and again such limitations have tended to be reflected in other cases. And, thirdly, there has, I think, been a misunderstanding of the judgment of Atkin LJ in *R* v *Electricity Commissioners, ex parte LEJC Co.*

In cases of the kind with which I have been dealing the Board of Works or the Governor or the club committee was dealing with a single isolated case. It was not deciding, like a judge in a law suit, what were the rights of the person before it. But it was deciding how he should be treated – something analogous to a judge's duty in imposing a penalty. No doubt policy would play some part in the decision – but so it might when a judge is imposing a sentence. So it was easy to say that such a body is performing a quasi-judicial task in considering and deciding such a matter, and to require it to observe the essentials of all proceedings of a judicial character – the principles of natural justice.

Sometimes the functions of a minister or department may also be of that character, and then the rules of natural justice can apply in much the same way. But more often their functions are of a very different character. If a minister is considering whether to make a scheme for, say, an important new road, his primary concern will not be with the damage which its construction will do to the rights of individual owners of land. He will have to consider all manner of questions of public interest and, it may be, a number of alternative schemes. He cannot be prevented from attaching more importance to the fulfilment of his policy than to the fate of individual objectors, and it would be quite wrong for the courts to say that the minister should or could act in the same kind of way as a board of works deciding whether a house should be pulled down. And there is another important difference. As explained in *Local Government Board* v *Arlidge* a minister cannot do everything himself. His officers will have to gather and sift all the facts, including objections by individuals, and no individual can complain if the ordinary accepted methods of carrying on public business do not give him as good protection as would be given by the principles of natural justice in a different kind of case.

We do not have a developed system of administrative law – perhaps because until fairly recently we did not need it. So it is not surprising that in dealing with new types of cases the courts have had to grope for solutions, and found that old powers, rules and procedure are largely inapplicable to cases which they were never designed or intended to deal with. But I see nothing in that to justify our thinking that our old methods are any less applicable today than ever they were to the older types of case. And, if there are any *dicta* in modern authorities which point in that direction, then, in my judgment, they should not be followed . . . [Lord Reid considered the exclusion of natural justice in many instances of war-time legislation and concluded:]

So I would not think that any decision that the rules of natural justice were excluded from war-time legislation should be regarded as of any great weight in dealing with a case such as this case, which is of the older type, and which involves the interpretation of an Act passed long before modern modifications of the principles of natural justice became necessary . . .

The matter has been further complicated by what I believe to be a misunderstanding of a much-quoted passage in the judgment of Atkin LJ in *R v Electricity Commissioners, ex parte LEJC Co.* He said: " . . . the operation of the writs [of prohibition and *certiorari*] has extended to control the proceedings of bodies which do not claim to be, and would not be recognised as, courts of justice. Wherever any body of persons having legal authority to determine questions affecting the rights of subjects, and having the duty to act judicially, act in excess of their legal authority, they are subject to the controlling jurisdiction of the King's Bench Division exercised in these writs." . . .

In [that case] the commissioners had a statutory duty to make schemes with regard to electricity districts and to hold local inquiries before making them. They made a draft scheme which in effect allocated duties to one body which the Act required should be allocated to a different kind of body. This was held to be *ultra vires*, and the question was whether prohibition would lie. It was argued that the proceedings of the commissioners were purely executive and controllable by Parliament alone. Bankes LJ said: "On principle and on authority it is in my opinion open to this court to hold, and I consider that it should hold, that powers so far-reaching, affecting as they do individuals as well as property, are powers to be exercised judicially, and not ministerially or merely, to use the language of Palles CB, as proceedings towards legislation." So he inferred the judicial element from the nature of the power. I think that Atkin LJ did the same. Immediately after the passage which I said has been misunderstood, he cited a variety of cases and in most of them I can see nothing "superadded" (to use Lord Hewart's word) to the duty itself. Certainly Atkin LJ did not say that anything was superadded. And a later passage in his judgment convinces me that he, like Bankes LJ, inferred the judicial character of the duty from the nature of the duty itself . . . There is not a word in Atkin LJ's judgment to suggest disapproval of the earlier line of authority which I have cited. On the contrary, he goes further than those authorities. I have already stated my view that it is more difficult for the courts to control an exercise of power on a large scale where the treatment to be meted out to a particular individual is only one of many matters to be considered. This was a case of that kind, and, if Atkin LJ was prepared to infer a judicial element from the nature of the power in this case, he could hardly disapprove such an inference when the power relates solely to the treatment of a particular individual . . .'

Comment

(1) *Ridge* v *Baldwin* is regarded as a landmark case. The judgment of Lord Reid indicates the development of a line of authority, based on a misunderstanding of the

dicta of Atkin LJ in the *Electricity Commissioners* case, which sought to confine the application of natural justice to judicial and quasi-judicial functions. This led to sterile debate and distinctions as to the nature of different functions, and caused problems where there were activities that bore characteristics of both administrative and adjudicative functions: see, for example, *Franklin* v *Minister of Town & Country Planning* (designation of New Town, and determination of objections). *Ridge* v *Baldwin* rejects this approach, and returns the law to consideration of the consequences of the action taken. If these infringe rights, then a duty to act judicially will be implied, by that meaning a duty to observe judicial standards as defined by the Courts. In retrospect *Ridge* v *Baldwin* is part of judicial rejection of classifications as means of deciding whether the courts can intervene: see the *GCHQ* case, p.215.

(2) The rejection of the classification approach as a precondition of judicial implication of standards does not mean that the nature of the function is unimportant: it may well be decisive in determining the standard of procedural fairness that is to be implied – that of a court or tribunal will be much stricter than those of a minister determining the award of an ex gratia payment: see, for example, *R* v *Secretary of State for Home Affairs, ex parte Harrison*, and the *dicta* of Woolf J in *R* v *Amber Valley, ex parte Jackson*.

(3) Subsequent case law has developed beyond interference with rights, into the standards to be observed when there is interference with legitimate expectations. The following extracts summarize this development.

R v *Secretary of State for the Home Department, ex parte Ruddock*

[1987] 1 WLR 1482 · Queen's Bench Division

The applicants sought declarations that the Secretary of State had improperly authorized the interception of the telephone calls of one of the applicants. The Secretary of State in response gave written evidence that no warrant had been issued which failed to comply with the published guidelines for interception of telephone calls. On the question of the existence of legitimate expectation, the Court concluded that there was a legitimate expectation that the criteria would be applied but that there was no evidence that they had not been so applied.

Taylor J: '. . . [Counsel for the applicant] relies upon an alleged breach of the criteria which he says the applicant legitimately expected to be faithfully applied. The issue can be put as follows. Did the publication of the criteria and repeated acknowledgment by successive Home Secretaries of their binding effect give rise to a legitimate expectation enforceable by judicial review that no warrant would issue outside those criteria? [Counsel for the Secretary of State] says the doctrine of legitimate expectation relates only to cases where the applicant's expectation is of being consulted or given the opportunity to make representations before a certain decision adverse to him is made. Since there can be no question of such consultation or opportunity to be heard before a warrant to intercept is issued, [he] contends that the doctrine of legitimate expectation does not apply in this field.

Since the phrase was introduced by Lord Denning MR in *Schmidt* v *Secretary of State for Home Affairs* there has been a number of cases in which the doctrine has been applied, culminating in the *GCHQ* case where it was ultimately overridden by a plea of national security. There, as in many of the cases, the expectation was one of consultation . . . [Taylor J cited from the judgments of Lord Diplock and Roskill in *GCHQ*, and then cited Lord Fraser:] "But even where a person claiming some benefit or privilege has no legal right to it, as a matter of private law, he may have a legitimate expectation of receiving the benefit or privilege, and, if so, the courts will protect his expectation by judicial review as a matter of public law. This subject has been fully explained by my noble and learned friend, Lord Diplock, in *O'Reilly* v *Mackman* and I need not repeat what he has so recently said. Legitimate, or reasonable, expectation may arise either from an express promise given on behalf of a public authority or from the existence of a regular practice which the claimant can reasonably expect to continue." . . .

It is true that Lord Diplock went on to indicate that one of the rules of natural justice he had in mind in that case was *audi alteram partem*: the applicant's right to be consulted or heard. But it is significant that he stated the doctrine in terms of a duty to act fairly, as did Lord Roskill in the *GCHQ* case.

In *Attorney-General of Hong Kong* v *Ng Yuen Shiu* Lord Fraser said: "When a public authority has promised to follow a certain procedure, it is in the interest of good administration that it should act fairly and should implement its promise, so long as implementation does not interfere with its statutory duty."

The same principle is to be found in two later cases. *Re Findlay* was an application for judicial review by Findlay and four other convicted prisoners who complained of a change of policy by the Home Secretary causing loss of their expectations of parole. Their applications failed. Lord Scarman said:

> But what was their legitimate expectation? Given the substance and purpose of the legislative provisions governing parole, the most that a convicted prisoner can legitimately expect is that his case will be examined individually in the light of whatever policy the Secretary of State sees fit to adopt provided always that the adopted policy is a lawful exercise of the discretion conferred upon him by the statute. Any other view would entail the conclusion that the unfettered discretion conferred by the statute upon the minister can in some cases be restricted so as to hamper, or even to prevent, changes of policy. Bearing in mind the complexity of the issues which the Secretary of State has to consider and the importance of the public interest in the administration of parole, I cannot think that Parliament intended the discretion to be restricted in this way.

I emphasise the phrase "in the light of whatever policy the Secretary of State sees fit to adopt" because it is implicit in that passage that the applicants could legitimately expect to be considered under the current policy. The complaint which failed was that the policy had been changed and the applicants should be excepted from the new one. If a complaint had been made out, however, that the applicants were being treated in a manner less favourable than the new policy required, the legitimate expectation defined by Lord Scarman would surely have been breached. This would have been so despite the lack of any right in the applicants to be consulted.

In *R v Secretary of State for the Home Department, ex parte Asif Khan*, the Secretary of State had issued a circular setting out the criteria he would apply in admitting children into the United Kingdom for adoption. The applicant sought judicial review of a refusal to admit a relative's child he wished to adopt on the grounds that the criteria had not been followed. In allowing the application on appeal, Dunn LJ said:

> Mr Latham submitted on behalf of the Home Secretary in this case that there were no statutory provisions or rules, that the Secretary of State had an unfettered discretion, and that he was entitled to take into account a pre-eminent policy consideration, namely that leave would only be granted to bring a child here for adoption where there was to be a genuine transfer of parental responsibility on the ground of the natural parents' inability to care for the child.
>
> If the Home Secretary had done no more than to state that it was a matter for his discretion whether or not the child could be brought here for adoption, I should find great force in that submission. But the Home Secretary did not do that. He caused the circular letter in common form to be sent to all applicants setting out the four criteria to be satisfied before leave could be given. Thereby, in my judgment, he in effect made his own rules and stated those matters which he regarded as relevant and would consider in reaching his decision. The letter said nothing about the natural parents' inability to care for the child as being a relevant consideration and did not even contain a general "sweeping up clause" to include all the circumstances of the case which might seem relevant to the Home Secretary.
>
> The categories of unreasonableness are not closed, and in my judgment an unfair action can seldom be a reasonable one. The cases cited by Parker LJ show that the Home Secretary is under a duty to act fairly, and I agree that what happened in this case was not only unfair but unreasonable. Although the circular letter did not create an estoppel, the Home Secretary set out therein for the benefit of applicants the matters to be taken into consideration, and then reached his decision on a consideration which on his own showing was irrelevant. In so doing, in my judgment, he misdirected himself according to his own criteria and acted unreasonably.

On those authorities I conclude that the doctrine of legitimate expectation in essence imposes a duty to act fairly. Whilst most of the cases are concerned, as Lord Roskill said, with a right to be heard, I do not think the doctrine is so confined. Indeed, in a case where *ex hypothesi* there is no right to be heard, it may be thought the more important to fair dealing that a promise or undertaking given by a minister as to how he will proceed should be kept. Of course such promise or undertaking must not conflict with his statutory duty or his duty, as here, in the exercise of a prerogative power. I accept Counsel's submission that the Secretary of State cannot fetter his discretion. By declaring a policy he does not preclude any possible need to change it. But then if the practice has been to publish the current policy, it would be incumbent upon him in dealing fairly to publish the new policy, unless again that would conflict with his duties. Had the criteria here needed changing for national security reasons, no doubt the Secretary of State could have changed them. Had those reasons prevented him also from publishing the new criteria, no doubt he could have refrained from doing so. Had he even decided to keep the criteria but depart from them in this single case for national security reasons, no doubt those reasons would have afforded him a defence to judicial review as in the *GCHQ* case.

It is no part of the Secretary of State's evidence or argument here, however, that the published criteria were inapplicable, either because they had been changed or abandoned or because for good reason (e.g. national security) it was justifiable to depart from them . . .'

Comment

(1)   The legitimate expectation can be of receiving a benefit or of being treated in a certain way (see *GCHQ*, p.215). It must not be confused with a mere hope of an advantage or benefit.

(2)   *Ruddock* demonstrates that there may be circumstances in which it would be unfair to change a policy adhered to without giving those affected a right to be heard.

(3)   In *R* v *Secretary of State for Transport, ex parte Richmond-on-Thames*, Laws J rejected an argument that the law protects legitimate expectations of a substantive, rather than procedural, kind. He also rejected the argument that the doctrine may limit the circumstances in which a policy could be changed to where the public interest requires it. *Dicta* of Lord Denning in *Re Liverpool Taxi Operators Association* should not be taken as support for the contrary. Laws J stated:

> The court is not the judge of the merits of the decision maker's policy . . . if (as must be the case) the public authority in question is the judge of the issue of whether 'the overriding public interest' justifies a change in policy, then the submission means no more than that a reasonable public authority, having regard only to relevant considerations, will not alter its policy unless it concludes that the public will be better served by the change. But that is no more than to assert that a change in policy, like any discretionary decision by a public authority, must not transgress *Wednesbury* principles.

(4)   In *McInnes* v *Onslow-Fane*, the plaintiff unsuccessfully sought a declaration that the British Boxing Board of Control had acted procedurally fairly in determining his application for a boxing manager's licence without being given an oral hearing or being told the reasons for refusal. Although the plaintiff had held licences to promote, train boxers and to act as Master of Ceremonies, he did not have a legitimate expectation of a licence. In such circumstances, the only duty was to act honestly. In giving judgment Sir Robert Megarry drew a distinction between three classes of case: forfeiture cases, legitimate expectation cases, and application cases. In the first two classes of case standards of procedural fairness would be implied which would be higher than in mere application cases such as this. He also pointed out that the phrase 'natural justice' is a flexible term, the requirements of which varied according to the particular circumstances. In particular:

> the courts must be slow to allow any implied obligation to be fair to be used as a means of bringing before the courts for review honest decisions of bodies exercising jurisdiction over sporting and other activities which those bodies are

far better fitted to judge than the courts . . . the concepts of natural justice and the duty to be fair must not be allowed to discredit themselves by making unreasonable requirements and imposing undue burdens.

(5) In *Re H.K. (An Infant)* the question arose as to whether the son of a Commonwealth citizen already resident in this country had any procedural expectations in respect of an immigration officer dealing with his entry into the United Kingdom. It was held that the immigration officer should inform the son of his impressions, so that the immigrant son could disabuse him of any misconceptions.

(6) Note that the issues in *Ruddock* arose prior to the Interception of Communications Act 1985.

(7) For discussion of issues of national security, see p.264.

Bias

Metropolitan Properties v *Lannon*

[1969] 1 QB 577 · Court of Appeal

The decision of a Rent Assessment Committee was quashed since the Chairman had indirect connections with one party to the proceedings.

Lord Denning MR: '. . . in considering whether there was a real likelihood of bias, the court does not look at the mind of the justice himself or at the mind of the Chairman of the tribunal, or whoever it may be, who sits in a judicial capacity. It does not look to see if there is a real likelihood that he would, or did in fact, favour one side at the expense of the other. The court looks at the impression which would be given to other people. Even if he was as impartial as could be, nevertheless if right minded persons would think that, in the circumstances, there was a real likelihood of bias on his part, then he should not sit. And if he does sit, his decision cannot stand. Nevertheless there must be a real likelihood of bias. Surmise or conjecture is not enough. There must be circumstances from which a reasonable man would think it likely or probable that the justice, or chairman . . . would or did favour one side unfairly at the expense of the other . . . Suffice it that reasonable people might think that he did.'

Comment

(1) Compare *R* v *Altrincham JJ, ex parte Pennington* where Lord Widgery suggested that the appropriate test might, on occasion, be to look for 'reasonable suspicion' of bias. See also *R* v *Liverpool JJ, ex parte Topping* ('Would a reasonable and fair-minded person sitting in a court and knowing all the relevant facts have a reasonable suspicion that a fair trial for the [appellant] was not possible?') approved in *R* v *Mulvihill*.

(2)   In *R* v *Inner West London Coroner, ex parte Dalliago*, apparent bias by a coroner in describing one of the relatives of the deceased as 'unhinged' was held to amount to 'apparent bias' and thus invalidated the verdict. See also *R* v *Gough*.

(3)   The nature of the activity may matter. Webster J in *Steeples* v *Derbyshire CC* said:

> Which of these tests is to be applied may depend . . . on the nature of the decision-making body in question. Where the body is a judicial body it may be that any doubt that justice is being done will suffice . . . at the other end of the scale, where the body in question is primarily administrative, it may be that its decisions are invalid (when in fact they are fair) only when they actually appear to be unfair.

(4)   For the relationship between a predetermined political view, or policy, and bias, see *Steeples* v *Derbyshire CC*, *R* v *Waltham Forest LBC*. It is unrealistic in an administrative setting to expect a body not to be predisposed to a particular proposal, or to have a policy thereon: see *Bushell* v *Secretary of State for the Environment*, p.338.

R v *Barnsley MDC, ex parte Hook*

[1976] 1 WLR 1052 · Court of Appeal

H was dismissed as a market-stallholder at Barnsley market, because of his conduct in urinating in public, albeit that this conduct occurred after the market had closed. The market manager, who initiated the disciplinary action, sat with the subcommittee that took the decision.

Lord Denning MR: '. . . I do not think that the right of a stallholder arises merely under a contract or licence determinable at will. It is a right conferred on him by the common law under which, so long as he pays the stallage, he is entitled to have his stall there: and that right cannot be determined without just cause . . . and then only in accordance with the provisions of natural justice. I do not mind whether the marketholder is exercising a judicial or an administrative function. A stallholder counts on this right in order to . . . earn his living . . . So it was quite right for the Committee to hold the hearings. I will assume that Mr Hook was given sufficient notice of the charge to be able to deal with it. But, nevertheless, each of the hearings was . . . vitiated by the fact that the market manager was there all the time. He was the only one who gave evidence . . . his evidence was given privately to the committee, not in the presence of Mr Hook or his representatives. Mr Hook was not himself in the room. His representatives were there, and they were heard. But when the Committee discussed the case and came to their decision, the market manager was there all the time . . . It is contrary to natural justice that one who is in the position of a prosecutor should be present at the deliberations of the adjudicating committee . . .

But there is one further matter: and that is that the punishment was too severe. It appears that there had been other [similar cases] and no such punishment had been inflicted . . . there are old cases which show that the court can interfere by certiorari if a punishment is altogether excessive and out of proportion to the occasion . . . [Mr Hook] is a man of good character and ought not to be penalised thus. On that ground alone . . . the decision . . . cannot stand. It is said to be an administrative decision, but even so, the court has jurisdiction to quash it. Certiorari would lie to quash not only judicial decisions but also administrative decisions . . .'

Comment

For the application of principles of procedural fairness, see *Ridge* v *Baldwin*, p.323. For development of proportionality as a basis of challenge, see p.299.

Statement of reasons

Doody v *Secretary of State for Home Affairs*

[1993] 3 All ER 92 · House of Lords

The applicants were serving mandatory life sentences imposed for murder. It had been the longstanding practice of Home Secretaries to request the Parole Board to consider the question of the granting of parole (i.e. the early release on licence) of such persons after the expiration of the period prescribed to reflect the sentencing concepts of retribution and deterrence. This prescribed period was set by the Home Secretary following recommendations by the trial judges. These recommendations were not automatically accepted. The applicants challenged the actions of the Secretary of State in not accepting the recommendations of their respective trial judges as to the prescribed periods to be applied in their cases, and argued that the Home Secretary's failure to give reasons was procedurally unfair. The House of Lords held that although the Home Secretary was entitled to depart from the recommendations of a trial judge, fairness demanded that he give reasons for his decision.

Lord Mustill: 'What does fairness require in the present case? My Lords, I think it unnecessary to refer by name or to quote from any of the often-cited authorities in which the courts have explained what is essentially an intuitive judgment. They are far too well-known. From them I derive the following. (1) Where an Act of Parliament confers an administrative power there is a presumption that it will be exercised in a manner which is fair in all the circumstances. (2) The standards of fairness are not immutable. They may change with the passage of time, both in the general and in their application to decisions of a particular type. (3) The principles of fairness are not to be applied by rote identically in every situation. What fairness demands is dependent on the context of the decision, and this is to be taken into account in all its aspects. (4) An essential feature of the context is the statute which creates the discretion, as regards both its language and the shape of the legal and administrative system within which the decision is taken. (5) Fairness will very often require that a person who may be adversely affected by the decision will have an opportunity to make representations on his own behalf either before the decision is taken with a view to producing a favourable result, or after it is taken, with a view to procuring its modification, or both. (6) Since the person affected usually cannot make worthwhile representations without knowing what factors may weigh against his interest fairness will very often require that he is informed of the gist of the case which he has to answer . . .

The respondents acknowledge that it is not enough for them to persuade the court that some procedure other than the one adopted by the decision-maker would be better or more fair. Rather, they must show that the procedure is actually unfair. The court must constantly bear in mind that it is to the decision-maker, not the court, that Parliament has entrusted not only the making of the decision, but also the choice as to how the decision is made . . . Accordingly, I prefer to begin by looking at the question in the round, and enquiring what requirements of fairness, germane to the present appeal attach to the Home Secretary's fixing of the penal element. As a general background to this task, I find in the more recent cases on judicial review a perceptible trend towards an insistence on greater openness, or if one prefers the contemporary jargon "transparency" in the making of administrative decisions . . .

[Lord Mustill examined the statutory framework, and continued:]

One further argument for the Secretary of State must be mentioned, namely that since the prisoner already knows all the circumstances of his offence, in the light of which the trial judge made his recommendation on the penal element, he can deduce without the need for any more information both the factual basis of the Secretary of State's decision, and the intellectual reasons why the penal element was fixed at a particular term of years. Although something akin to this argument has found favour in other cases, I am quite unable to accept it here. The prisoner does indeed know what primary materials were before the court, but he does not know what the judge and the Home Secretary made of them, nor does he know what other materials, not brought out at the trial, may have formed an element in the decision. That the choice of the penal element is not self-evident appears quite clearly from the number of occasions on which the Home Secretary's appraisal differs from that of the judges. Either there is something in the material before the Home Secretary which was not known to the judges, or the Home Secretary approaches his task in a way which is different from that adopted by the judiciary when passing sentence. In either event, the missing factor is hidden from view, and the prisoner can do no more than guess what it might be . . .

I accept without hesitation . . . that the law does not at present recognise a general duty to give reasons for an administrative decision. Nevertheless it is equally beyond question that such a duty may in appropriate circumstances be implied, and I agree with the analyses by the Court of Appeal in *R v Civil Service Appeal Board, ex parte Cunningham* of the factors which will often be material to such an implication. Turning to the present dispute I doubt the wisdom of discussing the problem in the contemporary vocabulary of "prisoner's rights", given that as a result of his own act the position of the prisoner is so forcibly distanced from that of the ordinary citizen, nor is it very helpful to say that the Home Secretary should out of simple humanity provide reasons for the prisoner, since any society which operates a penal system is bound to treat some of its citizens in a way that would, in the general be thought inhumane. I prefer simply to assert that within the inevitable constraints imposed by the statutory framework, the general shape of the administrative regime which ministers have lawfully built up around it, and the imperatives of the public interest, the Secretary of State ought to implement the scheme as fairly as he can. The giving of reasons may be inconvenient, but I see no ground at all why it should be against the public interest: indeed, rather the reverse. This being so, I would ask simply: Is refusal to give reasons fair? I would answer without hesitation that it is not . . . Is it fair that the mandatory life prisoner should be wholly deprived of the information which all other prisoners receive as a matter of course . . .

I can moreover arrive at the same conclusion by a different and more familiar route, of which *ex parte Cunningham* provides a recent example. It is not, as I understand it, questioned that the decision of the Home Secretary on the penal element is susceptible to judicial review. To mount an effective attack on the decision, given no more material than the facts of the offence and the length of the penal element, the prisoner has virtually no means of ascertaining whether this is an instance where the decision-making process has gone astray. I think it important that there should be an effective means of detecting the kind of error which would entitle the court to intervene, and in practice I regard it as necessary for this purpose that the reasoning of the Home Secretary should be disclosed . . . '

Comment

(1)   See also p.304.

(2)   Although the sentencing process is a judicial function, determination of how much of a term of imprisonment should be served is essentially executive in nature. In this context, the involvement of the judiciary in what is essentially an executive decision (albeit one that must be performed fairly) raises issues in relation to the separation of powers (see p.184).

(3)   In *R v Civil Service Appeal Board, ex parte Cunningham*, Lord Donaldson MR rejected the proposition that there was a general duty that a public law authority should always, or even usually, give reasons. However, where, as in that case, a body is carrying out a judicial function, natural justice required the Board to give reasons. This illustrates the fact that the nature of the function affects not only whether procedural fairness be implied (see *Ridge* v *Baldwin*, p.323) but also the nature of the procedural safeguards.

(4)   In *R v Higher Education Funding Council, ex parte Institute of Dental Surgery* (see below) Laws J accepted that Lord Mustill in *Doody* was not saying that reasons are called for wherever it is desired to know whether grounds for challenge exist:

Rather, he was holding that, in the situation of near total ignorance and impotence in which the prisoner found himself about something as vital to him as his prospects of liberty, such a duty arose . . .

(5)   Even in the absence of a statement of reasons, they may in fact become apparent if discovery occurs on judicial review. This does not, of course, assist in determining whether any grounds of challenge exist to justify the commencement of an application for judicial review.

(6)   Lord Mustill's comments about 'prisoner's rights' should be read with caution. Several cases, both in English courts and at the European Court of Human Rights

(as to which, see p.136) have demonstrated that prisoners do indeed have rights which the law must recognize and protect. The fact of incarceration does not remove standards that would otherwise be regarded as a minimum.

(7)   See also *R* v *Parole Board, ex parte Wilson*; *Re Findlay*.

R v *Higher Education Funding Council, ex parte Institute of Dental Surgery*

[1994] 1 All ER 651 · Divisional Court

The applicant academic institution sought judicial review of a decision taken by the Higher Education Funding Council in respect of the rating by the Council of the applicant's research work. It argued that the Council was under a duty to give reasons for its decision as to the research rating awarded to the applicant, and in the absence of reasons its decision was irrational. The application failed, there being, in the circumstances of the case, no duty to state reasons.

Sedley J: '. . . It seems both desirable and practical to test by a common standard both the fairness of not telling a person the reasons for a decision affecting him and the desirability of exposing any grounds of legal challenge. There are, moreover, reasons of principle for a unitary test. As the judgments in *Cunningham* show, one aspect of unfairness may be precisely the inability to know whether an error of law or of process has occurred. But since the latter is not a free-standing ground for requiring reasons (for if it were, it would apply universally), it can only be on grounds of fairness that it will arise; so that the need to know whether there has been an error of law or of process is rightly seen not as an alternative to the demands of fairness but as an aspect of them.

This approach places on an even footing the multiple grounds on which the giving of reasons may in any one case be requisite. The giving of reasons may among other things concentrate the decision-maker's mind on the right questions; demonstrate to the recipient that this is so; show that the issues have been conscientiously addressed and how the result has been reached; or alternatively alert the recipient to a justiciable flaw in the process. On the other side of the argument, it may place an undue burden on decision-makers; demand an appearance of unanimity where there is diversity; call for the articulation of sometimes inexpressible value judgments; and offer an invitation to the captious to comb the reasons for previously unsuspected grounds of challenge. It is the relationship of these and other material considerations to the nature of the particular decision which will determine whether or not fairness demands reasons . . . No doubt the common law will develop . . . case by case. It is not entirely satisfactory that this should be so, not least because experience suggests that in the absence of a prior principle irreconcilable or inconsistent decisions will emerge . . . At present, however, we cannot go beyond the proposition that, there being no general obligation to give reasons, there will be decisions for which fairness does not demand reasons . . .

It may be useful here to touch on an unresolved but potentially important question highlighted by the relief which [counsel] seeks in the form of mandamus to give reasons: is the giving of reasons, in a case where it is "the justice of the common law" which requires it, a free-standing duty enforceable by mandamus or simply . . .

a form of relief where independent grounds for it, such as irrelevant factors or irrationality, are established? If it is the latter then (pace the limited remedies in RSC ord.53) relief should consist of the remission of the matter for reasons to be given, and if adequate reasons are then not given the court will be not entitled to infer that there were none and that the decision was therefore irrational: see *Lonrho plc v Secretary of State for Trade and Industry.* Neither *R* v *Civil Service Appeal Board, ex parte Cunningham* nor *Doody* v *Secretary of State for the Home Department* gives an explicit answer. In the former case, however, a declaration was made and upheld on appeal that the refusal to give reasons was unlawful and *ultra vires*, strongly suggesting the existence of an independent legal obligation. In the latter case the House of Lords declared that the Home Secretary is obliged to give reasons for departing from the period recommended by the judiciary. If in such a case the maximum remedy was simple remission for the giving of reasons with the threat of quashing if none were given, mere non-compliance would frustrate the court's order without redress. The prisoner would lose by its quashing even the first review date set by the Home Secretary. This too powerfully suggests that the obligation to give reasons, where it is established, is an independent and enforceable legal obligation, and hence a ground of nullity where it is violated . . . '

Comment

(1)   In *Lonrho*, Lord Keith stated:

> The absence of reasons for a decision where there is no duty to give them cannot of itself provide any support for the suggested irrationality of the decision. The only significance of the absence of reasons is that if all other facts and circumstances appear to point overwhelmingly in favour of a different decision, the decision-maker who has given no reasons cannot complain if the court draws the inference that he has no rational reason for his decision.

(2)   Consider whether administrative burdens can ever justify a conclusion that reasons need not be stated. By definition, reasons for any rational decision must in fact exist.

(3)   Compare *R* v *Lambeth LBC, ex parte Walters* where the court held that English law had now reached the point where there was a general duty to give reasons whenever the administrative process was infused with the concept of fair treatment to those potentially affected.

Right to a hearing

Local Government Board v Arlidge

[1915] AC 120 · House of Lords

Viscount Haldane: '. . . what the procedure is to be in detail must depend upon the nature of the tribunal . . . Parliament must be taken, in the absence of any declaration to the contrary, to have intended it to follow the procedure which is its own, and is necessary if it is to be capable of doing its job effectively. I agree with the view expressed . . . [by Lord Loreburn in *Board of Education* v *Rice*] . . . that . . . in disposing of a question which was the subject of an appeal to it, the Board of Education was under a duty to act in good faith, and to listen fairly to both sides, in as much as that was a duty which lay on anyone who decided anything. But he went on to say that he did not think it was bound to treat such a question as though it were a trial. The Board had no power to administer an oath, and need not examine witnesses. It could, he thought, obtain information in any way it thought best, always giving a fair opportunity to those who were parties in the controversy to correct or contradict any relevant statement prejudicial to their view.'

Bushell v *Secretary of State for the Environment*

[1981] AC 75 · House of Lords

Lord Diplock: '. . . It [the case of *Johnson* v *Minister of Health*] contains a salutary warning against applying to procedures involved in the making of administrative decisions concepts that are appropriate to the conduct of ordinary civil litigation . . . The only [procedural requirement in the absence of regulations] . . . is that it must be fair to all those who have an interest in the decision . . . It is evident that an Inquiry of this kind and magnitude is quite unlike any civil litigation and that the inspector conducting it must have a wide discretion as to the procedures to be followed in order to achieve its objectives. These are to enable him to ascertain the facts that are relevant to each of the objections, to understand the arguments for and against them and, if he feels qualified to do so, to weigh their respective merits so that he may provide the Minister with a fair, accurate and adequate report on these matters.'

Comment

(1) In *R* v *Secretary of State for Transport, ex parte Gwent CC* there was an unsuccessful challenge to an order increasing the tolls on the Severn road bridge. The inspector had not erred by declining to consider government policy to place the burden of finance upon road users. What mattered was not whether there had been any procedural impropriety, but whether objectors had been treated fairly.

(2) The Franks Committee Report sought the adoption of qualities of 'openness, impartiality and fairness' into the inquiry processes.

R v *Secretary of State for the Home Department, ex parte Cheblak*

[1991] 2 All ER 319 · Court of Appeal

Shortly after the outbreak of the Gulf War in 1991, the Secretary of State decided to deport the applicant (a Lebanese citizen) on the grounds that his deportation would be 'conducive to the public good'. No appeal lay against such deportation, but the applicant had the opportunity to make representations to an independent advisory panel. The Home Secretary indicated that the reason for the deportation was the alleged links of the applicant with an organization which might take terrorist action.

The applicant sought to challenge the notice in an action for judicial review, alleging insufficient statement of reasons, a failure to have regard to all relevant factors, and irrationality. His application was dismissed, a conclusion upheld on appeal.

Lord Donaldson of Lymington: 'In essence Mr Cheblak seeks to invoke the jurisdiction of the court upon three grounds: (1) the failure to give more extensive reasons for the decision to deport, contrary to natural justice; (2) a failure to take account of all relevant circumstances as required by para. 167 of the Statement of Changes in Immigration Rules (HC Paper (1989–90) no. 251); (3) the irrationality of the decision to deport Mr Cheblak and to detain him pending deportation.

In my opinion he has no arguable case under any of these heads.

Failure to give further reasons

Although the notice of intention to deport only told Mr Cheblak that the ground and reasons for this decision were that his departure from the United Kingdom would be conducive to the public good for reasons of national security, as I have already mentioned this was later amplified by a statement that he was known to have links with an unspecified organisation which the Home Secretary believed could (or would) take terrorist action against Western targets if hostilities were to break out in the Gulf.

Mr Cheblak complains that this is wholly insufficient to enable him to meet the allegation that his departure from the United Kingdom would be conducive to the public good. In reply Mr Usher, a senior executive officer in the Home Office, has sworn an affidavit on behalf of the Home Secretary stating that "Further details cannot be disclosed because to do so would prove an unacceptable risk to national security".

There is no suggestion, still less any evidence, that either the Home Secretary or Mr Usher in so asserting are acting otherwise than in the utmost good faith. We are therefore, not for the first time, faced with a collision between two imperatives, the rights of the individual citizen, albeit a visitor to our shores, and the needs of national security. Of that Geoffrey Lane LJ said in *Hosenball*'s case

> There are occasions, though they are rare, when what are more generally the rights of an individual must be subordinated to the protection of the realm. When an alien visitor to this country is believed to have used the hospitality extended to him so as to present a danger to security, the Secretary of State has the right and, in many cases, has the duty of ensuring that the alien no longer remains here to threaten our security. It may be that the alien has been in the country for many years. It may be that he has built a career here in this country, and that consequently a deportation order made against him may result in great hardship to him. It may be that he protests that he has done nothing wrong so far as this country's security is concerned. It may be that he protests that he cannot understand why any action of this sort is being taken against him. In ordinary circumstances common fairness, you can call it natural justice if you wish, would demand that he be given particulars of the charges made against him; that he be given the names of the witnesses who are prepared to testify against him and, indeed, probably the nature of the evidence which those witnesses are prepared to give should also be delivered to him. But there are counter balancing factors.

Detection, whether in the realms of ordinary crime or in the realms of national security, is seldom carried out by cold analysis or brilliant deduction. Much more frequently it is done by means of information received. Courts of criminal jurisdiction have for very many years indeed, if not for centuries, given protection from disclosure to sources of information . . . [citations omitted] . . . The reasons for this protection are plain. Once a source of information is disclosed, it will cease thereafter to be a source of information. Once a potential informant thinks that his identity is going to be disclosed if he provides information, he will cease to be an informant. The life of a known informant may be made, to say the least, very unpleasant by those who, for reasons of their own, wish to remain in obscurity. Thus, take away the protection, and you remove the means of detection; and when the security of the country is involved, there may be added difficulties. It may well be that if an alien is told with particularity what it is said he has done, it will become quite obvious to him from whence that information has been received. The only persons who can judge whether such a result is likely is the person who has in his possession all the information available. That, in this case, is the Secretary of State himself. If he come to the conclusion that for reasons such as those which I have just endeavoured to outline he cannot afford to give the alien more than the general charge against him, there one has the dilemma. The alien certainly has inadequate information on which to prepare or direct his defence to the various charges which are made against him, and the only way that that could be remedied would be to disclose information to him which might probably have an adverse effect on the national security. The choice is regrettably clear: the alien must suffer, if suffering there be, and this is so on whichever basis of argument one chooses.

The problem may well appear insoluble if it is approached through the insular and blinkered eyes of those who regard the adversarial system of justice as the only one worthy of the name. But there are other systems which are widely accepted as just in other parts of the world, including the continent of Europe. There the judge or tribunal is not a passive spectator or referee and the essence of the system is not an adversarial contest, but a judicial investigation. The approach adopted by the Home Secretary's advisory panel is, perhaps, best described as an "independent quasi-judicial scrutiny". The members all have the necessary security clearance to enable them to take an active role in questioning and evaluating the weight of the evidence and information which formed the basis of the Home Secretary's initial decision. Similarly they seek to discover any countervailing evidence, information or represent-ations which the detainee may wish to put forward and evaluate its weight. Whilst that part of their task which involves the protection of the rights of the individual would be easier of performance if they could reveal to the detainee all that has become known to them, it is by no means impossible to perform it effectively where they cannot do so. Sufficient may already have been revealed by the Home Secretary himself to steer the detainee in the right direction and it is always possible for members of the panel to ask questions in a form which is itself not informative, but which leads the detainee on to giving as full an account as he wishes of his contacts and activities in the areas which are relevant to the Home Secretary's decision . . .

[Lord Donaldson then considered the other grounds of challenge, concluding that no illegality or irrationality was made out. He continued:]

This appeal and application have given rise to widespread anxiety and no less misunderstanding. The anxiety is understandable and commendable, since the maintenance of the rights of individuals depends, in part at least, upon there being a general belief in their fundamental importance and a willingness to campaign to uphold them. However, the misunderstanding is quite another matter and should, if possible, be reduced.

The judicial system in this country does not consist simply of the courts. It includes a multitude of specialist tribunals and panels (e.g. the City Takeover Panel), each with its own remit and procedures. This makes sense. Specialisation makes for better, cheaper and quicker decision-making. The hearings of some are open to the public. Others which are involved with intimate personal matters, such as mental health review tribunals, are not. Most permit representation by lawyers, but it is not self-evident that this is necessarily an advantage. The members of an experienced specialist tribunal or panel adopting a "hands on" approach may well be able to reach the right conclusion just as often, and a lot more cheaply and quickly, without as with such formal representation.

The judges of the courts do not "wash their hands" of matters referred to these tribunals and panels. In some cases Parliament has provided for an appeal to the courts on questions of law arising in the course of their work. But in all cases the courts retain a supervisory jurisdiction designed to ensure that their proceedings are fairly and properly conducted in accordance with the law. And it is the law and the rule of law which governs all. Judges take a judicial oath to "do right to all manner of people after the laws and usages of this realm without fear or favour, affection or illwill" (see the Promissory Oaths Act 1868, s.4). The "usages of this realm" is an old-fashioned phrase meaning in this context the customary procedures. Justice is not an abstract concept. It has to have a context and a content. The context is provided by the facts underlying particular disputes. The content is the law.

In individual cases injustice can arise from two quite different sources – human fallibility on the part of the judges or tribunal members and defects in the law. Human fallibility can never be eliminated, but its effects can be and are reduced by dedicated professionalism and by the system making provision for appeals. Defects in the law can be remedied by changing the law, but not by departing from it, an approach which would end by producing far more injustices than it cured. Judges are exhorted by commentators to be "robust". If what is meant is that judges should be very ready to re-examine the law in novel or changed circumstances, I agree that judges should indeed be "robust" and I hope that we are. But if what is meant is that in cases which arouse their sympathy, of which the present could well be one, they should depart from the law, I must disagree . . .

Two comments may perhaps be made. The first is that, although they give rise to tensions at the interface, "national security" and "civil liberties" are on the same side. In accepting, as we must, that to some extent the needs of national security must displace civil liberties, albeit to the least possible extent, it is not irrelevant to remember that the maintenance of national security underpins and is the foundation of all our civil liberties. The second is that it is not only national security which creates such tensions. So does the ordinary administration of justice. A citizen is charged with a very serious offence and remanded in custody. Later at his trial or on appeal he is acquitted. Only he will know for certain whether on the evidence he was extremely lucky to be acquitted, whether he was entitled to be acquitted because, although he did it, the prosecution could not prove it or whether he was wholly innocent. Since the system does not, and perhaps very seldom could, differentiate between these three categories, the wholly innocent accused, who alone has a real grievance at having been detained in prison pending his trial, has to accept his misfortune as part of the price of citizenship in a society in which the rule of law prevails.

The jurisdiction of the courts is not, and never has been, all-embracing. Thus they have no right to consider obligations arising under international treaties. In the case of national security, the responsibility is exclusively that of the government of the day, but its powers are limited by statute and the courts will intervene if it is shown that the minister responsible has acted otherwise than in good faith or has in any way overstepped the limitations upon his authority which are imposed by the law. No lack of good faith has been suggested in this case, but we have fully and speedily investigated the allegation that the Secretary of State has no power to detain Mr Cheblak.

The current system of independent scrutiny of the Home Secretary's decision to deport for reasons of national security, which has involved the creation of a specialist panel currently presided over by Lloyd LJ, was approved by Parliament 20 years ago. It replaced a statutory appeal system under the Immigration Appeals Act 1969. The appeal tribunal created under that Act was designed for an adversarial system of general application to all appeals against decisions to deport, each party presenting its evidence subject to cross-examination, with the tribunal giving a binding decision. However, where the Secretary of State certified that matters could not be disclosed to the appellant because of the interests of national security, the essential features and safeguards of the adversarial system disappeared, but it is not apparent that they were replaced by the safeguards of the present system with the additional responsibility which that system imposes upon the members of the panel.

I have no doubt that the advisory panel is susceptible of judicial review if, for example, it could be shown to have acted unfairly within its terms of reference. The fact that its decisions operate not as such, but as recommendations, may well be intended to reflect the ultimate personal responsibility of the Home Secretary in so sensitive and important a field, but whilst I strongly suspect that this represents a difference of form rather than of substance, it is not for me as a judge to inquire and the answer would only be clear if one knew the number of occasions, if any, upon which its recommendations have not been accepted. That legal representation is not permitted, although there would appear to be no objection to the prospective deportee being accompanied and assisted by a legally qualified friend, stems from the tribunal's terms of reference. If it is objectionable, as to which there may be more than one view, this is a matter for Parliament which approved the terms of reference and not for the courts. That the prospective detainee is not entitled to be given the fullest particulars of what is alleged against him would, in other circumstances, undoubtedly be objectionable as constituting a denial of natural justice. But natural justice has to take account of realities and something which would otherwise constitute a breach is not to be so considered if it is unavoidable. For reasons explained by Geoffrey Lane LJ in the extract from his judgment in *Hosenball*'s case which I have reproduced, this is not always avoidable, although I do not doubt that the panel will avoid it so far as is consistent with the needs of national security.

If there is a lesson to be drawn from these proceedings it is, I think, that detainees should try to have greater faith in the desire of the panel to safeguard their liberty to the maximum possible extent consistent with the risk to national security and should not first rush off to the courts which are, at best, a second line of defence in special circumstances.'

Comment

(1)   For the role of the courts on judicial review, see also p.210. For national security, see p.264.

(2)   See also *R* v *Secretary of State for the Home Department, ex parte Hosenball.* The applicant in that case was a citizen of the United States, resident in the UK, and working as a journalist. The Secretary of State decided to deport him on the grounds that such action would be conducive to the public good, as being in the interests of national security. The applicant availed himself of the right to make informal representations to the Advisory Panel. Although at the hearing held by that panel the applicant was allowed to give evidence and call witnesses, he was not informed of the allegations against him or the evidence upon which they were based. His application for *certiorari* to quash the decision of the Secretary of State was dismissed, as was his appeal. Where national security requires, the ordinary principles of natural justice will be modified.

(3)   Some comparisons may usefully be drawn with *Liversidge* v *Anderson*, p.12.

Hone v *Maze Prison Board of Prison Visitors*

[1988] AC 379 · House of Lords

The appellant sought judicial review of the decisions of the Board of Visitors, alleging that in denying them legal representation during disciplinary proceedings brought under the Prison Rules (Northern Ireland) 1982 there was a breach of natural justice. The applicant's appeals to the Northern Ireland Court of Appeal and the House of Lords were dismissed.

Lord Goff: '. . . the submissions on behalf of the appellants were as follows. The basic submission was that a convicted prisoner retains all his civil rights, except those which are taken away from him expressly or by necessary implication; and that an ordinary citizen charged with a criminal offence is entitled to legal representation before the tribunal which hears the charge against him. It was however accepted that, on an inquiry by the governor of a prison, a prisoner has no right to legal representation; such a right, it was submitted, applied only to hearings before boards of visitors, when the prisoner is charged with a criminal offence or the equivalent of a criminal offence . . . [Lord Goff decided that there was no material distinction between the relevant provisions of Northern Ireland and England and continued:] Since this is the first occasion upon which the present question has come before your Lordships' House, I propose to refer to certain aspects of them. The first of the authorities is the decision of the Court of Appeal in *R* v *Assessment Committee of St Mary Abbotts, Kensington.* In that case it was held that a householder who objected to a valuation list and wished his objection to be advanced before the assessment committee need not appear in person before the committee but could depute another person to do so on his behalf. This decision has been invoked on subsequent occasions in support of the proposition that any person appearing before a disciplinary tribunal is entitled to legal representation. The decision of the Court of Appeal in *Pett* v *Greyhound Racing Association Ltd* appeared, at first sight, to give some credence to that proposition. In that case the plaintiff claimed the right to legal representation at an inquiry by the association into a disciplinary matter, concerned with a serious charge against the plaintiff relating to the circumstances in which a greyhound of his was withdrawn from a race, it being alleged that traces of barbiturates were found in the dog's urine. On an interlocutory appeal Lord Denning MR, in holding that natural justice required that in matters affecting a man's reputation or livelihood or any matters of serious purport he should, if he wished, be legally represented, relied upon the *St Mary Abbotts* case; and Russell LJ, referred to his "common law right" to be so represented. However, on the substantive hearing (*Pett* v *Greyhound Racing Association Ltd (No. 2)*), Lyell J concluded that the only duty on the association was to observe the rules of natural justice, and distinguished the *St Mary Abbotts* case as being concerned not with legal representation before a tribunal but with a man employing an agent to communicate with a body performing an administrative act. He said:

> It appears to me that the Court of Appeal regarded the overseers as performing an administrative act in preparing the valuation lists . . . It has, so far as I am aware, never been suggested that the valuation officer in considering such objections is acting otherwise than in an administrative capacity. In view of the many authorities that domestic tribunals are subject only to the duty of observing what are called the rules of natural justice and any procedure laid down or necessarily to be implied from the instrument that confers their power, I am unable to follow the views expressed in the present case by the Court of Appeal, that the plaintiff is entitled to appear by an agent unless such right was expressly negatived by the rules of the club.

Subsequent cases have proceeded on the same basis. Thus in *Enderby Town FC Ltd* v *Football Association Ltd* Lord Denning MR rejected the suggestion that a man who is charged before a domestic tribunal is entitled as of right to be legally represented; on the contrary, he regarded that matter as being within the discretion of the tribunal. A similar suggestion was rejected by the Court of Appeal in *Fraser* v *Mudge* . . . There a prisoner asked for an injunction to restrain a board of visitors from inquiring into a charge against him of assaulting a prison officer unless he was represented by a solicitor and counsel of his choice. The case therefore raised the question whether, in such circumstances, the prisoner was entitled to legal representation as of right. Chapman J refused to grant the injunction, and his decision was affirmed by the Court of Appeal . . .

Subsequently, in *R* v *Secretary of State for the Home Department, ex parte Tarrant* a Divisional Court . . . accepted *Fraser* v *Mudge* as binding authority that, before a board of visitors, a prisoner charged with a disciplinary offence has no right to legal representation, though it was held that a board of visitors has a discretion to grant representation; and, in his . . . judgment, Webster J referred to considerations which he considered that every board of visitors should take into account when exercising its discretion whether to allow legal representation, or indeed the assistance of a friend or adviser, to a prisoner appearing before it on a disciplinary charge . . . counsel [for the appellants] had of necessity to submit that the decision of the Court of Appeal in *Fraser* v *Mudge* was wrong. In support of his submissions . . . he relied upon rule 30(2) of the Rules of 1982 . . . He stressed that a hearing before a board of visitors is a sophisticated hearing. In particular, he submitted, there is an oral hearing; a formal plea is entered; cross-examination is allowed and witnesses are called; the onus and standard of proof are the same as in a criminal trial; free legal aid is available; punishments are imposed; a plea in mitigation can be entered; and the board has greater powers of punishment than those exercised by magistrates' courts. He also, like others before him, invoked the *St Mary Abbotts* case as authority for the proposition that each appellant had a common law right to appoint a lawyer as his agent to appear before the board of visitors on his behalf.

I am unable to accept these submissions. I would first of all reject the argument founded upon the *St Mary Abbots* case as misconceived, for the very reasons given by Lyell J in *Pett* v *Greyhound Racing Association Ltd (No. 2)*, that the case is not in point since it was concerned only with the making of a communication to an administrative body. But, so far as [counsel's] wider submissions are concerned, I am unable to accept his second proposition that any person charged with a crime (or the equivalent thereof) and liable to punishment is entitled as a matter of natural justice to legal representation. No doubt it is true that a man charged with a crime before a criminal court is entitled to legal representation . . . No doubt it is also correct that a board of visitors is bound to give effect to the rules of natural justice. But it does not follow that, simply because a charge before a disciplinary tribunal such as a board of visitors relates to facts which in law constitute a crime, the rules of natural justice require the tribunal to grant legal representation. Indeed, if this were the case, then, as Roskill LJ pointed out in *Fraser* v *Mudge*, exactly the same submission could be made in respect of disciplinary proceedings before the governor of a prison. [Counsel] was at pains to escape from this conclusion by attempting to distinguish between a governor and a board of visitors, on the basis that there was no right of legal representation before the governor but an absolute right to legal representation before the board of visitors. I for my part am unable to accept this distinction. Each, both governor and board of visitors, is exercising a disciplinary jurisdiction; and, as the Rules of 1982 clearly demonstrate, each may do so in respect of offences against discipline which could in law constitute criminal offences. Each must also be bound by the rules of natural justice. The difference between them is not so much a legal as a practical difference . . . In the nature of things, it is difficult to imagine that the rules of natural justice would ever require legal representation before the governor. But though the rules of natural justice may require legal representation before a board of visitors, I can see no basis for counsel's submission that they should do so in every case as of right. Everything must depend on the circumstances of the particular case, as is amply demonstrated by the circumstances so carefully listed by Webster J in *R* v *Secretary of State for the Home Department, ex parte Tarrant* as matters which boards of visitors should take into account. But it is easy to envisage circumstances in which the rules of natural justice do not call for representation, even though the disciplinary charge relates to a matter which constitutes in law a crime, as may well happen in the case of simple assault where no question of law arises, and where the prisoner charged is capable of presenting his own case. To hold otherwise would result in wholly unnecessary delays in many cases, to the detriment of all concerned including the prisoner charged, and a wholly unnecessary waste of time and money, contrary to the public interest. Indeed, to hold otherwise would not only cause injustice to prisoners; it would also lead to an adventitious distinction being drawn between disciplinary offences which happen also to be crimes and those which happen not to be so, for the punishments liable to be imposed do not depend upon any such distinction.

[Lord Goff then considered the effect of art.6, ECHR:] It is to be observed that, under art.6 . . . a citizen is given the right to defend himself through legal assistance of his own choosing where he is charged with a criminal offence. If that provision were to be given a strict interpretation, it would lead to its application in all disciplinary proceedings where the facts charged constituted in law a crime; and, in the context of prison discipline, this would be equally applicable in disciplinary proceedings before a governor and in such proceedings before a board of visitors. It is not surprising, therefore, to discover that the provision has been the subject of interpretation by the European Court of Human Rights to ensure that its application does not exceed the bounds of common sense . . . [The] principles were applied by the court in *Campbell and Fell* v *United Kingdom*, where it was stated . . . (1) that the first matter to be ascertained is whether or not the text defining the offences in issue belongs, according to the domestic legal system, to criminal law, disciplinary law or both concurrently; (2) that, in any event, the indications so afforded by the national law have only a relative value; the very nature of the offence is a factor of greater import. In this connection, the court referred to the fact that some matters may be more serious than others, and that the illegality of some acts may not turn on the fact that they were committed in prison. However, the court then commented: "The court considers that these factors, whilst not of themselves sufficient to lead to the conclusion that the offences with which the applicant was charged have to be regarded as 'criminal' for Convention purposes, do give them a certain colouring which does not entirely coincide with that of a purely disciplinary matter"; (3) that it is necessary to have regard to the nature and degree of severity of the penalty which might be incurred; and that deprivation of liberty was "in general" a penalty that belonged to the "criminal" sphere.

Now in English law, the objective which is sought to be achieved is, in my opinion, indeed harmonious with art.6 of the Convention as interpreted by the European Court of Human Rights. It is only the technique which is different. In English law, we are fortunate in having available to us a discretionary power, so often employed when it is necessary to weigh the effect of different factors; and it is established that disciplinary tribunals have, in the exercise of their discretion, and having regard to a broad range of factors including those mentioned by the European Court, to decide whether natural justice requires that a person appearing before the tribunal should be legally represented. The European Court, being under the duty to apply principles embodied in the Convention, is striving, as I see it, to achieve the same flexibility by giving a liberal interpretation to the expression "criminal offence" in art.6. It follows that I cannot, for my part, see that recourse to the Convention can assist the appellants in the present case. The absolute right to legal representation now claimed by the appellants is not, as I understand the position, required by the Convention any more than it is required by English law . . .'

Comment

(1)   The value of legal representation was vividly expressed by Lord Denning MR in *Pett* v *Greyhound Racing Association*:

> It is not every man who has the ability to defend himself on his own. He cannot bring out the point in his own favour or the weaknesses in the other side. He may be tongue-tied or nervous, confused or wanting in intelligence. He cannot examine or cross-examine witnesses... [in a court] if justice is to be done, he ought to have the help of someone to speak for him; and who better than a lawyer who has been trained for the task? I should have thought, therefore, that when a man's reputation or livelihood is at stake, he not only has a right to speak by his own mouth. He also has a right to speak by counsel or solicitor.

No 'right' to legal representation was in fact found in the circumstances – see *Pett* v *Greyhound Racing Association (No. 2)*.

(2)   For the application of procedural standards generally in the prison context, see *R* v *Board of Visitors of Hull Prison, ex parte St Germain (No. 2)*.

(3)   In *R* v *Secretary of State for the Home Department, ex parte Tarrant* Nolan J indicated the following factors as appropriate to be taken into account in the exercise of the discretion discussed in *Hone*: (a) the seriousness of the charge and of the potential penalty; (b) whether any points of law were likely to arise; (c) the capacity of a particular prisoner to present his case; (d) the presence of procedural difficulties; (e) the need for reasonable speed in making an adjudication; (f) the need for fairness as between prisoners, and as between prisoner and prison officer.

(4)   For the status of the European Convention, see p.135.

15 Public interest immunity

Public interest immunity allows a successful claimant to withhold information, or the production of a document, despite the fact that that information or document may be necessary in legal proceedings. Formerly regarded as a privilege of the Crown (hence the old terminology, 'Crown privilege') modern authorities such as *D* v *NSPCC* (p.354) have demonstrated that the doctrine is wider than that. The term 'public interest immunity' reflects the fact that it is where withholding such matters can be justified in the public interest that the doctrine will apply: thus, claims can be made by bodies other than Crown bodies, although case law has carefully restricted this aspect of the doctrine. Nor does the term 'privilege' accurately reflect the doctrine: it cannot be a true privilege, since the court will be obliged to take the point itself even in the absence of a claim by the parties or a third party (*Duncan* v *Cammell, Laird*), though it is difficult to imagine such a claim being sustained in the light of the lack of claim by those whose task it is to protect the interest in question. The extent to which a claim of immunity can be waived is matter of judicial debate and disagreement.

Note that claims of immunity in respect of documents can be framed in terms of either a 'contents' claim, where the claim depends upon the contents of a particular document (or set of documents) or upon a 'class' claim, where the claim is made in the light of the type of documents in question. These may overlap, but the nature of the basis of claim may matter, since the Courts may be more reluctant to uphold a class rather than a contents claim (see *Conway* v *Rimmer*; and *ex parte Wiley*, p.360).

Of fundamental importance is a recognition that the doctrine creates constitutional difficulties. The availability of relevant material so that the administration of justice can be properly pursued is crucial to notions of accountability and answerability in law. Any procedural bars to discovery of documents held by the Crown were removed by s.28, Crown Proceedings Act 1948, which nevertheless preserves the operation of the doctrine: '. . . this section shall be without prejudice to any rule of law which authorises or requires the withholding of any document or the refusal to answer any question on the ground that the disclosure of the document or the answering of the question would be injurious to the public interest . . .'

It should also be noted that discovery is now available on an application for judicial review (see *O'Reilly* v *Mackman*, p.224), and may in reality be the only means available to an aggrieved person to discover the real basis of executive decision-making.

Conway v *Rimmer*

[1968] AC 910 · House of Lords

The appellant, a former probationary police constable, brought proceedings against a former superior for malicious prosecution, arising out of incidents whilst he was a probationer. During those proceedings he sought discovery of reports upon him as a probationer. Despite the wish of the respondent that the documents be produced the Home Secretary claimed Crown privilege in respect of those documents, on the grounds that they belonged to a class of documents that ought not to be disclosed. The House of Lords allowed discovery since it was unlikely that any harm would be done to the police service by disclosure of routine documents of this type.

Lord Reid: '. . . The question whether such a statement by a Minister of the Crown should be accepted as conclusively preventing any court from ordering production of any of the documents to which it applies is one of very great importance in the administration of justice. If the commonly accepted interpretation of the decision of this House in *Duncan* v *Cammell, Laird & Co. Ltd* is to remain authoritative the question of only one answer – the Minister's statement – is final and conclusive. Normally I would be very slow to question the authority of a unanimous decision of this House only 25 years old which was carefully considered and obviously intended to lay down a general rule. But this decision has several abnormal features.

Lord Simon thought that on this matter the law in Scotland was the same as the law in England and he clearly intended to lay down a rule applicable to the whole of the United Kingdom. But in *Glasgow Corporation* v *Central Land Board* this House held that that was not so, with the result that today on this question the law is different in the two countries . . . [H]ere we are dealing purely with public policy – with the proper relation between the powers of the executive and the powers of the courts – and I can see no rational justification for the law on this matter being different in the two countries.

Secondly, events have proved that the rule supposed to have been laid down in *Duncan*'s case is far from satisfactory. In the large number of cases in England and elsewhere which have been cited in argument much dissatisfaction has been expressed and I have not observed even one expression of wholehearted approval. Moreover, a statement made by the Lord Chancellor in 1956 on behalf of the Government . . . makes it clear that that Government did not regard it as consonant with public policy to maintain the rule to the full extent which existing authorities had held to be justifiable.

I have no doubt that the case of *Duncan* v *Cammell, Laird & Co. Ltd* was rightly decided. The plaintiff sought discovery of documents relating to the submarine

Thetis including a contract for the hull and machinery and plans and specifications. The First Lord of the Admiralty had stated that "it would be injurious to the public interest that any of the said documents should be disclosed to any person." Any of these documents might well have given valuable information, or at least clues, to the skilled eye of an agent of a foreign power. But Lord Simon LC took the opportunity to deal with the whole question of the right of the Crown to prevent production of documents in a litigation. Yet study of his speech leaves me with the strong impression that throughout he had primarily in mind cases where discovery or disclosure would involve a danger of real prejudice to the national interest. I find it difficult to believe that his speech would have been the same if the case had related, as the present case does, to discovery of routine reports on a probationer constable . . . Surely it would be grotesque to speak of the interest of the state being put in jeopardy by disclosure of a routine report on a probationer.

Lord Simon did not say very much about objections "based upon the view that the public interest requires a particular class of communications with, or within, a public department to be protected from production on the ground that the candour and completeness of such communications might be prejudiced if they were ever liable to be disclosed in subsequent litigation rather than on the contents of the particular document itself." But at the end he said that a Minister "ought not to take the responsibility of withholding production except in cases where the public interest would otherwise be damnified, for example, where disclosure would be injurious to national defence, or to good diplomatic relations, or where the practice of keeping a class of documents secret is necessary for the proper functioning of the public service." . . .

It is universally recognised that here there are two kinds of public interest which may clash. There is the public interest that harm shall not be done to the nation or the public service by disclosure of certain documents, and there is the public interest that the administration of justice shall not be frustrated by the withholding of documents which must be produced if justice is to be done. There are many cases where the nature of the injury which would or might be done to the nation or the public service is of so grave a character that no other interest, public or private, can be allowed to prevail over it. With regard to such cases it would be proper to say, as Lord Simon did, that to order production of the document in question would put the interest of the state in jeopardy; but there are many other cases where the possible injury to the public service is much less and there one would think that it would be proper to balance the public interests involved. I do not believe that Lord Simon really meant that the smallest probability of injury to the public service must always outweigh the gravest frustration of the administration of justice . . .

There are now many large public bodies, such as British Railways and the National Coal Board, the proper and efficient functioning of which is very necessary for many reasons including the safety of the public. The Attorney-General made it clear that Crown privilege is not and cannot be invoked to prevent disclosure of similar documents made by them or their servants, even if it were said that this is required for the proper and efficient functioning of that public service. I find it difficult to see why it should be necessary to withhold whole classes of routine "communications with or within a public department" but quite unnecessary to withhold similar communications with or within a public corporation. There the safety of the public may well depend on the candour and completeness of reports made by subordinates, whose duty it is to draw attention to defects. But, so far as I know, no one has ever suggested that public safety has been endangered by the candour or completeness of such reports having been inhibited by the fact that they may have to be produced if the interests of the due administration of justice should ever require production at any time . . .

The present position is so unsatisfactory that this House must re-examine the whole question in light of all the authorities.

Two questions will arise: first, whether the court is to have any right to question the finality of a Minister's certificate and, secondly, if it has such a right, how and in what circumstances that right is to be exercised and made effective.

A Minister's certificate may be given on one or other of two grounds: either because it would be against the public interest to disclose the contents of the particular document or documents in question, or because the document belongs to a class of documents which ought to be withheld, whether or not there is anything in the particular document in question disclosure of which would be against the public interest. It does not appear that any serious difficulties have arisen or are likely to arise with regard to the first class. However wide the power of the court may be held to be, cases would be very rare in which it could be proper to question the view of the responsible Minister that it would be contrary to the public interest to make public the contents of a particular document . . . In the present case your Lordships are directly concerned with the second class of documents . . . [Lord Reid cited cases from various jurisdictions:]

These cases open up a new field which must be kept in view when considering whether a Minister's certificate is to be regarded as conclusive. I do not doubt that it is proper to prevent the use of any document, wherever it comes from, if disclosure of its contents would really injure the national interest, and I do not doubt that it is proper to prevent any witness, whoever he may be, from disclosing facts which in the national interest ought not to be disclosed. Moreover, it is the duty of the court to do this without the intervention of any Minister if possible serious injury to the national interest is readily apparent. But in this field it is more than ever necessary that in a doubtful case the alleged public interest in concealment should be balanced against the public interest that the administration of justice should not be frustrated. If the Minister, who has no duty to balance these conflicting public interests, says no more than that in his opinion the public interest requires concealment, and if that is to be accepted as conclusive in this field as well as with regard to documents in his possession, it seems to me not only that very serious injustice may be done to the parties, but also that the due administration of justice may be gravely impaired for quite inadequate reasons.

It cannot be said that there would be any constitutional impropriety in enabling the court to overrule a Minister's objection. That is already the law in Scotland . . . And a limited citation of authority from the United States seems to indicate the same trend . . .

Lord Simon did not say that courts in England have no power to overrule the executive. He said in *Duncan*'s case: ". . . the decision ruling out such documents is the decision of the judge . . . It is the judge who is in control of the trial not the executive, but the proper ruling for the judge to give is as above expressed", that is, to accept the Minister's view in every case. In my judgment, in considering what it is "proper" for a court to do we must have regard to the need, shown by 25 years' experience since *Duncan*'s case, that the courts should balance the public interest in the proper administration of justice against the public interest in withholding any evidence which a Minister considers ought to be withheld.

I would therefore propose that the House ought now to decide that courts have and are entitled to exercise a power and duty to hold a balance between the public interest, as expressed by a Minister, to withhold certain documents or other evidence, and the public interest in ensuring the proper administration of justice. That does not mean that a court would reject a Minister's view: full weight must be given to it in every case, and if the Minister's reasons are of a character which judicial experience is not competent to weigh, then the Minister's view must prevail. But experience has shown that reasons given for withholding whole classes of documents are often not of that character. For example a court is perfectly well able to assess the likelihood that, if the writer of a certain class of document knew that there was a chance that his report might be produced in legal proceedings, he would make a less full and candid report than he would otherwise have done.

I do not doubt that there are certain classes of documents which ought not to be disclosed whatever their content may be. Virtually everyone agrees that Cabinet minutes and the like ought not to be disclosed until such time as they are only of historical interest. But I do not think that many people would give as the reason that premature disclosure would prevent candour in the Cabinet. To my mind the most important reason is that such disclosure would create or fan ill-informed or captious public or political criticism. The business of government is difficult enough as it is, and no government could contemplate with equanimity the inner workings of the government machine being exposed to the gaze of those ready to criticise without adequate knowledge of the background and perhaps with some axe to grind. And that must, in my view, also apply to all documents concerned with policy making within departments including, it may be, minutes and the like by quite junior officials and correspondence with outside bodies. Further, it may be that deliberations about a particular case require protection as much as deliberations about policy. I do not think that it is possible to limit such documents by any definition. But there seems to me to be a wide difference between such documents and routine reports. There may be special reasons for withholding some kinds of routine documents, but I think that the proper test to be applied is to ask, in the language of Lord Simon in *Duncan*'s case, whether the withholding of a document because it belongs to a particular class is really "necessary for the proper functioning of the public service."

It appears to me that, if the Minister's reasons are such that a judge can properly weigh them, he must, on the other hand, consider what is the probable importance in the case before him of the documents or other evidence sought to be withheld. If he decides that on balance the documents probably ought to be produced, I think that it would generally be best that he should see them before ordering production and if he thinks that the Minister's reasons are not clearly expressed he will have to see the documents before ordering production. I can see nothing wrong in the judge seeing documents without their being shown to the parties. Lord Simon said (in *Duncan*'s case) that "where the Crown is a party . . . this would amount to communicating with one party to the exclusion of the other." I do not agree. The parties see the Minister's reasons. Where a document has not been prepared for the information of the judge, it seems to me a misuse of language to say that the judge "communicates with" the holder of the document by reading it. If on reading the document he still thinks that it ought to be produced he will order its production . . .'

Comment

(1)   The case is important because of its rejection of the decision in *Duncan* v *Cammell Laird* that a certificate of a Minister was conclusive, and not to be questioned by a court. In one sense that view, not strictly necessary for the decision on the facts in *Duncan*, placed the Crown above the law, and opened the way for potential abuse. The danger was recognized by the Courts in subsequent case law (see, for example, *Ellis* v *Home Office*) and also led to practical concessions being made by the Lord Chancellor in 1956.

(2)   Note the distinction drawn by Lord Reid between 'class' and 'contents' claims, and the reluctance of the Court to challenge executive assessment of 'contents'.

(3)   Lord Reid rejects the candour argument, a rejection mirrored in subsequent authorities. However, Lord Wilberforce, dissenting, in *Burmah Oil* v *Governor and Company of the Bank of England* stated:

> One such ground [to support a claim of privilege] is the need for candour in communication between those concerned with policy making. It seems now rather fashionable to decry this, but if as a ground it may at one time have been exaggerated, it has now . . . received an excessive dose of cold water. I am certainly not prepared – against the view of the Minister – to discount the need, in the formation of such very controversial policy as that with which we are here involved, for frank and uninhibited advice from the Bank to the government, from and between civil servants and between ministers.

The comments of Lord Reid as to access to high level governmental papers, such as Cabinet minutes and the like, should be compared with those in *Jonathan Cape*, p.45. The justification given by Lord Reid underpins the constitutional conventions of cabinet and ministerial responsibility. Compare the attitude of Lord Fraser in *Air Canada*, p.358.

(4)   In *Balfour* v *Foreign and Commonwealth Office* the Court of Appeal indicated that in a case where a minister claims immunity on the basis of national security, the courts should refuse to inspect the documents for which such immunity is claimed. For national security, see p.264.

(5)   In *Rogers* v *Home Secretary* (see p.355 *sub nom R* v *Lewes JJ*) Lord Reid stated:

> The ground put forward has been said to be Crown privilege. I think that expression is wrong and may be misleading. There is no question of any privilege in the ordinary sense of the word. The real question is whether the public interest requires that the letter shall not be produced and whether that public interest is so strong as to override the ordinary right and interest of a litigant that he shall be able to lay before a court of justice all relevant evidence . . .

(6) Confidentiality is not of itself a ground sufficient to sustain a claim of immunity – but may be a material factor in determining such a claim. In *Alfred Crompton* v *Commissioners of Customs & Excise*, Lord Cross stated:

> What the Court has to do is to weigh on the one hand the considerations that suggest that it is in the public interest that the documents in question should be disclosed and on the other hand those which suggest that it is in the public interest that they should not be disclosed and to balance one against the other.

But, said Lord Scarman in *Science Research Council* v *Nasse*, with a slightly different emphasis:

> Though I agree ... [that] ... a court may refuse to order production of a confidential document if it takes the view that justice does not require its production, I do not see the process of decision making as a balancing act. If the document is necessary for fairly disposing of the case, it must be produced, notwithstanding its confidentiality. Only if the document should be protected by public interest immunity, will there be a balancing act. And then the balance will not be between 'ethical or social' values of a confidential relationship involving the public interest and the document's relevance in the litigation, but between the public interest represented by the state and its public service, i.e. the executive government, and the public interest in the administration of justice . . .

D v *National Society for the Prevention of Cruelty to Children*

[1978] AC 171 · House of Lords

The NSPCC, an independent society established by Royal Charter for the protection of children, is authorized under statute to bring proceedings for the care of children. The respondent brought an action against the Society, alleging injuries arising from the Society's negligence in failing properly to investigate a complaint made against the respondent. The Society resisted an application for discovery of documents which would disclose the identity of the complainant, on the grounds that secrecy was essential if sources of information were not to dry up. The House of Lords reversed a ruling by the Court of Appeal ordering discovery, and upheld the claim of immunity of the Society.

Lord Diplock: '. . . To assist them to carry out the purposes of their charter and their functions as a person authorised to take care proceedings under s.1 of the Children and Young Persons Act 1969, the NSPCC invite the help of the general public in telling the Society's officers of any child of whom they know who may be suffering because of misfortune, ignorance, neglect or ill-treatment. The leaflets, which the Society distributes widely to enlist the public's aid, contain the promise "Your name, and the information you give for the purpose of helping children, will be treated as confidential." The uncontradicted evidence of the director of the NSPCC is that the work of the Society is dependent upon its receiving prompt information of suspected child abuse and that, as might be expected, the principal sources of such information are neighbours of the child's family or doctors, schoolteachers, health visitors and the like who will continue to be neighbours or to maintain the same relationship with the suspected person after the matter has been investigated and dealt with by the NSPCC. The evidence of the director is that without an effective promise of confidentiality neighbours and others would be very hesitant to pass on to the Society information about suspected child abuse. There is an understandable reluctance to "get involved" in something that is likely to arouse the resentment of the person whose suspected neglect or ill-treatment of a child has been reported by the informant, however true the information may be. Unless the NSPCC can guarantee the anonymity of its informants, its ability to learn of cases where children are at risk would be drastically reduced.

The fact that information has been communicated by one person to another in confidence, however, is not of itself a sufficient ground for protecting from disclosure in a court of law the nature of the information or the identity of the informant if either of these matters would assist the court to ascertain facts which are relevant to an issue upon which it is adjudicating: *Alfred Crompton Amusement Machines Ltd* v *Customs and Excise Commissioners (No. 2)*. The private promise of confidentiality must yield to the general public interest that in the administration of justice truth will out, unless by reason of the character of the information or the relationship of the recipient of the information to the informant a more important public interest is served by protecting the information or the identity of the informant from disclosure in a court of law.

The public interest which the NSPCC relies upon as obliging it to withhold from the plaintiff and from the court itself material that could disclose the identity of the Society's informant is analogous to the public interest that is protected by the well established rule of law that the identity of police informers may not be disclosed in a civil action, whether by the process of discovery or by oral evidence at the trial: *Marks* v *Beyfus*. The rationale of the rule as it applies to police informers is plain. If their identity were liable to be disclosed in a court of law, these sources of information would dry up and the police would be hindered in their duty of preventing and detecting crime. So the public interest in preserving the anonymity of police informers had to be weighed against the public interest that information which might assist a judicial tribunal to ascertain facts relevant to an issue upon which it is required to adjudicate should be withheld from that tribunal. By the uniform practice of the judges which by the time of *Marks* v *Beyfus* had already hardened into a rule of law, the balance has fallen upon the side of non-disclosure except where upon the trial of a defendant for a criminal offence disclosure of the identity of the informer could help to show that the defendant was innocent of the offence. In that case, and in that case only, the balance falls upon the side of disclosure.

My Lords, in *R* v *Lewes Justices, ex parte Secretary of State for the Home Department* this House did not hesitate to extend . . . to persons from whom the Gaming Board received information for the purposes of the exercise of their statutory functions under the Gaming Act 1968 immunity from disclosure of their identity analogous to that which the law had previously accorded to police informers. Your Lordships' sense of values might well be open to reproach if this House were to treat the confidentiality of information given to those who are authorised by statute to institute proceedings for the protection of neglected or ill-treated children as entitled to less favourable treatment in a court of law than information given to the Gaming Board so that gaming may be kept clean . . .

For my part I would uphold the decision of Croom-Johnson J and reverse that of the Court of Appeal. I would do so upon what in argument has been referred to as the "narrow" submission made on behalf of the NSPCC. I would extend to those who give information about neglect or ill-treatment of children to a local authority or the NSPCC a similar immunity from disclosure of their identity in legal proceedings to that which the law accords to police informers. The public interests served by preserving the anonymity of both classes of informants are analogous; they are of no less weight in the case of the former than in that of the latter class, and in my judgment are of greater weight than in the case of informers of the Gaming Board to whom immunity from disclosure of their identity has recently been extended by this House.

In the Court of Appeal, as in this House, counsel for the NSPCC advanced, as well as what I have referred to as the narrow submission, a broad submission that wherever a party to legal proceedings claims that there is a public interest to be served by withholding documents or information from disclosure in those proceedings it is the duty of the court to weigh that interest against the countervailing public interest in the administration of justice in the particular case and to refuse disclosure if the balance tilts that way. This broad submission, or something rather like it confined to information imparted in confidence, was adopted in his dissenting judgment by Lord Denning MR, but as I have already indicated there is the authority of this House that confidentiality of itself does not provide a ground of non-disclosure; nor am I able to accept the proposition that the basis of all privilege from disclosure of documents or information in legal proceedings is to prevent the breaking of a confidence. For my part, I think this House would be unwise to base its decision in the instant case upon a proposition so much broader than is necessary to resolve the issue between the parties.

The majority of the Court of Appeal rejected both the broad and narrow submissions. In essence their ground for doing so was that "public interest" as a ground for withholding disclosure of documents or information was but another term for what had before *Conway* v *Rimmer* been called "Crown Privilege" and was available only where the public interest involved was the effective functioning of departments or other organs of central government. "Crown Privilege" they regarded as having always been so confined; *Conway* v *Rimmer* did not extend the ambit of Crown Privilege: all it did was to decide that a claim by a minister of the Crown that documents were of a class which in the public interest ought not to be disclosed was not conclusive but that it was for the court itself to decide whether the public interest which would be protected by non-disclosure outweighed the public interest in making available to the court information that might assist it in doing justice between the litigants in the particular case.

This narrow view as to the scope of public interest as a ground for protecting documents and information from disclosure was supported in argument before this House by copious citations of passages taken from judgments in previous cases in the course of which documents for which a claim to non-disclosure had been made described as relating to essential functions of government, to the performance of statutory duties, to the public service or to the interests of the state. From this your Lordships were invited to infer that the document in question would not have been entitled to protection from disclosure unless it fell within the description used in the particular case . . .

I see no reason and I know of no authority for confining public interest as a ground for non-disclosure of documents or information to the effective functioning of departments or organs of central government. In *Conway* v *Rimmer* the public interest to be protected was the effective functioning of a county police force; in *Re D. (an Infant)* the interest to be protected was the effective functioning of a local authority in relation to the welfare of boarded-out children. In the instant case the public interest to be protected is the effective functioning of an organisation authorised under an Act of Parliament to bring legal proceedings for the welfare of children. I agree with Croom-Johnson J that this is a public interest which the court is entitled to take into consideration in deciding when the identity of the NSPCC's informants ought to be disclosed. I also agree that the balance of public interest falls on the side of non-disclosure . . .'

Comment

(1) The view of Lord Hailsham that the categories of classes attracting immunity are not closed can be compared with the views expressed in *Science Research Council* v *Nasse*. Lord Fraser said:

> . . . I accept that proposition, but any extension can only be made by adding new categories analogous to those already existing, just as in that case immunity was extended to a new category of informers to the NSPCC by analogy with informers to the police who were already entitled to immunity . . .

Lord Scarman said:

> . . . I would not . . . go as far as [Lord Hailsham in *D* v *NSPCC*] when he said 'The categories of public interest are not closed' . . . I do not find anything in *Conway* v *Rimmer* or the cases therein cited which would extend public interest immunity in this way. On the contrary, the theme of Lord Reid's speech is that the immunity arises only if 'disclosure would involve a danger of real prejudice to the national interests' . . .

(2) The analogy relied upon in *D* v *NSPCC* is that which entitles the police to withhold the name of police informers: see *Marks* v *Beyfus*. There are limits on that doctrine. In *R* v *Hennessy* the Court of Appeal indicated that in an appropriate case cross examination ought to be allowed, despite the fact that it might lead to the identification of informants, because of the greater interest in the establishment of an accused person's innocence. In *R* v *Agar* the Court of Appeal held that the public interest in ensuring a fair trial for the appellant outweighed the public interest in protecting the identity of the informer, since in that case the identity of the informer was necessary to determine whether the appellant had been entrapped into the offence. The effect of these rulings can be dramatic: see *R* v *Langford* where serious criminal charges had to be dropped in order to protect the identity of informants, the trial court having applied the ruling in *Agar*. The protection extends, for the same reason, to the identity of the owner or occupier of premises used for police surveillance: see *R* v *Rankine*.

(3) The police informer analogy was relied upon in *Rogers* v *Secretary of State for the Home Department* (complaints to Gaming Board). In *Neilson* v *Laugharne* it was held that public interest immunity applied to statements during the course of a

formal investigation of police misconduct under s.49, Police Act 1964; see also *Hehir* v *Commissioner of Police for the Metropolis*. The position now is governed by the House of Lords decision in *ex parte Wiley*, p.360.

(4)   In the light of the important powers available to local authorities in respect of the welfare of children, and their impact upon individuals, debate as to the extent of public interest immunity in respect of child care records is important. In *Re D (An Infant)* it was held that local authority records for child care investigations were immune from disclosure in wardship proceedings, a principle held to be of general application in *Gaskin* v *Liverpool City Council*. See now *Re M (A Minor)* (1990) where Butler-Sloss LJ stated:

> There is therefore a long line of authority establishing the principle of public interest immunity in the case of social work records and records of similar organisations . . . social work and analogous records are therefore in my view in a special category of immunity, justified by the particular circumstances of the welfare of children.

Compare *Brown* v *Matthews*.

(5)   The Courts have rejected attempts to claim public interest immunity in respect of journalistic sources: see *British Steel* v *Granada TV*. However, now see s.10, Contempt of Court Act 1981; *X Ltd* v *Morgan Grampian Ltd*, p.24.

Air Canada v *Secretary of State for Trade & Industry*

[1983] 2 AC 394 · House of Lords

In proceedings against the Secretary of State the appellants sought discovery of various documents which would show, it was claimed, improper motives for the actions of the Secretary of State in giving certain financial instructions to the British Airports Authority. The documents were of various types: Category A documents comprised high level ministerial papers relating to the formulation of government policy; Category B documents were inter-departmental communications between civil servants. On appeal, the House of Lords held that the appellants had failed to show that the documents contained material which would give substantial support to their case.

Lord Fraser: '. . . In considering the present law of England on what has come to be called public interest immunity, in relation to the production of documents, it is not necessary to go further back than *Conway* v *Rimmer* . . . I do not think that even Cabinet minutes are completely immune from disclosure in a case where, for example, the issue in a litigation involves serious misconduct by a Cabinet Minister. Such cases have occurred in Australia (see *Sankey* v *Whitlam*) and in the United States (see *Nixon* v *United States*) but fortunately not in the United Kingdom: see also the New Zealand case of *Environmental Defence Society Inc.* v *South Pacific Aluminium Ltd (No. 2)*. But while Cabinet documents do not have complete immunity, they are entitled to a high degree of protection against disclosure. In the present case the documents in category A do not enjoy quite the status of Cabinet minutes, but they approach that level in that they may disclose the reasons for Cabinet decisions and the process by which the decisions were reached. The reasons why such documents should not normally be disclosed until they have become of purely historical interest were considered in *Burmah Oil Co. Ltd* v *Governor and Company of the Bank of England* where Lord Wilberforce said this:

> One such ground is the need for candour in communication between those concerned with policy making. It seems now rather fashionable to decry this, but if as a ground it may at one time have been exaggerated, it has now, in my opinion, received an excessive dose of cold water. I am certainly not prepared – against the view of the minister – to discount the need, in the formation of such very controversial policy as that with which we are here involved, for frank and uninhibited advice from the Bank to the government, from and between civil servants and between ministers ... Another such ground is to protect from inspection by possible critics the inner working of government while forming important governmental policy. I do not believe that scepticism has invaded this, or that it is for the courts to assume the role of advocates for open government. If, as I believe, this is a valid ground for protection, it must continue to operate beyond the time span of a particular episode. Concretely, to reveal what advice was then sought and given and the mechanism for seeking and considering such advice, might well make the process of government more difficult now. On this point too I am certainly not prepared to be wiser than the minister.

Although Lord Wilberforce dissented from the majority as to the result in that case, I do not think that his statement of the reasons for supporting public interest immunity were in any way in conflict with the views of the majority ...

We were referred to some observations in reported cases to the effect that the court should have all relevant information before it whichever party it might help ... As a general rule that is, of course, true, but it is subject to some qualification. The very existence of legal professional privilege and of public interest immunity constitutes qualification. The importance of the general rule was emphasised by all the noble and learned lords who delivered reasoned speeches in *D* v *NSPCC* but none of them was considering the present question, or the difference between the inspection stage and the production stage. Nor was any of them contemplating the possibility of a person being compelled to disclose information in his own favour which he preferred to keep private. In an adversarial system such as exists in the United Kingdom, a party is free to withhold information that would help his case if he wishes – perhaps for reasons of delicacy or personal privacy. He cannot be compelled to disclose it against his will. It follows in my opinion that a party who seeks to compel his opponent, or an independent person, to disclose information must show that the information is likely to help his own case. It would be illogical to apply a different rule at the stage of inspection from that which applies at the stage of production. After all, the purpose of inspection by the court in many cases, including the present, would be to let the court see whether there is material in favour of disclosure which should be put in the scales to weigh against the material in favour of immunity. Inspection is with a view to the possibility of ordering production, and in my opinion inspection ought not to be ordered unless the court is persuaded that inspection is likely to satisfy it that it ought to take the further step of ordering production ...

I do not think it would be possible to state a test in a form which could be applied in all cases. Circumstances vary greatly. The weight of the public interest against disclosure will vary according to the nature of the particular documents in question; for example, it will in general be stronger where the documents are Cabinet papers than when they are at a lower level. The weight of the public interest in favour of disclosure will vary even more widely, because it depends upon the probable evidential value to the party seeking disclosure of the particular documents, in almost infinitely variable circumstances of individual cases. The most that can usefully be said is that, in order to persuade the court even to inspect documents for which public interest immunity is claimed, the party seeking disclosure ought at least to satisfy the court that the documents are very likely to contain material which would give substantial support to his contention on an issue which arises in the case, and that without them he might be "deprived of the means of . . . proper presentation" of his case: see *Glasgow Corporation* v *Central Land Board* . . .

When the claim is a "class" claim judges will often not be well qualified to estimate its strength, because they may not be fully aware of the importance of the class of documents to the public administration as a whole. Moreover, whether the claim is a "class" claim or a "contents" claim, the court will have to make its decision on whether to order production, after having inspected the documents privately, without having the assistance of argument from counsel. It should therefore, in my opinion, not be encouraged to "take a peep" just on the off chance of finding something useful. It should inspect documents only where it has definite grounds for expecting to find material of real importance to the party seeking disclosure . . .'

Comment

(1)   The view taken as to the burden on the party seeking disclosure reflects that of Lord Wilberforce in *Burmah Oil* v *Governor and Company of the Bank of England*, p.353.

(2)   Compare the view of Lord Fraser re high level papers with that of Lord Reid in *Conway* v *Rimmer*. For an example of the Court ordering production of high level papers, see *Williams* v *Home Office*, where McNeil J ordered the production of ministerial policy documents relating to the control unit regime in Wakefield Prison.

R v *Chief Constable of the West Midlands Police, ex parte Wiley*

[1994] 3 All ER 420 · House of Lords

W and S applied to the Divisional Court for judicial review of the decision by the respondent Chief Constable not to give an undertaking not to use documents which arose out of investigations by the Police Complaints Authority in civil proceedings contemplated by the applicants. In addition, S sought a declaration and an injunction against the use by the Chief Constable of the documents, or any information contained in them, in the civil action contemplated by S against the Chief Constable. The Divisional Court granted the relief sought, a decision that was upheld by the Court of Appeal, which held that the public interest immunity that existed in respect of police complaints proceedings extended to the information acquired during that process. The House of Lords allowed the appeal brought by the Chief Constable, and discharged the declaration and injunction granted to S. A class claim in respect of documents created during the process of the police complaints process was not justified, although a contents claim might sometimes succeed. Even if the claim of immunity for the documents in question was justified, such immunity extended to the documents, and their disclosure, not the use of information obtained from the documents. The parts of the speeches extracted relate to general issues relating to claims of public interest immunity.

Lord Templeman: 'Whenever disclosure in litigation is under consideration, the first question is whether a document is sufficiently relevant and material to require disclosure in the interests of justice. In civil proceedings a document need only be disclosed if disclosure is necessary "for disposing fairly of the cause or matter or for saving costs": see RSC ord.24, r.8. In criminal proceedings a document need only be disclosed if it is relevant and material for the establishment of the guilt or innocence of the accused.

In civil proceedings, the relevance and materiality of a document depend on the issues between the parties established by the written proceedings. In criminal proceedings there is as yet no provision for written pleadings. Prosecution authorities know which documents are relevant to the prosecution but they cannot know for certain which documents will be relevant to the defence. In recent cases the Court of Appeal has quashed convictions because of the failure on the part of the police to disclose documents which, subsequently to the convictions, were held to be relevant and material to the establishment of the guilt or innocence of the accused. In order to avoid criticism and a miscarriage of justice one way or the other, the police authorities now feel obliged to disclose documents of doubtful relevance and materiality. In civil proceedings also, pleadings may be amended, and the issues which finally arise at trial may not be perceived or understood at the pleadings stage. The result in both criminal and civil proceedings is that masses of documents of no or doubtful relevance or materiality are made available and are presented to judge and jury. The indiscriminate and undisciplined preparation and presentation of documents for trial increase the length and cost of the trial and sometimes enable a litigant to snatch an undeserved victory under a cloak of confusion and obscurity which baffles judge and jury . . .

If a document is not relevant and material it need not be disclosed and public interest immunity will not arise. In cases of doubt as to relevance and materiality the directions of the court can be obtained before trial . . . If a document is relevant and material then it must be disclosed unless it is confidential and unless a breach of the confidentiality will cause harm to the public interest which outweighs the harm to the interests of justice caused by non-disclosure. It has been said that the holder of a confidential document for which public interest immunity may be claimed is under a duty to assert the claim, leaving the court to decide whether the claim is well-founded. For my part, I consider that when a document is known to be relevant and material, the holder of the document should voluntarily disclose it unless he is satisfied that disclosure will cause substantial harm. If the holder is in doubt he may refer the matter to the court. If the holder decides that a document should not be disclosed then that decision can be upheld or set aside by the judge. A rubber stamp approach to public interest immunity by the holder of a document is neither necessary nor appropriate.

If public interest immunity is approached by every litigant on the basis that a relevant and material document must be disclosed unless the disclosure will cause substantial harm to the public interest, the distinction between a class claim and a contents claim loses much of its significance. As a general rule the harm to the public interest of the disclosure of the whole or part of a document dealing with defence or national security or diplomatic secrets will be self evident and will preclude disclosure. On the other hand it is difficult to see how the disclosure of documents generated by the activities of the Police Complaints Authority can cause any harm. [They] may produce documents dealing with "sensitive police material relating to . . . policy and operational matters". It is unlikely that such matters will be relevant or material to criminal or civil proceedings but in a proper case a claim to public interest immunity could be asserted for the whole or part of a document in order to preserve those secrets which, if disclosed, would hamper the police in the investigation and prevention of crime. We were also told that public interest immunity might be claimed for the contents of the report of the investigating officer dealing with the complaint against the police. The report itself, as distinct from the documents generated by the inquiry, will not usually be relevant or material or admissible in criminal or civil proceedings. If [it is] . . . I do not see any sufficient reason for casting the cloak of secrecy over the report . . .'.

Comment

(1)   The views of Lord Templeman in respect of class claims were not universally shared by other members of the court. In particular, Lord Slynn wished to reserve his position as to whether some more narrow class claim could be sustained in the context of police complaints cases. The approach taken by Lord Templeman highlights the dangers of permitting class claims save in the most clear of cases. A class claim effectively puts the individual merits of the claim beyond the scrutiny of the court: see Lord Reid in *Conway* v *Rimmer*, p.349.

(2)   Note also the opinion of Lord Templeman that the Crown is not obliged to assert a claim of immunity, a position that runs counter to evidence given by Ministers to the Scott inquiry into the 'arms for Iraq' affair.

(3)   The position in respect of claims of public interest immunity in criminal cases was considered in *R* v *Keane*, where the Court of Appeal held that the trial court has to strike a balance between the weight of the public interest in non-disclosure against the importance of the documents for the defence. For the duty in respect of the disclosure and production of documents in criminal cases, see *R* v *Ward*; *R* v *Johnson, Davis and Rowe*.

16 Police discretion

Although the powers, functions and role of constables have changed over the centuries, the office has retained its peculiar legal status the significance of which remains of immense importance. Modern cases establish that a constable is not an employee or agent of either the local authority or the Chief Constable. In *Fisher* v *Oldham Corporation* it was held that the Watch Committee (whose modern counterpart is the police authority) were not vicariously responsible for the torts of a constable – they were not in the relationship of master and servant. On the other hand, another aspect of the absence of servant–master relationship was that the Committee could not instruct the constable how to carry out his tasks, e.g. whether to arrest or release any particular person.

Nor is a constable a Crown servant; he is an office holder under the Crown. Although a constable can often be said to be a Crown servant this does not mean that there exists the relationship of master and servant with the obligations of obedience to orders and vicarious liability which that would entail.

In *Attorney-General for New South Wales* v *Perpetual Trustee Co. Ltd*, the Privy Council said of a constable that:

> . . . he is to be regarded as a servant or minister of the King because . . . the administration of justice, both criminal and civil, and the preservation of order and prevention of crime by means of what is now called police, are among the most important functions of government, and by the constitution of this country these functions do of common right belong to the Crown.

But it was also said in that case that 'If ever he is called a servant, it is in the same sense in which any holder of a public office may be called a servant of the Crown or of the State'. In that case the defendant had negligently injured a constable who was then paid certain illness benefits by the Crown. The Crown attempted to recover from the defendant compensation in respect of these benefits. Had the Crown and the constable been in the relationship of master and servant the Crown would have been entitled to recover but the Privy Council confirmed the approach in *Fisher* v *Oldham Corporation* and held that a constable is not a servant of the Crown.

Although the matter was put graphically in *R* v *Chief Constable of Devon & Cornwall, ex parte CEGB* (p.412), 'the police are no one's lackeys', because of the public law nature of the office, police discretion is subject to review by the courts – see *Holgate-Mohammed* v *Duke* (p.373) and *R* v *Commissioner of Police for the Metropolis, ex parte Blackburn (No. 1)* (p.368).

The Police Act 1964, passed in response to the Report of the 1962 Royal Commission on the Police, creates a statutory framework regulating the organization, structure and supervision of the modern police force. It also provides for the funding of the police by police authorities with the benefit of a grant of 50 per cent from the Home Office. In most of England and Wales the police authorities are committees of the county council; within the Metropolitan Police District the police authority is the Home Secretary. Disciplinary procedures are now provided for in the Police and Criminal Evidence Act 1984. Although the Police and Magistrates' Courts Act 1984 has made extensive provision relating to arrangements for local policing, police authorities and discipline, it has not altered the constitutional position of police constables or the basis on which their discretion must be exercised.

Section 48, Police Act 1964

(1) The chief officer of police for any area shall be liable in respect of torts committed by constables under his direction and control in the performance or purported performance of their functions in like manner as a master is liable in respect of torts committed by his servants in the course of their employment, and accordingly shall in respect of any such tort be treated for all purposes as a joint tortfeasor.

Comment

(1) Section 48 creates vicarious liability and remedies the defect identified in *Fisher* v *Oldham Corporation*. The chief officer may be sued even if the identity of the individual constable is unknown. Under s.48(2) a police authority must indemnify a chief officer in respect of costs and damages; under s.48(4) a police authority may indemnify an individual officer at its discretion.

(2) The effect of the use of 'functions' and not 'duties' is that a police officer who is found to be acting outside the execution of his duty for the purposes of the offences in s.51 of the Act (p.379) may none the less be treated as within the performance or purported performance of his functions.

(3)   It is only in respect of torts which are committed as a police officer to which s.48 will apply; for example, a chief officer will not be vicariously liable for a police constable who, off duty, carelessly drops a pot of paint on a passer-by. A police officer may, in an extreme case, be treated as having gone off on 'a frolic of his own' even though he purports to be acting as a constable. In *Makanjuola* v *Metropolitan Police Commissioner* a police officer tricked his way into a flat using his warrant card and coerced the occupant into a sexual act. The police officer had been expressly restricted to desk duties. It was held that the chief officer was not vicariously liable since the sexual coercion was not a wrongful or unauthorized mode of doing what was authorized. By contrast, the court suggested that the entry to premises obtained by showing an identity card had been in the purported performance of his functions as a constable.

(4)   In *Rookes* v *Barnard* Lord Devlin said that exemplary damages might be awarded in respect of:

> ... oppressive, arbitrary or unconstitutional action by servants of the government. I should not extend this category ... to oppressive action by private corporations or individuals. Where one man is more powerful than another, it is inevitable that he will try to use his power to gain his ends; and if his power is much greater than the other's, he might perhaps be said to be using it oppressively. If he uses his power illegally, he must pay for his illegality in the ordinary way; but he is not to be punished simply because he is the more powerful. In the case of the government it is different, for the servants of the government are also the servants of the people and the use of their power must always be subordinate to their duty of service.

'Servants of the government' includes the police, and a claim for exemplary damages will be entertained even though there is nothing oppressive or arbitrary provided that it can be said to be 'unconstitutional' – see *Holden* v *Chief Constable of Lancashire*.

Harris v Sheffield United Football Club

[1988] 1 QB 77 · Court of Appeal

The South Yorkshire Police Authority claimed £51,699 for what it claimed were 'special police services' (within the meaning of s.15, Police Act 1964) requested by the defendant Football Club at their ground between August 1982 and November 1983. The Club claimed that the officers had been sent to the ground in pursuance of their general duty to maintain law and order and protect life and property, and that since outbreaks of violence at the ground were likely the officers had not been provided as a special police service, and accordingly there was no consideration to support the contract alleged by the Authority. The Club also contended that even if the services were special police services there had not been a request for their services. The Court of Appeal held that the services provided did amount to special police services and that a request could be implied from the circumstances.

Neill LJ: '. . . Viscount Cave LC [in *Glasbrook Bros* v *Glamorgan CC* said] "No doubt there is an absolute and unconditional obligation binding the police authorities to take all steps which appear to them to be necessary for keeping the peace, for preventing crime, or for protecting property from criminal injury; and the public, who pay for this protection through the rates and taxes, cannot lawfully be called upon to make a further payment for that which is their right".

Later in his speech Viscount Cave LC applied this statement of principle to the facts: "If in the judgment of the police authorities, formed reasonably and in good faith, the garrison was necessary for the protection of life and property, then they were not entitled to make a charge for it, for that would be to exact a payment for the performance of a duty which clearly was owed to the appellants and their servants; but if they thought the garrison a superfluity and only acceded to [the owners' agent's] request with a view to meeting his wishes, then in my opinion they were entitled to treat the garrison duty as special duty and to charge for it".

It will be apparent . . . that if the words by Viscount Cave LC in the *Glasbrook* case were applied as though they were the words of a statute the case for the club would be very strong if not overwhelming. Thus it is not in dispute that at all material times since about 1970 the chief constable has been of the opinion that the attendance of police officers at Bramall Lane on the occasion of league and cup matches has been necessary for the maintenance of law and order and the protection of life and property. In the *Glasbrook* case, however, the House of Lords was considering a very different situation from that before the court in the present case. The question before the House was whether a charge could be made where the precautions taken were more extensive than those which the police authorities considered to be necessary. But the emergency which required the presence, if not of a garrison of police officers, of at least a number of officers to watch the situation with other officers held in reserve, arose in the context of an industrial dispute and not because the colliery company had voluntarily chosen to invite a large number of people to their premises to watch a football match or other spectacle . . . I see the force of the argument that the court must be very slow before it interferes in any way with a decision of a chief constable about the disposition of his forces. The question posed in the instant case, however, is not whether the chief constable ought to have sent officers to Bramall Lane or as to the number of officers which were necessary; that the presence of officers was necessary is not in dispute. The question is whether, having regard to his general duty to enforce the law, the provision of these officers can properly be considered as the provision of special police services for which the police authority was entitled to make a charge. In answering this question I do not propose to attempt to lay down any general rules as to what are or are not "special police services", because in my judgment it is necessary to look at all the circumstances of the individual case. I would, however, venture to suggest that the following matters require to be taken into account. (1) Are the police officers required to attend on private premises or in a public place? Though in *Glasbrook Brothers Ltd* v *Glamorgan CC* the fact that the garrison was to be stationed on private premises was not treated as conclusive, the fact that the police will not as a general rule have access to private premises suggests that prima facie their presence on private premises would constitute special police services. (2) Has some violence or other emergency already occurred or is it immediately imminent? I can at present see no basis for an argument that the attendance of police officers to deal with an outbreak of violence which has actually occurred or is immediately imminent could constitute the provision of special police services, even though officers who would otherwise be off duty had to be deployed. (3) What is the nature of the event or occasion at which the officers are required to attend? It is to be noted that in *Wathen* v *Sandys* . . . the sheriff was not entitled to charge the candidates for the provision of constables at the polling booth because he was under a duty to procure the peace of the county. But a distinction can be drawn between public events such as elections which perhaps lie at one end of a spectrum, and private events such as weddings which lie at the other end. At various points in the middle may lie events such as football matches to which the public are invited and which large numbers of the public are likely to attend. It may also be relevant to inquire whether the event or occasion forms part of a series or whether it is a single occasion or event. Someone who stages events which require the regular attendance of police officers will be placing an exceptional strain on the resources of the police, particularly if the events take place at weekends or on public holidays. (4) Can the provision of the necessary amount of police protection be met from the resources available to the chief constable without the assistance of officers who would otherwise be engaged either in other duties or would be off duty? It was argued on behalf of the club that though it was relevant to take account of the total number of men available it was not permissible to take into consideration the fact that the use of "off-duty" officers might increase the payment of overtime. I am unable to accept this argument. The chief constable when deciding how to deploy his forces is subject not only to the constraints imposed by the number of men available, but also financial constraints. The payment of overtime on particular occasions may mean that on other occasions reductions have to be made in the ordinary services provided by the police or sacrifices have to be made in the provision of equipment.

Bearing these considerations in mind I return to the present case. The club has responsibilities which are owed not only its employees and the spectators who attend but also to the football authorities to take all reasonable steps to ensure that the game takes place in conditions which do not occasion danger to any person or property. The attendance of the police is necessary to assist the club in the fulfilment of this duty. The matches take place regularly and usually at weekends during about eight months of the year. Though the holding of the matches is of some public importance because of the widespread support in the local community both for the game and the club, the club is not under any legal duty to hold the matches. The charges which the police authority seek to make, and have made, relate solely to the officers on duty inside the ground and not to those in the street or other public places outside. There is clear evidence that the chief constable would be unable to provide the necessary amount of protection for Bramall Lane and also to discharge his other responsibilities without making extensive use of officers who would otherwise have been off duty. Substantial sums by way of overtime have therefore to be paid. The arrangements for the attendance of the officers are made to guard against the possibility, and for some matches the probability, of violence; the officers are not sent to deal with an existing emergency, nor can it be said that any outbreak of violence is immediately imminent.

In my judgment, looking at all these factors I am driven to the conclusion that the provision of police officers to attend regularly at Bramall Lane throughout the football season does constitute the provision of special police services. Nor in my opinion is it to the point that the club has stated that they do not expect the police to carry out any duties other than to maintain law and order. The resources of the police are finite. In my view if the club wishes on a regular basis to make an exceptional claim on police services to deal with potential violence on its premises, then however well intentioned and public spirited it may be in assembling the crowd at Bramall Lane, the services which it receives are "special police services" within the meaning of s.15(1) of the Police Act 1964.'

Comment

(1)   In *Glasbrook Bros* v *Glamorgan CC* there was a strike of miners. The mine owners were dissatisfied with the amount of police protection. They requested more officers and required that they should be billeted at the site. The police authority acceded to the request and sought to make a charge for these officers. The House of Lords held that a charge could be made if the amount of protection requested by the colliery exceeded that which the senior police officer reasonably considered to be necessary in the circumstances.

(2)   The local authority would almost certainly have taken action under legislation relating to safety at sports grounds if the club had tried to stage the game without police attendance. The police might also have placed restrictions on the club under the terms of s.14, Public Order Act 1986 (p.423).

R v Commissioner of Police for the Metropolis, ex parte Blackburn (No. 1)

[1968] 2 QB 118 · Court of Appeal

The Metropolitan Police Commissioner had issued a policy statement in which he directed his officers that observations on gambling clubs would not take place unless there was a suspicion that the clubs were being frequented by criminals. The reasons behind the policy were the uncertainty of the law, the expense and the manpower involved. The applicant claimed that illegal gambling was taking place and sought an order of mandamus to compel the Commissioner to reverse the policy statement. The Court of Appeal held that the Commissioner owed a public duty to enforce the law and that in the exercise of his discretion as to how to carry out that duty he could be controlled by the courts. Accordingly, in an appropriate case an order of mandamus would lie. But, since the Commissioner had instituted a reversal of the policy in the light of a decision which clarified the gambling laws and since, at the close of proceedings, he had undertaken to withdraw the earlier policy, an order of mandamus would not be granted.

Lord Denning MR: '. . . The office of Commissioner of Police within the Metropolis dates back to 1829 when Sir Robert Peel introduced his disciplined force. The commissioner was a justice of the peace specially appointed to administer the police force in the metropolis. His constitutional status has never been defined either by statute or by the courts. It was considered by the Royal Commission on the Police in their report in 1962 (Cmnd. 1728). But I have no hesitation in holding that, like every constable in the land, he should be, and is, independent of the executive. He is not subject to the orders of the Secretary of State, save that under the Police Act 1964, the Secretary of State can call upon him to give a report, or to retire in the interests of efficiency. I hold it to be the duty of the Commissioner of Police of the Metropolis, as it is of every chief constable, to enforce the law of the land. He must take steps so to post his men that crimes may be detected; and that honest citizens may go about their affairs in peace. He must decide whether or not suspected persons are to be prosecuted; and, if need be, bring the prosecution or see that it is brought. But in all these things he is not the servant of anyone, save of the law itself. No Minister of the Crown can tell him that he must, or must not, keep observation on this place or that; or that he must, or must not, prosecute this man or that one. Nor can any police authority tell him so. The responsibility for law enforcement lies on him. He is answerable to the law and to the law alone. That appears sufficiently from *Fisher* v *Oldham Corporation*, and *Attorney-General for New South Wales* v *Perpetual Trustee Co. Ltd.*

Although the chief officers of police are answerable to the law, there are many fields in which they have a discretion with which the law will not interfere. For instance, it is for the Commissioner of Police of the Metropolis, or the chief constable, as the case may be, to decide in any particular case whether inquiries should be pursued, or whether an arrest should be made, or a prosecution brought. It must be for him to decide on the disposition of his force and the concentration of his resources on any particular crime or area. No court can or should give him direction on such a matter. He can also make policy decisions and give effect to them, as, for instance, was often done when prosecutions were not brought for attempted suicide. But there are some policy decisions with which, I think, the courts in a case can, if necessary, interfere. Suppose a chief constable were to issue a directive to his men that no person should be prosecuted for stealing any goods less than £100 in value. I should have thought that the court could countermand it. He would be failing in his duty to enforce the law . . .

I turn to see whether it is shown that the Commissioner of Police of the Metropolis has failed in his duty. I have no doubt that some of the difficulties have been due to the lawyers and the courts. Refined arguments have been put forward on the wording of the statute which have gained acceptance by some for a time. I can well understand that the commissioner might hesitate for a time until those difficulties were resolved; but, on the other hand, it does seem to me that his policy decision was unfortunate. People might well think that the law was not being enforced, especially when the gaming clubs were openly and flagrantly being conducted as they were in this great city. People might even go further and suspect that the police themselves turned a blind eye to it. I do not myself think that was so. I do not think that the suggestion should even be made. But nevertheless the policy decision was, I think, most unfortunate.

The matter has, I trust, been cleared up now. On December 19, 1967, the House of Lords . . . made it quite clear that roulette with a zero was not rendered lawful simply by the "offer of the bank". Following that decision . . . the commissioner issued a statement in which he said: "It is the intention of the Metropolitan Police to enforce the law as it has been interpreted." That implicitly revoked the policy decision of April 22, 1966; and the commissioner by his counsel gave an undertaking to the court that that policy decision would be officially revoked. We were also told that immediate steps are being taken to consider the "goings-on" in the big London clubs with a view to prosecution if there is anything unlawful. That is all that Mr Blackburn or anyone else can reasonably expect.'

Comment

(1)   Salmon LJ recognized that the police must be subject to the law and that their duty to enforce the law was subject to review by the courts. He gave the example of a chief officer giving an instruction to his officers not to take steps to prosecute any housebreaker. Such an instruction would be a breach of duty – 'it would be so improper that it could not amount to exercise of discretion'.

(2)   The Police Act 1964 contains extensive provisions by which the police authority and the Home Secretary may call the chief officer to account for the policing in a particular area. The Act also provides for the appointment and dismissal of chief officers.

(3)   See *Holgate-Mohammed* v *Duke*, p.373. The chief officer's exercise of his discretion may be challenged by way of judicial review under the *Wednesbury* principles – see p.291. In considering the proper distribution by a chief officer of his force he is entitled to have regard to the wide variety of pressures and demands placed upon it, provided that this does not amount to an abdication of his functions. In *R* v *Commissioner of Police for the Metropolis, ex parte Blackburn (No. 3)* mandamus did not issue to compel enforcement of the Obscene Publications Act because the chief officer had remedied defects in the organization of his vice squad and increased its numbers. In *R* v *Oxford, ex parte Levey*, the chief officer had properly formulated a policy for policing Toxteth, Liverpool, even though his policy meant that police officers gave up the hot pursuit of thieves who had stolen jewellery from Mr Levey. The chief constable in formulating his policy had been entitled to take into account the Scarman Report into the Brixton Disorders provided he kept the policy under review.

(4)   In *R* v *Inland Revenue Commissioners, ex parte Mead*, Stuart Smith LJ considered that a decision to prosecute an adult was potentially subject to judicial review, although there were other avenues of challenge which might be more appropriate, e.g. abuse of process (see p.23). Since the Revenue had considered the case against the taxpayer on its merits fairly and dispassionately to see that the criteria for prosecution had been satisfied, and had not acted in bad faith or for ulterior, extraneous or improper purposes, the taxpayer's application was dismissed.

In *R* v *Chief Constable of Kent County Constabulary, ex parte L (a minor)* the Divisional Court held that:

> . . . in respect of juveniles, the decision of the Crown Prosecution Service to continue or discontinue criminal proceedings is reviewable . . . but only where it can be demonstrated that the decision was made regardless of or clearly contrary to a settled policy of the Director of Public Prosecutions evolved in the public interest, for example, the policy of cautioning juveniles, a policy which the CPS are bound to apply, where appropriate, to the exercise of their discretion to continue or discontinue criminal proceedings.

The juvenile's case failed on the merits.

In *Welsh* v *Chief Constable of Merseyside* it was held that policy considerations did not preclude an action in negligence in respect of the administrative responsibilities or practices of the Crown Prosecution Service to keep the court informed as to the state of an adjourned criminal case. However in *Elguzouli-Daf* v *Commissioner of Police of the Metropolis* the Court of Appeal rejected the imposition of a general duty of care on the CPS and regarded *Welsh* as an exceptional case depending on the assumption by the CPS of responsibility to a particular defendant.

Lindley v *Rutter*

[1981] 1 QB 128 · Divisional Court

The defendant had been arrested for being drunk and disorderly. She was placed in a police cell and refused to permit a policewoman to search her. Assisted by another policewoman the first officer searched the defendant and removed her brassiere; during the search and seizure the defendant struggled violently. The policewomen were under the impression that the search and removal were necessary, in the case of all female prisoners placed in cells, under standing orders from the Chief Constable. The defendant was charged with assaulting a constable acting in the execution of her duty contrary to s.51(1), Police Act 1964 (see p.379). The Divisional Court upheld the appeal of the defendant and held that the policewomen had failed to exercise their discretion properly in that they had failed to consider whether the search and seizure were justified. That failure had taken the policewomen outside the execution of their duty.

Donaldson LJ: '... The only matter in issue is whether WPc Fry was acting in the execution of her duty.

The wording of this offence is liable to be misunderstood by the public, but it is difficult to suggest an alternative form of words. However, I must make it clear that there is no suggestion that WPc Fry was acting otherwise than in accordance with what she believed to be her duty. The issue is whether what she did was justifiable in law. Police constables of all ranks derive their authority from the law and only from the law. If they exceed that authority, however slightly, technically they cease to be acting in the execution of their duty and have no more rights than any other citizen. This is a most salutary principle upon which all our liberties depend and it is not to be eroded merely because, as in this case, the limits of the constable's authority may not have been clearly defined and WPc Fry was acting in the bona fide belief that she was authorised to act as she did. These considerations may well provide an answer to criticism of the officer concerned. They do not deprive the aggrieved citizen of any of her rights ... [The court then considered the common law power of search and seizure:]

It is the duty of the courts to be ever zealous to protect the personal freedom, privacy and dignity of all who live in these islands. Any claim to be entitled to take action which infringes these rights is to be examined with very great care. But such rights are not absolute. They have to be weighed against the rights and duties of police officers, acting on behalf of society as a whole. It is the duty of any constable who lawfully has a prisoner in his charge to take all reasonable measures to ensure that the prisoner does not escape or assist others to do so, does not injure himself or others, does not destroy or dispose of evidence and does not commit further crime such as, for example, malicious damage to property. This list is not exhaustive, but it is sufficient for present purposes. What measures are reasonable in the discharge of this duty will depend upon the likelihood that the particular prisoner will do any of these things unless prevented. That in turn will involve the constable in considering the known or apparent disposition and sobriety of the prisoner. What can never be justified is the adoption of any particular measures without regard to all circumstances of the particular case.

This is not to say that there can be no standing instructions. Although there may always be special features in any individual case, the circumstances in which people are taken into custody are capable of being categorised and experience may show that certain measures, including searches, are prima facie reasonable and necessary in a particular category of case. The fruits of this experience may be passed on to officers in the form of standing instructions. But the officer having custody of the prisoner must always consider, and be allowed and encouraged to consider, whether the special circumstances of the particular case justify or demand a departure from the standard procedure either by omitting what would otherwise be done or by taking additional measures. So far as searches are concerned, he should appreciate that they involve an affront to the dignity and privacy of the individual. Furthermore, there are degrees of affront involved in such a search. Clearly going through someone's pockets or handbag is less of an affront than a body search. In every case a police officer ordering a search or depriving a prisoner of property should have a very good reason for doing so.

In the instant case, WPc Fry might have been justified in searching the defendant if she had had doubts whether she was suffering from the effects of drink or drugs and thought that a search might have resolved that doubt. But, of course, there was no reason whatsoever to believe that the defendant's condition was attributable to anything other than intoxication. Again, a search would have been justified if, bearing in mind the defendant's condition, including her reaction to being in custody, WPc Fry or the station officer had had any reason for thinking that the defendant might have some object on her with which she might accidentally or intentionally injure herself or others.

The forcible removal of her brassiere was understandably regarded by the defendant as peculiarly offensive. Such conduct would require considerable justification. It was inherently unlikely that possession of the brassiere could lead to accidental injury. If it was to be used intentionally for this purpose, other clothing would probably have served as well. Indeed, there would have had to have been some evidence that young female drunks in general were liable to injure themselves with their brassieres or that the defendant has shown a peculiar disposition to do so. It would obviously be a justification if the defendant had by words or conduct threatened to do so. But that is not this case.

The justices have found that WPc Fry was acting in accordance with the standing orders of the chief constable which applied to any female person arrested and placed in a cell in whatever circumstances and for whatever reason. They have made no finding that the constable gave any consideration to whether the search was necessary for any lawful purpose or whether the removal of the brassiere was in fact necessary for the defendant's own protection. It is impossible to justify such a standing instruction or WPc Fry's conduct if based upon it. Accordingly, WPc Fry was not acting in the execution of her duty and the defendant was entitled to use reasonable force to resist. In fact, she used more force than was necessary and so was guilty of a common assault upon WPc Fry. However, she was not guilty of the very much more serious offence of assaulting WPc Fry in the execution of her duty, since the constable was exceeding her duty . . .'

Comment

(1)   The officer had misunderstood the Chief Constable's Standing Order; it did not purport to exclude her discretion. Compare *R* v *Chief Constable of Avon and Somerset Constabulary, ex parte Robinsons* where the Court refused to interfere with the issuing of a circular by the Chief Constable concerning the access of solicitors' clerks to prisoners. The circular left the decision whether or not to permit access to the individual officers concerned and did not attempt to fetter their discretion or to create any absolute rules. See also *Middleweek* v *Chief Constable of Merseyside.*

(2)   Section 54, Police and Criminal Evidence Act 1984 (p.398) replaces the common law power to search an arrested person but the principle that the constable should exercise a discretion properly remains good.

Holgate-Mohammed v *Duke*

[1984] AC 437 · House of Lords

Section 2(4) of the Criminal Law Act 1964 provided that 'Where a constable, with reasonable cause, suspects that an arrestable offence has been committed, he may arrest without warrant anyone whom he, with reasonable cause, suspects to be guilty of the offence.' Acting under s.2(4) a police officer arrested the plaintiff in connection with the theft of property. He had reasonable cause to suspect that the plaintiff had committed the offence but he did not have sufficient evidence to charge her. The decision to arrest was taken in order that the plaintiff might be interviewed at the police station and in the belief that she would be more likely to confess during such questioning rather than in questioning at her home without an arrest having been made. After questioning the plaintiff was released and no charges were brought. The plaintiff sued for false imprisonment and succeeded at first instance where the Court held (1) that the police constable had had reasonable suspicion that the plaintiff had committed the offence but (2) that since the sole reason for arresting had been to subject her to questioning at the police station rather than under caution at her home, the arrest had been an improper exercise of discretion. The House of Lords dismissed the appeal of the plaintiff and held that a police officer arresting under s.2(4) was exercising an executive discretion which was capable of challenge on the basis of the *Wednesbury* principles. Applying those principles the House of Lords held that arrest in order to facilitate enquiry into the offence was a relevant consideration.

Lord Diplock: '. . . [T]he condition precedent [namely reasonable suspicion] to Detective Constable Offin's power to take the appellant into custody and the power of the other constables at Southsea Police Station to detain her in custody was fulfilled; and, since the wording of the subsection under which he acted is "may arrest without warrant," this left him with an executive discretion whether to arrest her or not. Since this is an executive discretion expressly conferred by statute upon a public officer, the constable making the arrest, the lawfulness of the way in which he has exercised it in a particular case cannot be questioned in any court of law except upon those principles laid down by Lord Greene MR in *Associated Provincial Picture Houses Ltd* v *Wednesbury Corporation*, that have become too familiar to call for repetitious citation. The *Wednesbury* principles . . . are applicable to determining the lawfulness of the exercise of the statutory discretion of a constable under s.2(4) of the Criminal Law Act 1967, not only in proceedings for judicial review but also for the purpose of founding a cause of action at common law for damages for . . . false imprisonment . . .

The first of the *Wednesbury* principles is that the discretion must be exercised in good faith. The judge in the county court expressly found that Detective Constable Offin in effecting the initial arrest acted in good faith. He thought that he was making a proper use of his power of arrest. So his exercise of that power by arresting Mrs Holgate-Mohammed was lawful, unless it can be shown to have been "unreasonable" under *Wednesbury* principles, of which the principle that is germane to the instant case is: "He [sc. the exerciser of the discretion] must exclude from his consideration matters which are irrelevant to what he has to consider." . . .

Detective Constable Offin . . . thought (with obvious justification) that even if the jeweller were to succeed in picking out Mrs Holgate-Mohammed on a properly conducted identification parade, such evidence would be too weak to justify convicting her of committing the crime of burglary in December 1979. In these circumstances, if she had in fact committed the offence of which there were reasonable grounds at the time of her arrest for suspecting her to be guilty, the only kind of admissible evidence probative of her guilt that would be likely to be procurable would be a confession obtained from Mrs Holgate-Mohammed herself.

Detective Constable Offin thought that she would be more likely to confess to what he had reasonable cause to believe to be the truth, if she were arrested and taken for questioning to the police station. In other words, the reason why Detective Constable Offin arrested her was that he held the honest opinion that the police inquiries were more likely to be fruitful in clearing up the case if Mrs Holgate-Mohammed were compelled to go to the police station to be questioned there. It is relevant to add that officers who had been concerned, as Detective Constable Offin had not, in the original investigations in December 1979 would have been available, and there would be facilities for recording any statements that Mrs Holgate-Mohammed decided to make.

The circuit judge, however, described Detective Constable Offin's reason for making the arrest in somewhat emotive phraseology . . . as being "to subject her to the greater stress and pressure involved in arrest and deprivation of liberty in the belief that if she was going to confess she was more likely to do so in a state of arrest." Yet despite his use of the expressions "stress" and "pressure," the judge went on to find that the questioning to which Mrs Holgate-Mohammed was subjected at the police station was conducted with complete propriety. "There was not," he said, "any suggestion of verbal bullying at the police station or anything approaching it." Indeed, it would appear that Mrs Holgate-Mohammed's solicitor, who had been sent for at her request, was present for part of the time at least and made no complaint of the arrest or the nature of the questioning or the length of time for which she was being detained.

So, applying *Wednesbury* principles, the question of law to be decided by your Lordships may be identified as this: "Was it a matter that Detective Constable Offin should have excluded from his consideration as irrelevant to the exercise of his statutory power of arrest, that there was a greater likelihood (as he believed) that Mrs Holgate-Mohammed would respond truthfully to questions about her connection with or knowledge of the burglary, if she were questioned under arrest at the police station, than if, without arresting her, questions were put to her by Detective Constable Offin at her own home from which she could peremptorily order him to depart at any moment, since his right of entry under s.2(6) of the Criminal Law Act 1976, was dependent on his intention to arrest her?"

My Lords, there is inevitably the potentiality of conflict between the public interest in preserving the liberty of the individual and the public interest in the detection of crime and the bringing to justice of those who commit it. The members of the organised police forces of the country have, since the mid-19th century, been charged with the duty of taking the first steps to promote the latter public interest by inquiring into suspected offences with a view to identifying the perpetrators of them and of obtaining sufficient evidence admissible in a court of law against the persons they suspect of being the perpetrators as would justify charging them with the relevant offence before a magistrates' court with a view to their committal for trial for it . . .

That arrest for the purpose of using the period of detention to dispel or confirm the reasonable suspicion by questioning the suspect or seeking further evidence with his assistance was said by the Royal Commission on Criminal Procedure in England and Wales (1981) (Cmnd. 8092) at paragraph 3.66 "to be well established as one of the primary purposes of detention upon arrest." That is a fact that will be within the knowledge of those of your Lordships with judicial experience of trying criminal cases; even as long ago as I last did so, more than 20 years before the Royal Commission's Report. It is a practice which has been given implicit recognition in rule 1 of successive editions of the Judges' Rules, since they were first issued in 1912. Furthermore, parliamentary recognition that making inquiries of a suspect in order to dispel or confirm the reasonable suspicion is a legitimate cause for arrest and detention at a police station was implicit . . . in s.43(3) of the Magistrates' Courts Act 1980 . . . So whether or not to arrest Mrs Holgate-Mohammed and bring her to the police station in order to facilitate the inquiry into the case of the December burglary was a decision that it lay within the discretion of Detective Constable Offin to take.'

Comment

(1)   As well as an application for judicial review, the legality of the exercise of discretion can be questioned in civil proceedings for false imprisonment, assault, battery, malicious prosecution or as a defence to a charge of assaulting or wilfully obstructing a police constable in the execution of his duty. In *Plange* v *Chief Constable, South Humberside Police* the Court of Appeal ordered a re-trial of a claim for damages for false imprisonment on the basis that it would be in breach of the *Wednesbury* principles (as explained in *Holgate-Mohammed* v *Duke*) for a constable to arrest for an offence when knowing full well that there was no

possibility of a charge. The court said that it would be highly unlikely that a plaintiff would be able to establish that fact but that the plaintiff should be able to seek to do so.

(2) The Police and Criminal Evidence Act 1984 now governs the powers referred to by Lord Diplock. The Act provides extensive powers of arrest (ss.24 and 25 – see p.394) and detention. There is still an executive discretion, and arrest for an identified offence with a view to questioning is implicit in the Act and accompanying Codes of Practice which replaces the Judges' Rules. For cases on arrest, see p.399.

(3) Section 43(3), Magistrates' Courts Act 1980, which previously governed detention after arrest, has been repealed and replaced by Part IV, Police and Criminal Evidence Act 1984. This now permits detention for up to 96 hours in the most serious of cases, subject to periodic review and authorization by magistrates' courts. The 1984 Act clearly envisages that the period of detention after arrest will be used primarily for questioning.

(4) As to the extent of questioning *prior to arrest* and the relationship of that to the formulation of reasonable suspicion, see *Castorina* v *Chief Constable of Surrey*.

Hill v *Chief Constable of West Yorkshire*

[1989] AC 53 · House of Lords

The House of Lords was asked to decide whether the police in investigating the crimes of S (a serial killer) owed the last victim a duty of care for the purposes of the tort of negligence. It was held that there was no general duty of care owed to individual members of the public in the investigation of crime, and there were no special factors leading to a specific duty being owed to this victim.

Lord Templeman: ' . . . The question for determination in this appeal is whether an action for damages is an appropriate vehicle for investigating the efficiency of a police force. The present action will be confined to narrow albeit perplexing questions, for example whether, discounting hindsight, it should have been obvious to a senior police officer that Sutcliffe was a prime suspect, whether a senior police officer should not have been deceived by an evil hoaxer, whether an officer interviewing Sutcliffe should have been better briefed and whether a report on Sutcliffe should have been given greater attention. The court would have to consider the conduct of each police officer, to decide whether the policeman failed to attain the standard of care of a hypothetical average policeman. The court would have to decide whether an inspector is to be condemned for failing to display the acumen of Sherlock Holmes and whether a constable is to be condemned for being as obtuse as Dr Watson. The appellant will presumably seek evidence, for what it is worth, from retired police inspectors, who would be asked whether they would have been misled by the hoaxer and whether they would have identified Sutcliffe at an earlier stage. At the end of the day the court might or might not find that there had been negligence by one or more members of the police force. But that finding would not help anybody or punish anybody.

It may be, and we all hope that the lessons of the Yorkshire Ripper case have been learned, that the methods of handling information and handling the press have been improved, and that co-operation between different police officers is now more highly organised. The present action would not serve any useful purpose in that regard. The present action could not consider whether the training of the West Yorkshire police force is sufficiently thorough, whether the selection of candidates for appointment or promotion is defective, whether rates of pay are sufficient to attract recruits of the required calibre, whether financial restrictions prevent the provision of modern equipment and facilities or whether the Yorkshire police force is clever enough and, if not, what can and ought to be done about it. The present action could only investigate whether an individual member of the police force conscientiously carrying out his duty was negligent when he was bemused by contradictory information or overlooked significant information or failed to draw inferences which later appeared to be obvious. That kind of investigation would not achieve the object which the appellant desires. The efficiency of a police force can only be investigated by an inquiry instituted by the national or local authorities which are responsible to the electorate for that efficiency.

Moreover, if this action lies, every citizen will be able to require the court to investigate the performance of every policeman. If the policeman concentrates on one crime, he may be accused of neglecting others. If the policeman does not arrest on suspicion a suspect with previous convictions, the police force may be held liable for subsequent crimes. The threat of litigation against a police force would not make a policeman more efficient. The necessity of defending proceedings, successfully or unsuccessfully, would distract the policeman from his duties.

This action is in my opinion misconceived and will do more harm than good. A policeman is a servant of the public and is liable to be dismissed for incompetence. A police force serves the public, and the elected representatives of the public must ensure that the public get the police force they deserve. It may be that the West Yorkshire police force was in 1980 in some respects better and in some respects worse than the public deserve. An action for damages for alleged acts of negligence by individual police officers in 1980 could not determine whether and in what respects the West Yorkshire police force can be improved in 1988. I would dismiss the appeal.'

Comment

(1)   Any duty owed was a public law duty. The case was not a simple one where there could be identified a close link between victim, criminal and the police. Police officers may be liable in a range of torts, e.g. trespass to the person, and there may also be liability in negligence in an appropriate case, e.g. *Rigby* v *Chief Constable of Northamptonshire*, *Knightley* v *Johns*. *Hill* v *Chief Constable of West Yorkshire* was applied in *Alexandrou* v *Oxford*, *Osman* v *Ferguson*, and *Ancell* v *McDermott*.

(2)   See also *Hughes* v *NUM* where it was held that in organizing the deployment of forces at a scene of grave public disorder the senior police officers did not owe a duty of care to individual officers who came under attack from rioters. This decision was based upon public policy considerations. In *Knightley* v *Johns*, at the scene of a traffic accident there was found to be such a duty since there had been a failure to follow specific and narrowly defined standing orders.

(3)   In *R* v *Croydon JJ, ex parte Dean*, the defendant was told by the police that he would be a prosecution witness in a case of murder and was led by the police to believe that he would not be prosecuted for attempting to prevent the apprehension of the murderer. Subsequent prosecution of the defendant was held to be an abuse of process – see p.23.

17 Police powers

Parliament has made extensive inroads into the liberty of the citizen to be free from interference by the police with his personal or property rights; for example, the Police and Criminal Evidence Act 1984 provides a broad range of investigative powers. However, in reliance upon the principle in *Entick* v *Carrington*, the common law does intervene to prevent unauthorized interferences. The scope of a citizen's liberties or a police constable's powers may be tested in civil proceedings (e.g. an action in trespass to the person or land), in criminal proceedings (where the defence may suggest that the police officer had acted illegally), or in proceedings for judicial review. Such issues are frequently raised in connection with the offence of wilfully obstructing or assaulting a constable acting in the execution of his duty (e.g. *Lindley* v *Rutter*, p.371).

Section 51, Police Act 1964

(1) Any person who assaults a constable in the execution of his duty, or a person assisting a constable in the execution of his duty, shall be guilty of an offence . . .

(3) Any person who resists or wilfully obstructs a constable in the execution of his duty, or a person assisting a constable in the execution of his duty, shall be guilty of an offence . . .

Comment

The feature common to both subsections is that the police officer must be shown to have been acting in the execution of his duty. Even if it is shown that there was an assault or a wilful obstruction, should the police officer have gone outside the execution of his duty no offence contrary to s.51 will have been committed. A police officer who acts unlawfully towards the defendant will be acting outside the execution of his duty: see *Davis* v *Lisle*, p.388, *Collins* v *Wilcock*, p.383, and *Lindley* v *Rutter*, p.371.

The police and personal liberty

Rice v *Connolly*

[1966] 2 QB 414 · Divisional Court

The defendant appeared to two constables to be acting suspiciously in an area where there had been several burglaries. The constables approached the defendant and questioned him about his presence on the street and asked him his name and address. Eventually the defendant replied 'Rice, Convamore Road' (which was true). He refused to give his full name and address or to accompany the police officers to a police box. He was arrested, taken to the police box and questioned. He was subsequently charged with wilfully obstructing the police officers in the execution of their duty. The obstruction was alleged to be the refusal to answer police questions. The Court upheld his appeal against conviction.

Lord Parker CJ: 'What the prosecution have to prove is that there was an obstructing of a constable; that the constable was at the time acting in the execution of his duty and that the person obstructing did so wilfully. To carry the matter a little further, it is in my view clear that "obstruct" under s.51(3) of the Police Act, 1964, is the doing of any act which makes it more difficult for the police to carry out their duty . . . It is also in my judgment clear that it is part of the obligations and duties of a police constable to take all steps which appear to him necessary for keeping the peace, for preventing crime or for protecting property from criminal injury. There is no exhaustive definition of the powers and obligations of the police, but they are at least those, and they would further include the duty to detect crime and to bring an offender to justice.

Pausing there, it seems to me quite clear that the defendant was making it more difficult for the police to carry out their duties, and that the police at the time and throughout were acting in accordance with their duties. The only remaining ingredient, and the one upon which in my judgment this case revolves, is whether the obstructing of which the defendant was guilty was a wilful obstruction. "Wilful" in this context not only in my judgment means "intentional" but something which is done without lawful excuse, and that indeed is conceded by [counsel] for the prosecution . . . Accordingly, the sole question here is whether the defendant had a lawful excuse for refusing to answer the questions put to him. In my judgment he had. It seems to me quite clear that though every citizen has a moral duty or, if you like, a social duty to assist the police, there is no legal duty to that effect, and indeed the whole basis of the common law is the right of the individual to refuse to answer questions put to him by persons in authority, and to refuse to accompany those in authority to any particular place; short, of course, of arrest.

[Counsel] has pointed out that it is undoubtedly an obstruction, and has been so held, for a person questioned by the police to tell a "cock-and-bull" story; to put the police off by giving them false information, and I think he would say: well, what is the real distinction? It is a very little way from giving false information to giving no information at all. If that does in fact make it more difficult for the police to carry out their duties, then there is a wilful obstruction.

In my judgment there is all the difference in the world between deliberately telling a false story – something which on no view a citizen has a right to do – and preserving silence or refusing to answer – something which he has every right to do. Accordingly, in my judgment, looked upon in that perfectly general way, it was not shown that the refusal of the defendant to answer the questions or to accompany the police officer in the first instance to the police box was an obstruction without lawful excuse . . .'

Comment

(1)   The police officer had not infringed the respondent's rights by merely asking questions. Contrast the actions of the constable in *Collins* v *Wilcock*, p.383. For the limited powers to stop and search a suspect see, for example, ss.1–4, Police and Criminal Evidence Act 1984 and s.23, Misuse of Drugs Act 1971.

(2)   There were conflicting *dicta* concerning the manner of refusal to cooperate. James J said: '. . . I would not go so far as to say that there may not be circumstances in which the manner of a person together with his silence could amount to an obstruction within the section'. But Marshall J said: 'In order to uphold this conviction it appears to me that one has to assent to the proposition that where a citizen is acting merely within his legal rights, he is thereby committing a criminal offence. Nor can I see that the manner in which he does it can make any difference whatsoever.' For a case which James J preferred, see *Ricketts* v *Cox*. The manner of the citizen's refusal to cooperate may amount to an offence under s.4 or s.5 of the Public Order Act 1986 – see *DPP* v *Orum*, p.429.

(3)   Advising a person to remain silent will not be a s.51 offence unless the conduct goes beyond what is reasonable and amounts to conduct which interferes with the police asking questions. See *Green* v *DPP*, which appears to be an application of *Ricketts* v *Cox*.

(4)   The duties of police officers were stated by the Court in very general terms and do not describe the scope of the powers of a police officer. The police officer did not need a power to question Mr Rice since there is nothing unlawful about one citizen questioning another. The right of the citizen is to decline to answer; he cannot be compelled to provide evidence against himself (unless there is a specific legal requirement to answer in certain instances, e.g. in connection with road traffic matters or withholding information about acts of terrorism). This right to silence exists both before and after arrest; the Police and Criminal Evidence Act 1984 creates safeguards to remind the citizen and the police of this right. Police questioning during detention is permitted within limits by the Police and Criminal Evidence Act 1984 – see *Holgate-Mohammed* v *Duke*, p.373.

A court may now draw whatever inference it considers appropriate from a failure in certain circumstances to mention facts later relied upon, or from a failure to explain various matters when requested to do so by the police. See Criminal Justice and Public Order Act 1994, ss.34–38. It should be noted that a person's right to silence is a fundamental right recognized as part of the rights protected by art.6 ECHR (see p.138).

(5) There is no power to arrest for a s.51 wilful obstruction unless there is a reasonable apprehension of a breach of the peace – see *Gelberg* v *Miller, Wershoff* v *Metropolitan Police Commissioner*; but see also the general power of arrest in s.25, Police and Criminal Evidence Act 1984.

Lewis v Cox

[1984] 3 WLR 875 · Divisional Court

The defendant's friend, Marsh, had been arrested and placed in a police vehicle. The defendant opened the door and asked Marsh where he was being taken. A police officer warned him about his conduct but the defendant opened the door a second time. The defendant was then arrested and charged with wilfully obstructing the police officer in the execution of his duty. The magistrates acquitted the defendant. The Court allowed the appeal by the prosecutor and remitted the case to the magistrates with a direction to convict. The motive of the defendant in interfering with the police officer was irrelevant.

Kerr LJ: '... The act must not only have been done deliberately, but with the knowledge and intention that it will have this obstructive effect. But in the absence of a lawful excuse, the defendant's purpose or reason for doing the act is irrelevant, whether this be directly hostile to, or "aimed at", the police, or whether he has some other purpose or reason. Indeed, in the majority of cases the intention to obstruct the police will not be simply "anti-police", but will stem from some underlying reason or objective of the defendant which he can only achieve by an act of intentional obstruction. This may be to assist an offender, which could be termed "hostile" to the police. Equally, the motivation could be public-spirited, for instance, by intervening on behalf of someone whom the defendant believes to be innocent, as in *Hills* v *Ellis*. Or it may be for some neutral reason, for instance because the defendant considers that something else should have a higher priority than the duty on which the police officer is immediately engaged. In all such cases, if the defendant intentionally does an act which he realises will, in fact, have the effect of obstructing the police in the sense defined above, he will in my view be guilty of having done so "wilfully", with the necessary *mens rea*. In the absence of a lawful excuse, the defendant's underlying intention, reason or purpose for intentionally obstructing the police is irrelevant, because the intention to obstruct is present at the same time.'

Comment

(1) The defendant might have been prosecuted successfully for an offence contrary to s.5, Public Order Act 1986; see p.419.

(2) There was no power of arrest (see above) unless there was a reasonable apprehension of a breach of the peace or unless s.25, Police and Criminal Evidence Act 1984 applied, p.394.

(3) In *Hills* v *Ellis*, the defendant had intervened in the lawful arrest of a person he believed was the victim of an assault, rather than the perpetrator, by taking hold of

the arresting police officer. This was held to be a wilful obstruction contrary to s.51(3), the absence of hostile motive was irrelevant. McCullough J:

> Hostility suggests emotion and motive, but motive and emotion are alike irrelevant in criminal law. What matters is intention, that is what state of affairs the defendant intended to bring about. What motive he had while so intending is irrelevant.
>
> What is meant by 'an intention to obstruct?' I would construe 'wilfully obstructs' as doing deliberate actions with the intention of bringing about a state of affairs which, objectively regarded, amount to an obstruction . . . i.e. is, making it more difficult for the police to carry out their duty. The fact that the defendant might not himself have called that state of affairs an obstruction is, to my mind, immaterial. This is not to say that it is enough to do deliberate actions which, in fact, obstruct; there must be an intention that those actions should result in the further state of affairs to which I have been referring.

(4)   In *Hills* v *Ellis*, if the arrest had been unlawful then the police officer would have been acting outside the execution of his duty.

(5)   *Blackburn* v *Bowering* concerned the offence of assaulting an officer of the court in the execution of his duty, contrary to s.149(1)(b), County Courts Act 1984. The Court of Appeal held, *obiter*, that it was a defence to a charge under s.51(1), Police Act 1964 that the defendant had a mistaken but genuine, even if unreasonable, belief that the person against whom force was used was not a police officer and that no more than reasonable force in self-defence had been used.

Collins v *Wilcock*

[1984] 1 WLR 1172 · Divisional Court

The police had developed a system of cautioning women suspected of soliciting for the purposes of prostitution. After two such cautions a woman was likely to be charged under the Sexual Offences Act 1959 and the cautions admitted as evidence of her character. The system was not statutory or provided for by the common law but was recognized by the Act which permitted application to a court for removal of a caution. The defendant, D, and another woman, who was a known prostitute, were suspected of soliciting men for the purposes of prostitution. D refused to be questioned by the police officers and began to walk away. In order to obtain information which would allow her to caution D, a woman police officer followed her and asked questions but D refused to cooperate. The police officer took D by the arm but D reacted violently. D was arrested and charged with assaulting a constable in the execution of her duty. The Divisional Court upheld D's appeal against conviction on the basis that there was an unjustified detention by the police officer which had taken her outside the execution of her duty and that the Sexual Offences Act 1959 did not authorize detention.

Goff LJ: '. . . we think it important to observe that in this case it is found as a fact that the police officer took hold of the defendant by the left arm to restrain her. Before considering the question as drawn, we think it right to consider whether, on the facts found in the case, the magistrate could properly hold that the police officer was acting in the execution of her duty. In order to consider this question, it is desirable that we should expose the underlying principles.

The law draws a distinction, in terms more easily understood by philologists than by ordinary citizens, between an assault and a battery. An assault is an act which causes another person to apprehend the infliction of immediate, unlawful, force on his person; a battery is the actual infliction of unlawful force on another person. Both assault and battery are forms of trespass to the person. Another form of trespass to the person is false imprisonment, which is the unlawful imposition of constraint upon another's freedom of movement from a particular place. The requisite mental element is of no relevance in the present case.

We are here concerned primarily with battery. The fundamental principle, plain and incontestable, is that every person's body is inviolate. It has long been established that any touching of another person, however slight, may amount to a battery. So Holt CJ held in *Cole* v *Turner* that "the least touching of another in anger is a battery." The breadth of the principle reflects the fundamental nature of the interest so protected . . . The effect is that everybody is protected not only against physical injury but against any form of physical molestation.

But so widely drawn a principle must inevitably be subject to exceptions. For example, children may be subjected to reasonable punishment; people may be subjected to the lawful exercise of the power of arrest; and reasonable force may be used in self-defence or for the prevention of crime. But, apart from these special instances where the control or constraint is lawful, a broader exception has been created to allow for the exigencies of everyday life. Generally speaking, consent is a defence to battery; and most of the physical contacts of ordinary life are not actionable because they are impliedly consented to by all who move in society and so expose themselves to the risk of bodily contact. So nobody can complain of the jostling which is inevitable from his presence in, for example, a supermarket, an underground station or a busy street; nor can a person who attends a party complain if his hand is seized in friendship, or even if his back is, within reason, slapped . . . Although such cases are regarded as examples of implied consent, it is more common nowadays to treat them as falling within a general exception embracing all physical contact which is generally acceptable in the ordinary conduct of daily life. We observe that, although in the past it has sometimes been stated that a battery is only committed where the action is "angry, revengeful, rude, or insolent". . . we think that nowadays it is more realistic, and indeed more accurate, to state the broad underlying principle, subject to the broad exception.

Among such forms of conduct, long held to be acceptable, is touching a person for the purpose of engaging his attention, though of course using no greater degree of physical contact than is reasonably necessary in the circumstances for that purpose . . . But a distinction is drawn between a touch to draw a man's attention, which is generally acceptable, and a physical restraint, which is not . . . Furthermore, persistent touching to gain attention in the face of obvious disregard may transcend the norms of acceptable behaviour, and so be outside the exception. We do not say that more than one touch is never permitted; for example, the lost or distressed may surely be permitted a second touch, or possibly even more, on a reluctant or impervious sleeve or shoulder, as may a person who is acting reasonably in the exercise of a duty. In each case, the test must be whether the physical contact so persisted in has in the circumstances gone beyond generally acceptable standards of conduct; and the answer to that question will depend upon the facts of the particular case.

The distinction . . . is of importance in the case of police officers. Of course, a police officer may subject another to restraint when he lawfully exercises his power of arrest; and he has other statutory powers . . . with which we are not concerned. But, putting such cases aside, police officers have for present purposes no greater rights than ordinary citizens. It follows that, subject to such case, physical contact by a police officer with another person may be unlawful as a battery, just as it might be if he was an ordinary member of the public. But a police officer has his rights as a citizen, as well as his duties as a policeman. A police officer may wish to engage a man's attention, for example if he wishes to question him. If he lays his hand on the man's sleeve or taps his shoulder for that purpose, he commits no wrong. He may even do so more than once; for he is under a duty to prevent and investigate crime, and so his seeking further, in the exercise of that duty, to engage a man's attention in order to speak to him may in the circumstances be regarded as acceptable: see *Donnelly* v *Jackman*. But if, taking into account the nature of his duty, his use of physical contact in the face of non-co-operation persists beyond generally acceptable standards of conduct, his action will become unlawful; and if a police officer restrains a man, for example by gripping his arm or his shoulder, then his action will also be unlawful, unless he is lawfully exercising his power of arrest. A police officer has no power to require a man to answer him, though he has the advantage of authority, enhanced as it is by the uniform which the state provides and requires him to wear, in seeking a response to his inquiry. What is not permitted, however, is the unlawful use of force or the unlawful threat, actual or implicit, to use force; and, excepting the lawful exercise of his power of arrest, the lawfulness of a police officer's conduct is judged by the same criteria as are applied to the conduct of any ordinary citizen of this country.

We have been referred by counsel to certain cases directly concerned with charges of assaulting a police officer in the execution of his duty, the crucial question in each case being whether the police officer, by using physical force on the accused in response to which the accused assaulted the police officer, was acting unlawfully and so not acting in the execution of his duty. In *Kenlin* v *Gardiner*, it was held that action by police officers in catching hold of two schoolboys was performed not in the course of arresting them but for the purpose of detaining them for questioning and so was unlawful . . . Similarly, in *Ludlow* v *Burgess*, it was held that "this was not a mere case of putting a hand on [the defendant's] shoulder, but it resulted in the detention of [the defendant] against his will," so that the police officer's act was "unlawful and a serious interference with the citizen's liberty" and could not be an act performed by him in the execution of his duty: see *per* Lord Parker CJ.

In *Donnelly* v *Jackman*, the police officer wished to question the defendant about an offence which he had cause to believe that the defendant had committed. Repeated requests by the police officer to the defendant to stop and speak to him were ignored. The officer tapped him on the shoulder; he made it plain that he had no intention of stopping to speak to him. The officer persisted and again tapped the defendant on the shoulder, whereupon the defendant turned and struck him with some force. The justices convicted the defendant of assaulting the officer in the execution of his duty, and this court dismissed an appeal from that conviction by way of case stated. The court was satisfied that the officer had not detained the defendant, distinguishing . . . *Kenlin* v *Gardiner* as a case where the officers had in fact "detained" the boys. It appears that they must have considered that the justices were entitled to conclude that the action of the officer, in persistently tapping the defendant on the shoulder, did not in the circumstances of the case exceed the bounds of acceptable conduct, despite the fact that the defendant had made it clear that he did not intend to respond to the officer's request to stop and speak to him; we cannot help feeling that this is an extreme case.

Finally, in *Bentley* v *Brudzinski*, it was found by the justices . . . that the police officer, having caught up with the defendant, said "Just a minute"; then, not in any hostile way but merely to attract attention, he placed his right hand on the defendant's left shoulder. The defendant then swore at the police officer and punched him in the face; and a struggle ensued. The justices considered that the act of the police officer amounted to an unlawful attempt to stop and detain the defendant, and so dismissed any information against the defendant alleging that he assaulted the police officer in the execution of his duty. This court dismissed the prosecutor's appeal by way of case stated; it appears that they considered that, having regard to all the facts of the case as found by the justices, they were entitled to hold that the police officer's act was performed not merely to engage the attention of the defendant, but as part of a course of conduct in which the officer was attempting unlawfully to detain the defendant . . .

[The prosecution] submitted that the purpose of the police officer was simply to carry out the cautioning procedure and that, having regard to her purpose, her action could not be regarded as unlawful. Again, we cannot accept that submission. If the physical contact went beyond what is allowed by law, the mere fact that the police officer had the laudable intention of carrying out the cautioning procedure in accordance with established practice cannot . . . have the effect of rendering her action lawful . . .

The fact is that the [constable] took hold of the defendant by the left arm to restrain her. In so acting, she was not proceeding to arrest the defendant; and since her action went beyond the generally acceptable conduct of touching a person to engage his or her attention, it must follow, in our judgment, that her action constituted a battery on the defendant, and was therefore unlawful. It follows that the defendant's appeal must be allowed, and her conviction quashed . . .

Furthermore, the word "detaining" can be used in more than one sense. For example, it is a commonplace of ordinary life that one person may request another to stop and speak to him; if the latter complies with the request, he may be said to do so willingly or unwillingly, and in either event the first person may be said to be "stopping and detaining" the latter. There is nothing unlawful in such an act. If a police officer so "stops and detains" another person, he in our opinion commits no unlawful act, despite the fact that his uniform may give his request a certain authority and so render it more likely to be complied with. But if a police officer, not exercising his power of arrest, nevertheless reinforces his request with the actual use of force, or with the threat, actual or implicit, to use force if the other person does not comply, then his act in thereby detaining the other person will be unlawful. In the former event, his action will constitute a battery; in the latter event, detention of the other person will amount to false imprisonment. Whether the action of a police officer in any particular case is to be regarded as lawful or unlawful must be a question to be decided on the facts of the case.'

Comment

(1)   In *Donnelly* v *Jackman* Talbot J said:

> When one considers the problem: was this officer acting in the course of his duty, one ought to bear in mind that it is not every trivial interference with a citizen's liberty that amounts to a course of conduct sufficient to take the officer out of the course of his duties.

(2)   The test adopted in *Collins* v *Wilcock* was approved by Lord Goff in the House of Lords in *F* v *West Berkshire Area Health Authority*.

Police and entry to premises

An occupier of land may grant either an express or an implied licence to a person to enter his land. Areas such as the front drive of a house offer to those who have lawful business at the house an implied licence to approach the house – see *Davis* v *Lisle*, p.388, *Robson* v *Hallett* and *Halliday* v *Nevill*. *Entick* v *Carrington* emphasizes rights in property both real and personal. But, these rights are not absolute, and are subject to statutory interference. In *McLorie* v *Oxford* it was said: 'That an Englishman's home is his castle is one of the few principles of law known to every citizen and was affirmed as early as 1604 in *Semayne's* case . . . and reaffirmed as recently as 1980 in *Morris* v *Beardmore*. The rule is of course subject to exceptions, but they are few and it is for the police to justify a forcible entry.' The principle has been breached extensively and the scope of powers of entry and search afforded to 'officialdom', e.g. the Inland Revenue, arguably is far broader than the scope of police powers.

Although the common law grants extensive powers to enter premises to deal with breaches of the peace (see p.409) the remainder of the powers available to the police and agencies are now matters of statute, for example see Police and Criminal Evidence Act 1984, p.392. The role of the Courts thus becomes one of interpretation – see *R* v *IRC, ex parte Rossminster*, p.11, and *Morris* v *Beardmore*, p.389. The Courts may well draw a distinction between the sanctity of the home and that of business premises, and offer greater protection to the home. Parliament has recognized that certain confidential professional matters are to be granted special protection against searches – see the special procedure and excluded material provisions of the Police and Criminal Evidence Act 1984, ss.8–16.

Davis v *Lisle*

[1936] 2 KB 434 · Divisional Court

Police officers saw a vehicle in the street outside garage premises; the vehicle was moved into the garage and the police officers went into the garage and began to ask questions. The defendant garage owner then came into the premises and ordered the police officers to leave. One of the police officers tried to produce his warrant card and the defendant used force to eject him. The defendant was prosecuted for assaulting a constable in the execution of his duty and with wilful damage to the police officer's tunic. The defendant's appeal to the Divisional Court was upheld and the conviction was quashed since the police officers had become trespassers when they had failed to leave and had therefore ceased to be acting in the execution of their duty.

Lord Hewart CJ: 'It is necessary, I think, to distinguish two things. Whether these officers at the material time were acting in the execution of their duty is one question and it is quite a different question whether that which the appellant did was justified by the view which he took that the officers were trespassers . . . It may well be that it may have to be determined hereafter. The point which is raised here with regard to the appellant's first two convictions is whether the officers were at the material time acting in the execution of their duty. In my opinion, they were not, and there are no grounds on which they can be held to have been so acting. The only ground which is put forward in support of the contention that they were so acting seems to me to be quite beside the point. I feel a difficulty in envisaging the legal proposition that because the police officers had witnessed an offence being committed on the highway they were acting in the execution of their duty in entering and remaining on private premises because the offenders then were on those premises. Admittedly, the officers had no warrant entitling them to search the premises. It is one thing to say that the officers were at liberty to enter this garage to make an enquiry, but quite a different thing to say that they were entitled to remain when, not without emphasis, the appellant had said: "Get outside. You cannot come here without a search warrant." From that moment on, while the officers remained where they were, it seems to me that they were trespassers and it is quite clear that the act which the respondent was doing immediately before the assault complained of was tantamount to putting forward a claim as of right to remain where he was. The respondent was in the act of producing his warrant card. That was after the emphatic order to "get out" had been made. [Counsel] . . . has admitted that, if the finding in the case that the respondent was in the act of producing his warrant card is fairly to be construed as meaning that he was asserting his right to remain on the premises, it is not possible to contend that at that moment the respondent was acting in the execution of his duty. I think it is quite clear that the act of producing his warrant card constituted the making of such a claim. I cannot think that there is any ambiguity about it . . .

In my opinion, it is not possible to maintain the conclusion that at the material time the respondent was acting in the execution of his duty as a constable. But that conclusion by no means disposes of everything contained in this case. It does not dispose of the question whether the assault which was in fact committed was justified. We have not the materials before us which would enable us to determine that question. Nor was the appellant prosecuted for assault. He was prosecuted for assaulting and obstructing a police officer in the execution of his duty. Furthermore, the conclusion to which I have come does not affect the third conviction – that of damaging a tunic by "wilfully and maliciously tearing" it. On that part of the case no question arises whether at that moment the officer was acting in the execution of his duty and I see no reason why we should interfere with that conviction.'

Comment

(1) In *Halliday* v *Nevill* the High Court of Australia said:

> Nor . . . will the implied licence ordinarily be restricted to presence on the open driveway or path for the purpose of going to the entrance of the house. A passer-by is not a trespasser if, on passing an open driveway with no indication that entry is forbidden or unauthorised, he or she steps upon it either unintentionally or to avoid an obstruction such as a vehicle parked across the footpath. Nor will a passer-by be a trespasser if, for example, he or she goes upon the driveway to recover some item of his or her property which has fallen or blown upon it or to lead away an errant child. To adapt the words of Lord Parker in *Robson* v *Hallett*, the law is not such an ass that the implied or tacit licence in such a case is restricted to stepping over the item of property or around the child for the purpose of going to the entrance and asking the householder whether the item of property can be reclaimed or the child led away. The path or driveway is, in such circumstances, held out by the occupier as the bridge between the public thoroughfare and his or her private dwelling upon which a passer-by may go for a legitimate purpose that in itself involves no interference with the occupier's possession nor injury to the occupier, his or her guests or his, her or their property.

(2) The occupier who wishes to keep out everyone or specific groups must display a prominent notice to that effect. For the requirements of revocation of express or implied licence, see *Snook* v *Mannion* where the use of foul and abusive language was held, on the facts, to be insufficient to indicate an unequivocal statement that the police officers should leave.

(3) In *Robson* v *Hallett*, Diplock LJ made it clear that a police officer does not become a trespasser immediately upon revocation of a licence. A person who leaves expeditiously and by a reasonable route will not be a trespasser. The constable in that situation will therefore remain within the execution of his duty. A police officer whose licence is revoked must be able to point to the exercise of some power to justify remaining. In order to exercise such a power the officer need not leave the premises and re-enter – see *Robson* v *Hallet*.

Morris v Beardmore

[1981] AC 446 · House of Lords

The House of Lords considered whether the Road Traffic Act permitted a police officer to remain on or enter premises once a licence had been revoked, and whether in such a case a request for a sample of breath would nonetheless be lawful. The House of Lords refused to imply such terms into the legislation.

Lord Diplock: '. . . s.8(2) contains no express provision prohibiting a constable from requiring a person to undergo a breath test when the constable is only able to communicate the requirement to that person as a result of his violation of that person's common law right to prevent other persons from entering or remaining on his property without his permission. But, with respect, the boot is on the other leg; if Parliament intends to authorise the doing of an act which would constitute a tort actionable at the suit of the person to whom the act is done, this requires express provision in the statute . . . The presumption is that in the absence of express provision to the contrary Parliament did not intend to authorise tortious conduct; and this presumption . . . owes nothing to the European Convention on Human Rights . . .

I have considered whether, even if it must be accepted in accordance with this presumption that Parliament did not "authorise" a constable to enter a person's home against his will in order to require him to take a breath test, it nevertheless intended the requirement made in such circumstances to be a lawful one; so that non-compliance with it would constitute a criminal offence, leaving as the sole remedy for the unlawful conduct of the constable a civil action for tort against him . . .

[I]f this be right it must apply not only to comparatively venial trespasses such as that committed in the instant case, but also to cases where entry to the private house of the person sought to be breathalysed has been obtained by the police by forcing doors or windows or overcoming reasonable force lawfully exerted by that person or on his behalf to remove them from the premises. I find it quite impossible to suppose that Parliament intended that a person whose common law right to keep his home free from unauthorised intruders had been violated in this way should be bound under penal sanctions to comply with a demand which only the violation of that common law right had enabled the constable to make to him . . .'

Lord Scarman: '. . . Had Parliament intended to empower a policeman to enter or remain on the private premises of a suspect against his will . . . Parliament could . . . have included in the relevant legislation an express power or right of entry. But in s.8 . . . Parliament has not done so; and it is not the task of the judges, exercising their ingenuity in the field of implication, to go further in the invasion of fundamental private rights and liberties than Parliament has expressly authorised . . . When one compares, as one must, the silence of Parliament in this section with the elaborate provisions and safeguards enacted for breach of private premises and seizure of evidence in [*R v IRC, ex parte Rossminster* and *Re Racal Communications*] . . . it becomes inconceivable that Parliament in its breathalyser legislation could have authorised, by implication, the entry into a private suspect's house, against his will and . . . at a time when, according to the cherished principle of English criminal law, the suspect was entitled to be presumed innocent . . . I have deliberately used an adjective which has an unfamiliar ring in the ears of common lawyers. I have described the right of privacy as "fundamental". I do so for two reasons. First, it is apt to describe the importance attached by the common law to the privacy of the home. It is still true, as was said by Lord Camden CJ in *Entick* v *Carrington* that: "No man can set his foot upon my ground without my licence, but he is liable to an action, though the damage be nothing . . . if he admits the fact, he is bound to shew by way of justification, that some positive law has empowered or excused him."

Second, the right enjoys the protection of the European Convention for the Protection of Human Rights and Fundamental Freedoms . . .'

Swales v *Cox*

[1981] 1 QB 849 · Divisional Court

Police reasonably suspected C of having committed an arrestable offence and followed him to the house of the respondent. For a brief period C prevented the police from opening the door. When the police opened the door the respondent, S, physically obstructed the police when they tried to move towards C and at one stage held on to the police officers who had seized C. S was charged with wilfully obstructing the police constables in the execution of their duty. There was a power of arrest under s.2 of the Criminal Law Act 1967 and s.2(6) provided that: 'For the purposes of arresting a person . . . a constable may enter (if need be, by force) and search any place where that person is . . .' The Court held that turning the handle of the door was the use of force and that it had to be justified by reference to necessity, and that normally there would be no necessity in the absence of a prior request to be permitted to enter. Accordingly, although the police had a power of arrest, they had not properly exercised their power of entry.

Donaldson LJ: '. . . First of all, let me define what I think is meant by "force." In the context of outside premises of course there is no problem about force unless there is a gate or something of that sort. The constable simply enters the place and is authorised to do so by s.2(6). But if he meets an obstacle, then he uses force if he applies any energy to the obstacle with a view to removing it. It would follow that, if my view is correct, where there is a door which is ajar but is insufficiently ajar for someone to go through the opening without moving the door and energy is applied to that door to make it open further, force is being used. *A fortiori* force is used when the door is latched and you turn the handle from the outside and then ease the door open. Similarly, if someone opens any window or increases the opening in any window, or indeed dislodges the window by the application of any energy, he is using force to enter, and in all those cases a constable will have to justify the use of force.

The first hurdle which he will have to overcome in justifying force will be by providing an answer to the question: "Why did you not ask to be allowed in?" That "an Englishman's home is his castle" is perhaps a trite expression, but it has immense importance in the history of this country, and it still has immense importance. Anybody who seeks to enter by force has a very severe burden to displace. There will undoubtedly be cases where it can be displaced. One has only to think of the cases which occasionally do arise today where a criminal is at large and the public, for example, are warned not to approach him because he is known to be a very dangerous man. If a constable is following such a man into premises, it may be essential for his own protection that he shall give no warning of his approach by asking the leave of the criminal to enter the premises. That of course is an extreme case, and there will be all sorts of other circumstances in between.

For my part, I think it would be wholly wrong to add to the provisions of the statute. The statute says that force can be used "if need be". All I am saying is that those words are of immense weight and importance, and if the question arises of "Was it necessary?" the constable will have to prove that it really was necessary before he will be able to justify an entry by force in the sense in which I have indicated . . .'

Comment

Section 117, Police and Criminal Evidence Act 1984 now governs the use of force for the purposes of, *inter alia*, entry, and s.24 provides the power of arrest for arrestable offences.

Police and Criminal Evidence Act 1984

17. (1) Subject to the following provisions of this section . . . a constable may enter and search any premises for the purpose—
    (a) of executing—
        (i) a warrant of arrest issued in connection with or arising out of criminal proceedings; or
        (ii) a warrant of commitment issued under section 76 of the Magistrates' Courts Act 1980;
    (b) of arresting a person for an arrestable offence;
    (c) of arresting a person for an offence under—
        (i) section 1 . . . of the Public Order Act 1936;
        (ii) any enactment contained in sections 6 to 8 or 10 of the Criminal Law Act 1977 . . .;
        (iii) section 4 of the Public Order Act 1986 . . .
    (d) of recapturing a person who is unlawfully at large and whom he is pursuing; or
    (e) of saving life or limb or preventing serious damage to property.
    (2) Except for the purpose specified in paragraph (e) of subsection (1) above, the powers of entry and search conferred by this section—
    (a) are only exercisable if the constable has reasonable grounds for believing that the person whom he is seeking is on the premises; and
    (b) are limited, in relation to premises consisting of two or more separate dwellings, to powers to enter and search—
        (i) any parts of the premises which the occupiers of any dwelling comprised in the premises use in common with the occupiers of any other such dwelling; and
        (ii) any such dwelling in which the constable has reasonable grounds for believing that the person whom he is seeking may be.
    (3) The powers of entry and search conferred by this section are only exercisable for the purposes specified in subsection (1)(c)(ii) above by a constable in uniform.
    (4) The power of search conferred by this section is only a power to search to the extent that is reasonably required for the purpose for which the power of entry is exercised.
    (5) Subject to subsection (6) below, all the rules of common law under which a constable has power to enter premises without a warrant are hereby abolished.

(6) Nothing in subsection (5) above affects any power of entry to deal with or prevent a breach of the peace.

18. (1) Subject to the following provisions of this section, a constable may enter and search any premises occupied or controlled by a person who is under arrest for an arrestable offence, if he has reasonable grounds for suspecting that there is on the premises evidence, other than items subject to legal privilege, that relates—
    (a) to that offence; or
    (b) to some other arrestable offence which is connected with or similar to that offence.

   (2) A constable may seize and retain anything for which he may search under subsection (1) above.

   (3) The power to search conferred by subsection (1) above is only a power to search to the extent that is reasonably required for the purpose of discovering such evidence.

   (4) Subject to subsection (5) below, the powers conferred by this section may not be exercised unless an officer of the rank of inspector or above has authorised them in writing.

   (5) A constable may conduct a search under subsection (1) above—
    (a) before taking the person to a police station; and
    (b) without obtaining an authorisation under subsection (4) above,
    if the presence of that person at a place other than a police station is necessary for the effective investigation of the offence.

   (6) If a constable conducts a search by virtue of subsection (5) above, he shall inform an officer of the rank of inspector or above that he has made the search as soon as practicable after he has made it . . .

19. (1) The powers conferred by subsections (2), (3) and (4) below are exercisable by a constable who is lawfully on any premises.

   (2) The constable may seize anything which is on the premises if he has reasonable grounds for believing—
    (a) that it has been obtained in consequence of the commission of an offence; and
    (b) that it is necessary to seize it in order to prevent it being concealed, lost, damaged, altered or destroyed.

   (3) The constable may seize anything which is on the premises if he has reasonable grounds for believing—
    (a) that it is evidence in relation to an offence which he is investigating or any other offence; and
    (b) that it is necessary to seize it in order to prevent the evidence being concealed, lost, altered or destroyed.

   (4) The constable may require any information which is contained in a computer and is accessible from the premises to be produced in a form in which it can be taken away and in which it is visible and legible if he has reasonable grounds for believing—
    (a) that—
        (i) it is evidence in relation to an offence which he is investigating or any other offence; or

    (ii) it has been obtained in consequence of the commission of an offence; and

  (b) that it is necessary to do so in order to prevent it being concealed, lost, tampered with or destroyed.

(5) The powers conferred by this section are in addition to any power otherwise conferred.

(6) No power of seizure conferred on a constable under any enactment (including an enactment contained in an Act passed after this Act) is to be taken to authorise the seizure of an item which the constable exercising the power has reasonable grounds for believing to be subject to legal privilege.

23. In this Act—

 'premises' includes any place and, in particular, includes—

  (a) any vehicle, vessel, aircraft or hovercraft;

  (b) any offshore installation; and

  (c) any tent or movable structure . . .

24. (1) The powers of summary arrest conferred by the following subsections shall apply—

  (a) to offences for which the sentence is fixed by law;

  (b) to offences for which a person of 21 years of age or over (not previously convicted) may be sentenced to imprisonment for a term of five years (or might be so sentenced but for the restrictions imposed by section 33 of the Magistrates' Courts Act 1980); and

  (c) to the offences to which subsection (2) below applies, and in this Act 'arrestable offence' means any such offence.

 (2) The offences to which this subsection applies are—

  (a) offences for which a person may be arrested under the customs and excise Acts, as defined in section 1(1) of the Customs and Excise Management Act 1979;

  (b) offences under the Official Secrets Acts 1911 and 1920 that are not arrestable offences by virtue of the term of imprisonment for which a person may be sentenced in respect of them;

  (c) offences under section . . . 22 (causing prostitution of women) or 23 (procuration of girl under 21) of the Sexual Offences Act 1956;

  (d) offences under section 12(1) (taking motor vehicle or other conveyance without authority etc.) or 25(1) (going equipped for stealing, etc.) of the Theft Act 1968; and

  (e) any offence under the Football (Offences) Act 1991;

  (f) an offence under s.2 of the Obscene Publications Act 1959 (publication of obscene matter);

  (g) an offence under s.1 of the Protection of Children Act 1978 (indecent photographs and pseudo-photographs of children);

  (h) an offence under s.165, Criminal Justice and Public Order Act 1994 (sale of tickets for designated football matches by unauthorised persons);

  (i) an offence under s.19 of the Public Order Act 1986 (publishing, etc. material intended or likely to stir up racial hatred).

(3) Without prejudice to section 2 of the Criminal Attempts Act 1981, the powers of summary arrest conferred by the following subsections shall also apply to the offences of—

    (a) conspiring to commit any of the offences mentioned in subsection (2) above;

    (b) attempting to commit any such offence [other than an offence under section 12(1) of the Theft Act 1968];

    (c) inciting, aiding, abetting, counselling or procuring the commission of any such offence;

and such offences are also arrestable offences for the purposes of this Act.

(4) Any person may arrest without a warrant—

    (a) anyone who is in the act of committing an arrestable offence;

    (b) anyone whom he has reasonable grounds for suspecting to be committing such an offence.

(5) Where an arrestable offence has been committed, any person may arrest without a warrant—

    (a) anyone who is guilty of the offence;

    (b) anyone whom he has reasonable grounds for suspecting to be guilty of it.

(6) Where a constable has reasonable grounds for suspecting that an arrestable offence has been committed, he may arrest without a warrant anyone whom he has reasonable grounds for suspecting to be guilty of the offence.

(7) A constable may arrest without a warrant—

    (a) anyone who is about to commit an arrestable offence;

    (b) anyone whom he has reasonable grounds for suspecting to be about to commit an arrestable offence.

25. (1) Where a constable has reasonable grounds for suspecting that any offence which is not an arrestable offence has been committed or attempted, or is being committed or attempted, he may arrest the relevant person if it appears to him that service of a summons is impracticable or inappropriate because any of the general arrest conditions is satisfied.

   (2) In this section 'the relevant person' means any person whom the constable has reasonable grounds to suspect of having committed or having attempted to commit the offence or of being in the course of committing or attempting to commit it.

   (3) The general arrest conditions are—

    (a) that the name of the relevant person is unknown to, and cannot be readily ascertained by, the constable;

    (b) that the constable has reasonable grounds for doubting whether a name furnished by the relevant person as his name is his real name;

    (c) that—

       (i) the relevant person has failed to furnish a satisfactory address for service; or

       (ii) the constable has reasonable grounds for doubting whether an address furnished by the relevant person is a satisfactory address for service;

      (d) that the constable has reasonable grounds for believing that arrest is necessary to prevent the relevant person—

         (i) causing physical injury to himself or any other person;

         (ii) suffering physical injury;

         (iii) causing loss of or damage to property;

         (iv) committing an offence against public decency; or

         (v) causing an unlawful obstruction of the highway;

      (e) that the constable has reasonable grounds for believing that arrest is necessary to protect a child or other vulnerable person from the relevant person.

(4) For the purposes of subsection (3) above an address is a satisfactory address for service if it appears to the constable—

      (a) that the relevant person will be at it for a sufficiently long period for it to be possible to serve him with a summons; or

      (b) that some other person specified by the relevant person will accept service of a summons for the relevant person at it.

(5) Nothing in subsection (3)(d) above authorises the arrest of a person under sub-paragraph (iv) of that paragraph except where members of the public going about their normal business cannot reasonably be expected to avoid the person to be arrested.

(6) This section shall not prejudice any power of arrest conferred apart from this section.

28. (1) Subject to subsection (5) below, where a person is arrested, otherwise than by being informed that he is under arrest, the arrest is not lawful unless the person arrested is informed that he is under arrest as soon as is practicable after his arrest.

(2) Where a person is arrested by a constable, subsection (1) above applies regardless of whether the fact of the arrest is obvious.

(3) Subject to subsection (5) below, no arrest is lawful unless the person arrested is informed of the ground for the arrest at the time of, or as soon as is practicable after, the arrest.

(4) Where a person is arrested by a constable, subsection (3) above applies regardless of whether the ground for the arrest is obvious.

(5) Nothing in this section is to be taken to require a person to be informed—

      (a) that he is under arrest; or

      (b) of the ground for the arrest,

if it was not reasonably practicable for him to be so informed by reason of his having escaped from arrest before the information could be given.

30. (1) Subject to the following provisions of this section, where a person—

      (a) is arrested by a constable for an offence; or

      (b) is taken into custody by a constable after being arrested for an offence by a person other than a constable,

at any place other than a police station, he shall be taken to a police station by a constable as soon as practicable after the arrest.

(2) ... the police station to which an arrested person is taken under subsection (1) above shall be a designated police station ...

(7)   A person arrested by a constable at a place other than a police station shall be released if a constable is satisfied, before the person arrested reaches a police station, that there are no grounds for keeping him under arrest . . .

(10) Nothing in subsection (1) above shall prevent a constable delaying taking a person who has been arrested to a police station if the presence of that person elsewhere is necessary in order to carry out such investigations as it is reasonable to carry out immediately . . .

32. (1)   A constable may search an arrested person, in any case where the person to be searched has been arrested at a place other than a police station, if the constable has reasonable grounds for believing that the arrested person may present a danger to himself or others.

(2)   Subject to subsections (3) to (5) below, a constable shall also have power in any such case—

   (a) to search the arrested person for anything—
      (i) which he might use to assist him to escape from lawful custody; or
      (ii) which might be evidence relating to an offence; and
   (b) to enter and search any premises in which he was when arrested or immediately before he was arrested for evidence relating to the offence for which he has been arrested.

(3)   The power to search conferred by subsection (2) above is only a power to search to the extent that is reasonably required for the purpose of discovering any such thing or any such evidence.

(4)   The powers conferred by this section to search a person are not to be construed as authorising a constable to require a person to remove any of his clothing in public other than an outer coat, jacket or gloves.

(5)   A constable may not search a person in the exercise of the power conferred by subsection (2)(a) above unless he has reasonable grounds for believing that the person to be searched may have concealed on him anything for which a search is permitted under that paragraph.

(6)   A constable may not search premises in the exercise of the power conferred by subsection (2)(b) above unless he has reasonable grounds for believing that there is evidence for which a search is permitted under that paragraph on the premises.

(7)   In so far as the power of search conferred by subsection (2)(b) above relates to premises consisting of two or more separate dwellings, it is limited to a power to search–

   (a) any dwelling in which the arrest took place or in which the person arrested was immediately before his arrest; and
   (b) any parts of the premises which the occupier of any such dwelling uses in common with the occupiers of any other dwellings comprised in the premises.

(8)   A constable searching a person in the exercise of the power conferred by subsection (1) above may seize and retain anything he finds, if he has reasonable grounds for believing that the person searched might use it to cause physical injury to himself or to any other person.

(9) A constable searching a person in the exercise of the power conferred by subsection (2)(a) above may seize and retain anything he finds, other than an item subject to legal privilege, if he has reasonable grounds for believing—

(a) that he might use it to assist him to escape from lawful custody; or

(b) that it is evidence of an offence or has been obtained in consequence of the commission of an offence.

54. (1) The custody officer at a police station shall ascertain and record or cause to be recorded everything which a person has with him when he is—

(a) brought to the station after being arrested elsewhere or after being committed to custody by an order or sentence of a court; or

(b) arrested at the station or detained there under section 47(5) above.

(2) In the case of an arrested person the record shall be made as part of his custody record.

(3) Subject to subsection (4) below, a custody officer may seize and retain any such thing or cause any such thing to be seized and retained.

(4) Clothes and personal effects may only be seized if the custody officer—

(a) believes that the person from whom they are seized may use them—

(i) to cause physical injury to himself or any other person;

(ii) to damage property;

(iii) to interfere with evidence; or

(iv) to assist him to escape; or

(b) has reasonable grounds for believing that they may be evidence relating to an offence.

(5) Where anything is seized, the person from whom it is seized shall be told the reason for the seizure unless he is—

(a) violent or likely to become violent; or

(b) incapable of understanding what is said to him.

(6) Subject to subsection (7) below, a person may be searched if the custody officer considers it necessary to enable him to carry out his duty under subsection (1) above and to the extent that the custody officer considers necessary for that purpose.

(6A) A person who is in custody at a police station or is in police detention otherwise than at a police station may at any time be searched in order to ascertain whether he has with him anything which he could use for any of the purposes specified in subsection (4)(a) above.

(6B) Subject to subsection (6C) below, a constable may seize and retain, or cause to be seized and retained, anything found on such a search.

(6C) A constable may only seize clothes and personal effects in the circumstances specified in subsection (4) above.

(7) An intimate search may not be conducted under this section.

(8) A search under this section shall be carried out by a constable.

(9) The constable carrying out a search shall be of the same sex as the person searched.

117. Where any provision of this Act—

(a) confers a power on a constable; and

(b) does not provide that the power may only be exercised with the consent of some person, other than a police officer,

the officer may use reasonable force, if necessary, in the exercise of the power.

Comment

(1)   The Act is supplemented by Codes of Practice (revised April 1991) which indicate to the police and citizen how the powers should be exercised. The Act creates a statutory scheme in respect of the detention of arrested suspects and creates judicial checks and balances to keep the detention under review. The Act also provides extensive powers to stop and search suspects.

(2)   The means of redress for breaches of the Act may well be civil action, for example for false imprisonment or trespass to land, or a complaint under the police complaints procedure created under the Act. Often the real remedy for an individual lies in seeking the exclusion of evidence obtained in breach of the Act or Codes of Practice. See, in particular, the requirements in s.76 in respect of confessions and the discretion to exclude evidence under s.78.

(3)   The powers of arrest in s.24 are similar to earlier statute and common law – see *Walters* v *WH Smith & Son Ltd*, *Holgate-Mohammed* v *Duke*, p.373. A citizen who arrests under s.24(4)(a) or s.25(5) does so under some peril. If it transpires that an arrestable offence neither is being committed nor has been committed, then arrest will be unlawful. In *R* v *Self* the defendant to a charge of assault to escape lawful arrest was entitled to be acquitted where he was able to demonstrate that he had not stolen certain goods. Thus, the arrest by a citizen assisting a store detective was not a lawful arrest, and the force used by the defendant to resist it could not amount to resisting lawful arrest. Presumably, since there had been no lawful arrest he would in turn by entitled to sue for battery and false imprisonment. See also *Walters* v *WH Smith*.

In *Davidson* v *Chief Constable of North Wales*, a store detective could not arrest the plaintiff under s.24(4) because the suspected offence was no longer being committed. Instead, she gave information to police officers as a result of which they arrested the plaintiff, who was able to show that the goods in her possession had been paid for. The plaintiff sued, *inter alia*, the store detective's employer. It was held that the employer was not liable in false imprisonment since the store detective had merely supplied information and had not directed or procured or requested the police to arrest the plaintiff. See also *Martin* v *Watson*.

(4)   Section 28 modifies the common law rule established in *Christie* v *Leachinsky* as to the notification of the grounds of arrest. Now, despite the fact that the ground (and fact) of arrest is obvious, a police officer is still required to state it. In *DPP* v *Hawkins* because of the violent struggle at the time of the initial arrest it had not been reasonably practicable to inform the defendant of the ground of arrest. It subsequently became practicable to do so at the police station but there was a

failure to do so. The court rejected a suggestion that the assault on a police constable at the time of the arrest was not an assault on a constable in the execution of his duty. The failure to state the ground did not operate retrospectively to invalidate the arrest. The arrest would be unlawful only from the moment of failure to state the ground.

(5)   In *Lewis* v *Chief Constable of the South Wales Constabulary*, the initial taking into custody of the two plaintiffs was unlawful since at that moment the arresting officers had failed to state the reasons for arrest in breach of s.28. At a later stage during custody, the reasons were stated. As from that moment the detention became a lawful arrest and the plaintiffs were entitled to damages for the brief period of false imprisonment. The prior period of unlawful detention was not 'cured' by the later statement of reasons. Of course, in *DPP* v *Hawkins* the situation was the opposite. There the initial failure to state reasons was justifiable as not being practicable; the arrest there became unlawful as from the moment at which it became practicable to give the required reasons.

(6)   For search of prisoners, see *Lindley* v *Rutter*, p.371. For use of force to enter premises see *Swales* v *Cox*, p.391.

18 Public order

One of the prime duties of the police is the maintenance of public order. The ancient common law powers to deal with actual or reasonably apprehended imminent breaches of the peace remain of significant importance despite the provisions of the Public Order Act 1986. The common law powers are preventive in nature and are available to the police (and to the citizen) irrespective of whether or not an offence has occurred. The common law imposes an obligation upon both police and citizen to deal with breaches of the peace (see *Lavin* v *Albert*, p.402).

The freedom to protest is circumscribed by the preventive power of the police and by statutory offences such as wilful obstruction of the highway. Despite the terms of the ECHR, Article 11 (see p.139), there are no rights to assemble and protest. These are residual freedoms which exist only to the extent that they are not affected by any positive law such as obstruction of the highway. In addition, the civil law may in an appropriate case restrict the freedom to protest (see *Hickman* v *Maisey*, p.436).

R v *Howell*

[1982] QB 416 · Court of Appeal

Police officers attempted to disperse a group of people who had spilled on to the street from a party; the group was noisy, shouting abuse and had disturbed neighbours who were gathered in the street. It was alleged that during the course of arrest the defendant had struck a police officer. The defendant alleged that there had not been a breach of the peace before the arrest and that the force used, if any, had been in resistance to an unlawful arrest. The Court of Appeal (a) defined a breach of the peace, (b) concluded that the trial court had directed itself properly, and (c) confirmed that there was a power of arrest for threatened breaches of the peace.

Watkins LJ: '. . . We hold that there is power of arrest for breach of the peace: where (1) a breach of the peace is committed in the presence of the person making the arrest or (2) the arrestor reasonably believes that such a breach will be committed in the immediate future by the person arrested although he has not yet committed any breach or (3) where a breach has been committed and it is reasonably believed that a renewal of it is threatened.

The public expects a police officer not only to apprehend the criminal but to do his best to prevent the commission of crime, to keep the peace, in other words. To deny him, therefore, the right to arrest a person whom he reasonably believes is about to breach the peace would be to disable him from preventing that which might cause serious injury to someone or even to many people or property. The common law, we believe, whilst recognising that a wrongful arrest is a serious invasion of a person's liberty, provides the police with this power in the public interest.

In those instances of the exercise of this power which depend upon a belief that a breach of the peace is imminent it must ... be established that it is not only an honest albeit mistaken belief but a belief which is founded on reasonable grounds ...

A comprehensive definition of the term "breach of the peace" has very rarely been formulated so far as ... we have been able to discover ... The older cases are of considerable interest but they are not a sure guide to what the term is understood to mean today, since keeping the peace in this country in the latter half of the 20th century presents formidable problems which bear upon the evolving process of the development of this breach of the common law. Nevertheless ... we cannot accept that there can be a breach of the peace unless there has been an act done or threatened to be done which either actually harms a person, or in his presence his property, or is likely to cause such harm, or which puts someone in fear of such harm being done. There is nothing more likely to arouse resentment and anger in him, and a desire to take instant revenge, than attacks or threatened attacks upon a person's body or property ...

We are emboldened to say that there is a breach of the peace whenever harm is actually done or is likely to be done to a person or in his presence to his property or a person is in fear of being so harmed through an assault, an affray, a riot, unlawful assembly or other disturbance.'

Comment

(1)   Lord Denning in *R* v *Chief Constable for Devon & Cornwall, ex parte CEGB* did not adopt the definition of breach of the peace (see p.412); but in *Parkin* v *Norman* the Court of Appeal reverted to the *Howell* test. A breach of the peace can occur on private premises even though no member of the public is present or likely to come onto the premises: see *McConnell* v *Chief Constable of the Greater Manchester Police.*

(2)   Following an arrest or detention for breach of the peace the perpetrator may be brought before a magistrates' court and be bound over to keep the peace or be of good behaviour, for example under the Justice of the Peace Act 1361. For a full review, see Law Commission Working Paper no. 103 and see also *Hughes* v *Holley.*

Lavin v Albert

[1982] AC 546 · House of Lords

A tried to 'jump the queue' at a bus stop. L, an off-duty and plain clothes police constable, was at the head of the queue. L had reasonable grounds for believing a breach of the peace to be imminent unless he obstructed A from boarding the bus out of turn. A's conduct while he was being restrained by L, during the course of which L said that he was a constable, was found by the magistrates to amount to a continuing breach of the peace. After being told that L was a constable, a statement which the magistrates found that A in his excited state honestly but unreasonably disbelieved, A struck him five or six times. A was arrested and charged with assault on a constable in the execution of his duty. The House of Lords held that a constable who reasonably believes that a breach of the peace is about to take place is entitled to detain any person without arrest to prevent that breach of the peace in circumstances which reasonably appear to him to be proper and that the detention of A was lawful. Accordingly the belief of A was irrelevant since L was acting in the execution of his duty.

Lord Diplock: '... What had been overlooked ... is that to the well-established principle referred to by the learned judge there is an equally well-established exception, not confined to constables, that is applicable to the instant case. It is: that every citizen in whose presence a breach of the peace is being, or reasonably appears to be about to be, committed has the right to take reasonable steps to make the person who is breaking or threatening to break the peace refrain from doing so; and those reasonable steps in appropriate cases will include detaining him against his will. At common law this is not only the right of every citizen, it is also his duty, although, except in the case of a citizen who is a constable, it is a duty of imperfect obligation ... Even if Albert's belief that Lavin was a private citizen and not a constable had been correct, it would not have made his resistance to Lavin's restraint of him lawful.'

Comment

(1)   Where a constable properly exercises his common law powers, the person who wilfully obstructs or assaults him will be guilty of an offence contrary to s.51, Police Act 1964 (p.379). Ignorance that the person seeking to preserve the peace is a constable will be relevant only where the charge is one of wilful obstruction.

(2)   The powers to deal with breaches of the peace are shared by police and the ordinary citizen but, as Lord Diplock said in *Lavin* v *Albert* (and also in *Attorney-General for Northern Ireland's Reference No. 1 of 1975*, p.404), the citizen is not under an absolute duty to preserve the peace, it is a duty of 'imperfect obligation'. This suggests that a reasonable excuse, e.g. illness or disability, will excuse the citizen or that the obligation cannot be enforced by action. A citizen who wrongfully fails to assist a police officer to deal with a breach of the peace when called upon to do so will be guilty of a common law offence: see *R* v *Brown*. On the other hand a police officer who in certain circumstances fails to carry out his duty may well be guilty of the offence of misfeasance in a public office: see *R* v *Dytham* where a police officer stood by whilst a vicious attack was made upon a victim who subsequently died.

(3)   The ancient cases establishing the obligations of the citizen stem from a time

when there was a police force totally different in character and training from the modern force and many of the statements as to the obligation of the magistracy are now out of date. Duties were formerly placed on the magistracy and the army, and failure to perform those duties might have led to criminal charges: see *R v Pinney*. In *Charge to the Bristol Grand Jury* the court said:

> And whilst I am stating the obligation imposed by the law on every subject of the realm, I wish to observe, that the law acknowledges no distinction in this respect between the soldier and the private individual. The soldier is still a citizen, lying under the same obligation and invested with the same authority to preserve the peace of the King as any other subject. If the one is bound to attend the call of the civil magistrate, so also is the other; if the one may interfere for that purpose when the occasion demands it, without the requisition of the magistrate, so may the other too; if the one may employ arms for that purpose, when arms are necessary, the soldier may do the same. Undoubtedly the same exercise of discretion which requires the private subject to act in subordination to and in the aid of the magistrate, rather than upon his own authority, before recourse is had to arms, ought to operate in a still stronger degree with a military force. But, where the danger is pressing and immediate; where a felony has actually been committed or cannot otherwise be prevented; and from the circumstances of the case no opportunity is offered of obtaining a requisition from the proper authorities; the military subjects of the King, like his civil subjects, not only may, but are bound to do their utmost, of their own authority, to prevent the perpetration of outrage, to put down riot and tumult, and to preserve the lives and property of the people.

Attorney-General for Northern Ireland's Reference No. 1 of 1975

[1977] AC 105 · House of Lords

A British soldier, the defendant in the subsequent trial, was part of a heavily equipped army patrol in a rural part of Northern Ireland which had often been the scene of terrorist activity. In daylight, the patrol came across a youth in a field; he was challenged but he ran away. The defendant fired a snap shot at the youth who was only 20 yards away; the youth was killed. The defendant did not believe that the youth was armed but he did honestly and reasonably believe that he was dealing with a member of the Provisional IRA who was seeking to run away. The defendant did not believe that the youth had been involved in acts of terrorism or was likely to be involved in any immediate act of terrorism. The defendant was charged with murder and his defence was that he had used reasonable force in the prevention of crime under s.3, Criminal Law (Northern Ireland) Act 1967. The defendant was acquitted. The Attorney-General for Northern Ireland sought clarification of the law using the Attorney-General's Reference procedure. The House of Lords held that the facts were sufficient to raise an issue for the tribunal of fact as to whether the Crown had established beyond reasonable doubt that the defendant's act constituted unreasonable force.

Lord Diplock: '. . . My Lords, to kill or seriously wound another person by shooting is prima facie unlawful. There may be circumstances, however, which render the act of shooting and any killing which results from it lawful; and an honest and reasonable belief by the accused in the existence of facts which if true would have rendered his act lawful is a defence to any charge based on the shooting. So for the purposes of the present reference one must ignore the fact that the deceased was an entirely innocent person and must deal with the case as if he were a member of the Provisional IRA and a potentially dangerous terrorist, as the accused honestly and reasonably believed him to be.

The facts to be assumed for the purposes of the reference are not capable in law of giving rise to a possible defence of "self-defence." The deceased was in fact, and appeared to the accused to be, unarmed. He was not attacking the accused: he was running away. So if the act of the accused in shooting the deceased was lawful it must have been on the ground that it was done in the performance of his duty to prevent crime or in the exercise of his right to stop and question the deceased under s.16 or to arrest him under s.12 of the Northern Ireland (Emergency Provisions) Act 1973.

There is little authority in English law concerning the rights and duties of a member of the armed forces of the Crown when acting in aid of the civil power; and what little authority there is relates almost entirely to the duties of soldiers when troops are called upon to assist in controlling a riotous assembly. Where used for such temporary purposes it may not be inaccurate to describe the legal rights and duties of a soldier as being no more than those of an ordinary citizen in uniform. But such a description is in my view misleading in the circumstances in which the army is currently employed in aid of the civil power in Northern Ireland. In some parts of the province there has existed for some years now a state of armed and clandestinely organised insurrection against the lawful government of Her Majesty by persons seeking to gain political ends by violent means – that is, by committing murder and other crimes of violence against persons and property. Due to the efforts of the army and police to suppress it the insurrection has been sporadic in its manifestations but, as events have repeatedly shown, if vigilance is relaxed the violence erupts again. In theory it may be the duty of every citizen when an arrestable offence is about to be committed in his presence to take whatever reasonable measures are available to him to prevent the commission of the crime; but the duty is one of imperfect obligation and does not place him under any obligation to do anything by which he would expose himself to risk of personal injury, nor is he under any duty to search for criminals or seek out crime. In contrast to this a soldier who is employed in aid of the civil power in Northern Ireland is under a duty, enforceable under military law, to search for criminals if so ordered by his superior officer and to risk his own life should this be necessary in preventing terrorist acts. For the performance of this duty he is armed with a firearm, a self-loading rifle, from which a bullet, if it hits the human body, is almost certain to cause serious injury if not death.

The use of force in the prevention of crime or in effecting the lawful arrest of suspected offenders is now regulated by s.3 of the Criminal Law Act (Northern Ireland) 1967 as follows:

(1) A person may use such force as is reasonable in the circumstances in the prevention of crime, or in effecting or assisting in the lawful arrest of offenders or suspected offenders or of persons unlawfully at large. (2) Subsection (1) shall replace the rules of the common law as to the matters dealt with by that subsection.

That section states the law applicable to the defence raised by the accused at the trial of his case.

In the instant reference the relevant purpose for which it is to be assumed that force was used by the accused is the prevention of crime. That is the purpose for which the power to stop and question is conferred upon soldiers by s.16 of the Northern Ireland (Emergency Provisions) Act 1973; and it has not been suggested that shooting to kill or seriously wound would be justified in attempting to effect the arrest under s.12 of a person who, though he was suspected of belonging to a proscribed organisation (which constitutes an offence under s.19), was not also believed on reasonable grounds to be likely to commit actual crimes of violence if he succeeded in avoiding arrest.

What amount of force is "reasonable in the circumstances" for the purpose of preventing crime is, in my view, always a question for the jury in a jury trial, never a "point of law" for the judge.

The form in which the jury would have to ask themselves the question in a trial for an offence against the person in which this defence was raised by the accused, would be: Are we satisfied that no reasonable man (a) with knowledge of such facts as were known to the accused or reasonably believed by him to exist (b) in the circumstances and time available to him for reflection (c) could be of opinion that the prevention of the risk of harm to which others might be exposed if the suspect were allowed to escape justified exposing the suspect to the risk of harm to him that might result from the kind of force that the accused contemplated using?

To answer this the jury would have first to decide what were the facts that did exist and were known to the accused to do so and what were mistakenly believed by the accused to be facts. In respect of the latter the jury would have had to decide whether any reasonable man on the material available to the accused could have shared that belief . . .

The jury would have also to consider how the circumstances in which the accused had to make his decision whether or not to use force and the shortness of the time available to him for reflection, might affect the judgment of a reasonable man. In the facts that are to be assumed for the purposes of the reference there is material upon which a jury might take the view that the accused had reasonable grounds for apprehension of imminent danger to himself and other members of the patrol if the deceased were allowed to get away and join armed fellow-members of the Provisional IRA who might be lurking in the neighbourhood, and that the time available to the accused to make up his mind what to do was so short that even a reasonable man could only act intuitively. This being so, the jury in approaching the final part of the question should remind themselves that the postulated balancing of risk against risk, harm against harm, by the reasonable man is not undertaken in the calm analytical atmosphere of the courtroom after counsel with the benefit of hindsight have expounded at length the reasons for and against the kind and degree of force that was used by the accused; but in the brief second or two which the accused had to decide whether to shoot or not and under all the stresses to which he was exposed.

In many cases where force is used in the prevention of crime or in effecting an arrest there is a choice as to the degree of force to use. On the facts that are to be assumed for the purposes of the reference the only options open to the accused were either to let the deceased escape or to shoot at him with a service rifle. A reasonable man would know that a bullet from a self-loading rifle if it hit a human being, at any rate at the range at which the accused fired, would be likely to kill him or to injure him seriously. So in one scale of the balance the harm to which the deceased would be exposed if the accused aimed to hit him was predictable and grave and the risk of its occurrence high. In the other scale of the balance it would be open to the jury to take the view that it would not be unreasonable to assess the kind of harm to be averted by preventing the accused's escape as even graver – the killing or wounding of members of the patrol by terrorists in ambush, and the effect of this success by members of the Provisional IRA in encouraging the continuance of the armed insurrection and all the misery and destruction of life and property that terrorist activity in Northern Ireland has entailed. The jury would have to consider too what was the highest degree at which a reasonable man could have assessed the likelihood that such consequences might follow the escape of the deceased if the facts had been as the accused knew or believed them reasonably to be.'

Comment

(1) The constitutional arrangements for calling for the assistance of military personnel are obscure as is the relationship between the duties of the military as citizens and their duty under military law; see the *Report of an Inquiry into the Featherstone Riots* (1893) C 7234. The government of the day may well call for or permit the military to intervene in a wide range of circumstances, for example to rescue terrorist hostages or to seal off an airport during a terrorist action. See also *Charge to Bristol Grand Jury*, p.404.

(2) Specialized emergency provisions to deal with terrorism are apt to be long-lived; see, for example, the Prevention of Terrorism (Temporary Provisions) Act 1989, the successor to the 1974 Act of the same name, which was itself modelled on the Prevention of Violence (Temporary Provisions) Act 1939 which lasted until 1954. Of even longer parentage is the Northern Ireland (Emergency Provisions) Act 1978 (as amended) which was the successor to the Civil Authorities (Special Powers) Act (NI) 1922 which lasted until repealed by the Northern Ireland (Emergency Provisions) Act 1973. All these Acts effected far-reaching changes to the normal powers or procedures available to the police, army and executive government – for example detention without trial; prolonged detention for questioning; abolishing trial by jury for certain offences and substituting trial by single judge (the so-called 'Diplock Courts'); creation of wide powers of search; proscription of certain organizations; exclusion orders prohibiting persons from entering parts of the United Kingdom even when citizens and without order of a court.

(3) The arrangements for the use of the military to assist in dealing with other forms of emergency are more formalized and are contained in the Emergency Powers Act 1920, s.1(1):

If at any time it appears to His Majesty that there have occurred, or are about to occur, events of such a nature as to be calculated, by interfering with the supply and distribution of food, water, fuel, or light, or with the means of locomotion, to deprive the community, or any substantial portion of the community, of the essentials of life, His Majesty may, by proclamation . . . declare that a state of emergency exists . . .

Troops may be used even though there is no proclamation, and there may be specific statutory provisions to deal with emergencies such as the East Coast flooding of 1953, the prison officers' dispute of 1980, and the droughts of 1975 and 1976.

(4)   In *R* v *MacNaughton*, a soldier was acquitted on a charge of attempted murder; he had shot a suspect who had been arrested and who had then attempted to escape over a fence. The court took into account, *inter alia*, the potentially hostile terrain and the risk that soldiers who might run in pursuit might be hit by their own colleagues, and the need to keep the patrol in its formation. Lowry J said:

> . . . in these circumstances one does not weigh the conduct of the accused in jeweller's scales. The law does not expect serving soldiers to be supermen . . . the law only expects them to be reasonable men . . . The security forces have not a free hand to do as they like just because of civil disturbances in the community or to disregard the law and to claim the same immunity as if they were on the battlefield. If there were convincing evidence that [the victim] was set up to be deliberately shot that would be reprehensible and . . . the accusation of attempted murder would clearly lie.

See also *R* v *Clegg*, p.437, and *Lynch* v *Fitzgerald*, Meredith J:

> . . . it is lawful to use only a reasonable degree of force for the protection of oneself or any other person against the unlawful use of force, and that such repelling force is not reasonable if it is either greater than is requisite for the purpose or disproportionate to the evil to be prevented.

Duncan v Jones

[1936] 1 KB 218 · Divisional Court

The respondent was about to speak to a crowd gathered on the street in the vicinity of an Unemployed Training Centre; no obstruction of the highway was alleged. The previous year there had been disturbances in the Centre after a similar meeting. The manager of the Centre called the police who reasonably apprehended a breach of the peace and instructed the respondent to move her meeting to a place 175 yards away but she refused and began to address the crowd. She was arrested and charged with wilful obstruction of a police officer acting in the execution of his duty. The magistrates found that Mrs Duncan must have known of the probable consequences of her holding the meeting, namely a disturbance and possible breach of the peace, and was not unwilling that those consequences would ensue. Her appeal against conviction was dismissed.

Lord Hewart CJ: 'There have been moments during the argument in this case when it appeared to be suggested that the Court had to deal with a grave case involving what is called the right of public meeting. I say "called", because English law does not recognize any special right of public meeting for political or other purposes. The right of assembly, as Professor Dicey puts it, is nothing more than a view taken by the Court of the individual liberty of the subject. If I thought that the present case raised a question which has been held in suspense by more than one writer on constitutional law – namely, whether an assembly can properly be held to be unlawful merely because the holding of it is expected to give rise to a breach of the peace on the part of persons opposed to those who are holding the meeting – I should wish to hear much more argument before I expressed an opinion. This case, however, does not even touch that important question.

Our attention has been directed to the somewhat unsatisfactory case of *Beatty* v *Gillbanks.* The circumstances of that case and the charge must be remembered, as also must the important passage in the judgment of Field J, in which Cave J concurred. Field J said: "I entirely concede that everyone must be taken to intend the natural consequences of his own acts, and it is clear to me that if this disturbance of the peace was the natural consequence of acts of the appellants they would be liable, and the justices would have been right in binding them over. But the evidence set forth in the case does not support this contention; on the contrary, it shows that the disturbances were caused by other people antagonistic to the appellants, and that no acts of violence were committed by them." Our attention has also been directed to other authorities where the judgments in *Beatty* v *Gillbanks* have been referred to, but they do not carry the matter any further, although they more than once express a doubt about the exact meaning of the decision. In my view, *Beatty* v *Gillbanks* is apart from the present case. No such question as that which arose there is even mooted here . . .

The case stated which we have before us indicates clearly a causal connection between the meeting of May, 1933, and the disturbance which occurred after it – that the disturbance was not only *post* the meeting but was also *propter* the meeting . . .'

Thomas v *Sawkins*

[1935] QB 249 · Divisional Court

A public meeting in a private hall was held to protest about the Incitement to Disaffection Bill then before Parliament. Several police officers under the control of an inspector insisted upon being present at the meeting despite the protests of the organizers. T, the organizer, took hold of the inspector with a view to ejecting him. S, another police officer, removed T's arm. T prosecuted S for assault but the case was dismissed. On appeal the Court held that the police had been exercising a power to enter and remain on the premises.

Lord Hewart CJ: '. . . it is said that it is an unheard-of proposition of law, and that in the books no case is to be found which goes the length of deciding, that, where an offence is expected to be committed, as distinct from the case of an offence being or having been committed, there is any right in the police to enter on private premises and to remain there against the will of those who, as hirers or otherwise, are for the time being in possession of the premises. When, however, I look at the passages which have been cited from *Blackstone's Commentaries* and from the judgments in *Humphries* v *Connor* and *O'Kelly* v *Harvey* and certain observations of Avory J in

Lansbury v *Riley*, I think that there is quite sufficient ground for the proposition that it is part of the preventative power, and, therefore, part of the preventative duty, of the police, in cases where there are such reasonable grounds of apprehension as the justices have found here, to enter and remain on private premises. It goes without saying that the powers and duties of the police are directed, not to the interests of the police, but to the protection and welfare of the public.

It was urged in one part of the argument of [counsel] that what the police did here amounted to a trespass. It seems somewhat remarkable to speak of trespass when members of the public who happen to be police officers attend, after a public invitation, a public meeting which is to discuss as one part of its business the dismissal of the Chief Constable of the county. It is elementary that a good defence to an action for trespass is to show that the act complained of was done by authority of law, or by leave and licence.

I am not at all prepared to accept the doctrine that it is only where an offence has been, or is being, committed, that the police are entitled to enter and remain on private premises. On the contrary, it seems to me that a police officer has *ex virtute officii* full right so to act when he has reasonable ground for believing that an offence is imminent or is likely to be committed . . .'

Avory J: 'I am of the same opinion. I think that it is very material in this particular case to observe that the meeting was described as a public meeting, that it was extensively advertised, and that the public were invited to attend. There can be no doubt that the police officers who attended the meeting were members of the public and were included in that sense in the invitation to attend. It is true that those who had hired the hall for the meeting might withdraw their invitation from any particular individual who was likely to commit a breach of the peace or some other offence, but it is quite a different proposition to say that they might withdraw the invitation from police officers who might be there for the express purpose of preventing a breach of the peace or the commission of an offence . . .

In my view, the right was correctly expressed in *R* v *Queen's County Justices*, where Fitzgerald J said: "The foundation of the jurisdiction [to bind persons to be of good behaviour] is very remote, and probably existed prior to the statute of 1360–61; but whatever its foundation may be, or by whatever language conveyed, we are bound to regard and expound it by the light of immemorial practice and of decision, and especially of direct modern decision. It may be described as a branch of preventive justice, in the exercise of which magistrates are invested with large judicial discretionary powers, for the maintenance of order and the preservation of the public peace." . . . In principle I think that there is no distinction between the duty of a police constable to prevent a breach of the peace and the power of a magistrate to bind persons over to be of good behaviour to prevent a breach of the peace . . . In my opinion, no express statutory authority is necessary where the police have reasonable grounds to apprehend a breach of the peace, and in the present case I am satisfied that the justices had before them material on which they could properly hold that the police officers in question had reasonable grounds for believing that, if they were not present, seditious speeches would be made and/or that a breach of the peace would take place. To prevent any such offence or a breach of the peace the police were entitled to enter and to remain on the premises . . .'

Comment

Although the facts of the case concern a public meeting, the reasoning is wide enough to encompass all meetings (and other activities) whether public or private. *Thomas* v *Sawkins* was approved and applied in *McLeod* v *Metropolitan Police Commissioner* where the court thought it important that the police should 'act with great care and discretion' and should be satisfied that 'there is a real and imminent risk of a breach of the peace'.

Piddington v *Bates*

[1961] I WLR 162 · Divisional Court

A police officer indicated that there should not be more than two pickets at each gate of certain premises. The defendant tried to picket a gate and pushed past a police officer. His appeal against conviction for wilful obstruction was dismissed on the basis that the police officer had reasonable grounds to apprehend a breach of the peace.

Lord Parker CJ: '. . . [T]he question here is whether the constables in question were acting in the course of the execution of their duty when they were obstructed . . . It seems to me that the law is reasonably plain. First, the mere statement by a constable that he did anticipate that there might be a breach of the peace is clearly not enough. There must exist proved facts from which a constable could reasonably anticipate such a breach. Secondly, it is not enough that his contemplation is that there is a remote possibility; there must be a real possibility of a breach of the peace. Accordingly, in every case, it becomes a question of whether, on the particular facts, it can be said that there were reasonable grounds on which a constable charged with this duty reasonably anticipated that a breach of the peace might occur . . .
    As I have said, every case must depend upon its exact facts, and the matter which influences me in this case is the matter of numbers. It is, I think, perfectly clear from the wording of the case, although it is not expressly so found, that the police knew that in these small works there were only eight people working. They found two vehicles arriving, with 18 people milling about the street, trying to form pickets at the doors. On that ground alone, coupled with the telephone call which, I should have thought, intimated some sense of urgency and apprehension, the police were fully entitled to think as reasonable men that there was a real danger of something more than mere picketing to collect or impart information or peaceably to persuade. I think that in those circumstances the [constable] had reasonable grounds for anticipating that a breach of the peace was a real possibility. It may be, and I think this is the real criticism, that it can be said: Well, to say that only two pickets should be allowed is purely arbitrary; why two? Why not three? Where do you draw the line? I think that a police officer charged with the duty of preserving the Queen's peace must be left to take such steps on the evidence before him he thinks are proper. I am far from saying that there should be any rule that only two pickets should be allowed at any particular door. There, one gets into an arbitrary area, but so far as this case is concerned I cannot see that there was anything wrong in the action of the [constable].
    Finally, I would like to say that all these matters are so much matters of degree

that I would hesitate, except on the clearest evidence, to interfere with the findings of magistrates who have had the advantage of hearing the whole case and observing the witnesses. . .'

R v *Chief Constable of Devon and Cornwall, ex parte CEGB*

[1982] 1 QB 458 · Court of Appeal

The CEGB had statutory powers to enter a site to survey it for suitability as to use as a site for a nuclear power station. Local demonstrators were prevented by injunction from interfering with the work or entering the site. Demonstrators from further afield obstructed the work but rendered the civil remedy unavailable by keeping their identities secret. Their tactic also frustrated the use of the summary offence under the Town and Country Planning Act 1971 which did not carry a specific power of arrest. The CEGB were reluctant to engage in physical confrontation and asked the police to assist in ejecting the trespassing demonstrators. The police maintained a watch on the site but refused to intervene on the basis that there was no actual or apprehended breach of the peace. The CEGB sought an order of mandamus requiring the Chief Constable to instruct his officers to remove or assist in the removal of the demonstrators. The Court of Appeal held that it was not an appropriate case for the grant of an order of mandamus. The Court of Appeal also indicated its views as to the existence of an actual or apprehended breach of the peace.

Lord Denning MR: '. . . It is common ground that, although the statute gives no power to arrest obstructors, nevertheless the police have power to arrest them if there is a breach of the peace or the reasonable apprehension of it . . . But the question is whether the obstructors were guilty of a breach of the peace, or whether there was any apprehension of it . . .

In our present case the police have taken the view that there has been no breach of the peace, nor that there is any apprehension of it . . .

The board and their contractors are entitled to manhandle the obstructors so as to move them out of the way. Every person who is prevented from carrying out his lawful pursuits is entitled to use self-help, so as to prevent any unlawful obstruction . . . He must, of course, not use more force than is reasonably necessary: but there is no doubt whatever that he can use force to do it.

I go further, I think that the conduct of these people, their unlawful obstruction, is itself a breach of the peace. There is a breach of the peace whenever a person who is lawfully carrying out his work is unlawfully and physically prevented by another from doing it. He is entitled by law peacefully to go on with his work on his lawful occasions. If anyone unlawfully and physically obstructs the worker – by lying down or chaining himself to a rig or the like – he is guilty of a breach of the peace. Even if this were not enough, I think that their unlawful conduct gives rise to a reasonable apprehension of a breach of the peace. It is at once likely that the lawful worker will resort to self-help by removing the obstructor by force from the vicinity of the work so that he obstructs no longer. He will lift the recumbent obstructor from the ground. This removal would itself be an assault and battery – unless it was justified as being done by way of self-help . . . So also the lifting up of a recumbent obstructor would be a battery unless justified as being done in the exercise of self-help. But in deciding whether there is a breach of the peace or the apprehension of it, the law does not go into the rights and wrongs of the matter – or whether it is justified by self-help or not. Suffice it that the peace is broken or is likely to be broken by one or another of those present. With the result that any citizen – and certainly any police officer – can intervene to stop the breach.

If I were wrong on this point, if there was here no breach of the peace nor apprehension of it, it would give a licence to every obstructor and every passive resister in the land. He would be able to cock a snook at the law as these groups have done. Public works of the greatest national importance could be held up indefinitely. This cannot be. The rule of law must prevail . . .

Notwithstanding all that I have said, I would not give any orders to the chief constable or his men. It is of the first importance that the police should decide on their own responsibility what action should be taken in any particular situation . . .

The decision of the chief constable not to intervene in this case was a policy decision with which I think the courts should not interfere. All that I have done in this judgment is to give the "definitive legal mandate" which he sought. It should enable him to reconsider their position. I hope he will decide to use his men to clear the obstructors off the site or at any rate help the board to do so . . .'

Lawton LJ: '. . . A statutory body can use the minimum of force reasonably necessary to remove those obstructing the exercise of its statutory powers from the area where work has to be carried out. This is the common law remedy of abatement by self-help . . . There are many reasons why self-help should be discouraged. Disputes are likely to arise as to whether the minimum amount of force reasonably necessary was used. In my judgment, based on my understanding of human nature and a long experience of the administration of criminal justice, the most important reason for not using self-help, if any other remedy can be used effectively, is that as soon as one person starts to, or makes to, lay hands on another, there is likely to be a breach of the peace. Those obstructing may assert that they will allow themselves to be removed without resisting; but, when the manhandling starts, particularly if a man has to lay hands on a woman, struggling and uproar are likely to begin. I should have expected most police constables to appreciate that this is so; and as they have a duty to deal with breaches of the peace which actually occur or which they have reasonable cause for suspecting are about to occur, those who see what is happening should act either by trying to persuade those obstructing to stop doing so or arresting them if they persist in their unlawful conduct. In many cases those who persist to the point of having to be arrested will commit some other offence in doing so such as obstructing or assaulting police officers in the execution of their duty: see s.51 of the Police Act 1964. If no other offence is committed, the police constable making the arrest should take the person arrested before the local magistrates to show cause why he should not be bound over, with or without sureties, to keep the peace and be of good behaviour: see s.115 of the Magistrates' Courts Act 1980 . . .

I was surprised to read, and I would like to think that the chief constable was too, that a senior police officer could have been of the opinion that the situation which he described was not likely to cause a breach of the peace . . . What matters, however, is not the chief inspector's errors in law, but his assessment of what was likely to happen. The unlawful obstruction was going on in his area: his officers were reporting to him what they had seen: he may himself have watched what was happening. Although he may have put too much stress on keeping on good terms with those in the area who did not want a nuclear power station built there, there is nothing in his report or in the other evidence to suggest that his assessment of the situation was not his honest opinion. The chief constable was entitled to accept it and he did. This led him to state in the affidavit which he swore in opposition to the board's application for an order of mandamus that he was not satisfied that the demonstrators had any intention of using violence or committing breaches of the peace.

The issue was further befogged by the chief constable averring, on legal advice, first that he was not satisfied "that force should be used in the present circumstances either by the board or by anyone else" and, secondly, that the board should deal with the problem by taking further proceedings. If the chief constable was purporting to tell the board when it could use self-help, he had no right to do so anymore than the board had any right, if it ever thought it had, to call upon the chief constable to provide muscle power to remove those who were obstructing the exercise of its statutory powers. Police constables are no one's lackeys; but they do have a duty to preserve the peace no matter how unpopular that may make them with some sections of the community . . . The board knows that any police officers who may be watching what is going on cannot act unless they see a breach of the peace or have reasonable cause for suspecting that there is a real and imminent risk of one occurring or that those present, being three or more in number, by their conduct show an intention to use violence or behave in a tumultuous way. If those obstructing do allow themselves to be removed without struggling or causing uproar (which to me seems unlikely, but I may be wrong) the police will have no reason for taking action, nor should they . . .'

Templeman LJ: '. . . The police on the spot must decide when to intervene. I consider that they will be fully justified in intervening if the board enter the site with the intention of completing the survey and the obstructors decline to leave. But in any event the police will be entitled to intervene if an obstructor resists being carried away from the site or runs to another part of the site or tries to enter the site or tries to return to the site, thus obliging the board's representatives to seize him so that he may be permanently excluded. Such conduct by an obstructor, whether he calls himself a passive resister or not, will create an imminent and serious danger of a breach of the peace for which the obstructor will be responsible and liable to arrest or removal by the police . . . But it is for the police and the board to co-operate and to decide upon and implement the most effective method of dealing with the obstructors. The court cannot tell the police how and when their powers should be exercised, for the court cannot judge the explosiveness of the situation or deal with the individual problems which will arise as a result of the activities of the obstructors. This court can and does confirm that the police have powers to remove and arrest passive resisters in the circumstances which prevail at the site when the board resume their work to complete their survey. This court can and does indicate that the time has come for the board and the police to exercise their respective powers so that the survey may be completed . . .'

Comment

(1) Note the contrasting views taken in the *CEGB* case of when the police might properly intervene. The common law requires the police to deal with actual or reasonably apprehended imminent breaches of the peace by reasonable methods but

gives little guidance as to the weighing of competing interests. It tends to favour the maintenance of the peace rather than, say, freedom of expression. This can lead to difficult issues of principle.

In *Humphries* v *Connor* an orange lily worn by the plaintiff to demonstrate allegiance to a political cause was removed by a constable in order to prevent a breach of the peace when the wearing of it suggested the outbreak of violence on the part of opponents. The plaintiff sued for damages and the defendant constable pleaded that he was under a duty to seize the item; the court agreed and held that the constable's power to seize the item stemmed from his duty to preserve the peace. Hayes J:

> ... The law has not ventured to lay down what precise measures shall be adopted by him in every state of facts which calls for his interference. But it has done far better; it has announced to him, and to the public ... that he is not only at liberty, but is bound, to see that the peace be preserved, and that he is to do everything that is necessary for that purpose, neither more nor less ...

Fitzgerald J sounded a note of caution:

> ... the doubt which I have is, whether a constable is entitled to interfere with one who is not about to commit a breach of the peace, or to do, or join in any illegal act, but who is likely to be made an object of insult or injury by other persons who are about to break the Queen's peace ... I do not see where we are to draw the line. If a constable is at liberty to take a lily from one person, because the wearing of it is displeasing to others, who may make it an excuse for a breach of the peace, where are we to stop? It seems to me that we are making, not the law of the land but the law of the mob supreme, and recognising in constables a power of interference with the rights of the Queen's subjects, which, if carried into effect to the full extent of the principle, might be accompanied by constitutional danger.

(2) The plaintiff in *Humphries* v *Connor* could now be charged under s.4 or s.5 of the Public Order Act 1986. If she were to be charged under s.5 the defence of reasonableness in s.5(3) might apply.

(3) In *Moss* v *Maclachlan*, the police in Nottinghamshire operated road blocks at which they checked vehicles leaving the motorway in the close proximity of pits which were still working during the miners' strike. The defendants were miners who were intending to picket at one of four pits within five miles of the road-check. They were stopped by the police but refused to obey the instruction of the police to turn back. They were arrested and charged with wilfully obstructing the police constables in the execution of their duty. Their appeals against conviction were dismissed; the police officers were acting in the execution of their duty since they reasonably apprehended an imminent breach of the peace and the steps taken were reasonable. Skinner LJ:

> The situation has to be assessed by the senior police officers present. Provided they honestly and reasonably form the opinion that there is a real risk of a breach

of the peace in the sense that it is in close proximity both in place and time, then the conditions exist for reasonable preventive action including, if necessary, the measures taken in this case . . . The possibility of a breach must be real to justify any preventive action. The imminence or immediacy of the threat to the peace determines what action is reasonable. If the police feared that a convoy of cars travelling towards a working coal field bearing banners and broadcasting, by sight or sound, hostility or threats towards working miners might cause a violent episode, they would be justified in halting the convoy to enquire into its destination and purpose. If, on stopping the vehicles, the police were satisfied that there was a real possibility of the occupants causing a breach of the peace one-and-a-half miles away, a journey of less than five minutes by car, then in our judgment it would be their duty to prevent the convoy from proceeding further and they have the power to do so.

(4)   Note the scope for the interaction of the common law powers with the powers found in ss.12–14 of the Public Order Act 1986.

Beatty v Gillbanks

(1892) 9 QBD 308   ·   Divisional Court

The appellants were Salvation Army members whose parades through Weston-super-Mare had been violently opposed by the so-called 'Skeleton Army'. Despite having been ordered by magistrates not to march (for which the magistrates had no power) the Salvation Army members marched and were, as expected, opposed by a tumultuous and shouting mob. The appellants refused to disperse when told to do so by a police officer and they were arrested. The appellants were bound over to keep the peace by magistrates who found that their activity amounted to an unlawful assembly. The Divisional Court upheld the appeal on the basis that there was no unlawful assembly.

Field J: '. . . There is no doubt that they and with them others assembled together in great numbers, but such an assembly to be unlawful must be tumultuous and against the peace. As far as these appellants were concerned there was nothing in their conduct when they were assembled together which was either tumultuous or against the peace. But it is said, that the conduct pursued by them on this occasion was such as, on several previous occasions, had produced riots and disturbance of the peace and terror to the inhabitants, and that the appellants knowing when they assembled together that such consequences would again arise are liable to this charge.

Now I entirely concede that every one must be taken to intend the natural consequences of his own acts, and it is clear to me that if this disturbance of the peace was the natural consequence of acts of the appellants they would be liable, and the justices would have been right in binding them over. But the evidence set forth in the case does not support this contention; on the contrary, it shews that the disturbances were caused by other people antagonistic to the appellants, and that no acts of violence were committed by them . . .

What has happened here is that an unlawful organisation has assumed to itself the right to prevent the appellants and others from lawfully assembling together, and the finding of the justices amounts to this, that a man may be convicted for doing a lawful act if he knows that his doing of it may cause another to do an unlawful act. There is no authority for such a proposition . . .'

Comment

(1) At that time, but not now, it was necessary for the prosecution to establish that the appellants had committed a criminal offence in order for the magistrates to exercise their binding over jurisdiction. The magistrates therefore had to identify the necessary elements of unlawful assembly even though they had no jurisdiction to try that offence. Unlawful assembly has been abolished and has effectively been replaced by s.2, Public Order Act 1986, which is narrower in scope since it requires the use or threat of unlawful violence.

(2) If the appellants were now charged with wilful obstruction of a police officer acting in the execution of his duty, they would be convicted: see *Duncan* v *Jones*, p.408. It is said that the two cases conflict but the simple fact is that two different offences were under consideration.

(3) Can A's threat of violence against B be used as an excuse by the police to stop B exercising his liberties? This is the question identified by Fitzgerald J in *Humphries* v *Connor* (p.415). How ought the common law to deal with the situation which faced the United States' courts in connection with a proposed march by the American Nazi Party through the suburb of Chicago known as Skokie. Most of the 70,000 inhabitants were Jewish and included many survivors or relatives of those persecuted by the Nazis during World War II, and they threatened violence to keep the marchers out. The United States courts gave pre-eminence to the peaceful exercise of the freedom of expression and assembly (even with inherently objectionable symbols such as the swastika), although the march did not in fact go ahead. As to statute, see Public Order Act 1986, ss.11–16.

Public Order Act 1986

1. (1) Where 12 or more persons who are present together use or threaten unlawful violence for a common purpose and the conduct of them (taken together) is such as would cause a person of reasonable firmness present at the scene to fear for his personal safety, each of the persons using unlawful violence for the common purpose is guilty of riot.
   (2) It is immaterial whether or not the 12 or more use or threaten unlawful violence simultaneously.
   (3) The common purpose may be inferred from conduct.
   (4) No person of reasonable firmness need actually be, or be likely to be, present at the scene.
   (5) Riot may be committed in private as well as in public places.
   (6) A person guilty of riot is liable on conviction on indictment to imprisonment for a term not exceeding ten years or a fine or both.

2. (1) Where 3 or more persons who are present together use or threaten unlawful violence and the conduct of them (taken together) is such as would cause a person of reasonable firmness present at the scene to fear for his personal safety, each of the persons using or threatening unlawful violence is guilty of violent disorder.

   (2) It is immaterial whether or not the 3 or more use or threaten unlawful violence simultaneously.

   (3) No person of reasonable firmness need actually be, or be likely to be, present at the scene.

   (4) Violent disorder may be committed in private as well as in public places.

   (5) A person guilty of violent disorder is liable on conviction on indictment to imprisonment for a term not exceeding 5 years or a fine or both, or on summary conviction to imprisonment for a term not exceeding 6 months or a fine not exceeding the statutory maximum or both.

3. (1) A person is guilty of affray if he uses or threatens unlawful violence towards another and his conduct is such as would cause a person of reasonable firmness present at the scene to fear for his personal safety.

   (2) Where 2 or more persons use or threaten the unlawful violence, it is the conduct of them taken together that must be considered for the purposes of subsection (1).

   (3) For the purposes of this section a threat cannot be made by the use of words alone.

   (4) No person of reasonable firmness need actually be, or be likely to be, present at the scene.

   (5) Affray may be committed in private as well as in public places.

   (6) A constable may arrest without warrant anyone he reasonably suspects is committing affray.

   (7) A person guilty of affray is liable on conviction on indictment to imprisonment for a term not exceeding 3 years or a fine or both, or on summary conviction to imprisonment for a term not exceeding 6 months or a fine not exceeding the statutory maximum or both.

4. (1) A person is guilty of an offence if he—
   (a) uses towards another person threatening, abusive or insulting words or behaviour, or
   (b) distributes or displays to another person any writing, sign or other visible representation which is threatening, abusive or insulting,
   with intent to cause that person to believe that immediate unlawful violence will be used against him or another by any person, or to provoke the immediate use of unlawful violence by that person or another, or whereby that person is likely to believe that such violence will be used or it is likely that such violence will be provoked.

   (2) An offence under this section may be committed in a public or a private place, except that no offence is committed where the words or behaviour are used, or the writing, sign or other visible representation is distributed or displayed, by a person inside a dwelling and the other person is also inside that or another dwelling.

(3) A constable may arrest without warrant anyone he reasonably suspects is committing an offence under this section.

(4) A person guilty of an offence under this section is liable on summary conviction to imprisonment for a term not exceeding 6 months or a fine not exceeding level 5 on the standard scale or both.

4A. (1) A person is guilty of an offence if, with intent to cause a person harassment, alarm or distress, he—

(a) uses threatening, abusive or insulting words or behaviour, or disorderly behaviour, or

(b) displays any writing, sign or other visible representation which is threatening, abusive or insulting,

thereby causing that or another person harassment, alarm or distress.

(2) An offence under this section may be committed in a public or a private place, except that no offence is committed where the words or behaviour are used, or the writing, sign or other visible representation is displayed, by a person inside a dwelling and the person who is harassed, alarmed or distressed is also inside that or another dwelling.

(3) It is a defence for the accused to prove—

(a) that he was inside a dwelling and had no reason to believe that the words or behaviour used, or the writing, sign or other visible representation displayed, would be heard or seen by a person outside that or any other dwelling, or

(b) that his conduct was reasonable.

(4) A constable may arrest without warrant anyone he reasonably suspects is committing an offence under this section.

(5) A person guilty of an offence under this section is liable on summary conviction to imprisonment for a term not exceeding 6 months or a fine not exceeding level 5 on the standard scale or both.

5. (1) A person is guilty of an offence if he—

(a) uses threatening, abusive or insulting words or behaviour or disorderly behaviour, or

(b) displays any writing, sign or other visible representation which is threatening, abusive or insulting,

within the hearing or sight of a person likely to be caused harassment, alarm or distress thereby.

(2) An offence under this section may be committed in a public or a private place, except that no offence is committed where the words or behaviour are used, or the writing, sign or other visible representation is displayed, by a person inside a dwelling and the other person is also inside that or another dwelling.

(3) It is a defence for the accused to prove—

(a) that he had no reason to believe that there was any person within hearing or sight who was likely to be caused harassment, alarm or distress, or

(b) that he was inside a dwelling and had no reason to believe that the words or behaviour used, or the writing, sign or other visible representation displayed, would be heard or seen by a person outside that or any other dwelling, or

        (c) that his conduct was reasonable.

   (4) A constable may arrest a person without warrant if—

        (a) he engages in offensive conduct which the constable warns him to stop, and

        (b) he engages in further offensive conduct immediately or shortly after the warning.

   (5) In subsection (4) 'offensive conduct' means conduct the constable reasonably suspects to constitute an offence under this section, and the conduct mentioned in paragraph (a) and the further conduct need not be of the same nature.

   (6) A person guilty of an offence under this section is liable on summary conviction to a fine not exceeding level 3 on the standard scale.

6. (1) A person is guilty of riot only if he intends to use violence or is aware that his conduct may be violent.

   (2) A person is guilty of violent disorder or affray only if he intends to use or threaten violence or is aware that his conduct may be violent or threaten violence.

   (3) A person is guilty of an offence under s.4 only if he intends his words or behaviour, or the writing, sign or other visible representation, to be threatening, abusive or insulting, or is aware that it may be threatening, abusive or insulting.

   (4) A person is guilty of an offence under s.5 only if he intends his words or behaviour, or the writing, sign or other visible representation, to be threatening, abusive or insulting, or is aware that it may be threatening, abusive or insulting or (as the case may be) he intends his behaviour to be or is aware that it may be disorderly.

   (5) [Relates to intoxication.]

   (6) [Relates to intoxication.]

   (7) Subsections (1) and (2) do not affect the determination for the purposes of riot or violent disorder of the number of persons who use or threaten violence.

7. (1) No prosecution for an offence of riot or incitement to riot may be instituted except by or with the consent of the Director of Public Prosecutions . . .

8. . . . 'dwelling' means any structure or part of a structure occupied as a person's home or as other living accommodation (whether the occupation is separate or shared with others) but does not include any part not so occupied, and for this purpose 'structure' includes a tent, caravan, vehicle, vessel or other temporary or movable structure;

'violence' means any violent conduct, so that—

        (a) except in the context of affray, it includes violent conduct towards property as well as violent conduct towards persons, and

        (b) it is not restricted to conduct causing or intended to cause injury or damage but includes any other violent conduct (for example, throwing at or towards a person a missile of a kind capable of causing injury which does not hit or falls short).

9. (1)   The common law offences of riot, rout, unlawful assembly and affray are abolished.

11. (1)   Written notice shall be given in accordance with this section of any proposal to hold a public procession intended—
   (a) to demonstrate support for or opposition to the views or actions of any person or body of persons,
   (b) to publicise a cause or campaign, or
   (c) to mark or commemorate an event,
   unless it is not reasonably practicable to give any advance notice of the procession.

(2)   Subsection (1) does not apply where the procession is one commonly or customarily held in the police area (or areas) in which it is proposed to be held or is a funeral procession organised by a funeral director acting in the normal course of his business.

(3)   The notice must specify the date when it is intended to hold the procession, the time when it is intended to start it, its proposed route, and the name and address of the person (or of one of the persons) proposing to organise it.

(4)   Notice must be delivered to a police station—
   (a) in the police area in which it is proposed the procession will start, or
   (b) where it is proposed the procession will start in Scotland and cross into England, in the first police area in England on the proposed route.

(5)   If delivered not less than 6 clear days before the date when the procession is intended to be held, the notice may be delivered by post by the recorded delivery service; but section 7 of the Interpretation Act 1978 (under which a document sent by post is deemed to have been served when posted and to have been delivered in the ordinary course of post) does not apply.

(6)   If not delivered in accordance with subsection (5), the notice must be delivered by hand not less than 6 clear days before the date when the procession is intended to be held or, if that is not reasonably practicable, as soon as delivery is reasonably practicable.

(7)   Where a public procession is held, each of the persons organising it is guilty of an offence if–
   (a) the requirements of this section as to notice have not been satisfied, or
   (b) the date when it is held, the time when it starts, or its route differs from the date, time or route specified in the notice.

(8)   It is a defence for the accused to prove that he did not know of, and neither suspected nor had reason to suspect, the failure to satisfy the requirements or (as the case may be) the difference of date, time or route.

(9)   To the extent that an alleged offence turns on a difference of date, time or route, it is a defence for the accused to prove that the difference arose from circumstances beyond his control or from something done with the agreement of a police officer or by his direction.

(10) A person guilty of an offence under subsection (7) is liable on summary conviction to a fine not exceeding level 3 on the standard scale.

12. (1)   If the senior police officer, having regard to the time or place at which and the circumstances in which any public procession is being held or is intended to be held and to its route or proposed route, reasonably believes

that—

    (a) it may result in serious public disorder, serious damage to property or serious disruption to the life of the community, or

    (b) the purpose of the persons organising it is the intimidation of others with a view to compelling them not to do an act they have a right to do, or to do an act they have a right not to do,

he may give directions imposing on the persons organising or taking part in the procession such conditions as appear to him necessary to prevent such disorder, damage, disruption or intimidation, including conditions as to the route of the procession or prohibiting it from entering any public place specified in the directions.

(2) In subsection (1) 'the senior police officer' means—

    (a) in relation to a procession being held, or to a procession intended to be held in a case where persons are assembling with a view to taking part in it, the most senior in rank of the police officers present at the scene, and

    (b) in relation to a procession intended to be held in a case where paragraph (a) does not apply, the chief officer of police.

(3) A direction given by a chief officer of police by virtue of subsection (2)(b) shall be given in writing.

(4) A person who organises a public procession and knowingly fails to comply with a condition imposed under this section is guilty of an offence, but it is a defence for him to prove that the failure arose from circumstances beyond his control.

(5) A person who takes part in a public procession and knowingly fails to comply with a condition imposed under this section is guilty of an offence, but it is a defence for him to prove that the failure arose from circumstances beyond his control.

(6) A person who incites another to commit an offence under subsection (5) is guilty of an offence.

(7) A constable in uniform may arrest without warrant anyone he reasonably suspects is committing an offence under subsection (4), (5) or (6).

(8) A person guilty of an offence under subsection (4) is liable on summary conviction to imprisonment for a term not exceeding 3 months or a fine not exceeding level 4 on the standard scale or both.

(9) A person guilty of an offence under subsection (5) is liable on summary conviction to a fine not exceeding level 3 on the standard scale.

(10) A person guilty of an offence under subsection (6) is liable on summary conviction to imprisonment for a term not exceeding 3 months or a fine not exceeding level 4 on the standard scale or both, notwithstanding section 45(3) of the Magistrates' Courts Act 1980 (inciter liable to same penalty as incited). . .

13. (1) If at any time the chief officer of police reasonably believes that, because of particular circumstances existing in any district or part of a district, the powers under section 12 will not be sufficient to prevent the holding of public processions in that district or part from resulting in serious public disorder, he shall apply to the council of the district for an order prohibiting for such period not exceeding 3 months as may be specified in the

application the holding of all public processions (or of any class of public procession so specified) in the district or part concerned.

(2) On receiving such an application, a council may with the consent of the Secretary of State make an order either in the terms of the application or with such modifications as may be approved by the Secretary of State.

(3) Subsection (1) does not apply in the City of London or the metropolitan police district.

(4) If at any time the Commissioner of Police for the City of London or the Commissioner of Police of the Metropolis reasonably believes that, because of particular circumstances existing in his police area or part of it, the powers under section 12 will not be sufficient to prevent the holding of public processions in that area or part from resulting in serious public disorder, he may with the consent of the Secretary of State make an order prohibiting for such period not exceeding 3 months as may be specified in the order the holding of all public processions (or of any class of public procession so specified) in the area or part concerned.

(5) An order made under this section may be revoked or varied by a subsequent order made in the same way, that is, in accordance with subsections (1) and (2) or subsection (4), as the case may be.

(6) Any order under this section shall, if not made in writing, be recorded in writing as soon as practicable after being made.

(7) A person who organises a public procession the holding of which he knows is prohibited by virtue of an order under this section is guilty of an offence.

(8) A person who takes part in a public procession the holding of which he knows is prohibited by virtue of an order under this section is guilty of an offence.

(9) A person who incites another to commit an offence under subsection (8) is guilty of an offence.

(10) A constable in uniform may arrest without warrant anyone he reasonably suspects is committing an offence under subsection (7), (8) or (9).

(11) A person guilty of an offence under subsection (7) is liable on summary conviction to imprisonment for a term not exceeding 3 months or a fine not exceeding level 4 on the standard scale or both.

(12) A person guilty of an offence under subsection (8) is liable on summary conviction to a fine not exceeding level 3 on the standard scale.

(13) A person guilty of an offence under subsection (9) is liable on summary conviction to imprisonment for a term not exceeding 3 months or a fine not exceeding level 4 on the standard scale or both, notwithstanding section 45(3) of the Magistrates' Courts Act 1980.

14. (1) If the senior police officer, having regard to the time or place at which and the circumstances in which any public assembly is being held or is intended to be held, reasonably believes that—

(a) it may result in serious public disorder, serious damage to property or serious disruption to the life of the community, or

(b) the purpose of the persons organising it is the intimidation of others with a view to compelling them not to do an act they have a right to do, or to do an act they have a right not to do,

he may give directions imposing on the persons organising or taking part in the assembly such conditions as to the place at which the assembly may be (or continue to be) held, its maximum duration, or the maximum number of persons who may constitute it, as appear to him necessary to prevent such disorder, damage, disruption or intimidation.

(2) In subsection (1) 'the senior police officer' means—

    (a) in relation to an assembly being held, the most senior in rank of the police officers present at the scene, and

    (b) in relation to an assembly intended to be held, the chief officer of police.

(3) A direction given by a chief officer of police by virtue of subsection (2)(b) shall be given in writing.

(4) A person who organises a public assembly and knowingly fails to comply with a condition imposed under this section is guilty of an offence but it is a defence for him to prove that the failure arose from circumstances beyond his control.

(5) A person who takes part in a public assembly and knowingly fails to comply with a condition imposed under this section is guilty of an offence, but it is a defence for him to prove that the failure arose from circumstances beyond his control.

(6) A person who incites another to commit an offence under subsection (5) is guilty of an offence.

(7) A constable in uniform may arrest without warrant anyone he reasonably suspects is committing an offence under subsection (4), (5) or (6).

(8) A person guilty of an offence under subsection (4) is liable on summary conviction to imprisonment for a term not exceeding 3 months or a fine not exceeding level 4 on the standard scale or both.

(9) A person guilty of an offence under subsection (5) is liable on summary conviction to a fine not exceeding level 3 on the standard scale.

(10) A person guilty of an offence under subsection (6) is liable on summary conviction to imprisonment for a term not exceeding 3 months or a fine not exceeding level 4 on the standard scale or both notwithstanding section 45(3) of the Magistrates' Courts Act 1980.

14A.(1) If at any time the chief officer of police reasonably believes that an assembly is intended to be held in any district at a place on land to which the public has no right of access or only a limited right of access and that the assembly—

    (a) is likely to be held without the permission of the occupier of the land or to conduct itself in such a way as to exceed the limits of any permission of his or the limits of the public's right of access, and

    (b) may result—

        (i) in serious disruption to the life of the community, or

        (ii) where the land, or a building or monument on it, is of historical, architectural, archaeological or scientific importance, in significant damage to the land, building or monument,

he may apply to the council of the district for an order prohibiting for a specified period the holding of all trespassory assemblies in the district or a part of it, as specified.

(2) On receiving such an application, a council may—

(a) in England and Wales, with the consent of the Secretary of State make an order either in the terms of the application or with such modifications as may be approved by the Secretary of State . . .

(3) Subsection (1) does not apply in the City of London or the metropolitan police district.

(4) If at any time the Commissioner of Police for the City of London or the Commissioner of Police for the Metropolis reasonably believes that an assembly is intended to be held at a place on land to which the public has no right of access or only a limited right of access in his police area and that the assembly—

(a) is likely to be held without the permission of the occupier of the land or to conduct itself in such a way as to exceed the limits of any permission of his or the limits of the public's right of access, and

(b) may result—

   (i) in serious disruption to the life of the community, or

   (ii) where the land, or a building or monument on it, is of historical, architectural, archaeological or scientific importance, in significant damage to the land, building or monument,

he may with the consent of the Secretary of State make an order prohibiting for a specified period the holding of all trespassory assemblies in the area or part of it, as specified.

(5) An order prohibiting the holding of trespassory assemblies operates to prohibit any assembly which—

(a) is held on land to which the public has no right of access or only a limited right of access, and

(b) takes place in the prohibited circumstances, that is to say, without the permission of the occupier of the land or so as to exceed the limits of any permission of his or the limits of the public's right of access.

(6) No order under this section shall prohibit the holding of assemblies for a period exceeding 4 days or in an area exceeding an area represented by a circle with a radius of 5 miles from a specified centre.

(7) An order made under this section may be revoked or varied by a subsequent order made in the same way . . .

(8) Any order under this section shall, if not made in writing, be recorded in writing as soon as practicable after being made.

(9) In this section and sections 14B and 14C—

'assembly' means an assembly of 20 or more persons;

'land' means land in the open air;

'limited', in relation to a right of access by the public to land, means that their use of it is restricted to use for a particular purpose (as in the case of a highway or road) or is subject to other restrictions; . . .

15. (1) The chief officer of police may delegate, to such extent and subject to such conditions as he may specify, any of his functions under sections 12 to 14A to a deputy or assistant chief constable; and references in those sections to the person delegating shall be construed accordingly.

(2) Subsection (1) shall have effect in the City of London and the metropolitan police district as if 'a deputy or assistant chief constable' read 'an assistant commissioner of police'.

16. ... 'public assembly' means an assembly of 20 or more persons in a public place which is wholly or partly open to the air;

'public place' means—

    (a) any highway, ... and

    (b) any place to which at the material time the public or any section of the public has access, on payment or otherwise, as of right or by virtue of express or implied permission;

'public procession' means a procession in a public place.

Comment

(1)   The Act replaces all but s.1 (wearing of uniforms for a political objective: see *O'Moran* v *DPP*, p.431), s.2 (unlawful drilling of personnel) and s.9 (definition) of the Public Order Act 1936. The Act is not comprehensive: there are many offences left untouched, e.g. obstruction of the highway, public nuisance, outraging public decency, seditious and criminal libel. The common law powers to deal with a breach of the peace were preserved by s.40 and will often overlap with the powers in ss.11–14.

(2)   The appellants in *Beatty* v *Gillbanks* (p.416) would not be guilty of an offence contrary to s.2 but the police would now be able to apply for a banning order under s.13. The power to ban processions only extends to banning classes of processions and does not permit a particular procession to be banned. The usual order is to ban all processions in the locality with certain exceptions, e.g. religious or ceremonial processions. Such a 'blanket' ban was upheld by the European Commission of Human Rights in *Christians Against Racism and Facism* v *UK*, and see *Kent* v *Metropolitan Police Commissioner* where the Court of Appeal refused to interfere with the exercise of the discretion of the chief officer in making such a ban on the basis that he had properly directed his mind to the issues.

(3)   Sections 4A and 14A were added by the Criminal Justice and Public Order Act 1994. This Act makes extensive provision for police preventive powers to control a wide range of behaviour including trespassory assemblies, see comment (4); raves, see comment (5); disruptive behaviour, see comment (6). The Act also replaces s.39 of the 1986 Act which dealt with unlawful mass trespassers, see s.61, and enables local authorities to give directions to unauthorized campers to leave land, see s.77.

(4)   Section 14B of the 1994 Act creates offences in connection with organizing or participating in a trespassory assembly, or incitement to an offence. A constable in uniform may arrest without warrant on reasonable suspicion that someone is committing an offence. Under s.14C a constable in uniform who is within the area to which the order applies and who reasonably believes that a person is on their way to a trespassory assembly, may stop the person and order him not to proceed in the direction of the assembly. Failure to comply is an offence for which there is a power of arrest without warrant upon reasonable suspicion. The offences in ss.14B and 14C are punishable summarily only.

(5)   Section 63 applies to 'raves', i.e. 'a gathering on land in the open air of 100 or more persons (whether or not trespassers) at which amplified music is played during the night (with or without intermissions) and is such as by reason of its loudness and duration and the time at which it is played, is likely to cause serious distress to the inhabitants of the locality.' The Act does not extend to licensed 'raves'.

Section 63(2) gives a superintendent of police power to order those preparing or gathering for a rave to leave land and remove their vehicles. It is an offence for a person who knows that a direction has been given to fail to leave land as soon as is reasonably practicable. There are also powers of entry to premises and seizure of vehicles or sound equipment. A court may forfeit sound equipment, and police may retain, dispose of or destroy vehicles.

Under s.65 a constable in uniform who reasonably believes that a person is on his way to a rave, in respect of which a direction has been given, may stop that person and direct him not to proceed in the direction of the rave. The power may only be exercised within 5 miles of the site of the rave.

(6)   Section 68 of the 1994 Act creates an offence of aggravated trespass which was introduced for the purpose of dealing with the interruption of such activities as fox or stag hunting and road or other construction – see for example the relevance of this to the facts in the *CEGB* case, p.412. The offence is committed by a person who trespasses on land in the open air and, in relation to any lawful activity which persons are engaging in or are about to engage in on that or adjoining land in the open air, does anything which is intended by him to intimidate those persons so as to deter them from engaging in that activity or to obstruct or disrupt the activity.

Under s.69(1) the senior police officer at the scene may direct anyone he reasonably believes is committing, has committed or intends to commit an offence under s.68, to leave the land. This power also extends to two or more persons he reasonably believes are trespassing on land in the open air with the common purpose of intimidating persons so as to deter them from engaging in a lawful activity, or of obstructing or disrupting a lawful activity. Failure to leave, or re-entry to, the land within three months is an offence. It is a defence to show that a person was not trespassing or had a reasonable cause for failing to leave the land as soon as practicable or for re-entering as a trespasser. A constable in uniform who reasonably suspects that a person is committing an offence under this section may arrest him without a warrant.

Brutus v Cozens

[1973] AC 854   ·   House of Lords

Demonstrators protesting about apartheid interrupted play at Wimbledon Tennis Championships. Several protesters blew whistles, distributed leaflets and invaded the playing area. The defendant was prosecuted under s.5 of the 1936 Public Order Act with using threatening, insulting or abusive words or behaviour whereby a breach of the peace was likely to be occasioned. The House of Lords upheld the appeal of the defendant against the decision of the Divisional Court and held that since 'insulting' bore no special meaning it was a matter of fact for the magistrates who had acquitted the defendant.

Lord Reid: '. . . The meaning of an ordinary word of the English language is not a question of law. The proper construction of a statute is a question of law. If the context shows that a word is used in an unusual sense the court will determine in other words what that unusual sense is. But here there is in my opinion no question of the word "insulting" being used in any unusual sense. It appears to me, to be intended to have its ordinary meaning. It is for the tribunal which decides the case to consider, not as law but as fact, whether in the whole circumstances the words of the statute do or do not as a matter of ordinary usage of the English language cover or apply to the facts which have been proved. If it is alleged that the tribunal has reached a wrong decision then there can be a question of law but only of a limited character. The question would normally be whether their decision was unreasonable in the sense that no tribunal acquainted with the ordinary use of language could reasonably reach that decision.

Were it otherwise we should reach an impossible position. When considering the meaning of a word one often goes to a dictionary. There one finds other words set out. And if one wants to pursue the matter and find the meaning of those other words the dictionary will give the meaning of those other words in still further words which often include the word for whose meaning one is searching.

No doubt the court could act as a dictionary. It could direct the tribunal to take some word or phrase other than the word in the statute and consider whether that word or phrase applied to or covered the facts proved. But we have been warned time and time again not to substitute other words for the words of a statute. And there is very good reason for that. Few words have exact synonyms. The overtones are almost always different.

Or the court could frame a definition. But then again the tribunal would be left with words to consider. No doubt a statute may contain a definition – which incidentally often creates more problems than it solves – but the purpose of a definition is to limit or modify the ordinary meaning of a word and the court is not entitled to do that.

So the question of law in this case must be whether it was unreasonable to hold that the appellant's behaviour was not insulting. To that question there could in my view be only one answer – No.

But as the Divisional Court have expressed their view as to the meaning of "insulting" I must, I think, consider it. It was said: ". . . in my view it is not necessary, and is probably undesirable, to try to frame an exhaustive definition which will cover every possible set of facts that may arise for consideration under [s.5]. It is, as I think, quite sufficient for the purpose of this case to say that behaviour which affronts other people, and evidences a disrespect or contempt for their rights, behaviour which reasonable persons would foresee is likely to cause resentment or protest such as was aroused in this case, and I rely particularly on the reaction of the crowd as set out in the case stated, is insulting for the purpose of this section."

I cannot agree with that. Parliament had to solve the difficult question of how far freedom of speech or behaviour must be limited in the general public interest. It would have been going much too far to prohibit all speech or conduct likely to occasion a breach of the peace because determined opponents may not shrink from organising or at least threatening a breach of the peace in order to silence a speaker whose views they detest. Therefore vigorous and it may be distasteful or unmannerly speech or behaviour is permitted so long as it does not go beyond any one of three limits. It must not be threatening. It must not be abusive. It must not be insulting. I see no reason why any of these should be construed as having a specially wide or a specially narrow meaning. They are all limits easily recognisable by the ordinary man. Free speech is not impaired by ruling them out. But before a man can be convicted it must be clearly shown that one or more of them has been disregarded.

We were referred to a number of dictionary meanings of "insult" such as treating with insolence or contempt or indignity or derision or dishonour or offensive disrespect. Many things otherwise unobjectionable may be said or done in an insulting way. There can be no definition. But an ordinary sensible man knows an insult when he sees or hears it.

Taking the passage which I have quoted, "affront" is much too vague a word to be helpful; there can often be disrespect without insult, and I do not think that contempt for a person's rights as distinct from contempt of the person himself would generally be held to be insulting. Moreover, there are many grounds other than insult for feeling resentment or protesting. I do not agree that there can be conduct which is not insulting in the ordinary sense of the word but which is "insulting for the purpose of this section." If the view of the Divisional Court was that in this section the word "insulting" has some special or unusually wide meaning, then I do not agree. Parliament has given no indication that the word is to be given any unusual meaning. Insulting means insulting and nothing else.

If I had to decide, which I do not, whether the appellant's conduct insulted the spectators in this case, I would agree with the magistrates. The spectators may have been very angry and justly so. The appellant's conduct was deplorable. Probably it ought to be punishable. But I cannot see how it insulted the spectators . . .'

Director of Public Prosecutions v Orum

[1989] 1WLR 88 · Divisional Court

The defendant was arguing in offensive terms with his girlfriend in a public place when he was approached by a police officer. The defendant was abusive towards the police officer and he was warned that he was causing a breach of the peace. The defendant continued and was arrested for breach of the peace by the police officer whom he assaulted in the back of the police van into which he was placed. The defendant was charged with an offence contrary to s.5 of the Public Order Act 1986 and with assaulting a police officer acting in the execution of his duty. It was held that a police officer might be a person who would be likely to be harassed, alarmed or distressed for the purposes of s.5(1), and that the arrest for breach of the peace was lawful, and accordingly the assault had been on a police officer acting in the execution of his duty.

Glidewell LJ: '. . . The main question which we have to answer is: can a police officer be a person who is likely to be caused harassment, alarm or distress by the threatening, abusive or insulting words or behaviour? It is apparent, as [counsel] concedes, that. . . the magistrates first have taken the view that they can discount any question of harassment, alarm or distress to people living in and presumably mostly asleep in the nearby dwelling houses, because there is no evidence that any such person was likely to be caused harassment.

Secondly, they appear to have totally discounted the effect of the defendant's conduct upon his girlfriend. What they concerned themselves with, and what we are asked to concern ourselves with, is the impact of that conduct upon either or both of the two police constables.

The magistrates seem to have been advised by their clerk that they could not properly – presumably as a matter of law – conclude that either of the constables was likely to be caused harassment, alarm or distress by the words or behaviour of the defendant . . .

I find nothing in the context of the Act of 1986 to persuade me that a police officer may not be a person who is caused harassment, alarm or distress by the various kinds of words and conduct to which s.5(1) applies. I would therefore answer the question in the affirmative, that a police officer can be a person who is likely to be caused harassment and so on. However, that is not to say that the opposite is necessarily the case, namely, it is not to say that every police officer in this situation is to be assumed to be a person who is caused harassment. Very frequently, words and behaviour with which police officers will be wearily familiar will have little emotional impact on them save that of boredom. It may well be that in appropriate circumstances, magistrates will decide (indeed, they might decide in the present case) as a question of fact that the words and behaviour were not likely in all the circumstances to cause harassment, alarm or distress to either of the police officers. That is a question of fact for the magistrates to be decided in all the circumstances: the time, the place, the nature of the words used, who the police officers are, who else was present and so on . . . [Counsel] for the prosecution, poses for our consideration a second question: if in fact a police officer is not likely to be caused harassment etc., does he then have any power to arrest under s.5(4)? Theoretically, the answer to that question may be "Yes", but in practice, in my view, it must almost invariably be "No". The reason is this. If an officer is not caused harassment, alarm or distress, it is difficult to see how he can reasonably suspect, if he is the only person present, that an offence against s.5(1) has been committed since such causation is a necessary element in the offence. If he does not reasonably suspect that such an offence has been committed, then he has no power of arrest under s.5(4).'

Comment

(1) *Brutus* v *Cozens* remains authority for the construction of an ordinary word of the English language. For the meaning of disorderly, harassment, alarm and distress in s.5 of the 1986 Act, the principle in *Brutus* v *Cozens* will apply.

(2) In *Jordan* v *Burgoyne*, a case on s.5 of the 1936 Act, the House of Lords took the view that the defendant had to take his 'victim' as he found him and that if the 'victim' was predisposed to violence then an offence would still be made out. The same principle will apply to s.4 of the 1986 Act in regard to the likelihood of provocation to immediate unlawful violence.

(3) In *R* v *Horseferry Road Metropolitan Stipendiary Magistrate, ex parte*

Siadatan the applicant sought to overturn a magistrates' decision not to issue a summons under s.4 in respect of the distribution to bookshops by Penguin Books Ltd of copies of the *Satanic Verses*. The Divisional Court rejected the application on the basis that the words 'such violence' in s.4 meant 'immediate unlawful violence' and referred back to the first use of that phrase and not the more grammatically correct 'unlawful violence'. The Court also indicated that 'immediate':

> ... does not mean 'instantaneous'; that a relatively short time interval may elapse between the act which is threatening, abusive or insulting and the unlawful violence. 'Immediate' connotes proximity in time and proximity in causation, that it is likely that violence will result within a very short period of time and without any intervening occurrence.

(4) In *Atkin* v *DPP* two Customs and Excise officers went to the defendant's house accompanied by a bailiff. The bailiff stayed in the car whilst the officers went into the defendant's farmhouse. The defendant said that 'if the bailiff gets out of the car he's a dead un' [sic]. The defendant was charged with an offence under s.4 of the Public Order Act 1986. On appeal against conviction it was held that 'uses towards another person' meant in the presence of and in the direction of another person directly, it did not mean concerning or in regard to another person. Accordingly no offence had been made out because the person who had used the words and the person towards whom the words had been used were both inside a dwelling and thus fell outside the scope of the Act (see s.4(2)).

(5) The importance of s.6 was confirmed in *Director of Public Prosecutions* v *Clarke* which concerned the display of photographs of foetuses outside an abortion clinic to police officers and a passer-by in a car. On a s.5 charge, the magistrates found that this was both abusive and insulting, and not reasonable, but found that there had been no intention that it should be insulting or abusive.

On appeal the Divisional Court said that what had to be shown was that the display was abusive or insulting, and then, applying s.6(4), that that had been the intention of the defendant.

> A picture might cause harassment or alarm or distress without being threatening or abusive or insulting, and vice versa. Even if ... the respondents must have been aware that the pictures might cause alarm or distress, it by no means follows that they intended them to be threatening or abusive or insulting, or that they were aware that they might be so.

DPP v *Clarke* also confirmed that the defence of reasonableness in s.5(3)(c) is an objective one and must take into account all the circumstances.

O'Moran v *DPP*

[1975] QB 864 · Divisional Court

By s.1 of the Public Order Act 1936 it is an offence in any public place or at any public meeting to wear uniform signifying association with any political organization or with the promotion of any political object. The defendants were amongst a group of mourners at an IRA funeral and were dressed in dark sweaters, trousers and berets. The defendants' appeals against conviction under s.1 were rejected.

Lord Widgery CJ: '. . . "Wearing" in my judgment implies some article of wearing apparel. I agree with the submission made in argument that one would not describe a badge pinned to the lapel as being a uniform worn for present purposes. In the present instance, however, the various items relied on, such as the beret, dark glasses, the pullovers and the other dark clothing, were clearly worn and therefore satisfy the first requirement of the section . . . It seems to me that in deciding whether a person is wearing a uniform different considerations may apply according to whether he is alone or in company with others. If a man is seen walking down Whitehall wearing the uniform of a policeman or a soldier, it is unnecessary to prove that that is uniform of any sort because it is so universally recognised or known as being the clothing worn by a member of the metropolitan police or the Army, as the case may be, that it is described as uniform on that account, and judges can take judicial notice of the fact that it is uniform in that sense. If a man was seen walking down Whitehall wearing a black beret, that certainly would not be regarded as uniform unless evidence were called to show that that black beret, in conjunction with any other items appropriate to associate with it, had been used and was recognised as the uniform of some body. In other words, the policeman or the soldier is accepted as wearing uniform without more ado, but the isolated man wearing a black beret is not to be regarded as wearing a uniform unless it is proved that the beret in its association has been recognised and is known as the uniform of some particular organisation, proof of which would have to be provided by evidence in the usual way . . . Where an article such as a beret is used in order to indicate that a group of men are together and in association, it seems to me that that article can be regarded as uniform without any proof that it has been previously used as such. The simple fact that a number of men deliberately adopt an identical article of attire justifies in my judgment the view that that article is uniform if it is adopted in such a way as to show that its adoption is for the purposes of showing association between the men in question. Subject always to the *de minimis* rule, I see no reason why the article or articles should cover the whole of the body or a major part of the body, as was argued at one point, or indeed should go beyond the existence of the beret by itself. In this case the articles did go beyond the beret. They extended to the pullover, the dark glasses and the dark clothing, and I have no doubt at all in my own mind that those men wearing those clothes on that occasion were wearing uniform within the meaning of the Act. . .

The next point, and perhaps the most difficult problem of all, is the requirement of the section that the uniform so worn shall signify the wearer's association with any political organisation. This can be done in my judgment in two ways. The first I have already referred to. It is open to the prosecution, if they have the evidence and wish to call it, to show that the particular article relied upon as uniform has been used in the past as the uniform of a recognised association, and they can by that means, if the evidence is strong enough, and the court accepts it, prove that the black beret, or whatever it may be, is associated with a particular organisation. In my judgment it is not necessary for them to specify the particular organisation because in many instances the name of the organisation will be unknown or may have been recently changed. But if they can prove that the article in question has been associated with a political organisation capable of identification in some manner, then that would suffice for the purposes of the section. . .

Alternatively, in my judgment the significance of the uniform and its power to show the association of the wearer with a political organisation can be judged from the events to be seen on the occasion when the alleged uniform was worn. In other words, it can be judged and proved without necessarily referring to the past history at all, because if a group of persons assemble together and wear a piece of uniform such as a black beret to indicate their association one with the other, and furthermore by their conduct indicate that that beret associates them with other activity of a political character, that is enough for the purposes of the section. . .'

Comment

Section 3, Prevention of Terrorism (Temporary Provisions) Act 1989, makes it an offence to wear in a public place any item of dress or in any public place to wear, carry or display any article in such a way or in such circumstances as to arouse reasonable apprehension that the wearer is a member or supporter of a proscribed organization. Section 1 of the Act gives the Secretary of State power to make statutory instruments banning organizations which appear to him to be concerned in terrorism, or in promoting or encouraging terrorism, occurring in the United Kingdom and connected with the affairs of Northern Ireland; the proscribed organisations are the IRA and INLA.

Hirst & Agu v *Chief Constable of West Yorkshire*

(1987) 85 Cr App R 143 · Divisional Court

The defendants were picketing a furrier's shop and stood either in the doorway of the shop or on the highway distributing leaflets and holding placards; large groups of passers-by were attracted. They were prosecuted for wilful obstruction of the highway contrary to s.137, Highways Act 1980, which provides that: 'If a person, without lawful authority or excuse, in any way wilfully obstructs the free passage along a highway he shall be guilty of an offence.' Their appeal against conviction was upheld since the magistrates had failed to consider the reasonableness of their use of the highway.

Glidewell LJ: '. . . recent authority, which is binding on us, is that in *Nagy* v *Weston*, a decision of this Court. In that case the defendant parked a hot dog van in St Giles Street, Oxford. He was convicted under s.121(1) of the Highways Act 1959, which is in identical terms to the present section. The conviction was upheld, but Lord Parker CJ, giving a judgment with which the other two members of the Court agreed, put the position in a way which in my view establishes the major authority for the consideration of questions arising under this section. He first of all quoted the case stated which concluded with the words: "The question for the opinion of the High Court is whether we correctly interpreted the meaning of the words 'wilfully obstruct'. and whether the facts of the case are capable as a matter of law of justifying a conviction."

Lord Parker proceeded "In my judgment, the answer to those questions is clearly yes. Counsel for the appellant concedes . . . that any occupation of part of a road, thus interfering with people having the use of the whole of the road, is an obstruction. He also concedes that wilful obstruction is when the obstruction is caused purposely or deliberately. He goes on, however, to say that, before anyone can be convicted of this offence, two further elements must be proved, first that the defendant had no lawful authority or excuse, and, secondly, that the user to which he was putting the highway was an unreasonable user. For my part I think that excuse and reasonableness are really the same ground, but it is quite true that it has to be proved that there was no lawful authority. It is really difficult to think of any argument that could be used in the present case to the effect that the appellant had lawful authority to obstruct the highway if what happened was an obstruction. It is undoubtedly true – counsel for the appellant is quite right – that there must be proof that the user in question was an unreasonable user. Whether or not the user amounting to an obstruction is or is not an unreasonable use of the highway is a question of fact. It depends on all the circumstances, including the length of time the obstruction continues, the place where it occurs, the purpose for which it is done, and, of course, whether it does in fact cause an actual obstruction as opposed to a potential obstruction. So far as this case is concerned, the magistrates, in the finding that I have already read, have clearly found that, in the circumstances, there was an unreasonable use of the highway. Indeed on the facts stated, it is difficult to see how they could conceivably arrive at any other conclusion. I would dismiss the appeal."

That statement of the law was approved by Lord Denning MR in the Court of Appeal in the case of *Hubbard and Others* v *Pitt and Others*. It is however right to remind oneself that Lord Denning in that case, first of all, was dissenting from the other two members of the Court and, secondly, that the passage in question is in any case *obiter* . . .

In *Waite* v *Taylor* . . . a busker . . . had been juggling with fire sticks in a pedestrian precinct. May LJ said . . . ". . . I have reached the conclusion that the underlying principle in all these cases can be relatively simply stated. In so far as a highway is concerned members of the public have the right to pass and re-pass along it. That does not, however, mean that one must keep moving all the time. However, if one does stop on a highway then prima facie an obstruction occurs, because by stopping you are on a piece of the very highway that somebody else may wish to pass and re-pass along. Where, however, your stopping is really part and parcel of passing and re-passing along the highway and is ancillary to it (such as a milkman stopping to leave a milk bottle on a doorstep) then this is not an obstruction within the meaning of the subsection with which we are concerned. On the other hand, where stopping on the highway cannot properly be said to be ancillary to or part and parcel of the exercise of one's right to pass and re-pass along that highway, then the obstruction becomes unreasonable and there is an obstruction contrary to the provisions of the subsection." . . .

Now it is clear in the present case that the Crown Court did not consider whether the defendants' user of the highway was reasonable or not, because that Court, considering itself bound by *Waite* v *Taylor*, decided that handing out leaflets and holding banners was not incidental to the lawful use of the highway to pass and re-pass and, therefore, that the reasonableness of that activity was not relevant.

As I have already said, in my judgment *Nagy* v *Weston* is the leading modern authority and it does not apply so rigid a test as that found in the judgment of May LJ in *Waite* v *Taylor* . . . In *Nagy* v *Weston* itself, the activity being carried on . . . could not in my view be said to be incidental to the right to pass and re-pass along the street. Clearly, the Divisional Court took the view that it was open to the magistrates to consider, as a-question of fact, whether the activity was or was not reasonable. On the facts the magistrates had concluded that it was unreasonable (an unreasonable obstruction) but if they had concluded that it was reasonable then it is equally clear that in the view of the Divisional Court the offence would not have been made out . . .

As counsel pointed out to us in argument, if that is not right, there are a variety of activities which quite commonly go on in the street which may well be the subject of prosecution under s.137. For instance, what is now relatively commonplace, at least in London and large cities, distributing advertising material or free periodicals outside stations, when people are arriving in the morning. Clearly, that is an obstruction; clearly, it is not incidental to passage up and down the street because the distributors are virtually stationary. The question must be: is it a reasonable use of the highway or not? In my judgment that is a question that arises. It may be decided that if the activity grows to an extent that it is unreasonable by reason of the space occupied or the duration of time for which it goes on that an offence would be committed, but it is a matter on the facts for the magistrates . . .

Some activities which commonly go on in the street are covered by statute, for instance, the holding of markets or street trading, and thus they are lawful activities because they are lawfully permitted within the meaning of the section. That is lawful authority. But many are not and the question thus is (to follow Lord Parker's *dictum*): have the prosecution proved in such cases that the defendant was obstructing the highway without lawful excuse? That question is to be answered by deciding whether the activity in which the defendant was engaged was or was not a reasonable user of the highway.

I emphasise that for there to be a lawful excuse for what would otherwise be an obstruction of the highway, the activity in which the person causing the obstruction is engaged must itself be inherently lawful. If it is not, the question whether it is reasonable does not arise. So an obstruction of the highway caused by unlawful picketing in pursuance of a trade dispute cannot be said to be an activity for which there is a lawful excuse. But in this case it is not suggested that the activity itself – distributing pamphlets and displaying banners in opposition to the wearing of animal furs as garments – was itself unlawful.

I suggest that the correct approach for justices who are dealing with the issues which arose and arise in the present case is as follows. First, they should consider: is there an obstruction? Unless the obstruction is so small that one can consider it comes within the rubric *de minimis*, any stopping on the highway, whether it be on the carriageway or on the footway, is prima facie an obstruction. To quote Lord Parker: "Any occupation of part of a road thus interfering with people having the use of the whole of the road is an obstruction."

The second question then will arise: was it wilful, that is to say, deliberate? Clearly, in many cases a pedestrian or a motorist has to stop because the traffic lights are against the motorists or there are other people in the way, not because he wishes to do so. Such stopping is not wilful. But if the stopping is deliberate, then there is wilful obstruction.

Then there arises the third question: have the prosecution proved that the obstruction was without lawful authority or excuse? Lawful authority includes permits and licences granted under statutory provision, as I have already said, such as for market and street traders and, no doubt, for those collecting for charitable causes on Saturday mornings. Lawful excuse embraces activities otherwise lawful in themselves which may or may not be reasonable in all the circumstances mentioned by Lord Parker in *Nagy* v *Weston*. In the present case the Crown Court never considered this question. In my judgment . . . they were wrong not to do so, and I would, therefore, allow the appeal.'

Comment

(1) 'Wilful' simply means intentional – see *Arrowsmith* v *Jenkins*: 'If anybody, by an exercise of free will, does something which causes an obstruction, then an offence is committed'.

(2) There is a right to pass and repass over highways; that is the purpose for which highways were dedicated. There is no right to assemble on the highway; there is a freedom to do so only to the extent that the assembly does not infringe any law; the same principles apply to an ice-cream queue as to a political gathering or an industrial picket. Thus, meetings are prima facie unlawful and processions are prima facie lawful.

In *Hickman* v *Maisey*, the plaintiff owned land upon which he permitted another to exercise race-horses. The defendant, a racing tout, would observe the horses from a highway running across the land. It was held that this use of the highway constituted a trespass to the land and the plaintiff was entitled to an injunction and damages:

> . . . Many authorities show that prima facie the right of the public is merely to pass and repass along the highway; but I quite agree with what Lord Esher MR said in *Harrison* v *Duke of Rutland* . . . namely, that, though highways are dedicated prima facie for the purposes of passage, 'things are done upon them by everybody which are recognised as being rightly done and as constituting a reasonable and usual mode of using a highway as such'; and 'if a person on a highway does not transgress such reasonable and usual mode of using it' he will not be a trespasser; but, if he does 'acts other than the reasonable and ordinary user of a highway as such' he will be a trespasser . . . But I cannot agree with the contention of the defendant's counsel that the acts which this defendant did, not really for the purpose of using the highway as such, but for the purpose of carrying on his business as a racing tout to the detriment of the plaintiff by watching the trials of race-horses on the plaintiff's land, were within such an ordinary and reasonable user of the highway . . . and in *Harrison* v *Duke of Rutland* . . . the plaintiff went upon a highway, the soil of which was vested in the defendant, while a grouse drive was taking place on adjoining land of the defendant, for the purpose of interfering with the drive, which the keepers prevented him from doing by force. The plaintiff . . . brought an action for assault . . . and the defendant counterclaimed in trespass . . . it was clear . . . that he was not using the highway for the purpose of passing or repassing . . . but solely for the purposes of interfering with the defendant's enjoyment of his right of shooting . . . and it was held therefore that the plaintiff's user of the highway was a trespass. I cannot see any real distinction between that case and the present.

(3)   Misuse of the highway may amount to torts such as trespass, public nuisance or private nuisance in respect of which the owner of the highway or adjoining occupiers may be able to obtain an injunction to terminate the conduct, and damages to compensate for any loss. In *Hubbard* v *Pitt*, Lord Denning regarded the picket of an estate agent's premises (by people opposed to the sale of properties to people from outside the area) as being a reasonable user of the highway and thus not a tort. At first instance it was said to be the tort of nuisance. The majority of the Court of Appeal dealt with the case on the basis of the exercise of their discretion to grant an interlocutory injunction (which was in fact granted).

(4)   Where there is a protest on the highway the police may have resort to their preventive powers under s.14, Public Order Act 1986, or at common law. Equally, they may resort to arrest for substantive criminal offences, e.g. for activities contrary to ss.4 or 5 of the 1986 Act or wilful obstruction of the highway (see the power of arrest in s.25, Police and Criminal Evidence Act, 1984). The scope of police powers to deal with protests is really quite immense.

Postscript

R v Clegg [1995] 1 All ER 334

In *R* v *Clegg* the House of Lords considered the case of a soldier convicted of the murder of a passenger in a car driven by a 'joyrider'. As the car accelerated through a checkpoint, C had fired four shots from a high-velocity rifle. The first three shots were found by the judge to have been fired in self-defence or in defence of another soldier. The fourth shot, a significant cause of death, was held to have been fired after the car had passed the checkpoint and when the soldiers were no longer in danger. The judge held that there was no evidence to support a defence under s.3 of the Criminal Law (Northern Ireland) Act 1967 that C had fired to prevent crime or to arrest the driver. The Court of Appeal considered that the defence could have been raised, but that, if it had been raised, it would have failed since the force used would have been 'grossly disproportionate to the mischief to be averted', i.e. the arrest of a 'joyrider' not suspected of involvement in terrorist offences.

Although the House of Lords noted the special position of soldiers operating in Northern Ireland, identified by Lord Diplock in the *Attorney-General for Northern Ireland's Reference* case (p.404), and in particular the absence of scope for graduated force to be deployed, their Lordships upheld the conviction for murder.

The House of Lords held that existing law did not permit a verdict of manslaughter instead of murder where excessive force was used in self-defence, and that there was no distinction between that situation and force used to prevent crime or to prevent arrest. In such matters there was no distinction to be drawn between, on the one hand, a soldier acting in the course of his duties and, on the other hand, an ordinary citizen.

Equally important was the decision of the House of Lords not to create new law in a case where Parliament had already legislated and where it was important for Parliament to weigh competing arguments.